ABOUT THE COVER

Clockwise from upper left: This is a scanning-electron micrograph taken from the fracture surface of a specimen cut from a carbon-fiber-reinforced plastic bicycle tube, showing the fractured graphite fibers that have been pulled out of the epoxy matrix of the tube. See Figure 13.28 on page 338.

This shows some of the important components of the knee joint: the lateral and medial menisci, the collateral and cruciate ligaments, and the articular cartilage. Not shown here are the quadriceps and patella ligaments. See Figure 1 on page 375.

This is a transmission electron micrograph of a quenched-and-tempered 4130 (Cr-Mo) steel. This is the steel commonly used for high-quality bicycle frames. The dark particles are carbides that provide the strength of this alloy. See Figure 9.9 on page 204.

This shows the tread, plies, and belts of a radial tire. The plies are a fabric usually made from polyester or nylon cord. The belts are generally made from cold-drawn, high-carbon steel wire. The tread is compounded from a mix of rubbers. See Figure14.3 on page 350.

ACKNOWLEDGEMENTS

I wish to acknowledge the contributions of the generation of students at the University of Pennsylvania who, by their comments and advice, helped to shape this book and the course in introductory-level materials science and engineering for which it was used. In addition, the work of Mr. Ransom Weaver in designing and supervising the production of the multimedia content on the CD-ROM and of Ms Kathy McLaughlin in preparing the book for printing has been invaluable and is gratefully acknowledged. The students who produced various parts of the animations on the CD were Seamus Woods, Lu Wang, Joyeeta Dutta, Sudeshna Dutta, Eric Hewett, Jennifer Connolly, Wee-Quan Jung, Asha Maliakel, and Alan Pachence.

Figures 17.13 - 17.17, 17.20, 17.23 and 17.27 were originally published in Sentralnervesystemet, Bygning Og Funksjon. Copyright © by Tano; used here with permission.

Finally, I dedicate this book to my wife, Helen, who patiently provided constant care and feeding, as well as expert proof reading, throughout this process.

Charles McMahon
Philadelphia
December, 2004

Printed in Canada
ISBN 0-9646598-5-9

Merion Books
Philadelphia, PA
www.merionmedia.com

Distributed by:
Enfield Publishing & Distribution Co.
Lebanon, NH
www.enfieldbooks.com

Structural Materials

A textbook with animations

C.J. McMahon, Jr.

Professor of Materials Science and Engineering
University of Pennsylvania

Interactive Design by Ransom Weaver

Topics Treated in CD-ROM Tutorials

Structural Materials

CORROSION PROTECTION

MECHANICAL BEHAVIOR

MATERIALS STRUCTURES

DISLOCATIONS AND PLASTIC FLOW

ANNEALING

METAL FATIGUE

PHASE DIAGRAMS

CARBON STEELS

HARD MATERIALS

PRECIPITATION HARDENING

BICYCLE CONSTRUCTION

POLYMERS

COMPOSITES

TIRES

FLEXIBLE CONNECTIVE TISSUE

RIGID CONNECTIVE TISSUE: BONE

SKELETAL MUSCLE

C.J. McMahon, Jr.

University of Pennsylvania

Interactive Design by Ransom Weaver

ISBN 0-9646589-8-3

www.merionmedia.com

CORROSION PROTECTION 21'

1-1 Wooden wheels
1-2 Tension-spoked wheel
1-3 Wheel building
1-4 Radial vs. tangential spoking
1-5 Spoke attachment
1-6 Cyclic loading of spokes
1-7 Stainless vs. carbon steel
4'51"

2-1 Corrosion of iron
2-2 Oxygen-concentration cell
2-3 Pitting corrosion
2-4 Galvanic protection
2-5 Galvanic series
2-6 Sacrificial anode
2-7 Galvanized steel
2-8 Chromium plating
2-9 Perforation and pitting
2-10 Passivation
2-11 Stainless steel
10'17"

3-1 Substitutional solid solution
3-2 Interstitial solid solution
3-3 BCC structure
3-4 Definition of a phase
3-5 FCC structure
3-6 Austenitic stainless steel
3-7 Chromium carbide
5'54"

MECHANICAL BEHAVIOR 35.3'

1-1 Small-scale vs. large-scale deform'n
1-2 Wire drawing
1-3 The tensile test
1-4 Engineering vs. true stress
1-5 Engineering vs. true strain
1-6 Shear stress, strain
6'36"

2-1 Hooke's law
2-2 Young's moduli
2-3 Poisson contraction
2-4 E, G, and ν
2-5 Interatomic energies
2-6 Binding-energy curve
2-7 Force-displacement curve
2-8 Elastic modulus
2-9 High vs. low E
2-10 Stored elastic energy
9'55"

3-1 Plastic yielding
3-2 Tensile test, small scale deform'n
3-3 Define yield stress
3-4 σ_y, stainless and carbon steel
3-5 The edge dislocation
3-6 Strain hardening
3-7 Shear stress in tensile specimen
3-8 Schmid factor
3-9 Maximum shear stress
8'26"

4-1 Tensile test, large-scale deform'n.
4-2 Necking, UTS
4-3 Necking criterion
4-4 Stainless vs. carbon steel
4-5 Rupture
4-6 Triaxial tension in neck
4-7 Tensile ductility
4-8 Wire-drawing die
4-9 Biaxial stresses
4-10 Comb'd. tension & compression
4-11 Annealed vs. cold-drawn wire
10'20"

MATERIALS STRUCTURES 19.3'

1-1 Metallography
1-2 Ginding and polishing
1-3 Etching
1-4 Metallographic microscope
1-5 Vertical illuminator
1-6 Reflection contrast
1-7 Bubble raft
1-8 High-angle grain boundaries
1-9 Low-angle grain boundaries
1-10 Non-etching boundaries
1-11 Close packing
5'57"

2-1 FCC stacking
2-2 FCC unit cell
2-3 HCP stacking
2-4 FCC, HCP metals
2-5 CP planes and directions
2-6 CP planes in FCC
2'50"

3-1 Miller indices
3-2 Intercepts
3-3 Reciprocals
3-4 (001) plane
3-5 Origin of axes
3-6 Cube planes: {100}
3-7 (111) plane
3-8 {111} planes
3-9 Fractional intercepts
3-10 (212) plane
3-11 (110), (011), (101) planes
3-12 PLANE GAME
6'37"

4-1 <100> directions
4-2 <110> directions
4-3 <111> directions
4-4 [hkl] direction & (hkl) plane
4-5 Directions in a plane
4-6 CP directions in a CP plane
4-7 Cubic crystals
4-8 FCC vs. BCC
4-9 DIRECTION GAME
3'56"

DISLOCATIONS AND PLASTIC FLOW 77'

1-1 Deformability vs. strength
1-2 Strain hardening
1-3 Deformation of spokes
1-4 Plastic vs. elastic def'm
1-5 Slip
1-6 Slip vector
1-7 Slip directions
1-8 Slip planes
1-9 Close-packed planes
1-10 FCC slip systems
6'45"

2-1 Kink in a rug
2-2 Edge dislocation
2-3 Burgers vector b
2-4 Extra half plane
2-5 Glide vs. climb
2-6 Positive vs. negative edge
2-7 Bubble model
2-8 Plane strain: edge
2-9 Anti-plane strain
2-10 Screw dislocation
2-11 Compare edge and screw
2-12 Glide of screw
2-13 Cross slip
2-14 Mixed dislocation
2-15 Definition of a dislocation
2-16 Dislocation sign; annihilation
2-17 Dislocation loop
2-18 Shear by a dln loop
2-19 Sign and b in a dln loop
10'56"

3-1 TEM
3-2 Dlns in TEM
3-3 Diffraction contrast
3-4 Electron scattering by atom
3-5 Scattering by group of atoms
3-6 Reinforced scattering
3-7 Scattered beam
3-8 Bragg's law
3-9 Scattering at a dln
3-10 Dln motion in TEM
5'

4-1 Peierls stress
4-2 Slip in BCC
4-3 Ionic & covalent crystals
4-4 Strain hardening & dlns
4-5 Grain-size effect
4-6 Solid-solution hardening
4-7 Precipitation hardening
6'18"

5-1 Stress fields of dlns
5-2 Nature of a stress field
5-3 Stress at a point
5-4 Components of stress
5-5 Normal vs. shear stresses
5-6 Normal stresses
5-7 Shear stresses
5-8 Nine components
5-9 Six independent components
5-10 Equilibrium condition
5-11 Hydrostatic compression
5-12 Stress field of screw dln 1
5-13 Stress field of screw dln 2
5-14 Stress field of screw dln 3
5-15 Cartesian vs. cylindrical coord.
5-16 σ_z=Gb/2πr
5-17 Screw dln vs. substitutional solute
5-18 Stress field of edge dln 1
5-19 Stress field of edge dln 2
5-20 Stress field of edge dln 3
5-21 Stress field of edge dln 4
5-22 Interactions of edge dlns
5-23 Edge dln vs. substitutional solute 1
5-24 Edge dln vs. substitutional solute 2
5-25 b of mixed dln
20'40"

6-1 Elastic strain energy
6-2 Energy of screw dln I
6-3 Energy of screw dln II
6-4 SE/L=Gb^2
6-5 Energy of edge dln
6-6 Dln bowing
6-7 Line tension
5'30"

7-1 Dislocation density
7-2 Dislocation interactions
7-3 Parabolic hardening
7-4 Plastic strain & dln density 1
7-5 Plastic strain & dln density 2
7-6 Plastic strain & dln density 3
7-7 Plastic strain & dln density 4
7-8 Plastic strain & dln density 5
7-9 Necessity of dln multiplication
7-10 Multiplication mechanism
7-11 Force on a dln I
7-12 Force on a dln II
7-13 F/L=τ•b
7-14 Line tension = Gb^2
7-15 Loop bowing 1
7-16 Loop bowing 2
7-17 Loop bowing 3
7-18 Frank-Read source 1
7-19 Frank-Read source 2
7-20 F-R sources in TEM
7-21 Double cross slip
7-22 Double cross slip and F-R source
7-23 Dln density vs. dln spacing
7-24 Flow stress $\approx \rho^{1/2} \approx \varepsilon_p{}^{1/2}$
7-25 Parabolic vs. linear hardening
22'

ANNEALING 56.5'

1-1 Wire drawing
1-2 Strain hardening
1-3 Cold-worked state
1-4 Energy, enthalpy
1-5 Spontaneous reaction
1-6 Order vs. disorder
1-7 Entropy
1-8 Gibbs free energy
1-9 Stored energy of CW
7'50"

2-1 Hardness test
2-2 Rockwell hardness
2-3 Recrystallization
2-4 Strain-free grains
2-5 Nucleation of new grain
2-6 Growth of new grains
2-7 Temperature dependence
2-8 Maxwell-Boltzmann dist'n
2-9 Exponential dependence
2-10 Reaction rate
2-11 Arrhenius equation
2-12 Activation energy
2-13 S-curve
2-14 Recrystallization temperature
10'10"

3-1 Recovery
3-2 Dislocation climb
3-3 Electrical resistivity
3-4 Eq'm vacancy conc'n
3-5 Entropy effect
3-6 G=H-TS
3-7 Boltzmann entropy
3-8 Microstates
3-9 Microstates/macrostate
3-10 S=klnW
3-11 dG/dn = 0
3-12 H_f, Vacancy conc'n
3-13 Cu at 1000K
3-14 Vacancy sources, sinks
3-15 Kinetics of recovery
3-16 Effect of temperature
3-17 Driving force for recovery
15'20"

4-1 Grain growth
4-2 Soap-cell growth
4-3 Bubble pressure
4-4 Mechanism of GG
4-5 Atom neighbors in GB
4-6 GB triple junctions
4-7 Eq'm at triple junct.
4-8 GB curvature
4-9 Growth vs shrinkage
4-10 Kinetics of GG
4-11 Parabolic growth
4-12 Solute effects
4-13 Desegregation
4-14 Particle effects
4-15 GB pinning
4-16 Particle coarsening
4-17 Hardness vs. GG
4-18 Σ of annealing
14'35"

5-1 CS spoke, longi. section
5-2 Transverse section
5-3 Anneal 700°C, 3h, 24h
5-4 Ferrite, carbide
5-5 Carbide coarsening
5-6 H_2O droplet I
5-7 H_2O droplet II
5-8 Anneal 950°C, FC
5-9 Pearlite
5-10 Cold drawing of CS
8'40"

METAL FATIGUE 37.5'

1-1 BCC iron
1-2 Slip systems
1-3 Screw dln mobility
1-4 Toughness
1-5 Cleavage fracture
5'

2-1 Solute atoms
2-2 Solutes vs. dlns
2-3 Substitutional solutes
2-4 Solid-solution strengthening
2-5 Interstitials in FCC
2-6 Interstitials in BCC
2-7 Interstitials vs. screw dlns in BCC
5'28"

3-1 Solute segregation
3-2 Interstitial diffusion
3-3 Dislocation pinning
3-4 Discontinuous yielding
3-5 Lüders bands
3-6 Decarburization
3-7 Strain-aging
3-8 Upper, lower yield stress
3-9 Substitutional diffusion
3-10 Diffusion coefficient
7'33"

4-1 Fatigue failure
4-2 Coffin-Manson law
4-3 Persistent slip bands
4-4 Stress concentrations
4-5 Pedal stems
4-6 Fatigue fracture surface
4-7 Plastic blunting
4-8 Critical-size crack
4-9 Rotating-beam test
4-10 S-N diagram
4-11 Scatter in N
4-12 Failure control
4-13 Surface hardening
4 14 Fatigue design
4-15 Variable loading
14'35"

5-1 Loading of spokes
5-2 Spoke failure
5-3 Fracture surface
5-4 Fatigue striations
5-5 Fatigue limit
5-6 Role of dln pinning
5-7 CS vs. SS spokes
5-8 Corrosion protection
5'

PHASE DIAGRAMS 79.3'

1-1 Brazing
1-2 Soldering
1-3 Wetting
1-4 Wetting agent
1-5 Contact angle
1-6 Surface energy
1-7 Surface tension
1-8 Equilibrium shape
1-9 To promote wetting
1-10 Flux
1-11 Capillary action
1-12 Brazing clearance
9'36"

2-1 Melting temperature
2-2 Road salt
2-3 NaCl + H_2O
2-4 $CaCl_2$ + H_2O
2-5 Phases
2-6 Two-phase mixtures
2-7 Eutectic reaction
2-8 Solid+liquid slush
2-9 Phase diagrams
2-10 NaCl vs. H_2O
7'36"

3-1 Simple eutectic
3-2 Solid phases
3-3 Solid solutions
3-4 Liquid solutions
3-5 Miscibility of metals
3-6 Atom-size effect
3-7 Intermetallic compounds
3-8 Two-phase regions
3-9 Solubility limit
3-10 Saturated α
3-11 Sugar + H_2O
3-12 Saturated β
3-13 Tie line
3-14 Alloy composition
3-15 Lever rule
3-16 Relative amounts of α & β
3-17 Wt% vs. At%
3-18 Eutectic freezing
3-19 Eutectic microstructure
3-20 Composition of each phase
3-21 Amount of each phase
16'20"

4-1 Eutectic morphology
4-2 Three-phase equilibrium
4-3 Mushy α + liquid
4-4 Solidification
4-5 Dendrites
4-6 Use of lever rule
4-7 Liquidus and solidus
4-8 Eutectic solidification
4-9 Primary α
4-10 Precipitation of β in α
4-11 Hypoeutectic vs. hypereutectic
4-12 Recap simple eutectic
11'

5-1 Pb-Sn diagram
5-2 Cooling curves
5-3 Eutectic alloy
5-4 α & β in eutectic
5-5 Lamellar microstructure
5-6 Solute redistribution
5-7 Eutectic cells
5-8 Pb-30%Sn alloy
5-9 Freezing of Pb-30%Sn
5-10 Freezing continued
5-11 Primary α vs. eutectic α
10'20"

6-1 Dendritic morpholgy
6-2 Interface stability
6-3 Stability continued
6-4 Examples of dendrites
6-5 Eutectic divorcement
6-6 Pb-10%Sn alloy
6-7 Slow cooling of Pb-10%Sn
6-8 Finding the solvus line
6-9 Normal cooling of Pb-30%Sn
6-10 Non-equilibrium eutectic
6-11 Non-equilibrium solidus
6-12 Sterling silver
6-13 Pb-90%Sn alloy
11'6"

7-1 Two-phase equilibrium
7-2 Chemical potential
7-3 C(P-1) equations
7-4 T, p, & compostion
7-5 P(C-1)+2 variables
7-6 Degrees of freedom
7-7 Phase rule
7-8 Three-phase equilibrium
7-9 Checking phase diagrams
7'

8-1 Brazing bike frames
8-2 Pb-Sn?
8-3 Creep
8-4 Ag-Cu alloys
8-5 Lugs for brazing
8-6 Cu-Zn alloys
8-7 Cu-40%Zn
8-8 Brazed joint
8-9 Microstructure of joint
8-10 Ordering of β brass
8-11 Furnace brazing
8-12 Fillet brazing
6'24"

CARBON STEELS 37'

1-1 Carbon-steel microstructure
1-2 Kinetics
1-3 Furnace-cooled spoke
1-4 Ferrite & pearlite
1-5 Fe-C phase diagram
1-6 Steels
1-7 Graphite
1-8 Cementite
1-9 Fe-Fe_3C diagram
1-10 Eutectoid transformation
1-11 Austenitization
1-12 Hypoeutectoid steel
1-13 Proeutectoid ferrite
1-14 FC 1040 microstructure
1-15 Prior-austenite gb
1-16 Pearlite growth
9'

2-1 Driving force
2-2 Diffusion kinetics
2-3 Transformation diagram
2-4 IT diagram
2-5 1080 IT diagram
2-6 Pearlite formation
2-7 S-curve
2-8 G vs T diagram for γ
2-9 G vs T for α+Fe_3C
2-10 Driving-force limitation
2-11 Diffusion limitation
2-12 C-curve
2-13 Pearlite spacing
2-14 Upper bainite
2-15 Lower bainite
2-16 1040 IT diagram
2-17 Ferrite-start curve
2-18 Transformation at 750°C
2-19 Transformation at 675°C
2-20 Kinetics of ferrite growth
12'

3-1 Continuous cooling
3-2 CT diagram
3-3 Dilatometer
3-4 Dilatometer curve
3-5 DTA curve
3-6 1080 steel wire experiment
3-7 Jominy bar
3-8 Jominy bar and CT diagram
3-9 Finding the P_S point
3-10 1040 steel CT diagram
3-11 FC vs. AC spokes
3-12 FC curve on CT diagram
3-13 AC curve on CT diagram
3-14 Widmanstättin ferrite
3-15 Cold-drawn 1040
9'

4-1 Martensite
4-2 FCC to BCT
4-3 Tetragonality
4-4 Driving force for martensite
4-5 Defects in martensite
4-6 Homogeneous shear
4-7 Twinning
4-8 Retained austenite
4-9 M_s & M_f vs. %C
4-10 Tempering
4-11 Hardness of martensite
7'

HARD MATERIALS 79.7

1-1 Friction
1-2 Wear
1-3 Metal surfaces
1-4 Energy levels
1-5 Energy bands
1-6 Metallic bonding
1-7 Cold welding
1-8 Frictional force
1-9 Effect of hardness
1-10 Coefficient of friction
1-11 Static vs. sliding
1-12 To reduce friction
1-13 Adhesive wear
1-14 Abrasive wear
1-15 To reduce wear
1-16 Boundary lubrication
1-17 Grease and oil
1-18 Hydrodynamic lubrication
1-19 High-velocity shear
14'

2-1 Hardened steel
2-2 52100 steel
2-3 Hardness of martensite
2-4 Bicycle chain
2-5 4340 vs. 1040 steel
2-6 Hardenability
2-7 Jominy curves
2-8 Austenite stabilizers
2-9 Carbide formers
2-10 Hardness vs. toughness
2-11 Tempering
2-12 Stages of tempering
2-13 Alloy carbides
2-14 4130 steel
2-15 Precipitation hardening
2-16 Tool steels
9'24"

3-1 Quench cracking
3-2 Thermal stresses
3-3 Tempered glass
3-4 Transformation stresses
3-5 Slow quenching
3-6 Retained austenite
3-7 Small vs. large parts
13'

4-1 Surface hardening
4-2 Carburizing
4-3 Hard case, tough core
4-4 Diffusion
4-5 Fick's 1st law
4-6 Mass balance
4-7 dC/dt = -dJ/dx
4-8 Fick's 2nd law
4-9 Boundary conditions
4-10 Error function
4-11 Table of erf z
4-12 Use of the table
4-13 √Dt
4-14 D, Q, D_0
4-15 Carburizing a cog
14'50"

5-1 Cracks
5-2 Brittle fracture
5-3 Stress concentration factor
5-4 Elliptical hole
5-5 Griffith approach
5-6 Surface energy
5-7 Energy release
5-8 Energy balance
5-9 Energy vs. crack length
5-10 Critical size
5-11 LEFM
5-12 Fracture energy, G
5-13 K_c
5-14 Plane stress vs. plane strain
5-15 K_{1c}
5-16 Strength vs. toughness
5-17 Concept of K
15'6"

6-1 Ceramics
6-2 Brittleness
6-3 Covalent crystals
6-4 Ionic crystals
6-5 Polycrystals
6-6 Mixed bonding
6-7 Crystal-structure rules
6-8 Making ceramics
6-9 Sintering
6-10 Grain-boundary diffusion
6-11 Driving force
6-12 Glass phase
6-13 Liquid-phase sintering
6-14 Silicates
6-15 Clay
6-16 Si_3N_4
6-17 α- Si_3N_4
6-18 β- Si_3N_4
6-19 Hot pressing
6-20 Ceramic bearings
13'24"

PRECIPITATION HARDENING 36.5'

1-1 Bike rims
1-2 Wilm experiment
1-3 Al-Cu system
1-4 Pptn hardening
1-5 Particle effects
1-6 Al-Li alloy TEM
1-7 Dark vs. bright field
1-8 Orowan mechanism
1-9 Multiple loops
1-10 Particle spacing
1-11 Heat treatment
1-12 Solution treatment
1-13 Homogeneous pptn
1-14 Particle strength
12'50"

2-1 Particle growth
2-2 Pptn thermodynamics
2-3 Driving force for pptn
2-4 ΔG of pptn
2-5 Critical radius
2-6 Particle stability
2-7 Derive r*
2-8 Undercooling effect
2-9 Hetergeneous nucleation
2-10 Grain boundary pptn
9'5"

3-1 Interfacial energy
3-2 Structural vs chemical components
3-3 Incoherent interface
3-4 Metastable ppts
3-5 GP zones
4'8"

4-1 Al-Ag system
4-2 Al-Cu GP zones
4-3 Al-Cu θ' and θ"
4-4 Semi-coherent interface
4-5 Al-Cu pptn sequence
4-6 Al-Cu hardness curves
4-7 Natural aging
6'33"

5-1 Al-alloy designations
5-2 Temper designations
5-3 Al-Mg-Si system
5-4 6061-T6 alloy
4'

BICYCLE CONSTRUCTION 33'

1-1 Materials vs. geometry
1-2 Important material properties
1-3 A typical bike frame
1-4 Pin-jointed model
1-5 Extra link needed
1-6 Forces in each link
1-7 Tension, compression, bending
1-8 Axial stresses
1-9 Bending in front section
1-10 Compressive forces
1-11 Bending forces
1-12 Free-body model
1-13 Bending-moment diagram
12'43"

2-1 Stresses in bent beam
2-2 Pure bending
2-3 Bending-moments
2-4 I-beams, tubes, etc.
2-5 Stress distribution
2-6 Bending moment vs. depth
2-7 Integrated bending moment
2-8 I, moment of inertia
2-9 Strain distribution
2-10 σ=My/I, σ_{max}=Mh/2I
2-11 I of rectangular beam
2-12 I of cylinder
2-13 I for tube
13'26"

3-1 I of front section
3-2 Stresses in front section
3-3 Stressed in impact
3-4 Bottom-bracket shell
3-5 Bending stress
3-6 Consequences of bending
5'40"

4-1 Frame materials
4-2 Joining of tubes
4-3 Tube design
4-4 Stiffness vs. diameter
4-5 Properties of frame alloys
4'

5-1 Brazing with Cu-40Zn
5-2 Low-carbon steel
5-3 Cr-Mo steel
5-4 Compare tube thickness
5-5 Lugs
5-6 Investment casting
5-7 Porosity in castings
5-8 Lug from sheet steel
5-9 TIG welding
5-10 Lack-of-penetration defect
5-11 Microstructure of Cr-Mo steel
5-12 Microstructure of HAZ
5-13 Butted tubing
10'40"

6-1 Aluminum-alloy tubes
6-2 Use of adhesive bonding
6-3 Advantages of Al alloys
6-4 HAZ in TIG-welded Al
6-5 Need for post-weld heat treat
6-6 Example of LOP defect
6-7 Advantages of Ti-alloy
6-8 Allotropic transformation in Ti
6-9 Furnace-cooled Ti-3Al-2.5V
6-10 α and β stabilizers
6-11 α/β microstructure
6-12 Cold-drawn Ti-3Al-2.5V
6-13 TIG welding Ti alloys
6-14 Weld-joint microstructure
6-15 Bonded multi-material frame
10'

POLYMERS 40.5'

1-1 Tires
1-2 Rubber
1-3 Elastomers
1-4 Polyethylene
1-5 Polymer melt
1-6 Paraffins
1-7 Plastic behavior
1-8 Glassy behavior
1-9 Thermoplastic
1-10 Injection molding
7'6"

2-1 PE polymerization initiation
2-2 Addition polymerization
2-3 Viscosity of a linear polymer
2-4 Molecular weight
2-5 Melting, freezing
2-6 Crystallization of PE
2-7 Spherulites
2-8 HDPE vs LDPE
2-9 Branching
2-10 Volume vs. temperature
2-11 Glass transition
2-12 PE behavior
2-13 PS behavior
2-14 PS glass transition
2-15 Viscous behavior
13'40"

3-1 Viscoelasticity
3-2 Voight model, creep
3-3 Maxwell model, stress relaxation
3-4 Strain rate effects
3-5 Viscoelastic modulus
3-6 VE modulus vs. temperature
3-7 PS as a vinyl polymer
3-8 Tacticity
3-9 Amorphous vs. crystalline PS
3-10 Cross links
3-11 Effect of cross links
3-12 Elastomeric behavior
3-13 Entropy vs. enthalpy
3-14 Elastomeric restoring force
12'18"

4-1 Conjugated dienes
4-2 Effects of double bonds
4-3 Cis vs. trans
4-4 Gutta percha
4-5 Vulcanization
4-6 Thermosets
4-7 Effect of ozone on rubber
4-8 Synthetic rubbers
4-9 Crystallization in rubber
4-10 Heat effects in rubber elasticity
7'30"

COMPOSITES 67'

1-1 Fiber reinforced composites
1-2 Single fiber
1-3 Bonded fibers
1-4 Fiber vs. matrix
1-5 Continuous fibers
1-6 Composite modulus
1-7 Longitudinal loading
1-8 Stress distribution
1-9 Rule of mixtures
1-10 Design of stiffness
1-11 Transverse loading
1-12 Strain distribution
1-13 Bounds of moduli
1-14 Wood, plywood
1-15 Crack arrest in matrix
1-16 Short fibers
1-17 Discontinuous fibers
1-18 Single-fiber model
1-19 Fiber loading
1-20 Stick model
1-21 Transfer length
16'

2-1 Natural fibers
2-2 Collagen
2-3 Cellulose acetate
2-4 Rayon
2-5 Nylon
2-6 Cold drawing
2-7 Hydrogen bonding
2-8 Kevlar I
2-9 Kevlar II
2-10 Graphitizing polymers
2-11 Graphite fibers
2-12 Graphite-fiber composites
2-13 Comparison of fibers
2-14 Spectra
11'

3-1 Silica-based glass
3-2 SiO_4^{4-} tetrahedron
3-3 Fused quartz
3-4 Network modifiers
3-5 Pyrex
3-6 Thermal shock
3-7 Glass fibers
3-8 Neck-less drawing
3-9 Freshly drawn fibers
3-10 Stress in bent fibers
3-11 Surface damage
3-12 Surface protection
3-13 Piano wire
3-14 Patenting
3-15 Steel tire cord
12'

4-1 Network polymers
4-2 Bakelite I
4-3 Bakelite II
4-4 Bakelite III
4-5 Hard rubber
4-6 Epoxy prepolymer
4-7 Curing of epoxy
4-8 Epoxy resins
4-9 Glassy behavior
7'

5-1 Adhesive joints
5-2 Adhesive bonding
5-3 Joint strength
5-4 Surface preparation I
5-5 Surface preparation II
5-6 Loading of joints
5-7 Pre-mixed epoxies
5-8 Curing reactions
4'

6-1 CFRP composites
6-2 CFRP bike frame
6-3 Bonded joint in frame
6-4 Al-Si casting I
6-5 Al-Si casting II
6-6 Al-Si casting III
6-7 SEM of epoxy adhesive
6-8 SEM operation
6-9 Depth of focus
6-10 Back-scattered image
6-11 X-ray analysis
6-12 X-ray map
6-13 Filler in epoxy
6-14 Porosity in epoxy
6-15 CFRP tube
6-16 Fiber lay-up
6-17 Tube design
6-18 Tube construction
6-19 Frame design
6-20 CFRP brittleness
6-21 Damage tolerance
6-22 Monocoque frames
6-23 Lotus pursuit bike
6-24 CFRP wheels
6-25 DuPont wheel
17'

TIRES 48'

1-1 Tires as composites
1-2 Functions of tires I
1-3 Functions of tires II
1-4 Treads
1-5 Belts, plies, beads, and sidewalls
1-6 Liner, apex, shoulder belt
5'

2-1 Tire-cord materials
2-2 Polyesters
2-3 PET
2-4 Cord yarn
2-5 Cord fabric
2-6 Calendering
2-7 Steel-wire cord
2-8 Brass plating of steel wire
4'

3-1 Polymers for tires
3-2 Bulk polymerization of dienes I
3-3 Bulk polymerization of dienes II
3-4 Emulsion polymerization I
3-5 Emulsion polymerization II
3-6 Emulsion polymerization III
3-7 Styrene butadiene rubber SBR
3-8 Role of styrene
3-9 SBR random copolymers
3-10 Reactivity ratios I
3-11 Reactivity ratios II
3-12 Conversion limit of SBR
3-13 Butyl rubber
3-14 Cationic polymerization I
3-15 Cationic polymerization II
11'

4-1 Modifiers
4-2 Polymer blends for tires
4-3 Isomers of polybutadiene
4-4 Importance of T_g
3'

5-1 Stabilizers
5-2 Importance of sulfur content
5-3 Antioxidents
5-4 Carbon black
5-5 Nanoscale dispersion of black
5-6 Structure of black
5-7 Furnace black
5-8 Bonding of rubber to black
5-9 Reinforcement by black
5-10 Strain softening
5-11 Tread-wear resistance
5-12 Silica filler
8'

6-1 Vulcanization of NR
6-2 Effects of vulcanization
6-3 Scorch time
6-4 Accelerated vulcanization I
6-5 Accelerated vulcanization II
6-6 Accelerator reaction
6-7 Delayed action
6-8 Cu-S bonding
6-9 Sulfur/accelerator ratio
7'

7-1 Mixing
7-2 Blending
7-3 Incorporation
7-4 Processing after mixing
7-5 Extrusion
7-6 Tire molding
5'

8-1 Block copolymers
8-2 Phase separation
8-3 Thermoplastic elastomers
8-4 Microstructures
8-5 Anionic polymerization
8-6 Living ends
8-7 PS-PB-PS triblock copolymers
5'

FLEXIBLE CONNECTIVE TISSUE 42'

1-1 Introduction
1-2 Knee joint
1-3 Synovial capsule
1-4 Synovial fluid
1-5 Articular cartilage
4'

2-1 Cartilage microstructure
2-2 Collagen/polypeptides
2-3 Amino acids
2-4 Polypeptide structure
2-5 Polypeptide chains
2-6 Amino acids in collagen
2-7 Type-II collagen
2-8 Staggered chains and cross links
2-9 Zones of cartilage
2-10 Deep zone
2-11 Ground substance
2-12 Role of proteoglycans
2-13 Recap of cartilage microstructure
2-14 Ion transport in cartilage
2-15 Viscoelasticity in cartilage
2-16 Health of cartilage
2-17 Stiffness variation
2-18 Lack of healing response
16'

3-1 The menisci
3-2 Microstructure of meniscus
3-3 Behavior of meniscus
3-4 Variation of properties
3-5 Poor healing response
4'

4-1 Quadriceps/patella tendon
4-2 Microstructure of tendon
4-3 Fibroblast
4-4 Mitochondria
4-5 Architecture of tendon
4-6 Sheathed tendon
4-7 Straight tendon
4-8 Tensile behavior
4-9 Variability of tendon
4-10 Viscoelastic behavior
4-11 Dependence on age
4-12 Types of injury
4-13 Rupture of tendon
4-14 Healing of tendon
4-15 Avascular tendons
10'

5-1 Ligaments in knee
5-2 Elastin
5-3 Fascicle configuration
5-4 Insertion into bone
5-5 Tensile behavior
5-6 Stress-strain curve
5-7 Viscoelastic behavior
5-8 Tensile properties
5-9 Effect of immobilization I
5-10 Effect of immobilization II
5-11 Injuries
5-12 Healing of MCL & LCL
5-13 Repair of ACL & PCL
8'

RIGID CONNECTIVE TISSUE: BONE 35'

1-1 Skeletal bone
1-2 Calcium storage
1-3 The diaphysis
1-4 The epiphysis
3'

2-1 Microstructure
2-2 Osteoblasts
2-3 Osteocytes
2-4 Calcification
4'

3-1 Cartilage model
3-2 Development I
3-3 Development II
3-4 Development III
3-5 Development IV
4'

4-1 Remodeling I
4-2 Remodeling II
4-3 Remodeling III
4-4 Calcium regulation
4-5 Radiography of osteons
4'

5-1 Bending moment of femur
5-2 Sagittal plane
5-3 Stress-strain curve
5-4 Viscoelastic behavior
5-5 Tensile modulus
5-6 Stronger in compression
5-7 Transverse loads
5-8 Creep of bone
5-9 Creep rupture
5-10 Cyclic loading
5-11 Wolff's Law
5-12 Bone-growth mechanisms
5-13 Coffin-Manson behavior
5-14 Fatigue in compression
5-15 Fatigue cracking
5-16 Spongy bone
5-17 Elastic modulus in compression
5-18 Failure of spongy bone
13'

6-1 Bone mass vs. age
6-2 Diaphysis of femur vs. age
6-3 UTS of compact bone
6-4 Degradation of spongy bone
3'

7-1 Fracture experiments
7-2 Growth of microcracks
7-3 Transverse crack deflection
7-4 Healing of fracture I
7-5 Healing of fracture II
4'

SKELETAL MUSCLE 43'

1-1 Mechanics
1-2 Architecture
1-3 Strength
2'

1-1 Muscle fibers
2-2 Sarcomeres
2-3 Fine structure
2-4 Thick and thin filaments
2-5 Myosin and actin
2-6 Recap microstructure
4'

3-1 Actin structure
3-2 Myosin structure
3-3 Myosin head
3-4 Sarcoplasmic reticulum
3-5 ATP
3-6 Cross-bridge cycle I
3-7 Cross-bridge cycle II
3-8 Cross-bridge cycle III
3-9 Molecular motor
7'

4-1 Fuel for contraction
4-2 Anaerobic metabolism
4-3 Aerobic metabolism
4-4 Metabolism of fat
4'

5-1 Motor neurons
5-2 Muscle twitch
5-3 Fast-twitch fibers
5-4 Red vs. white muscle
5-5 Schwann cells
5-6 Synapse
5'

6-1 Action potential
6-2 Ion channels
6-3 Two gradients
6-4 Na-K ion pump
6-5 Depolarization
6-6 Repolarization
6-7 Multiple nerve impulses
6-8 Action-potential transmission
6-9 Transmission at a synapse
6-10 Fused twitches
9'

7-1 Myotendonous junction
7-2 Stress-strain curve
7-3 Muscle-force curve
7-4 Torque on a joint
7-5 Strength training I
7-6 Strength training II
7-7 Endurance training
7-8 Oxidative metabolism
6'

8-1 Contusion
8-2 Heterotopic bone
8-3 Laceration
8-4 Muscle strain
8-5 Incomplete tears
8-6 Atrophy
8-7 Benefit of stretching
8-8 Muscle soreness
8-9 Cramping
6'

CONTENTS

1 CORRORSION AND CORROSION PROTECTION 1
1.1 Corrosion of Steels. 1
1.2 Corrosion Protection of Steel. 2
1.3 Constitution of Stainless Steel. 4
1.4 Case Study:the Bicycle Wheel. 7
Summary 9
Glossary/Vocabulary 9
Exercises 11

2 MECHANICAL BEHAVIOR 13
2.1 Types of Stress and Strain 13
2.2 Small-Scale *vs*. Large-Scale Deformation. 16
2.3 Measurement of Stress *vs*. Strain — The Tensile Test 18
2.4 Elastic Behavior. 20
2.5 Plastic Behavior. 23
2.6 Large-Scale Plastic Flow — The Stress-Strain Curve. 28
Summary 32
Appendix 2.1 The Load Cell. 33
Appendix 2.2 Criterion for Necking in a Tensile Test 33
Glossary/Vocabulary 34
Exercises 38

3 MICROSTRUCTURE AND CRYSTAL STRUCTURE. 40
3.1 Metallographic Sample Preparation. 40
3.2 Optical Microscopy 40
3.3 Imaging of Grain Boundaries by Reflection Contrast. 41
3.4 The Structure of a Perfect FCC Crystal. 43
3.5 Crystallographic Indices of Planes 44
3.6 Direction Indices 47
Summary 48
Appendix 4.1 The Scalar Product of Two Vectors 49
Glossary/Vocabulary 49
Exercises 51

4 SLIP, DISLOCATIONS, AND STRAIN HARDENING 52
4.1 Slip in FCC Crystals 53
4.2 Types of Dislocation 55
4.2.1 The Edge Dislocation 55
4.2.2 The Screw Dislocation 56
4.2.3 Mixed Dislocations 58
4.2.4 General Characteristics of Dislocations 61
4.3 Imaging of Dislocations 62
4.4 The Stress Field of a Dislocation 63
4.4.1 General Aspects of Stress Fields 63
4.4.2 The Stress Field of a Screw Dislocation 64
4.4.3 The Stress Field of an Edge Dislocation 66
4.4.4 Mixed Dislocations 67
4.4.5 Energy of a Dislocation 67
4.5 Mechanism of Strain Hardening 68
4.5.1 Plastic Strain and Dislocation Density 69
4.5.2 Yielding and Dislocation Multiplication 70
4.5.3 The Physical Basis of Strain Hardening 74
Summary 77
Appendix 4.1 Bragg's Law of Diffraction 78
Appendix 4.2 Stress Field of an Edge Dislocation 79
Glossary/Vocabulary 81
Exercises 85

5 ANNEALING OF COLD-WORKED METALS 87
5.1 Thermodynamic Principles 87
5.2 Stages of Annealing 90
5.3 Recrystallization 90
5.3.1 Mechanism of Recrystallization 90
5.3.2 Kinetics of Recrystallization 91
5.4 Recovery 94
5.5 Grain Growth 97
5.5.1 Mechanism of Grain Growth 97
5.5.2 Kinetics of Grain Growth 99
5.5.3 Softening During Grain Growth 102
5.6 Annealing of Carbon-Steel Spokes 103
5.6.1 The As-Received Condition 103
5.6.2 The Annealed Condition 104
5.6.3 The "Fully-Annealed" Condition 106
Summary 107
Appendix 5.1 Measurement of Hardness 108
Appendix 5.2 The Equilibrium Concentration of Lattice Vacancies 109
Glossary/Vocabulary 110
Exercises 115

6 CARBON STEEL: PLASTIC DEFORMATION AND FATIGUE RESISTANCE 116
6.1 Slip in BCC Iron 116
6.2 Interaction of Solute Atoms with Dislocations 117
6.3 Segregation of Solutes to Dislocations 119
6.3.1 Substitutional Diffusion 119
6.3.2 Interstitial Diffusion 120
6.4 The Nature of Metal Fatigue 122
6.5 The S-N Curve 124
6.5.1 Analysis of the Failure of a Stainless Steel Spoke 126
6.6 The Fatigue Limit of Carbon Steel 128
Summary 129
Appendix 6.1 Brittle Fracture in Carbon Steel 130
Appendix 6.2 Crystal Symmetry 132
Glossary/Vocabulary 134
Exercises 137

7 PHASE DIAGRAMS 138
7.1 Soldering and Brazing 138
7.2 Low-Melting Alloys for Soldering; Phase Diagrams 140
7.2.1 Lowering of the Melting Temperature; Salt-Water Mixtures 141
7.2.2 A Hypothetical Simple-Eutectic Phase Diagram 142
7.2.3 The Lead-Tin System (Soft Solder) 147
7.2.4 Microstructures of Hypoeutectic Lead-Tin Alloys 153
7.2.5 The Microstructure of a Hypereutectic Pb-Sn Alloy . . . 157
7.3 The Phase Rule 158
7.4 Brazing Alloys 159
Summary 163
Appendix 7.1 The Allotropic Transformation of Tin 163
Appendix 7.2 The Phase Rule 164
Glossary/Vocabulary 166
Exercises 170

8 PHASE TRANSFORMATIONS IN CARBON STEEL 172
8.1 The Iron-Carbon Phase Diagram 173
8.2 Eutectoid Decomposition 175
8.2.1 Isothermal Transformation 175
8.2.2 Transformation during Cooling 179
8.3 Transformations in a Hypoeutectoid Steel Spoke 181
8.3.1 The "Equilibrium" Condition 181
8.3.2 Isothermal Transformation 181
8.3.3 Transformations during Cooling of a 1040 Steel Spoke 183
8.3.4 Processing of Spokes 184
8.4 The Martensite Transformation 185
8.4.1 Hardening of Steel 185
Summary 190
Glossary/Vocabulary 191

Exercises . . . 194

9 FRICTION AND WEAR; HARD MATERIALS . . . 196
9.1 Friction . . . 196
9.2 Wear . . . 198
9.3 Lubrication . . . 199
9.4 The Use of Hardened-Steel Components . . . 200
9.4.1 The Hardness of Martensite . . . 201
9.4.2 Hardenability of Steel . . . 202
9.4.3 Tempering of Steel . . . 203
9.4.4 Heat Treatment of Steels . . . 205
9.4.5 Surface Hardening . . . 207
9.5 Cracks in Solids . . . 211
9.6 The Use of Ceramics for Bearings . . . 213
9.6.1 Crystal Structures . . . 214
9.6.2 Dislocation Motion and Ductility . . . 215
9.6.3 Forming of Ceramics, Sintering . . . 216
9.6.4 Silicon Nitride Bearings . . . 219
Summary . . . 223
Appendix 9.1 Twinning in Crystals . . . 223
Appendix 9.2 Linear-Elastic Fracture Mechanics . . . 225
Glossary/Vocabulary . . . 228
Exercises . . . 234

10 PRECIPITATION HARDENING . . . 236
10.1 Mechanism of Precipitation Hardening . . . 237
10.2 Requirements for Precipitation Hardening . . . 239
10.3 Principles of Precipitation . . . 240
10.4 Factors that Control γ . . . 242
10.5 Stages of Precipitation Hardening . . . 246
10.6 Fabrication of Wheel Rims . . . 247
Summary . . . 250
Appendix 10.1 Strengthening Effects of Precipitate Particles . . . 250
Glossary/Vocabulary . . . 252
Exercises . . . 255

11 THE BICYCLE FRAME . . . 256
11.1. Alloys for Bicycle Frames; General Considerations . . . 256

11.2 Comparisons of Steel, Aluminum-Alloy, and Titanium-Alloy Frames . . . 260
11.2.1 Road Bikes. . . 260
11.2.2 Mountain Bikes . . . 260
11.3 Steel Frames. . . 261
11.3.1 Effects of Brazing on Steel Tubing. . . 261
11.3.2 Lugs; the Fabrication of Complex Shapes . . . 264
11.3.3 Fabrication of Steel Frames by Welding. . . 266
11.3.4 Butted Tubing . . . 269
11.4 Joining of Light-Metal Frames . . . 269
11.4.1 Al-Alloy Frames . . . 269
11.4.2 Titanium Alloy Frames . . . 272
11.4.3 Hybrid Frames. . . 276
Summary. . . 276
Appendix 11.1 The Ideal Case: Pure Bending. . . 277
Appendix 11.2 Bending *vs.* Axial Loading . . . 282
Appendix 11.3 Buckling of a Thin Strut under Axial Compression. . . 283
Glossary/Vocabulary. . . 285
Exercises. . . 288
12 POLYMERIC MATERIALS . . . 289
12.1 Characteristics of Polymers . . . 289
12.2 Polyethylene. . . 293
12.2.1 Molecular Structure. . . 293
12.2.2 Crystallization . . . 294
12.2.3 The Glass Transition . . . 296
12.3 Viscoelasticity . . . 297
12.4 Rubber . . . 301
Summary. . . 305
Appendix 12.1 Secondary Bonds. . . 306
Appendix 12.2 Architecture of Some Simple Polymers 308
Glossary/Vocabulary. . . 309
Exercises. . . 314
13 COMPOSITE MATERIALS; RIGID MATRIX . . . 315
13.1 Principles of Fiber Reinforcement. . . 316
13.1.1 Longitudinally Stressed Fibers in a Continuous-Fiber Composite . . . 317
13.1.2 Transversely Stressed Fibers. . . 318
13.1.3 Discontinuous Fibers. . . 321
13.1.4 Composite Behavior . . . 321
13.2 Fibers For Reinforcement . . . 322
13.2.1 Organically Based Fibers . . . 322
13.2.2 Inorganically Based Fibers . . . 327
13.3 Network Polymers for Composites and Adhesives. . . 330
13.3.1 Formation of Network Polymers. . . 330
13.3.2 Adhesive Bonding. . . 332

13.4 Carbon-Fiber Reinforced Composite Frames 333
13.4.1 Case Study of a Hybrid Composite Frame 333
13.4.2 Monocoque Frames 338
13.4.3 Composite Wheels 340
Summary 342
Glossary/Vocabulary 343
Exercises 347

14 COMPLEX MULTISCALE COMPOSITES: TIRES 349
14.1 Tire Construction 350
14.2 Reinforcement Materials 351
14.3 Tire Cord 353
14.3.1 Textile-Fiber Cord 353
14.3.2 Steel-Wire Cord 354
14.4 The Rubber Matrix 354
14.4.1 Polymerization of Dienes 354
14.4.2 Emulsion Polymerization 355
14.4.3 Anionic Polymerization 357
14.4.4 Styrene Butadiene Rubber 357
14.4.5 Butyl Rubber 359
14.5 Rubber Compounding 360
14.6 Reinforcement of Rubber by Nanoscale Particles 361
14.6.1 Carbon Black 361
14.6.2 Silica and Silicates 363
14.7 Vulcanization 364
14.8 Rubber Processing 366
14.8.1 Mixing 366
14.8.2 Extrusion 367
14.8.3 Calendering 367
14.9 Tire Molding 368
14.10 Failure of Tires in Service 368
14.11 Triblock Copolymers by Anionic Polymerizatin 369
Summary 371
Glossary/Vocabulary 372
Exercises 374

15 FLEXIBLE CONNECTIVE TISSUE 375
15.1 Cartilage 376
15.1.1 Microstructure of Articular Cartilage 375
15.1.2 Collagen 377
15.1.3 Zones of Articular Cartilage 380
15.1.4 Ground Substance 381
15.1.5 Mechanical Behavior of Cartilage 382
15.1.6 Injury in Cartilage 383
15.2 The Meniscus 384
15.2.1 Microstructure of the Meniscus 384
15.2.2 Mechanical Behavior of the Meniscus 385
15.2.3 Injury to the Meniscus 385

15.3 Tendon 385
15.3.1 Microstructure of Tendon 386
15.3.2 Mechanical Behavior of Tendon 387
15.3.3 Injury, Healing, and Repair of Tendon 389
15.4 Ligament 390
15.4.1 Microstructure of Ligament 390
15.4.2 Mechanical Behavior of Ligament 391
15.4.3 Injury and Healing of Ligament 393
Summary 394
Glossary/Vocabulary 395
Exercise 399

16 RIGID CONNECTIVE TISSUE: BONE 400
16.1 Microstructure of Mature Compact Bone 401
16.1.1 Growth of Bone at the Cellular Level 402
16.2 Formation of Long Bones during Development 403
16.3 Remodeling of Bone 404
16.4 Mechanical Behavior of Bone 407
16.5 Effects of Aging 412
16.6 Fracture and Repair 414
Summary 416
Glossary/Vocabulary 417
Exercises 419

17 SKELETAL MUSCLE 421
17.1 Muscles and Muscle Fibers 421
17.2 Microstructure of Muscle 422
17.2.1 Muscle Fibers 422
17.2.2 Sarcomeres 424
17.3 Contraction of a Muscle Fiber 426
17.4 Energetics of Muscle Contraction 427
17.5 The Stimulus for Muscle Contraction 429
17.5.1 Motor Neurons 429
17.5.2. The Membrane Potentia 431
17.5.3 The Action Potential 433
17.5.4 Synaptic Transmission 435
17.6 Mechanical Behavior of Muscle 436
17.7 Training Effects 438
17.8 Injury and Healing of Muscle 439
Summary 441
Glossary/Vocabulary442
Exercises 446

Appendix 1 Conversion of Units 447

Appendix 2 Physical Constants 448

Appendix 3 SI Prefixes 448

Appendix 4 Physical Properties of Common Metals 449
Appendix 5 Elastic Constants of Common Metals 449
Appendix 6 Ionic Radii (Å) 450
Appendix 7 Specific Modulus Values 451
Appendix 8 Properties of Some Engineering Materials 452
Glossary Locator. 453
Index 458
Periodic Table of the Elements 470

1

CORROSION AND CORROSION PROTECTION

We begin our study of engineering materials with the subject of corrosion and how we can protect against it. Corrosion is one of the principal ways in which metallic materials fail, and it is one of the best understood. Moreover, it is commonly treated in introductory courses in chemistry, so we can start here by building on the experience of most students. In addition, an understanding of the elements of corrosion at this level is of immediate applicability to some problems of everyday life. We use the bicycle wheel to illustrate one such application.

1.1 Corrosion of Steels

Corrosion involves the ionization of metal atoms and the loss of these ions into solution or into a corrosion product. Since the ionization reaction means giving up electrons, a flow of electrons away from the site of this reaction must occur to avoid a build-up of negative charge. Thus, corrosion is an electrochemical reaction.

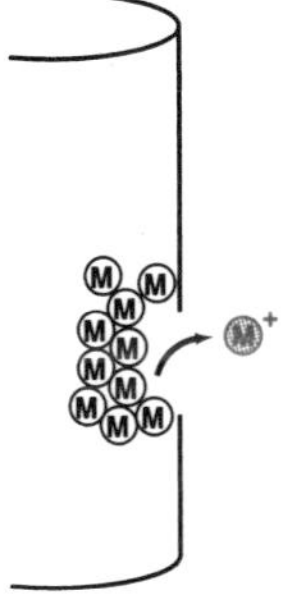

The site where the loss of metal occurs is called the anode, or anodic region, and the electrons flow through the metal to a site, called a cathode, where they are consumed in a cathodic reaction. In the case of iron, the anodic reaction is usually

$$Fe \longrightarrow Fe^{++} + 2e^-$$

and the cathodic reaction, in the presence of water and sufficient oxygen, is usually

$$H_2O + 1/2\ O_2 + 2e^- \longrightarrow 2\ OH^-$$

The corrosion product, rust, forms from

$$Fe^{++} + 2\ OH^- \longrightarrow Fe(OH)_2$$

The actual electrochemical mechanism can be appreciated if one considers how a rust pit forms. A pit begins at some inhomogeneity on the surface, such as an impurity particle, and the above reactions occur. The pit-type geometry forms because the anodic reaction continues to occur underneath the rust cover, as shown in Fig. 1.1.

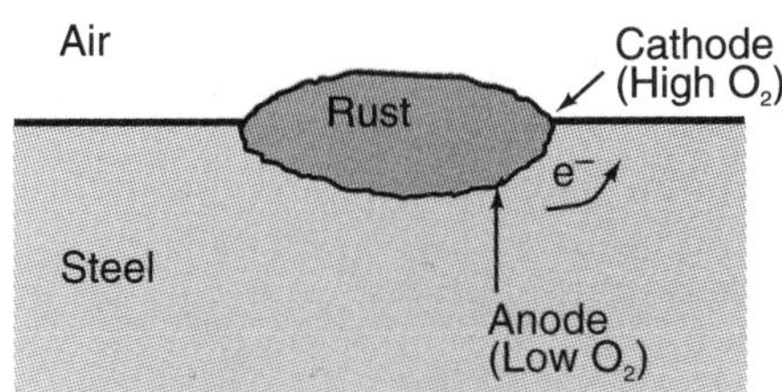

Fig. 1.1 Corrosion occurs under the rust, where the oxygen content is lower. The result is the formation of a pit.

It is useful to consider the formation of a rust pit in some detail, because it helps one understand the electrochemical nature of corrosion more clearly. The important questions are: where is the anode and where is the cathode? Since the cathodic reaction employs water and oxygen to use up electrons, it must occur where the water and oxygen are available. This locates the cathode at the surface of the steel at the periphery of the rust. The anode is then at a location where water and oxygen are less concentrated, which is underneath the rust. Thus, iron is ionized under the rust, and the electrons flow to the surface alongside the rust, to be consumed in the cathodic reaction. Hence, material loss proceeds underneath the rust, and the result is a pit.

1.2 Corrosion Protection of Steel

Carbon steel can be protected from corrosion by coating it with a more reactive "sacrificial" metal. If the coating is zinc, the product is referred to as *galvanized* steel; it can be made, for example, by dipping the steel into a bath of molten

zinc. A sacrificial metal is one that undergoes the anodic reaction in preference to another, more "noble" metal. That is, the sacrificial metal has a greater tendency to lose electrons. This tendency can most usefully be expressed in what is called a "Galvanic series." Table 1.1 gives such a series for some metals and alloys in sea water. This table gives only relative positions, rather than quantitative differences, because it is not based upon a standardized testing condition.

Table 1.1 Galvanic Series in Sea Water

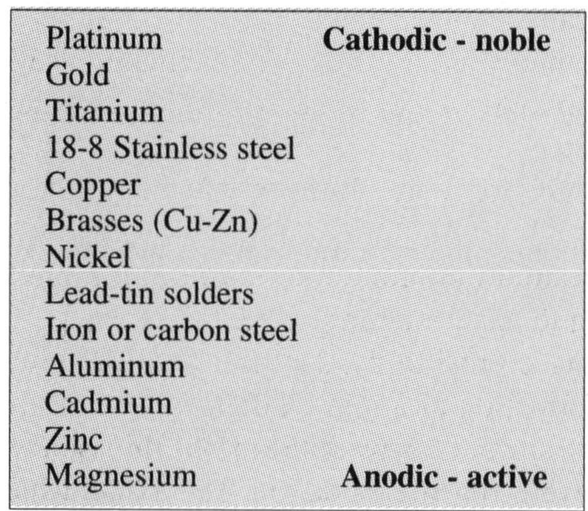

Platinum	**Cathodic - noble**
Gold	
Titanium	
18-8 Stainless steel	
Copper	
Brasses (Cu-Zn)	
Nickel	
Lead-tin solders	
Iron or carbon steel	
Aluminum	
Cadmium	
Zinc	
Magnesium	**Anodic - active**

The meaning of Table 1.1 is that zinc or cadmium, being more active than iron or carbon steel in this series, will, if electrically connected to iron, act as the

anode, and the electrons released will then flow to the iron, which will be forced to serve as the cathode, as shown in Fig. 1.2. The cathode does not dissolve, so the iron remains intact as long as any of the more active metal remains close by.

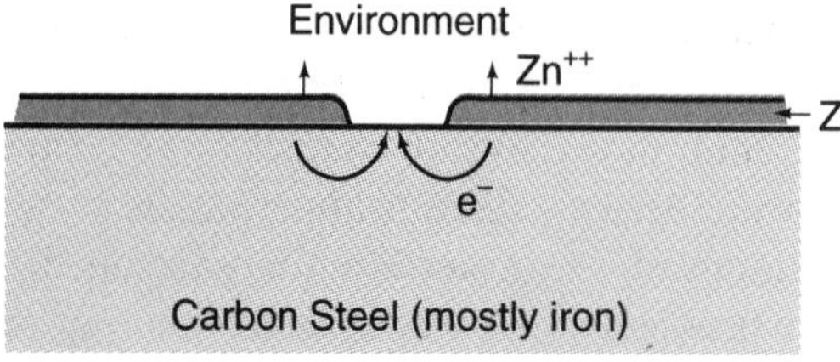

Fig 1.2 The release of electrons by the more active zinc layer causes the iron to be cathodic.

One might think to protect the carbon steel by chromium plating, which gives a brighter surface than does zinc. However, the chromium plating is not sacrificial. Chromium plating is actually mostly nickel (plated over a thin layer of copper, used to make a better bond with the steel), as shown in Fig. 1.3. The relatively thick nickel layer is then covered by a very thin layer of chromium to keep the surface bright.

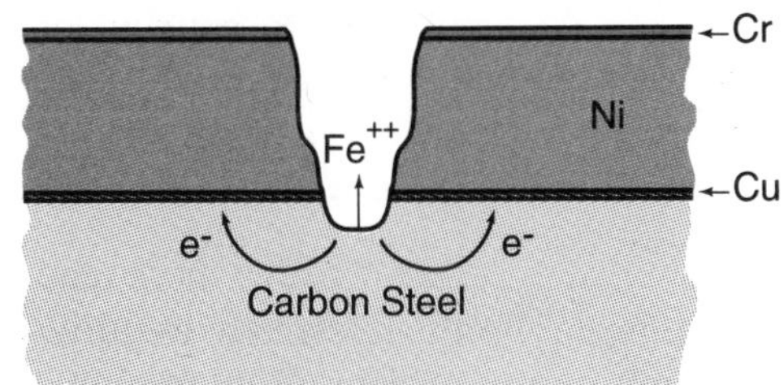

Fig. 1.3 If the coating on a chromium-plated steel is breached, the exposed carbon steel can become a very active anode, and a pit can form.

If this coating is breached locally (e.g., by mechanical damage), the iron is exposed in a small area that is surrounded mainly by nickel. Since nickel is noble with respect to iron (Table 1.1), it acts as a cathode and the iron as an anode; therefore, a rust pit forms. It tends to form quickly, since the cathode:anode area ratio is large; this gives a high *current density* at the anode.

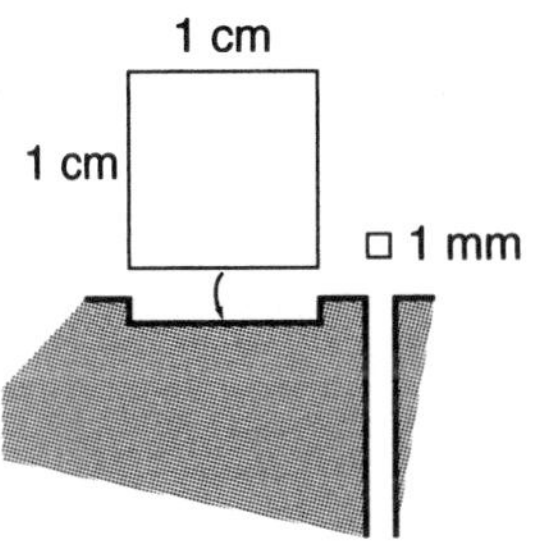

The electrons that leave the anode area represent the corrosion current. In the case where iron atoms become ferrous ions, two electrons leave for every ion created. One could calculate the weight loss by measuring the corrosion current and knowing the atomic weight of iron. For example, a current of about $3x10^{15}$ electrons would remove one atom layer from an anode area of $1cm^2$. However, if the anode area were confined to $1mm^2$, the same current would make a pit 100 atom layers deep. Thus, for a given area of cathode, the smaller the anode area is, the deeper the pit.

A rust pit is undesirable for cosmetic reasons, but it can also serve as a stress concentrator, leading to early fatigue failure, for example.

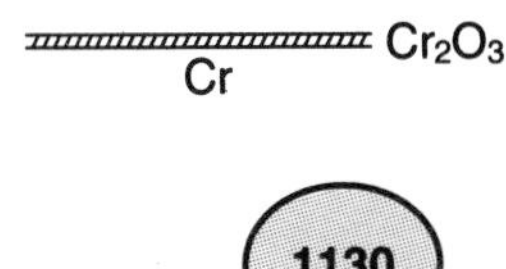

Chromium resists corrosion by a process called *passivation.* Passivation involves the rapid formation of a thin oxide layer by the chemical combination of oxygen atoms with surface atoms of the metal; this isolates the metal from the environment and prevents further oxidation. The oxide, which is so thin that it is transparent, must be highly stable, well-bonded to the metal, and free of pores and other defects. Once formed, it must have an extremely slow rate of thickening. With chromium, the protecting oxide is Cr_2O_3.

Passivation is also responsible for the corrosion resistance of metals like aluminum and titanium, which also form very stable oxides. That is, the driving force to form the oxide is large. Once formed, the oxide is very difficult to reduce. (That is why these metals are relatively expensive to produce; it requires large amounts of energy to reduce the oxide ores to produce the free metal.)

A solid piece of chromium would retain its passivated character even if the surface oxide were scratched away. This is because there is always more of the chromium below to form oxide and re-establish the protection. Only factors that inhibit the oxide formation would cause problems. Chloride ions act this way, so

$FeCr_2O_4$
Fe, Cr Alloy

salt water environments are dangerous to metals protected by passivating oxides.

Stainless steel works on the same principle as a piece of solid chromium. There are enough chromium atoms dispersed in the crystal lattice of stainless steel to provide an oxide sufficiently rich in chromium to passivate the surface.

In contrast to stainless steel, the problem with so-called chromium plating is that, once the underlying carbon steel is exposed, a protective oxide does not re-form over it; therefore, any defect in the plating will ultimately lead to a tiny rust pit. (The rust can be cleaned off by abrasion, but the reaction will continue, and more rust will eventually erupt from the pit. The process can be retarded somewhat by applying a coating, such as a wax, which tends to seal off the pits.) Clearly, stainless steel is far superior to chromium-plated carbon steel.

1.3 Constitution of Stainless Steel

In stainless steel, which is usually more than 70% iron, the chromium exists in *solid solution* in the iron, meaning that the chromium atoms simply substitute for iron atoms in the crystal structure, as indicated in Fig. 1.4. This is called a

substitutional solid solution. The solid solubility can be large when the solute atom is nearly the same size as the host atom and not too different chemically. Another kind of solid solution occurs with solute atoms that are very much smaller than the host atom and are thus able to fit into the interstices between the

1160 host atoms in its crystal (cf. Fig. 1.4). This is called an *interstitial* solid solution. The classical example is carbon in iron, which will be discussed in great detail later.

A solid solution is an example of a solid *phase*. A phase can be defined as a homogeneous body of matter having a distinct structure (i.e., atomic arrangement) and that can, at least in principle, be mechanically separated from a surrounding phase (or phases).

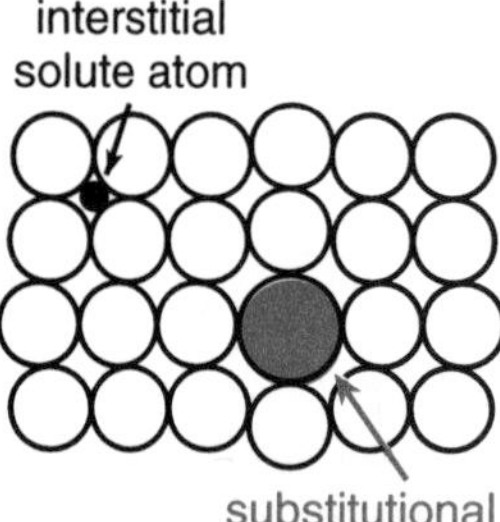

Fig. 1.4 Stainless steel is a solid solution, having both substitutional solutes (Cr and Ni) and interstitial solutes (C and N). The latter are usually treated as impurities in stainless steels.

Example 1.1:

Q. How many phases are present in a glass of ice water?

A. Three: liquid, solid, and vapor.

Q. Is the number of phases changed if something is dissolved in the water?

A. No, but the water becomes a liquid solution, and the ice would become a solid solution, if the substance dissolves in it.

It has been found empirically that at least 12 wt% chromium in solid solution is necessary to make stainless steel. However, it turns out that an Fe-12 % Cr alloy tends to have low *ductility* and *toughness,* so it would not be easy to make a wire spoke out of it. Ductility refers to the ability of a piece of metal to be stretched (permanently) by plastic deformation. (It is related to malleability, the ability to be processed (by rolling) into thin sheets.) Toughness refers to the resistance of a material to the propagation of a crack; it is the opposite of brittleness.

The low ductility and toughness of Fe-Cr alloys at ordinary temperatures is related to their crystal structure, which is the same as in pure iron: *body-centered cubic,* or BCC, as shown in Fig. 1.5. To get around the low-ductility problem, it
was found possible to change the crystal structure of an Fe-Cr alloy by adding a 1200
sufficient amount of nickel. Alloys will be discussed later, but that is why the nickel is present; it does not play an important role in the corrosion protection.

The most common stainless steel is the "18-8" austenitic stainless steel, meaning it contains 18 wt% chromium and 8 wt% nickel and has the *face-centered cubic,* or FCC, crystal structure of the phase called *austenite,* named in honor of W. C. Roberts-Austen, an early pioneer in the study of steels. It is illustrated in Fig. 1.6. One attractive feature of this crystal structure is that it is almost always ductile and can be readily cold-drawn into wire, ideal for making bicycle spokes, for example.

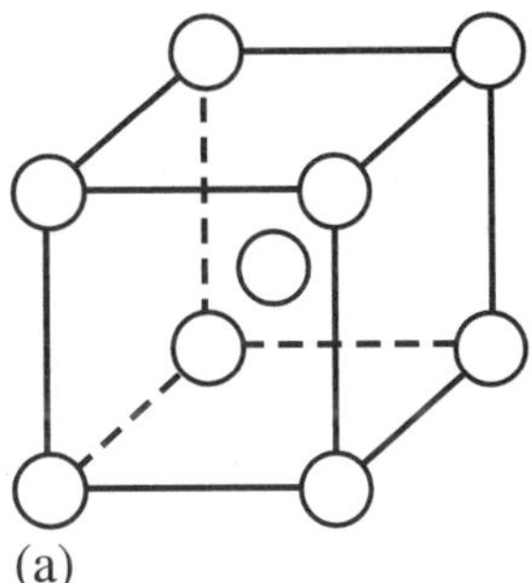
(a)

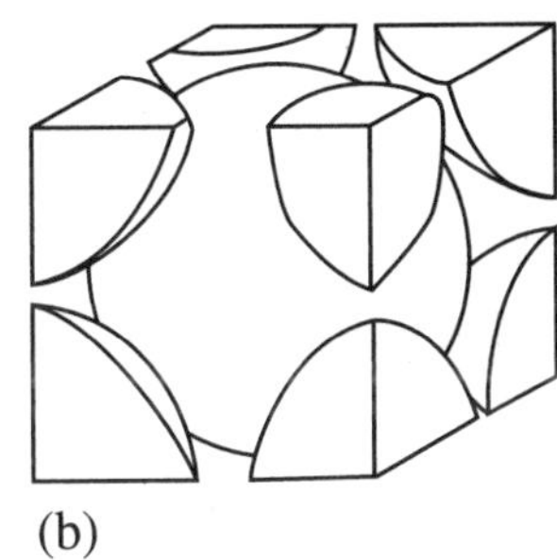
(b)

Fig. 1.5. The BCC unit cell, expressed as (a) a ball-and-stick model, showing the locations of the atom centers, and (b) a hard-sphere model, showing that atoms touch along the diagonals of the cubic unit cell (i.e., the body diagonals).

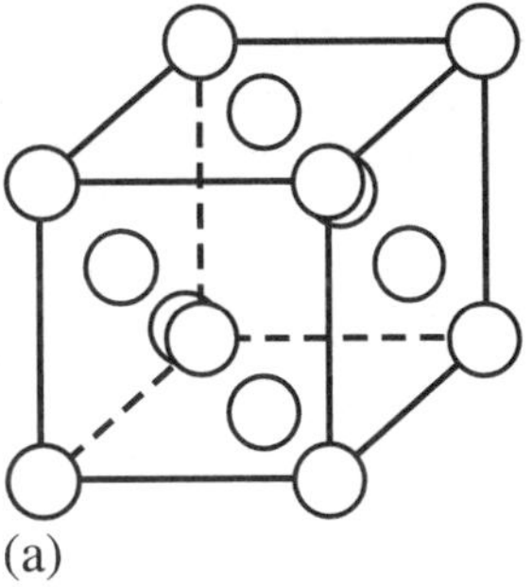
(a)

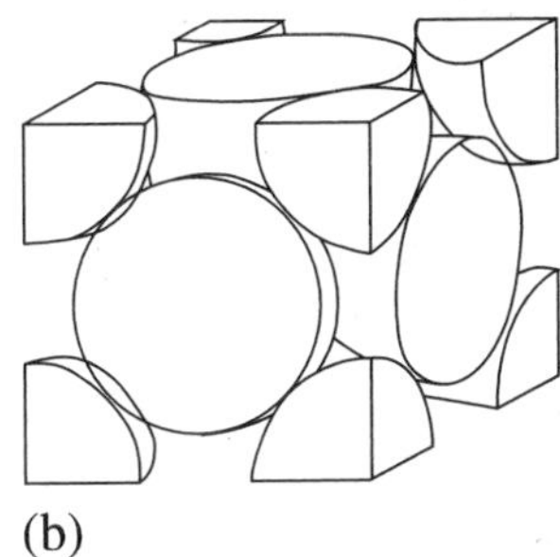
(b)

Fig. 1.6 The FCC unit cell. The atoms touch along each of the face diagonals.

Example 1.2:

Q. In a cubic crystal (e.g., BCC or FCC) the lattice parameter a is the length of an edge of the unit cell. Calculate the length of the diagonal of a face and of the cube (the body diagonal).

A. Face diagonal: $\sqrt{a^2 + a^2} = a\sqrt{2}$

Body diagonal: $\sqrt{a^2 + a^2 + a^2} = a\sqrt{3}$

Example 1.3

Q. Calculate the packing density of a BCC crystal; i.e., the percentage of the unit cell occupied by atoms, assuming the hard-sphere model.

A. In a BCC unit cell the atoms touch along the body diagonal. Let the atomic radius be r. Then $4r = \sqrt{3}a$, and the volume of the unit cell is

$$a^3 = \frac{64r^3}{3\sqrt{3}}$$

There are two atoms per unit cell:

1/8 per corner x 8 corners = 1, plus the center atom = 2

Therefore, the total volume of atoms is $2 \times 4/3\ \pi\ r^3$, and

$$\text{the packing density} = \frac{\text{volume of atoms}}{\text{volume of unit cell}} = \frac{8/3\ \pi\ r^3}{64/3\sqrt{3}r^3} = 0.68$$

Thus, 68% of the BCC unit cell is occupied by solid matter, according to the hard-sphere model.

Example 1.4

Q. In an 18-8 stainless steel, what is the atomic % chromium?

A. 18-8 stainless steel contains 18 wt% chromium and 8 wt% nickel.

Approximate atomic weights (from the Periodic Table, inside back cover):

Fe 56

Cr 52

Ni 59

Consider 100g of the stainless steel; it has 18g Cr, 8g Ni, and 74g Fe.

$$\text{Approximate atomic \% Cr} = \frac{18/52}{74/56 + 18/52 + 8/59} = 19$$

1.4 Case Study: The Bicycle Wheel

The modern bicycle wheel functions in a fundamentally different way from the traditional wagon wheel. As depicted in Fig. 1.7(a), the load on a wagon wheel is supported by the compression of the bottom spoke, with the rim transmitting lesser compressive loads to the adjacent spokes. The spokes in the upper part of the wheel carry none of the load. The spokes must be thick enough to resist failure by buckling, which occurs when the compressive load on a thin rod, or column, reaches a critical value such that even a slight deviation from pure axial alignment of the load causes instability and collapse of the column.

In comparing the bicycle wheel to the wagon wheel, an illustrative analogy would be that the former is to the latter as a suspension bridge is to a cathedral. The wagon wheel and the cathedral are both restricted to compressive loading of their components, whereas the suspension bridge and the bicycle wheel both employ stretched wires to support their loads. The analogy is imperfect, however, in that the loaded hub of the bicycle wheel is not simply suspended from the upper spokes, like a roadway is hung from its suspension cables. Rather, the spokes in a bicycle wheel are pre-tensioned during construction of the wheel, like the strings on a guitar.

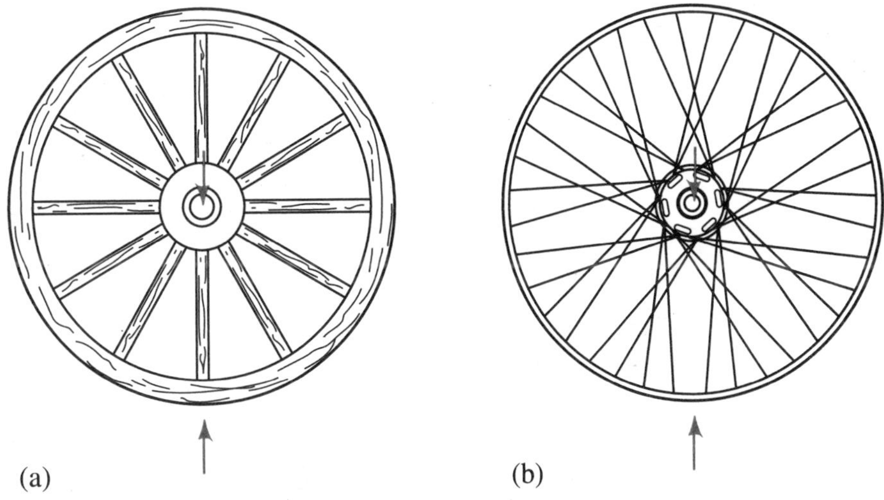

Fig. 1.7 (a) A wagon wheel, showing that the load is carried by the compression of the bottom spoke. (b) A modern bicycle wheel. (From J. Brandt, *The Bicycle Wheel,* Avocet, Menlo Park, CA, 1981, pp. 11 and 12.)

Figure 1.8 illustrates the geometry of a conventional spoke and a nipple and the method of their attachment to the hub and rim of a wheel. The tensioning of each spoke is carried out by turning the nipple with a spoke wrench. When a wheel is properly tensioned, the rim is loaded in uniform circumferential compression, such that it is not distorted out of its plane. In this case the wheel is said to be "true."

In contrast to the wagon wheel, when a bicycle wheel is loaded, the tension in the bottom few spokes is decreased significantly, and the tension in all the rest of the spokes is increased by a small amount. The important point is that all the spokes remain stressed in tension; no spoke is ever in compression. In fact, it is physically impossible for a spoke to be loaded in compression, due to the method of attachment to the rim (cf. Fig. 1.8). This is essential, of course, because the spokes are thin wires, and the critical load for buckling would be very small.

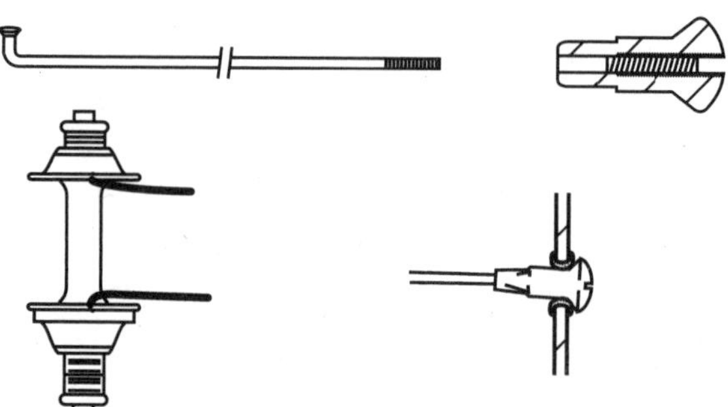

Fig. 1.8 Schematic illustration of a spoke and a nipple and of the method of their attachment to the hub and rim of a wheel. (Adapted from J. Brandt, loc. cit.)

The tensile stress in each spoke is considerable. A typical tensioning load is 90 kg, and a typical spoke diameter is 1.6 mm. This gives a tensile stress of about 440 MPa, which is around one-half the value needed for permanent deformation (i.e., the elastic limit). (The primary strengthening mechanism for spokes is the subject of Chapter 4.)

It must also be recognized that the stress on a given spoke in a rotating wheel varies with time and also varies with the actions of the rider and the conditions of the road surface. For example, if the rider is coasting (i.e., not pedaling) on a smooth surface, a given spoke would be partially unloaded every time this spoke became the bottom spoke. The effect of a pot-hole in the road would be to accentuate this unloading. This cyclic behavior is illustrated schematically in Fig. 1.9. Cyclic loading can lead to failure by fatigue.

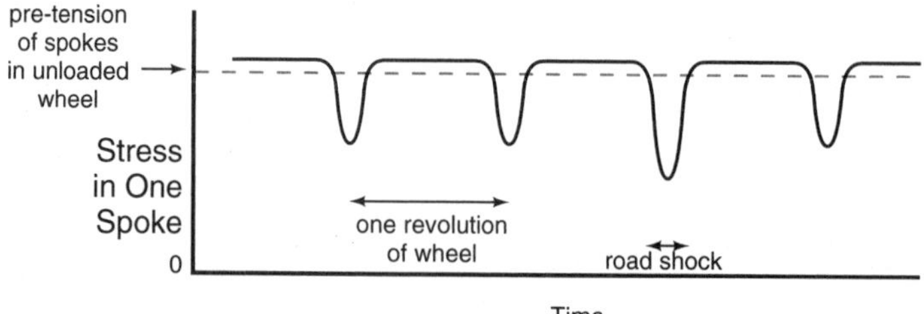

Fig. 1.9 Schematic illustration of the variation of the stress on a particular spoke with time as a wheel rotates, including the effect of a pot-hole in the road surface. (After C.J. Burgoyne and R. Dilmaghanian, J. Eng. Mech., ASCE, Vol. 119, March 1993, p. 439.)

Fatigue is a process of gradual fracture of a component subjected to a cyclic, or repeated, load. In this process a fine crack nucleates at the surface (usually) and grows to a size that produces sudden failure. (This is what happens when one breaks a short piece of wire from a longer piece by repeated bending back and forth.) The mechanism of fatigue failure and how it can be resisted are dealt with in Chapter 6. Obviously, as a bicycle wheel turns, the spokes go through cycles of greater and lesser tension (cf. Fig. 1.9); hence, they are subject to fatigue failure. Such a failure in the front wheel can cause the rider to be pitched over the handlebars, if the broken spoke falls across the front fork and causes the wheel to jam.

The choice of carbon *vs.* stainless steel spokes hinges on which factor is considered more important: resistance to corrosion or resistance to fatigue failure. The available means of corrosion protection for carbon steel are only transitory, as we have seen. However, carbon steel has an advantage over stainless steel in that it is more resistant to the other common mode of spoke failure, fatigue.

Cyclists who ride thousands of miles per year are more concerned about fatigue failure than about corrosion, so they sometimes choose carbon steel spokes. They re-lace their wheels with new spokes so frequently that there is not enough time for significant corrosion to develop in the carbon steel spokes (which are temporarily protected by coatings of cadmium or zinc).

Summary

Corrosion involves loss of metal atoms at an anode and consumption of the resulting electrons at a cathode. Carbon-steel spokes are temporarily protected from corrosion by coatings of cadmium or zinc, which act as sacrificial anodes. Stainless steel spokes are self-protecting by the formation of a passive surface layer comprising a very thin mixed-Fe-Cr oxide. This requires the presence of chromium atoms in solid solution in the iron; a minimum of 12wt% chromium in solid solution is required for this protection; bicycle spokes normally contain about 18wt%. About 8wt% nickel is also added (making "18-8" stainless steel, which is the most common variety) for the purpose of converting the crystal structure from BCC to FCC. The latter is much more amenable to mechanical processing by wire drawing. The permanent corrosion resistance of the stainless steel makes it preferable to the more fatigue-resistant carbon steel for most riders.

Glossary/Vocabulary - Chapter 1

Anodic reaction — In corrosion, the reaction at the anode involves the conversion of metal atoms to ions, with the concomitant release of electrons. Examples: $Fe \dashrightarrow Fe^{++} + 2e^-$ and $Zn \dashrightarrow Zn^{++} + 2e^-$

Body-centered cubic, BCC — This is a crystal structure with a cubic unit cell and with a lattice site on each corner and one in the center of the cube. Iron is BCC at temperatures up to 910°C. Chromium and molybdenum are BCC at all temperatures up to the melting point.

Cathodic reaction — In corrosion, the reaction at the cathode is one in which electrons are consumed. Example: $H_2O + 1/2\ O_2 + 2e^- \dashrightarrow 2OH^-$

Coordination number — This is the number of atoms that surround a given atom in a crystal, or the average number in a disordered solid or a liquid. The coordination number in a BCC crystal is eight. In an FCC or HCP crystal it is twelve.

Cyclic loading — The repeated loading of a specimen or component is called cyclic loading. Bicycle spokes are cyclically loaded, going from high tension to lower tension once for each revolution of the wheel.

Face-centered cubic, FCC	This is a crystal structure with a lattice site at each corner of the cubic unit cell and one in the center of each face. Iron is FCC at temperatures between 910 and 1394°C. Aluminum, gold, silver, nickel, and copper are all FCC.
Galvanic series	A listing of metals and alloys in order of their tendency to be active (anodic) vs. noble (cathodic) in a particular environment, such as sea water. Zinc and cadmium are active with respect to iron in the galvanic series in sea water.
Hard-sphere model	A model of a structure, like a crystal structure, in which atoms are depicted as hard spheres, as opposed to a ball-and-stick model. The hard-sphere model is appropriate for ionic crystals and for metallic crystals in which directional bonding is negligible. The ball and stick model is more appropriate for covalently bonded crystals or molecules. Hard-sphere models are normally used for FCC, BCC, and HCP crystals.
Noble *vs.* active	A noble metal is one from which it is difficult to remove electrons. Thus, a noble metal resists the anodic reaction. The opposite is an active metal. Metals at the top of the Galvanic series, like gold and platinum, are noble.
Packing density	The fraction of the volume of a unit cell that is occupied by atoms (assuming a hard-sphere model) is called the packing density. The packing density of a BCC unit cell is 0.68.
Passivated surface	The formation of a continuous (i.e., complete) surface layer of oxide, which isolates a metal from an aggressive environment and is self-healing when disrupted, is said to passivate the surface. That is, it converts an initially active metal into a passive state. The oxide layer must remain very thin; i.e., the kinetics of thickening must be very slow. Aluminum is passivated by formation of Al_2O_3. Titanium is passivated by formation of TiO_2. Chromium is passivated by Cr_2O_3
Phase	A phase is a physically distinct body of matter that is, in principle, mechanically separable from surrounding matter. It may be gaseous, liquid, or solid. In a mixture of solid phases, each has a particular structure (i.e., atomic arrangement) and composition. Ice in water is a two-phase mixture. (Three, if we count the vapor phase above the mixture.) Austenitic stainless steel is a single-phase alloy; a solid solution is a phase.
Pitting corrosion	Pitting is the result of localization of corrosion. That is, the anode remains localized and is surrounded by a cathodic region. The opposite case is general corrosion, wherein anodic and cathodic regions are distributed more or less uniformly over a surface. Pitting can occur under the rust formed over a local anodic region, because the oxygen concentration is higher alongside the rust, making the latter regions cathodic.
Sacrificial anode	A relatively active metal when connected electrically to a less-active metal acts as a sacrificial anode, because it suffers corrosion in preference to the less-active metal. This occurs as long as the electrons so produced can flow to the less-active metal, which serves as the cathode. Examples: Zinc plating or cadmium plating on carbon steel.

Solid solution A crystalline solid, like a metal, may contain foreign atoms within its crystal structure, either substitutionally or interstitially. This constitutes a solid solution. The foreign atom (either an impurity or an alloying element) is the solute, and the host element is the solvent. Chromium and nickel are substitutional solute elements in austenitic stainless steel. Carbon is an interstitial solute in steel. That is, it is too small to substitute for an iron atom on the crystal lattice, so it resides in an interstice (the space left by a group of touching atoms).

Stainless steel Any steel that contains a minimum of 12% chromium in solid solution is considered "stainless" in that it does not rust when exposed to water and oxygen. The reason is that the surface is passivated by the formation of a mixed Fe-Cr oxide. Normally, stainless steel contains at least 18%Cr to allow for the precipitation of some of the chromium by carbon. (Cr is a strong carbide-former.) Fe+18%Cr would make a ferritic stainless steel (BCC); when carbon is added to allow martensitic hardening (cf. Chapter 8), it can be used for knives and razor blades. Fe+18%Cr+8%Ni would make an austenitic stainless steel (FCC); this is used for flatware and automobile trim, for example.

Exercises

1.1 Aside from cost considerations, is gold plating a good way to protect iron against corrosion? Explain your answer.

1.2 How would this differ from zinc coating (galvanizing) the iron?

1.3 What is the risk of connecting a new copper water pipe to an existing iron pipe? How can this risk be reduced, while continuing to use the same two dissimilar pipes?

1.4 Copper and brass are often plated with nickel, as are the brass nipples used to attach spokes to wheel rims. (Further examples are plumbing fixtures such as faucets.) Explain the purpose of the nickel and describe how it functions.

1.5 When a piece of carbon steel is exposed to humid air, rust forms all over the surface. Therefore, localized anodes and cathodic regions must exist on the surface of the piece. Speculate on what might cause this.

1.6 The decorative steel straps on the steel plates bordering the South Street bridge near the University of Pennsylvania campus (Fig. 1.10) have bulged out as a result of crevice corrosion behind them. From the discussion of pitting corrosion, explain in terms of oxygen concentrations why the rust formed under the straps. (This represents a direct conversion of chemical energy into mechanical work.)

Fig. 1.10. Decorative steel straps on steel plates that border the South Street bridge leading to the Penn campus. The straps have buckled out from the rust that formed beneath them owing to crevice corrosion.

1.7[1] Zinc anodes weighing 100g are attached to the steel hull of a ship to protect it from corrosion. If an average corrosion current of 0.01A is measured through each anode, how long will they last? Suggest a reason why zinc anodes are normally used for this purpose, instead of, say, magnesium or cadmium; give a concrete basis for your answer. (See Appendix 2 at back of book for useful data.)

1.8 Explain why using copper rivets in a steel plate would cause less of a corrosion problem than steel rivets in a copper plate.

1.9 Write the anode reactions and use simple sketches to show the path of flow of electrons for corrosion under the following three conditions:

(a) A zinc-coated carbon-steel spoke with a gap in the coating.

(b) A nickel-coated carbon-steel spoke with a gap in the coating.

(b) Two overlapping carbon-steel plates held together by a carbon-steel bolt and nut. (No coatings on any of them.)

1.10 How would you evaluate the feasibility of making stainless-type steel spokes using an Fe-Al alloy or an Fe-Ti alloy, in the event of a scarcity of chromium.

1.11 What is the total number of atoms contained within an FCC unit cell? What is the packing density (i.e., the fraction of the unit-cell volume occupied by atoms, using the hard-sphere model)? Note: The atoms touch along face diagonals.

1.12 A common carbon steel used for spokes contains 0.4wt% carbon. Convert this to atomic % carbon. (Use the Periodic Table for atomic weights.)

1.13 Aluminum costs more per ton than does steel, but aluminum has virtually replaced steel for beverage containers. Give as many factors as you can think of that could explain this replacement.

[1] Contributed by Professor D. L. Callahan, Rice University.

2

MECHANICAL BEHAVIOR

2.1 Types of Stress and Strain

In order to analyze mechanical deformation, it is necessary to determine the relevant loads and to convert each load into a *stress,* meaning load per unit area. The various types of stress, and the corresponding strains, are defined in this section.

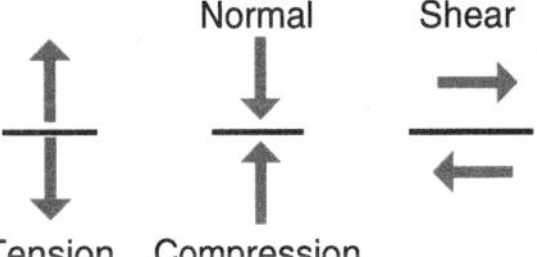

The basic types of stress are normal and shear. A normal stress may be either tensile or compressive.

Using the example of a bicycle wheel, a spoke in a tensioned wheel is loaded axially (i.e. along its length) by a tensile force and is said to be loaded in simple tension. The tensile stress is defined as the force, F, divided by the area, A, or

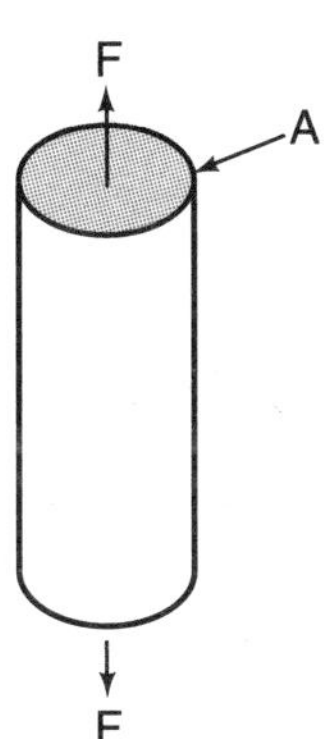

$$\sigma = \frac{F}{A}$$

where the lower-case Greek letter sigma, σ, is used to designate a normal stress, that is, a stress that acts perpendicular, or normal, to the plane of interest. This tensile stress is considered to act uniformly across the cross-section. Since the force in the spoke is constant along its length, so is the tensile stress. As noted in Chapter 1, a typical tensioning load of 90 kg applied to a spoke of 1.6mm diameter would produce a tensile stress of about 440 MPa.

The primary design concern would be that the stress in a spoke be kept below the level that would stretch it permanently. That is, the spoke should behave elastically. This means that the distortion caused by the load would be completely reversed when the load is removed. A body that behaves elastically follows *Hooke's law.*

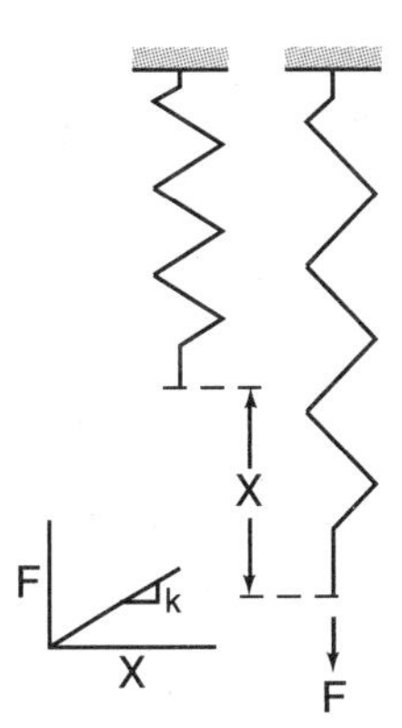

The original formulation of Hooke's law in 1679 stated that the distortion of an elastic body is proportional to the force applied. This is the behavior of a spring, which follows the law (or equation)

$$F = k\,x$$

where F is the applied force, x is the extension of the spring, and k is called the *spring constant.*

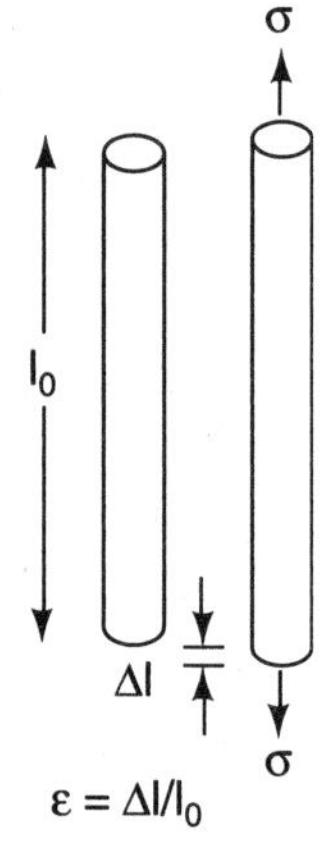

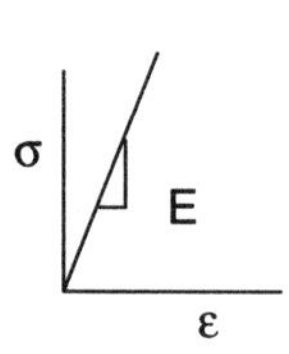

This law applies equally well to a spoke, but here the extension would be much smaller than for a spring; i.e., the spring constant for the spoke would be very much larger. One would say that the spoke is much more elastically stiff than a spring. The form of Hooke's law applied here uses stress instead of force, and, instead of extension, uses the extension per unit length, or strain, of the spoke. To denote strain the lower-case Greek letter epsilon, ε, is used, and Hooke's law is written as

$$\sigma = E\,\varepsilon$$

where E is known as the *elastic modulus,* or *Young's modulus,* in honor of Thomas Young, who first recognized this relationship more than one hundred years after Robert Hooke's original observation. This equation applies to any normal stress, either tensile or compressive. In general, tension and compression can be treated as differing only in the sign of the stress; tensile stresses are conventionally taken to be positive, and compressive stresses are, therefore, taken as negative.

Stress and strain, instead of force and displacement, are used to take account of the dimensions of a body. In Section 2.4 the physical origins of ε and E will be considered. Irreversible distortion, or plastic deformation, which occurs when the elastic limit is exceeded, is discussed in Section 2.5 and in Chapter 4.

If a spoke is loaded in bending, then both tensile and compressive stresses are present. For example, in Fig. 2.1 the top of the spoke is in compression, and the bottom is in tension. (Obviously, somewhere in between the stress must pass through zero.) Bending loads are extremely important in any structure, because they produce much higher tensile (and compressive) stresses than are usually found in axial loading (cf. Appendix 11.2). This is a matter of common experience. If one wishes to break a stick, one loads the stick in bending, e.g., across the knee, rather than by pulling on it axially, because less force is needed in bending to reach the fracture stress of the stick.

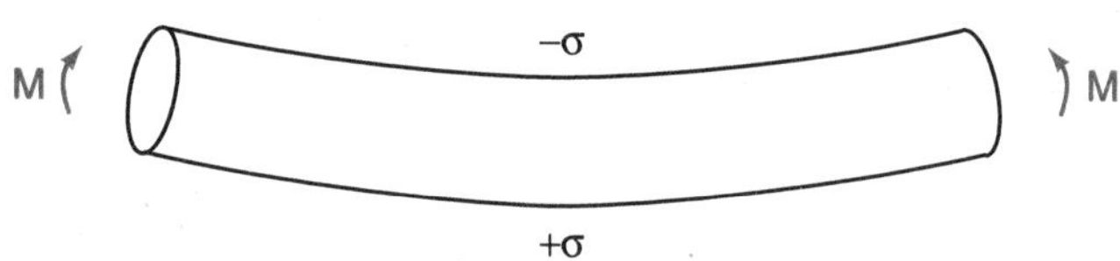

Fig. 2.1 Illustration of a spoke loaded by a bending moment M.

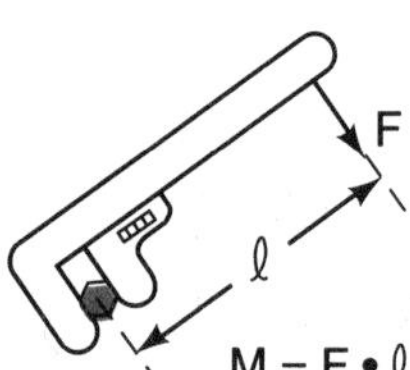

The bending of the spoke in Fig. 2.1 was accomplished by a *bending moment,* M, which is equal to a force multiplied by the length of the *moment arm* through which the force acts. The moment arm is the perpendicular distance from the line of action of the force to the point about which the force acts to rotate the body. A moment is analogous to the torque exerted on a bolt by a wrench.

In addition to tensile and compressive stresses, there may also be shear stresses in a bent structural member, such as a beam. This is illustrated in the cantilever beam in Fig. 2.2(a) and by the division of the beam into two *free-bodies* in Fig. 2.2(b). A free-body is a portion of a structure that is isolated so that one can denote all the forces that act on that part of the structure. Since the downward force, F, must be balanced by an equal and opposite force, there must exist a force F acting upward in the plane of the joint between the beam and the wall.

Similarly, the requirement for a balance of vertical forces means that there must be the forces shown acting on the faces of the cut between the two free bodies in Fig. 2.2(b). (The cut could have been made on any transverse plane.) The right-hand free body exerts a downward force on the left-hand one, and the left-hand free body exerts an upward force on the right-hand one. These forces acting in a plane (instead of perpendicular to it as in the case of a normal stress) are known as shearing forces; they act on every transverse plane in this beam.

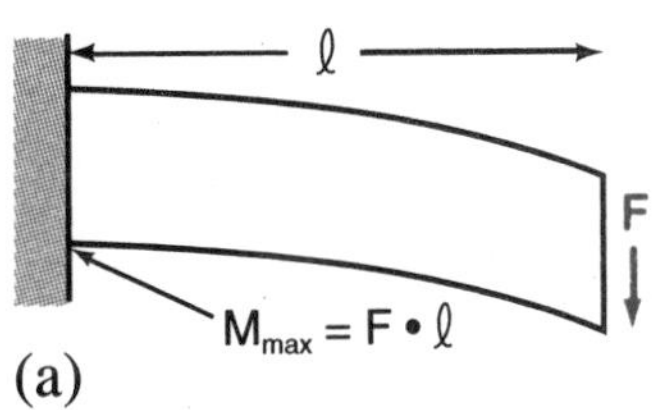

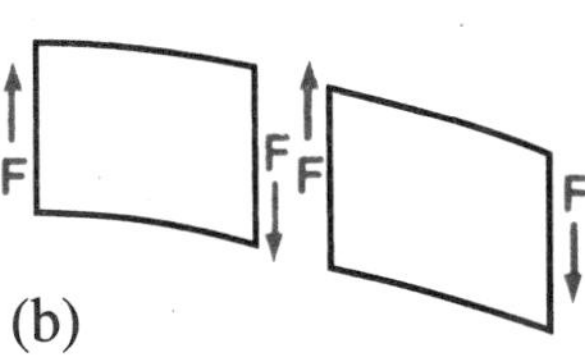

Fig. 2.2 (a) A cantilever beam loaded by the force F at a distance ℓ from the built-in end. (b) Division of the beam into two free bodies by cutting along an arbitrarily selected transverse plane.

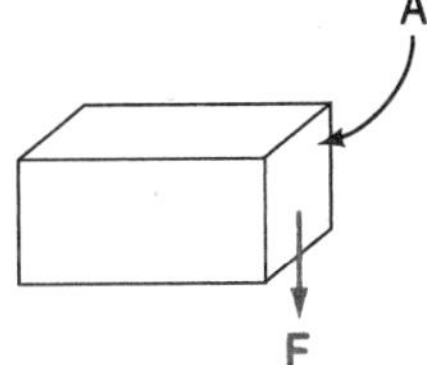

A shear stress is denoted by the Greek letter tau, τ, and is defined as the shearing force divided by the area of the plane on which it acts: $\tau = F/A$, analogous to a normal stress.

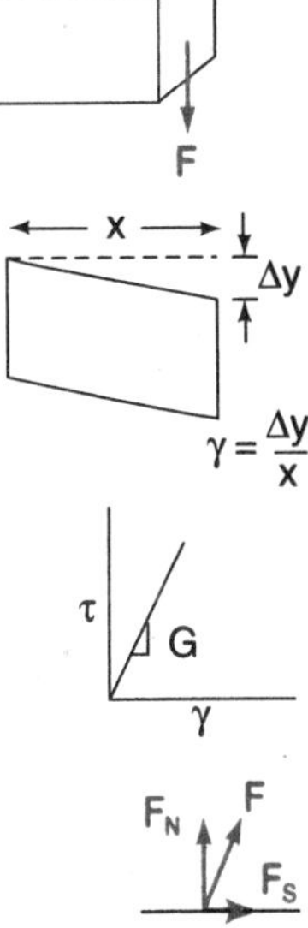

The shear strain, denoted by the Greek letter gamma, γ, is defined as the tangent of the angle of shear, which is equal to the displacement in the direction of the stress per unit length normal to the stress.

Hooke's law for elastic deformation in shear is

$$\tau = G\gamma$$

where G is the shear modulus.

Any force acting on a plane can be resolved into its normal and shearing components to give a normal stress and a shear stress.

Before proceeding further, one should reflect upon the physical significance of the various types of stress. A tensile stress can lead to fracture in a body that has a tendency to be brittle, i.e., one that can be broken with very little plastic deformation. This does not happen in a well-behaved metallic alloy, but it can, for example, in a carbon-fiber-reinforced plastic (CFRP), as will be seen in Chapter 13. In other words, a tensile stress tends to cause a crack to propagate if the plane of the crack lies nearly normal to the stress. Conversely, a compressive stress would tend to close a crack; therefore, one does not have to worry nearly so much about compressive stresses.

To illustrate the significance of this point, consider the construction methods of masonry structures like cathedrals and aqueducts, for example. Stone and mortar are brittle materials and are likely to contain crack-like flaws; they must not be loaded in tension. Our predecessors learned this the hard way, and they developed design features, like arches, that ensured that all joints would be in compression. The only ancient materials that could be loaded safely in tension were bone, wood, rope, and leather, all of which depend on the presence of strong fibers. Even here, tension can be applied only in the fiber direction; these materials are weak in the direction perpendicular to the fibers.

A material in which the properties vary with direction is said to be *anisotropic,* while one in which the properties are the same for all directions is called *isotropic.* In present-day structures like bicycles, airplanes, bridges, etc., one relies mainly on metallic materials to carry tensile stresses safely, and these are usually approximately isotropic. However, fiber-reinforced composites are being applied increasingly where minimizing weight is important, and these materials are often anisotropic.

Shear stresses of sufficient magnitude tend to deform materials plastically. Plastic deformation is an alternative to fracture; that is, an applied force can do work on a solid by either fracture or plastic shear. Many metallic materials tend to be *ductile,* as opposed to brittle, because of their ability to deform plastically and, thus, to resist fracture. One challenge in developing better metallic materials is to devise methods for strengthening them against plastic deformation in order to carry higher applied stresses, without restricting the plasticity so much that they become brittle. The approaches used to strengthen metallic materials will be dealt with in much of this book.

2.2 Small-Scale *vs.* Large-Scale Deformation

Materials engineers tend to approach the subject of mechanical behavior from the perspective of either large-scale or small-scale deformation. Spokes can serve to illustrate this very well. When a spoke is in use on a bicycle, one is concerned with small-scale deformation, which extends from the elastic range through the early stages of plastic deformation. When the bicycle is in use, a large-scale plastic strain would result only from some traumatic event. On the other hand, during manufacture of spokes, in which steel rods are drawn into wires by pulling them through dies, the imposed plastic strains are obviously quite large, and one is not at all concerned with elastic behavior or with the early stages of plastic flow. This dual perspective is reflected in the two ways used to define stress and strain.

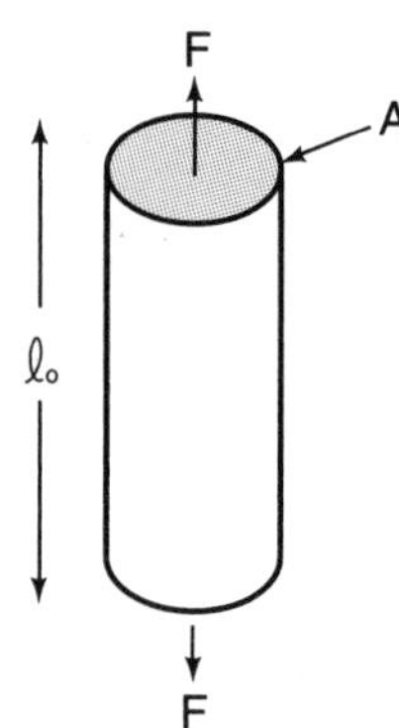

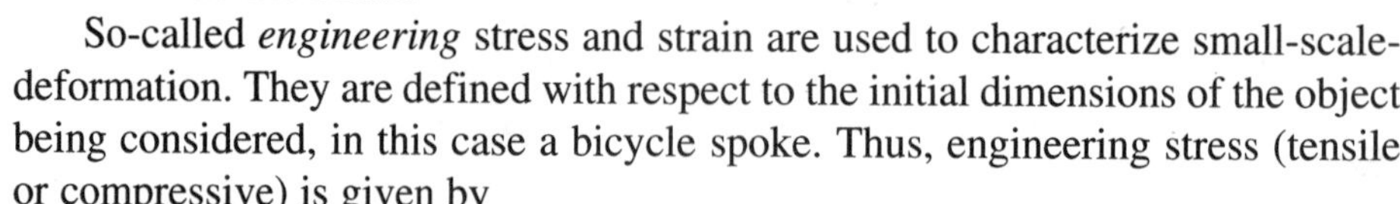

So-called *engineering* stress and strain are used to characterize small-scale-deformation. They are defined with respect to the initial dimensions of the object being considered, in this case a bicycle spoke. Thus, engineering stress (tensile or compressive) is given by

$$\sigma = \frac{F}{A_0}$$

and engineering strain by

$$\varepsilon = \frac{\Delta l}{l_0}$$

(If the loading were compressive, Δl, ε, F, and σ would all be given a negative sign.)

These definitions are applicable when one is interested in elastic behavior; i.e., in the application of Hooke's law: $\sigma = E\varepsilon$. They also are used when referring to the *yield* stress, which is the stress used to characterize the onset of plastic flow. (See Section 2.3.) Note that, while stress has dimensions of force per unit area (N/m^2 or pascals, Pa), strain is dimensionless. Thus, Young's modulus has the same units as stress.

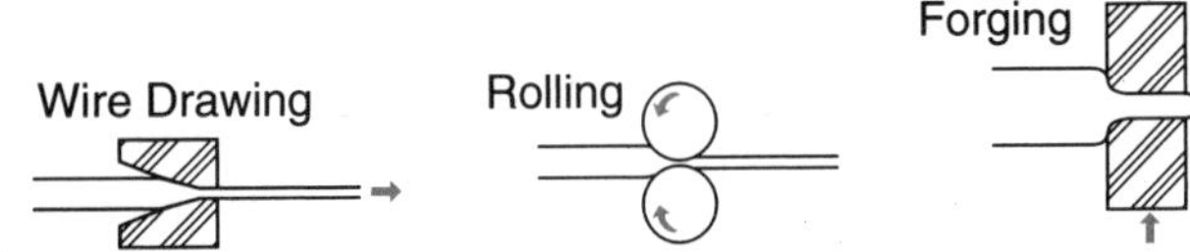

Fig. 2.3 Examples of metal-forming operations that entail large plastic strains.

At the other extreme, manufacturing operations like wire-drawing, rolling, or forging, employ large plastic strains, as illustrated in Fig. 2.3. Here, the changes in dimensions are so large that the initial dimensions lose their relevance. Therefore, *true* stress and strain should be used; these employ the instantaneous dimensions of the object:

$$\text{true stress} = \frac{F}{A}$$

and

$$\text{true strain} = \sum_{l_0}^{l_f} \frac{\Delta l}{l}$$

where A is the instantaneous area, l is the instantaneous length, and the summation is made over all $\Delta l/l$ from the initial length (l_0) to the final length (l_f). Of course, the summation is evaluated as an integral:

$$\text{true strain} = \int_{l_0}^{l_f} \frac{dl}{l} = \ln \frac{l_f}{l_0}$$

Since the focus in this book is on small-scale deformation, rather than on deformation processing, engineering stress and strain can be used throughout.

With regard to elastic behavior, it should be noted that Young's modulus, E, defined by Hooke's law, is a property of the material; it depends on the interatomic bonding forces, as will be seen below. Materials that are elastically stiff have a high E. For example, as seen in Table 2.1, steel is three times as stiff as aluminum. Therefore, bicycle spokes are made of steel, but the rims are made from aluminum to minimize weight.

Example 2.1

Q. What is the elastic strain in a carbon-steel spoke stressed to 350 MPa ?

A. From Table 2.1, E for carbon steel is 210 GPa. Therefore,

$$\varepsilon = \sigma/E = 350 \text{ MPa}/210\text{GPa} = 1.67\times10^{-3} \text{ or } 0.167\%$$

Q. Does it matter whether some plastic yielding has occurred during the loading?

A. No. The elastic strain depends only on the stress and Young's modulus.

A note on units is in order here. As in most present-day texts, the units employed in this book are mainly the Système Internationale (SI) units (kilograms, meters, newtons, etc.). However, an occasional exception is made in which English units (pounds, inches, etc.) are used. These are still the units in wide use in the U. S., and many test results are reported in these units; hence, it is necessary to be bilingual in this sense. One can translate from one set of units to the other using the conversion tables in the back of the book. For example, since one pound is equal to 4.448 newtons, and one inch equals 25.4 millimeters, or 0.0254 meters, one pound per square inch (psi), converted to SI units, is

$$1 \text{ psi} = \frac{4.448}{(0.0254)^2} = 6894 \text{ N/m}^2$$

In the context of materials deformation, one normally deals with thousands of psi, which is denoted ksi. The counterpart in SI units is the mega-newton per square meter, MN/m^2, or mega-pascal, MPa. The important conversion factor is, therefore,

$1\text{MPa} = 10^6 \text{ Pa}$

$$1 \text{ ksi} = 6.9 \text{ MPa}$$

GPa = Gigapascal

$1\text{GPa} = 10^9 \text{ Pa}$

Table 2.1 Young's modulus of materials used in bicycles.

Material	Young's Modulus GPa	psi
Iron	210	~30x10^6
Carbon and low-alloy steels	210	~30x10^6
18-8 stainless steel	210	~30x10^6
Aluminum	70	~10x10^6
Titanium	116	~17x10^6
Glass (for fibers)	76	~11x10^6
Carbon fibers Type 1	390	~56x10^6
Type 2	250	~36x10^6
Kevlar	130	~18x10^6
Rubbers	0.01 - 0.1	~10^3 - 10^4
Epoxies	2 - 5.5	~3 - 8x10^5

2.3 Measurement of Stress *vs.* Strain — The Tensile Test

The tensile test gives important information about the mechanical properties of a material. In the case of a bicycle spoke, it is necessary to know Young's modulus in order to know how much tensile stress is generated from a given strain imposed by tightening a nipple (cf. Fig.1.8). It is also important to avoid permanent deformation of the spoke during tensioning of the wheel. Thus, the applied tensile stress should not be more than about half the yield stress. The yield stress is defined as the stress at which the deformation becomes inelastic (i.e., partly permanent) by some specified amount.

A tensile test is carried out on a machine that can exert sufficient force to stretch the specimen of interest; for a spoke a capacity of about one thousand pounds is needed. One end of the specimen is attached through a suitable linkage to a load cell, and the other is attached to a movable cross-head, which is driven by either large screws or by a hydraulic piston. A screw-driven machine is illustrated schematically in Fig.2.4(a). The elongation of the specimen can be measured by an extensometer, which is a displacement transducer, or a device that converts a displacement to an electrical signal. The voltage outputs from the load cell and the extensometer are sent to the Y and X terminals, respectively, of an X-Y recorder and the small-scale-deformation portion of the stress-strain curve is displayed, as illustrated in Fig. 2.4(b). Most load cells and extensometers employ electrical-resistance strain gauges, the operation of which is described in Appendix 2.1.

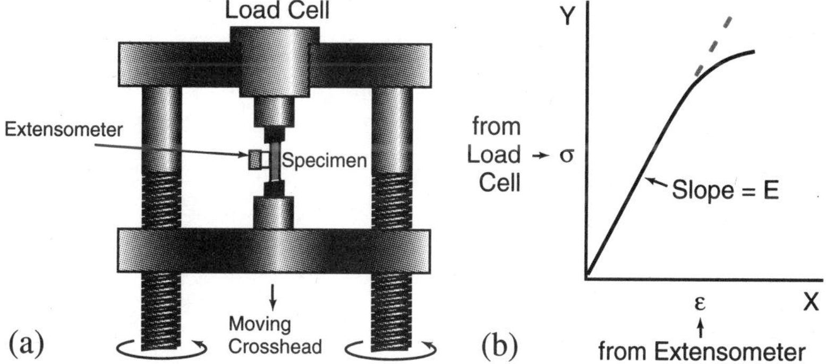

Fig. 2.4 (a) Schematic representation of tensile-testing apparatus. (From H. W. Hayden, W. G. Moffat, and J. Wulff, *The Structure and Properties of Materials Vol. III,* John Wiley & Sons NY, 1965, p.2.) (b) Initial portion of σ-ε curve plotted by an X-Y recorder, showing plastic yielding, causing the departure from linear elastic behavior.

In the stress-strain curve shown in Fig. 2.4(b), Young's modulus, E, is simply the slope of the initial, linear portion of the curve. The yield stress is less-obviously characterized, since the transition from elastic to inelastic behavior occurs gradually. In order to have a material parameter that can be defined unambiguously, it is conventional to select some small amount of permanent (i.e., plastic) deformation as the indicator that the purely elastic behavior has come to an end. For example, a plastic offset (from the elastic line) of 0.002 inch in a one-inch gauge section (i.e., a plastic strain of 0.2 percent) could be selected; this gives the 0.2% yield stress. Obviously, the definition of the yield stress is arbitrary in the sense that the plastic strain must be specified.

The initial parts of the stress-strain curves of the two common types of bicycle spoke are shown in Fig. 2.5; the yield stress (arrows) is defined by the 0.2% plastic offset criterion. The differences between carbon steel and stainless steel spokes will be discussed in detail later. For the present, note that the yield strength and the elastic modulus are similar for the two types. Therefore, one can substitute one for the other in a bicycle wheel without compromising the mechanical integrity of the wheel.

In the design of a bicycle wheel it is necessary to use Young's modulus to calculate the amount of distortion that would occur when the wheel is loaded. Also, the yield stress must be known to ensure that the spokes are not deformed plastically by any reasonable loading condition. Thus, the tensile test has played an important role in the development of bicycle spokes and wheels.

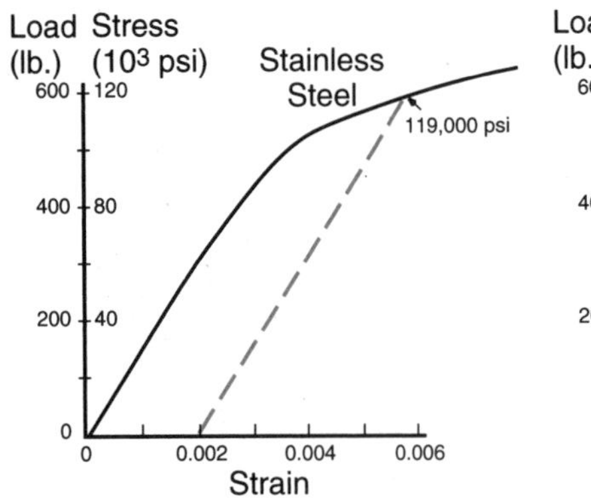

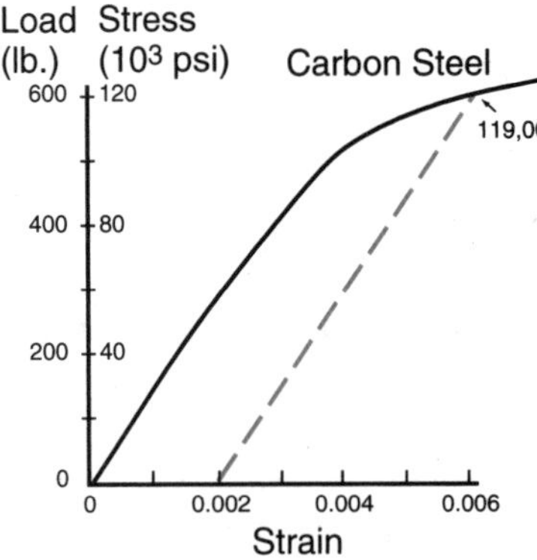

Fig. 2.5 The initial stress-strain curves of a carbon-steel and a stainless-steel spoke; the strain was measured with a strain-gauge extensometer and displayed on an XY recorder.

Example 2.2

Q. For the stress-strain curve of the stainless-steel spoke shown in Fig. 2.5, show how the 0.2% yield stress and the total strain at this stress are calculated. The spoke diameter is 2mm (0.08in).

A. The load at which the stress-strain curve crosses the line representing a plastic strain of 0.002 is 2578 N (600 lb). (Note that this line has a slope equal to E, 210 GPa (30x10^{6}psi). Since the cross-sectional area is 3.14mm^2 (0.005in^2), the yield stress is:

$$\frac{\text{load at 0.2\% plastic offset}}{\text{original cross-sectional area}} = \frac{2578\text{N}}{3.14\text{x}10^{-6}\text{m}^2} = 821\text{MPa (119,000psi)}$$

The total strain (ε_t) = elastic strain (ε_e) + plastic strain (ε_p). At yielding, ε_p = 0.002 and ε_e = 821 MPa/210 GPa = 0.004. Therefore, ε_t = 0.006.

2.4 Elastic Behavior

Table 2.1 indicates that carbon steel, which is usually more than 90 volume-percent iron (the rest being iron carbide), has essentially the same Young's modulus as stainless steel, which is about 70 volume-percent iron (the rest being mainly chromium and nickel dispersed in solid solution in the iron). Thus, the modulus is determined by the majority (or solvent) element in these iron-based alloys. On the other hand, Table 2.1 shows that aluminum has a Young's modulus only one-third that of iron. To understand the physical basis for differences in E from one material to another, elastic strain must be examined on the atomic scale.

2080 Elastic deformation is easiest to envision in terms of a two-dimensional array of atoms, as shown in Fig. 2.6. Note that this deformation may be viewed equivalently either as a vertical separation of atoms or as shearing of the rows of atoms oriented at ±30° to the horizontal. This shearing occurs because a solid reacts to a stretching force so as to minimize the increase in volume that accompanies a tensile strain. Thus, the solid contracts laterally as it stretches, and this contraction is accomplished by the shears depicted in Fig. 2.6

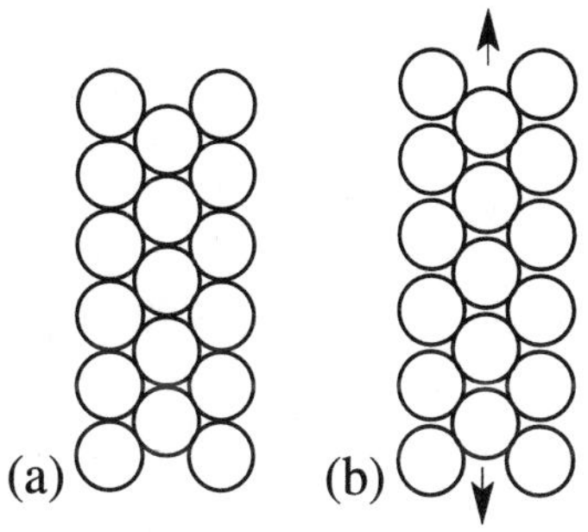

Fig. 2.6 (a) A portion of a close-packed plane of atoms; each atom touches six neighbors. This is the densest possible packing of spheres of equal size. (b) An (exaggerated) elastic strain is produced in this plane by the application of a tensile stress.

The amount of contraction per unit tensile strain is a property of the material and is called *Poisson's ratio.* If the tensile strain occurs along the y axis and the lateral contraction along the x axis, the Poisson's ratio, usually denoted by the Greek letter nu, ν, is expressed as follows:

$$\nu = \frac{-\varepsilon_x}{\varepsilon_y}$$

Values of ν for metals are generally in the range 0.3 to 0.35.

Since the property of a material that expresses the resistance to elastic shear is the shear modulus, and since a tensile strain with a Poisson contraction necessitates elastic shearing, there must be a relationship connecting the three material constants E, G, and ν. For an isotropic solid this relationship is

$$G = \frac{E}{2(1+\nu)}$$

Most crystals are not isotropic, so the relationship is more complicated and varies with the crystallographic directions involved, but solids made up of a large number of small crystals having random orientations can be approximated as isotropic. This is the case for metallic materials used in bicycles, so the above expressions can be applied here.

Elastic strain is produced when the applied stress works against the interatomic bonding forces; i.e., the forces that cause the atoms to condense into a crystal. Interatomic bonding is actually the resultant of two opposing forces: an attractive force that works over a long range (relative to the atom diameter) and a repulsive, short-range force that comes into play when the atoms are close together. The corresponding attractive, repulsive, and resultant energies, from which the forces are derived, are shown schematically in Fig. 2.7(a).

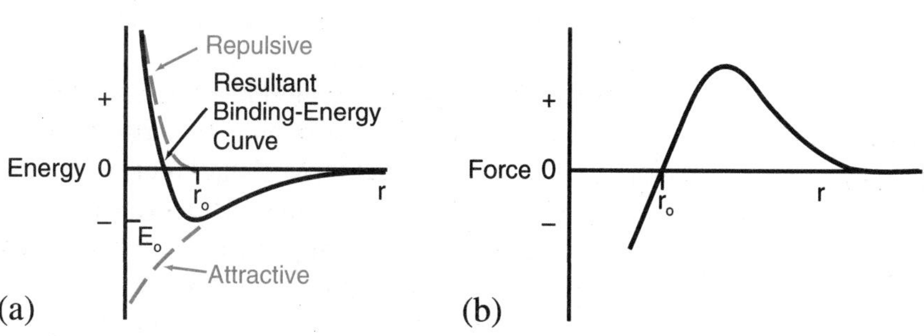

Fig. 2.7 (a) An interatomic bonding energy curve as the resultant of an attractive and a repulsive energy. The equilibrium separation of atoms is r_0, and the binding energy is E_0. (b) The force *vs.* displacement curve (i.e., the "stress-strain" curve for the pair of atoms), from the first derivative of the energy curve in (a).

The nature of the attractive energy depends on the type of bond being formed. For example, in an ionic crystal like NaCl, it is simple Coulombic attraction between the ions of opposite charge. The simplest metals are, essentially, positive ions surrounded by a sea of negative charge; i.e., the valence, or "free," electrons. Therefore, metallic bonding is more complicated, but the shape of the attractive-energy curve is roughly similar to the simple ionic case. The steeply rising repulsive energy comes into play when the ion cores are pressed so closely together that they begin to overlap; this drastically raises the energies of the electrons in the overlap regions. It is because of this steep repulsive energy that ionic or metallic crystals can be modeled as arrays of hard spheres.

The binding energy is the sum of the attractive and repulsive energies. The interatomic force is just the derivative of that energy with respect to the distance of atomic separation, as shown in Fig. 2.7(b). Since Young's modulus is proportional to the slope of the force *vs.* displacement in a tensile test, it must be proportional to the slope of the interatomic force *vs.* displacement curve shown in Fig. 2.7(b) at the equilibrium atomic separation (where the force passes through zero). (Note that elastic strains involve very small interatomic displacements; they are on the order of 10^{-3} times the atomic diameter or less. Thus, the displacements in Fig. 2.6 are highly exaggerated.)

Three points about elastic behavior should be emphasized:

1. Hooke's Law ($\sigma = E\varepsilon$) is only true for small displacements; at very large elastic strains the σ–ε behavior would be nonlinear. That is, the force *vs.* displacement curve shown in Fig. 2.7(b) is approximately linear only in the vicinity of $r = r_0$.

2. E is the same in tension and compression for small strains.

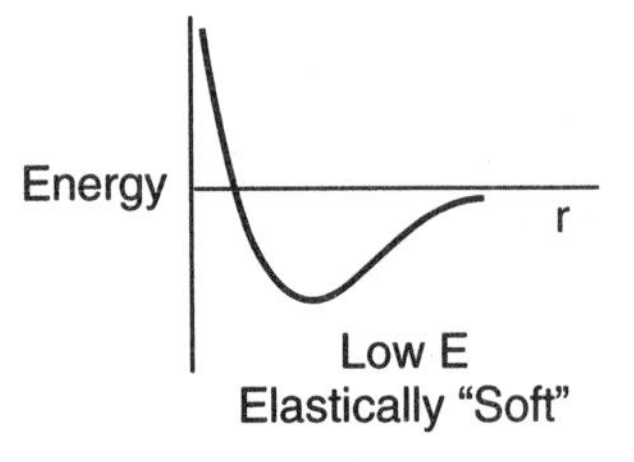

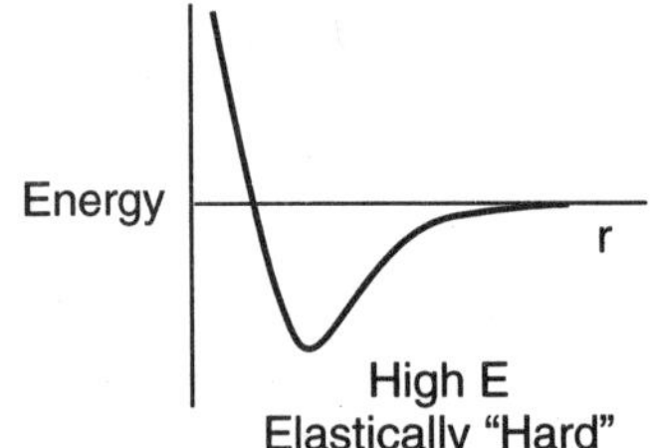

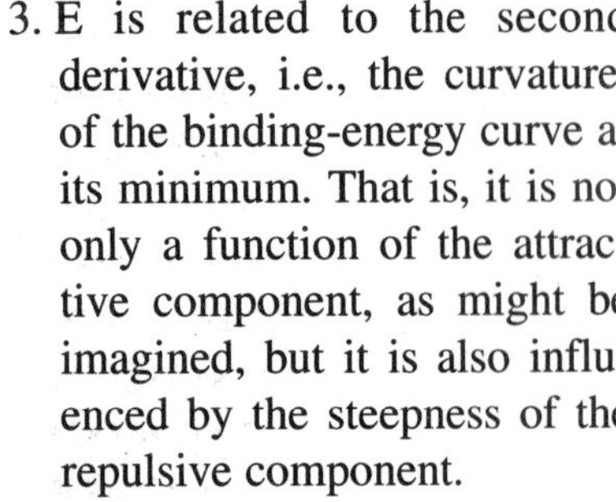

3. E is related to the second derivative, i.e., the curvature, of the binding-energy curve at its minimum. That is, it is not only a function of the attractive component, as might be imagined, but it is also influenced by the steepness of the repulsive component.

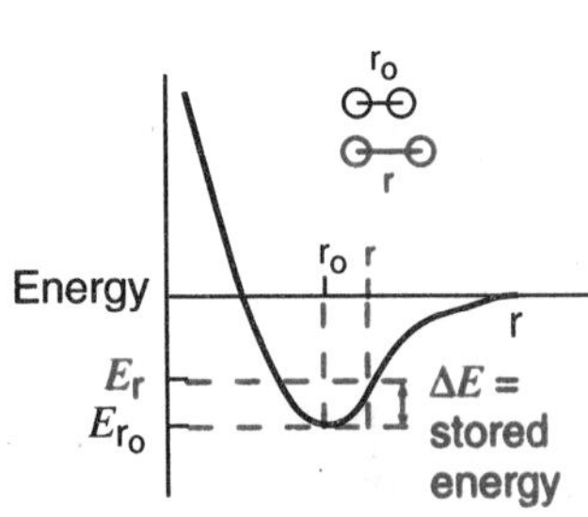

As shown in Fig. 2.6, an elastic strain decreases the packing density of the atomic array. That is, the volume per atom is increased, as is the average interatomic spacing (r in Fig. 2.7). This must involve an increase in energy of the crystal, because it was originally in a state of minimum energy. This is equivalent to saying that the crystal is no longer at the minimum in the binding energy curve in Fig. 2.7(a). Thus, there is stored elastic energy in an elastically deformed solid, just as there is stored energy in a stretched spring. The amount of stored energy is simply the product of the average force times the displacement, or the area under the force *vs.* displacement curve, as shown in Fig. 2.8.

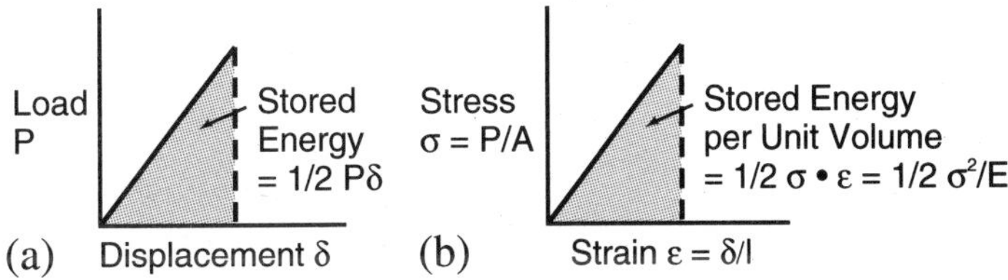

Fig. 2.8 (a) The stored elastic energy is the area under an elastic load-displacement curve. (b) The stored energy per unit volume is the area under the σ–ε curve.

Since stress is force/area and strain is displacement/length, the area under the σ-ε curve is stored-energy/volume. (Force x displacement = energy, and length x area = volume.) Strain energy is of great importance in some areas of materials science, but the stored energy in the spokes in a bicycle wheel plays no direct role in the functioning of the bicycle. It is just a consequence of the fact that the spokes are tensioned.

Example 2.3

Q. Calculate the stored elastic energy per unit volume in the spoke loaded to the 0.2% yield stress in Example 2.2.

A. Stored energy/volume = $1/2\ \sigma^2/E = 1/2(821\text{MPa})^2/210\text{GPa} = 1600\text{x}10^3\text{Pa}$

Therefore, the stored energy/volume = 1600 kJ/m^3.

$$1\text{Pa} = \frac{1\text{N}}{\text{m}^2} = \frac{1\ \text{N-m}}{\text{m}^3} = \frac{1\text{J}}{\text{m}^3}$$

2.5 Plastic Behavior

As already noted, when the applied stress becomes sufficiently high, a metallic material, like a steel, departs from linear elastic behavior, because plastic deformation begins. The stress-strain relationship is no longer described by Hooke's Law. (However, the elastic strain at a given stress, even in the non-linear region, is still obtained from Hooke's law.) Because the accumulation of plastic strain is so gradual, the yield stress is arbitrarily defined at a certain amount of plastic strain, as shown in Fig. 2.5.

Plasticity in a crystalline solid is fundamentally different from elastic deformation. As indicated schematically in Fig. 2.9, plastic flow occurs by a shearing of a crystal along a certain crystallographic plane in a certain crystallographic direction. This process is called *slip*. The planes and directions will be discussed later, but the important points for the moment are the following:

1. Plastic displacement occurs by the shearing of one part of the crystal relative to another in units of the interatomic spacing along the direction of slip.

2. Plastic strain is permanent; it does not reverse itself when the stress is removed. That is, the block of crystal in Fig. 2.9(b) is in a new position of equilibrium; there is no restoring force tending to return it to the configuration of 2.9(a).

3. Slip does not change the symmetry of the crystal; the crystal structure is the same after slip as before.

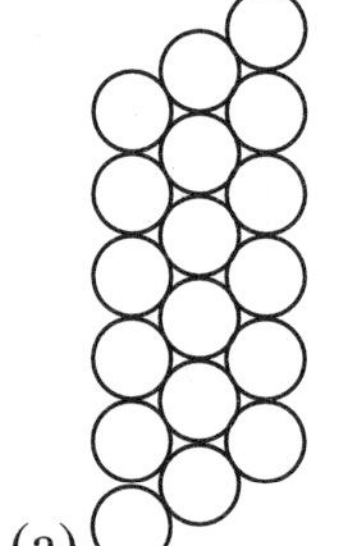

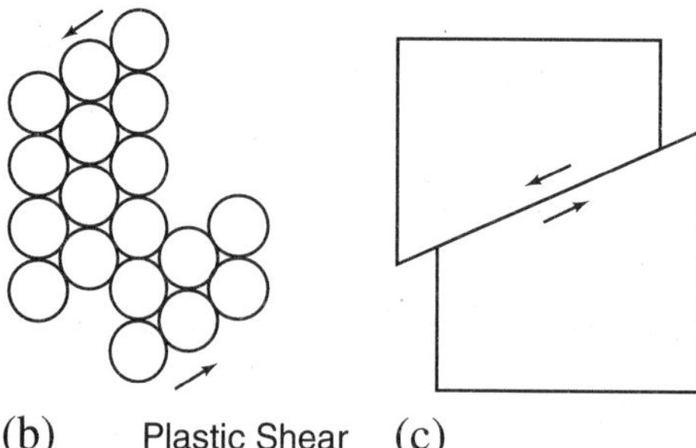

Fig. 2.9 Schematic representation of plastic shear in a crystal. (a) is the original block of atoms. (b) is the block after plastic shear. (c) represents shear strain in a continuum block.

One can observe the effects of slip by examining under a microscope the surface of a deformed piece of polycrystalline brass, shown in Fig. 2.10. The piece was heated to a high temperature to produce coarsening of the crystallites, called *grains,* and then polished to a mirror-like finish before being squeezed in a vise. The explanation of how this microscopic image is formed is given in the next chapter; here, we are only concerned with the slip lines that appear in individual grains. These lines are manifestations of the steps formed in the surface of these grains due to the intense plastic offset that has occurred there. Obviously, in this material the plastic strain is concentrated in well-defined, narrow bands.

If the surface of a pre-polished tensile specimen of the coarse-grained brass were to be observed with a microscope during a tensile test, one would find that the process of yielding takes place in the following way: First, very faint slip lines (meaning small surface steps) occur in a few isolated grains. At this stress, the deviation from linear elasticity is hardly detectable with an ordinary displacement transducer, since these only detect displacements equivalent to strains of 10^{-5} or greater. As the stress is further increased, the slip lines in the isolated grains become more apparent. That is, the slip steps become larger, and more slip lines occur in these and other grains. At some point the deviation from linear behavior appears on the X-Y recorder. When the plastic strain reaches 10^{-3} (0.1%), most of the grains will contain observable slip lines.

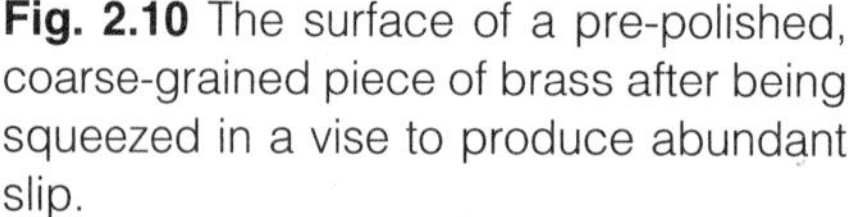
Fig. 2.10 The surface of a pre-polished, coarse-grained piece of brass after being squeezed in a vise to produce abundant slip.

It might be imagined that slip occurs by the sliding of one part of a crystal over another in the manner of rigid blocks, the way a pack of cards can be sheared. However, it can be shown that this would require an extraordinarily high stress, and it is now known that slip actually occurs progressively, rather than all at once. A useful analogy is the displacement of a rug on a floor when one creates a ripple in the rug and then pushes the ripple across the rug to the far side, as shown 2170
in Fig. 2.11. The amount of displacement achieved in this manner is equal to the amount of rug in the ripple (b in Fig. 2.11) . The displacement is achieved with far less force than would be required to move the whole rug at once. The ripple in the rug is analogous to a linear defect in a crystal called a *dislocation.* An illustration of one of the two basic kinds of dislocation is given in Fig. 2.12.

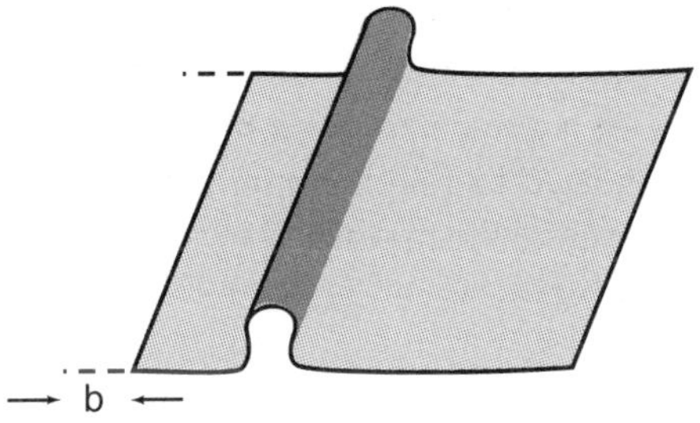

Fig. 2.11 A rug may be given a shear displacement with respect to the floor by propagating a ripple across it.

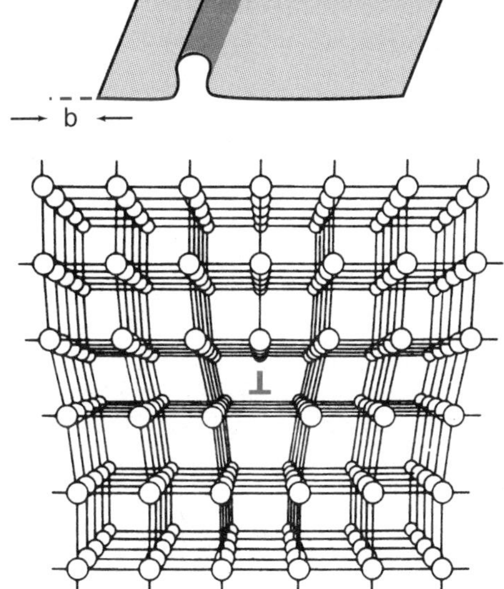

Fig. 2.12 An edge dislocation in a crystal. The dislocation comprises the bottom edge of the extra plane of atoms contained in the upper half of the crystal. (From A. G. Guy, *Elements of Physical Metallurgy,* Addison-Wesley, Reading, MA,1959, p. 110.)

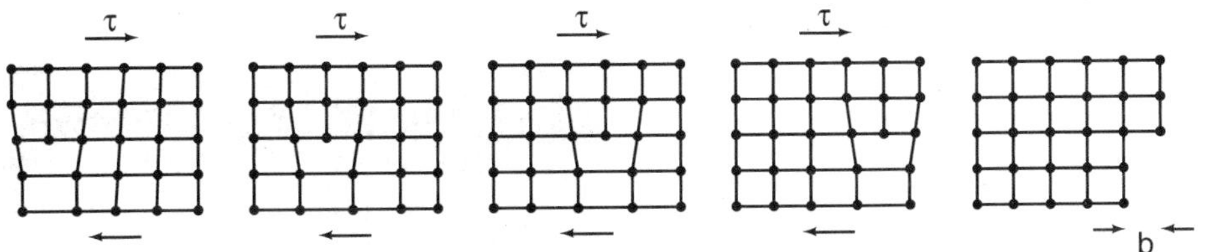

Fig. 2.13. The glide of an edge dislocation under the influence of a shear stress τ.

The plastic shear in crystalline solids occurs by the motion of dislocations, as illustrated by Fig. 2.13. One must understand a certain amount about dislocations to comprehend how crystalline solids deform and how they can be strengthened (i.e., made more resistant to deformation). This is particularly important in bicycle spokes, since they are manufactured by plastic deformation (i.e., wire drawing), and this large-scale plastic deformation gives them most of their strength, a process known as *strain hardening.* Strain hardening is the increase in yield stress imparted to a material by plastic deformation; it results from an increase in the density of dislocations.

Also, the superior fatigue resistance, or resistance to fracture from repeated stressing, of carbon steel spokes can only be understood in terms of the special interaction between dislocations and interstitial atoms, like carbon, in carbon steel. This will be made clear in subsequent chapters. For now, the following points about dislocations need to be made.

1. The component of stress that causes dislocations to "glide" along a particular plane in a crystal, producing slip, is a shear stress. This shear stress lies in the plane of glide and acts in the direction along which slip occurs, as indicated in Fig. 2.13. The magnitude of the shear stress is the shearing force divided by the area of the plane on which it acts.
2. After a metallic material is heated to a high temperature (but not so high as to melt it) and cooled to room temperature, it contains a relatively small number of dislocations. When plastic deformation occurs by the motion (glide) of these dislocations, the dislocations multiply (by a process to be described later), and, therefore, the separation distance between dislocations becomes progressively smaller.
3. The region in a crystal around the dislocation line is obviously distorted; i.e., the atoms are displaced from their equilibrium positions. Thus, there must be a stress field and an associated stored elastic energy associated with the dislocation. It will be shown later that, if similar dislocations approach each other, their stress fields will interact to cause mutual repulsion. The repulsive force will be shown to be inversely proportional to the dislocation spacing, just as with two electrically charged particles of like sign. Since dislocation multiplication decreases their average spacing, it must increase their average mutual repulsion. This makes glide more difficult, and more stress must be applied to cause a continuation of dislocation motion. Thus, plastic deformation results in strain hardening.

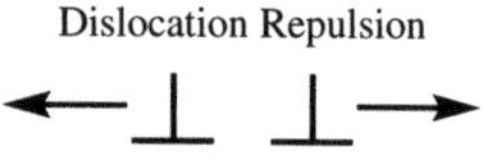

2190 The shear stress that causes dislocation motion can be related to an applied tensile stress in the following way: Consider a cylindrical rod, like a spoke, having a cross-sectional area A_0, subjected to a tensile force P. This tensile force can be resolved into components that lie in, and perpendicular to, any plane. These are the shear and normal forces and can be designated S and N, respectively. The area of this arbitrary plane is denoted as A.

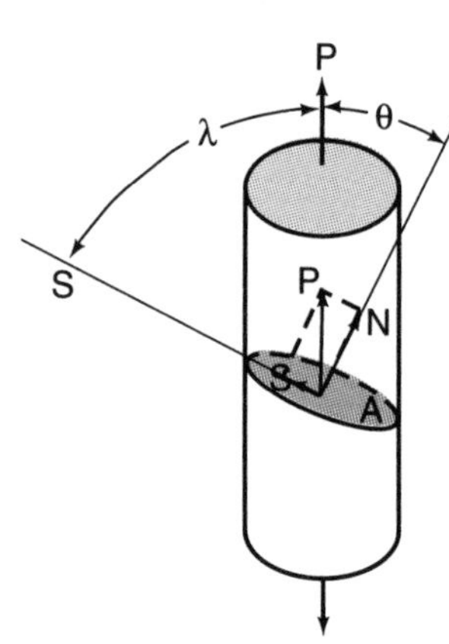

The orientation of the plane is specified by the angle, θ, between the tensile axis and the plane normal. The complementary angle, λ, is between the tensile axis and the vector S.

The area A is given by:

$$A = A_0/\cos\theta$$

The force vector, S, which is the shearing force on the arbitrary plane, is given by:

$$S = P\cos\lambda$$

The shear stress, τ, on that plane is defined as S/A and is given by:

$$\tau = P \cos \lambda / A_0 / \cos \theta = (P/A_0) \cos \lambda \cos \theta$$

Since P/A_0 is by definition σ, the resolved shear stress can be written: 2200

$$\tau = \sigma \cos \lambda \cos \theta$$

This expression is known as the *Schmid* equation. It can be shown (cf. Problem 2.8) that the maximum value of τ, i.e., of $\cos \lambda \cos \theta$, occurs when $\lambda = \theta = 45°$, or when $\cos \lambda = \cos \theta = \sqrt{2}/2$. This maximum value is, therefore, $\tau = \sigma/2$.

Figure. 2.14 shows three orientations of the arbitrary plane. Of the three, (a) would have the maximum shear stress, because λ and θ are both close to 45°. In (b), where θ is small, the resolved shearing force S is small; hence, so is τ. In (c), where θ is large, S is large, but the plane would have a very large area; hence τ is small. The latter result may appear counterintuitive, until it is remembered that stress is defined as force per unit area.

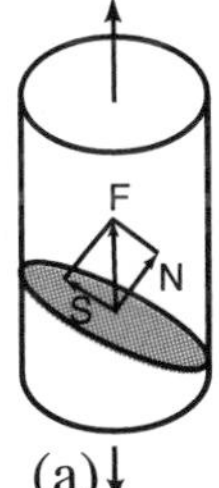

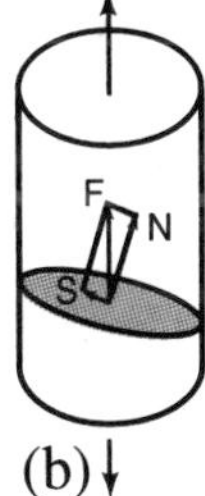

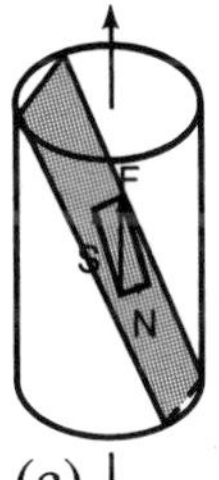

Fig. 2.14 Resolution of a tensile force (F) into shear (S) and normal (N) force components on three arbitrary planes.

Returning to the description of the yielding process, it should now be apparent why a few isolated grains in a polycrystalline tensile specimen would yield before the others. These are the grains with the highest shear stress on the particular crystallographic plane on which dislocation motion is easiest. (The crystallography of slip will be discussed in Chapter 4.)

Example 2.4

Q. Calculate the shear stress on the planes and directions defined by the following λ and θ values for an applied tensile stress of 100 MPa. (Assume that the shear direction, tensile axis, and shear plane normal are coplanar, as would be the case in a continuum solid.)

λ	θ
15°	75°
40	50
75	15

A. Use Schmid eqn: $\tau = \sigma \cos \lambda \cos \theta$
For σ = 100 MPa,

λ	θ	τ (MPa)
15°	75°	25
40	50	49
75	15	25

2.6 Large-Scale Plastic Flow — The Stress-Strain Curve

One often wants to know more about the mechanical behavior of a material than just the Young's modulus and the yield stress. Much useful information is contained in the total stress-strain curve, obtained by continuing the tensile test until the specimen fails. The strain involved is usually well beyond the range of most extensometers, so in the complete tensile test the extension of the specimen is measured in a comparatively crude manner. This is generally adequate, since there is no need for high precision when the strains are very large.

The total engineering stress-strain curve is actually plotted in the form of a load-elongation curve. The curves have the same shape because of the definition of engineering stress and strain (i.e., load and elongation divided by constants, A_0 and l_0, respectively). The curve is often plotted on a strip-chart recorder, which can record only one input signal. This comes from the load cell of the machine, and it goes to the Y axis. The chart is driven at a constant rate, so the measure along the X axis is simply time. However, if the movable cross-head on the testing machine is also driven at a constant rate, then a distance along the X axis is proportional to the displacement of this cross-head. The rates of travel of the chart and the cross-head can each be set as one wishes. Examples of the stress-strain curve from each kind of spoke are shown in Fig. 2.15.

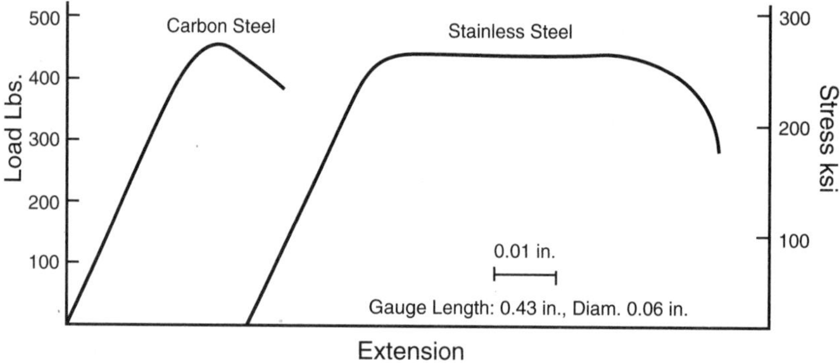

Fig. 2.15 Comparison of the tensile behavior of carbon-steel and stainless-steel spokes, showing the load plotted against the displacement of the movable cross-head of the machine. The load is proportional to the engineering stress (load/original area) and the displacement is proportional to the engineering strain (extension/the nominal gauge length of the specimen). Virtually all of the plastic extension occurs in this gauge section.

Several aspects of the engineering stress-strain curves are worth noting:

1. The initial linear portion represents elastic deformation, but the slope is not Young's modulus, because the displacement of the whole load train is being recorded, not just that of the gauge section of the specimen.
2. After yielding, a large amount of strain hardening can occur. It is this behavior that makes metals so useful; plastic flow leads not to immediate collapse or fracture, but to a stronger material.
3. Ultimately, the curve passes through a maximum. This maximum represents the ultimate load-bearing capacity of the specimen. It is called the *ultimate tensile strength,* UTS, and is the maximum load divided by the original area of the gauge section.

The maximum in the stress-strain curve occurs because the specimen gets thinner as it is plastically stretched; in this sense it becomes weaker. The strain hardening is initially more than sufficient to compensate for the thinning of the specimen, but ultimately it is not, because the rate of strain hardening decreases with strain. (The reason for this will be shown in Chapter 4.) At the point where the strain hardening is just balanced by the thinning, the specimen becomes "plastically unstable," and at some point along the gauge section the specimen begins to neck down. (The criterion for necking is given mathematically in Appendix 2.2.) Essentially all subsequent plastic flow is then concentrated in this necked region, and failure occurs there also, since this is now the region of maximum stress.

The neck is also a region in which damage accumulates in the form of internal cavities. These generally nucleate at impurity particles and grow with continued plastic flow. They finally link up to form a large internal crack-like flaw, which leads to final failure. The process of necking and failure is illustrated schematically in Fig. 2.16, and an example of failure by rupture is shown.

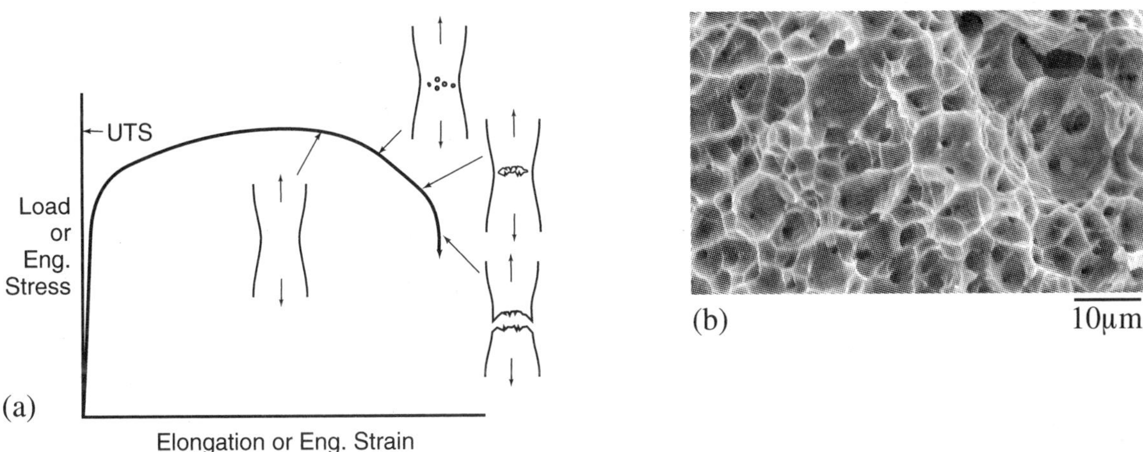

Fig. 2.16 (a) Schematic illustration of necking, cavity formation and coalescence, and rupture. (b) Fracture surface of a stainless steel spoke. (Scanning electron micrograph by Cliff Warner, Univ. of Penn.)

The reason the cavities grow in the center of the necked region is that the triaxial tension is greatest there. In a tensile specimen the state of stress in the center of a neck is a combination of simple, or uniaxial, tension (i.e., the tension applied by the machine), and transverse tension. The latter arises from the fact that the necked region tends to continue to thin down with the ongoing plastic flow, but the thicker regions alongside the neck do not, because very little further plastic flow occurs there. Thus, the thicker regions exert a constraint on the material in the neck. This constraint manifests itself as a transverse tensile stress, which is equal in all radial directions.

The stress state in the center of the neck is illustrated schematically in Fig. 2.17. The transverse tensile stress reaches a maximum in the center of the neck and falls to zero at the free surface, since a free surface is, by definition, free of normal components of stress (i.e., components of stress perpendicular to the surface). If the tensile test is interrupted just before failure and the specimen is then sectioned longitudinally and examined under a microscope, it is found that cavities have formed internally in the region of the neck, as shown schematically in Fig. 2.16(a). The cavities are large near the central axis and diminish in size toward the surface of the neck.

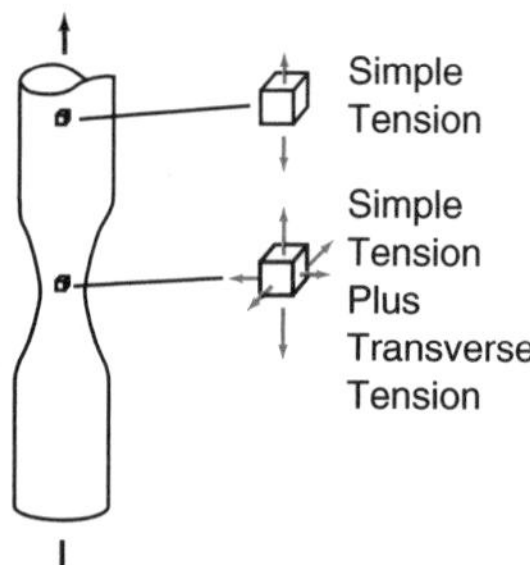

Fig. 2.17 The state of stress in the center of a neck contains a transverse component, caused by plastic constraint.

The type of failure involving hole growth is called *rupture*. It is a displacement-controlled (as opposed to a stress-controlled) mode of failure, because it results from the damage that accumulates with strain. That is how ductile materials fail.

Ductility is normally expressed in one of two ways: The preferred way is the *percent reduction in area,* %RA, which is simply the total reduction of area divided by the original area times 100. That is,

$$\%RA = \frac{A_0 - A_f}{A_0} \times 100$$

where A_0 is the original cross-sectional area of the gauge section and A_f is the final area in the neck. This parameter best expresses the resistance of the material to rupture. For example, the cleaner the material, i.e., the lower the concentration of impurity particles (which serve as nuclei for cavities), the greater is the %RA.

The less-preferred measure of ductility is the *percent elongation,* %elong, which represents the total plastic extension of the specimen (measured from the stress-strain curve) divided by the original nominal gauge length. That is,

$$\%elong = \frac{l_f - l_0}{l_0} \times 100$$

where l_0 is the original length of the gauge section, and l_f is the final length. Percent elongation is easier to determine, but it is less precise, and its physical meaning is less clear, since it combines the uniform elongation before necking with the elongation that occurs only in the neck. This makes the percent elongation a function of the original gauge length, which is not the case with the %RA.

In the operation of a bicycle, the ductility of the spokes is not usually a consideration, except that some ductility is obviously required. However, during the wire-drawing operation used to make spokes, the ductility is clearly very important. If the wire cannot be greatly elongated and thinned, then extensive wire drawing cannot
2280 be carried out. The drawing process relies heavily on the fact that the wire-drawing dies exert a transverse compression on the wire, as illustrated in Fig. 2.18.

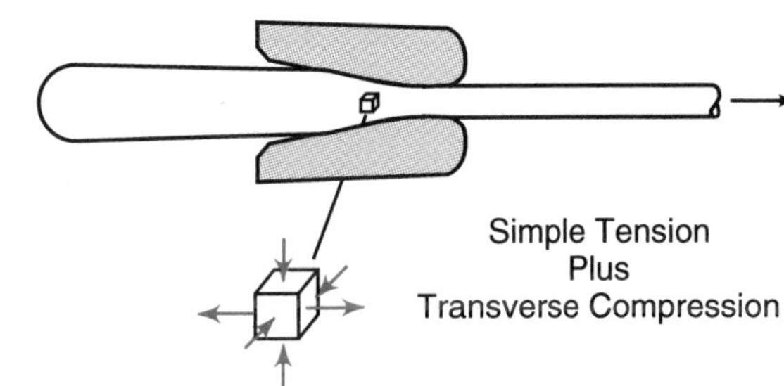

Fig. 2.18 Schematic representation of a wire being drawn through a die. The die exerts transverse compression and allows large tensile elongation without rupture.

The transverse compression plays two important roles. First, it inhibits the growth of any cavities that may form in the wire. That is, it has an effect opposite to that of the transverse tension from plastic constraint in the neck of a tensile specimen. Secondly, the transverse compression acts to elongate the wire by squeezing it, just as one can elongate a roll of clay by making a fist around it and squeezing. The effect can be understood mathematically by considering the two-dimensional cases shown in Fig 2.19.

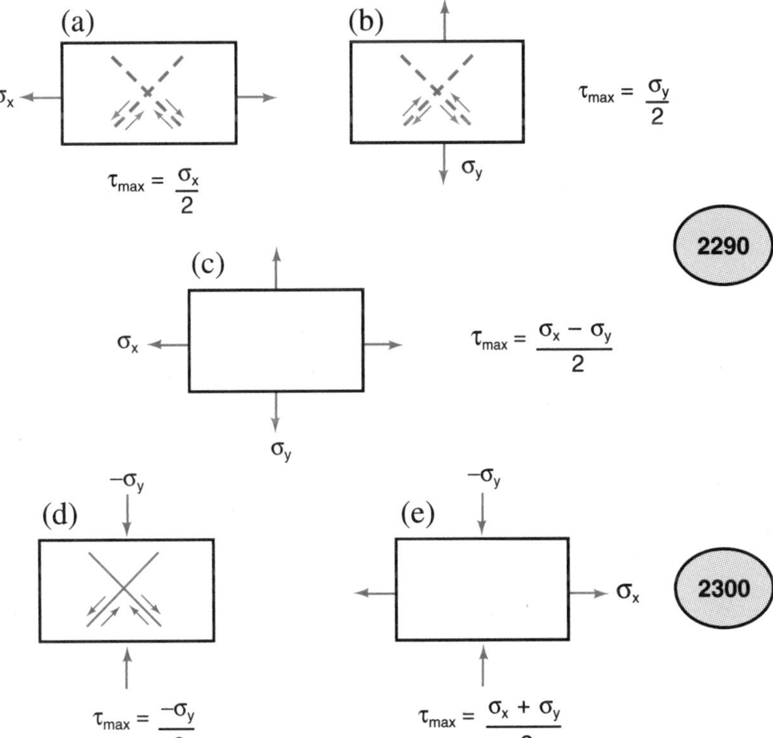

2290

2300

Fig. 2.19 Illustrations of the maximum shear stresses that arise from various combinations of tensile and compressive stresses. (a) Longitudinal tension only. (b) Transverse tension only; note that the sign of the shear stress is reversed from (a). (c) Combination of (a) and (b); note that the maximum shear stress is reduced by the transverse tension. (d) Transverse compression only; note that the sign of the shear stress is the same as in (a). (e) Combination of (a) and (d); note that the shear stress is greatest in this case, which is analogous to the case of wire drawing.

Because the transverse compression imposed by the wire-drawing die increases the maximum shear stress in the wire, plastic flow is enhanced; hence elongation and thinning of the wire proceed more readily. Of course, the frictional force exerted by the dies must be overcome by the drawing force, and the drawing force must also overcome the strain hardening effect. After a certain amount of drawing, the wire must be softened by *annealing,* meaning heating so as to soften it, before more drawing can be done. Otherwise, the drawing force would become so large that the wire would neck while it is being drawn. (Annealing will be discussed in Chapter 5.)

The strain hardening produced by wire drawing is the primary means of strengthening bicycle spokes. The effect of the wire drawing on the tensile strength of a stainless steel spoke is illustrated in Fig. 2.20; here, the stress-strain curve of an as-drawn stainless-steel spoke is compared to that of an annealed spoke. Note that the wire-drawing process produces a level of strain hardening much greater than can be achieved in a tensile test. This is a direct result of the enhancement of plastic flow caused by the transverse compression from the drawing die.

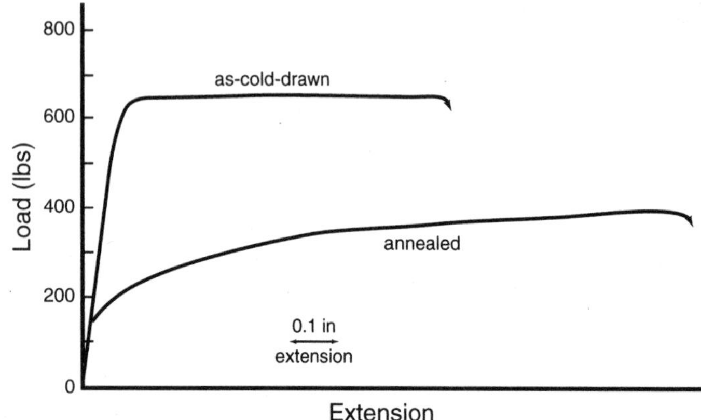

Fig. 2.20 Stress-strain curves of an as-cold-drawn stainless steel spoke and the same kind of spoke after being annealed.

Summary

Solids can be loaded by normal stresses (either tension or compression) or by shear stresses, or they can be subjected to a bending moment, which produces a non-uniform stress field comprising a mixture of tension, compression, and sometimes shear. The tensile stress in a spoke must be kept well below the yield stress; i.e., the loading must be in the elastic range. The stress created by a given amount of strain (imposed by turning the threaded nipple) can be calculated by means of Hooke's law, with knowledge of Young's modulus. Both the yield stress and Young's modulus can be measured in the tensile test by employing an extensometer, which is used in the study of small-scale deformation. Here, engineering stress and strain are always used.

When the consideration is production of spokes, rather than their use in a wheel, large-scale-deformation behavior is the relevant issue. This is exemplified by the tensile test carried out beyond the point of necking to fracture to measure the UTS and the % RA or the % elongation. The transverse tension in the neck of the specimen, imposed by the constraint of the un-necked regions, leads to void formation in the interior of the neck. The growth and coalescence of the voids produces failure by rupture. By contrast, a wire-drawing die imposes transverse compression, which has two effects: Void formation is suppressed, and the shear stress is increased. The latter produces enhanced plastic flow in the die, which in turn has two effects: It facilitates the reduction in wire diameter at a drawing force below that corresponding to the UTS of the wire, and it produces much more strain hardening than does deformation by simple tension. Thus, wire drawing serves both to fabricate the spokes from rod stock and to strengthen it for use in a wheel.

Appendix 2.1 - The Load Cell

Load cells have wide applications; one is the common bathroom scale. Most operate on the principle of the resistance strain gauge.

The electrical resistance of a wire, R, is given by the product of the resistivity of the material, ρ, times the length of the wire, divided by its cross-sectional area: $R = \rho\ell/A$. When the wire is stretched, ℓ increases and A decreases; this means R must increase. Thus, if a wire carrying a constant current, *i,* is stretched, the voltage drop along the wire must change, according to Ohm's law:

$$V = iR$$

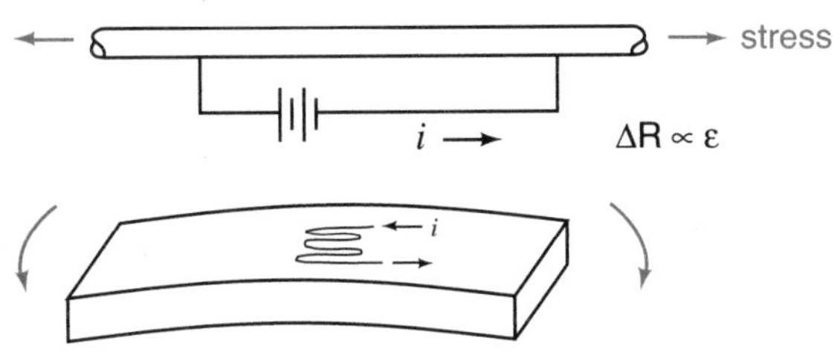

In a load cell a strain gauge comprising a long, folded wire is bonded to a beam that is bent as the load is applied.

As the beam bends, the wire of the strain gauge is stretched. The effect of the change in its resistance is measured by the use of a Wheatstone-bridge circuit in which the strain gauge is one of the legs. With the appropriate electronics, the effect is indicated as a voltage in the millivolt range. This is, in turn, calibrated (by application of known weights to the beam to which the gauge is bonded) to read out as a load. Obviously, the load cell must be powered by a constant-current source.

The allowable load range for a given load cell must be such that the beam deforms only elastically.

Appendix 2.2 - Criterion for Necking in a Tensile Test

The mathematical criterion for reaching a maximum in the load *vs.* elongation curve is that the variation in load becomes zero. Load, P, is stress, σ, times area, A. Therefore, at maximum P:

$$dP = 0 = \sigma dA + A d\sigma$$

or

$$\frac{d\sigma}{\sigma} = -\frac{dA}{A}$$

Physically, $d\sigma/\sigma$ can be interpreted as the fractional increase in load due to strain hardening, and $-dA/A$ as the fractional decrease in cross-section as the specimen is plastically elongated. Before necking, the former exceeds the latter:

$$\frac{d\sigma}{\sigma} > -\frac{dA}{A}$$

and the specimen is plastically stable. After necking, strain hardening continues in the necked region, but it is insufficient to compensate for the thinning in the neck. That is,

$$\frac{d\sigma}{\sigma} < -\frac{dA}{A}$$

Necking occurs when $d\sigma/\sigma = -dA/A$. This is known as the *Considère criterion.*

Glossary/Vocabulary - Chapter 2

% elong — This means the percent elongation to failure in a tensile specimen. It includes the uniform elongation (i.e., up to the point of necking) as well as the elongation after necking, which is confined to the necked region. A stainless-steel spoke exhibits much greater % elong than a carbon-steel spoke because of its greater capacity for strain hardening.

%RA — This means the percent reduction in area at the point of failure in a tensile specimen. It is the most useful measure of ductility. It is given by $(A_f - A_0)/A_0 \times 100$, where A_f is the final (minimum) area, e.g., in the neck, and A_0 is the original area. The %RA obviously increases as void-forming particles are eliminated from a material.

Binding-energy curve — This is a plot of the energy of a solid vs. the distance of separation of its constituent atoms. The equilibrium interatomic spacing in a crystal occurs at the minimum in the curve. The binding energy is given by the depth of the minimum. The minimum is the result of the competing forces of attraction and repulsion between the atoms. The sharpness of the curvature at the minimum is a measure of the elastic modulus of the crystal, and the binding energy is manifested by the temperature of melting.

Deformation processing — This is the forming of metals by such processes as forging, rolling, wire drawing, etc. Hot working causes only a shape change; cold working causes strain hardening in addition to the shape change. Both are considered deformation processing.

Dislocation — A dislocation is a linear defect in a crystal. Conceptually, a crystal can be dislocated if one part is sheared partly over the other part. The boundary between the sheared and not-sheared regions is the dislocation. Dislocations are of three types: edge, screw, and mixed. Plastic deformation of crystals occurs mainly by slip, which involves the motion of dislocations. That is, slip occurs progressively, rather than all at once, similar to the displacement of a rug by the motion of a ripple in the rug.

Dislocation glide — This is the term for the motion of a dislocation on a slip (or glide) plane of a crystal. It is the mechanism of slip.

Ductility — Ductility is a measure of the ability of a material to be deformed plastically without breaking. The most common measure of ductility is the percent reduction of area of a specimen in a tensile test prior to failure. An alternative measure is the percent elongation. Ductility is usually inversely related to strength. A stainless-steel spoke exhibits more ductility than a carbon-steel spoke, partly because of the carbides in the latter, which promote void formation in the neck of a tensile specimen. A martensitically hardened steel would exhibit low ductility.

Elastic limit — The elastic limit is a stress beyond which a body becomes permanently deformed. That is, it no longer behaves elastically. In a tensile test, the stress-strain curve becomes non-linear at the elastic limit. (The detection of the elastic limit depends on the precision of the measurement of elongation.)

Elastic modulus — See Young's modulus.

Engineering stress — This is defined as load divided by the area of the original cross section. The yield stress and the ultimate tensile stress are always given in terms of engineering stress.

Engineering strain Like engineering stress, engineering strain is defined in terms of original dimensions. In the case of normal strains (tensile or compressive), the engineering strain is the change in length divided by the original (gauge) length. The strain used to define yielding is always expressed as engineering strain.

Extensometer This is a type of displacement transducer, with which a mechanical motion is converted to an electrical signal. The extensometer is attached to the gauge section of a tensile specimen, and, when the specimen is extended, the extensometer experiences a displacement, which is converted to a voltage signal by way of an electrical device, like an electrical-resistance strain gauge. A common extensometer is a clip gauge, which has knife edges spaced, say, 0.5inch apart that are attached to the specimen and so define the gauge length. When these are displaced, the thin beam-like arms attached to them are bent, and the bending is indicated by the change in resistance in the strain gauge bonded to one arm.

Gauge length This is the reference length on a tensile specimen used to specify strain. When an extensometer is used, it is the length over which the extensometer measures a length change. When one is not used, the gauge length is taken to be the length over which the cross section is of uniform area; i.e., the length between the shoulders of the specimen. In the U.S., the gauge length of tensile specimens is commonly 0.5 or 1 inch.

Hooke's law A solid in which the amount of deformation is proportional to the applied force is said to exhibit linear elastic behavior and to follow Hooke's law. It was first defined for springs, and the proportionality between force and displacement is expressed by the spring constant. Later it was defined in terms of stress and strain, and the relevant parameter, for example in tensile deformation, is Young's modulus. A solid in which the amount of deformation is proportional to the applied force is said to exhibit linear elastic behavior and to follow Hooke's law.

Isotropic A body is isotropic with respect to some property if the value of the property is independent of the direction along which it is measured. A glassy (amorphous) material is isotropic with respect to all properties.

Necking The maximum in the stress-strain curve occurs because the reduction in cross-sectional area becomes too great to be compensated for by strain hardening. At that point the specimen becomes plastically unstable, meaning that some region of the gauge section begins to thin down more than any other region. After that, the thinning becomes concentrated and a neck forms in that region, followed finally by failure there by rupture. Because stainless-steel (FCC) spokes strain harden to a greater extent than carbon-steel (BCC) spokes, they are more resistant to necking. This is manifested by a more prolonged maximum in the stress-strain curve.

Necking criterion This is also known as the Consideré criterion. Since necking begins at the maximum of the stress-strain curve, it occurs when the variation in load is zero; that is, $dP = d\sigma A = 0$. This leads to the criterion that necking occurs when $d\sigma/\sigma = -dA/A$; that is, when the fractional increase in flow stress due to strain hardening is just balanced by the fractional decrease in cross section due to the plastic extension of the specimen.

Normal stress	A stress is, by definition, a force divided by the area of the surface upon which the force acts. A normal stress is one in which the force lies perpendicular to the surface. It may be either tensile or compressive. It tends to change the volume of a body, rather than its shape. A bicycle spoke is subjected to tension; this represents a stress normal to the cross-section of the spoke.
Plastic constraint	The material in the neck of a tensile specimen is constrained to some extent from continuing to deform plastically, because the transverse stress components reduce the net shear stress in the neck. Since these transverse stresses are caused by the un-necked regions, the latter are said to exert plastic constraint on the necked region. The same kind of constraint exists in any case where one part of a specimen tends to deform plastically more than a neighboring part.
Plastic strain	When a material is deformed beyond its elastic limit, part of the deformation becomes permanent, or irreversible. That part of the deformation is called plastic deformation. When expressed as displacement per unit length, it is plastic strain. A material loaded to the 0.2% yield stress has undergone a plastic strain of 0.002, or 0.2%.
Poisson's ratio	Most materials contract laterally as they are extended; this contraction, when expressed per unit lateral dimension (e.g., thickness), represents a negative strain. The lateral strain divided by the longitudinal strain for elastic deformation is called Poisson's ratio. It is given by $\nu = -\varepsilon_x/\varepsilon_z$. Poisson's ratio for most metals is about 1/3.
Rupture	Rupture is tensile failure by prolonged plastic deformation. In a tensile specimen, it occurs in a necked region. Most specimens contain particles of either a second phase or impurities, and voids form around these particles when triaxial tension is applied, as in a neck. Rupture occurs with the growth and coalescence of these voids. In the absence of such particles, necking would continue, and rupture would occur when the cross section is reduced to zero area. Rupture in a stainless steel spoke occurs as a result of voids that form around particles of oxide, sulfide, etc.
Schmid factor	This is the factor $\cos\lambda \cos\theta$ in the Schmid equation. The maximum value of the Schmid factor is 0.5.
Schmid law	Strictly speaking, the Schmid law states that crystals should slip on the slip planes that are subjected to the largest shear stress. The maximum shear stress is given by $\tau = \sigma \cos\lambda \cos\theta$, where σ is the applied tensile stress, and λ and θ are the angles between the tensile axis and the slip-plane normal and slip direction, respectively. This equation is also sometimes referred to as the Schmid law. The maximum possible shear stress would occur when λ and θ both equal 45 degrees.
Shear modulus	This is the slope of a plot of shear stress vs. elastic shear strain for an elastic body. It is a material property. The shear modulus is approximately 3/8 of Young's modulus for most metals.
Shear strain.	Shear strain is defined as a displacement per unit length perpendicular to the displacement. This is equivalent to the tangent of the angle of shear. It tends to change the shape of a body, rather than its volume.

Shear stress	A stress is, by definition, a force divided by the area of the surface upon which the force acts. In the case of a shear stress, the force lies parallel to the surface. A skier exerts a shear stress on the surface of snow.
Slip	Slip is a mechanism of plastic deformation of a crystalline solid. It occurs by the motion, or glide, of dislocations. It occurs along the most closely packed planes and in close-packed directions.
Slip band	Also called a slip line, a slip band is an intense, essentially two-dimensional region of plastic shear, in which many dislocations are generated and move a considerable distance, until they reach a surface or are blocked by some obstacle, like a grain boundary or a second phase.
Spring constant	The slope of the plot of force vs. displacement for an elastic body. A stiff spring has a large spring constant.
Stored elastic energy	When a body is deformed elastically, energy is stored in the distorted interatomic bonds. That is, the bonds act like springs. The amount of energy stored per unit volume is equal to the area under the stress-strain curve. Since the area under an elastic stress-strain curve is given by 1/2 $\sigma\varepsilon$, it is also given by $\sigma^2/2E$, using Hooke's law, $\sigma = E\varepsilon$.
Strain gauge	This is a device to measure the extension of a specimen, as in a tensile test, for example. It comprises a thin metal wire or thin metallic film, arranged in a kind of back-and-forth pattern to increase its length, and bonded to the surface of the specimen (and insulated from the specimen). (The pattern is placed across the direction of the elongation of the specimen.) The electrical resistance of the gauge increases as the specimen and the bonded gauge are stretched, and this is monitored by making the gauge part of a bridge circuit.
Strain hardening	Strain hardening is the name given to the increase in resistance to plastic deformation that results from the process of plastic deformation itself. It is one of the hallmarks of metallic behavior. Stress-strain curves of metallic materials normally exhibit a rise in the "flow stress" after the yield stress is passed. That is, the metal is strengthened by plastic deformation. This is a common mechanism used to strengthen structural materials, such as bicycle spokes. Strain hardening is the result of dislocation multiplication during plastic flow.
Stress-strain curve	This is the output of a tensile test; it is a plot of load vs. extension, which is similar in shape to an engineering stress-*vs.*-strain plot, because stress and strain are related to load and extension through constant factors. The complete stress-strain curve of a metallic material shows the initial elastic range, the strain-hardening range, and the final failure, usually preceded by necking, which begins as the curve passes through a maximum.
Tensile test	This is a test of the mechanical behavior of a material in which a rod- or sheet-like specimen is gripped at each end and extended. The load *vs.* extension is plotted on an X-Y recorder if an extensometer is used, and on a strip-chart recorder if one is not used. An extensometer is generally used to measure Young's modulus and the yield stress (small-scale deformation), and the load-*vs.*-extension curve on a strip-chart recorder is used to measure UTS and the percent elongation.

True strain	Like true stress, the true strain is defined with respect to actual dimensions, which change with plastic strain. For tensile strain, it is the integral from l_0 to l_f of dl/l, which equals ln l_f/l_0. True strain is always larger than engineering strain, but the difference is negligible in small-scale deformation
True stress	This is defined as load divided by the actual, or current, area of the cross section to which the load is applied. This area changes with plastic deformation. It is normally only used in discussions of deformation processing, in which the plastic strains are large. In a tensile test, the true stress is higher than the engineering stress, because the cross-sectional area decreases with plastic strain.
Ultimate tensile strength (UTS)	The UTS is the maximum in the stress-strain curve. It is an engineering stress given by the maximum load divided by the original cross-sectional area. Thus, it is a conservative measure of the maximum load-bearing capacity of a tensile specimen. The UTS of a steel bicycle spoke is approximately 150ksi, or 1050MPa
Wire drawing	Wire is made by starting with a rod, usually produced on a rolling mill with grooved rolls, and by pulling the rod through a series of dies containing holes of successively smaller diameter. Bicycle spokes are produced by wire drawing.
Wrought product	This is a metal object formed by deformation processing, like rolling, wire-drawing, forging, etc. The process can involve either hot working or cold working. This is in contrast to a cast object or to one formed by sintering. The spokes of a bicycle wheel and the tubes of the frame are wrought products.
X-Y recorder	This a device for plotting curves generated by two voltage inputs, one on each of the X and Y axes. A stress-strain curve for small-scale deformation is normally plotted on an X-Y recorder. The load signal is applied to the Y-axis and the signal from the extensometer to the X-axis.
Yield stress	This is the stress required to give a specified amount of plastic strain in a tensile test, usually 0.1 or 0.2 %. The 0.2% yield stress of steel bicycle spokes is about 120ksi, or 840MPa.
Young's modulus	This is the slope of a stress-strain curve in the elastic region. It is the same for tension and compression in the linear elastic region. It is a material constant.

Exercises

2.1 For small-scale deformation, engineering stress and strain are good approximations for true stress and strain. Explain why.

2.2 A carbon-steel spoke with an elastic modulus of 210 GPa is loaded to a tensile stress of 240 MPa. The total strain is found by means of an extensometer to be 0.3%. Calculate how much plastic strain has occurred.

2.3 Calculate the stored elastic energy per unit volume in the spoke in Problem 2.2. How can this be related to the binding-energy curve (cf. Fig. 2.7.)?

2.4 If the UTS of a stainless steel spoke is 1725 MPa (250ksi), what is the *elastic* strain at this UTS? (Use the engineering stress approximation.)

2.5 What is the average (plastic) shear strain in a crystal in which one out of every twenty atom planes (on average) is displaced in shear by 4 atom spacings? (The type of shear is shown in Fig. 2.9 and at right.)

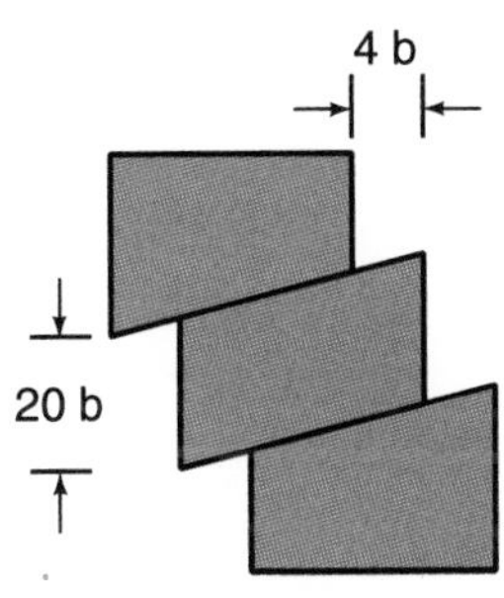

2.6 To the extent that the elastic strain is negligibly small, there is no volume change associated with plastic strain. Explain. (cf. Fig. 2.9).

2.7 What is the maximum shear stress on a plane the normal of which lies at 35° to the tensile axis, when a force of 4450N (1000lb) is applied to a bicycle spoke with a diameter of 2mm?

2.8 Prove mathematically that the maximum shear stress in a tensile specimen is half the applied tensile stress. (Hint: express θ in terms of λ, since their sum is 90°, and then maximize τ with respect to λ by differentiation.)

2.9 Write an expression for the maximum shear stress in a spoke as it is being drawn through a die when the longitudinal stress is σ_l and the radial stress from the die is σ_r.

2.10 Explain why wire drawing produces more strain hardening in a spoke than can be produced in a tensile test; cf. Fig. 2.20. (Assume the starting condition in both cases is an annealed wire.)

2.11 It can be seen from Fig. 2.20 that the load needed to produce plastic flow in the cold-drawn spoke in a tensile test is above 600lb. However, the load required for reduction of the wire diameter during cold drawing of the spoke was significantly lower. Explain why.

2.12 A tensile sample has an initial gauge diameter of 11.3mm, and gauge length of 50mm. After the sample fractures, the diameter at the neck is 9.6mm.

a. Express the ductility as percent reduction in area.

b. What can you say about the ductility expressed as percent elongation?

2.13 A stainless steel bicycle spoke 1.8mm in diameter is loaded in service with a tensile force of 1300N.

a. What is the tensile force in pounds?
b. What is the tensile stress in the spoke?
c. Compare the tensile stress to the expected yield strength.
d. What is the elastic strain in the spoke?
e. If the spoke is 25.30 cm long when unstressed, how long is it when the maximum load is applied?

2.14 In producing wire for bicycle spokes, fairly long lengths of wire are pulled through a wire-drawing die as in Fig. 2.18. If the wire emerging from the die has a diameter of 0.125 inch, and the force required to pull the wire through the die at a constant rate is 1200 lb,

a. What is the tensile stress in the wire?
b. If the length of the wire (measured from the die to the point where the force is applied) is 35.2 ft with the force applied; by how much will the wire shorten if the force is removed?

3

MICROSTRUCTURE AND CRYSTAL STRUCTURE

3.1 Metallographic Sample Preparation

As shown in Fig. 2.20, there is a dramatic difference in the tensile behavior between an annealed and a cold-drawn stainless steel spoke. To begin to explore the reasons for this difference, one can examine the microstructure of the spokes in an optical microscope; this process is called *optical metallography.* In order to do a metallographic examination, it is necessary to cut, mount, polish, and etch the specimen to be examined. This process is outlined in Fig. 3.1.

1. Piece to be analyzed is cut to reveal the desired section.
2. Cut piece is mounted in plastic (e.g., Bakelite® or Lucite®).

3. Specimen surface is ground flat on a series of abrasive papers having ever-finer sizes of silicon carbide (SiC) particles.

4. The ground specimen is polished on a series of polishing wheels using ever-finer grits of diamond dust or Al_2O_3 suspended in oil or water, respectively, to produce a mirror-like surface.
5. The sample is etched in an appropriate reagent, often a dilute acid.

Fig. 3.1 Process for preparing a metallographic specimen; for example, a longitudinal and a transverse cross-section of a bicycle spoke.

3.2 Optical Microscopy

When the preparation is completed, the specimen may be examined in a metallurgical microscope, a schematic example of which is shown in Fig. 3.2. The special characteristic of this microscope is that it is configured for the observation of opaque specimens. (Geologists use the same kind of microscope for rocks and minerals; they call it a petrographic microscope.) One can see that the illumination is directed from the light source down through the objective lens to the specimen. The light that is reflected directly back from the specimen passes again through the objective lens and then up through the half-silvered reflector and the eyepiece. (Obviously, there is a considerable loss of intensity from the light's having to pass twice through the reflector, but this is unavoidable and is compensated for by the use of a bright, well-focussed lamp as the light source.)

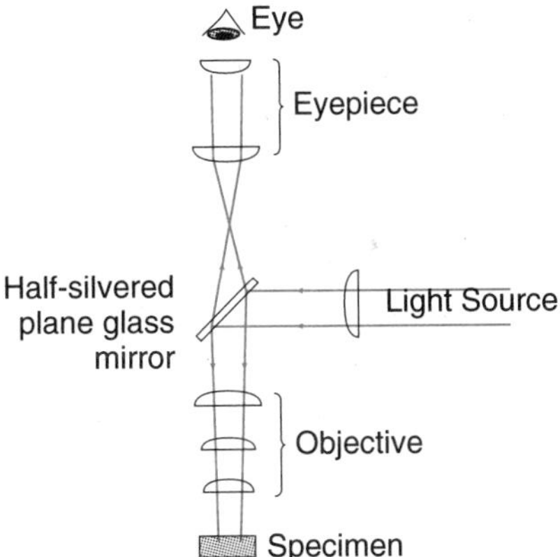

Fig. 3.2 Schematic representation of a metallurgical microscope.

One can observe the microstructure through the eyepiece, or, by mounting a camera over the eyepiece, one can make a photomicrograph (not a microphotograph) of the specimen. This was done for the specimen of a cold-drawn stainless-steel spoke; the results are shown in Fig. 3.3.

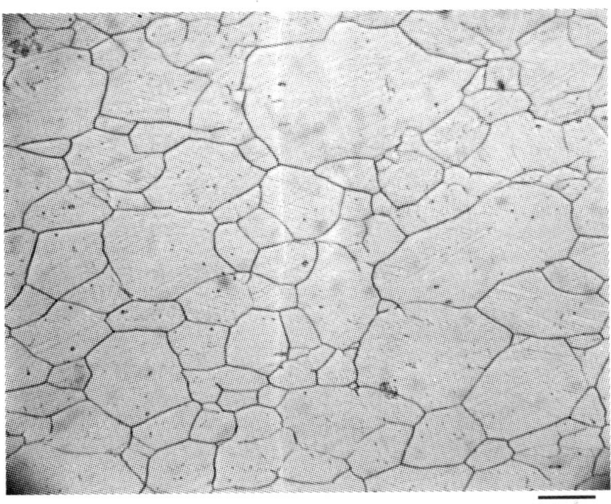

Fig. 3.3 Microstructure of a stainless steel bicycle spoke in the cold-drawn (i.e., as-received) condition.

3.3 Imaging of Grain Boundaries by Reflection Contrast

The microstructure of the stainless steel spoke in Fig. 3.3 shows a polycrystalline aggregate, the nature of which can be understood by using a two-dimensional analog of a polycrystal that can be produced by a bubble raft, as shown in Fig. 3.4. This is made by blowing bubbles of equal size in a soap solution held in a broad, flat container. The bubbles coalesce into two-dimensional arrays floating on the surface of the solution, and they tend to form ordered regions in which each bubble has six neighbors. Such a region is analogous to a close-packed plane of atoms in a crystal; this configuration is the densest possible packing of spheres of equal size. With continued blowing of bubbles, the regions grow until they merge. This process is analogous to the solidification of a polycrystalline material (like stainless steel).

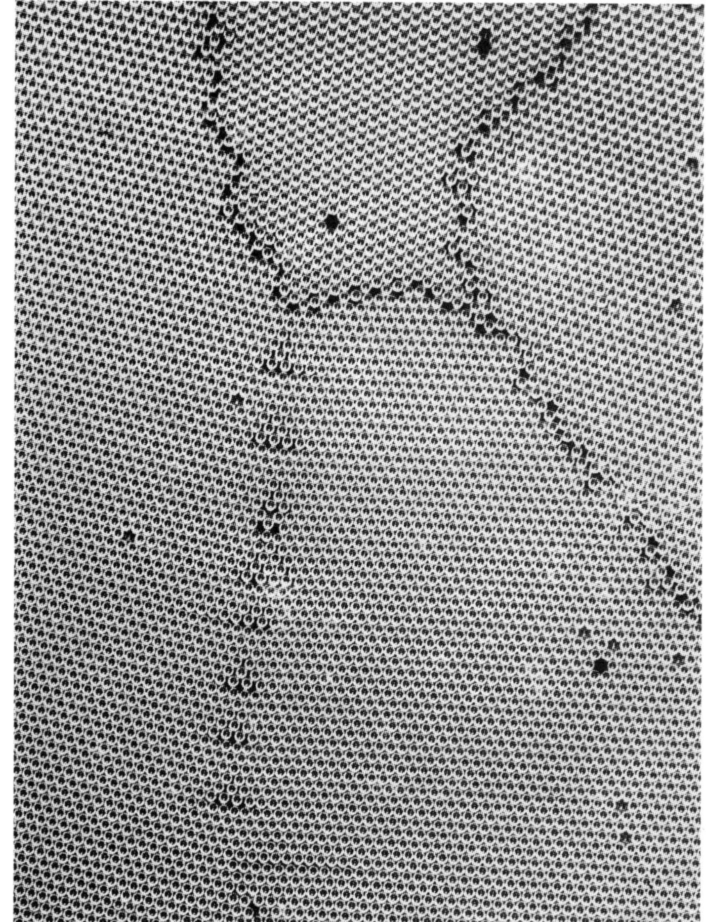

Fig. 3.4 A two-dimensional analog of a polycrystal, made with a bubble raft, showing the varying degrees of atomic disorder at grain boundaries. (From P. G. Shewmon, *Transformations in Metals,* McGraw-Hill, N.Y. 1969, p. 26.)

The arrangement of the "atoms" in the boundaries of the two-dimensional "grains" of the bubble raft depends on the degree of misorientation of the two contiguous grains and the orientation of the boundary. However, two things are clear:

1. In a two-dimensional grain, each atom touches 6 neighbors; however, the atoms along the grain boundaries have, on the average, fewer than 6 touching neighbors. Since the arrangement of atoms inside the grain is the minimum-energy configuration, atoms along a grain boundary (or on a surface) must be in a higher energy state than atoms fully within a grain. Thus, there is associated with grain boundaries in a solid an extra energy per unit area (in three dimensions) that is analogous to the surface energy of a solid or liquid.

2. Some boundaries are more disordered and loosely packed than others. Therefore, the grain boundary energy varies from one boundary to another.

Since atoms along grain boundaries are in a relatively high energy state, they go into solution more readily than atoms fully within grains when the specimen is etched in a chemical reagent. For this reason, grooves tend to develop along grain boundaries, the depth of which depends on the duration of etching attack and the atomic arrangements in the boundary. This grooving causes light to be scattered, rather than reflected back through the objective lens, when the etched sample is viewed in the microscope. This scattering delineates the grain boundaries, as illustrated by Fig. 3.5.

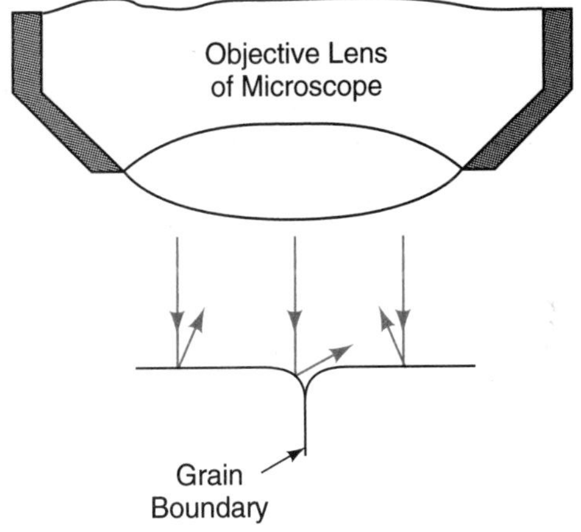

Fig. 3.5 The groove formed by etching makes a grain boundary appear as a dark line. (From W. D. Callister, Jr., *Materials Science and Engineering,* John Wiley, NY, 1985, p. 61. Reprinted by permission of John Wiley & Sons, Inc.)

3.4 The Structure of a Perfect FCC Crystal

As discussed in Chapter 1, the austenitic stainless steel used for bicycle spokes has an FCC crystal structure, the unit cell of which has already been illustrated in Fig.1.6. A hard-sphere model extending over a few dozen of these unit cells is shown in Fig. 3.6(a). This kind of model is quite reasonable for many metallic crystals, because the attractive (bonding) forces are very nearly nondirectional (being provided by the interaction between the positive ion cores and the "sea" of negative charge of the delocalized, or "free," valence electrons). Also, the steeply-rising repulsive force is felt only at close atomic spacings. Thus, a metal crystal can be approximated as a densely packed array of mutually attracting hard spheres.

The FCC structure represents the highest possible packing density for spheres of equal size, because it comprises close-packed planes stacked one on top of the other. One of the close-packed planes is illustrated in Fig. 3.6(c); this is revealed by removing a few of the corner atoms. An FCC crystal is constructed by stacking close-packed planes in a particular sequence, which can be described by considering the three sets of atom positions shown in Fig. 3.7. If one places the first close-packed plane in the A sites, the second in the B sites, and the third in the C sites, and repeats this ABC stacking indefinitely, the result is the FCC crystal shown in Fig. 3.6.

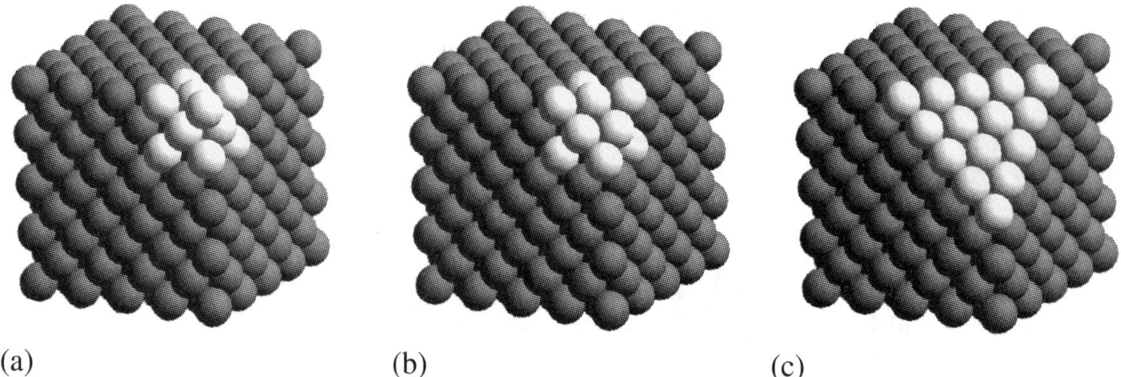

Fig. 3.6 Hard-sphere model of an FCC crystal, showing (a) a unit cell, (b) one sphere removed to show a close-packed plane, and (c) more spheres removed to enlarge the close-packed plane.

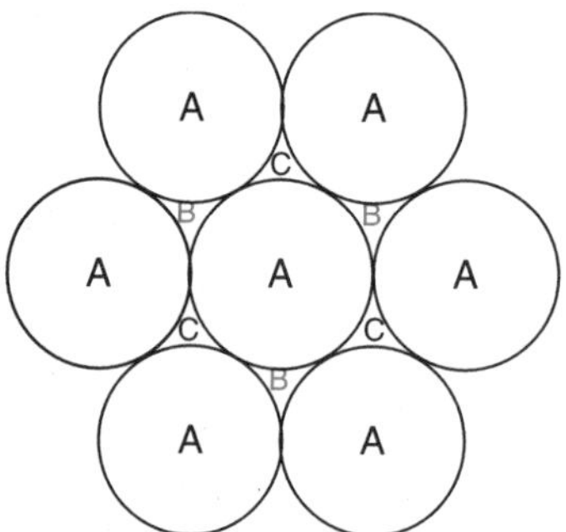

Fig. 3.7 A close-packed plane has three sets of sites, A, B, and C, as shown.

It can be seen that each atom has 12 neighbors in a close-packed crystal: six around it in a close-packed plane and three touching it in the adjacent planes above and below. This is the crystal structure one would expect in an ideal metal, which reaches its minimum energy condition by achieving the maximum density.

The FCC crystal structure is characteristic of platinum, gold, silver, copper, aluminum, and nickel, for example. The reason the stainless steel has this crystal structure is that it contains at least 8wt% nickel. This allows the high-temperature form of iron, which is also FCC, to be retained at low temperatures. If it were not for this alloying, the steel would be body-centered-cubic, BCC (cf. Fig. 1.5), at lower temperatures. Chromium is also BCC, so it is completely compatible with the normal low-temperature form of iron. Note that the BCC crystal structure has no close-packed planes; thus, it is less densely-packed than the FCC structure. (When all atoms in a crystal are the same size, the packing density depends only on the crystal structure.) In the case of the transition metals, like iron and chromium, the BCC crystal structure implies that the bonding has a directional component.

3.5 Crystallographic Indices of Planes

Close-packed planes are important in an FCC crystal, not only because of the way they are stacked, but also because slip occurs preferentially on close-packed planes. Therefore, these planes play an important role in plastic deformation of stainless steel spokes, for example. In order to be able to discuss slip planes and slip directions in metals, it is necessary to learn the system of notation used to designate particular planes and directions. Here, the discussion is confined to cubic crystals; that is, the system of notation to be described applies equally well to FCC or BCC crystals.

Returning to Fig. 3.6(b), it is apparent that the choice of corners from which to remove atoms was arbitrary; any one of eight corners could have been chosen. However, if the corner diagonally across the cubic array from the top-right-front corner had been chosen, the exposed close-packed plane would be parallel to that seen in Fig. 3.6(b). Crystallographically, these planes are considered equivalent. Therefore, one can say that there are only four distinct close-packed planes in the FCC crystal lattice: the ones revealed by removing atoms from any of the four top corners of the cubic block shown in Fig. 3.6(a).

The notation developed to identify planes in cubic crystals is the system of *Miller indices,* which is described by the following procedure. For simplicity one can think of a simple cubic lattice, made of the three perpendicular sets of parallel lines that define the unit cell, as shown in Fig. 3.8.

1. Select any lattice point as the origin of coordinates; use a right-handed set of Cartesian coordinates x,y,z, as shown in Fig. 3.8.
2. As an example, consider the shaded face of the unit cell in Fig. 3.8.
3. Write down the *intercepts* of the plane in units of the *lattice parameter.* (The lattice parameter is the length of an edge of the unit cell.) In this case the intercepts are ∞, 1, ∞. Because the plane is parallel to the x and z axes, it is considered to intercept them at infinity. 3175
4. Take the *reciprocals* of this set of intercepts. These are the Miller indices of the plane. Thus, 1/∞, 1/1, 1/∞ becomes 010.
5. To indicate the specific plane, enclose the set of indices in parentheses: (010). Note that the indices are <u>not</u> separated by commas.

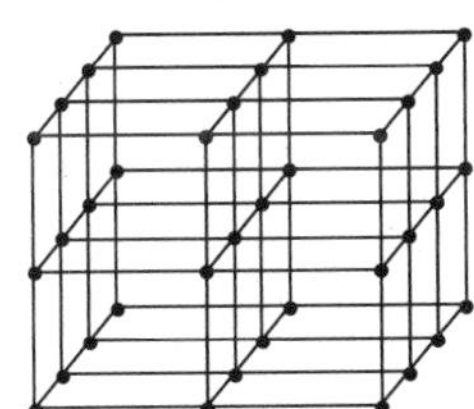

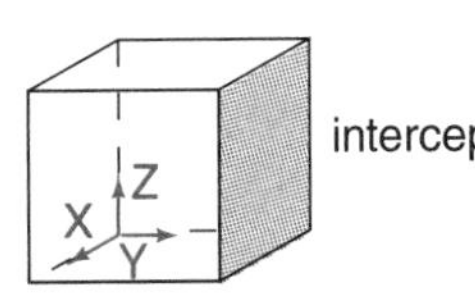

Fig. 3.8 A simple cubic lattice and the unit cell, showing the plane to be identified and the origin of coordinates chosen for this purpose.

Any face of a cubic unit cell can be represented by some permutation of 0, 1, and 0. The top plane, using the axes shown in Fig. 3.8, is (001); the front plane is (100). To index the rear plane, simply move the origin to a front corner; the indices of the plane are then ($\bar{1}$00). This, of course, is parallel to the front plane and is crystallographically equivalent to (100). (Any two planes whose Miller indices are related by multiplying through by -1 are equivalent.)

To refer to cube planes in general, curly brackets are used. Thus, {100} means any cube face, and it includes all the specific cube-plane indices. Note that, by convention, minus signs are written above a negative index, and the index is called *bar* one, *bar* two, etc.

Note also that Miller indices are always expressed as sets of integers. Hence, fractional reciprocal intercepts are always cleared by multiplication through by the lowest common denominator. For example, consider the plane shown shaded in Fig. 3.9(a), the intercepts of which are 1, 2, and 1. The reciprocals are 1, $^1/_2$, and 1, and these are multiplied through by 2 to get the Miller indices: (212).

Note further that, when any set of Miller indices is multiplied through by any number, the result is a plane parallel to the original; an example is shown in Fig. 3.9(b).

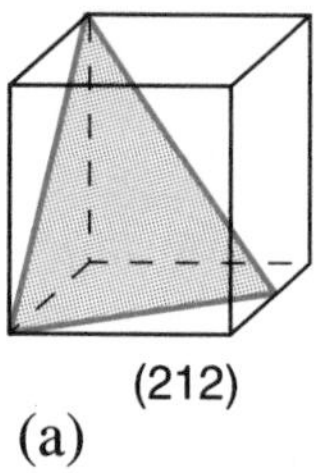

(a) (212)

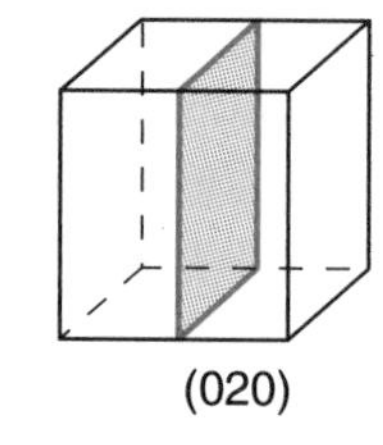

(b) (020)

Fig. 3.9 (a) The (212) plane. (b) The (020) plane is parallel to the (010) plane.

The above procedure is valid for all cubic lattices. The fact that the BCC and FCC lattices have lattice points at the body center and at the face centers, respectively, of the unit cells is irrelevant.

Returning to the FCC crystal depicted in Fig. 3.6(b), the close-packed plane shown there can be represented in either of the ways depicted in Fig. 3.10. One would normally give the Miller indices as (111).

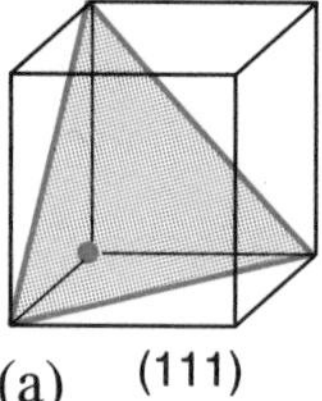

(a) (111)

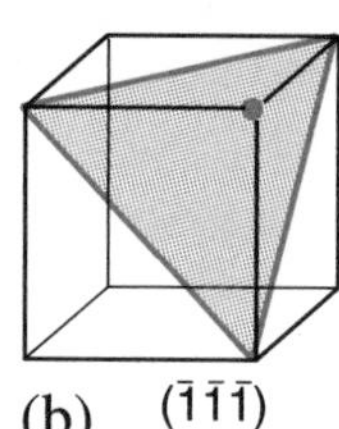

(b) $(\bar{1}\bar{1}\bar{1})$

Fig. 3.10 (a) The (111) plane. (b) The $(\bar{1}\bar{1}\bar{1})$ plane. Each is referred to the origin indicated by the filled dot. These planes are equivalent, since they are related by a -1 multiplication, and the choice of the origin is arbitrary.

Example 3.1

Q. Sketch the other three close-packed planes in the FCC crystal shown in Fig. 3.6 and give their Miller indices.

A. The three planes can be revealed by removing atoms from the other three top corners of the block in Fig. 3.6. If the (111) plane, which is already indexed, is considered as the southeast (SE) corner, then the others are as shown below:

SW corner

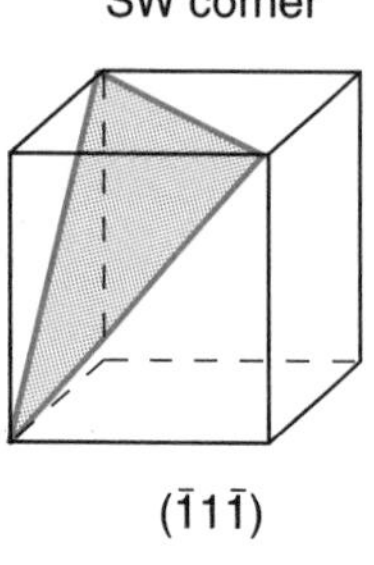

$(\bar{1}1\bar{1})$

NW corner

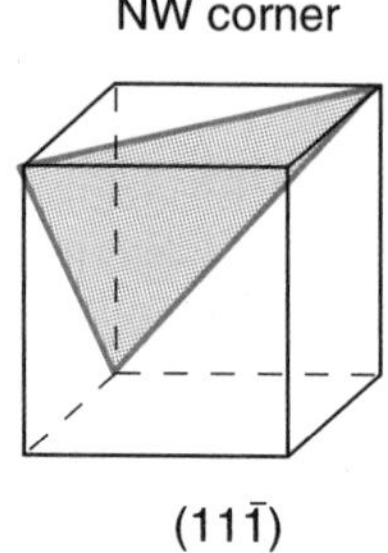

$(11\bar{1})$

NE corner

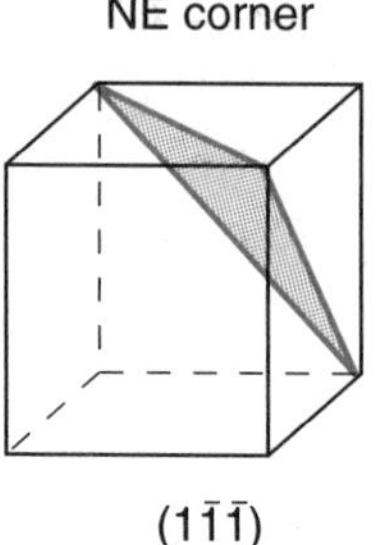

$(1\bar{1}\bar{1})$

The origin is always chosen for convenience; obviously, the plane must not pass through the origin. The Miller indices are given for each plane.

Note that none of the four sets of indices: (111), ($\bar{1}1\bar{1}$), ($11\bar{1}$) and ($1\bar{1}\bar{1}$) can be obtained by a -1 multiplication of any of the others. Therefore, they are distinct planes. These are the only {111}-type planes in the FCC crystal lattice; the ones revealed by removing atoms from the bottom corners of the block in Fig. 3.6 are parallel to, and therefore equivalent to, the ones shown above.

Another important plane in cubic crystals is parallel to a cube axis and passes through a cube face. This family of planes has the indices {110}. Two examples are shown in Fig. 3.11.

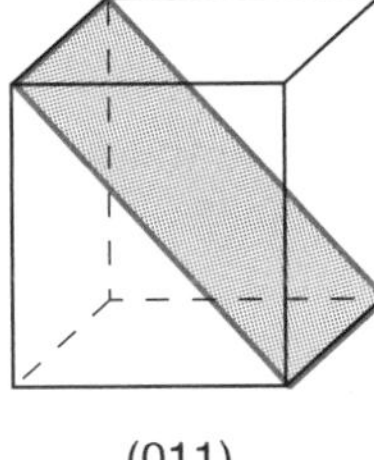

(011)

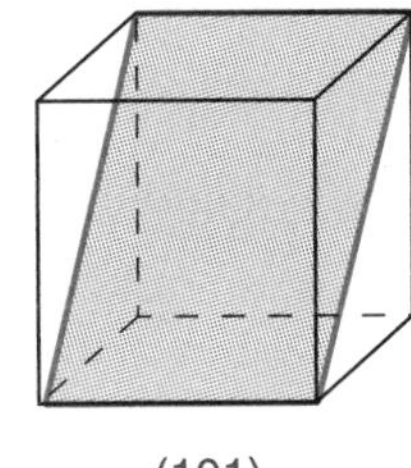

(101)

Fig. 3.11 Two examples of {110} planes.

Example 3.2

Q. Referring to Fig. 3.11, sketch the other four {110}-type planes in a cubic lattice and give their indices.

A. The four planes are shown below, with their indices:

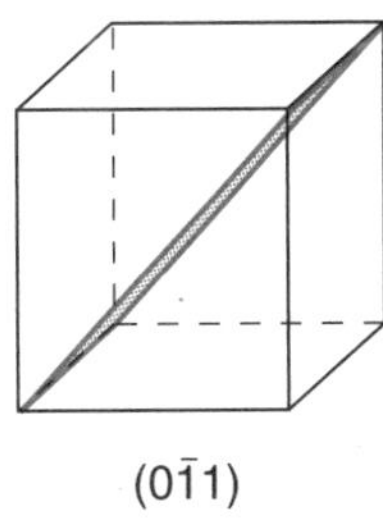

(0$\bar{1}$1)

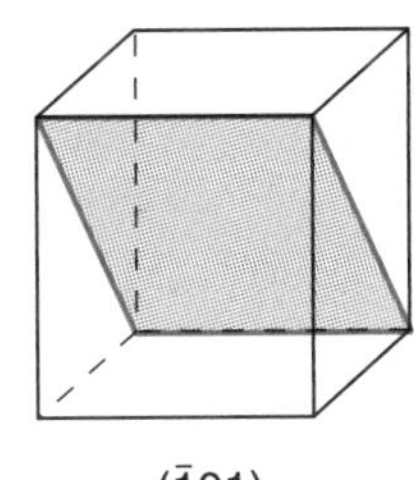

($\bar{1}$01)

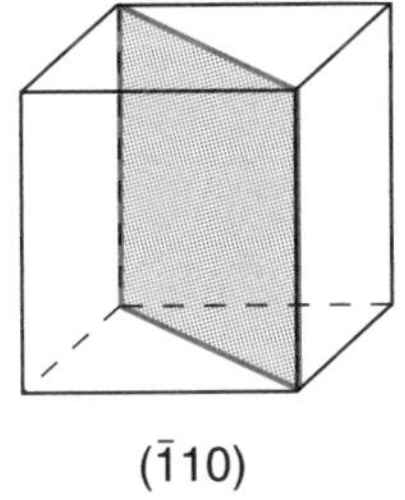

($\bar{1}$10)

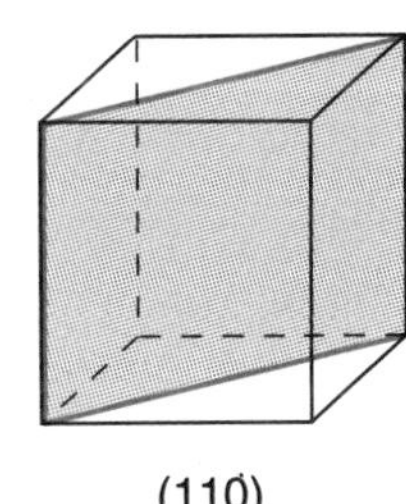

(110)

3.6 Direction Indices

It is also important to have a system for denoting directions in crystals. For example, it is necessary to describe slip in terms of a slip plane and a slip direction. Direction indices are nothing more than the smallest set of indices that describes a vector in units of the lattice parameter, using the cube axes as the coordinate system. For specific directions square brackets are used: [ ]. For example, the cubic axes are [100], [010], and [001]. To refer to these axes generically, angled brackets are used: < >. For example, [100] means the direction along the x axis, and <100> means any of the three axial directions.

A great convenience in the cubic lattice is the fact that the [hkl] direction is perpendicular to the (hkl) plane. Examples are shown in Fig. 3.12. (This is only true for cubic crystals.) Note that multiplying direction indices through by -1 simply gives the reverse direction; it is crystallographically equivalent to the original. The body diagonals of a cube have <111> indices, and the face diagonals have <110> indices. Table 3.1 summarizes the convention regarding brackets around indices.

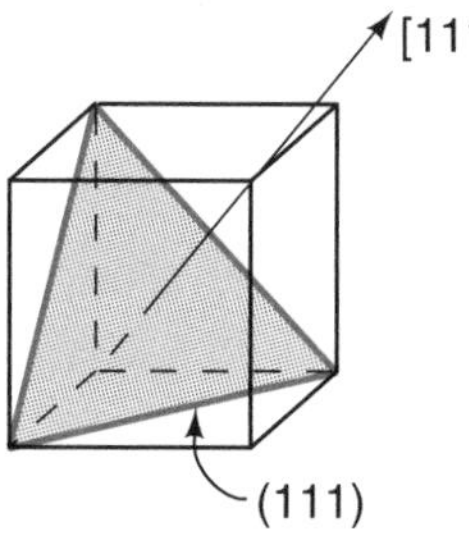

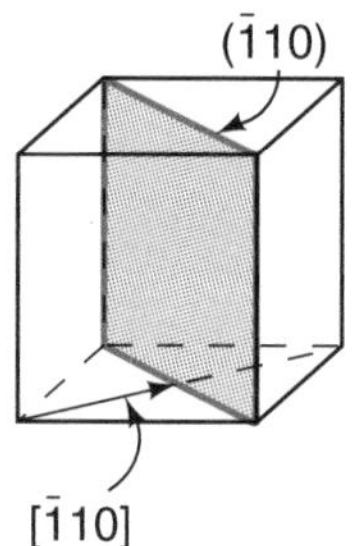

Fig. 3.12 Examples of [hkl] directions lying perpendicular to (hkl) planes.

Table 3.1 Convention for brackets around indices.

	Planes (Miller indices)	Directions
Specific	( )	[ ]
Generic	{ }	< >

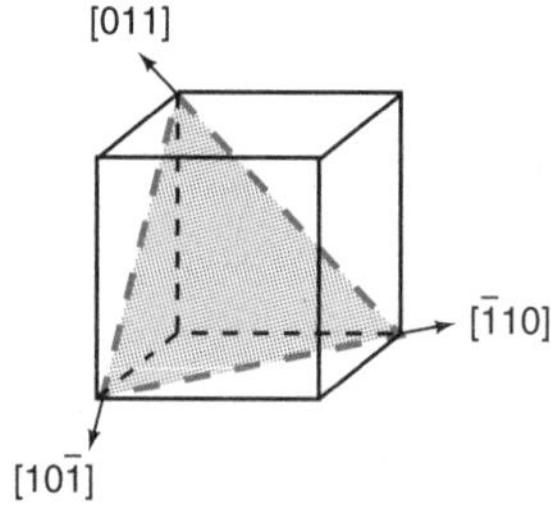

Example 3.3

Q. Show that three <110> directions lie in the (111) plane and give their indices.

A. The directions are sketched in the unit cell shown here; they could also have been represented by their opposites: [$\bar{1}$01], [1$\bar{1}$0], and [01$\bar{1}$].

Summary

Properties of materials depend on structure on several dimensional scales. What is commonly referred to as the microstructure is the arrangement of phases and grains as perceived with the optical (metallographic) microscope. Specimen preparation usually involves grinding, polishing, and etching, and the microstructure is imaged by means of reflection contrast.

On the atomic scale, the crystal structure of solids can be analyzed by means of x-ray diffraction (cf. Appendix 4.1), utilizing crystallographic notation to specify various planes and directions. This notation is introduced here for the cubic lattices, and the FCC structure characteristic of stainless-steel spokes is used as the working example.

Appendix 3.1 - The Scalar Product of Two Vectors

The *scalar,* or *dot,* product of two vectors **A** and **B** is defined by the equation

$$\mathbf{A} \bullet \mathbf{B} = |\mathbf{A}|\,|\mathbf{B}| \cos \theta$$

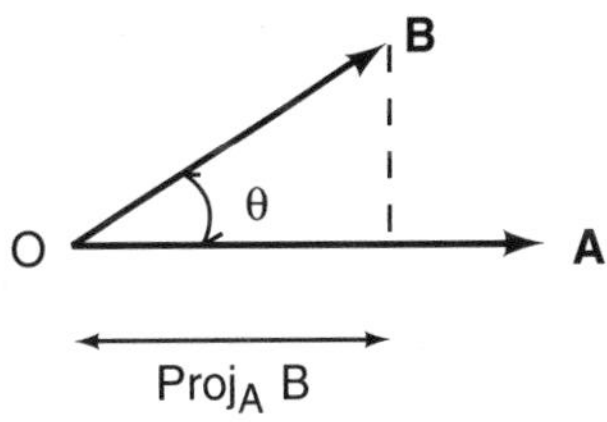

where θ is the angle between **A** and **B**.

Thus, the dot product may be interpreted geometrically as the length of **A** times the length of the projection of **B** onto **A**. In the present context, the usefulness of the dot product lies in the fact that, if **A** and **B** are perpendicular, cos θ = 0, and the dot product is zero.

The dot product can be calculated by writing the vectors in terms of their components,

$$\mathbf{A} = a_1\mathbf{i} + a_2\mathbf{j} + a_3\mathbf{k}$$

$$\mathbf{B} = b_1\mathbf{i} + b_2\mathbf{j} + b_3\mathbf{k}$$

and multiplying the components, as follows:

$$\mathbf{A} \bullet \mathbf{B} = a_1b_1 + a_2b_2 + a_3b_3$$

Thus, the $[1\bar{1}0]$ direction lies in the (111) plane, because

$$1 \times 1 + \bar{1} \times 1 + 0 \times 1 = 0$$

Glossary/Vocabulary - Chapter 3

Bravais lattice	A space lattice is also called a Bravais lattice, of which there are 14. That is, there are only 14 unique ways to arrange an ordered array of points in space so that every point has identical surroundings. Every crystal structure belongs to one of the 14 Bravais lattices. Most metals crystallize in one of three Bravais lattices: FCC, BCC, or hexagonal.
Close-packed direction	This is a direction in a crystal along which atoms touch. There are three close-packed directions in a close-packed plane. Slip usually occurs along close-packed directions.
Close-packed plane	A plane of atoms (all of equal size and considered as hard spheres) in which each atom is surrounded and touched by six neighbors is called close packed, because that represents the maximum possible areal (i.e., two-dimensional) packing density. An FCC crystal can be made by stacking close-packed planes of atoms in a sequence ABCABCA.....
Crystal lattice	This is properly called a space lattice. The points of a space lattice are defined by the intersections of three sets of parallel, equally spaced straight lines that divide space into contiguous equal-sized parallelepipeds. The lattice points are the positions occupied by atoms, or groups of atoms, in crystals.

Direction indices This is the system used to designate a direction in a crystal lattice. It is given by the components of any vector expressed in units of the basic lattice vectors. A cube edge is a <100> direction. A cube body diagonal is a <111> direction. A face diagonal is a <110> direction.

Grain boundary The interface between two crystals, or grains, in a polycrystalline aggregate is called a grain boundary. It is a two-dimensional crystalline defect. In a polycrystal, the grain boundaries comprise a multiply connected, two-dimensional surface embedded in the material.

Grain-boundary energy This is the interfacial energy associated with the interface between two grains in a polycrystal. It is the excess energy per unit area of boundary arising from the fact that the atoms along the boundary are not in their minimum-energy configuration. That is, they are not surrounded by the same number of atoms as would be the case in the interior of a grain, and the neighboring atoms are not all in the "right" positions. Another way to view this is that there is excess free volume associated with a grain boundary, compared with the interior of a grain. The excess energy should be essentially proportional to this excess free volume.

Lattice parameter The dimensions of the unit cell of a crystal lattice are given in terms of the lattice parameter. For the most general case, the unit cell would have three lattice parameters, denoted *a, b,* and *c*. A cubic crystal has only one lattice parameter, *a*, the length of the cube edge.

Metallography This is the process used to examine the microstructure of a solid specimen. It is usually taken to include specimen preparation and the examination of the specimen under a microscope. For a metallic material, metallography usually involves cutting a specimen, mounting it in plastic, polishing to a mirror-like flatness, and etching in some reagent that selectively attacks the microstructure.

Miller indices This is the three-digit system used to denote the planes in cubic crystal lattices. The indices {hkl} represent the reciprocals of the intercepts of the plane with the three axes, x,y,z, respectively, with fractions cleared. The cube faces are denoted as {100} planes. The slip planes in FCC metals are {111} planes and in BCC metals usually {110} planes.

Photomicrograph In materials science, this is a photograph taken through a metallurgical microscope of a metallographically prepared specimen. The prefix photo implies that light (i.e., an optical microscope) is used, as opposed to, say, electrons, as for an electron micrograph. A photomicrograph of a stainless-steel spoke would reveal the microstructure of a single-phase polycrystalline aggregate; i.e., it would show grains and grain boundaries.

Polycrystalline material A solid comprising an aggregate of individual crystals, or grains, is called polycrystalline, or a polycrystal. The individual grains may be oriented randomly in space, or there may be a preferred crystallographic orientation. This is the normal condition for a metal or alloy that solidifies from the liquid state, because during freezing, individual crystals nucleate at different points in the liquid and grow until they impinge upon one another.

Unit cell This is the basic unit of a crystal structure. It is repeated in three dimensions and displays the symmetry of the crystal structure. Most metals have BCC, FCC, or HCP unit cells.

Exercises

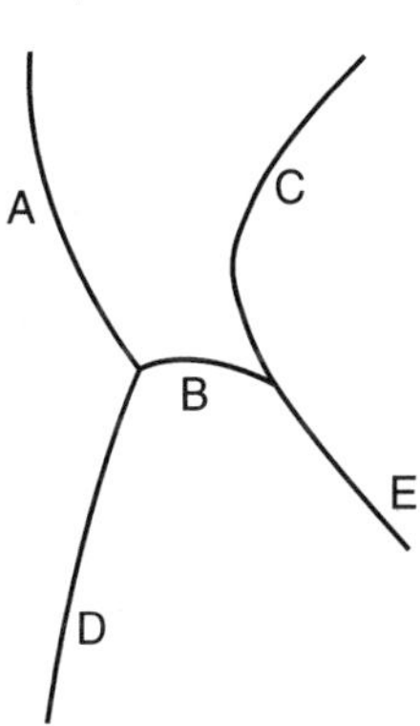

3.1 Referring to Fig. 3.4, how would you expect the grain boundaries (denoted A, B, C, D, and E in the sketch to the right) to rank in order of grain boundary energy; use three groups: high, medium, and low energy, and explain your rankings.

3.2 A two-dimensional analog of the atomic packing density is the number of atoms per unit area on a crystallographic plane. (Only atoms whose centers lie on the plane are included in the number.) Calculate the areal packing density on the (001), (011), and (111) planes in the FCC and in the BCC structures.

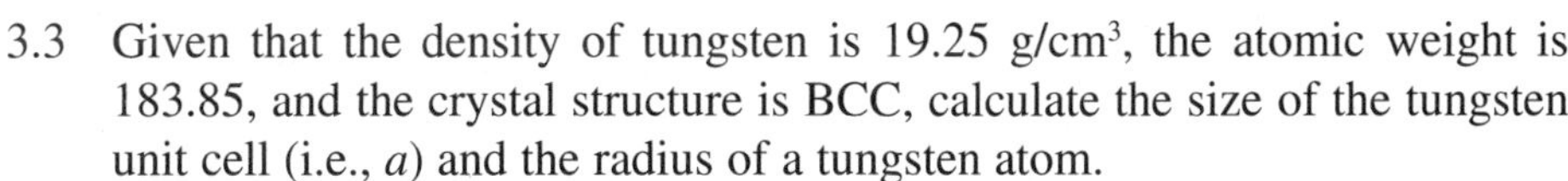

3.3 Given that the density of tungsten is 19.25 g/cm^3, the atomic weight is 183.85, and the crystal structure is BCC, calculate the size of the tungsten unit cell (i.e., *a*) and the radius of a tungsten atom.

3.4 Given the fact that platinum is FCC with atomic weight 195, calculate the mass of one unit cell. Then, given the density = 21.5 g/cm^3, calculate the size of the unit cell and the diameter of a Pt atom. Finally, calculate the areal density of packing of Pt atoms on a close-packed (111) plane. (Consider the plane to pass through the centers of the atoms.)

3.5 A simple cubic unit cell has an atom of radius r at each corner of the cube. Each edge of the cube has length 2r. Calculate the atomic packing density of this structure.

3.6 Sketch a unit cell, and show the following:

$$[100]\ [110]\ [120]\ [0\bar{1}0]\ [01\bar{1}]\ [012]$$

and

$$(001)\ (1\bar{1}\bar{2})\ (1\bar{1}1)$$

3.7 Show by means of a sketch that the (112) and (111) planes both contain the $[\bar{1}10]$ direction.

3.8 Using the fact that the [hkl] direction is perpendicular to the (hkl) plane in a cubic lattice and the concept of a scalar product of two vectors (i.e., a dot product; cf. Appendix 3.1), show that the $[\bar{1}10]$ direction must lie in both the (112) and (111) planes. (Pay attention to the difference between plane and direction indices; i.e. ( ) vs. [ ].)

3.9 Find the three {110} planes that contain the $[\bar{1}\bar{1}1]$ direction. Illustrate this with a sketch and prove your answer by means of dot products.

3.10 Draw a unit cell and show a (115) and a (112) plane.

4

SLIP, DISLOCATIONS, AND STRAIN HARDENING

The stress-strain curves of the stainless-steel spokes shown in Fig. 2.20 exemplify the unique behavior of metallic structural materials. This is the only class of materials that exhibits both large-scale plastic flow and strain hardening. Strain hardening is not only a primary strengthening mechanism in metals, but it is the reason why stable plastic flow is possible (cf. Appendix 2.2). This behavior of metals can be contrasted with that of other crystalline materials, like oxides, carbides, nitrides, etc., which generally exhibit negligible plasticity. These are brittle materials because they are likely to contain crack-like defects, and these cracks cannot be rendered harmless by plasticity (which blunts the tip of a sharp crack). In viscous amorphous materials, plastic flow can occur, but strain hardening cannot. In order to understand these differences, a knowledge of the properties and behavior of crystal dislocations is required.

Some of the specific questions to be addressed in this and later chapters are the following:

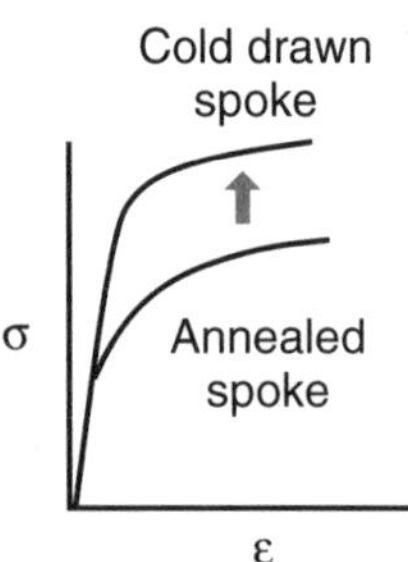

1. How does strain hardening occur, and why does it saturate; i.e., why does the rate of strain hardening decrease with strain?

2. Besides strain hardening, how else can one make a high-strength metallic alloy? That is, how can one inhibit the motion of dislocations, so that a high applied stress is required for plastic flow? Applications are high-strength, thin-walled steel tubing or high-strength aluminum alloys for lightweight bicycle frames, for example.

3. Why do carbon-steel spokes have a fatigue limit, whereas stainless-steel spokes do not? (At stresses below the fatigue limit, fatigue failure does not occur, regardless of the number of stress cycles applied.)

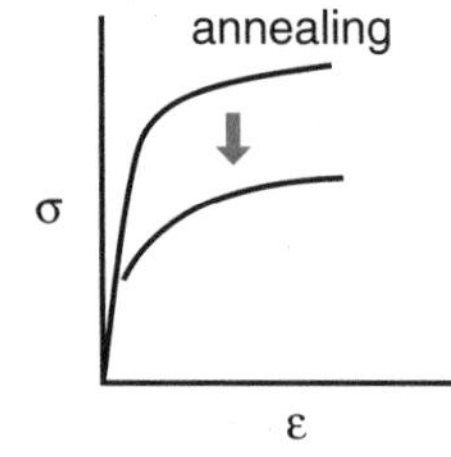

4. Why do strain-hardened materials like spokes soften when heated to around half the melting temperature (on the absolute scale, degrees Kelvin)?

5. Why do high-strength (precipitation-hardened) aluminum alloys soften at even lower temperatures?

4.1 Slip in FCC Crystals

In metallic crystals, slip tends to take place on planes with the closest packing and in directions of closest packing on those planes. The simplest to understand are FCC metals, of which stainless steel is a good example. Face-centered cubic crystals are made of stacked close-packed planes (cf. Figs. 3.6 and 3.7), and each close-packed plane contains three directions, called *close-packed directions,* along which atoms touch. These directions are illustrated in Fig. 4.1(a).

When slip occurs on a close-packed plane, it means that the adjacent (parallel) plane is translated along one of the close-packed directions. The slip displacements occur in units of the interatomic spacing. For example, one unit of slip is depicted by the vector marked "b" in Fig. 4.1(a). If the plane shown were designated as an A plane (cf. Fig. 3.7) and the next plane up is called a B plane, then one would say that the slip vector b represents the translation of an atom from one B site to the next. In an FCC crystal the close-packed planes are {111} planes, as seen earlier. One of these, the (111) plane, is shown in Fig. 4.1(b), along with the three close-packed directions, i.e., the <110> directions, in that plane.

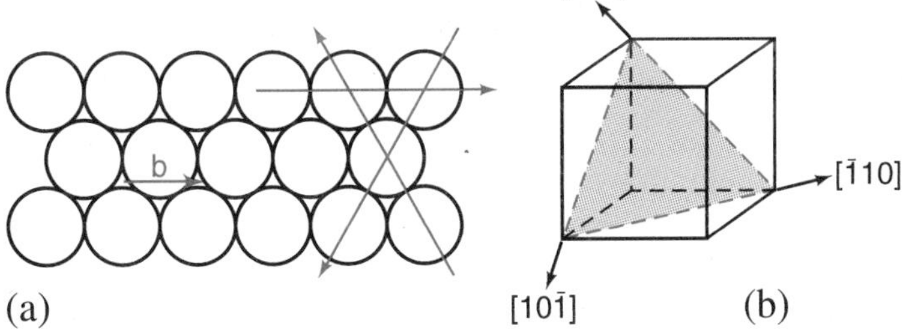

Fig.4.1 (a) A close-packed plane of hard spheres, showing three close-packed directions and a slip vector. (b) An FCC unit cell showing a slip plane and three slip directions in that plane.

The reason close-packed directions are preferred for slip is that this requires the least work. One could say, rather loosely, that the "bumps" are smaller in such a direction. A bit more scientifically, one would say that shear of one plane of atoms over another periodically decreases the packing density of the crystal in that region, as the atoms move from one set of low-energy sites to the next. Any decrease in density requires an input of energy, i.e., work. The decrease in density during slip is obviously smallest along a close-packed direction; hence, work is minimized. (This simple explanation is appropriate for close-packed metals, but other factors become important for more complex crystal structures.)

Example 4.1

Q. Show that the three slip vectors illustrated in Fig. 4.2(a) can be expressed as $\frac{a}{2}[\bar{1}10]$, $\frac{a}{2}[10\bar{1}]$, and $\frac{a}{2}[0\bar{1}1]$, where a is the lattice parameter.

A. The vectors can be drawn to span atom centers or to span interstices (the spaces between atoms), as indicated in Fig. 4.2(a), and they can also be depicted in a unit cell, as shown in Fig. 4.2(b). The vector in the $[\bar{1}10]$ direction has the components $-\frac{a}{2}$, $\frac{a}{2}$, 0. Factoring out the $\frac{a}{2}$, one writes $\frac{a}{2}[\bar{1}10]$. The other two vectors are treated similarly.

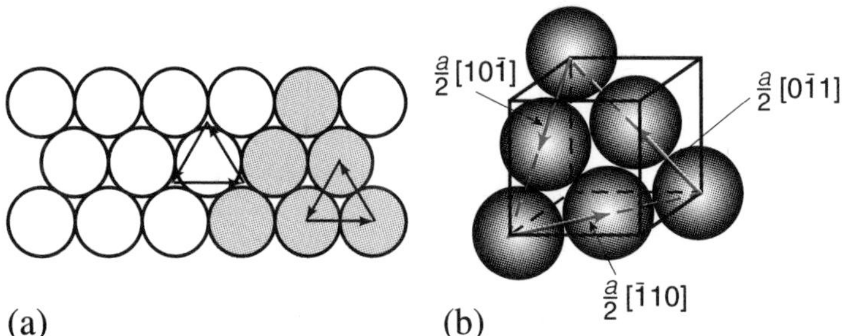

Fig. 4.2 (a) The slip vectors in a close-packed plane may be drawn spanning either interstices or atom centers. (b) The same vectors are shown in a unit cell.

The reason a close-packed plane is usually chosen for slip, if one is available in the crystal structure, is essentially the same as for the choice of a close-packed direction: The "bumps" are smaller. This can be illustrated by comparing the packing of a {111} and a {100} plane in an FCC crystal, as shown in Fig. 4.3. Possible slip vectors are shown in each case. Not only are the slip vectors longer for the {100} plane, but the vertical displacements that occur when an adjacent plane is translated along this vector are larger than for the {111} plane. When two adjacent planes are in their normal, equilibrium relationship, they are in a minimum-energy configuration. When they are translated past each other, they pass through states of increased energy, as indicated schematically in Fig. 4.3(b). The difference between a minimum and a maximum in the plot of energy *vs.* displacement represents the work done during slip of one interatomic distance. The minimum work is done when slip occurs on a close-packed plane in a close-packed direction. The force necessary for slip would be the maximum slope of the energy *vs.* displacement curve. This is obviously greater for the non-close-packed plane in Fig. 4.3.

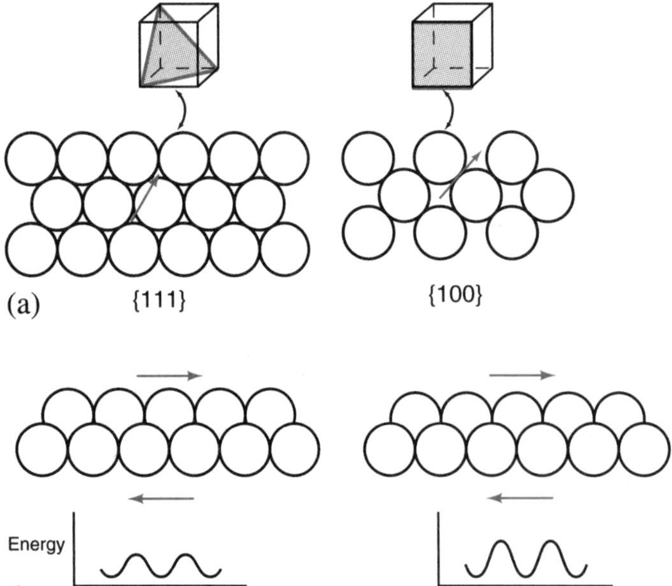

Fig. 4.3 Comparison of the atomic packing on {111} *vs.* {100} planes in an FCC crystal, showing (a) plan views of these planes and their locations in a unit cell, (b) two adjacent planes in an elevation view, and the variation in energy as the upper plane is translated over the lower plane in the direction of the vectors shown.

A combination of a slip plane and slip direction lying in that plane is called a *slip system;* the slip systems in an FCC metal are referred to generically as {111}<110>. As already noted in Chapter 2, slip occurs not by whole blocks of crystal sliding past one another, but by the passage of dislocations. In other words, slip is a consecutive, rather than a simultaneous, process. In the rest of this chapter, the properties of dislocations that are important for the understanding of plastic yielding, strain hardening, and other strengthening mechanisms, as well as the fatigue limit in carbon-steel spokes, are described. Some details about dislocation properties and behavior are contained in Appendix 4.2 and the worked examples throughout the chapter.

4.2 Types of Dislocation

There are two basic types of dislocation: *edge* and *screw.* They can each produce slip on any slip system, but they have very different geometries and behaviors. Dislocations can also be of mixed type (edge and screw combined).

4.2.1 The Edge Dislocation

The edge dislocation has already been illustrated in Figs. 2.12 and 2.13. One can imagine the creation of an edge dislocation by the process shown in Fig. 4.4. The top half of the block of crystal is sheared to the right with respect to the bottom half, but the displacement does not occur all at once over the whole plane of shear. Rather, the sheared region spreads from left to right, leaving a step on the left-hand face of the block. The boundary between the sheared (i.e., slipped) and unsheared portions of the plane of shear (i.e., slip plane) is defined as the dislocation line.

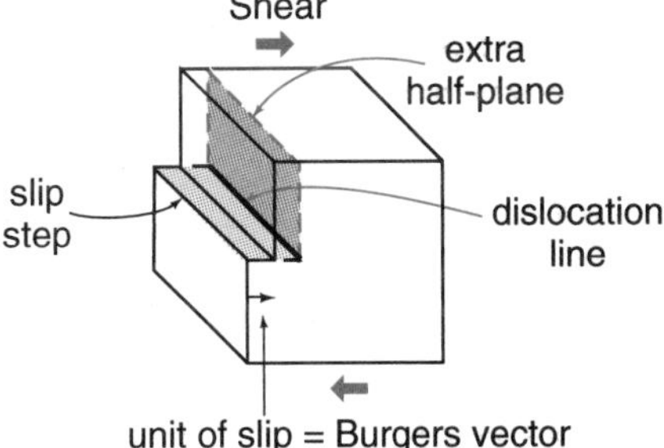

Fig. 4.4 Slip has occurred in the darkly shaded region of this block of crystal. The boundary between the slipped and unslipped region is called a dislocation; it is a linear crystal defect. In this case an edge dislocation has been created.

The partial shearing of the block in Fig. 4.4 has left N vertical planes of atoms in the upper half of the block squeezed into the space occupied by N-1 planes in the lower half of the block. The extra half-plane in the upper part is found at the end of the sheared region. As the sheared region continues to spread, the location of the extra half-plane moves to the right, as seen in Fig. 4.5*. When the shear is complete, the extra half-plane appears as a step on the right-hand side of the block (cf. Fig. 4.5c). The bottom edge of the extra half-plane locates the line of the edge dislocation.

*Note that the extra half-plane is a configuration, like the ripple in the rug in Fig. 2.11. When we say that the dislocation moves, we mean that the configuration moves; we do not mean to imply that a particular half-plane of atoms is transported from one side of the crystal block towards the other.

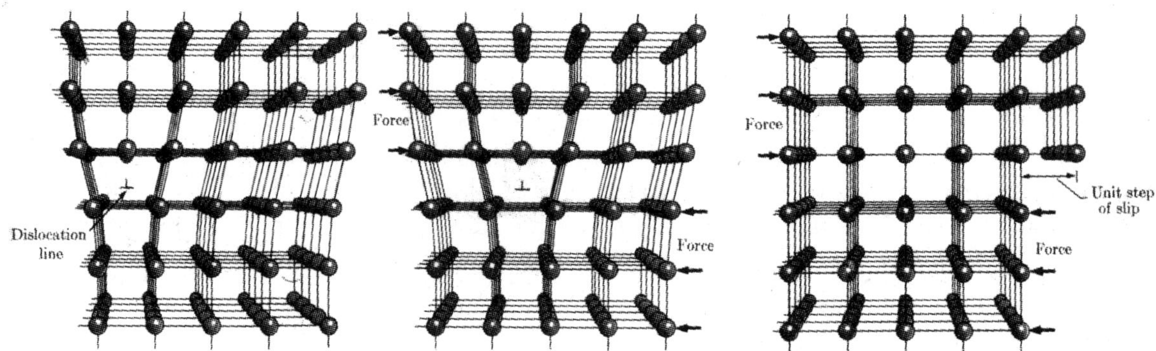

Fig. 4.5 An atomistic representation of an edge dislocation at several stages of the glide process, which produces slip. In the final panel the dislocation has emerged at the surface, leaving a slip step, and the crystal is left dislocation-free. (From A. G. Guy, *Elements of Physical Metallurgy,* Addison-Wesley, Reading, MA, 1959, p. 109.)

An important property of a dislocation is the slip vector, or *Burgers vector.* The Burgers vector denotes the magnitude and direction of slip produced when
4130 the dislocation glides. It also indicates the size of the slip step produced when an edge dislocation exits the crystal face, as in Figs. 2.13 and 4.5. An edge dislocation has the following important characteristics:

1. The Burgers vector is perpendicular to the dislocation line.
2. Glide occurs in the direction of the Burgers vector.
3. The glide plane of an edge dislocation is fixed. It is defined by the dislocation line and the Burgers vector. Because the edge dislocation involves extra material, it can only move off its glide plane if atoms are added to, or subtracted from, the extra half-plane. (This would be a non-conserva-

4140 tive process, and it must involve diffusion of atoms (i.e., an elevated temperature) as will be seen in Chapter 5.)

It is important to reiterate that slip does not change the geometry (i.e., the symmetry) of a crystal. A crystal is the same after the passage of a dislocation as it was before. This means that the Burgers vector must produce an "identity translation." Thus, the Burgers vector of a slip dislocation in an FCC crystal must connect one atomic site with the next along the slip direction, as illustrated in Fig. 4.2(a). The Burgers vector of a slip dislocation in an FCC crystal is designated as $a/2$ <110>; this nomenclature is clarified by Example 4.1. Three examples of Burgers vectors are shown in Fig. 4.2(b).

4.2.2 The Screw Dislocation

The other basic type of dislocation, the screw dislocation, can be formed by shearing the kind of block shown in Fig. 4.4, but in a direction 90° from that used

4170 to form the edge dislocation. This is illustrated in Fig. 4.6. In this case the slip step is on the side face of the block.

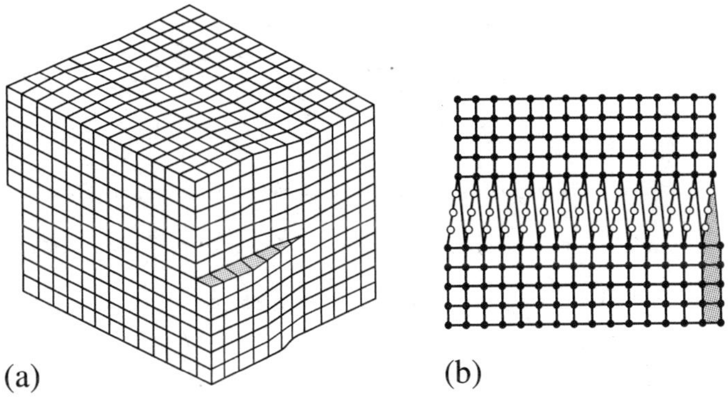

Fig. 4.6 (a) Illustrates the type of shear that produces a screw dislocation. (b) Shows the displacement of atoms in the core of the screw dislocation. (Adapted from W.T Read, Jr., *Dislocations in Crystals*, McGraw-Hill, N.Y., 1953, p. 17.)

There is no extra half-plane of atoms associated with a screw dislocation.
Rather, the atoms in the zone along the dislocation line (i.e., in the core of the 4180
dislocation) are displaced into a helical configuration. The atomic planes perpendicular to the dislocation line are distorted from a stack of parallel planes into a spiral ramp (like the threads of a screw) in the dislocation core. Looking vertically downward on the slip plane, the core would appear as shown in Fig. 4.6 (b). 

The special characteristics of a screw dislocation are:

1. The Burgers vector is parallel to the dislocation line.
2. Glide occurs in the direction perpendicular to the Burgers vector, as shown in Fig. 4.7, but the Burgers vector is still, by definition, in the direction of shear.

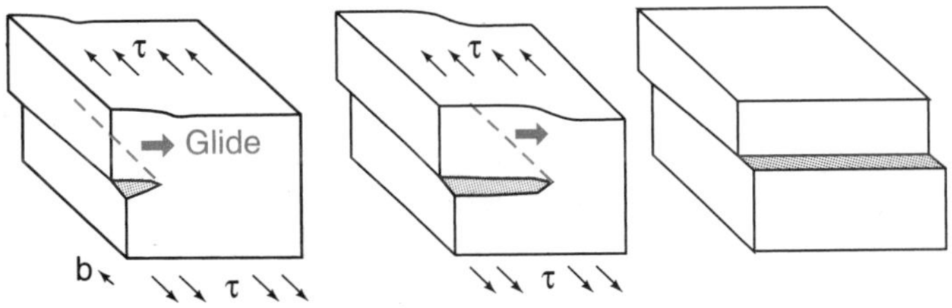

Fig. 4.7 Slip by glide of a screw dislocation. Note: τ still lies along b, but the direction of glide is now perpendicular to τ and b.

3. Since the Burgers vector and the dislocation line are parallel, they do not
define a glide plane. Therefore, from a purely geometrical standpoint, a 

screw dislocation can glide on any of the infinite number of planes that contain the Burgers vector. Thus, if a crystal had no preferred slip planes (e.g., close-packed planes), the slip step could be quite wavy, as shown in Fig. 4.8(a). In most materials, however, there are preferred slip planes
(like {111} planes in FCC stainless steel), and the slip steps from screw 

dislocations are made up of straight segments, as shown in Fig. 4.8 (b).

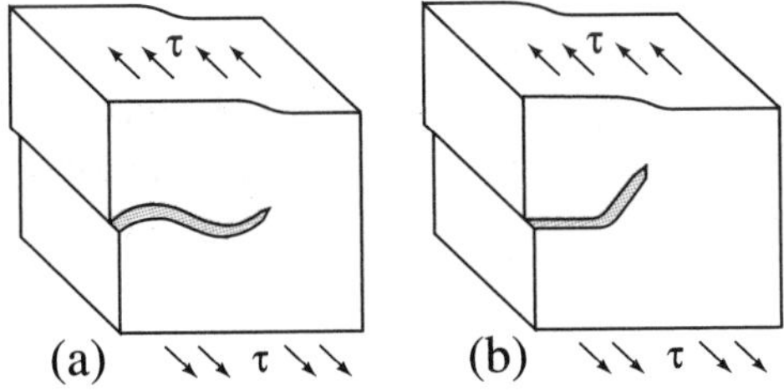

Fig. 4.8 Schematic illustration of slip steps that would occur when a screw dislocation glides on more than one plane. In (a), no particular slip plane is preferred. (b) represents the case of FCC crystals in which close-packed planes are preferred.

4.2.3 Mixed Dislocations

A mixed dislocation is simply one for which the Burgers vector is neither parallel nor perpendicular to the dislocation line, but somewhere in between. One can be constructed by shearing a block of crystal starting at a corner, as shown in Fig. 4.9. The shear along one edge of the block produces a dislocation that varies continuously from pure edge to pure screw. That is, the angle between the Burgers vector and the dislocation line varies from 90° at point A to 0° at point B. Figure 4.10 shows that the glide of this dislocation (i.e., the spreading of the slipped region) produces the same kind of shear of the block as would occur with a pure edge or pure screw dislocation.

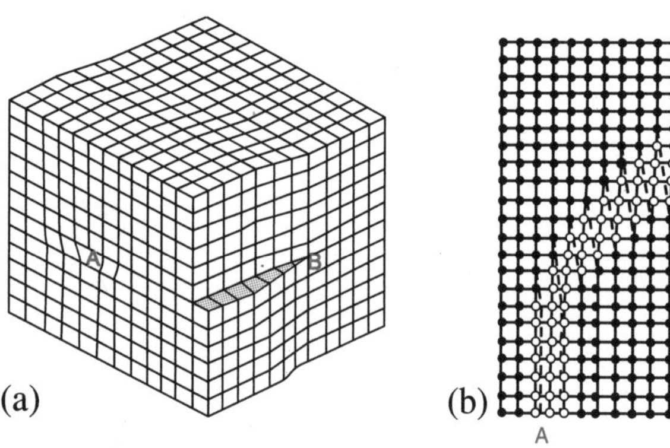

Fig. 4.9 (a) Illustrates a crystal sheared to produce a mixed dislocation, which runs from A to B. (b) Shows the displacements of atoms in the core of the dislocation, which is pure edge at A and pure screw at B. (Adapted from W. T. Read, Jr., *Dislocations in Crystals,* McGraw-Hill, N.Y., 1953, p. 18.)

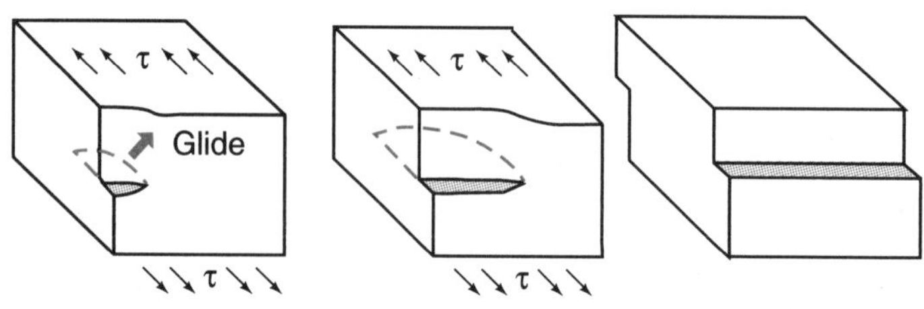

Fig. 4.10 Slip by glide of a mixed dislocation.

The important characteristics of the three dislocation types can be summarized as follows:

Type	Angle between b and Dislocation Line	Direction of Shear	Direction of Glide	b in FCC Crystal
Edge	90°	along b	perpendicular to the line	*a*/2<110>
Screw	0°	"	"	"
Mixed	varied	"	"	"

Example 4.2

Q. What happens in a crystal in which the extra half-plane of an edge dislocation lies below the glide plane, as in Fig. 4.11 (using a T sign to indicate the dislocation, as shown).

A. The shear in the crystal occurs in the opposite sense to the case in which the half-plane lies above the glide plane. One can assign a positive sense to an edge dislocation with half-plane up and a negative sense to one with half-plane down. Note that a dislocation of negative sign glides in a direction opposite to that for a positive dislocation upon the application of a shear stress. This is illustrated in Fig. 4.11.

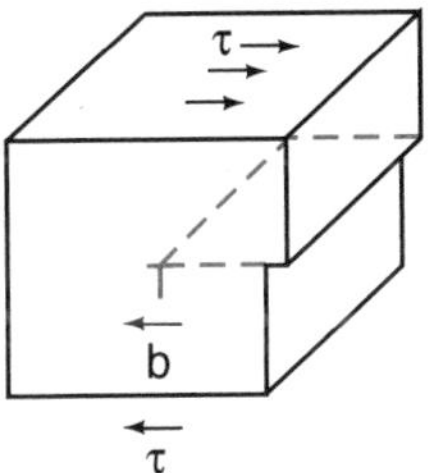

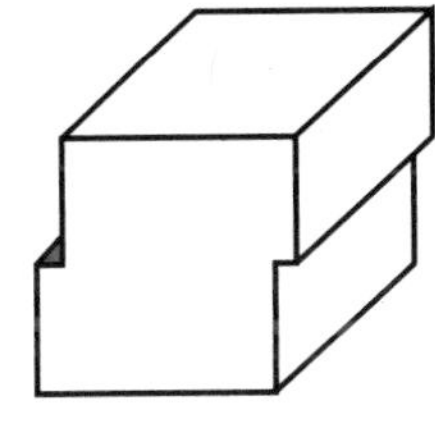

Fig. 4.11 A negative edge dislocation subjected to the same positive shear stress as applied in Figs. 4.4 and 4.5. Note that the negative dislocation glides in the opposite direction to the ones shown in those figures.

Example 4.3

Q. What happens in a crystal with two edge dislocations of opposite sign on the same glide plane? of the same sign?

A. If the two are of opposite sign, the application of a shear stress of one sense will drive them apart, as in Fig. 4.12(a), and a shear stress of the reverse sense will bring them together, whereupon they will annihilate each other, as in Fig. 4.12(b). If they are of the same sign, they will both move in the same direction upon the application of a shear stress, but there will be a mutual repulsion between them. (This will be elaborated upon in Section 4.5.) The dislocations of opposite sign experience a mutual attraction.

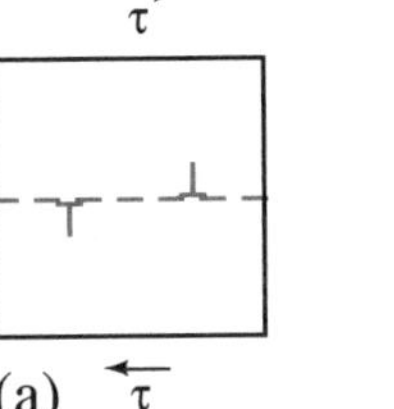

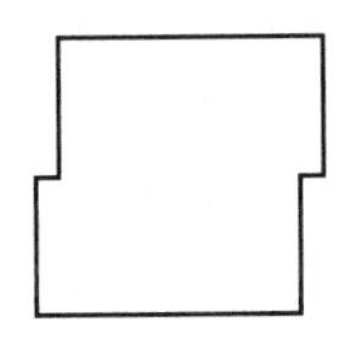

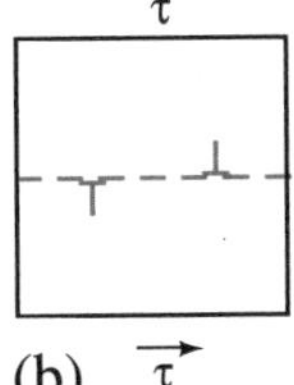

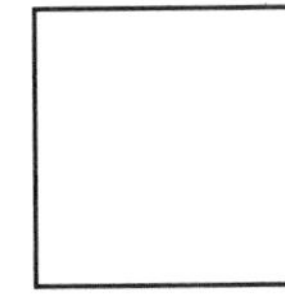

Fig. 4.12 (a) A pair of edge dislocations of opposite sign, showing the result of the application of a positive shear stress to this pair of dislocations; slip steps are formed on opposite side of the crystal block as each dislocation emerges at the surface. (b) Shows the result of the application of a negative shear stress.

Example 4.4

Q. Can one speak of positive and negative screw dislocations?

A. Yes. Fig. 4.13 shows what this means. Note that the assignment of which is called positive and which negative is completely arbitrary. It is only important that the assignment be consistent.

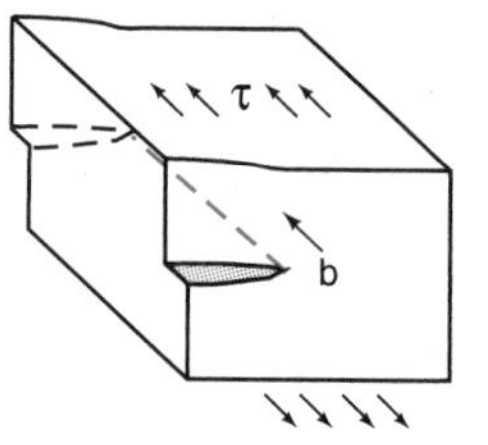

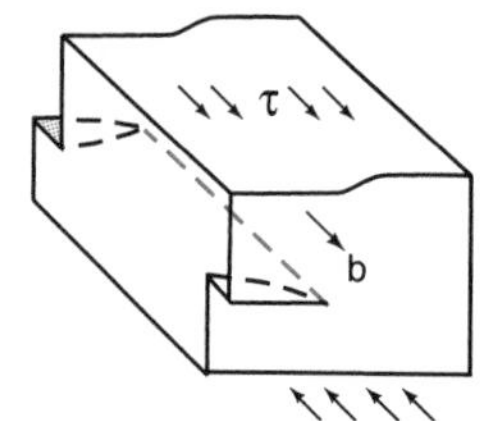

Fig. 4.13 Screw dislocations of opposite sign.

Example 4.5

Q. What would happen if, when a shear stress is applied to a crystal block, slip started in the center of the block, instead of at an edge?

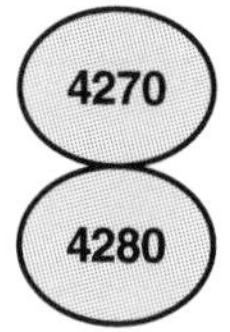

A. By definition, the boundary between slipped and unslipped regions of a slip plane is a dislocation line. If the slipped region is contained entirely inside the crystal, the dislocation line must form some kind of loop that closes on itself. Fig. 4.14(a) gives an example, drawn under the approximation that all parts of the dislocation line have the same elastic-strain energy; this means that the loop would be circular. Note that all parts of the loop have the same b, since the same kind of slip has occurred throughout the slipped region. Note, also, that diametrically opposed portions of the loop are dislocations of the same type, but of opposite sign. In Fig. 4.14(a), the loop is + edge at 12:00 o'clock and - edge at 6:00 o'clock, + screw at 3:00 o'clock and - screw at 9:00 o'clock. At all other positions the dislocation line is of mixed character.

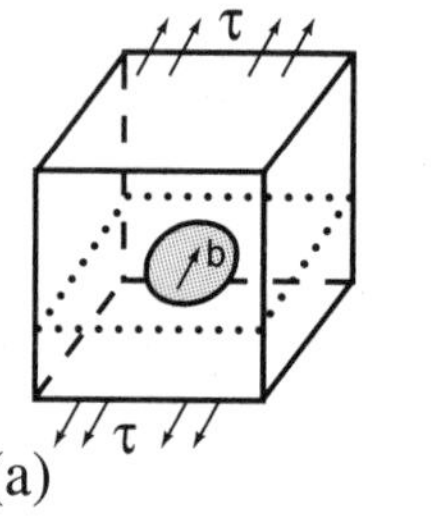

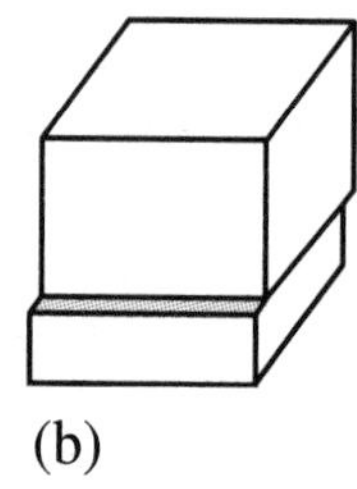

Fig. 4.14 (a) A dislocation loop created by shear starting inside a crystal. (b) The sheared block after the loop has exited at the surfaces.

Example 4.6

Q. What would happen if the shear stress on the crystal block in Fig. 4.14(a) were continuously increased?

A. The loop would continue to expand and would finally emerge from the side surfaces, leaving slip steps on the front and back sides, as shown in Fig. 4.14(b).

Example 4.7

Q. What would happen if the shear stress on the block in Fig. 4.14(a) were suddenly removed, assuming that the intrinsic resistance to dislocation glide in that crystal is very small?

A. The loop would shrink by inward glide, owing to the mutual attraction of diametrically opposed segments (parallel dislocations of opposite sign). Finally, the loop would self-annihilate.

4.2.4 General Characteristics of Dislocations

It is important to maintain perspective about dislocations and not get bogged down in details. They are analogous to ripples in rugs (cf. Fig. 2.11). When a ripple moves (i.e., "glides"), the rug is translated over the floor, like one part of a crystal block over another. Moving a rug like this is much easier than moving it all at once, because the resistance to ripple glide is much smaller than the frictional force opposing the motion of the whole rug. The same is true for a dislocation in metals. Considering the atomistic representation of an edge dislocation (Fig. 4.5), one can see that the crystal planes are elastically warped in opposite directions on either side of the dislocation line. The restoring forces arising from the distorted interatomic bonds would tend to make these planes straighten up. Thus, the dislocation "feels" two equal and opposite forces. An applied shear stress causes an imbalance of these forces, and in a soft FCC crystal (e.g., pure copper) even a small imbalance is sufficient to cause glide.

The ease of dislocation glide in any metallic crystal depends on two factors:

1. The nature of the intrinsic interatomic bonding forces, and
2. The types and densities of barriers, such as foreign atoms, particles having a different crystal structure, other dislocations, etc. (These are factors extrinsic to the crystal *per se*.)

The bonding force in a simple FCC metal is essentially non-directional. Thus, dislocation glide, which involves changing the angular relationships between rows of atoms, is relatively easy. Therefore, pure copper, silver, gold, platinum, and aluminum, for example, are plastically "soft." On the other hand, BCC transition metals, like iron, chromium, molybdenum, and tungsten, have more complicated bonding. In these metals, edge dislocations still glide fairly easily, but the cores of screw dislocations are highly distorted. The small displacements of atoms in the direction of b along the screw dislocation line are more like a spiral staircase in BCC crystals than like the spiral-ramp configuration in FCC crystals. This makes screws relatively immobile in BCC metals (like iron) at low temperatures. At higher temperatures, thermal vibrations of atoms "smear out" the steps in the screw dislocation core, and glide becomes easier; i.e., BCC metals become more deformable as temperature is increased, and this causes their tendency toward brittleness to decrease.

In a covalently bonded crystal like silicon, the bonding is completely directional, and even edge dislocation glide is impossible below temperatures of around 800°C (silicon melts at 1410°C). Thus, silicon is brittle, except at very high temperatures.

A new factor comes into play in ionic crystals. Not only are there size differences between positive and negative ions, but the ions are constrained to lie in an ordered array, with negative ions surrounded by positive ions, and vice versa. Since dislocation glide would break up the order on many of the potential glide planes, slip occurs on few systems, and polycrystalline ionic solids are generally brittle.

The extrinsic barriers to dislocation glide are the means whereby crystalline solids, particularly metals, are strengthened. These must be employed carefully, since, when plasticity is inhibited, ductility and toughness usually suffer. Bicycle technology employs a variety of strengthening mechanisms. In spokes the most important one is dislocation density; i.e., strain hardening. To understand strain hardening one needs to learn how dislocations interact. They do so by virtue of their stress fields. Before moving to this topic, it is useful to consider how dislocations in crystals can be observed directly.

4.3 Imaging of Dislocations

The true role of dislocations in crystals was not widely recognized until the application of the electron microscope to solids in the 1950s. To prepare a sample for transmission electron microscopy (TEM), one first cuts a thin slice of a metal or alloy; the slice is then thinned further by electrolytic dissolution to a fraction of a micrometer. This is thin enough that an electron beam accelerated by a voltage of around 100kV can pass through it. The essential features of a standard electron microscope are illustrated in Fig. 4.15(a), and some dislocations in a thin foil of stainless steel are shown in Fig. 4.15(b).

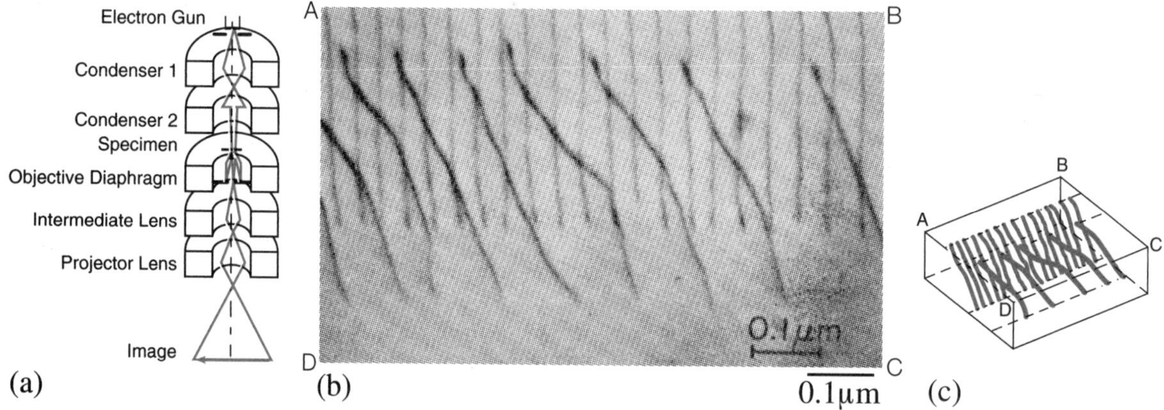

Fig. 4.15 (a) Schematic illustration of essential features of a transmission electron microscope. (b) Dislocations in a thin foil of stainless steel. (c) Illustration of the foil which produced the image shown in (b). ((b) and (c) from D. Hull and D. J. Bacon, *Introduction to Dislocations,* 3rd ed., Pergamon Press, Oxford, 1984, p. 34. Reproduced by permission of Butterworth-Heinemann Ltd.)

The dislocations in the slice of stainless steel have been revealed by a process called *diffraction contrast* (as opposed to the process of reflection contrast through surface roughening in optical microscopy). Since the electron beam has a wavelength smaller than the interatomic spacing in a crystal, the beam can be diffracted by the crystal lattice. (The law of diffraction was first worked out by Sir Lawrence Bragg in 1912, and it is explained in Appendix 4.1.) Because some atomic planes are bent in the vicinity of a dislocation (cf. Fig.4.5), the electron beam is diffracted at a different angle than in the undistorted crystal remote from the dislocation line. Thus, this part of the diffracted beam is not focused on the photographic plate, and the dislocation line appears dark.

The arrays of parallel dislocations in Fig. 4.15(b) are actually segments of dislocations that have been captured by the sectioning of the specimen, and the segments run from the bottom surface of the foil to the top, in the manner shown in Fig. 4.15(c).

4.4 The Stress Field of a Dislocation

The fact that metals deform plastically by way of dislocation motion was deduced long before there was direct evidence that dislocations actually exist in crystals. One of the originators of the dislocation concept, G. I. Taylor, also conceived the first theory of strain hardening. In it he recognized that plastic deformation involves the multiplication of dislocations (which means that their average spacing must decrease), and that there is a mutual repulsion between parallel dislocations of like sign. This repulsion exists because the displacements of the atoms in the crystal in the vicinity of the dislocation line give rise to a stress field. The stress can be calculated through Hooke's law, if the displacements are known.

4.4.1 General Aspects of Stress Fields

The stress field of a dislocation is, in a certain sense, analogous to the electric field around a charged particle. Just as the strength of the electric field 4390
depends upon the distance from the charged particle, the stress field of a dislocation depends on the distance from the dislocation. Therefore, one must be able to deal with the value of a stress field at some point in a solid. The way to do this for an edge dislocation is to imagine an infinitesmal cube centered on the point of interest, as shown in Fig. 4.16. The z coordinate of the cube is aligned with the dislocation line.

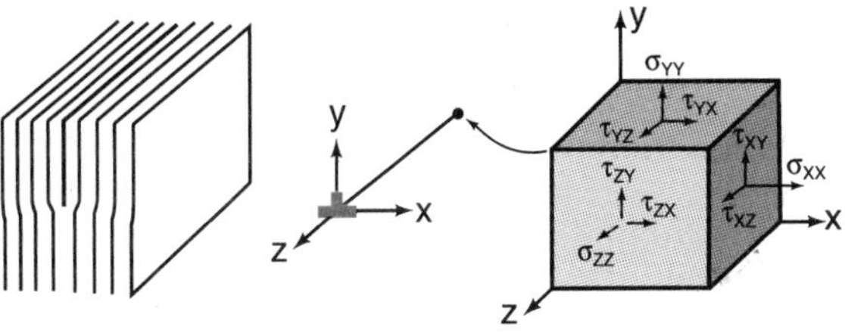

Fig. 4.16 Illustration of the components of stress at some point remote from a dislocation line by consideration of the stresses acting on the surface of an infinitesmal cube centered at that point.

The components of the stress field are defined as the stresses that act on the surface of the cube; all the possible positive components of stress are shown on the cube in Fig 4.16. Each of these has an equal and opposite component acting on the respective opposite faces.

The scheme used to designate the various stress components involves a double subscript, the first to indicate the **plane** on which the stress acts, and the second to indicate the **direction** in which it acts. Thus, σ_{xx} represents a normal stress on a plane perpendicular to the *x* axis and acting in the positive *x* direction. ($-\sigma_{xx}$ would act in the negative *x* direction.) Similarly, τ_{yz} is a shear stress on a plane perpendicular to the *y* axis and acting in the *z* direction. A bit of thought will quickly lead to the conclusion that Fig 4.16 does, in fact, show all of the possible (positive) components of stress on the surface of the cube. These stress components can be represented in the following matrix:

$$\begin{matrix} \sigma_{xx} & \tau_{xy} & \tau_{xz} \\ \tau_{yx} & \sigma_{yy} & \tau_{yz} \\ \tau_{zx} & \tau_{zy} & \sigma_{zz} \end{matrix}$$

It is easy to show that there are only six independent components in this matrix, since:

$$\tau_{xy} = \tau_{yx} \qquad \tau_{xz} = \tau_{zx} \qquad \tau_{yz} = \tau_{zy}$$

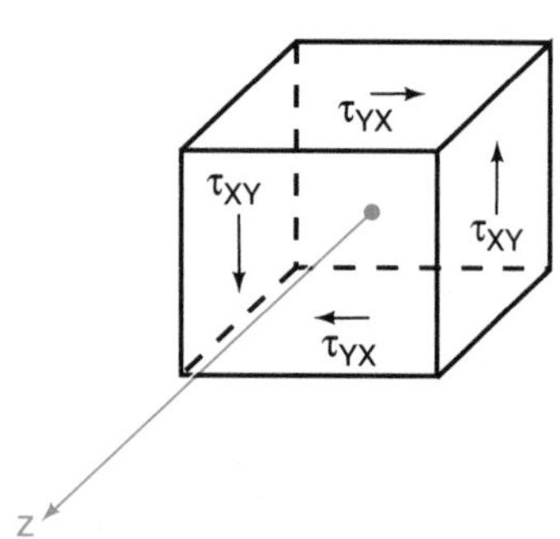

These relationships stem from the fact that the cube is stationary and at equilibrium. For example, let the origin of coordinates be in the center of the cube, let the faces be of unit area (so that stresses are numerically equal to forces), and consider the moments that tend to spin the cube about the *z* axis. The forces τ_{xy} and $-\tau_{xy}$ would tend to spin it counter-clockwise, and the forces $\pm\tau_{yx}$ would tend to spin it clockwise. Since the cube does not spin, and the moment arms of these forces are all equal to half the length of the cube edge, the respective force components must be equal; thus, $\tau_{xy} = \tau_{yx}$. The other relationships can be proved by considering moments about the other two axes.

It is important to point out that, in some cases, some of the terms in the matrix are equal to zero. An example is the stress field around a substitutional solute atom in an alloy like stainless steel. If the solute atom is too large for its lattice site (i.e., larger than the host atoms), then the solute atom is compressed symmetrically in three dimensions by the surrounding host atoms.

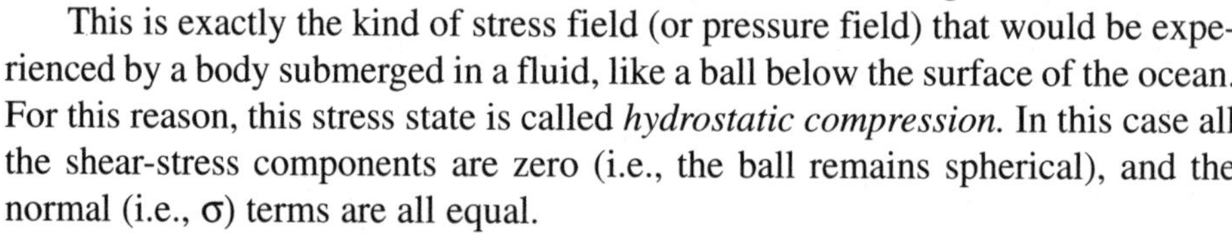

This is exactly the kind of stress field (or pressure field) that would be experienced by a body submerged in a fluid, like a ball below the surface of the ocean. For this reason, this stress state is called *hydrostatic compression.* In this case all the shear-stress components are zero (i.e., the ball remains spherical), and the normal (i.e., σ) terms are all equal.

Even before the existence of dislocations in crystals was first postulated, the stress fields in distorted blocks (as in Figs. 4.4 and 4.6) had been determined in the context of continuum elasticity theory. The case of the screw dislocation is particularly straightforward, and the stress field can be calculated easily.

4.4.2 The Stress Field of a Screw Dislocation

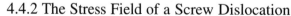

The stress field of a screw dislocation can be demonstrated by considering a cylindrical block of radius r and length L, as shown in Fig. 4.17. In a thought experiment, the block is slit longitudinally through to its central axis and displaced axially by an amount b before re-joining the faces of the slit. The block is now elastically strained, and the strain is obviously greatest along the central axis where the shearing was terminated. The strain field in the block gives rise to a stress field (through Hooke's law).

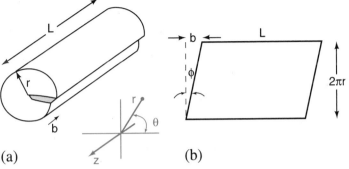

Fig. 4.17 (a) Creation of a screw dislocation along the axis of a cylindrical block. (b) The shear strain produced in the cylindrical surface at a distance r from the core of the dislocation.

The stress field in the dislocated cylinder approximates that of a screw dislocation in a crystal. The approximation arises from the use of an isotropic elastic continuum to represent a crystal, which, of course, is made up of discrete atoms. This kind of approximation is made routinely in materials science, because continuum elastic theory is very well developed, and atomistic calculations are still rather new and complex.

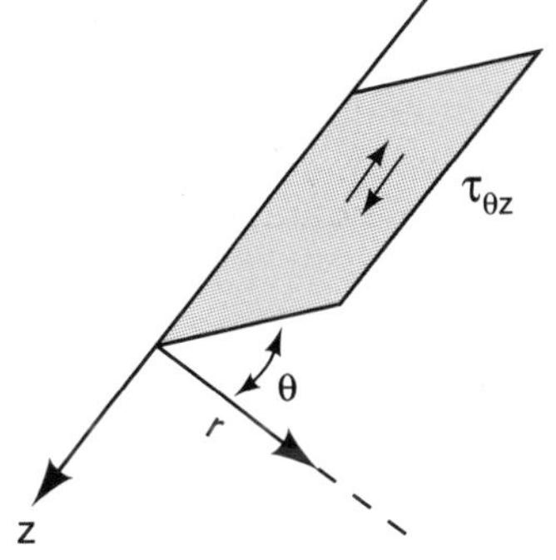

Because the screw-dislocated cylinder has (obviously) cylindrical symmetry, it is more convenient to use cylindrical coordinates instead of Cartesian (*x,y,z*) coordinates to express the components of the stress field. In cylindrical coordinates, the axis of symmetry is designated as the *z* axis, and any point is given by its *z* coordinate along with its radial coordinate, r, and its angular coordinate, θ.

Planes are denoted in the same way as in Cartesian coordinates: The *z* plane is perpendicular to the *z* axis; the "r plane" is the cylindrical surface perpendicular to any radius. The θ plane contains the *z* axis and is perpendicular to the angular coordinate, θ.

Applying this scheme to the dislocated cylinder in Fig. 4.17, it is clear that a θ plane has been sheared in the *z* direction. Therefore, the necessary shear stress is $\tau_{\theta z}$.

To determine the stress field in the cylinder, it is necessary first to calculate the strain and then to use the version of Hooke's law that applies to shear deformation:

$$\tau = G\gamma$$

where G is the shear modulus, or the slope of the plot of the shear stress, τ, *vs.* the elastic shear strain, γ. The strain is found by mentally unwrapping the outer surface of the cylinder so it becomes a flat sheet. One can see in Fig. 4.17 (b) that what was originally a rectangle of dimensions L x 2πr has been sheared by an amount b into a parallellogram.

Applying this to a screw dislocation in a crystal, b would be the Burgers vector of the dislocation. The shear strain is defined by tan ϕ, where ϕ is the angle of shear. Thus,

$$\gamma = \tan\phi = \frac{b}{2\pi r}$$

and Hooke's law gives

$$\tau = \frac{Gb}{2\pi r}$$

This shear stress $\tau_{\theta z}$ is the same on all radial (θ) planes. That is, the stress field would be the same regardless of which θ plane was picked to be slit and sheared in the *z* direction. Note, also, that the shear stress varies as 1/r. That is, the stress in the body is large near the dislocation line, and it falls off with the radial distance from the dislocation.

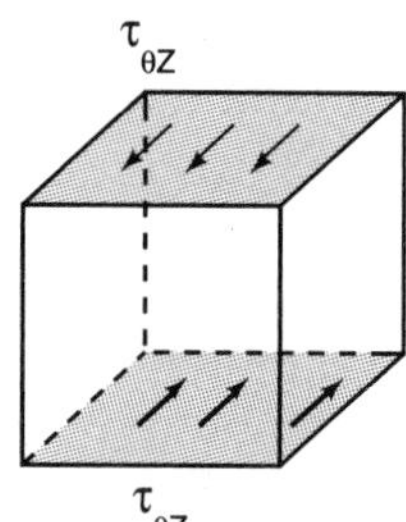

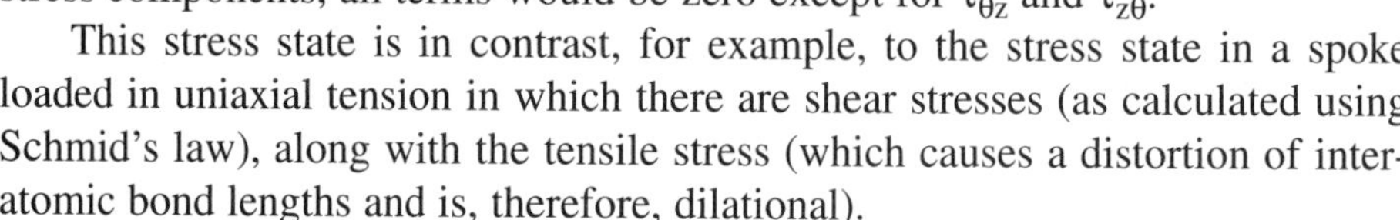

The stress field of a screw dislocation is very simple; it is pure shear and does not involve any dilational terms. That is, to a first approximation, there is only a shape change in the block; there is no volume change. In the matrix of stress components, all terms would be zero except for $\tau_{\theta z}$ and $\tau_{z\theta}$.

This stress state is in contrast, for example, to the stress state in a spoke loaded in uniaxial tension in which there are shear stresses (as calculated using Schmid's law), along with the tensile stress (which causes a distortion of interatomic bond lengths and is, therefore, dilational).

It is clear that the stress field of a screw dislocation would go to infinity as r goes to zero; this is physically unrealistic. Continuum elasticity theory is not capable of giving the actual stress level in the dislocation core. This problem is circumvented by using the continuum theory to give the stress field outside the core only. The core is defined by a cut-off radius, r_0, which is a few atomic diameters. Problems involving the core region must be handled by atomistic calculations, but these are not necessary for most problems in dislocation mechanics.

4.4.3 The Stress Field of an Edge Dislocation

Since an edge dislocation involves an extra half-plane of material and is, therefore, not axi-symmetric (i.e., the same for all values of θ), its stress field is more complicated than that of a screw. It is obvious from inspection of Fig. 4.5 that the material above the glide plane is in a state of compression and that below in a state of expansion. Thus, for an edge dislocation there must be dilational stress terms as well as shear stresses. However, all these terms contain the factor Gb/r, so the stress field of an edge dislocation shares certain features with that of a screw, including the 1/r fall-off of stress with distance from the dislocation line.

The expressions for the various terms of the stress field of an edge dislocation are given in Appendix 4.2. These expressions employ Cartesian coordinates because of the symmetry involved. For the present purpose it is not necessary to examine the details of these equations, except for two important points. The first is that the stress field of the edge dislocation has normal-stress, or dilational, components as well as a shear-stress component. This means that edge dislocations (and mixed dislocations) interact with other defects that have a dilational component to their stress fields. By "interact" is meant either to be attracted to, in cases where the stress fields have terms of opposite sign and thereby tend to cancel each other (as with charged particles of opposite sign), or to be repelled by, in cases where the stress field terms have the same sign and thereby reinforce each other.

A classic example is the interaction of an edge dislocation and a misfitting substitutional solute atom. An oversize solute atom would exert a repulsive force on an edge dislocation if the solute were on the same side of the glide plane as the extra half-plane of the dislocation. This can be understood by consideration of the model of the edge dislocation shown in Fig. 4.5, in which one can see that the atoms in the vicinity of the extra half-plane are squeezed together. This creates a compressive stress field, which interacts with the compressive stress field around the oversized solute in a repulsive manner in the same way that two negatively charged particles would repel each other. This kind of interaction is obviously important in the context of strengthening mechanisms.

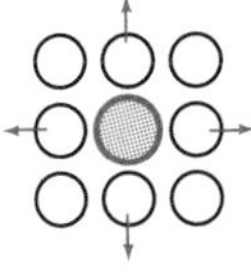

It is important to emphasize that two defects can interact elastically only if their respective stress fields contain matching non-zero components. This can be made clear by considering the cases of an edge dislocation, a misfitting substitutional solute atom, and a screw dislocation. The edge will interact with the solute, but the screw will not, as seen by the matchup of the stress matrices:

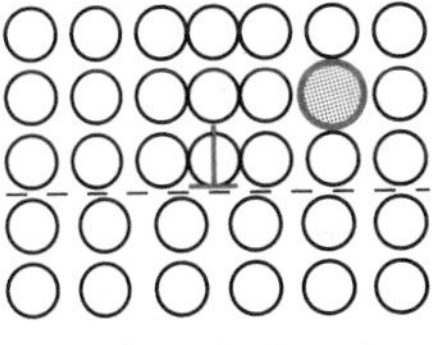

repulsive interaction

$$\begin{matrix} \sigma_{xx} & \tau_{xy} & 0 \\ \tau_{yx} & \sigma_{yy} & 0 \\ 0 & 0 & \sigma_{zz} \end{matrix} \qquad \begin{matrix} \sigma_{xx} & 0 & 0 \\ 0 & \sigma_{yy} & 0 \\ 0 & 0 & \sigma_{zz} \end{matrix} \qquad \begin{matrix} 0 & 0 & \tau_{xz} \\ 0 & 0 & \tau_{yz} \\ \tau_{zx} & \tau_{zy} & 0 \end{matrix}$$

EDGE — SOLUTE — SCREW

EDGE/SOLUTE: **Interaction**; SOLUTE/SCREW: **No Interaction**

The second important point is that the shear component of the stress field of an edge dislocation, although not axisymmetric, does depend on 1/r, as in the case of a screw dislocation. Thus, the general feature of strain hardening, which is the interaction between the shear-stress fields of parallel dislocations of like sign, is essentially the same for all kinds of dislocations.

4.4.4 Mixed Dislocations

The stress field of a mixed dislocation can be estimated by treating it as a superposition of stress fields of two dislocations having Burgers vectors b_E and b_S which would add up to the resultant b of the mixed dislocation, as shown in Fig. 4.18.

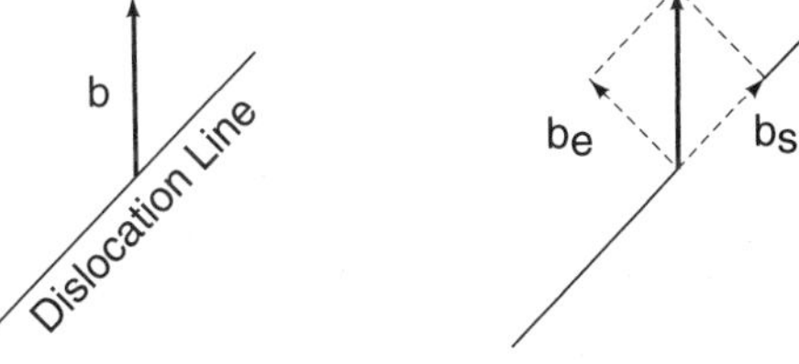

Fig. 4.18 The Burger's vector of a mixed dislocation can be resolved into screw and edge components.

4.4.5 Energy of a Dislocation

As shown in Section 2.4, any solid under stress contains strain energy, which is the energy stored in the distorted atomic bonds. Since the crystal lattice around a dislocation line is distorted, there must be energy associated with any dislocation. It is possible to derive an expression for the strain energy per unit length of a dislocation outside the core region, because the stress field is known. The screw dislocation serves as the simplest case.

Consider the cylinder in Fig. 4.17 that contains a screw dislocation. The stress field is given by $\tau = Gb/2\pi r$, and the strain field is given by $\gamma = b/2\pi r$. From Section 2.4 the strain energy per unit volume is given by the area under the stress strain curve for a specimen in simple tension (in which the stress is uniform all the way through the specimen). This area is $\sigma \cdot \varepsilon/2$. For a solid in pure shear the analogous expression is $\tau \cdot \gamma/2$. Since the stress in the cylinder in Fig. 4.17 is not uniform (i.e., it varies with 1/r), the term $\tau \cdot \gamma/2$ must be integrated over the volume of the cylinder. Thus,

$$\text{Strain energy} = 1/2 \int_V \tau\gamma \, dV$$

One can substitute for τ by using Hooke's law, $\tau = G\gamma$, and use the fact that, for a cylinder, $dV = 2\pi r dr$ times L, the length of the cylinder. Hence,

$$\text{Strain energy} = 1/2 \int_V G\,\gamma^2 \, dV = 1/2\, L \int_{r_0}^{r} G\left(\frac{b}{2\pi r}\right)^2 2\pi r \, dr$$

When the integral is evaluated, the result is

$$\text{Strain energy/unit length of dislocation} = \frac{Gb^2}{4\pi} \ln \frac{r}{r_0}$$

The result of such a calculation for an edge dislocation turns out to be almost the same, in spite of the more complicated stress field. Hence, for any dislocation, edge, screw, or mixed, it is sufficient to make the following approximation: Since the energy increases with ln r, most of the energy is in the region near the dislocation, and one can account for almost all the energy if r is set equal to $10^4\, r_0$. Then,

$$\ln r/r_o = \ln 10^4 = 2.3 \log 10^4 = 4(2.3), \text{ and } \frac{4\,(2.3)}{4\pi} \text{ is approximately one.}$$

Therefore,

$$\text{Strain energy/unit length} \approx Gb^2$$

The relatively small contribution to the total energy from the region $r < r_0$ does not affect the approximation greatly.

Note that more strain energy is stored in a stiffer material (higher G), as one might expect, and that the energy of a dislocation increases with the square of the Burgers vector. This is why the dislocations observed in crystals tend to be those with the minimum Burgers vector.

4.5 Mechanism of Strain Hardening

The essence of strain hardening can be summarized as follows: As plastic strain proceeds, the dislocation density increases, and as the separation between dislocations decreases, the force of mutual repulsion between neighboring dislocations gets larger. This means that more stress must be applied to the material for plastic flow to continue.

To understand this phenomenon thoroughly, it is necessary to examine first the relationship between plastic strain and dislocation density, then the process of yielding and dislocation multiplication, and finally the nature of the force between neighboring dislocations. The result will be that the rate of strain hardening decreases as strain increases in a material. Thus, the flow stress, or the stress needed to maintain plastic flow, will be found to vary parabolically with plastic strain:

$$\sigma_{fl} \propto \varepsilon_{pl}^{1/2}$$

4.5.1 Plastic Strain and Dislocation Density

Here it will be shown that, in a metal undergoing plastic strain, the dislocation density increases with strain in an approximately linear fashion. First, it is necessary to show the relationship between plastic strain and the motion of a dislocation. Then, a simple expression can be written to relate plastic strain to the motion of a number of dislocations over some average distance.

Consider first a cubic unit volume of crystal and allow one dislocation to glide completely through this volume. The plastic offset would be equal to the Burgers vector of the dislocation, b. If this happened in every unit of volume in the crystal, the average shear strain would be the displacement, b, divided by the spacing of the glide planes, assuming one glide plane per unit volume, or

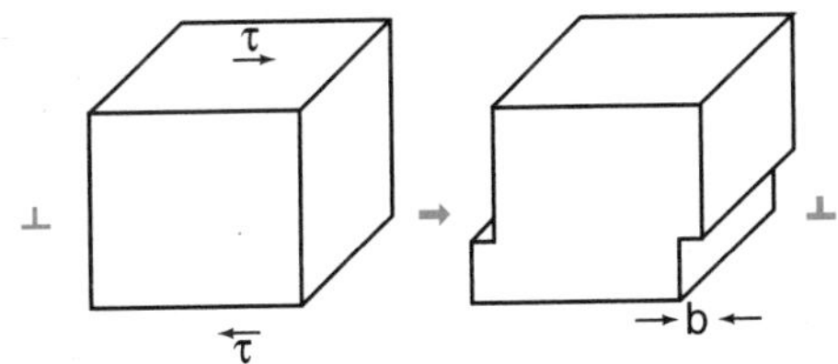

$$\gamma_p = b/1$$

Now consider such a unit volume containing one dislocation, and let the dislocation glide by a small amount dx. The plastic offset is now only a fraction of b, and this fraction is dx/1, which is the portion of the length of the glide plane traversed by the dislocation when it glides by the amount dx. If this happened in every unit of volume in the crystal, the average shear strain would be the displacement, bd$x$/1, divided by the spacing of the glide planes (i.e., unity).

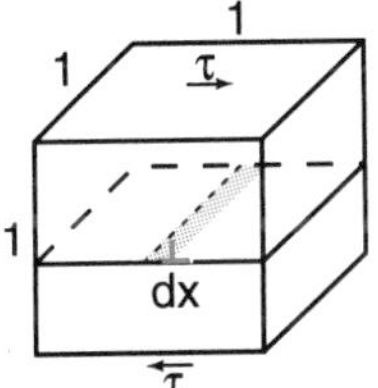

$$d\gamma_p = b\,dx$$

The tensile strain would be given approximately by

$$d\varepsilon_p = 0.7\ b\ dx$$

if it is assumed that the glide planes lie, on the average, at about 45° to the tensile axis.

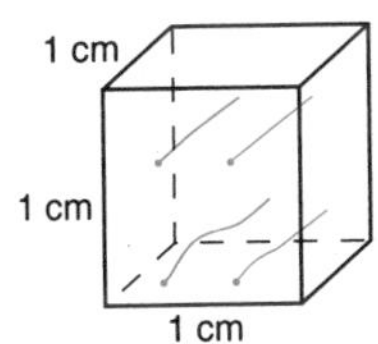

Dislocation density, ρ, is defined as the total dislocation length per unit volume, or, equivalently for a small volume in which all dislocations can be considered to be parallel, the number of dislocations passing through a unit of area.

Now consider a unit volume of material having a dislocation density ρ, and during an increment of plastic strain let each dislocation move by dx. The plastic shear strain, $d\gamma_p$, would be ρbdx. Integrating from zero plastic tensile strain, the result would be

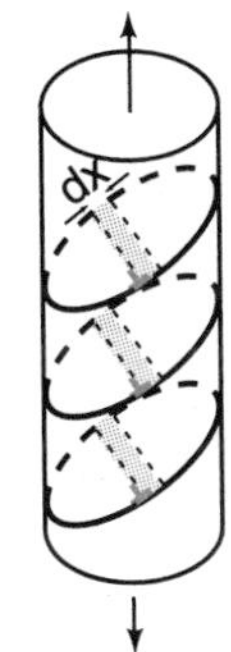

$$\varepsilon_p = 0.7\ \rho\ b\ \overline{x}$$

where $\overline{x}$ is the average distance moved by the dislocations. In a polycrystalline metal, $\overline{x}$ can be set approximately equal to some fraction of the grain size. (It decreases during plastic strain, but to a much smaller degree than the increase in ρ.) Therefore, the dislocation density must increase approximately linearly with plastic strain. That is, dislocations must multiply during plastic strain.

The need for dislocation multiplication can be illustrated by a simple example. A typical ductile metal can elongate plastically on the order of 50% in a normal tensile test. An annealed metal, after having been made into a tensile specimen, would have a dislocation density of less than 10^6 cm of dislocation per cm^3 (or 10^6 dislocations per cm^2 of area). Considering a tensile specimen with a two-millimeter-diameter gauge section (roughly, like a spoke) in which the average slip plane is oriented at 45° and in which the grain size is 0.1mm (which is fairly large for a typical structural alloy), assume that the average distance of dislocation glide is one-tenth of the grain size. The amount of plastic tensile strain that would be possible from motion of the pre-existing population of dislocations, assuming that they were all mobile and all contributed to the plastic strain, would be given approximately by:

$$\varepsilon_p = 0.7 \rho b \bar{x}$$

Let b be 2.5 x 10^{-8}cm, which is about right for a common metal, like iron or copper. Thus,

$$\varepsilon_p = 0.7 \text{ x } 10^6/\text{cm}^2 \text{ x } 2.5 \text{ x } 10^{-8}\text{cm x } 0.001\text{cm}$$

$$= 0.0018\%$$

Therefore, the initial dislocation population could only account for a tiny fraction of the amount of plastic strain actually observed. The conclusion must be that, to achieve the amounts of plastic strains observed in tensile tests, ρ must increase by at least several orders of magnitude during the test. In the above example, ρ would have to increase by more than a factor of $3\text{x}10^4$ to account for the 50% strain that would occur in the test.

4.5.2 Yielding and Dislocation Multiplication

To understand these processes, it is first necessary to have an accurate idea of what the initial dislocation structure in an annealed crystalline solid would look like.

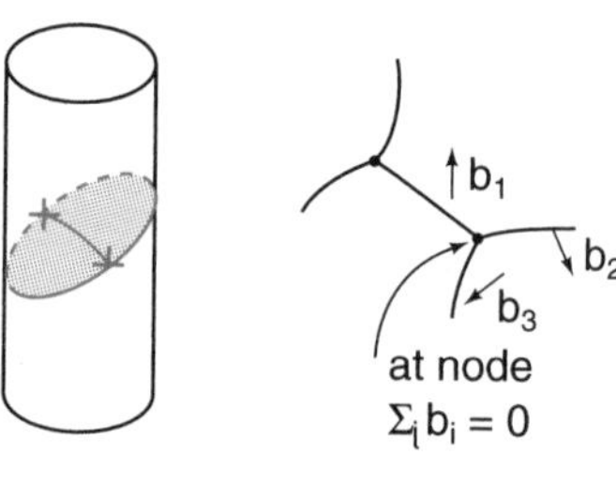

A dislocation is a linear defect with a beginning and an end. Because a dislocation represents the boundary between slipped and not-yet-slipped portions of a crystal, it cannot end inside the crystal except at some other defect. This other defect could be, for example, a surface (either the external surface or that of an internal void), a grain boundary, the interface of a particle of a second phase, or another dislocation line. In the latter case, a three-dislocation node is formed, and the Burgers vectors of the three must sum to zero.

The proper mental picture of a dislocation, therefore, is a linear defect that may be pinned at each end, like a stretched rubber band. As seen in Section 4.4.5, the dislocation has an energy per unit length, or a line tension, of approximately Gb^2. Thus, as with the rubber band, a force must be applied to the dislocation to make it bow out into a loop, thereby increasing its length (and total energy).

Such a force is exerted by a shear stress, which has a vector component parallel to the Burgers vector of the dislocation. That is, dislocation glide is caused only by that component of a shear stress that lies along the Burgers vector of the dislocation.

Because a dislocation is not a physical entity, but is, rather, a configuration of matter, the idea of a force on a dislocation needs to be defined carefully. It is useful to speak of a force acting on a dislocation, because a dislocation can move under the influence of a shear stress, and work is done by this motion. However, the magnitude of the force for a given shear stress is derived in a somewhat roundabout way. The method is simply to calculate the work done on a crystal when a dislocation moves, and then to take the derivative of that work with respect to the distance moved and call that the force. (Work = force x displacement.) This is done as follows:

Consider a block of crystal containing a dislocation to which a shear stress, τ, is applied, as shown in Fig. 4.19. The area of the glide plane is A. If the dislocation were to glide across this entire glide plane, from one side to the other, the two parts of the crystal would be displaced with respect to each other by b, the Burgers vector of the dislocation, Fig. 4.19(b). The work done by the shear stress, which lies along the direction of b, would then be the force times the displacement, or

$$\text{WORK} = \tau\, A\, b$$

If, on the other hand, the dislocation were to glide over only a small portion of the glide plane, Fig. 4.19(c), then only a fraction of this work would be done. Let the distance of glide be dx. The area swept out is then Ldx. The fractional amount of work done, dW, should then be Ldx/A times the total possible work, τAb. Thus,

$$dW = (Ldx/A)\,(\tau Ab) = \tau Lbdx$$

If the force on the dislocation is defined to be dW/dx, then this force is Lτb, and one can write the force per unit length of dislocation as

$$\text{Force per unit length} = \tau b$$

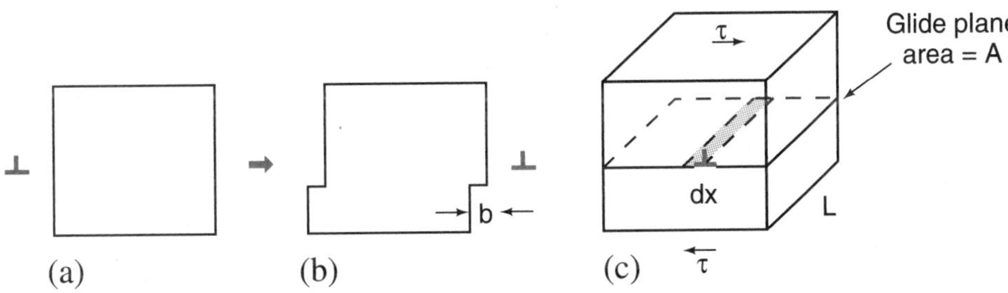

Fig. 4.19 (a) and (b) A dislocation before and after passing through a volume of crystal; the passage causes a shear displacement of b. (c) A dislocation in that volume that glides only by an amount dx; the shear displacement is now only a fraction of b.

Note that this force acts normal to the dislocation line at every point along the line (i.e., in the direction of glide). In this sense it is analogous to the force on a bubble due to the internal pressure of the air trapped inside the bubble. (Note that, strictly speaking, the force per unit length should be written as the dot-product of two vectors: $\boldsymbol{\tau}\cdot\mathbf{b}$.)

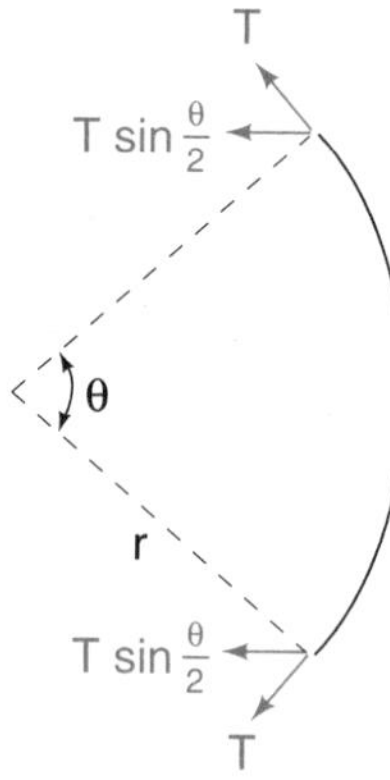

Returning to the case of a dislocation segment pinned at both ends, the shear stress necessary to bow-out a dislocation segment of length S can now be derived by considering the equilibrium between the restoring force, acting to the left, that results from the line tension ($T = Gb^2$ per unit length)* and the force exerted by the shear stress τ, acting to the right, given by τbS.

The segment has a radius of curvature equal to r, and it subtends an arc θ, expressed in radians. Therefore,

$$\theta = \frac{S}{r}$$

The total force acting to the left is the sum of the horizontally resolved components of the line tension at each end of the segment, given by

$$T \sin \frac{\theta}{2}$$

The approximation that $\sin \theta/2 \approx \theta/2$, when θ is given in radians, can be used, and the force balance can then be written

$$\tau bS = 2\,T \sin \frac{\theta}{2} = T\theta = \frac{TS}{r} = \frac{Gb^2S}{r}$$

The final result is that the shear stress needed to bow out a dislocation segment to a radius r is, approximately,

$$\tau = \frac{Gb}{r}$$

Obviously, the shear stress necessary to bow out a loop increases as the radius of the loop decreases. Conversely, if the shear stress is removed, the loop should become straight again, owing to the restoring force.

With these basic ideas about dislocation behavior in hand, it is now possible to understand the mechanism of dislocation multiplication, which was conceived independently by two theorists, F. C. Frank and W. T. Read, around 1950. A useful mental image of this simple but brilliant idea can be gotten by visualizing the ripples generated when a pebble is dropped into a quiet pond. The appearance of dislocation loops emanating from a dislocation source on a glide plane would be similar to the circular ripples that radiate from the point of impact of the pebble on the surface of the water.

Dislocation multiplication starts with a segment of dislocation of length L that can bow-out between pinning points, and it follows a process illustrated schematically in Fig. 4.20. In order for the segment to become a loop, the stress must increase as the radius of curvature decreases, according to $\tau \approx Gb/r$. When the loop reaches a semi-circular shape, further bowing-out proceeds with an increasing radius. Therefore, past this point, the applied stress of ~Gb/L/2 is more than necessary to hold the loop in place, and the loop expands in an unstable manner. The unstably expanding loop folds back on itself and transforms into a full circle when the two parts touch, as shown, because these two parts annihilate each other, being of opposite sign. The complete loop encloses a segment like the original one, lying between the two pinning points. A further increase in the stress causes the complete loop to expand and the residual segment to bow out as before. The process then repeats over and over, giving a set of concentric loops expanding away from the source. A similar process occurs at many locations in a metallic material, gradually filling the material with new dislocations.

* Note: Gb^2 = energy per unit length = force

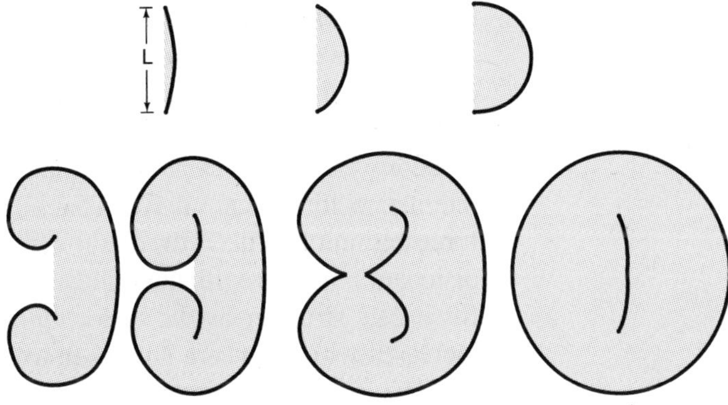

Fig. 4.20 Stages of bowing out of a segment of dislocation into a loop which then becomes unstable and produces a full loop and the starting configuration over again. This is known as the Frank-Read process.

The early stages of plastic flow in an annealed metallic material can now be described. It is now known that dislocations are emitted from grain boundaries during the process of yielding. This is illustrated schematically in Fig. 4.21(a), in which the dislocation is emitted as an elongated loop that, here, is mainly of screw type. The region of slip plane swept out by the loop is represented by shading. The unique feature of a screw dislocation, as noted earlier, is that it is not constrained to glide on any one plane. Rather, it can change planes, as shown previously in Fig. 4.8, by a process known as *cross slip*. This can happen along a portion of the emitted screw dislocation, as shown in Fig. 4.21(b), and it can happen a second time, returning the dislocation to the original slip plane, as shown in Fig. 4.21(c). The total process shown here is known as *double cross slip*.

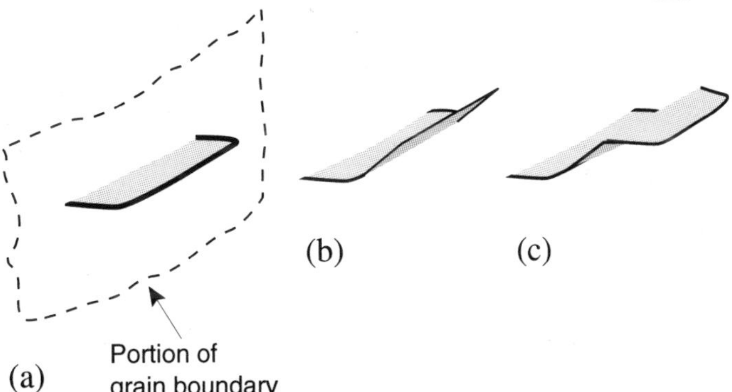

Fig. 4.21 (a) A dislocation loop, mainly screw, emitted from a grain boundary in the early stages of yielding. (b) A segment of the emitted screw dislocation has cross slipped onto another {111} plane. (c) This segment cross slips again back to the original {111} plane; the segment is now pinned at its end points and is constrained to bow out as a loop.

The dislocation configuration formed by this process is of particular importance, because it creates a segment of dislocation that is pinned at its end points. This is the starting configuration for dislocation multiplication by the Frank-Read mechanism. The reason the segment is pinned is that the parts of the dislocation left on the first cross-slip plane are edge in character (because they lie perpendicular to the Burgers vector) and, therefore, cannot glide in any direction except parallel to b. This means that the segment that has undergone double cross slip is constrained to bow out in a new loop, with its end points anchored in place.

4.5.3 The Physical Basis of Strain Hardening

Since every dislocation has a stress field with a shear stress component, one dislocation may exert a force on another dislocation. The most relevant situation is that of dislocations that lie more or less parallel to one another. If two such dislocations are of the same sign, they have similar stress fields, and the mutual interaction force is repulsive. That is, the stress field of one dislocation exerts a force per unit length (= τb) on the other. Since the shear stress component for any dislocation is approximately Gb/r, the interaction force varies as 1/r. That is, the force gets stronger as the dislocation spacing decreases. Thus, the flow stress increases with $1/\bar{r}$ where $\bar{r}$ is taken to be the average dislocation spacing.

The average spacing is given by

$$\bar{r} = \frac{1}{\sqrt{\rho}}$$

where ρ is the dislocation density, because ρ is defined as the total length of dislocation line per unit volume, which is equivalent to the number of dislocations
4790 passing through a unit of area for the case of parallel dislocations. Thus, $1/\rho$ is area per dislocation, and the square root of the area per dislocation is the dislocation spacing.

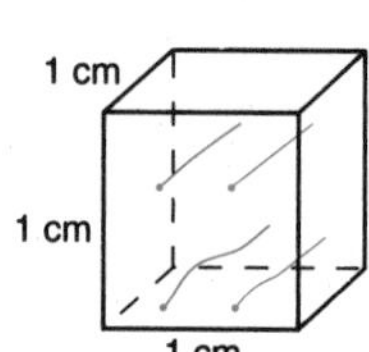

The relationship between the average spacing and the dislocation density can be illustrated by considering a unit volume of material (e.g., a 1-cm cube) that contains four more or less parallel dislocations. The dislocation density is

$$\rho = 4 \text{ cm/cm}^3 = 4 \text{ dislocations/cm}^2$$

and the average spacing is

$$\bar{r} = 1/2 \text{ cm/dislocation} = \frac{1}{\rho^{1/2}}$$

It was demonstrated earlier that ρ varies approximately linearly with plastic strain, ε_{pl}. Since flow stress varies with $1/\bar{r}$, it must vary as $\rho^{1/2}$. Therefore, the conclusion is that in a material with uniformly spaced parallel dislocations,

$$\sigma_{fl} \propto \varepsilon_{pl}^{1/2}$$

which means that the plastic part of the stress-strain curve is parabolic. This is equivalent to saying that strain hardening proceeds at a decreasing rate as plastic strain increases, or the strain-hardening effect tends to saturate, as shown schematically in Fig. 4.22. This effect is observed in Fig. 2.20 for the stainless-steel spokes.

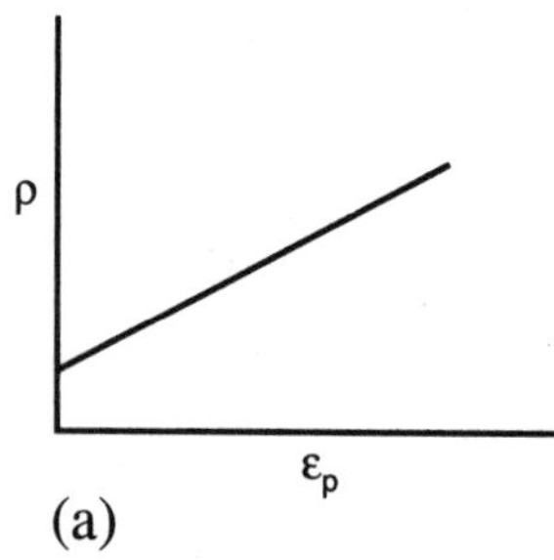

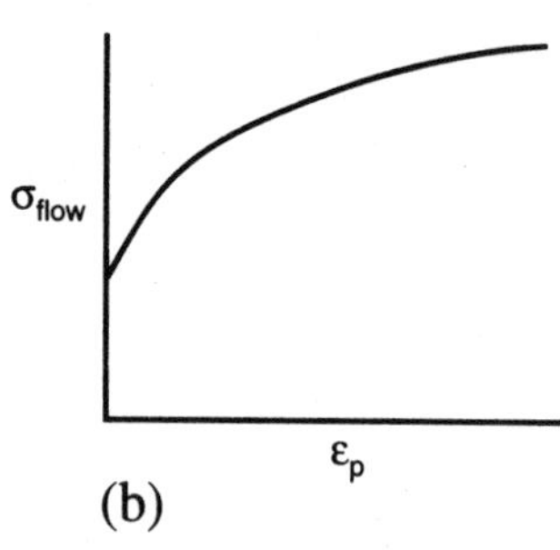

Fig. 4.22 The linear variation of dislocation density with plastic strain (a) leads to (b) a parabolic stress-strain curve.

Example 4.8

Q. Write each individual slip system in the set {111}<110> for an FCC crystal.

A. For the (111) plane (cf. Fig. 4.1(b)) the result is

$$(111)[\bar{1}10]$$
$$(111)[10\bar{1}]$$
$$(111)[0\bar{1}1]$$

For the rest the result is

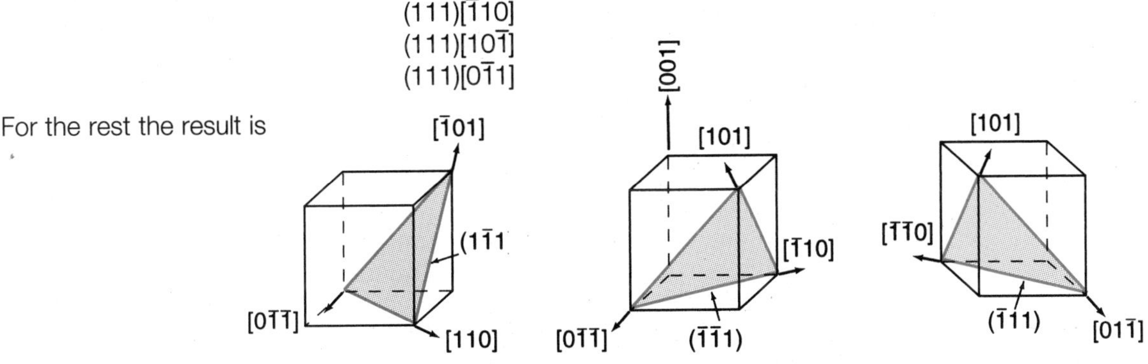

Example 4.9

Q. If the slip step left by a cross-slipping screw dislocation in an FCC crystal is made up of segments on the (111) and $(\bar{1}\bar{1}1)$ planes, as shown below, what must be the Burgers vector of the dislocation?

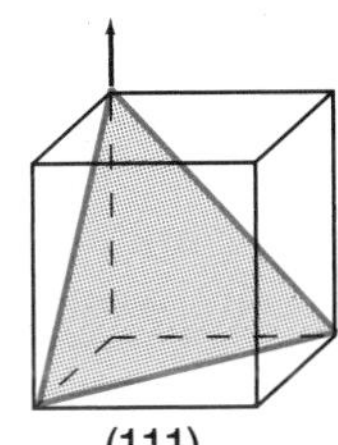

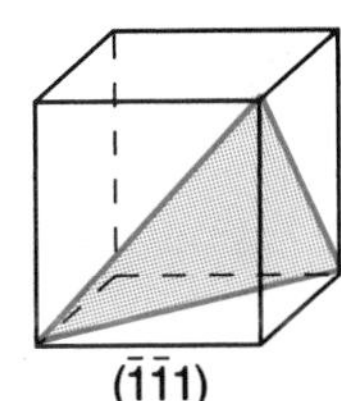

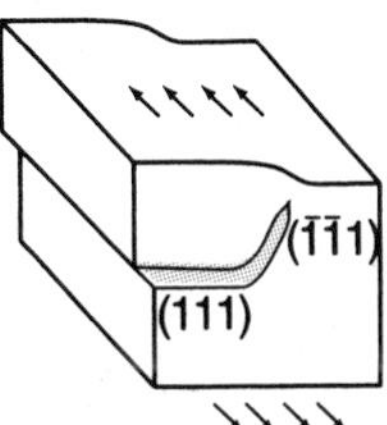

A. The Burgers vector must be of the type $a/2$ <110>, since it is an FCC crystal. The only <110> direction that lies in both of the observed glide planes is the $[\bar{1}10]$ direction (or, equivalently, $[1\bar{1}0]$.) Therefore, the Burgers vector must be $a/2\ [\bar{1}10]$ or $a/2\ [1\bar{1}0]$.

Example 4.10

Q. Prove that the $[\bar{1}10]$ direction lies in both the (111) and $[\bar{1}\bar{1}1]$ planes.

A. In a cubic crystal the [hkl] direction is normal to the (hkl) plane. Therefore, the normals to the two {111} planes are in the [111] and $[\bar{1}\bar{1}1]$ directions, respectively. By definition, a plane normal is perpendicular to any vector in the plane. Therefore, the dot-product of a plane normal and any vector in the plane must be zero. Taking the dot-product, it is found that

$$[\bar{1}10]\cdot[111] = \bar{1}\text{x}1 + 1\text{x}1 + 0\text{x}1 = 0, \text{ and}$$
$$[\bar{1}10]\cdot[\bar{1}\bar{1}1] = \bar{1}\text{x}\bar{1} + 1\text{x}\bar{1} + 0\text{x}1 = 0$$

Therefore, the $[\bar{1}10]$ direction lies in both planes.

Example 4.11

Q. Consider an interaction between an oversize substitutional solute atom and an edge dislocation in which the solute atom could lie either above or below the glide plane, as indicated below. Which of the positions would produce a repulsive interaction and which would produce an attractive interaction?

A. The oversize solute atom puts the surrounding lattice into a compressive stress state that is spherically symmetrical, assuming the atom acts like a hard sphere and the crystal is elastically isotropic. This means that it has a stress field of purely hydrostatic compression. Therefore, if the solute atom lies above the glide plane (position A), the stress fields reinforce, and the interaction is repulsive. Conversely, in position B the interaction is attractive. Note that, in either position, glide of the dislocation past the solute would be inhibited.

Example 4.12

Q. What would the answer have been if the dislocation in Example 4.11 had been a screw instead of an edge?

A. There is no geometrically defined glide plane for a screw dislocation; also, the stress field is axi-symmetric. Therefore, the interaction depends only on r, not on θ. Also, the stress field of the screw has no normal components, while that of the substitutional solute has only normal components. Therefore, there is no interaction resulting from the solute-size effect.

Example 4.13

Q. Suppose that a substitutional solute atom alters the atomic bonding locally so as to reduce the shear modulus G. How would that affect the interactions between the solute and any dislocation?

A. Since the dislocation energy per unit length is proportional to G, this energy would be lower in the vicinity of the solute atom. Thus, the solute atom would attract the dislocation and could act as a local trap for the dislocation. This effect alone would tend to inhibit glide. (Obviously, the interaction would be repulsive if G were locally increased by the solute atom.) These effects can play a role in solid-solution hardening.

Example 4.14

Q. Calculate the force per unit length on an edge dislocation with Burgers vector $b = 2.5 \times 10^{-10}$m on the indicated slip plane in the mono-crystalline tensile specimen subjected to a tensile stress, $\sigma = 100$ MPa, shown below. (Note that the tensile axis (TA), the slip-plane normal (N), and the slip direction (b) are not co-planar.)

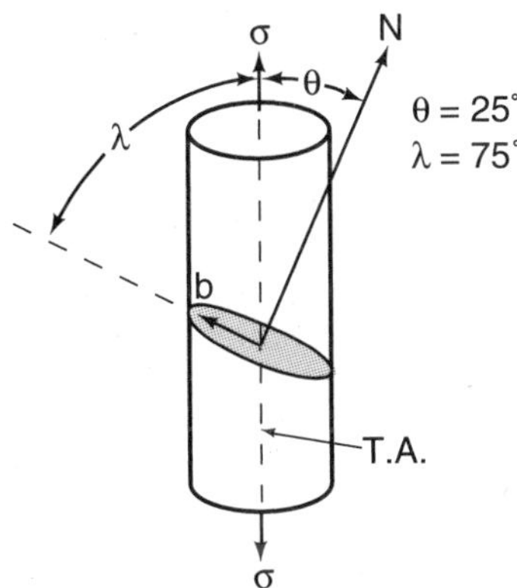

A. Since the force per unit length is given by τb, one simply needs to calculate τ in the direction of b. This is given by the Schmid relationship:

$$\tau = \sigma \cos \lambda \cos \theta$$

$$= 100\text{MPa} \cos 25 \cos 75 = 23.5 \text{ MPa}$$

Therefore, the force per unit length is

$$\tau b = 23.5\text{MPa} \,.\, 2.5 \times 10^{-10}\text{m}$$

$$= 58.6 \times 10^{-4}\text{N/m}$$

Summary

The process of plastic deformation can be summarized as follows: As the stress on a material is increased, dislocation loops are emitted from grain boundaries. Double cross-slip creates dislocation segments pinned at their end points, and the longest segments bow out first, followed by shorter and shorter segments as the stress rises. The response of the material, therefore, becomes gradually less elastic. (However, the plastic displacement in this early stage of plasticity is too small to be detected by the transducers generally used in tensile testing.) At a sufficiently high stress, dislocation multiplication takes place, and the plastic displacement increases rapidly; this constitutes yielding. The dislocation density continues to increase, and the dislocation interactions become more intense; this is strain hardening. The flow stress continues to rise until necking occurs; past this point, the load-elongation curve falls until rupture occurs.

Some important features of dislocations are the following:

- They create a stress field that is inversely proportional to the distance from the dislocation. That is, the stress field has a 1/r dependence.
- One dislocation, A, exerts a force (per unit length) on another dislocation, B, equal to the dot product of the shear stress of A acting at B and the Burgers vector of B. Thus, the force between parallel dislocations is inversely proportional to their spacing.
- Dislocations have an energy per unit length equal approximately to Gb^2. Thus, a strain-hardened material is in a high-energy state.

Appendix 4.1 - Bragg's Law of Diffraction

Because x-ray or electron beams can have wave lengths comparable to the atomic spacing in crystals, these beams can be diffracted by crystals. This was demonstrated with x-rays by von Laue in 1912, and the geometrical law governing diffraction by crystals was worked out by W. L. Bragg in the same year.

To understand this, recall that an x-ray or electron beam can be considered as an electric field that varies sinusoidally with time. When an atom in a crystal is encountered by an incident beam, the electrons are set into oscillation, and they, in turn, radiate energy in all directions. (Any accelerating electric charge radiates electromagnetic energy, as in a radio antenna, for example.)

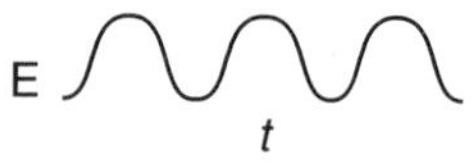

E

t

Incident beam; the electric field, E, varies with time.

The electrons in the atom are oscillated by E and energy radiates over 360°.

When an x-ray or electron beam hits a crystal and penetrates a micrometer or so, all atoms in this region are made to radiate energy in all directions. In certain directions this "scattered" radiation is in phase, and a "diffracted" beam results. In all other directions the scattered radiation is out of phase, and the beams cancel each other.

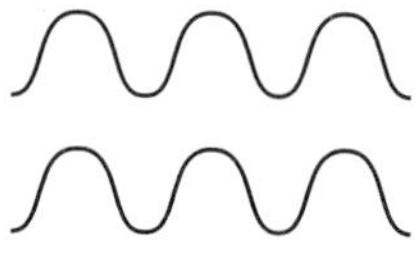

Two beams in phase

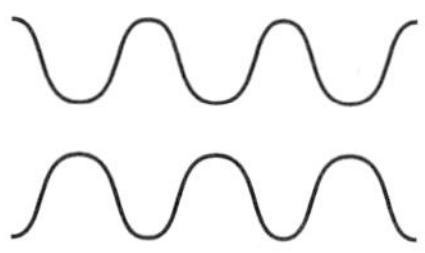

Two beams 180° out of phase

To derive Bragg's law, consider the top few atomic planes of a crystal, as in Fig. A4.1.1. A diffracted beam will result if the incident beam strikes the top plane at an angle θ, such that scattered beams from atom planes parallel to the top plane, with planar spacing d, are in phase with the incident beam. That is, the phase difference between the two must be an integral number of wave lengths. In Fig. A4.1.1, the incoming beams, with wave length λ and incident angle θ, are in phase along the plane front *xx'*. Consider beam 1 scattered from atom K and beam 2 scattered from atom L, giving scattered beams 1' and 2'. If the path difference MLN is nλ, where *n* is an integer, then beams 1' and 2' are in phase along the plane front yy' and they reinforce one another.

Fig. A4.1.1 Diffraction of an x-ray or electron beam from a crystal. Adapted from B.D. Cullity, *Elements of X-ray Diffraction,* Addision-Wesley, Reading, MA, 1956, p.120.)

From geometry,

$$ML = LN = d \sin \theta$$

Therefore, the diffraction condition is

$$n\lambda = 2d \sin \theta$$

Thus, for this combination of λ, d, and θ, Bragg's law is said to be satisfied. Whenever this occurs, a diffracted beam results. The intensity of the diffracted beam depends on the kinds of atoms present and their density (number per unit area); the intensity is not predicted by Bragg's Law.

Appendix 4.2 - Stress Field of an Edge Dislocation

The edge dislocation has a stress field that is more complicated than that of a screw dislocation. To derive the expressions for the stress components of an edge dislocation requires a knowledge of the theory of elasticity and of stress analysis. For present purposes it is sufficient merely to quote the results:

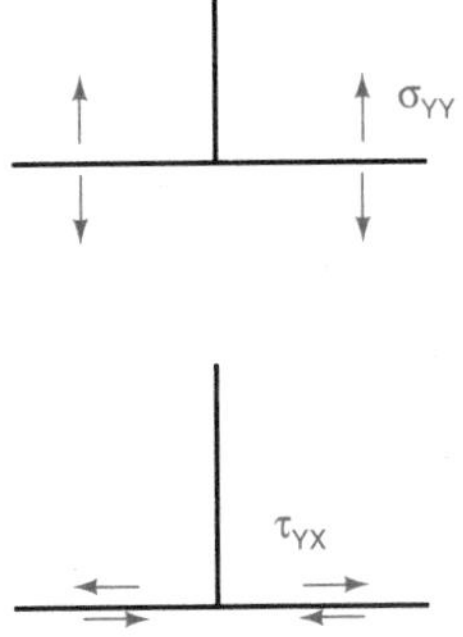

Normal Stresses:

$$\sigma_{xx} = -Dy \frac{(3x^2 + y^2)}{(x^2 + y^2)^2} \qquad \sigma_{yy} = Dy \frac{(x^2 - y^2)}{(x^2 + y^2)^2}$$

$$\sigma_{zz} = \nu(\sigma_{xx} + \sigma_{yy})$$

Shear Stress:

$$\tau_{xy} = \tau_{yx} = Dx \frac{(x^2 - y^2)}{(x^2 + y^2)^2}$$

The remaining components, $\tau_{xz} = \tau_{zx}$ and $\tau_{yz} = \tau_{zy}$, are zero. That is, there is no component of shear stress in the direction along the line of an edge dislocation.

The parameter ν is a material constant, called *Poisson's ratio* and is defined by:

$$\nu = \frac{-\varepsilon_{zz}}{\varepsilon_{xx}} = \frac{-\varepsilon_{yy}}{\varepsilon_{xx}}$$

for an isotropic material. For example, it characterizes the contraction of a solid along the two transverse axes, *y* and *z*, when the solid is stretched along the longitudinal axis, *x*. The value of ν for most interesting materials is in the range 0.3 to 0.35.

The parameter, D, is defined by:

$$D = \frac{Gb}{2\pi\,(1 - \nu)}$$

where G is the shear modulus and b is the Burgers vector of the dislocation.

Although the expressions for these stress components look quite different from the $\tau = Gb/2\pi r$ derived for the screw dislocation, there is an important similarity. First, the term $(1 - \nu)$ is about equal to 2/3. Thus, $D \approx Gb/4$. Secondly, the radial distance in the x,y plane from the dislocation line is

$$r = (x^2 + y^2)^{1/2}$$

and inspection of the functions of *x* and *y* in the three stress components shows that they have a 1/r character. Of course, they depend on whether *y* is positive or negative and whether *y* is greater than, less than, or equal to *x* at the point *x*, *y* where the stress state is to be calculated. Hence, the stress components change sign in various regions of the *x*, *y* plane; but, the magnitude of the stress at any point still varies approximately as $Gb/2\pi r$.

It was noted earlier that, for a screw dislocation, it is more convenient to use cylindrical coordinates r, θ, *z* instead of Cartesian coordinates *x*, *y*, *z*, as illustrated in Fig. A4.2.1. In this case the stress field of the screw dislocation is characterized by:

$$\tau_{\theta Z} = Gb/2\pi r$$

(This is equal to $\tau_{Z\theta}$, which exerts a twist to the end of the cylinder shown in Fig. 4.17; this is irrelevant for our purposes.)

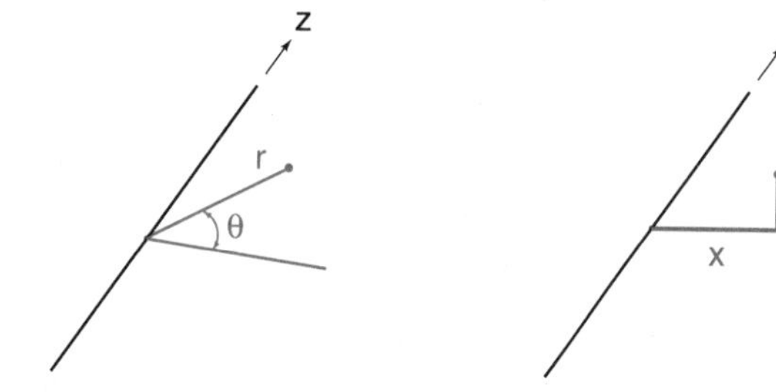

Fig. A4.2.1 Coordinate systems used for screw and edge dislocations

Finally, it should be emphasized that shear stress components produce shape changes, and normal stress components produce volume changes, or dilations.

Glossary/Vocabulary - Chapter 4

Bright-field technique	This is the technique normally used in transmission electron microscopy of crystalline solids, in which the image on the viewing screen is formed by a diffracted beam from the majority phase, as opposed to a second phase present in small amounts (cf. dark-field technique). The electron micrographs used, for example, to reveal dislocations in a deformed metal are made with the bright-field technique.
Bragg's Law	This is the basic law of diffraction of an electromagnetic wave, like an x-ray or an electron beam, from a crystal. It gives the diffraction angle, or Bragg angle, for the diffraction (in-phase scattering) of a beam of wavelength λ from planes of a crystal with an interplanar spacing of d, according to $n\lambda = 2d \sin \theta$, θ being the diffraction angle with respect to the scattering plane (2θ with respect to the incoming beam), and n is an integer. The basis for Bragg's law is that, for constructive, or in-phase, scattering, the scattered beams from successive layers of atoms must differ by integral numbers of wave lengths.
Burgers vector	The slip vector of a dislocation, which means the vector that describes how one plane of atoms is sheared over the one below when a dislocation glides, is called the Burgers vector. The Burgers vector of a slip dislocation in an FCC crystal is given by $a/2$ <110>, where a is the lattice parameter. In a BCC crystal, it is $a/2$ <111>.
Climb	Edge dislocations, or dislocations with edge component, because they have extra material associated with them, can move up or down (relative to the glide plane) only by losing or gaining atoms: i.e., by absorbing or emitting vacancies. This vertical movement (perpendicular to the glide plane) is called climb. Climb is important in recovery and in creep, because it allows the rearrangement of dislocations in response to internal stresses or to applied (external) stress.
Core of a dislocation	This is the highly distorted set of atoms that lie along the dislocation line, within a few atom diameters of the line. The ease of dislocation glide under an applied shear stress depends on the size and configuration of the core. Dislocations with a narrow or non-planar core, as in silicon, glide only at high stresses or at high temperatures. Dislocations in copper have a wide, planar core, and copper is therefore soft.
Cross slip	When a screw dislocation glides from one slip plane to another slip plane that intersects the first, the process is known as cross slip. The first slip plane is usually one with a maximum value of the Schmid factor. The cross-slip process is usually caused by some internal source of stress that reduces the net shear stress on the primary slip plane.
Double cross slip	This is an extension of the process of cross slip in which the screw dislocation shifts back to the primary slip plane. This is an important process in dislocation multiplication, because it is often a necessary prelude to the formation of a Frank-Read source.

Diffraction contrast	This is a mechanism that provides contrast in transmission electron microscopy of crystalline specimens. Regions in which the crystal structure is perturbed by some kind of defect produce diffraction of the electron beam at some angle other than the Bragg angle of the surrounding crystal. This diffracted radiation is blocked by the aperture of the microscope, and the region appears dark. Here, we refer to the case in which the specimen is being imaged by the direct electron beam; this is called the bright-field method.
Dilational stress	A dilational stress is one that changes the volume of a body, as opposed to its shape. Therefore, it is a normal stress, tensile or compressive. The stress field around an oversize or undersize solute atom in a crystal lattice is dilational.
Dislocation density	This is defined as the total length of dislocations per unit volume, usually one cm^3, or, alternatively, the total number of dislocations passing through unit area, usually one cm^2. The latter definition assumes that all dislocation lines are parallel, but the error is usually small, since the area observed is usually small. An annealed metal is usually assumed to have $<10^6$ dislocations per cm^2, and a cold worked metal often has as many as 10^{12} dislocations per cm^2.
Dislocation energy	Any defect that strains a crystal lattice is a source of strain energy. The strain energy per unit volume in a body under a single uniform stress is given by 1/2 the stress times the associated strain (i.e., the area under the stress-strain curve). The strain energy of a unit length of dislocation is given by the volume integral of 1/2 each component of stress times its associated strain term. The strain energy per unit length of a screw dislocation is $\frac{Gb^2}{4\pi} \ln \frac{r}{r_0}$, where G is the shear modulus and b is the Burgers vector.
Dislocation interactions	Since dislocations have elastic stress fields associated with them, one dislocation will interact with another through these stress fields, component by component. If the respective components are of the same sign, the interaction is repulsive. If they are of opposite sign, attractive. The interaction force is inversely proportional to their spacing. Two parallel screw dislocations with vectors of the same sign would repel each other. If the Burgers vectors are anti-parallel, they would attract and annihilate each other.
Dislocation loop	A curved dislocation (lying on a single crystallographic plane) that closes on itself is called a dislocation loop. If the Burgers vector lies in the plane of the loop, the loop can be expanded, causing slip, if a shear stress is applied in the direction of the Burgers vector. A segment of dislocation pinned at both ends, if acted upon by a shear stress parallel to its Burgers vector, would bow out and emit a loop by way of the Frank-Read mechanism.
Dislocation multiplication	During plastic strain, the dislocation density increases by orders of magnitude. The generally accepted mechanism is the Frank-Read source, in which a segment of dislocation pinned at both ends is caused to bow out by the application of a shear stress in the direction of its Burgers vector. When the segment reaches a semi-circular shape, it becomes unstable and rapidly expands into a complete loop, leaving a segment like the original one between the two pinning points. With the continued application of stress, the loop expands, and the process repeats itself over and over again. The process will continue until the outermost loop hits a barrier. After that, the loops pile up against the barrier and exert a back stress, which finally shuts down the source.

Dislocation-solute interactions Because dislocations and misfitting solute atoms each have elastic stress fields associated with them, they interact through these stress fields, component by component. The normal stress components of the stress field of an edge dislocation would interact with the corresponding normal stress components of an misfitting solute atom.

Edge dislocation An edge dislocation is one for which the slip vector, or Burgers vector, is perpendicular to the line of the dislocation, which lies along the bottom of an extra half-plane of atoms. The orthogonal combination of the Burgers vector and the dislocation line define the glide plane of the dislocation. Because the edge dislocation has extra atoms associated with it, it is constrained to move only in its glide plane, unless atoms are either added or taken away (non-conservative motion).

Force on a dislocation When a dislocation with Burgers vector b is acted upon by a shear stress τ in the direction of b, the dislocation acts as if it experiences a force per unit length equal to τb. Since a dislocation is actually a configuration of matter, rather than a body of matter, the force is a notional one, found by taking the derivative of the work done by the stress τ with respect to the distance that the dislocation glides.

Frank-Read mechanism See dislocation multiplication.

Hydrostatic compression This is a type of stress field in which there are three equal normal stresses acting in a negative sense and no shear stresses. It is called hydrostatic, because that is the state of stress on a body suspended in a fluid, in which the pressure is the same in all directions. An oversize substitutional solute atom in a crystal lattice is subjected to hydrostatic compression by the surrounding atoms.

Line tension Same as dislocation energy per unit length (above).

Mixed dislocation A mixed dislocation is one for which the slip vector, or Burgers vector, lies at some angle between zero and 90 degrees to the dislocation line. It has some extra atoms associated with it, but not as much as an edge dislocation. Since the dislocation line and Burgers vector are not parallel, a specific glide plane is defined, and conservative motion can take place only on that plane.

Parabolic hardening In a material in which dislocation multiplication during plastic strain takes place more or less uniformly through the straining volume of material, the plastic part of the stress-strain curve is parabolic. That is, the flow stress varies with the square root of the strain. This can be derived from the facts that the strength of dislocation interactions are inversely proportional to their spacing and that this spacing is given by the inverse square root of the dislocation density. (The latter increases approximately linearly with plastic strain.) Metals that cross slip easily generally exhibit classical parabolic hardening.

Peierls stress The shear stress necessary to move a straight dislocation through an otherwise perfect lattice at 0 K is called the Peierls stress, after Rudolph Peierls, who first calculated an approximate model for this stress, at the suggestion of Egon Orowan. The Peierls stress for FCC metals is normally rather low. The Peierls stress for the motion of edge dislocations in BCC metals is comparably low, but that for screw dislocations is high, and thermal activation is important for screw dislocation mobility in BCC metals.

Pinning Pinning means retarding the motion of something, usually a dislocation or a grain boundary. Segregated solute atoms can pin dislocations, and small particles of a second phase can pin grain boundaries (during annealing).

Primary slip plane This is the plane with the maximum value of the Schmid factor in a stressed crystal. In an FCC crystal loaded in tension along the [001] direction, there are four equally stressed {111} slip planes, with two equally stressed <110> slip directions. Thus, the Schmid factor is the same for all eight slip systems, and any one of them can serve as a primary slip plane.

Screw dislocation A screw dislocation is one for which the slip vector, or Burgers vector, lies parallel to the dislocation line. The core of the dislocation in a simple metal resembles a spiral ramp of atoms; hence the name.

Slip system A combination of a slip plane and a slip direction in that plane is called a slip system. The common slip system in FCC metals is {111}<110>, and in BCC metals {110}<111>.

Stress field of dislocation A dislocation distorts the crystal lattice and thereby sets up an elastic stress field that is centered on the dislocation and diminishes in intensity with distance from the center, much like the electric field around a charged particle. The value of the stress field at any point is given by nine components of stress that act on the faces of an infinitesmal cube centered on that point, three normal stresses and six shear stresses. (The normal stresses are parallel to the edges of the cube.) Only three of the shear stresses are independent. Some of these stress terms may be zero. The stress field of a screw dislocation is one of pure shear. That is, there are only two non-zero shear stress terms (out of six), and they are equal. All three normal-stress terms are zero. The shear stress is given by $Gb/2\pi r$, where G is the shear modulus, b the Burgers vector, and r the distance from the dislocation line.

Stress to bow a loop When a segment of dislocation that is constrained at each end (i.e., pinned) is acted upon by a shear stress parallel to its Burgers vector, the segment begins to bow out and form a loop between the pinning points. (This is the first step in the operation of a Frank-Read source.) The shear stress needed to bow out a loop increases with the curvature of the loop according to $\tau = Gb/r$, where G is the shear modulus, b is the Burgers vector of the dislocation, and r is the radius of curvature of the loop.

X-ray diffraction Because crystal lattices have dimensions on the same scale as the wave lengths of x-rays, constructive interference can occur when the atoms of the crystal scatter an incoming beam. This interference produces a diffracted beam, as when a light beam is diffracted by a ruled grating. Von Laue in 1912 showed that an x-ray beam is diffracted when passed through a crystal of copper sulfate. This demonstrated simultaneously the wave nature of x-rays and the fact that the crystal comprised a regular array of atoms.

Exercises

4.1 When a screw dislocation changes glide planes, the process is called cross slip. Determine the direction of the Burgers vector of the screw dislocations that can undergo the following types of cross slip:

From $(1\bar{1}1)$ to (111)

From $(1\bar{1}1)$ to $(\bar{1}11)$

4.2 It is physically possible to have dislocations with the Burgers vector *a*<100> in an FCC crystal. Compare the energy of such a dislocation with that of one with the common Burgers vector *a*/2<110>, using the approximation that energy per unit length is equal to Gb^2, and comment on why the former is rarely observed. Remember, for the vector $\mathbf{a} = a_1\mathbf{i} + a_2\mathbf{j} + a_3\mathbf{k}$,

$$|a| = \sqrt{(a_1^2 + a_2^2 + a_3^2)}$$

4.3 Consider a segment of dislocation pinned securely at each end as shown, with a Burgers vector as indicated. If the mobility of an edge dislocation in this material is much larger than the mobility of a screw dislocation (as in the case of iron at temperatures around 77K), the segment would not form a symmetrical loop when subjected to a shear stress in the direction of the Burgers vector. With the aid of a sketch, show the expected response of the segment to such a stress.

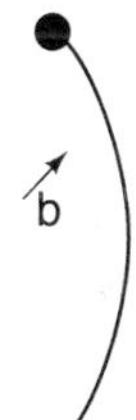

4.4 Show the connection between the dislocation loop pictured in Fig. 4.14 and the operation of a Frank-Read source.

4.5 List the strengthening mechanisms (i.e., ways to impede dislocation glide) that you have learned about so far, and explain briefly how they operate.

4.6 Consider the edge dislocation shown below, in which the extra half-plane is a (010) plane of the crystal. If the presence of this dislocation were to be revealed by diffraction contrast in the TEM, it would be a good idea to use the beam diffracted from (010) planes; explain why. What would be the result if the beam diffracted from (100) planes were used to form the image?

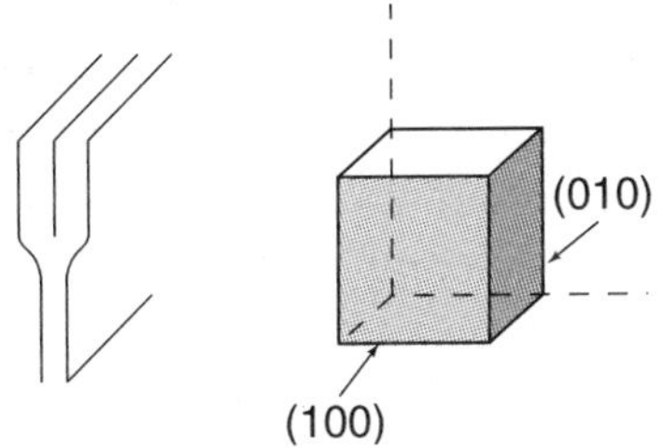

4.7 The energy per unit length of a screw dislocation = $Gb^2/4\pi(\ln r/r_0)$ obviously depends on the value chosen for r (i.e., the extent of the crystal around the dislocation within which the energy is stored). Make a plot of energy/length *vs.* r (not ln r). (Let $r_0 = 2b$, and express r in terms of b; i.e., $r = 10b$, 10^2b, etc.) Plot the energy in units of Gb^2, and extend the plot to $r=10^3b$.

4.8 An FCC crystal is subjected to a tensile stress, σ, of 140 MPa along the $[\bar{1}\bar{1}2]$ direction. Calculate the force per unit length on dislocations that lie on the $(\bar{1}\bar{1}1)$ plane and have the following Burgers vectors: $a/2[\bar{1}10]$ and $a/2[101]$. Let $a = 2.5\text{x}10^{-10}$m.

4.9 Imagine an isolated substitutional solute atom that causes a local reduction in the shear modulus of the crystal. By means of a schematic sketch showing the solute atom and a screw dislocation, show the nature of the expected interaction between them as the screw attempts to glide past the solute atom. Do the same for the case where the local shear modulus is increased.

4.10 Iron is BCC at room temperature, with $a = 0.28$ nm.

a. Calculate the length of the Burgers vector in iron.
b. Calculate the shear modulus in iron, given $\nu = 0.33$ and E = 210GPa
c. Calculate the approximate energy per unit length of a dislocation line in iron.

4.11 Consider a reaction in which two dislocations combine to make a third. Written in terms of the Burgers vectors, a potential reaction is

$$1/2\ [111] + 1/2\ [1\bar{1}\bar{1}] \longrightarrow [100]$$

Is this physically possible from the standpoint of vector addition? Is it energetically favorable or unfavorable? Explain your answer

5

ANNEALING OF COLD-WORKED METALS

Spoke manufacture involves drawing rods through a series of dies of decreasing hole size until wire of the desired diameter is produced. This cannot be done in one continuous series of draws, starting with thick rods, because the accumulation of strain hardening would become too great. The force needed to pull the wire through a die cannot exceed that corresponding to the UTS, or the wire will neck and rupture. Therefore, the wire must be softened periodically during the drawing process. This is accomplished by heating the wire above some threshold temperature in a process known as *annealing.* The annealing process involves some important internal changes in the wire that permit it to transform from a high-energy, *cold-worked* state to a lower energy state. (Cold-working a metallic material means deforming it plastically at a temperature low enough that the strain-hardened condition is retained indefinitely.) To understand the annealing process, it is necessary to think in terms of thermodynamics, the basic principles of which will be described before proceeding further.

5.1 Thermodynamic Principles

The cold-worked state is thermodynamically unstable because of the internal energy stored in the deformed grains, mainly in the form of dislocations (Gb^2 per unit length), but also as *point defects,* mainly excess lattice vacancies. A lattice vacancy is a lattice site from which an atom is missing. As will be shown later, this is a "natural" kind of defect in a crystalline solid. That is, at any temperature above absolute zero, a crystal at equilibrium will have a certain fraction of vacant lattice sites. The process of plastic flow results in a vacancy concentration higher than the equilibrium value. The return to equilibrium entails, in part, the "annealing out" of the excess vacancy concentration.

The central concept of thermodynamics is that of equilibrium. The equilibrium state of a system is the state that persists interminably, without change, regardless of attempts to perturb the system by small amounts. For example, water represents an equilibrium configuration of oxygen and hydrogen (at room temperature and one atmosphere of pressure). Shaking water in a container does not cause it to separate into its elements.

It is common experience that the attainment of equilibrium in any system involves a reduction of energy to a minimum value. Thus, water runs downhill to minimize its potential energy (in the gravitational field of the earth). The cold-worked condition is not at equilibrium, because it is not in a state of minimum energy. Although the cold-worked condition is unstable, it persists at low temperatures, because the processes that produce softening, which are lumped together under the term "annealing," must be *thermally activated.* That is, thermal energy is required for the several kinds of atomic rearrangements that must take place. This can be envisioned schematically with the aid of Fig. 5.1; the system can pass from the high-energy state to the more stable, low-energy state only if an activation energy is supplied. The net energy difference between the two states is the *driving force* for the reaction.

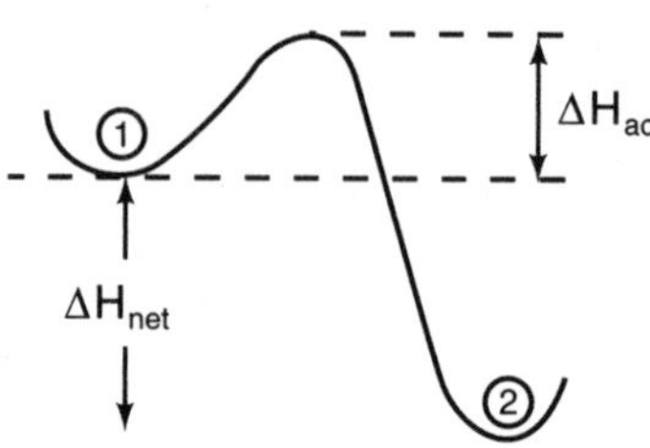

Fig. 5.1 Schematic illustration of the requirement of an activation energy to allow a system to pass from high-energy state 1 to a lower-energy state 2.

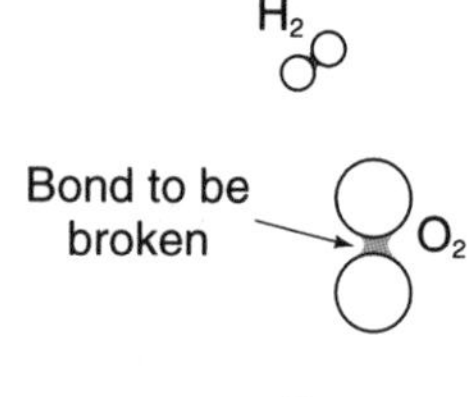

An analogy can be made to a container of oxygen and hydrogen gas at room temperature and pressure. Although water would be the equilibrium condition, some energy must be supplied to the gas mixture to break the bonds of the O_2 molecules so the oxygen atoms can react with the H_2 molecules. The energy released by this reaction is much larger than the activation energy needed to get it started. Thus, the invested activation energy is "paid back" once the reaction starts.

A minimum of energy is not the only factor that determines the equilibrium state. This can be illustrated by considering a box large enough to contain many gas molecules, but that contains only a few, as illustrated schematically in Fig. 5.2, which shows four possible configurations of the molecules.

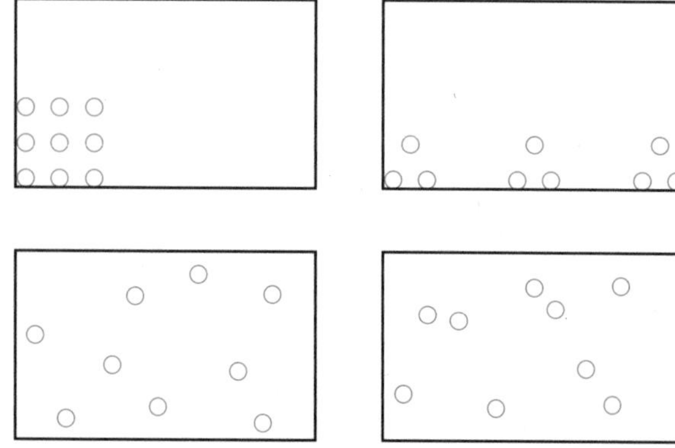

Fig. 5.2 Four possible arrangements of n molecules in a box large enough to contain N molecules, where N is much greater than n.

Assume that the temperature and pressure are constant. Ignore, for the moment, the influence of energy on the molecular arrangement, and let all arrangements have equal probability. It is intuitively obvious that the molecules are more likely to be found at random locations than in either of the two orderly arrangements shown. Thus, one would say that, if the molecules were stacked in an orderly array in one corner of the box, the system would not be at equilibrium, because there would be a tendency for it to transform spontaneously into a more probable configuration. This means that the criterion for equilibrium must somehow take probability into account.

Imagine that the box can be divided up into cells, each of which can contain one gas molecule, and the molecules are permitted to occupy any of the cells. There is a very large number of possible random, disorderly configurations and only a relatively small number of possible orderly arrangements. Therefore, one would conclude that, at equilibrium, the molecules will be arranged in some disorderly array. It does not matter which disorderly array, since they are all equivalent in the sense that they all lack order. (An orderly array is one for which there is some scheme whereby, if the position of one molecule is known, then the positions of all others can be calculated by some formula.) This does not mean that the molecules are never arranged in an orderly array. Ordering may indeed occur at some instant in time, but this arrangement does not persist. The equilibrium condition is the one that would be found at virtually any instant in time, and this would be characterized by a minimum of order. The thermodynamic variable that characterizes the state of disorder is *entropy,* denoted by S. Thus, all other things being equal, the equilibrium state is characterized by a maximum of entropy.

Suppose now that the temperature of the system is reduced to the point where the molecules condense from a gaseous to a crystalline state. The entropy has now been reduced to a very low value, because the energy part of the criterion for equilibrium has taken control. That is, because of the existence of the kind of 5070
binding energy illustrated in Fig. 2.7(a), the crystalline state is the most stable at a sufficiently low temperature. Therefore, the equilibrium criterion must be mediated somehow by temperature.

The universal criterion for equilibrium was deduced by J. Willard Gibbs and involves the minimization of a *free energy,* which is an energy modified to take probability into account. It is written

$$G = H - TS$$

where G is called the *Gibbs free energy,* T is the absolute temperature (degrees Kelvin), and H is called the *enthalpy.* The latter is equal to E + pV, where p means pressure, V means volume, and E is the *internal energy,* e.g., the binding energy of the molecules (cf. Fig. 2.7). In solids and liquids the volume is negligible compared to that in the gaseous state, and at one atmosphere the pV term is also negligible. That is, one can usually ignore changes in energy arising from changes in volume at one atmosphere pressure. Therefore, H can normally be considered equivalent to E for condensed systems.

Thus, equilibrium is characterized by a minimum value of G, and any spontaneous change in nature must involve a decrease in G. That is, a stable system is one for which G is a minimum. At zero Kelvin, this is equivalent to a minimum in energy. However, as the temperature is increased, entropy becomes more and more important. For example, at a certain temperature, the TS term becomes large enough to overcome the binding energy of the molecules in the box, and the gaseous state takes over.

These principles will now be applied to the process of annealing a cold worked bicycle spoke. The heat supplies the activation energy needed for various stages to occur so the spoke can find its way to a minimum free energy.

5.2 Stages of Annealing

The three stages of annealing are *recovery, recrystallization,* and *grain growth.* The latter two stages can be followed by measurement of *hardness,* which can be defined as the resistance of a material to indentation by a loaded indenter. Several common hardness tests are described in Appendix 5.1; their utility lies in their simplicity and speed and the fact that specimen preparation is minimal. Physically, hardness represents a generalized resistance of a material to plastic deformation under a rather complicated, but reproducible, state of stress. Therefore, it is a useful parameter for comparative purposes or for following trends of hardening or softening, but not for understanding phenomena at a fundamental level. The way hardness varies during cold working and annealing is shown schematically in Fig. 5.3.

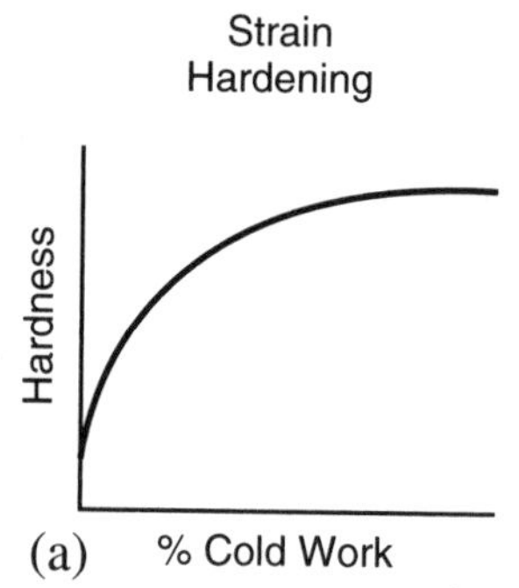

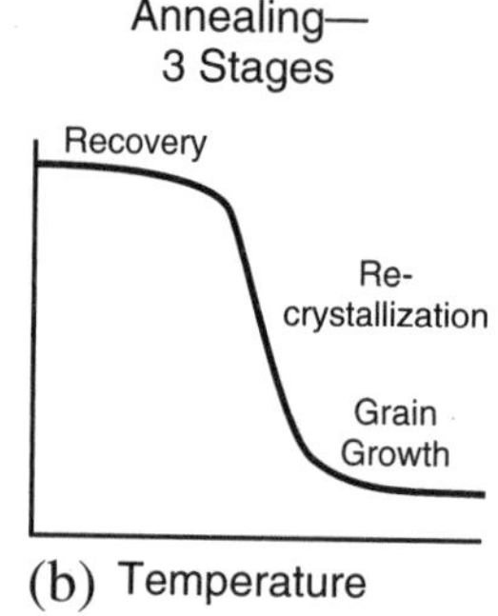

Fig. 5.3 Variation of hardness during (a) cold working and (b) annealing. (During annealing a fixed time at each temperature is assumed.)

5090

5.3 Recrystallization

5.3.1 Mechanism of Recrystallization

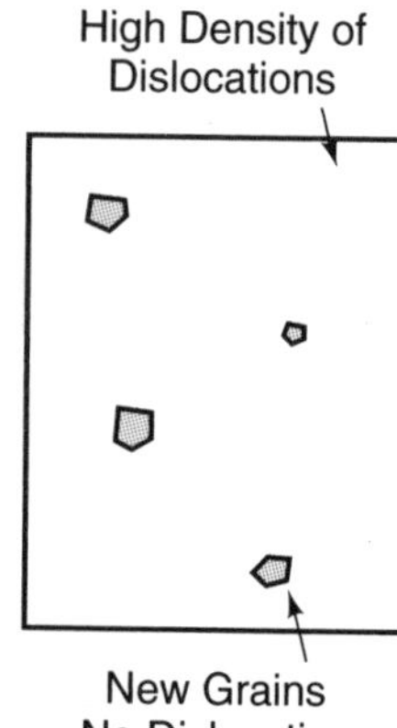

A dramatic change in a cold-worked material occurs in the recrystallization stage of the annealing process. Here the microstructure is transformed from deformed (i.e., hard) grains with a high dislocation density to equi-axed grains with a very low dislocation density. The new grains are soft, because the strain-hardening has been eliminated. This transformation is an example of a class of transformations that occur by nucleation and growth.

In recrystallization, new grains are nucleated in regions of particularly high dislocation density, and these grains grow by consuming the surrounding deformed, high-energy grains. The growth process involves simply the transfer of atoms across the boundaries of the new grains from the high-energy to the low-energy side.

Thus, the driving force is the difference in energy per atom between the old grain with many dislocations and the new grain with almost none. That is, the driving force is the stored energy of cold work. The recrystallization process can be observed by means of transmission electron microscopy, as illustrated by Fig. 5.4.

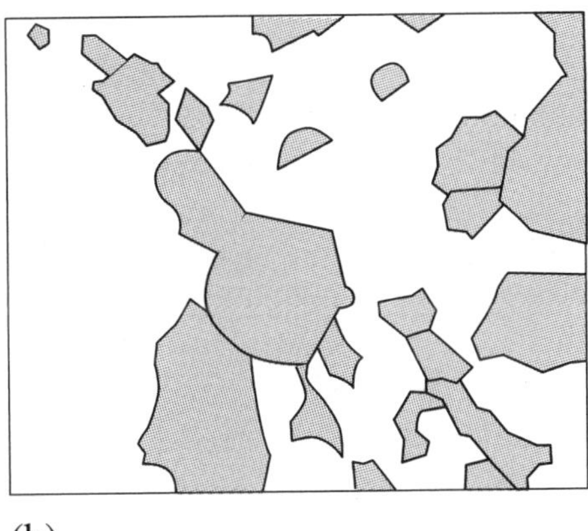

Fig. 5.4 (a) Recrystallized grains in cold-worked iron annealed 5 min at 500°C (From W. C. Leslie et al. in *Iron and Its Dilute Solid Solutions,* Interscience, NY, 1963, p. 164.) (b) Tracing of (a) showing new, dislocation-free grains and the surrounding matrix.

5.3.2 Kinetics of Recrystallization

Since the growth process requires atomic migration, the atoms near the boundary must acquire some kinetic energy. This is where the activation energy Δh_{ACT} comes in. (Lower-case h is used here to refer to energy per atom, whereas upper-case H will refer to energy per mole of atoms, meaning Avogadro's number of atoms.) The bonds holding an atom in the deformed grain must be broken before the atom can jump across the gap to the new, low-energy grain. The rate of such a process is equal to the number of attempts per second to cross the energy barrier times the probability that any given attempt will be successful. The number of attempts per second can be taken to be equal to the frequency of atomic vibration, ν, in the direction of the jump. The probability of success is essentially equal to the probability that the atom has the necessary kinetic energy, Δh_{ACT}.

The most probable distribution of energy among a collection of N particles, where N is large, can be calculated by the methods of statistical mechanics. A useful result is the Maxwell-Boltzmann distribution, depicted in Fig. 5.5, showing the probability that a particle has a given energy.

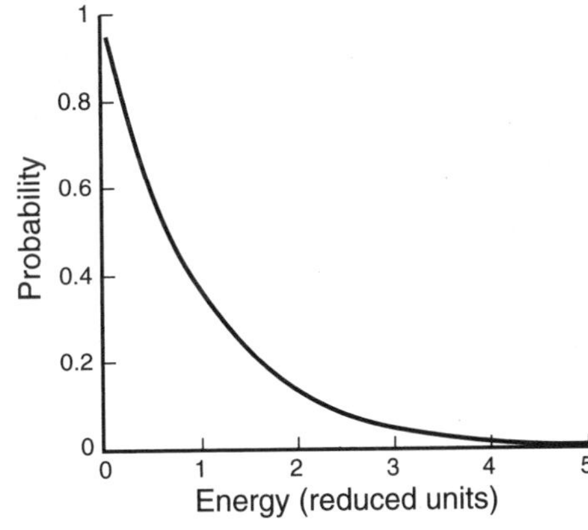

Fig. 5.5 The Maxwell-Boltzmann distribution of energy.

The important feature of this distribution is that the probability that a particle has a given energy decreases exponentially as the value of this energy increases. One is interested only in atoms with a kinetic energy toward the high end of the distribution, because Δh_{ACT} is not small. The kinetic energy of any particle depends on temperature. For example, the kinetic theory of gases shows that the average gas particle has a kinetic energy of 1/2 kT for each of the three orthogonal directions of motion of the particle, where k is Boltzmann's constant. In a collection of particles in which the energy is distributed according to the Maxwell-Boltzmann function, it can be shown that, at a temperature T (in degrees Kelvin), the probability that a particle has an energy Δh (e.g., the increase in energy per atom needed for a process) is given by

$$\text{Probability} = \exp - \left(\frac{\Delta h}{kT}\right)$$

Thus, the rate at which atoms cross the barrier to the new grain is given by:

$$\text{Rate} = \nu \exp - \left(\frac{\Delta h}{kT}\right)$$

which is the same as:

$$\text{Rate} = \nu \exp - \left(\frac{\Delta H}{RT}\right)$$

for one mole of jumping atoms, R being the gas constant = $N_o k$, where N_o is Avogadro's number. A process that follows this rate equation, known as the *Arrhenius equation,* is termed a thermally-activated process.

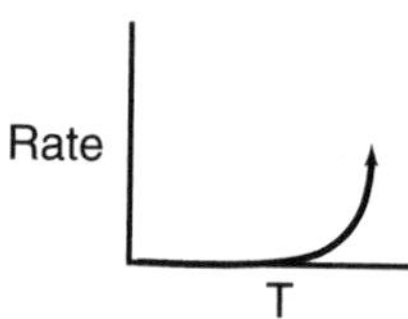

The exponential dependence on temperature results in a steeply rising rate of jumping of atoms from old to new grains over a small temperature range. This is reflected in Fig. 5.3(b), which indicates that recrystallization occurs within a fairly well-defined range of temperature.

Recrystallization is a substitution reaction. It occurs by nucleation and growth, following a classical pattern when the fraction transformed is plotted against time. This is shown schematically in Fig. 5.6, along with an example of interrupted recrystallization in cold-worked iron.

Recrystallization occurs sooner as the annealing temperature is raised in the temperature range of this process (because the rate varies exponentially with temperature). The physical explanation of the classical S-shaped curve is the following: The transformation occurs at the boundaries of the growing clusters of new grains (cf. Fig. 5.6b), which are scattered about the volume of the cold-worked material. As the clusters grow larger, so does the total area along their outer boundaries. Because the reaction occurs by atoms jumping across boundaries, the increase in boundary area causes the transformation to go faster. Also, additional new grains are nucleated as time passes. However, as time passes the clusters of new grains begin to impinge upon one another. Wherever this happens, the transformation must cease in the regions where overlap would otherwise occur. From this time on, the volume transformed per unit time must decrease. The fraction transformed goes asymptotically to unity as the last bit transforms.

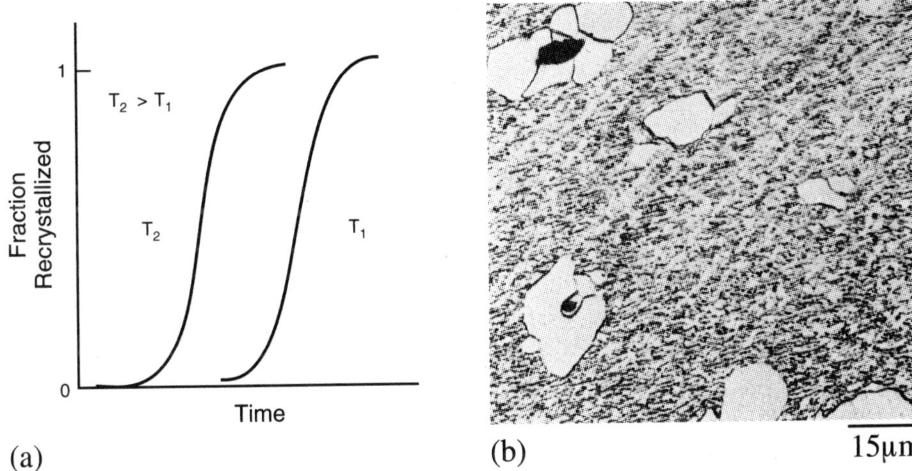

Fig. 5.6 (a) Kinetics of recrystallization, a substitution reaction that occurs more rapidly as temperature is increased. (b) Early stage of recrystallization in cold-worked iron, initiated at oxide inclusions; optical photomicrograph. (From W. C. Leslie et al. in *Iron and Its Dilute Solid Solutions,* Interscience, NY, 1963, p. 169.)

It should be pointed out that the apparent "recrystallization temperature" depends on the following factors:

1. The annealing time. The longer the time, the lower the temperature at which dramatic softening occurs (within a limited temperature range).
2. The amount of prior cold work. The more driving force available, the lower the recrystallization temperature. (Again, within limits.) 

3. The purity of the material. The growth stage occurs more easily in a pure, single-phase material. For example, high-purity aluminum can recrystallize at room temperature, whereas commercial-purity aluminum must be heated above 200°C.

Example 5.1

Q. In Fig. 5.6(a), it is indicated that recrystallization occurs in a shorter time if the annealing temperature is raised. Give a physical explanation for this.

A. The rate-controlling step in recrystallization is the transfer of atoms across the interface between the cold-worked matrix and the new, dislocation-free growing grain. Thus, the rate of growth of the new grains increases exponentially with temperature according to: 

$$\text{rate} = \text{constant x exp} -(\Delta H_{act}/RT)$$

where ΔH_{act} is the activation energy (cf. Fig. 5.1 and Appendix 5.2) needed to transfer one mole of atoms across the interface, and T is the absolute temperature (degrees Kelvin). R = 8.31J/mole-K.

Example 5.2

Q. Suppose that ΔH_{act} for the growth stage of recrystallization of a stainless-steel spoke were 170kJ/mole. Calculate the annealing temperature needed to double the rate of growth found at 1073K (=800°C). (This would approximately halve the time needed for recrystallization.)

A. The following relationship must be solved for T_2, given that T_1 = 1073K.

$$\frac{\text{Rate 2}}{\text{Rate 1}} = 2 = \frac{\exp-\left(\frac{170 \times 10^3}{8.31 \times T_2}\right)}{\exp-\left(\frac{170 \times 10^3}{8.31 \times T_1}\right)}$$

The constant in the rate equation cancels out. Rearranging,

$$2 \exp-\left(\frac{170 \times 10^3}{8.31 \times 1073}\right) = 1.05 \times 10^{-8} = \exp-\left(\frac{170 \times 10^3}{8.31 \times T_2}\right)$$

Taking the logarithm of both sides

$$-18.37 = -\frac{170 \times 10^3}{8.31 \times T_2}$$

giving

$$T_2 = 1113\text{K} = 840°\text{C}$$

Thus, the rate of recrystallization would double with an increase in annealing temperature from 800 to 840°C.

5.4 Recovery

It should not be supposed that nothing happens in advance of recrystallization in a cold-worked material. Prior to recrystallization, the cold-worked state undergoes a kind of relaxation process, called *recovery.* During recovery the excess concentration of point defects, mainly lattice vacancies, decays toward the equilibrium level. (The excess point defects are generated as a result of the intersection of dislocations gliding on different slip systems.) The equilibrium level of vacancies in a crystal at any temperature can be derived mathematically by means of elementary statistical mechanics, as shown in Appendix 5.2. Examples of lattice vacancies in a bubble raft are shown in Fig. 3.4.

The physical explanation of this derivation is the following: When a lattice vacancy is formed, the internal energy of the crystal is increased, because the atoms around the vacancy are displaced from their equilibrium lattice positions. That is, there is a stored elastic energy associated with a vacancy. This means that at zero Kelvin the free energy is minimized only if there are no vacancies. However, at a higher temperature, entropy must play a role. A perfect crystal can be envisioned as having lattice vacancies only on its outer surface. This is a highly ordered configuration of the vacancies. The entropy of the crystal would be increased if some of those vacancies were distributed randomly on lattice sites.

Therefore, to minimize G=H-TS at some temperature T, the vacancy concentration inside the crystal would rise until the increase in TS (decrease in -TS) begins to be offset by the increase in H. This is the equilibrium concentration, because it minimizes G.

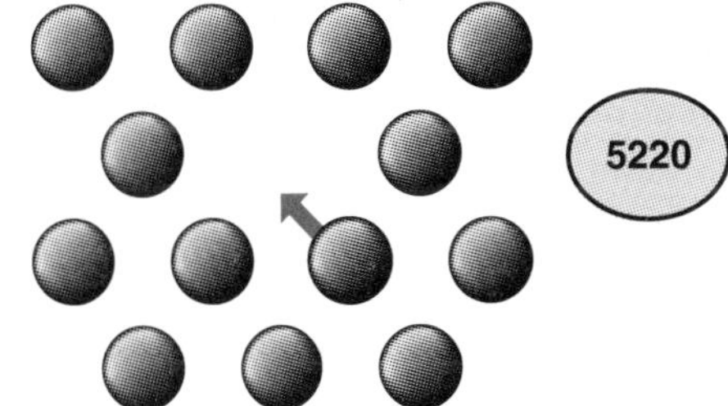

In actuality, the vacancy concentration can rise only if the temperature is high enough to provide thermal activation (in the form of kT) to permit atoms to change places with vacancies. This process is called *self-diffusion.* During self-diffusion, vacancies jump randomly about in a crystal, which is equivalent to saying that atoms jump randomly about through interchange with vacancies.

The result of the derivation in Appendix 5.2 is that the equilibrium vacancy concentration is

$$\text{vacancy concentration} = \exp - \left(\frac{\Delta H_f}{RT} \right)$$

where ΔH_f is the increase in the enthalpy (internal energy) of the crystal when one mole of vacancies is formed.

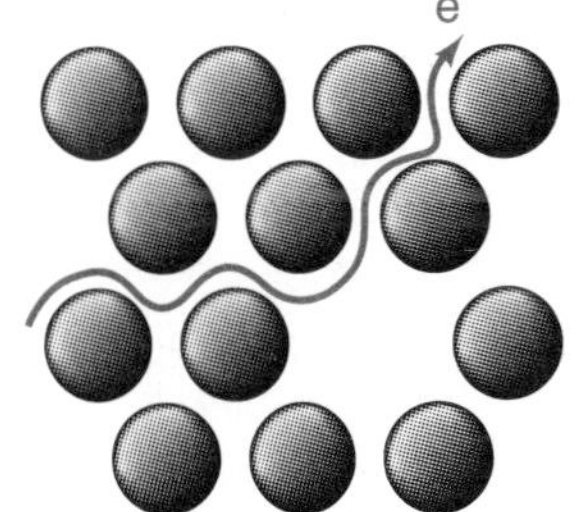

The recovery process may be studied in several ways. One utilizes the fact that vacancies contribute to electrical resistivity, because they interrupt the periodic variation of electron density in a metallic crystal lattice. Since they act as isolated scatterers, the increase in resistivity is essentially proportional to the vacancy concentration. Thus, one can follow the "annealing out" of vacancies by monitoring the drop in resistivity with time at a fixed temperature, as in Fig. 5.7.

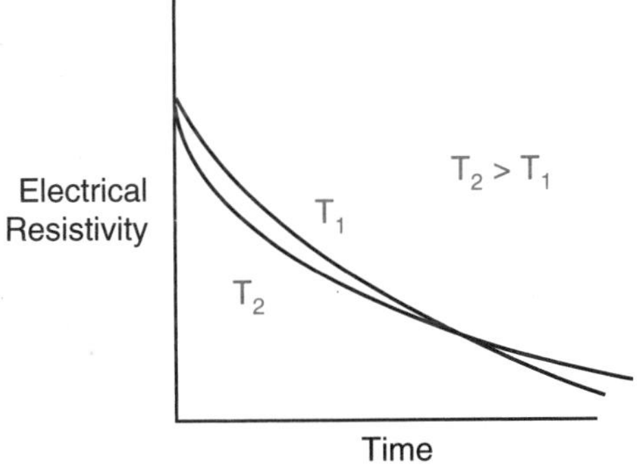

Fig. 5.7 Schematic representation of the kinetics of recovery. Note that both T_1 and T_2 are below the recrystallization temperature.

The question arises: Where do the vacancies go as they anneal out? Most go to dislocations with some edge component, because they can eliminate part of the extra material associated with an edge dislocation. This causes the dislocation to climb, a process illustrated in Fig. 5.8. One can think of the extra half-plane as being compressed along its sides by the surrounding crystal into which it is jammed (like a wedge into a piece of wood). When the dislocation climbs, the compressive stress σ_{xx} (cf. Appendix 4.2) does work, and it relaxes in the same way that the stress in a person's hand is relaxed when toothpaste squirts out of a tube. Thus, the driving force for recovery is, again, the stored energy of cold work.

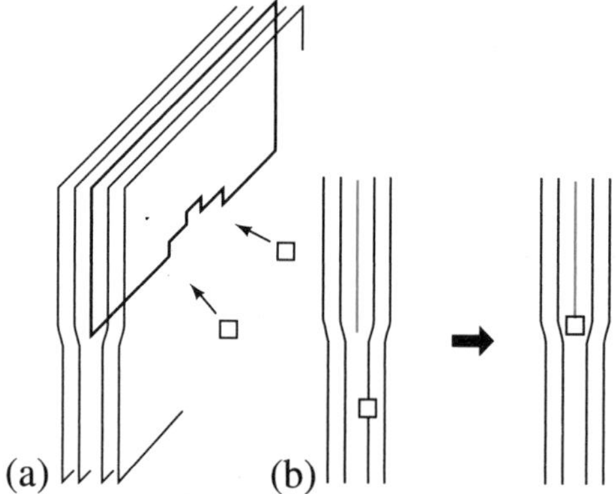

Fig. 5.8 Illustration of climb of an edge dislocation due to the absorption of vacancies, represented (a) in three dimensions and (b) in two dimensions.

The dislocation climb that occurs during recovery allows the tangled networks of dislocations resulting from cold work to rearrange into lower-energy configurations. An example is shown in Fig. 5.9. This rearrangement usually does not lower the dislocation density enough to produce a significant amount of softening, as reflected in the hardness plot of Fig. 5.3.

1.5μm (a) Iron, cold-rolled 16% at room temperature

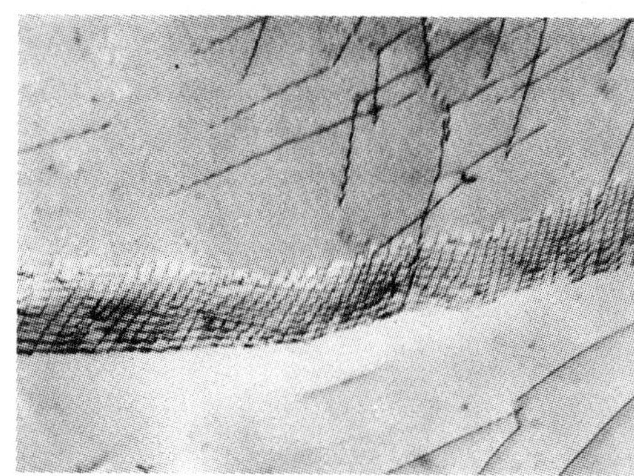

(b) Same, after 16h at 550°C 0.5μm

Fig. 5.9 Effect of recovery on dislocation cell structure in cold-rolled iron (A.S. Keh in *Direct Observation of Imperfections in Crystals,* J.B. Newkirk and J.H. Wernick, Eds., Interscience, NY, 1962, p. 213.)

Example 5.3

Q. In Fig. 5.7 it is indicated that recovery becomes more rapid if the temperature is raised. Why should this be so?

A. The annihilation of vacancies occurs by diffusion of vacancies to dislocations with some edge component. This diffusion occurs by successive interchanges between vacancies and atoms in the crystal lattice. In each interchange, a neighboring atom "jumps into" a vacant site. Since this requires thermal activation, the rate of jumping must increase exponentially with temperature.

Example 5.4

Q. In Fig. 5.7 the schematic curves for the two temperatures are drawn to cross at long annealing times. Explain why this should be expected.

A. The electrical resistivity is proportional to the vacancy concentration, and the equilibrium vacancy concentration increases exponentially with temperature (cf. Appendix 5.2). Therefore, the ultimate level of resistivity should be higher for the higher annealing temperature.

5.5 Grain Growth

5.5.1 Mechanism of Grain Growth

Just after the completion of recrystallization, a material usually has a fine grain size, especially if the amount of prior cold work was large (meaning that there were very many sites for nucleation of new grains). Since atoms in a grain boundary have higher energy than those in the crystal lattice, the total internal energy of a fine-grained material is larger than that of a coarse-grained material. This provides a driving force for grain growth.

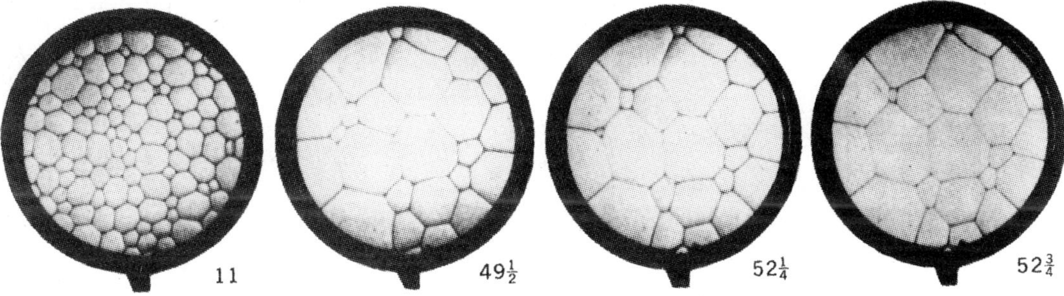

Fig. 5.10 Stages of bubble growth in a two-dimensional cell at the indicated times, in minutes. (C. S. Smith in *Metal Interfaces,* ASM, Metals Park, OH, 1952, p. 81.)

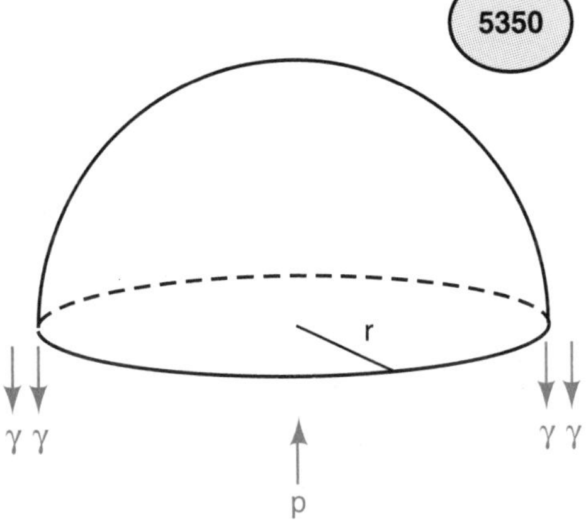

One can observe the analog of grain growth in a network of bubbles (e.g., of a soap solution), an example of which is shown in Fig. 5.10. The driving force here is the surface energy associated with the bubble walls. The mechanism of bubble growth depends on the fact that the pressure inside a small bubble is larger than that inside a large bubble, as demonstrated by the following argument.

Consider the equilibrium of forces on the upper half of a soap bubble. The force pulling the bubble down is due to the surface tension, γ, and is equal to $2\gamma 2\pi r$, since the bubble has 2 surfaces, and the length over which γ operates is $2\pi r$, the bubble circumference. The upward force due to the internal pressure, p, is $p\pi r^2$, since the pressure acts on the cross-sectional area.

At equilibrium

$$p\pi r^2 = 2\gamma 2\pi r$$

or

$$p = \frac{4\gamma}{r}$$

Because of the pressure gradient between a small bubble and a large one, air diffuses through the connecting wall, and the larger one grows at the expense of the smaller, as illustrated in Fig. 5.11(a).

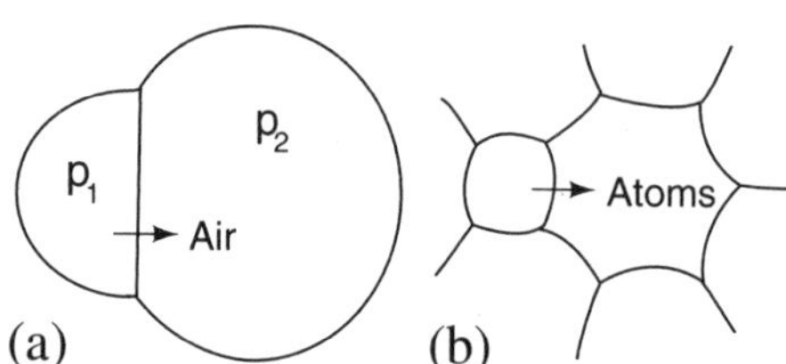

Fig. 5.11 (a) In a pair of soap bubbles the larger one grows at the expense of the smaller by diffusion of air through the connecting bubble wall, driven by the pressure difference. (b) In a polycrystal a large grain grows at the expense of its smaller neighbors by the jump of atoms from the smaller grains to the larger one.

In the case of a polycrystalline solid, the analog of the diffusion of air between bubbles is the transport of atoms across the boundaries from small grains to large grains, as indicated schematically in Fig. 5.11(b). Atoms along a grain boundary on the convex side have, on the average, fewer neighbors than
5360 those on the concave side, as indicated in Fig. 5.12(a). Thus, the average energy per atom of the former is slightly higher. (The minimum energy state is that in which an atom is completely surrounded by a crystal with atoms in their correct positions; in an FCC crystal each would have 12 neighbors.)

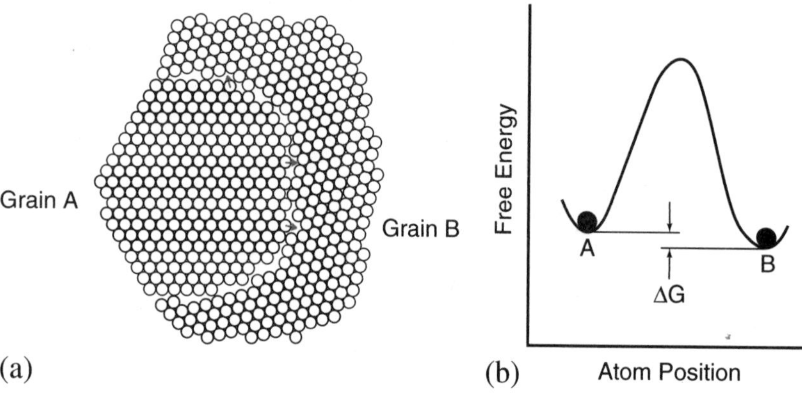

Fig. 5.12 Atoms at the boundary of the left-hand (convex) grain in (a) have, on average, fewer neighbors than those across the boundary on the concave side, causing an energy gradient across the boundary, as shown in (b).

At an elevated temperature the atoms along a grain boundary hop back and forth from one side to the other and tend to stick longer to the side on which they have more neighbors (i.e., lower energy). Hence, over time there is a net motion from the smaller grain to the larger. That is, the grain boundary tends to migrate towards its center of curvature, and the larger grain grows at the expense of the smaller. One can imagine the surface tension "squeezing" the high-energy atoms from the smaller to the larger grain, just as the high-pressure gas is squeezed from the smaller soap bubble into the larger.

The "grain boundaries" of a bubble network meet at dihedral angles of 120°. This is due to the necessity for equilibrium among surface tensions, which is given by

$$\gamma_{12} = \gamma_{23} \cos \theta/2 + \gamma_{13} \cos \theta/2$$

or, since in a soap froth,

$$\gamma_{12} = \gamma_{23} = \gamma_{13} = \gamma,$$

$$\gamma = 2\gamma \cos \theta/2$$

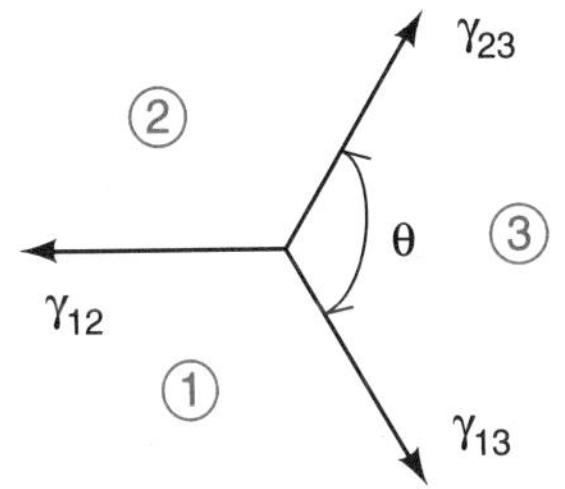

Thus,

$$\cos \theta/2 = 1/2, \therefore \theta = 120°$$

Thus, the walls of the bubbles in a soap froth must curve in such a way that all the dihedral angles equal 120°.

If the grain boundaries of a polycrystalline solid all had equal energy, as do the walls of a bubble network, they would also meet at 120° angles. In reality, the energies vary with the atomic structure of the boundary (cf. Fig. 3.4). However, for most boundaries in a polycrystalline aggregate of randomly oriented grains the variation is not large, and the bubble network can still be used as a model.

In a two-dimensional representation of a three-dimensional network, as shown in Fig. 5.13, the requirement that all triple points have 120° angles between the constituent boundaries, means that for grains with six sides, the boundaries are straight. For grains with three, four, or five sides, the sides are concave inward; i.e., the center of curvature lies toward the grain center. However, for grains with more than six sides, the sides are concave outward. Thus, according to Fig. 5.12, the larger grains should grow at the expense of the smaller grains, as long as there is enough thermal energy to activate the hopping of atoms across the boundary.

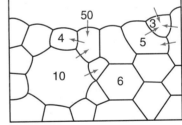

Fig. 5.13 Schematic representation of grain growth. Large grains (>6 sides) tend to grow, and small grains (< 6 sides) tend to shrink. (after J.E. Burke, from P.G. Shewmon, *Transformations in Metals,* McGraw-Hill, NY, 1969, p.120.)

5.5.2 Kinetics of Grain Growth

The kinetics of grain growth can be expressed by plotting the average grain diameter *vs.* time, as in Fig. 5.14.

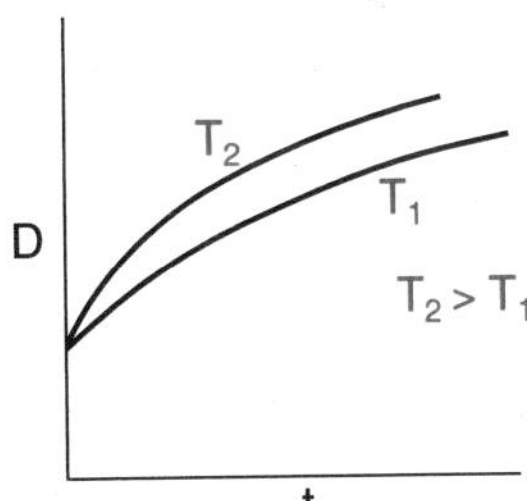

Fig. 5.14 Schematic illustration of the parabolic variation of average grain diameter D with time t during grain growth at different temperatures T_1 and T_2.

The shape of the curves can be explained by the following argument:

1. The driving force for growth is given by :

$$\frac{\gamma \text{ x grain-boundary area}}{\text{total grain volume}}$$

   where γ is the average grain-boundary energy per unit area.

2. If the average grain diameter is D, then the average grain-boundary area is proportional to D^2 and the average grain volume is proportional to D^3. Thus, the driving force is proportional to γ/D.

3. It is reasonable to set the rate of grain growth, dD/dt, proportional to the driving force (at a fixed temperature). Thus:

$$\frac{dD}{dt} = \frac{k\gamma}{D}$$

   where k is some constant depending on grain geometry, temperature (exponentially), and the material.

This equation, when integrated, yields a parabolic growth law:

$$D = k\gamma\, t^{1/2}$$

if the approximation is made that the grain size is very small (≈ 0) at time zero.

This analysis is idealized, because it ignores the effects of impurity atoms and particles of second phase, both of which cause grain growth to be slower than would be predicted otherwise. The impurity atoms are, in effect, unwanted elements in solid solution. The second-phase particles can be unwanted dirt, or they can be intentionally present, e.g., for purposes of inhibiting grain growth.

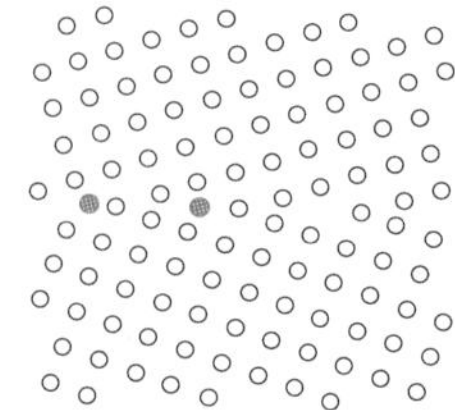

Solute elements tend to segregate (i.e., by diffusion) to grain boundaries at low temperatures, because the total internal energy of the polycrystal is thereby reduced. For example, an oversize solute often can fit into a grain boundary with less local distortion than within a grain, because the grain boundary can have an excess of free volume, because of looser atomic packing in the boundary (cf. Fig. 3.4). Alternatively, solutes that tend to develop directional bonds with the host atoms may be able to do that in a grain boundary, where the packing arrangement permits it. If the jumping rate of the segregated solute atom is slower than the host atoms, then grain boundary migration is retarded.

This drag on grain boundary mobility diminishes as temperature increases, because segregated solutes tend to leave the grain boundary and return to their random arrangements in solid solution at higher temperatures. The explanation for this is that solute segregation reduces the entropy of a polycrystal (i.e., makes it less randomly organized). This has an effect opposite to the reduction of internal energy that promoted the segregation in the first place. In other words, at low temperatures, H dominates and segregation occurs, but, as T increases, segregation diminishes, because -TS becomes more important. Thus, the minimization of G=H-TS requires that desegregation take place at elevated temperatures. This would have the effect of making the grain boundaries more mobile, and the parabolic growth kinetics would be more likely to be observed.

The effect of second-phase particles can be analyzed from the standpoint of interfacial energy. A particle has an interfacial area between itself and the matrix, whether it is within a grain or on a grain boundary. Since a grain boundary also has an energy per unit area associated with it, anything that reduces the total grain-boundary area must reduce the energy of the system. If a particle resides on a grain boundary, part of the area of the boundary is replaced by the cross-sectional area of the particle, as shown in Fig. 5.15.

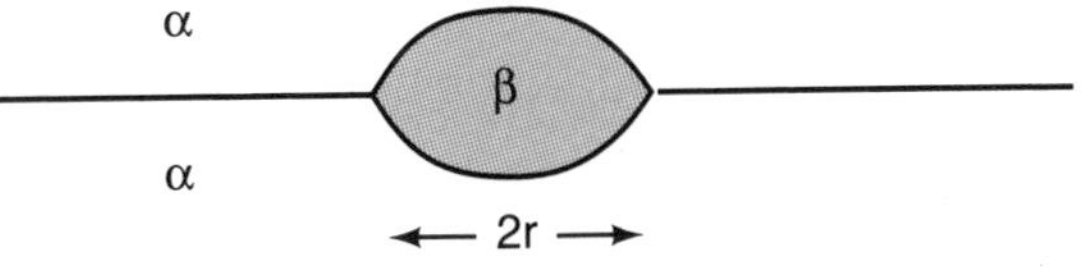

Fig. 5.15 A particle of the β phase on a grain boundary of the α phase reduces the total α grain boundary area.

Thus, the total interfacial energy is reduced by:

$$\gamma_{\alpha\alpha}\pi r^2$$

where $\gamma_{\alpha\alpha}$ is the average grain boundary energy of the matrix (α) phase. This amount of energy must be supplied to pull a grain boundary away from the particle.

The regions of grain boundary remote from the particle would tend to migrate in the normal way. The local pinning by the particle causes the boundary to become curved into a cusp, as shown in Fig. 5.16, thus causing the total grain boundary area to increase. When the depth of the cusp gets large enough, it becomes energetically favorable for the boundary to separate from the particle, 

and a local spurt of grain boundary migration then occurs.

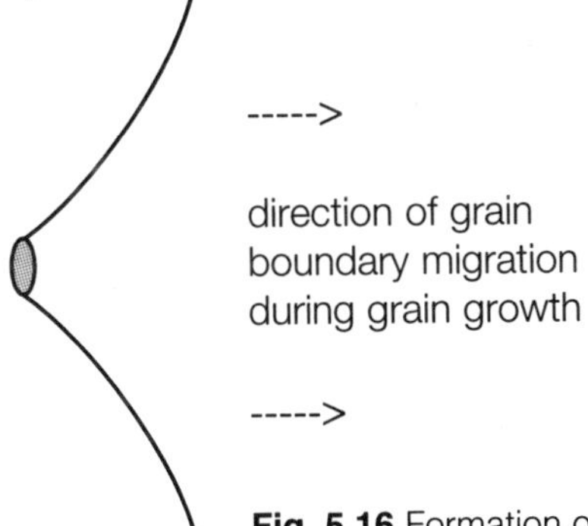

Fig. 5.16 Formation of a grain boundary cusp at a pinning particle.

Clearly, the more densely arrayed the particles are in the solid, the less bowing-out there will be between particles. (Note the analogy with dislocations.) Thus, an array of many fine particles will retard grain growth more effectively than fewer large ones.

The particle-pinning effect also tends to diminish as temperature is increased, owing to two effects. First, the solubility of a second phase tends to increase with temperature (the entropy effect again). As the volume fraction of particles is thereby reduced, there is less pinning. Second, the interfacial energy acts as a driving force to make particles coarsen. This occurs by the diffusion of the constituent solute element through the matrix from smaller particles to larger particles (cf. Section 5.6). With coarsening, the particle spacing increases, and again the pinning effect is reduced.

5.5.3 Softening During Grain Growth

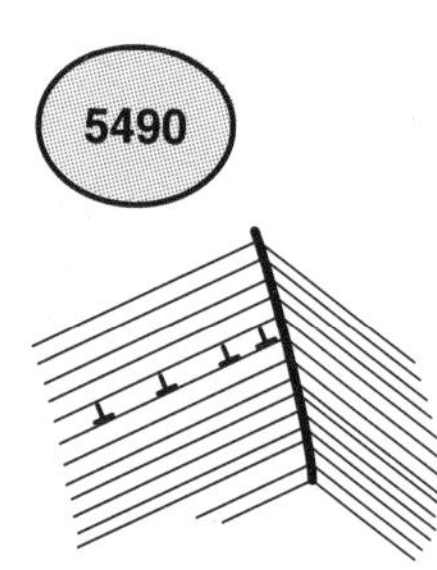

Grain growth produces gradual softening for two reasons. The more important reason is that irregularities on grain boundaries are prime sources of dislocations during deformation. Therefore, as the grain boundary area per unit volume decreases during grain growth, so does the density of dislocation sources per unit volume. Hence, the dislocation density at any stage in the deformation tends to be lower. (That is, the plastic strain is accomplished by fewer dislocations moving greater distances, on the average.) Thus, grain coarsening during annealing weakens the strain-hardening effect during subsequent deformation.

The other aspect of grain growth that produces softening is that grain boundaries act as barriers to slip bands because of the mismatch of slip systems from grain to grain. This effect tends to diminish in importance as plastic strain increases and the dislocation arrangements become more complicated, because slip bands are less well defined at large plastic strains.

Applying an understanding of annealing to bicycle spokes, one can appreciate that, since strain hardening is used to strengthen spokes, the wire drawing must be carried out well below the recrystallization temperature range. (Deformation in or above the temperature at which recrystallization occurs is called *hot working.*) Furthermore, one must not heat a spoke into the recrystallization range; otherwise, much of its strength would be lost, and premature failure could result.

Example 5.5

Q. How is grain growth different from the growth stage in recrystallization, since both involve growth of grains?

A. The driving force is different. In recrystallization, atoms hop from highly dislocated grains to undislocated grains. That is, they flow down a gradient of internal energy. In grain growth the atoms hop back and forth between undislocated grains. They simply tend to stick longer to the side with more nearest neighbors.

Example 5.6

Q. How does surface energy, γ, act to drive grain growth? What is the physical mechanism?

A. Surface energy (J/m^2) also has the units of surface tension (N/m), and the dihedral angles at three-grain junctions can be thought of as being governed by the equilibrium of surface-tension forces. This is what controls the curvature of a grain boundary, depending on the number of sides of the two neighboring grains. The sign of the curvature determines the direction of net drift of the hopping atoms.

5.6 Annealing of Carbon-Steel Spokes

The microstructure of a carbon-steel spoke comprises two phases: about 95% of the steel is almost-pure BCC iron (cf. Fig. 1.5), and the balance is iron carbide, Fe_3C, called *cementite,* which is a hard, brittle phase. Since the plastic deformation of carbon-steel spokes during wire drawing occurs almost entirely in the BCC-iron phase, known as *ferrite,* the presence of the cementite will be ignored for now. The ferrite is not quite pure iron; it contains carbon in addition to some other, less important, elements in solid solution. The carbon plays several important roles, as will be seen, but first the microstructure in the cold-drawn condition and after two kinds of annealing treatments will be examined.

5.6.1 The As-Received Condition

Photomicrographs of a longitudinal and a transverse section of a carbon-steel spoke in the as-received (i.e., cold-drawn) condition are shown in Fig. 5.17. The 5520
microstructure obviously consists of light-etching and dark-etching regions strung out in the direction of wire drawing, as seen in the longitudinal section. The distribution of light and dark constituents is non-directional when viewed in the transverse section, as might be expected from the cylindrical symmetry of the wire-drawing die (cf. Fig. 2.18).

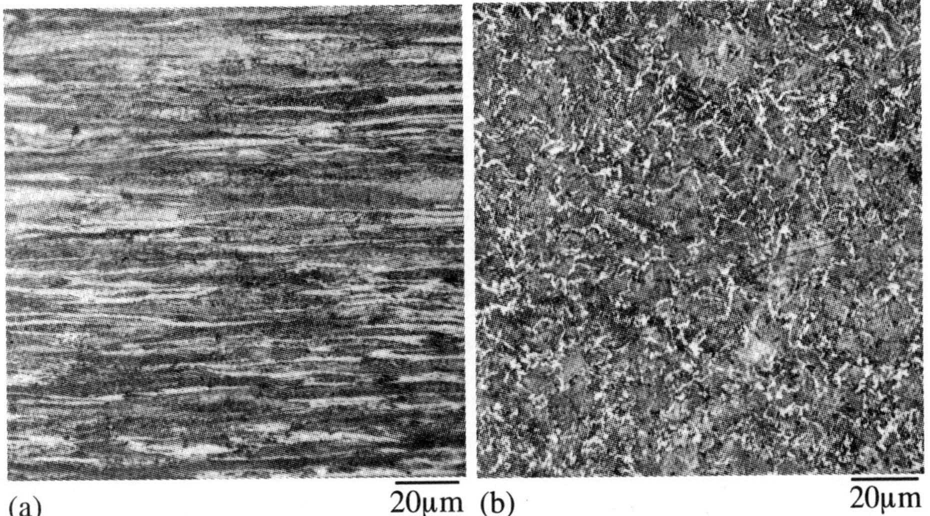

Fig. 5.17 Microstructure of an as-received carbon-steel spoke at 500X magnification. (a) longitudinal section; (b) transverse section. (Metallography by E. Anderson, Univ. of Penn.)

Recalling that the contrast in the optical microscope comes from surface roughness, as illustrated schematically in Fig. 5.18, one can interpret Fig. 5.17 as comprising one constituent that is essentially un-attacked by the etchant (i.e., is flat, reflects the incident light, and appears white) and another constituent that is heavily roughened by the etchant; therefore, it scatters the incident light and appears dark.

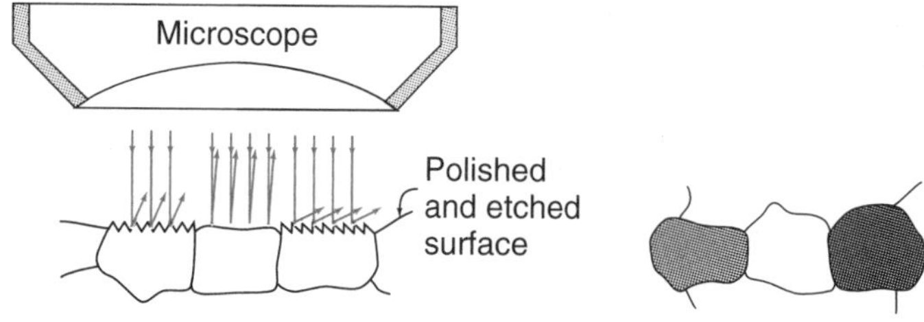

Fig. 5.18 Schematic representation of three regions in which etching produces different degrees of roughening. This gives variations from light to dark contrast in the image viewed in the microscope (From W.D. Callister, Jr., loc. cit., p. 60. Reprinted by permission of John Wiley & Sons, Inc.)

5.6.2 The Annealed Condition

The microstructure of the carbon steel spoke can be simplified by annealing. In order to recrystallize the steel, 700°C was chosen, since this temperature is greater than 0.5 T_{MP} in degrees Kelvin, and self-diffusion occurs rapidly above this temperature. Two annealing times were used: 3h and 24h. After the shorter annealing time, the microstructure, shown in Fig. 5.19(a) and (b), consisted of two phases. One is the fine-grained polycrystalline matrix comprising ferrite (BCC iron), and the other consists of particles of iron carbide, or cementite, Fe_3C, of less than 1µm diameter, which are strung out in the wire-drawing direction. It is apparent that the ferrite grain size in the transverse section of the recrystallized spoke, shown in Fig. 5.19(b), ranges from about 1 to 7µm, even though the annealing temperature is quite high. This is a good example of how a dispersed second phase can inhibit grain growth.

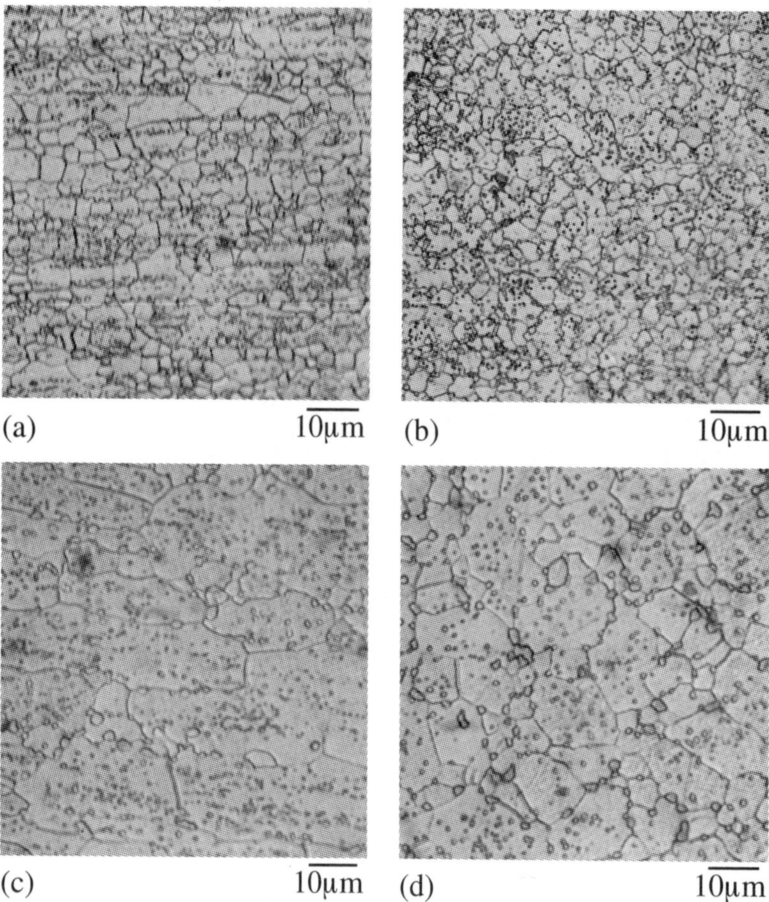

Fig. 5.19 Microstructure of a carbon steel spoke after annealing at 700°C for the indicated times, shown at 1000x magnification; (a) 3h, longitudinal section, (b) 3h, transverse section, (c) 24h, longitudinal section, (d) 24h, transverse section. (Metallography by E. Anderson, Univ. of Penn.)

The effect of prolonging the annealing time to 24h is shown in Fig. 5.19(c) and (d). Now the ferrite grain size in the transverse section ranges from about 5 to 25μm, and the cementite particles have coarsened substantially. Fig. 5.19(c) shows that the grain growth in the longitudinal direction during the extended anneal has been even larger.

Two distinct but interrelated phenomena are illustrated in Fig. 5.19. The first is that the cementite particles coarsen with time during annealing. That is, the average particle size increases. The number of carbides per unit volume decreases, and their spacing increases. (Of course, the total volume of carbide remains constant during coarsening.) The second phenomenon is grain growth in the ferrite phase. However, this growth is constrained to occur mainly in the longitudinal direction of the wire, owing to the presence of the longitudinal strings of cementite particles. As the spacing between the particles increases during coarsening, the constraint on grain growth in the ferrite is gradually reduced. Both phenomena are driven by interfacial energy: carbide coarsening by the ferrite/cementite interfacial energy, and ferrite grain growth by the energy of the ferrite/ferrite boundaries.

The evolution of the microstructures shown in Fig. 5.19 can be summarized as follows: During the anneal at 700°C, the cold-worked ferrite recrystallizes rapidly, but grain growth is inhibited by the fine distribution of cementite particles. This microstructure, however, contains a large amount of interfacial energy, which provides a driving force for the coarsening of the cementite and grain 5530
growth in the ferrite. The coarsening reaction proceeds by the diffusion of carbon atoms from small cementite particles to larger ones.

The reason for this flux of carbon is the curvature of the interface, as is the case with grain growth (cf. Fig. 5.12). The carbon atoms in solid solution in the ferrite next to a cementite particle can be thought of as analogous to atoms in the gaseous state above a solid. Then, the "partial pressure" of the carbon next to a small particle would be greater than that next to a larger one.

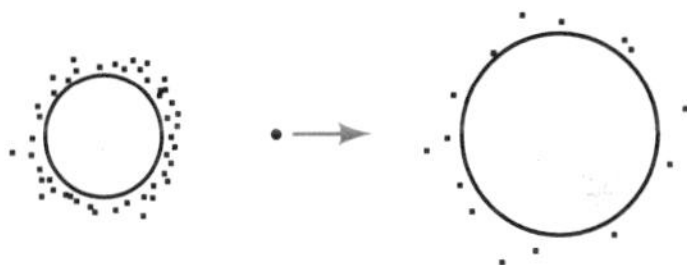

The reason for the greater carbon concentration around small particles is simply that the carbon at the surface of a smaller particle is less-completely surrounded by the cementite crystal structure and is, therefore, less-tightly bound. The difference in "partial pressure" translates to a difference in carbon concentration in the ferrite between small and large cementite particles, and this concentration gradient drives the diffusion of carbon from the smaller to the larger particles.

As the cementite particles coarsen they become fewer in number and, therefore, more widely spaced; the ferrite grain boundaries then have fewer barriers to pin them, and grain growth becomes increasingly less inhibited. This is especially true in the longitudinal direction, but the strings of carbide particles continue to inhibit grain growth in the lateral direction. Thus, the "memory" of the prior deformation processing persists in the annealed microstructure.

5.6.3 The "Fully-Annealed" Condition

When a carbon-steel spoke is heated to 950°C and slowly cooled (e.g., by switching off the furnace), the result, shown in Fig. 5.20, is completely unlike that found in Fig. 5.19. In the steel industry, this condition is called the "fully-annealed" condition, but in truth it should be called the "fully transformed" condition. Not only is there no memory of the elongated cold-drawn condition, but the steel is now divided into roughly equal volumes of light and dark constituents. The former is ferrite, and the latter is called *pearlite* and consists of alternate layers of ferrite and cementite. The layers are so finely spaced that most of the etched pearlite is dark. This is close to the condition that existed prior to the final cold-drawing operation, which produced the microstructure shown in Fig. 5.17. That is, during the cold drawing, the ferrite and pearlite constituents were deformed into cigar-shaped regions mixed on a fine scale. The explanation for the radical change in microstructure shown in Fig. 5.20 will be given in Chapter 8.

Fig. 5.20 Microstructure of a carbon steel spoke that has been "austenitized" at 950°C and furnace cooled. The light regions are ferrite, and the dark are pearlite, comprising lamellar ferrite and cementite. (Metallography by E. Anderson, Univ. of Penn.)

Summary

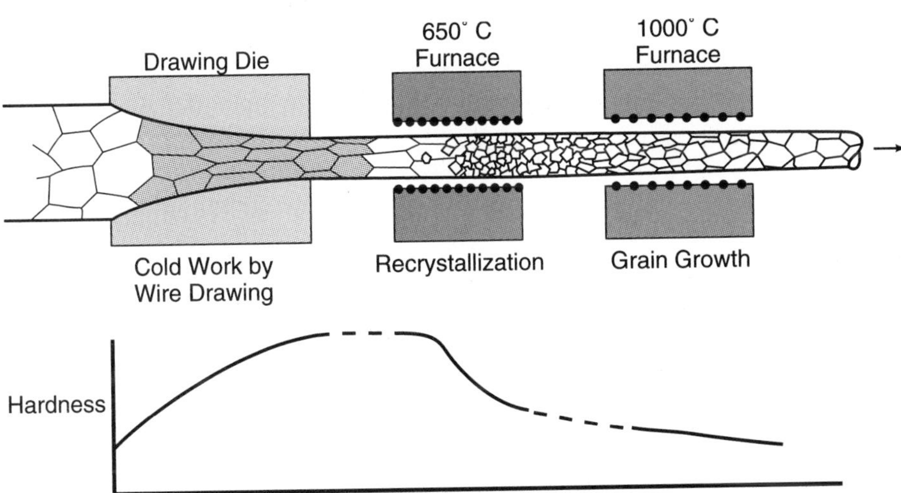

At certain stages of processing rod into wire for spokes it is necessary to soften the metal by annealing, because the wire can become so strain-hardened that there is danger of breakage during wire drawing. Most of the softening occurs in a rather narrow temperature range by the process of recrystallization, in which new dislocation-free grains nucleate and grow into the cold-worked matrix. This is a substitution reaction, and it follows the classical S-curve behavior (fraction transformed plotted *vs.* time for a fixed annealing temperature).

At temperatures below the recrystallization range, the cold-worked metal undergoes the process of recovery in which excess lattice vacancies anneal out, mainly by annihilation at dislocations, leading to dislocation climb and rearrangement. This process can be monitored by measurements of electrical resistivity (because vacancies scatter conduction electrons in a crystal lattice). It exhibits the isothermal kinetics of a decay reaction that occurs homogeneously throughout the solid, in contrast to the heterogeneous nature of recrystallization. The driving force for both recovery and recrystallization is the stored energy of cold work, which is essentially equal to the total length of dislocations times Gb^2.

At high annealing temperatures, after recrystallization is completed, the process of grain growth can occur. This is driven by the total interfacial energy associated with grain boundaries, and in the ideal case the grain size would increase with the square root of time at a constant annealing temperature. Of course, the rate would increase exponentially with temperature. The rate of grain growth can be decreased by the segregation of solute atoms to grain boundaries and by the presence of second-phase particles in grain boundaries. Both effects tend to diminish as the annealing temperature is raised. Concepts introduced in this chapter include self diffusion and the equilibrium concentration of lattice vacancies as a function of temperature. The connection between grain-boundary energy and the growth of large grains at the expense of small ones is also explained.

In a carbon-steel spoke, the presence of a second phase, cementite (Fe_3C), inhibits grain growth in the ferrite matrix after the latter recrystallizes. Extended annealing, however, produces coarsening of the cementite, and grain growth in the ferrite can then proceed. The starting condition before wire drawing was one that involved austenitization (cf. Chap. 8) and transformation during cooling to ferrite and pearlite, the latter being a mixture of ferrite and cementite. In steel-industry terminology this is called "full-annealing" if the cooling is slow and "normalizing" if air-cooling is used.

Appendix 5.1 - Measurement of Hardness

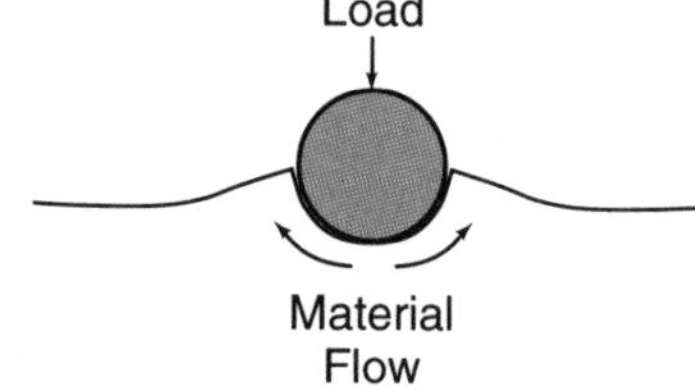

The term *hardness* is generally used to connote resistance to plastic deformation. (It is sometimes also used in the context of elastic behavior, as the opposite to elastically soft, or springy.) There exist a number of simple, common hardness tests, all of which characterize the resistance of a material to penetration by an indenter of a particular size and geometry under a known load.

As one can visualize, this is a rather complicated mode of plastic deformation, so the result of such a test cannot be interpreted in the same way as a uniaxial tensile test. Rather, it measures the combined effects of yielding and strain hardening in a multiaxial stress state. Thus, hardness data are used for purposes of comparison, rather than to probe a fundamental material property. The features of the various common hardness tests are summarized in Table A5.1.1.

Table A5.1.1 Features of Common Hardness Tests

Test Name	Indenter	Load(s)	Parameter Measured	Units of Hardness	Comments
Brinell	10 mm sphere	500, 1000 or 3,000 kg	Diameter of indentation; then calculate projected area*	kg/mm^2	Large indentation; a large volume of material is sampled.
Vickers, or Diamond Pyramid	Symmetrical diamond pyramid	1 g to 120 kg	Two axes of diamond-shaped indentation; then calculate projected area*	kg/mm^2	One of the most precise methods; can be used with very low loads to give microhardness.
Knoop	Elongated diamond pyramid	1 g to 120 kg	The major axis of the elongated indentation; then calculate projected area*	kg/mm^2	Measurement precision higher than Vickers, but subject to effects of anisotropy of material.
Rockwell	diamond cone or 1/16 in. sphere	60 to 150 kg	Machine measures depth of penetration and gives output on a dial	none	Quick and easy, but less precise.

*The calculations are tabulated and are available in handbooks; one can, therefore, read out the hardness number, given the measured diameter (for a given load).

Mineralogists use the Mohs scale, which ranks minerals in a relative way such that any mineral scratches the one below and is scratched by the one above. Diamond is at the top, and talc is at the bottom; silica glass ranks below hardened steel, but above gold, for example. This is still a measure of resistance to plastic deformation, but on a more extreme level, since a scratch is formed by a kind of plowing action in which a material is deformed to the point of failure in shear.

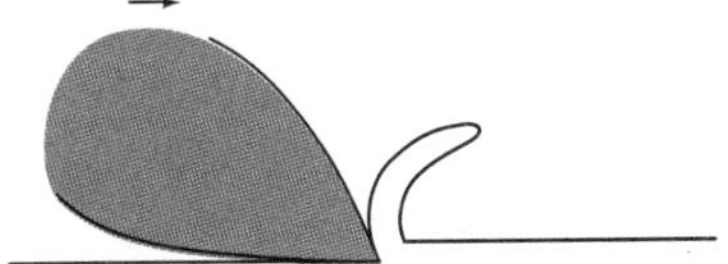

Fig. A5.1.1 Schematic illustration of deformation involved in a scratch-hardness test. It is akin to machining on a lathe.

Appendix 5.2 - The Equilibrium Concentration of Lattice Vacancies

Consider a crystal containing N atoms and n vacancies. An expression for the free energy associated with vacancies can be written as follows

$$G = H - TS = nh - TS$$

where h is the enthalpy (≈ local crystal-distortion energy) associated with each vacancy. (The perfect crystal is the zero-energy reference state.) It is desired to calculate the value of n for which G is a minimum; i.e., for which

$$\frac{dG}{dn} = 0$$

To do this, Boltzmann's statistical definition of entropy is employed,

$$S = k \ln W$$

where W is the number of "microstates per macrostate," or the number of distinguishable ways of arranging the N atoms and n vacancies on the N + n lattice sites. If the sites are filled one by one, starting with an empty lattice, there are N + n choices for the first move, N + n - 1 for the second, N + n - 2 for the third, and so on. For the first two, there are (N + n)(N + n - 1) combinations of arrangements. The total number of combinations for all arrangements is, then, (N + n)! However, since all atoms are indistinguishable, as are all vacancies, the number of distinguishable combinations is much less and can be written as:

$$W = \frac{(N + n)!}{n!\, N!}$$

because any of the n vacancies or N atoms can be interchanged with another vacancy or atom, respectively, without creating a new atom-vacancy arrangement. Therefore, the total number of combinations must be reduced by dividing by n! to account for the number of ways of arranging n vacancies on a given set of n lattice sites, and similarly for the N atoms on a given set of N lattice sites.

Stirling's approximation: $\ln x! \approx x\ln(x) - x$ can be used to write:

$$\ln W \approx (N + n)\ln(N + n) - (N + n) - n \ln(n) + n - N \ln(N) + N$$

Hence, the entropy associated with the presence of vacancies is

$$S = k\,[(N + n)\ln(N + n) - n\ln(n) - N\ln(N)]$$

Therefore,

$$G = nh - kT\,[(N+n)\ln(N + n) - n\ln(n) - N\ln(N)]$$

and for equilibrium G must be a minimum; therefore,

$$dG/dn = 0 = h - kT\,[\ln(N + n) + 1 - \ln(n) - 1]$$

or

$$h = kT\ln[(N+n)/n]$$

and, transposing, the vacancy concentration at equilibrium at temperature T is

$$\frac{n}{N+n} = \exp -\left(\frac{h}{kT}\right)$$

On a per-mole basis, one uses $R = kN_0$, where R is the gas constant and N_0 is Avogadro's number, and $H = N_0h$ is used to express the enthalpy of formation of one mole of vacancies. Since $n << N$, one can write

$$\frac{n}{N} \approx \exp -\left(\frac{H}{RT}\right)$$

As an example, $H \cong 23$ kcal/mole for copper, and the gas constant R has a value of approximately 2 cal/mol-K. At 1000K (727°C), therefore,

$$\frac{n}{N} \approx 10^{-5}$$

That is, one lattice site in 100,000 in copper is vacant at equilibrium at 1000K. (Copper melts at 1083°C.)

Glossary/Vocabulary - Chapter 5

Activation energy — The energy that must be supplied to a system in metastable equilibrium to allow it to pass to a state of lower energy is called the activation energy. The rate of a reaction at a given temperature varies exponentially with the inverse of the activation energy, in accordance with an Arrhenius equation.

Annealing — Annealing of metals means heating a cold-worked metal so as to remove the effects of strain hardening. It comprises the processes of recovery, recrystallization, and grain growth. When a steel rod is made into spokes by wire drawing, periodic annealing is required; otherwise, strain hardening would make the wire too hard to draw through the die.

Coarsening — Particles of a second phase tend to coarsen, that is, to become larger and fewer, by means of diffusion of solute from smaller to larger particles. This is driven by interfacial energy, the total of which is reduced by this process. If the second phase is a strengthening precipitate, the coarsening process leads to softening, because, as the particle spacing increases, they are less-effective barriers to dislocation motion.

Cold work	This means plastic deformation, as during deformation processing, like wire drawing, at a temperature below which any annealing would occur. Bicycle spokes are wire drawn at ambient temperatures; thus, they are cold worked.
Diamond-pyramid hardness, DPH	This is a hardness measured with a diamond-pyramid indenter. It is also known as the Vickers hardness. It is considered a highly precise test, and it can be used at loads ranging from 1g to 120kg. At the lower range, it is used in conjunction with a microscope for microhardness testing.
Driving force	A system tends to pass from a state of higher to one of lower Gibbs free energy as it progresses toward equilibrium. The gradient in energy provides the driving force for the reaction. The driving force for heat flow in a body with non-uniform temperature is the gradient in thermal energy within the body.
Effect of grain size on strength	The yield stress of a polycrystalline aggregate generally varies as $D^{-1/2}$ where D is the average grain diameter. This can be derived by assuming that grain boundaries are the sources of dislocations and that there is some average number of dislocation sources per unit grain-boundary area, and then proceeding with a strain-hardening-type of argument, knowing that the grain-boundary area per unit volume is proportional to 1/D.
Energy of formation	The energy of formation of a crystal defect is the increase in the total energy of the crystal that results from the formation of the defect. The energy of formation of a vacancy is the elastic strain energy associated with the local distortion of the crystal lattice as the atoms surrounding the vacancy adjust their positions to take account of the absence of a neighbor.
Energy of motion	This is the activation energy needed for the motion of a crystal defect. The energy of motion of a vacancy is the kinetic energy that must be imparted through thermal activation to some of the atoms surrounding a vacancy to allow the interchange of an atom with the vacancy.
Enthalpy	This is the thermodynamic variable obtained by adding the product of pressure and volume to the internal energy. That is, it is the internal energy plus any energy added to a system by expansion or contraction associated with external pressure, so-called "pV work." Thus, $H = E + pV$. In condensed systems at one atmosphere pressure, p is small, and volume changes are small, so H is essentially the same as E.
Entropy	Entropy is a thermodynamic variable that characterizes the state of disorder of a system. In statistical mechanics, it is defined as $k\ln W$, where W is the number of microstates per macrostate, and k is Boltzmann's constant. Except for the influence of internal energy, a system at equilibrium tends to a maximum in entropy at any temperature above zero Kelvin. That is because disorder becomes increasingly more probable than order as temperature increases.
Equilibrium	The equilibrium state of a system is that which persists interminably, without change. The system tends to return to that state after any attempt to perturb it. At equilibrium, the Gibbs free energy has a minimum value. A rocking chair comes to its equilibrium position when its center of mass is at a minimum distance from the floor.

Equilibrium in a cellular network The angles between the cell walls in a cellular network, like a soap froth, an assembly of fat cells, or the grains in a polycrystal, are governed by the equilibrium of the surface-tension forces set up by the interfaces that meet at a triple junction. If all the surface tensions are equal, the equilibrium dihedral angle is 120°. Whether the cell walls are convex or concave depends on the number of faces the cell has in three dimensions. In two dimensions, a cell with fewer than six sides will have concave sides, and one with more than six sides will have convex sides.

Gibbs free energy The minimization of Gibbs free energy is the general criterion for the attainment of equilibrium in a system. That is, any spontaneous process in nature occurs with a decrease in Gibbs free energy. It is denoted by G and is equal to enthalpy, H, minus entropy times the temperature in Kelvin: $G = H - TS$. At zero Kelvin, the minimization of G and H are synonymous.

Grain-boundary pinning The migration of grain boundaries can be inhibited by particles, because the energy of the system is reduced if the particle lies in the boundary. The reason for this is that there is less grain-boundary area in this case, because a portion of the boundary equal to the area subtended by the particle is missing. In order to move the boundary away from the particle, the amount of energy γA must be added to the system, where A is the subtended area and γ is the grain-boundary energy per unit area.

Grain growth In a fully recrystallized material, continued heating allows the process of grain growth, in which large grains grow at the expense of their smaller neighbors. This occurs as a result of the migration of grain boundaries in the direction of their centers of curvature, as atoms hop back and forth across the boundaries and tend to stick to the side with more neighbors per atom. The curvature of a grain boundary is determined by the number of sides, or facets, of a grain and by the fact that, on average, grain boundaries meet at dihedral angles of 120 degrees.

Hardness test Hardness means the resistance of a material to plastic deformation. It may be measured by making an indentation, using an indenter of particular geometry under a known load, and measuring the area or a linear dimension of the indentation, or the depth of indentation. The most common test for metals is the Rockwell test, which employs a machine that gives the Rockwell hardness number on an arbitrary scale (C, B, A, etc.) according to the depth of the indentation caused by a given load applied by one of several kinds of indenter.

Hot working Plastic deformation at a temperature at which recrystallization occurs immediately is called hot working. Large-scale deformation processing, as in a steel mill, is often carried out by hot working; for example, hot rolling or hot forging.

Internal energy This is the potential energy stored in a system by virtue of the interactions of the particles that comprise it. In a crystal at zero Kelvin, the internal energy is minimized when the effects of the attractive and repulsive interactions among the constituent particles just balance.

Kinetics Kinetics has to do with the rate, or time dependence of a reaction. This is in contrast to the relevant thermodynamics, which gives the direction of a reaction, but not its rate. Recrystallization exhibits S-curve kinetics, whereas recovery exhibits decay-type kinetics.

Maxwell-Boltzmann distribution	This is the distribution of kinetic energies in a collection of particles at equilibrium. It is a relation derived from statistical mechanics. In any reaction involving thermal activation, only the particles near the top of the distribution can participate. The number of particles with kinetic energy h is proportional to exp-(h/kT), so this means the number of particles with high energy at any temperature T decreases exponentially as h is increased. Conversely, the number with energy h increases exponentially with T.
Nucleation and growth	Many transformations are heterogeneous in that they occur by the nucleation of a new phase, or new condition, and the growth of the new at the expense of the surrounding old. Usually the rate is controlled by some kind of diffusion. Recrystallization, austenitic decomposition to ferrite or pearlite, and precipitation from solid solution are all nucleation-and-growth reactions.
Point defect	In a crystal lattice, a lattice vacancy, an interstitialcy, (i.e., an atom normally on a lattice site forced into an interstice), or a foreign atom (solute atom) are all defects of zero dimension, therefore point defects. The most important point defect is the vacancy, because it provides the mechanism for self diffusion or substitutional diffusion.
Recovery	Recovery is the first stage of the annealing process in a cold-worked metal. It involves the migration to sinks of point defects, mainly vacancies. The sinks where the vacancies are annihilated are mainly edge dislocations or those having an edge component (i.e., excess atoms). This annihilation causes the dislocations to climb, which then leads to glide and mutual annihilation of some of the dislocations. Out of this process, orderly arrays of dislocations are formed out of disorderly tangles. The progress of recovery can be followed by the decrease in electrical resistivity, since the resistivity varies more-or-less linearly with the vacancy concentration.
Recrystallization	If a cold-worked metal is heated to a high-enough temperature, new, dislocation-free grains nucleate in the regions of high dislocation density (i.e., large stored energy), and these grains grow at the expense of the surrounding dislocation-containing grains until the whole body is converted to grains with low dislocation density. This is called recrystallization. This is a substitution transformation, and it follows a classical S-shaped curve in a plot of fraction transformed vs. time.
S- curve	For a substitution transformation, a plot of fraction transformed vs. time has an S shape. The transformation takes place at the boundary between the new and the old regions, so it accelerates as the amount of this boundary increases. Later, it slows down as the transformed regions impinge on one another. Two well-known transformations that follow S-curve kinetics are recrystallization of a cold-worked metal and the eutectoid decomposition of austenite to pearlite.

Segregation of solute atoms	If solute atoms are able to migrate, i.e., if the lattice vacancies are mobile enough, then they can lower their energy (enthalpy) if they segregate to locations at which they can be accommodated with less strain of the lattice. This tendency is opposed by the fact that segregation lowers the entropy of the system, because it decreases the randomness. Therefore, the amount of segregation diminishes as the temperature is increased, because the term -TS is thereby decreased, and entropy becomes more important in lowering Gibbs free energy (G=H-TS). Solute atoms, which are usually either too large or too small for lattice sites, tend to segregate to grain boundaries and to dislocations.
Stored energy of cold work	The energy associated with dislocations, both the self energy per unit length of all the dislocations and the energy arising from the interactions between dislocations, comprises most of the stored energy of cold work. (The rest is the energy of point defects.) Of all the energy put into a metal during plastic deformation, only about 10% or so is stored in the material. The rest is converted into heat.
Substitution transformation	When one condition of a system is converted to another by the nucleation of the new condition at various locations and the growth of the new regions at the expense of the surrounding old regions, the system is said to undergo a substitution transformation, also called a nucleation-and-growth transformation. When the fraction transformed is plotted against time, the result is an S-shaped curve.
Thermal activation	A system in a metastable equilibrium can be activated toward a more-stable state by means of thermal excitation of the particles that comprise the system. That is, heat input supplies kinetic energy to the particles, allowing the system to relax to a state of lower energy. In self diffusion, thermal energy must be supplied to the atoms surrounding a vacancy to allow the atom-vacancy interchange to occur.
Thermodynamics	This is the branch of physical science that deals with the flow of energy. It sets the rules for the state of equilibrium at which all energy flows come to an end and the system in question persists in a changeless condition. An isolated body with an uneven distribution of temperature would eventually come to equilibrium by the flow of heat from the hot end toward the cold end.
Vacancy	A vacancy, or lattice vacancy, is a point defect in a crystal lattice that comprises simply a vacant lattice site, or a missing atom. If the temperature is high enough, a neighboring atom can exchange places with a vacancy. By this process, a vacancy tends to migrate in a random way about the lattice; this process is known as self diffusion.
Vacancy concentration at equilibrium	The fraction of lattice sites in a crystal that are vacant, i.e., from which an atom is missing, is the vacancy concentration. The equilibrium concentration can approach 10^{-4} close to the melting point. The vacancy concentration at equilibrium is non-zero at any temperature above zero Kelvin.

Exercises

5.1 Explain the difference between activation energy and driving force.

5.2 Why does hardness decrease during recrystallization much more than during grain growth?

5.3 Explain the driving forces for recrystallization and grain growth.

5.4 Explain why high-purity aluminum recrystallizes at a much lower temperature than commercial purity aluminum.

5.5 Explain from the standpoint of kinetics why recrystallization and recovery are fundamentally different kinds of transformations. Find an analog of each in nature or society.

5.6 With regard to Example 5.2, calculate the further increase in temperature needed to double the rate of recrystallization again.

5.7 Determine the geometry of a grain-boundary triple junction in which one of the three grain boundaries has an energy of one-half the average, while the other two are average.

5.8 Explain why the kinetics of grain growth become much more nearly parabolic (rate $\propto t^{1/2}$) as the annealing temperature is increased, whereas the time exponent is usually less than 1/2 at lower temperatures.

5.9 If grain boundaries are assumed to be the major sources of dislocations in a material, and if dislocation sources are uniformly distributed on grain boundaries, then the dislocation density, ρ, must be proportional to the grain boundary area per unit volume. Use this idea to show that the flow stress should vary with grain size according to

$$\sigma_{flow} = \sigma_0 + k\,D^{-1/2}$$

where σ_0 is the stress needed to overcome the effects of lattice friction, solute atoms, etc.; D is the average grain diameter, and k is a constant.

5.10 Figure 5.19 shows the evolution of the microstructure of a carbon steel spoke during annealing for times up to 24h. What would be the ultimate microstructure if the annealing were to be carried out *ad infinitum* (assuming cementite would not transform to graphite, which is the ultimately stable phase)?

5.11 What would you expect to happen if the transformed microstructure shown in Fig. 5.20 were to be similarly annealed at 700°C *ad infinitum?*

6

CARBON STEEL: PLASTIC DEFORMATION AND FATIGUE RESISTANCE

6.1 Slip in BCC Iron

Referring to the microstructure of a fully annealed carbon-steel spoke, shown in Fig. 5.21, it will be shown in Chapter 8 that the pearlite constituent is about 90% BCC ferrite and 10% carbide, so the steel as a whole is about 95% ferrite. Therefore, the mechanical behavior of the spoke depends mainly on the deformation behavior of the ferrite. The deformation properties of BCC metals differ markedly from those of FCC metals. The difference in both the crystal structure and deformation behavior is the result of a directional component of interatomic bonding, which is absent in FCC metals*. Another important factor is the unique behavior of interstitial solutes in BCC metals, particularly with regard to the interaction between interstitial atoms and dislocations. The classic example is that of carbon in iron, and this behavior plays a central role in the special fatigue behavior of carbon steel, which depends on the interaction between carbon atoms and dislocations. This topic will be covered in the present chapter. Another manifestation of this interaction is the dependence of hardness on carbon content in quenched (i.e., "hardened") steels, which will be described in Chapter 9.

As one can see from Fig. 1.5, the atoms in a BCC crystal touch along the body diagonals of the unit cell. Thus, the <111> directions are close-packed directions, and the Burgers vectors of the slip dislocations lie along these directions. However, the slip plane in a BCC crystal is less well defined. There is no close-packed plane; the {110} planes are the most nearly close packed, and these tend to be the slip plane of choice. However, other planes that contain a <111> direction, such as {112}, can also act as slip planes. For our purposes, the slip systems will be taken to be {110}<111>; an example is shown in Fig.6.1.

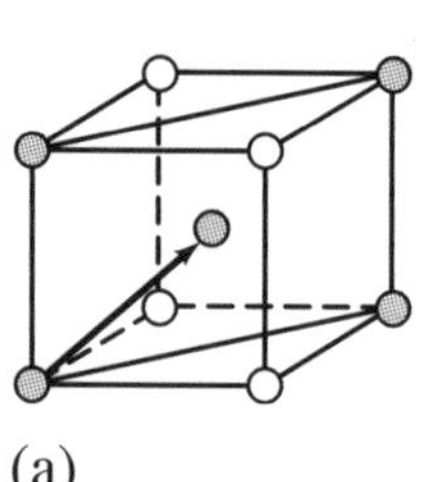

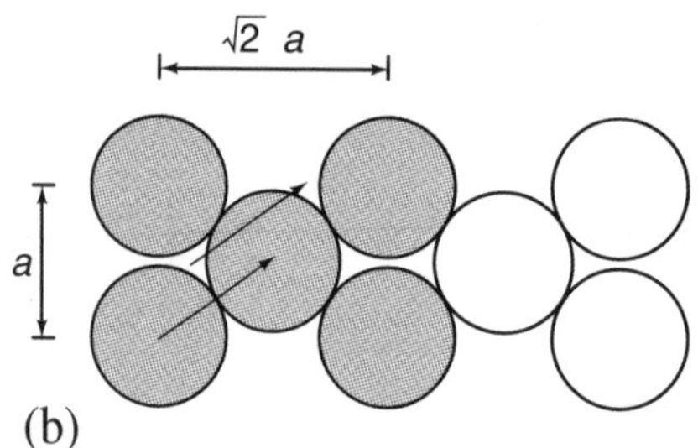

Fig. 6.1 Two representations of a BCC slip system: (a) in a unit cell, and (b) on a hard-sphere model of a {110} plane.

Except for the differences in the crystallography of slip, the previous discussion of dislocation behavior in FCC stainless steel applies to BCC iron. An additional characteristic of BCC transition metals like iron, however, is that, as mentioned in Section 4.2.4, the displacements of atoms along the core of a screw

* Except for iridium

dislocation do not take the smooth form of a helical ramp, but tend to be concentrated in certain radial planes (i.e., planes that contain the Burgers vector and intersect along the core of the dislocation). This is not important at higher temperatures, because thermal vibration of the atoms tends to wash out this kind of irregularity. However, at low temperatures this distortion of the core of screw dislocations restricts their mobility. As a result, plasticity is made more difficult (e.g., Frank-Read-loop expansion requires a much higher stress), and the yield stress increases steeply as the temperature is reduced. This is the reason for the ductile-brittle transition found in carbon steel at low temperatures. (cf. Appendix 6.1.)

Example 6.1

Q. Sketch each individual slip system in the set {110} <111> for a BCC crystal.

A.

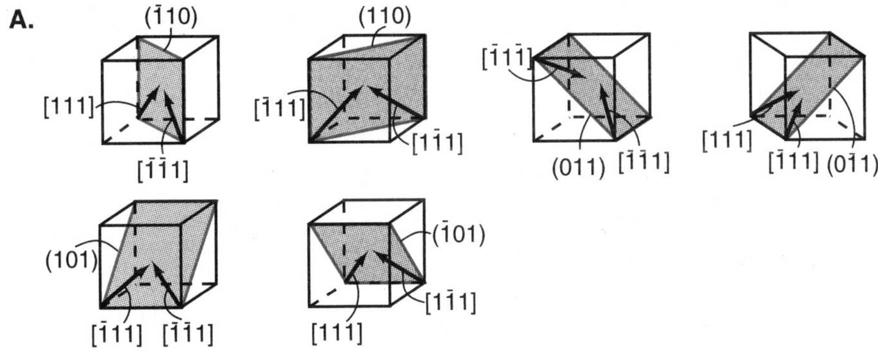

6.2 Interaction of Solute Atoms with Dislocations

As discussed earlier in Section 4.4.3, a dislocation can interact with a misfitting solute atom, because they both have elastic stress fields. If the stress fields have the same sign, the interaction is repulsive, and if they are of opposite sign, the interaction is attractive. This is easy to understand in the case of an edge dislocation. Figure 6.2 gives the four possible interactions. All of them decrease the mobility of an edge dislocation or a mixed dislocation. (A mixed dislocation has some edge character, meaning that there is some part of an extra half-plane associated with the dislocation.) This reduction in mobility means that additional stress must be applied to force a dislocation to glide through a crystal containing such solutes. This phenomenon is known as *solid-solution hardening*.

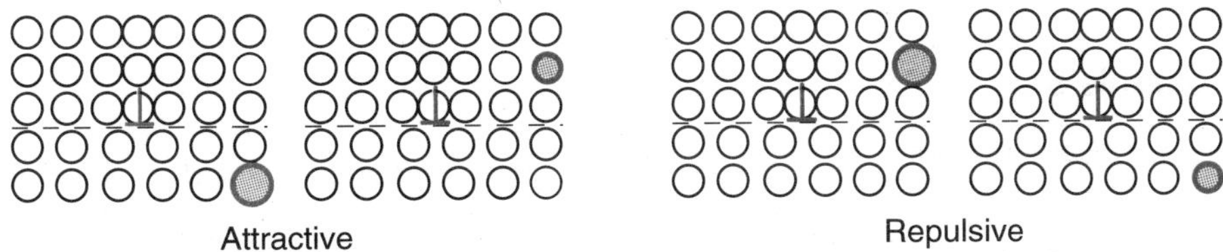

Fig. 6.2 The four possible interactions between misfitting substitutional solute atoms and dislocations with edge, or partly edge, character.

A pure screw dislocation has no extra material associated with it. Its stress field is one of pure shear; there are no dilational terms. Therefore, there is, to a first approximation, no interaction between a screw dislocation and a substitutional solute, since the solute has only a hydrostatic stress field (i.e., equal in all directions) but no shear component (cf. Section 4.4.3). In general, the same considerations are valid for an interstitial solute in an FCC lattice, since here again the distortion around the solute atom is spherically symmetrical. However, this is not the case for an interstitial solute in a BCC crystal, and this is of critical importance in carbon steel.

A special feature of an interstitial solute in a BCC crystal, like carbon or nitrogen in iron, is that the distortion is not purely dilational. There is a component of shape distortion of the site in which carbon atoms reside. That is, the site that produces the minimum overall strain energy in the lattice is located in the center of a cube face, as shown in Fig. 6.3. (The center of a cube edge is an equivalent site.) This site is called an octahedral site, because it has six surrounding iron atoms that lie at the apices of an octahedron (cf. Fig. 6.3). The site
6110 is not symmetrical, since the distance between one pair of iron atoms is a, the lattice parameter, whereas the distance between the other two pairs is $\sqrt{2}a$. When a carbon atom occupies this site, the latter two pairs are attracted inward, but the third pair is pushed outward. This converts the symmetry of the crystal from cubic to tetragonal in the vicinity of the carbon atom. (A tetragonal unit cell can be obtained by stretching or compressing a cube along one axis; see Appendix 6.2 for more on crystal symmetry.) Because of the localized shape change of the unit cell, the stress field of an interstitial atom in a BCC lattice contains non-zero shear-stress terms.

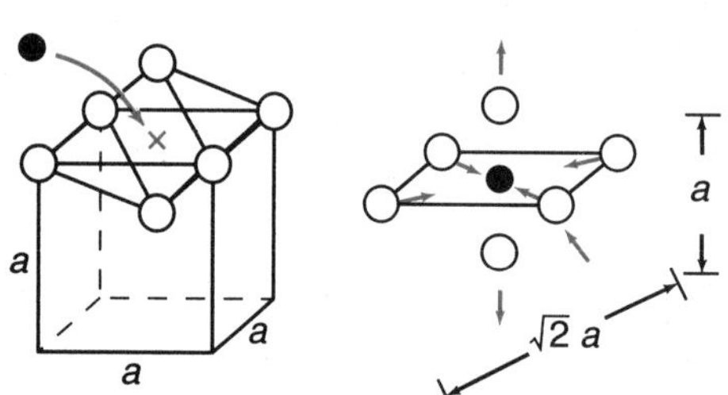

Fig. 6.3 An interstitial atom in the octahedral site of a BCC lattice produces a tetragonal distortion.

The result of this distortion is that carbon atoms in BCC iron are attracted even to pure screw dislocations. This has profound effects, which will be described after considering how the solutes get to the dislocations.

Example 6.2

Q. Show that the octahedral site in the center of the face of the BCC unit cell in Fig. 6.3 is equivalent to the center of an edge of the unit cell.

A. Since all the atoms in the crystal lattice are equivalent, the unit cell could have been centered on any atom. Two alternatives are shown. It can be seen that the center of the top face in one unit cell is the center of an edge in the other.

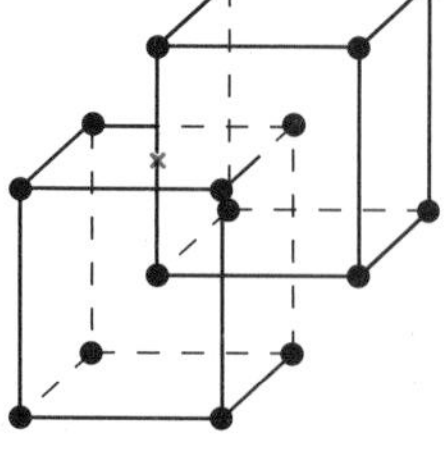

6.3 Segregation of Solutes to Dislocations

The driving force for the segregation of solutes to dislocations is the reduction of the overall elastic strain energy in the crystal lattice. That is, segregation produces a decrease in enthalpy, which in turn produces a decrease in free energy, G=H-TS, if temperature is low enough. This caveat is necessary, because segregation of randomly distributed solute atoms to dislocations increases the orderliness of the solute-atom arrangements and, therefore, decreases the entropy of the system. This would contribute to an increase in free energy, and it can only occur at low temperatures, where the TS term is small. The conclusion from thermodynamics, therefore, is that the influence of entropy tends to drive the solutes back into random solid solution as the temperature is increased. (This is true of any segregation process, including segregation of solutes to grain boundaries or the free surface.) Of course, if the temperature is so low that diffusion cannot occur in a reasonable time, then segregation is precluded, and equilibrium cannot be reached.

6.3.1 Substitutional Diffusion

In discussing solute segregation, one must distinguish between diffusion of substitutional *vs.* interstitial solutes. For substitutional solutes to diffuse, lattice vacancies are required. The process is illustrated in Fig. 6.4 and can be viewed either as vacancy migration or as the interchange of position between an atom and a vacancy. (If there is no solute involved, only host atoms, the process is called *self diffusion.*)

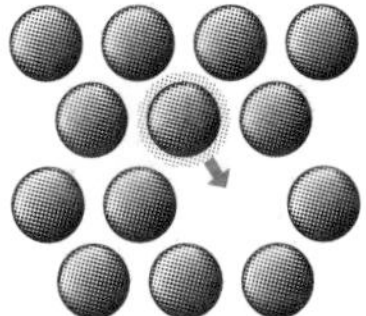

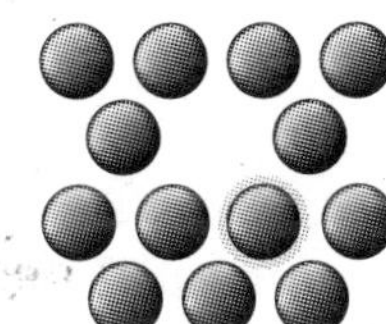

Fig. 6.4 Substitutional or self diffusion occurs by vacancy migration.

In order for one such jump to occur, there are two requirements. First, a site next to the solute atom must be vacant. Second, there must be enough kinetic energy in the cluster of atoms around the vacancy for the solute to leave its site and jump into the vacant site, overcoming the constraint of its neighbors. Thus, the probability of a successful jump is the product of two probabilities: the probability that one adjacent site is vacant (which is proportional to the concentration of vacancies in the lattice) and the probability that sufficient kinetic energy can be localized at the jumping atom. Both probabilities are exponential functions of temperature. That is why significant diffusion of substitutional solutes occurs only at elevated temperatures (meaning temperatures on the order of half the melting temperature in degrees Kelvin or higher).

The important features of substitutional diffusion can be summarized as follows:

1. The mechanism involves the interchange between atoms and vacancies. This occurs in a random manner, except that it can be biased by a gradient in strain energy (i.e., by a strain field, as near a dislocation).

2. The probability of any particular interchange depends on two factors: the probability that a site next to a particular atom is vacant (exp-(ΔH_f/RT), where ΔH_f is the energy of vacancy formation, and the probability that the atom has enough thermal energy to make the jump into the vacancy (exp-ΔH_m/RT), where ΔH_m is the activation energy for vacancy motion.

3. Thus, the rate of substitutional diffusion is proportional to

$$\exp-\left(\frac{\Delta H_f}{RT}\right)\exp-\left(\frac{\Delta H_m}{RT}\right) = \exp-\left[\frac{(\Delta H_f + \Delta H_m)}{RT}\right] = \exp-\left(\frac{Q}{RT}\right)$$

The term $Q = \Delta H_f + \Delta H_m$ is the activation energy for substitutional diffusion, or for self-diffusion.

6.3.2 Interstitial Diffusion

The situation for diffusion of interstitial solutes is different than for substitutional solutes, since no vacancy is required, as indicated by Fig. 6.5. The concentration of interstitial solutes is always so small that there is little likelihood that two adjacent interstitial sites are occupied. Therefore, the activation energy, Q, for interstitial diffusion contains only one term: the enthalpy of motion, or the kinetic energy required for the interstitial atoms to jump through the small "cage" formed by the host atoms that restrict the path to a neighboring interstitial site.

Fig. 6.5 Diffusion of interstitial solute atoms does not require the presence of lattice vacancies.

Since the vacancy concentration is irrelevant here, interstitial diffusion can occur at temperatures far below those needed for substitutional diffusion. For example, a carbon atom in iron at room temperature changes its interstitial site once per second, on the average. This means that all dislocations in iron will gradually become "decorated" with segregated carbon (or nitrogen) atoms.

The site for interstitial segregation to an edge dislocation is illustrated in Fig. 6.6. Since this is a minimum-energy configuration, the dislocations can become immobilized, or "pinned," if enough of this segregation occurs. That is, extra work must be done to free a pinned dislocation from an "atmosphere" of segregated carbon. This has a profound influence on the deformation behavior of iron and, in particular, on its resistance to fatigue failure, which is the topic of the following sections.

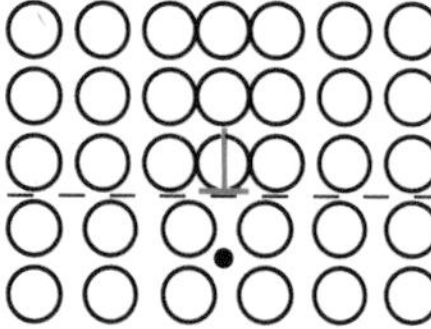

Fig. 6.6 An interstitial solute atom is attracted to the expanded lattice in the core of an edge dislocation.

Example 6.3

Q. There are three sets of octahedral sites in a BCC lattice, one set along each of the three coordinate axes of the unit cell, as shown below. These sets can be called x, y, and z sites, respectively. Deduce the effect of the application of a tensile stress along the [100] axis of a crystal of BCC iron that contains interstitial carbon in solid solution. Assume that the temperature is high enough for interstitial diffusion.

A. Any octahedral site occupied by a carbon atom is distorted by elongation along one of the three axes and contraction along the other two. A carbon atom in an x site causes the unit cell to elongate along the [100] axis. Therefore, the application of a tensile stress along the x axis would favor the x sites as sites for carbon atoms; the distortion of the unit cell would then be similar to the elastic strain caused by the applied stress. The carbon atoms, initially deployed at random among the three sets of sites (to maximize entropy), would then diffuse into x sites. As this occurred, the crystal would continue to extend in the [100] direction until all of the carbon atoms had reached x sites. If the stress were removed, the process would reverse until the carbon distribution again became random. The result would be a time-dependent strain, as shown at right. The stress can be applied or removed quickly, but the attainment of the extra strain, or its decay to zero, would take time, since diffusion is required. This kind of strain is called *anelastic* strain, because it is not plastic and is not governed by Hooke's law.

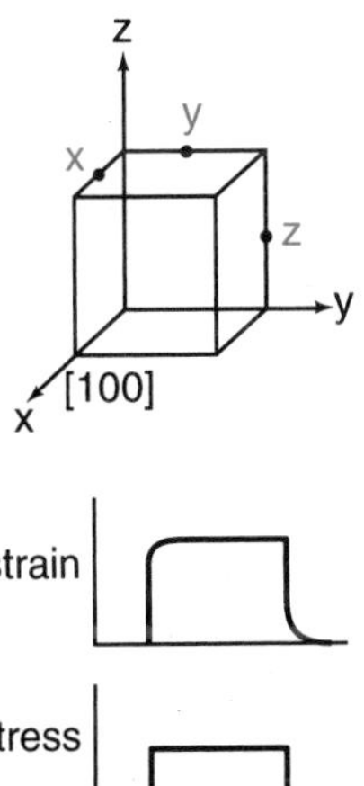

Example 6.4

Q. Lattice vacancies are equilibrium defects in crystals, meaning that, at a finite temperature, a certain fraction of lattice sites will be vacant, even though vacancies increase the internal energy of the crystal lattice. Why is this true for vacancies (and other point defects) but not for defects like dislocations or grain boundaries?

A. The entropy associated with point defects is very large, especially compared with that associated with line defects or planar defects. The reason is that the number of choices for the position of a vacancy is essentially equal to the number of atoms in the crystal. Because a very large number of atoms is associated with a dislocation or grain boundary, the choice of locations is much more limited. Therefore, the entropy effect associated with dislocations and grain boundaries is too low to offset the increase in enthalpy associated with them. Hence, the presence of dislocations or grain boundaries always raises the free energy of a material above its minimum value.

6.4 The Nature of Metal Fatigue

Fatigue is a common mode of failure in metallic materials that are subjected to repetitive loading. This is obviously the case with spokes, and fatigue is usually the life-limiting factor for spokes given high-mileage usage. For such usage, cyclists often select carbon steel spokes. The reason will be examined in some detail here, after it is established just what is meant by fatigue failure.

Anyone who has broken a piece of wire by bending it back and forth repeatedly has performed a rudimentary fatigue experiment. It is common experience that the greater the bending deflection on each cycle, the smaller the number of cycles needed to break the wire. It would take very many cycles, indeed, if the bending were so slight as to be almost entirely elastic. Such is the case for most cases of fatigue of mechanical components.

Research has shown that fatigue failure occurs by the formation of a crack, usually at the surface of a component but sometimes at an internal defect, and the growth of this crack by a small increment during each loading cycle. The crack begins in a region of concentrated plastic flow, as in an intense slip band, which gradually creates a microscopic fissure where it meets the surface. This process can be accelerated by corrosion. The number of cycles needed for crack nucleation can be greatly reduced by the presence of stress concentrations, such as sudden variations in cross-section, deep scratches, corrosion pits, etc., as indicated schematically in Fig. 6.7.

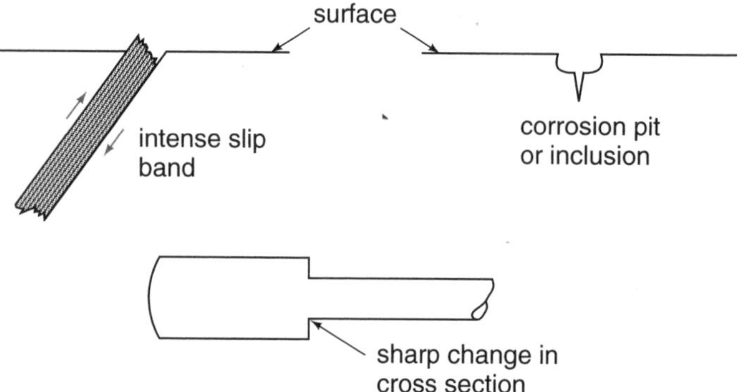

Fig. 6.7 Common sites of fatigue-crack initiation.

The most common mode of crack advance is the plastic opening, or blunting, that occurs on each loading cycle; this is illustrated by Fig. 6.8. This blunting simply increases the total surface area of the crack, and, when the crack closes during the unloading or compression part of the cycle, it is necessarily longer than before. All of this occurs on the microscopic scale, and it is usually not until late in the specimen or component life that the crack is large enough to detect visually. Since inspection procedures are seldom good enough to reveal growing fatigue cracks, there are many sudden, surprising failures of mechanical components annually. These occur when cracks become so large that the applied load is sufficient to cause rapid propagation during the final loading cycle.

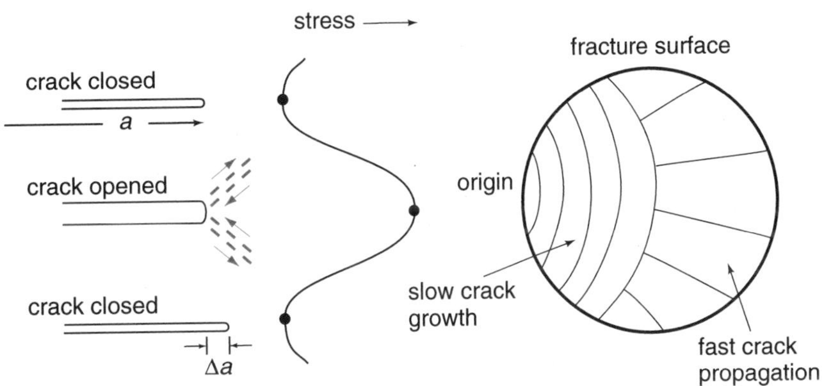

Fig. 6.8 Fatigue crack of length *a* grows by a plastic-blunting mechanism.

Since bicycle components are loaded cyclically, they are subject to fatigue failure. One common site of such failure is the connection of the pedal to the crank that turns the chainwheel. The pedal rotates on a stem that is normally screwed into the end of the crank. When the rider drives the pedal downward with his foot, the stem is loaded like a cantilever beam, and the maximum stress is found at the juncture of the stem and the crank. The stress is further concentrated here by the notch provided by the last screw thread, as shown schematically in Fig. 6.9.

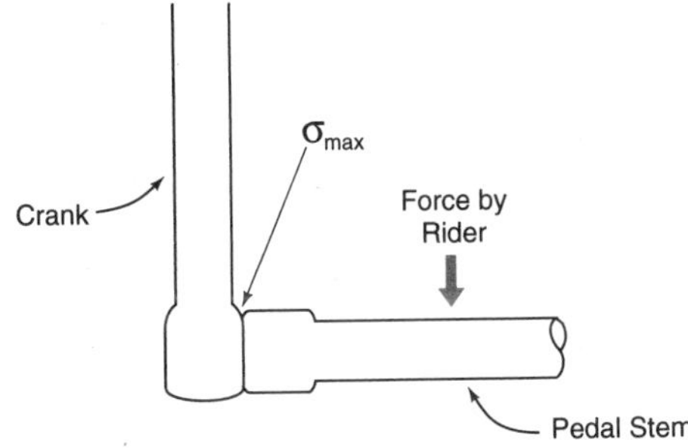

Fig. 6.9 Location of maximum tensile stress due to bending of the pedal stem under the downward force of the rider's foot.

An analogous configuration can be found in the oarlock of a racing shell. Here, every rowing stroke loads the pin on which the oarlock rotates in the same manner as a pedal stem. An example of a fatigue failure of such a stem is shown in Fig. 6.10.

Fig. 6.10 Fracture surface of an oarlock pin that failed in fatigue.

The fatigue crack in Fig. 6.10 started in a thread root at the point indicated by the arrow, and propagated initially in microscopic steps. The crack front had the classical thumbnail shape, and the slight rubbing of the two faces of the crack produced the smooth appearance. Variations in the oxide film (owing to variations in temperature and relative humidity) provide a record of the crack-front shape at several locations. As the crack progressed, the steps (one per rowing stroke) grew larger, and the fracture surface became more ragged. When the fatigue crack had progressed slightly more than half-way through the pin, the stem snapped off during the final stroke.

This kind of failure can be dangerous, because it usually comes without warning. Cracks are often obscured by other parts and are, therefore, difficult to inspect. This is the case with pedal stems and oarlock pins. With the sudden fracture of a heavily loaded part, injuries are likely to occur. Bicycle riders have been severely injured by falls after failure of a pedal stem. This kind of problem is often the fault of a manufacturer, on the grounds that the stress analysis during the design of the component was inadequate (i.e., not up to the state of the art). However, users of devices with heavily stressed components that are cyclically loaded can help protect themselves by being aware of the possibility of fatigue and by periodically inspecting, or even replacing, critical components.

6.5 The S-N Curve

The study of fatigue behavior was first systematized by A.Wöhler, a German railway engineer, in the 19th century. He showed that the fatigue life of any component could be characterized by plotting the number of cycles to failure as a function of the maximum tensile stress per cycle, assuming all cycles to be identical. (The latter is usually true only in the laboratory, but that is the source of most fatigue data.) Common lab tests include a rotating cylindrical beam subjected to a side-wise force, which produces a sinusoidal variation in tensile stress at any point on the surface, as shown in Fig. 6.11.

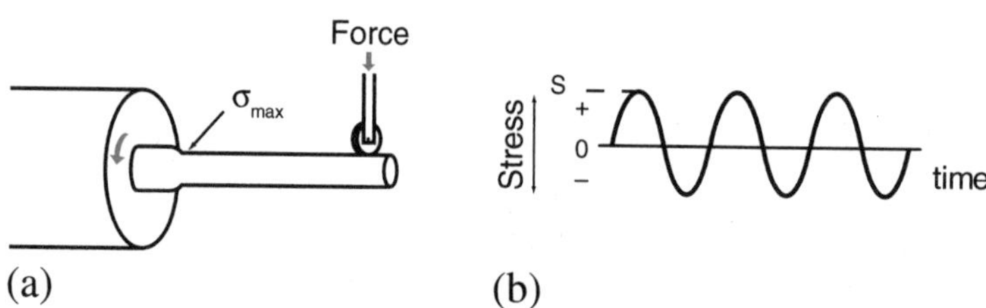

Fig. 6.11 (a) Schematic representation of the rotating-beam fatigue test. (b) Sinusoidal variation of stress with time at some point on the surface, when the rotation rate is constant.

The Wöhler curve, or S-N curve, conventionally shown with the independent variable, stress (S), along the ordinate (as in Fig. 6.12), has been a common basis for design against fatigue for many decades. One can test a given material in a particular condition of heat treatment, grain size, yield strength, etc. and determine the S-N curve. The intended life, or "design life," of a particular component, in terms of the number of cycles one can anticipate before the component is replaced or discarded is then established (often assumed) by the design engineer. From the S-N curve, the maximum allowable tensile stress can then be specified, under the assumption that all loading cycles will be identical.

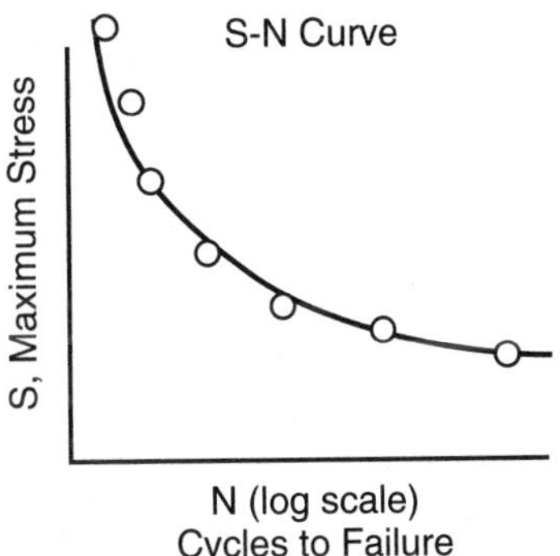

Fig. 6.12 The S-N, or Wöhler, curve; this is the most common representation of fatigue behavior.

The initiation and growth of a fatigue crack involves localized plastic deformation. Therefore, increasing the resistance of a material to plastic deformation, i.e., strengthening it, has the effect of raising the S-N curve to higher levels of stress. That is, it would require more cycles at a given stress to produce fatigue failure. Conversely, anything that reduces the yield strength would also reduce the fatigue resistance. This is particularly true for a reduction in the strength of surface regions, since that is where fatigue cracks typically start. In fact, surface regions are often specifically strengthened to improve fatigue resistance. A common way of doing this is "shot peening," which involves blasting a surface with small steel balls to strengthen it by strain hardening.

It should be noted that a large number of supposedly identical specimens run at the same maximum stress will usually show a distribution of fatigue life scattered about a mean value, as shown schematically in Fig. 6.13. In principle, the mean value should be used for the S-N curve shown in Fig. 6.12. This means that the earliest fatigue failures will occur at a life somewhat shorter than indicated by the curve.

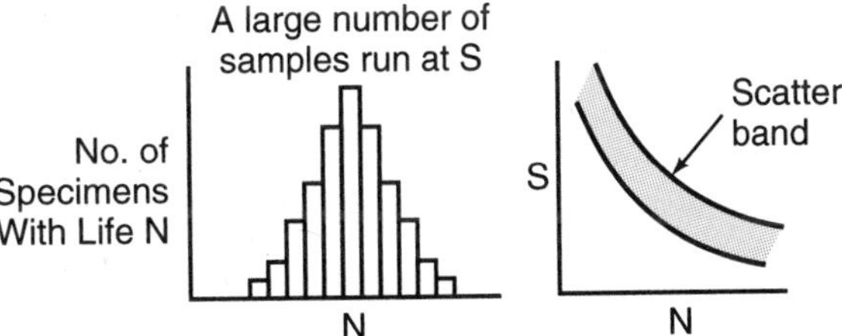

Fig. 6.13 There will be a distribution of fatigue lives at a given stress level; hence, an S-N curve should show a scatter band.

The problems encountered in designing against fatigue failure on the basis of S-N data are as follows:

1. The scatter in the fatigue life for a given stress (cf. Fig. 6.13) can be large. This may force the designer to choose between an unreasonably low design stress (e.g., an unreasonably large and heavy component) or some finite probability of fatigue during the life of the component. The remedy for this problem is to control the manufacturing process so that microstructure and properties vary as little as possible from one specimen to the next. This reduces the scatter of the S-N data and makes it easier to design for almost-zero failures.

2. It is often unreasonable to expect that all loading cycles will be identical. In this case fatigue data should be obtained under conditions of varying maximum stress to mimic the expected service conditions. This kind of testing can be complicated and expensive and carries with it a set of assumptions that may be inadequate. However, in some critical applications, like airplane wings, for example, there is no alternative.

3. In components of varying cross section, like a shaft with varying diameter or with screw threads or other stress concentrations (cf. Fig. 6.7), a careful stress analysis is required to estimate the stress-concentration factor at each discontinuity. It must be emphasized that the maximum tensile stress on the component, i.e., at the most severe stress concentration, is the stress that must be used in the S-N diagram to estimate the number of cycles to failure.

4. The effects of corrosion, superimposed on those of cyclic loading, are often extremely difficult to predict. Even if relevant laboratory data are available, the service conditions could vary unpredictably.

All of these problems necessitate periodic inspection of critical components or replacement of components that cannot be adequately inspected. Applying this to the bicycle would mean replacement of spokes after a certain number of miles ridden and periodic removal of the pedals for inspection of the roots of the screw threads where they attach to the cranks.

6.5.1 Analysis of the Failure of a Stainless Steel Spoke

A road bike with about 9000 miles on its wheels since the spokes were replaced was ridden over a bump in the pavement, and one of the spokes broke with a loud snapping noise. Inspection showed that the fracture took place at a thread root inside the nipple. Fig. 6.14(a) shows the nipple after it had been sectioned longitudinally to reveal the remaining piece of the spoke, and the fracture surface of the mating piece is shown in Fig. 6.14(b). The failure was obviously caused by a fatigue crack that began at the point indicated by the arrow and propagated more than halfway through the cross section before rapid failure occurred. On the fatigue portion of the fracture surface (lighter portion), coarse "thumbnail" marks denoting locations of crack arrest can be seen.

The fatigue portion was examined at higher magnifications in a scanning electron microscope (cf. Section 13.4.1), and the point of initiation of the fatigue crack is shown in Fig. 6.14(c). Crack-arrest striations on a finer scale can be seen here. Finally, at still higher magnification (Fig. 6.14d), striations demarking crack arrest with a spacing of 2 to 3 micrometers can be seen. The latter striations probably mark the progress of the fatigue crack during each revolution of the wheel. The larger striations probably correspond to road bumps of various magnitudes. The larger the bump, the greater the crack opening and the more pronounced the striation. The presence of the thumbnail pattern and the striations at high magnification are the classic hallmarks of a fatigue failure.

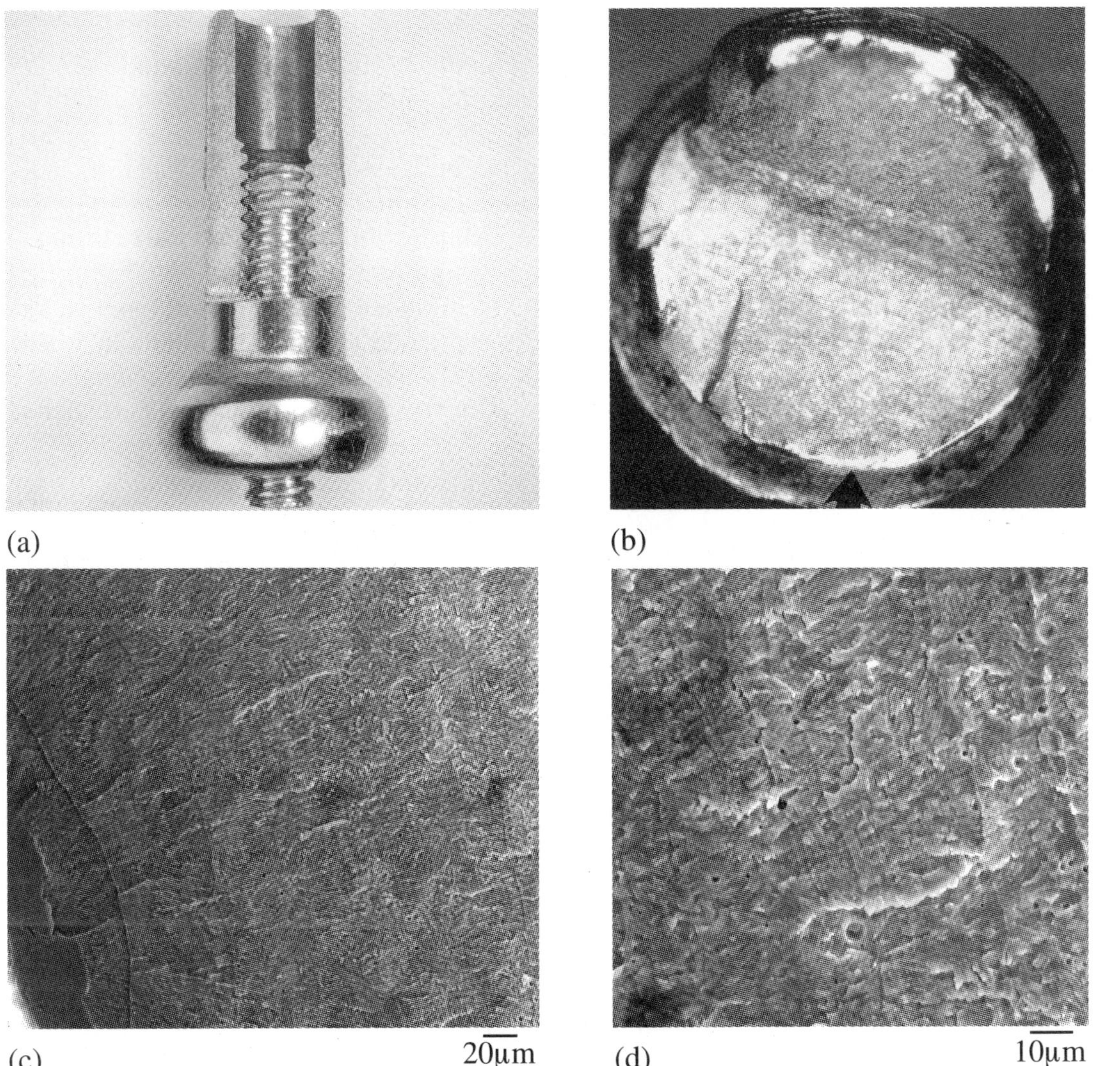

Fig. 6.14 (a) Sectioned nipple containing the end of a fractured stainless steel spoke. (b) The fracture surface of the mating piece; the arrow denotes the origin of the fatigue crack; the lighter portion is that over which the fatigue crack grew, and the darker portion is that which failed rapidly at the final bump in the road. (c) The origin of the fatigue crack at high magnification, showing crack-arrest striations. (d) Part of (c) at still higher magnification, showing striations with a 2-to-3 micrometer spacing. (Contributed by Cliff Warner, Univ. of Penn.)

6.6 The Fatigue Limit of Carbon Steel

There are two general classes of S-N behavior. In one class, which includes carbon steel, there is a threshold value of S below which the fatigue life becomes essentially infinite. This value is called the *fatigue limit.* This is shown schematically in Fig. 6.15. Thus, in principle, one can design against fatigue in a material with a fatigue limit simply by keeping the maximum stress below the fatigue limit. In the other class of behavior, which includes austenitic stainless steels, there is no threshold of any practical significance, which means that fatigue failure is an ultimate certainty once the requisite number of cycles is reached. The question to be addressed is: what is the reason for the fatigue limit in ferritic steels? It has to do with the interaction between carbon atoms and dislocations.

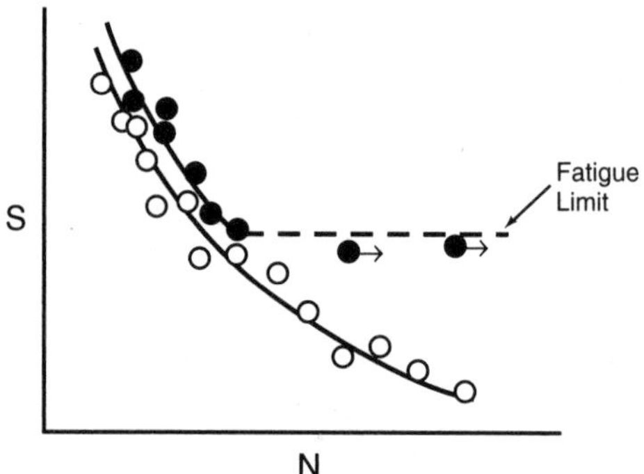

Fig. 6.15 Schematic illustration of S-N curves for materials with and without a fatigue limit.

It was explained in Section 6.2 that carbon atoms in solution in BCC metals occupy octahedral sites around which the lattice is distorted locally into a tetrahedral symmetry. Since this local shape change involves shear strains in addition to the dilational strains associated with the interstitial solute, the carbon atoms interact with all dislocations in the BCC lattice. The attraction between carbon atoms and dislocations in BCC iron is strong, and because diffusion of this interstitial atom is rapid at room temperature, carbon can migrate readily to dislocations. This causes the dislocations to become pinned in place so that they do not glide when a shear stress is applied.

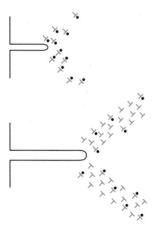

It has been shown by experiment that the fatigue limit can be removed from a low-carbon steel by a heat treatment in hydrogen, which removes carbon. (The carbon diffuses to the surface and reacts with the hydrogen to form methane, CH_4.) It is believed that the carbon produces the fatigue limit by pinning dislocations; this can prevent concentrated slip bands from forming, or it can stop the development of early-stage fatigue cracks. The pinning is present before the steel is cyclically loaded, and more pinning may occur by the diffusion of carbon to new dislocations formed after cyclic loading has started. Above the fatigue limit the stress is high enough to produce fresh (i.e., not pinned) dislocations and to cause them to multiply at a rate too rapid for them to be pinned by diffusion of carbon during the cyclic loading.

The fatigue behavior of carbon steel *vs.* stainless steel spokes is shown in Fig. 6.16. These results are for segments of spokes loaded in cantilever bending. This is not the same as in-service loading, but it permits a comparison of the material behavior. It can be seen that, for a given maximum load, the life of the carbon steel exceeded that of the stainless steel by a substantial amount. This difference increased as the load was reduced. At the lowest stress employed, the carbon steel appears to be approaching its fatigue limit; the testing could not be carried out long enough to establish what that limit is.

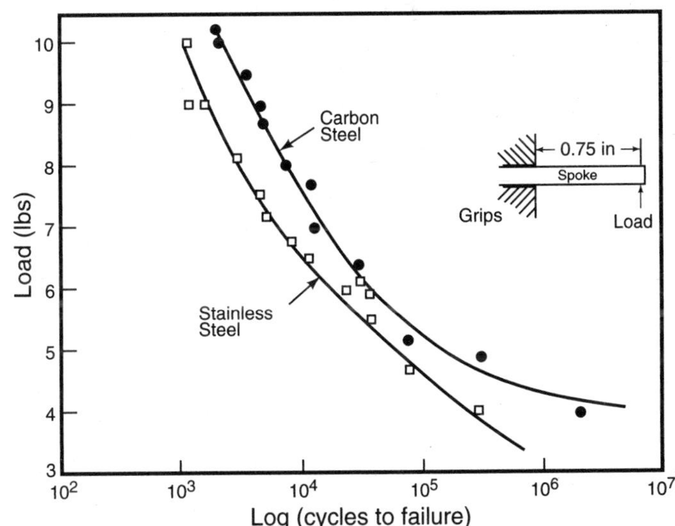

Fig. 6.16 Fatigue behavior of carbon steel and stainless steel spokes loaded in repeated cantilever bending.

The importance of a fatigue limit for design purposes is that, as long as the maximum cyclic stress is kept below this value, the life should be essentially infinite with respect to fatigue. Of course, any surface damage to a spoke that produces a stress concentrator, such as a deep scratch or a corrosion pit, can cause the local stress to exceed the fatigue limit. Thus, even with carbon steel, spokes must be inspected periodically for surface damage. Fatigue failures are to be avoided, especially in the front wheel, since the rider may be pitched over the handlebars if a broken spoke falls across the front fork and jams the wheel.

Summary

Carbon-steel spokes are 95% BCC iron, or ferrite, and as such their deformation behavior differs markedly from that of the FCC stainless steel spokes. Carbon-steel spokes would become brittle at very low temperatures because of the inherent low mobility of screw dislocations in the BCC lattice; they are ductile at room temperature owing to the presence of sufficient thermal energy to "smear out" the complicated core structure of the screw dislocations, which enables them to glide more readily. In addition, interstitial solutes occupy octahedral sites in the BCC lattice, and these are not spherically symmetrical. Therefore, the lattice is locally distorted into a BCT, or body-centered tetragonal, symmetry around the interstitial atom, such as with carbon in ferrite. The resulting stress field around the interstitial atom contains shear-stress terms, as well as the dilational terms found in the FCC lattice. The presence of the shear-stress terms means that interstitial atoms in a BCC lattice would interact with all dislocations, including pure screws. This effect leads to dislocation pinning and, therefore, to the fatigue limit observed in carbon steel at low cyclic stresses.

The process of fatigue was shown to be one of nucleation of cracks, usually at surfaces, as a result of plastic deformation, even on a very small and localized scale, and the growth of these cracks by way of the plastic-blunting mechanism. This growth can be arrested at low cyclic stresses by the diffusion of carbon atoms to the plastic zone at the tips of small cracks; this produces the fatigue limit. Interstitial diffusion was shown to be much faster than substitutional diffusion, owing to the fact that vacant lattice sites are not necessary for the former.

Appendix 6.1 Brittle Fracture in Carbon Steel

6040 Many metals and alloys undergo a ductile-to-brittle transition when cooled to relatively low temperatures. The underlying reason for this, in general, is that certain kinds of dislocation motion become difficult at low temperatures. In iron and other BCC metals, screw dislocation mobility decreases at low temperatures. This has to do with atomic displacements in the cores of screw dislocations in BCC metals, as discussed in Section 6.1. The result is a steeply rising yield stress with decreasing temperature and a corresponding decrease in ductility; the behavior of BCC iron is contrasted with that of FCC copper in Fig. A6.1.1.

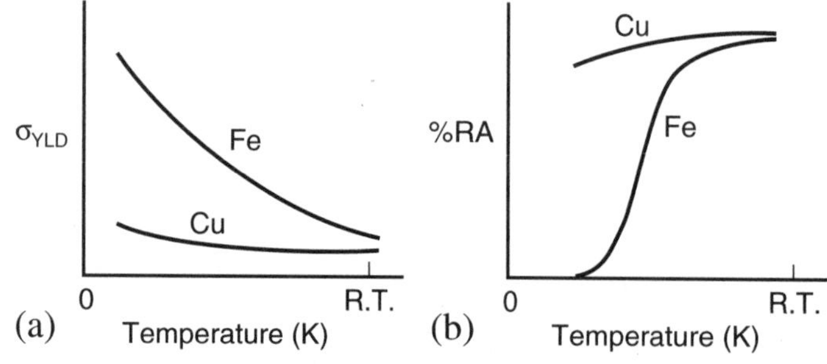

Fig. A6.1.1 Schematic representation of variation of (a) yield stress and (b) ductility with temperature in BCC iron and FCC copper.

The high yield stress at low temperatures in BCC metals makes it possible to attain levels of tensile stress at which the cohesive forces between atoms can be overcome, so that brittle fracture can occur. In a typical case, a few dislocations move and become blocked by some strong obstacle, such as a hard particle. This concentrates stress at the particle, and a microcrack can form, starting with cracking of the particle. This microcrack can propagate through the metal if the applied stress is high enough and if plastic flow at the crack tip is difficult; both of these conditions apply in iron, and therefore carbon steel, at low temperatures.

In iron and carbon steels the brittle fracture usually occurs by cleavage along {100} planes, giving a fracture appearance as shown in Fig. A6.1.2.

The tendency of carbon steel to behave in a brittle manner at low temperatures has been responsible for many catastrophic failures, even the fracture of entire ships. A well known example is that of the S.S. Schenectady, which split in two shortly after outfitting. As shown in Fig. A6.1.3, it fractured on a cold day while sitting alongside a pier in quiet water.

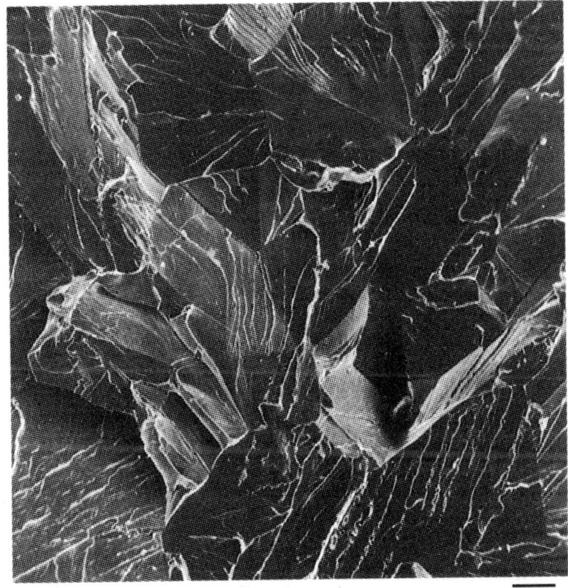
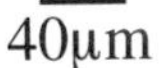

Fig. A6.1.2 An example of cleavage fracture in iron. The {100} cleavage cracks must change planes at every grain boundary. (This makes fine-grained steels tougher than coarse-grained steels.)

Fig. A6.1.3 The S.S. Schenectady after it fractured in half on a cold winter day while tied up at a fitting-out pier in calm weather. This is an example of brittle fracture of carbon steel presumably triggered by residual stresses from construction. (Final report of a board of investigation convened by order of the Secretary of the Navy to inquire into the design and methods of construction of welded steel merchant vessels, U.S. Gov't Printing Office, 1947, Fig. 11.)

Appendix 6.2 Crystal Symmetry

Most metals and alloys crystallize in simple structures, because the constituent atoms are the same or nearly the same in size, and the bonding is essentially metallic; i.e., positive ions share a delocalized pool of "free" electrons. Thus, the constraints of ionic compounds, in which negative ions must surround positive ions, and covalent solids, in which bond lengths and bond angles are important, are absent. The most common metallic structure is cubic, which has the highest symmetry.

For example, a cubic crystal has three 4-fold axes of rotational symmetry, which are the three cube axes. That is, one can rotate a cube by 90°, 180°, 270°, or 360° around any <100> axis and find that the atom positions are indistinguishable before and after the rotation. By the same token a <111> direction is a 3-fold rotation axis, and a <110> direction is a 2-fold rotation axis, as shown in Fig. A6.2.1.

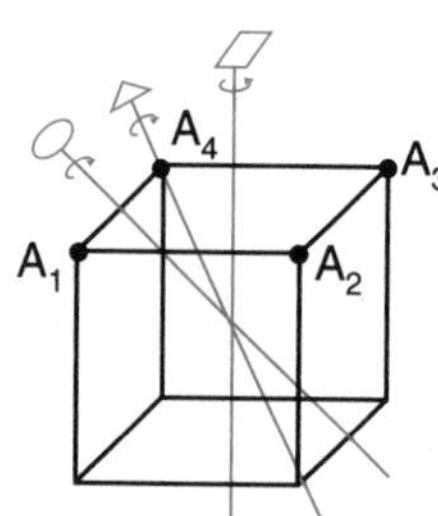

Fig. A6.2.1 Axes of rotational symmetry in a cubic crystal: □4-fold axis: A_1 becomes A_2; △3-fold axis: A_1 becomes A_3; 0 2-fold axis: A_1 becomes A_4. (From B. D. Cullity, *Elements of X-Ray Diffraction,* Addison-Wesley, Reading, MA, 1956, p.34.)

These statements are true for both FCC and BCC crystals, which correspond to two of the fourteen Bravais lattices. Figure A6.2.2 shows the unit cells of the lattices representing the fourteen possible ways of arranging points in space in a "space lattice," in which the unit cell is repeated in three dimensions. There are no others!

When a cubic unit cell is distorted along one axis, the result is a tetragonal lattice. It has lower symmetry than a cubic lattice: one 4-fold and two 2-fold axes of rotation.

Crystal symmetry has a profound effect on physical properties. For example, cubic crystals are isotropic with regard to heat flow, thermal expansion, and diffusion. All others are anisotropic: e.g., the rates of heat and mass flow vary with the crystallographic direction. In cubic crystals only three elastic constants are needed to describe all possible stress-strain relationships. In the triclinic lattice, which has the least symmetry, twenty-one are needed.

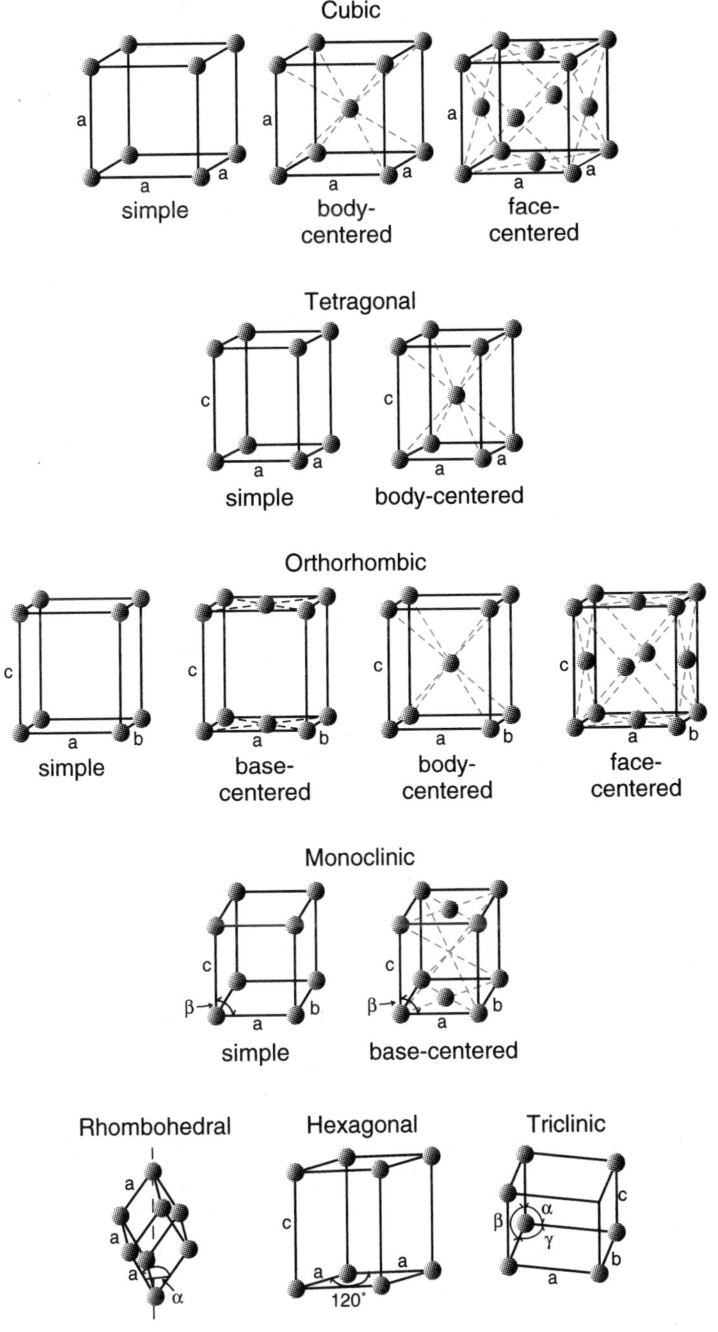

Fig. A 6.2.2 The fourteen Bravais lattices.

Glossary/Vocabulary - Chapter 6

Austenite	This is the name given to the FCC phase in the Fe-C alloy system. It was named in honor of the metallurgist Roberts-Austen. Any steel that is FCC at room temperature is called austenitic. Stainless steel with enough nickel to make it FCC is called austenitic stainless steel.
Brittle fracture	By this is usually meant a stress-controlled mode of fracture, like transcrystalline cleavage or intergranular decohesion, with little prior plastic deformation. Virtually all metallic materials, except FCC metals and alloys*, and all ceramic materials can undergo brittle fracture under some conditions. Amorphous polymers below their glass transition temperature also do. Brittle fracture is often associated with the behavior of ferritic steels at low temperatures, where the low mobility of screw dislocations causes the yield stress to increase greatly, thereby inhibiting stress relaxation at defects and other stress concentrations.
Cementite	This is a name given to iron carbide, Fe_3C, in the early days of the study of steels, because it was thought to bind together the grains of iron. Cementite is a rather brittle phase, and it can be cracked by slip bands. At low temperatures, this can lead to cleavage cracking in the surrounding ferrite.
Cleavage fracture	Cleavage fracture means the stress-controlled separation of a crystalline material along specific crystallographic planes. It is a form of brittle fracture. Cleavage fracture occurs in iron and ferritic steels at low temperatures; the cleavage plane in this and other BCC metals is the {100} plane.
Crystal symmetry	If the external faces of a crystal are developed, they display a definite symmetry of arrangement, and this symmetry is also displayed by the crystal lattice. The physical properties of the crystal in different crystallographic directions depend on this symmetry. Cubic crystals have three 4-fold rotational symmetry axes (<100>), four 3-fold rotational axes (<111>), and six 2-fold rotational axes (<110>), for example.
Ductile-brittle transition	Most materials undergo a transition from ductile behavior at high temperatures to brittle behavior at low temperatures when tested in a short-time test, like a tensile test or impact test. (The exception is FCC metals*.) The classical example is ferritic steel because of the wide use of this material. The transition usually involves an increase in flow stress with decreasing temperature and a change in the fracture mode from displacement-controlled (e.g., plastic rupture) to stress-controlled (e.g., cleavage or intergranular decohesion).
Fatigue crack nucleation	Fatigue cracks generally nucleate at a surface, at a stress concentrator if one is present. In the absence of a stress concentrator, they can nucleate at places where slip becomes concentrated and a surface discontinuity develops from the back-and-forth concentrated shear. Fatigue cracks typically nucleate at thread roots, corrosion pits, or sharp changes in cross section, for example.
Fatigue life	The number of cycles to failure in a cyclically loaded specimen or component is known as the fatigue life. It is commonly designated by the letter N. The most common representation of fatigue life is the S-N diagram, called the Wöhler diagram in Europe. It is a plot of the maximum stress per cycle, called S, *vs.* the number of cycles to failure.

* Except for iridium

Fatigue limit Some materials exhibit a fatigue limit such that, below a certain value of S, the fatigue life, N, is infinite. That is, fatigue cracks do not develop and grow below this value of S. The classical example is carbon steel, in which the fatigue limit is caused by the pinning of dislocations by carbon and nitrogen, preventing the concentrated slip that leads to fatigue-crack nucleation and growth.

Ferrite This is the name given to the BCC phase of iron or a BCC Fe-based solid solution. (It is also the name given to the magnetic oxides containing iron.) Ferrite is the majority phase in carbon steel.

Interstitial diffusion This is the diffusion of an interstitial solute. It occurs by the hopping of the solute from one interstice to another. The best-known example is diffusion of carbon in BCC iron and iron-based alloys, as in the segregation of carbon atoms to dislocations.

Interstitial solute A foreign atom that is too small to substitute for a host atom on its crystal lattice can often fit into an interstice, the space left by a contiguous cluster of atoms in the crystal, in which case it is called an interstitial solute. The common interstitial solutes in metals are C, N, H, and B.

Octahedral site An octahedral site in a crystal is the center of an octahedron formed by six surrounding atoms, four in a plane and one on each side of that plane. The center of the face of a BCC unit cell is an octahedral site; it is noteworthy because that is the site occupied by a carbon atom in solid solution in iron.

Pearlite This is the name given to the eutectoid micro-constituent in a carbon steel. That is, it is the product of eutectoid decomposition of austenite. It comprises alternating lamellae of ferrite and cementite. Pearlite is about 90% ferrite, 10% cementite. The thickness of the lamellae depends on the temperature at which they form.

Plastic blunting This is the principle mechanism of fatigue-crack growth. A tensile-stress cycle causes the tip of the crack to become blunt because of the plastic flow concentrated there. When the crack closes during the compression or unloading part of the cycle, it is necessarily longer because of the blunting during the previous opening. One can often detect striations on a fatigue-fracture surface by examination at high magnifications (e.g., in a scanning electron microscope). These mark the positions of the crack tip after each blunting cycle.

Self diffusion At temperatures on the order of half the (absolute) melting point or above, the interchange of atoms and vacancies occurs at a significant rate, and vacancies thereby execute a "random walk" through the crystal. This process is known as self diffusion. The rate of self diffusion can be measured by measuring the rate of diffusion of a radioactive isotope of an element in a crystal of that element.

Shot peening To enhance fatigue resistance, it is often the practice to harden a surface by blasting it with small steel balls, called shot. These put small plastic dents in the surface, a process called peening. This acts both to strain harden the surface and to put it in a state of residual compressive stress, both of which make fatigue-crack growth more difficult.

Solute segregation If solute atoms are able to migrate, then they can lower their energy (enthalpy) if they segregate to locations at which they can be accommodated with less strain of the lattice. This tendency is opposed by the fact that segregation lowers the entropy of the system, because it decreases the randomness. Therefore, the amount of segregation diminishes as the temperature is increased, because the term -TS is thereby decreased, and entropy becomes more important in lowering Gibbs free energy (G=H-TS). Solute atoms, which usually are either too large or too small for lattice sites, tend to segregate to grain boundaries and to dislocations.

Stress concentration In a stressed body, any local decrease in the area of a plane produces a local concentration of stress on that plane. A hole in a stressed plate produces a concentration of stress in the vicinity of the hole. This can be viewed as the need to "make up for" the absence of load-bearing material in the hole. The important stress concentrations come from elongated, sharply pointed holes, like cracks. A long hole means that there is a lot of non-load-bearing material, and a sharp point means that this must be made up for in a small volume of material.

Stress-concentration factor This is a geometrical factor by which one multiplies the nominal value of an applied stress to get the actual local stress at some stress concentrator, such as a notch or crack. That is, the factor depends on the geometry of the stress concentrator. The stress-concentration factor for an elliptical hole in a plate is$(1+\sqrt{a/\rho})$,where a is the length of the hole, and ρ is the radius of curvature at the tips of the hole. For a round hole, $a=\rho$, and the stress-concentration factor is 3. That is, the stress at the edge of the round hole is three times the nominal stress away from the hole. (See Section 9.5)

Substitutional diffusion This is the diffusion of a substitutional solute by interchange of atoms with vacancies. In a concentration gradient, there would be a net mass flow down the gradient resulting from the random motion of vacancies. Mechanistically, this is similar to self diffusion. However, it is more complex in that the rate of interchange of atoms with vacancies depends on the nature of the atom, so solute atoms and host atoms make this interchange at different rates.

Tetragonal distortion This is the distortion of a crystal lattice that is stretched along one axis. When this happens in a cubic lattice, it results in two lattice parameters, instead of one. Martensite that contains carbon is body-centered tetragonal (BCT), because the carbon trapped during quenching distorts what would otherwise be a BCC crystal (i.e., ferrite).

Tetrahedral site A tetrahedral site is the center of a tetrahedron formed by four contiguous atoms in a crystal lattice. A carbon solute atom in an FCC iron-based phase occupies a tetrahedral site.

Exercises

6.1 The lattice parameter (i.e., the unit-cell dimension) of BCC iron at room temperature is 2.87Å (0.287nm). Calculate the diameter of the largest interstitial atom that could fit into an octahedral site without distorting the lattice.

6.2 If the interstitial atom in Problem 6.1 could take the shape of an oblate spheroid, calculate the major and minor diameters of such a spheroid that would just fill the octahedral site in iron without distorting the lattice.

6.3 The diameter of a carbon atom in diamond or graphite is about 1.5Å. Assuming this value for a carbon atom in iron, calculate the two kinds of displacement of iron atoms that would occur when a hard-sphere carbon atom occupies an octahedral site such that all six iron atoms touch the carbon atom, which is assumed to be spherical.

6.4 Fig. 6.3 shows an interstitial carbon atom located in the center of the face of a BCC unit cell. Show that the position at the center of an edge of the unit cell is crystallographically equivalent. That is, the surrounding atoms are at the same distances and in equivalent directions.

6.5 Where in a bicycle spoke is a fatigue failure most likely to occur? Why?

6.6 Assume that, for a 26-inch diameter bicycle wheel, the predicted fatigue life of a spoke is 500,000 cycles; how far can it travel before fatigue failure is likely?

6.7 Sketch two stress-strain curves, one for a ductile material and one for a brittle material. Label the yield stress, the UTS, and the elongation at fracture.

6.8 Although fatigue is a fracture process, the rate of fatigue-crack propagation depends on the resistance to plastic deformation. That is, as the yield stress is decreased, fatigue cracks grow farther per cycle. Considering the mechanism of fatigue crack growth, explain this.

7

PHASE DIAGRAMS

7.1 Soldering and Brazing

Throughout most of the history of bicycles, frames have been made of steel tubes held together by brazed joints. Brazing differs from soldering only in the temperature range in which it is carried out. The term soldering is used for joints made below about 450°C and brazing for those made above that temperature. In both processes the parts to be joined remain solid, and only the filler metal is melted. The molten filler metal is drawn into the crevice of the joint by capillarity before it solidifies. (Capillarity is a phenomenon that depends on differences in interfacial energies; it is why liquids are absorbed by paper tissues and is described in more detail below.) In household plumbing systems made with copper tubing, joints are soldered with a Pb-Sn alloy known as "soft solder." The joints are made with copper fittings that form a sleeve around the tubing and provide a large amount of joint surface along which the molten solder can be drawn, as shown in Fig. 7.1.

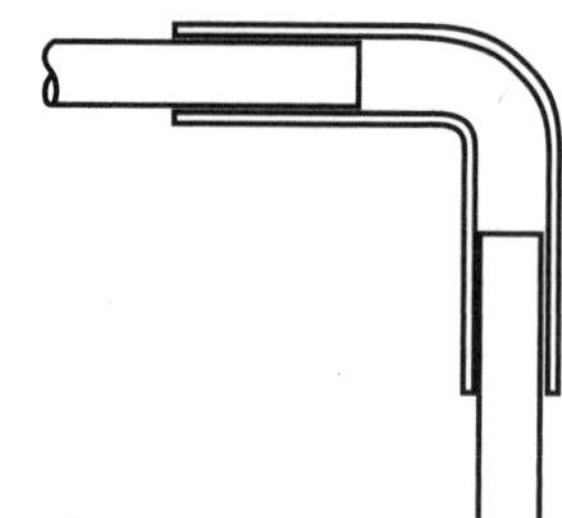

Fig. 7.1 Right-angle connection in a plumbing line to be soldered.

Capillary action can draw solder up into the joint if the solder "wets," or
7010 spreads out on, the surface of the copper. Figure 7.2 shows schematically two extremes of wetting and non-wetting. The extent of wetting can be characterized by the contact angle, θ. When wetting is nearly perfect, θ approaches zero, and the liquid spreads out on the solid, as is needed in soldering or brazing.

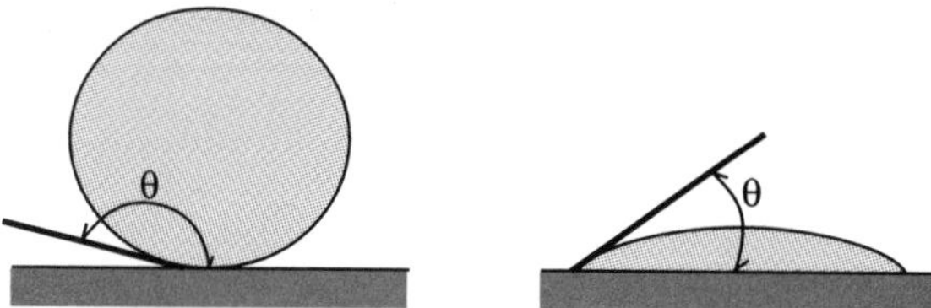

Fig. 7.2 A liquid droplet on a solid plate, showing (a) a small degree of wetting; the contact angle θ is large. (b) A large degree of wetting.

The value of θ depends on the energies of the various surfaces or interfaces involved. Atoms at the interface between two phases are in a higher energy state than atoms in the interior of either phase, because they are partly surrounded by the "wrong" structure and/or composition. The energy of an interface depends on the degree of "wrongness." For example, a metal/metal interface would have a lower energy than a metal/metal-oxide interface, because in the latter case one of the phases would have non-metallic bonding. A liquid-metal/solid-metal interface would be higher in energy than one between two solid metals because of the greater structural dissimilarity in the former.

An equilibrium of forces, similar to that discussed in Section 5.5, must exist along the triple junction where the three phases meet: the solid, liquid, and vapor (air). This equilibrium is depicted in Fig. 7.3.*

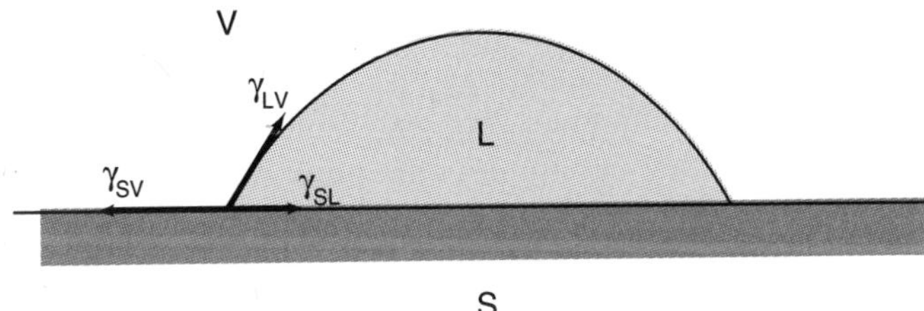

Fig. 7.3 Schematic representation of equilibrium of surface tensions at a solid-liquid-vapor triple junction.

The horizontal equilibrium condition is given by:

$$\gamma_{SV} = \gamma_{SL} + \gamma_{LV} \cos \theta$$

Hence, θ is given by:

$$\cos \theta = (\gamma_{SV} - \gamma_{SL})/\gamma_{LV}$$

For good wetting, θ should approach zero; therefore, cos θ should be as large as possible. That means it is necessary to maximize γ_{SV} and minimize γ_{SL}. (Normally, one cannot do much about γ_{LV} in soldering.**) It can be seen from Fig. 7.3 that γ_{SV} is the force tending to spread the liquid, and γ_{SL} is the force tending to pull it into a ball. In other words, wetting involves the substitution of a low-energy (solid/liquid) interface for a high-energy (solid/vapor) interface.

In order to achieve wetting, it is necessary to raise the energy of the solid surface. Oxidation of a copper surface reduces its γ_{SV}. Therefore, to raise the surface energy, it is necessary to remove the oxide and expose bare metal.

* In this figure only the horizontal components of the surface tension are considered; the vertical components are irrelevant, and to deal with the equilibrium of these components would require one to know how the solid is distorted on the atomic scale at the triple junction.

** This is not the case with water. Here one can use a wetting agent, like a soap, which lowers γ_{LV} and thereby promotes spreading of the water on a solid. Sometimes one wants to retard wetting; waxing an automobile reduces γ_{SV} and increases γ_{SL}, thereby causing water droplets to "ball-up," like solder on an oxidized copper surface.

An interface between the copper oxide and molten solder would have a high energy (γ_{SL}), because the liquid alloy and the oxide are so different chemically. This is the opposite of what is desired for wetting, but this problem is rectified when the oxide is removed. For copper plumbing, one applies hydrochloric acid to the tube and fitting in order to remove most of the oxide. The rest of the oxide is removed by applying a flux, which, when heated by a torch, can entrain the residual oxide in a liquid. This liquid does not mix with the liquid solder, and, being lighter in mass, it is swept away ahead of the solder as it spreads over the clean metal surface. The metal/metal interface formed when a liquid metal spreads on a clean solid metal has a low energy, owing to the ease of metallic-bond formation. Thus, the term (γ_{SV} - γ_{SL}) is maximized by cleaning the oxide off the copper and allowing the molten solder to spread on the cleaned surface.

The other factor in making a successful joint is the clearance between the two metal pieces. The requirement for a small clearance can be explained by a simple exercise in physics, as in Fig. 7.4. At equilibrium the upward capillary force, $2\gamma_{NET}$ x L, must be balanced by the downward force due to gravity, mg,
7080 where m is the mass of the liquid in the column, and g is the gravitational constant. Since m is given by density, ρ, times the volume of liquid in the column, thL, the force balance can be written:

$$\rho\, t\, h\, L\, g = 2\, \gamma_{NET}\, L$$

or

$$h = 2\, \gamma_{NET} / \rho\, g\, t$$

7100 That is, for a given ρ and γ_{NET}, h increases as t decreases. Therefore, one wants the spacing as small as possible while still allowing the liquid to flow into the joint.

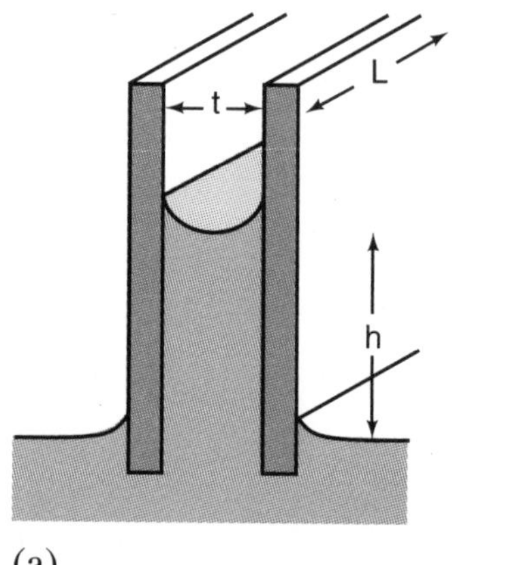

(a)

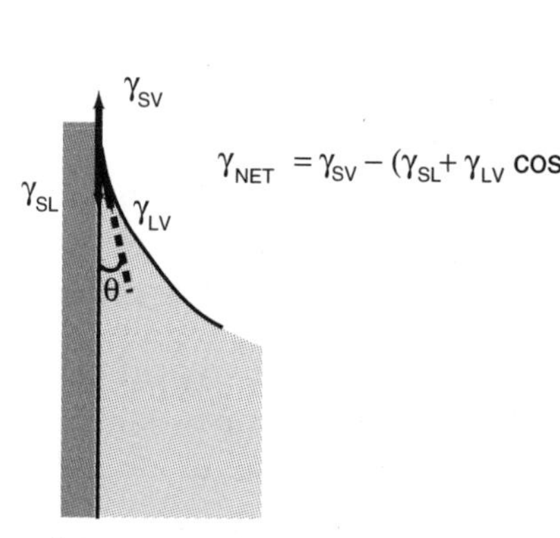

(b)

Fig. 7.4 (a) Two parallel solid plates, spaced t apart, are dipped in a liquid, which rises under the influence of the capillary force, γ_{NET}, given in (b), so that t rises to a height above the surrounding liquid.

7.2 Low-Melting Alloys for Soldering; Phase Diagrams

The most obvious characteristic one would desire for a soldering or brazing alloy is that it melt at the lowest possible temperature, consistent with the required mechanical properties of the joint. The reason for using an alloy in the first place, instead of a pure metal, is that the melting point of a substance can often be lowered by mixing in a second substance. This is employed during winter in the use of road salts, which lower the freezing point of water.

7.2.1 Lowering of the Melting Temperature; Salt-Water Mixtures

A very useful diagram that expresses the lowering of melting points is the *phase diagram.* Parts of the phase diagrams of the salt-water mixtures for the two common road salts are shown in Fig. 7.5. Both these diagrams exhibit what is known as a eutectic reaction, in which a liquid phase freezes at a single temperature to a mixture of two solid phases. This takes place at the *eutectic point,* which is the minimum in the liquid phase field, shown in Fig. 7.5. ("Eutectic" comes from the Greek *eu*, meaning well and *tekein* meaning to melt; thus, a eutectic alloy melts at the lowest possible temperature.

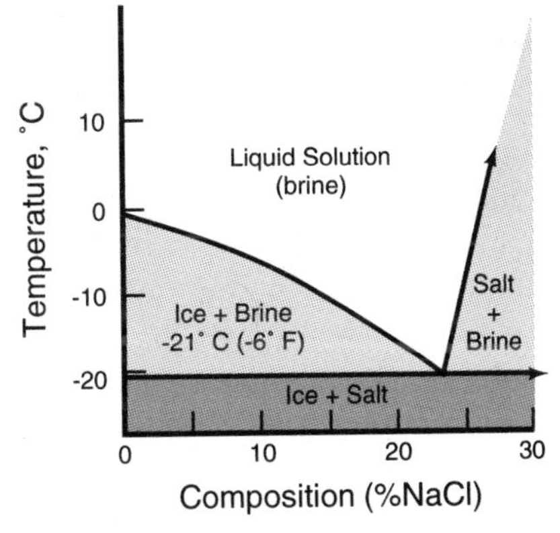

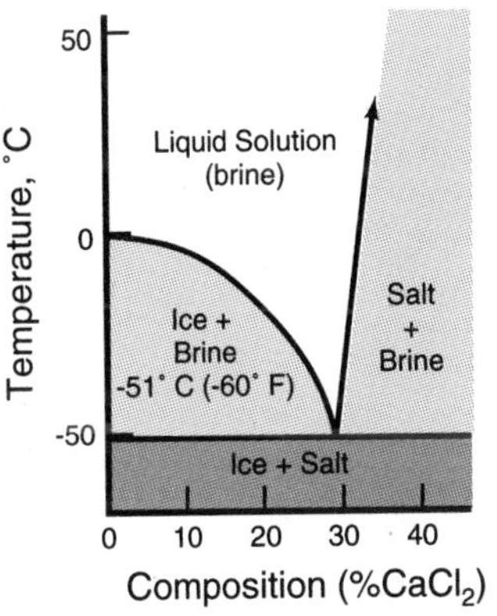

Fig. 7.5 Parts of the phase diagrams for the NaCl-water and $CaCl_2$-water systems.

It is easy to see why calcium chloride has replaced sodium chloride as the road salt of choice wherever its higher cost can be justified. When $CaCl_2$ is applied, slush (i.e., a solid-liquid mixture) would be stable down to a temperature of -60°F (-51°C). That is, the two-phase regions in the phase diagram extend down to that temperature. In contrast, the NaCl-water system becomes completely solid at -6°F (-21°C). No matter how much rocksalt is applied, the mixture would remain solid below that temperature.

The diagrams in Fig. 7.5 are examples of binary phase diagrams. That means they express the equilibrium configuration of two components at different temperatures. (The other relevant thermodynamic variable is pressure, which is taken to be fixed at one atmosphere in most phase diagrams.) The components may be either pure elements or stable compounds, as in Fig. 7.5. (By "stable" it is meant that the compounds do not break down into their constituent elements at the temperatures of interest.) Thus, phase diagrams are simply maps of the temperature and composition regions in which one, or more than one, phase is stable at equilibrium. In such a map, temperature is plotted on the vertical axis, and the composition, in terms of the amount of the second component, is plotted on the horizontal axis. The composition axis is used for two purposes:

1. To express the composition of the alloy, or mixture of components, as a whole. For example, the composition of the eutectic mixture of rocksalt and water is 23.3% NaCl and 76.7% water.

2. To express the composition of the phases present at any given temperature. For example, the NaCl brine that is in equilibrium with ice at -10°C has a composition of 15% NaCl, 85% water.

7.2.2 A Hypothetical Simple-Eutectic Phase Diagram

To illustrate how to "read" a phase diagram and use it to understand the microstructures of binary (i.e., two-component) mixtures, it is useful to consider the hypothetical system depicted in Fig. 7.6. This is a simple eutectic system with three phases: a liquid in which both components A and B are completely miscible, and two solid phases, denoted as α and β. The components could be either pure elements (e.g., metals) or stable compounds (e.g., oxides). The two solid phases are based on the two components. Each solid phase is a solid solution, and each has the crystal structure of the component upon which it is based. Because the discussion here is centered upon metallic alloys, it will be assumed that A and B are both pure metals; however, the principles to be discussed can be applied to any two-component system that forms a simple eutectic.

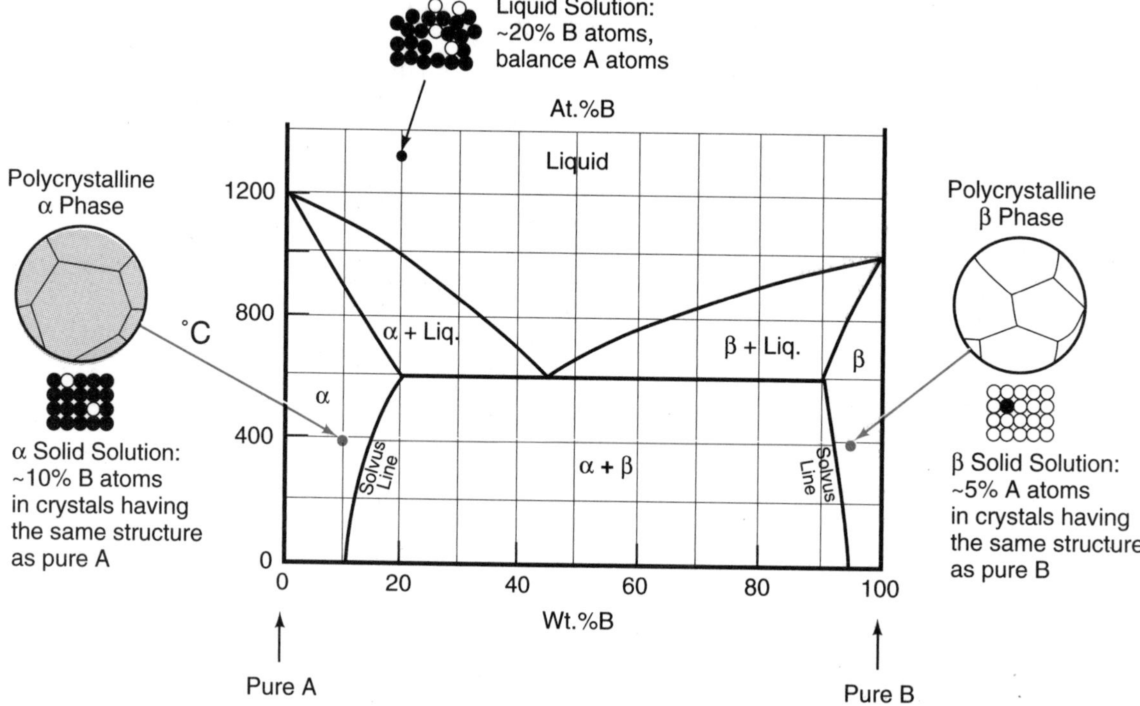

Fig. 7.6 Hypothetical simple-eutectic phase diagram for a system of components A and B.

Figure 7.6 shows that a certain amount of component B can be dissolved in component A to form an α-phase solid solution. Similarly, a β-phase solid solution can be formed by adding A atoms to pure B. This is common in metallic systems because of the flexibility of metallic bonding, in which positive ions are held together by a sea of negative charge comprising the delocalized valence electrons.

It is useful to contrast this with the case of the salt-water mixtures shown in Fig. 7.5. Here, the two solid phases are virtually equivalent to the two components; that is, neither salt nor ice exhibits any appreciable solid solubility for the other. The fact that chloride salts have negligible solubility in ice, and H_2O has negligible solubility in the salts, means simply that the crystal lattice of the salt cannot accommodate water molecules, and that of the ice cannot accomodate the ions of the salt. This should not be surprising. The ionic bonding in salt crystals operates by the electrostatic attraction between positive and negative ions, which are the result of electron transfer from the metal atom to the chlorine atom. In ice, there is no electron transfer, and, therefore, no charged particles. Ice is bonded by a special kind of secondary bond, called a *hydrogen bond*, between water molecules, which are themselves internally bonded by covalent bonding, or the sharing of electrons between hydrogen and oxygen atoms (cf. Appendix 12.1). Because the bonding of these solids is so different, they are incompatible in the solid state and exhibit essentially no mutual solid solubility.

This is in sharp contrast to the case of a metallic alloy, in which both components exhibit similar bonding. In such alloys, the solid solubility of one component for another depends on the size of the constituent atoms and on their degree of chemical similarity. If two metals are sufficiently dissimilar in the configuration of their valence electrons, then they may form *intermetallic compounds.* (See Fig. 7.21 for examples of such compounds in the Cu-Zn alloy system.) In the system depicted in Fig. 7.6, there are no such compounds, and the limitations on the solubility of B in α and A in β would then be mainly the result of the difference in the sizes of the A and B atoms.

It is apparent in Fig. 7.6 that the three single-phase fields are bounded within the diagram by two-phase fields. The boundary line between a one-phase and a two-phase field represents a solubility limit, or the locus of points at which the single phase becomes saturated with solute. For example, the boundary between the α- and α+β-phase fields (called a *solvus line*) represents the saturation of the α phase with component B. Thus, if a crystal of pure A were held at 400°C and B atoms were added to it, this crystal would become saturated if the concentration of B exceeded 15wt%, according to Fig. 7.6. Addition of more B atoms would result in the formation of the β phase. If the overall concentration of B atoms in the alloy were increased, the amount of β phase would increase, and the concentration of B atoms in the α phase would remain the same (i.e., it would be fixed at the saturation value for the temperature 400°C).

Exactly the same kind of argument with regard to the saturation of the β phase at 400°C could be made by starting with pure B at that temperature and continually adding A atoms. The β phase would become saturated with A atoms when the concentration exceeded 8wt%, according to Fig. 7.6. Continuing to add A atoms beyond the saturation point would simply increase the amount of α phase.

The concepts of saturation and of exceeding the solubility limit to form a two- 7250
phase mixture are familiar to anyone who cooks. For example, one can make syrup by dissolving sugar in water, and it is well known that more sugar can be dissolved as the water temperature is increased. Thus, the solubility limit of sugar in the "α" phase (i.e., the syrup) increases with temperature.

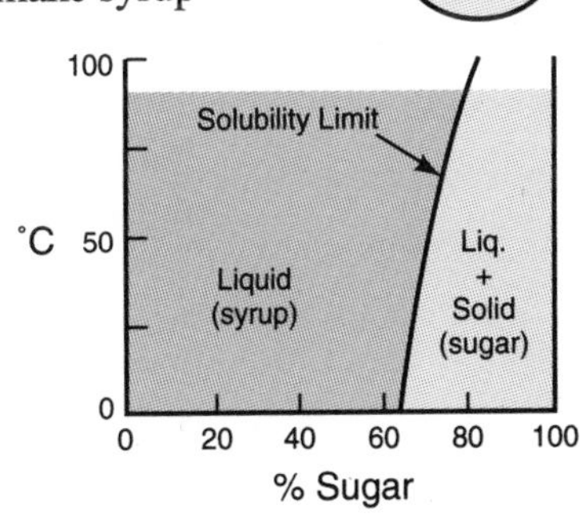

The solubility limit can be exceeded, i.e., the syrup can become supersaturated, by either adding too much sugar at any given temperature or by cooling a syrup of a given sugar concentration. In either case, the excess sugar separates as a second phase; that is, a two-phase region in the sugar-water phase diagram has been entered.

Returning to Fig. 7.6, shown again below as Fig. 7.7, and the discussion of varying the composition of an A-B alloy held at 400°C, it has been established that variations in the B content between 15 and 92wt% affect only the relative amounts of the α and β phases, and not their compositions. That is, for any alloy within this composition range, both phases are saturated with the respective solutes. It should be obvious that, when the alloy composition is just beyond 15% B, it is still almost all α, and, when it has reached, say, 90%B, it must be almost all β. The relative amount of each phase in any alloy containing between 15 and 92%B at equilibrium at 400°C can be found simply by noting the position of the alloy composition along the line in the two-phase region connecting the α and β solubility limits, 15%B and 92%B, respectively. This line is called a *tie line*. The change in the relative amounts of each phase along the tie line at 400°C is illustrated below. (Note that phase diagrams are determined by experimenting with alloys made by weighing out various mixtures of the components. Thus, they are normally expressed in concentrations given in weight percent. This can be converted to atom percent by use of the atomic weights of the components.)

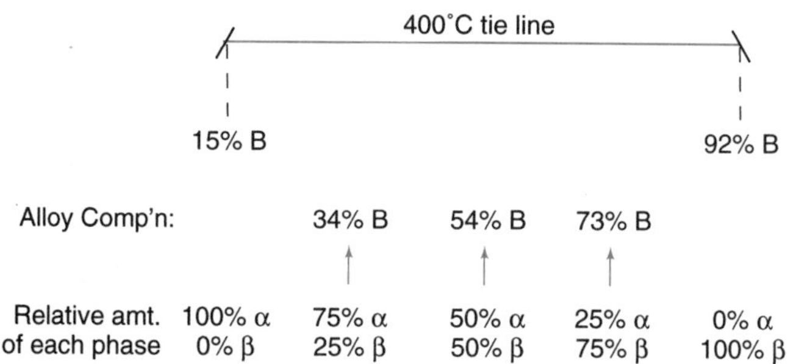

The microstructure, meaning the distribution of phases, of any alloy at any temperature can only be understood if one has reference to the relevant phase diagram. The method of doing this can be illustrated with Fig. 7.7. First, consider the eutectic alloy, A-45%B. This solidifies directly from the liquid state to a two-phase mixture of α and β, according to the phase diagram. The relative amount
7320 of each phase can be found by drawing a tie line just below the eutectic temperature, 600°C; i.e., in the two-phase region. The end points of the tie line are at 20
7350 and 90% B, respectively. To make things clear, consider a 100g sample of the eutectic alloy at 599°C. The amount of β is obtained by calculating how far the
7340 alloy composition (45%B) is along the line from 20 to 90%. Thus,

$$\text{Amount of } \beta = \frac{45-20}{90-20} \text{ times } 100\text{g} = 35.7\text{g}$$

The amount of α must, therefore, be 64.3g. This can be checked by seeing if it is in agreement with the compositions of the alloy and of each phase. The alloy must have 45g of B in it, and

$$\text{Amount of B in } \beta \text{ phase} = 0.90 \text{ x } 35.7\text{g} = 32.1\text{g},$$
$$\text{Amount of B in } \alpha \text{ phase} = 0.20 \text{ x } 64.3\text{g} = 12.9\text{g}$$

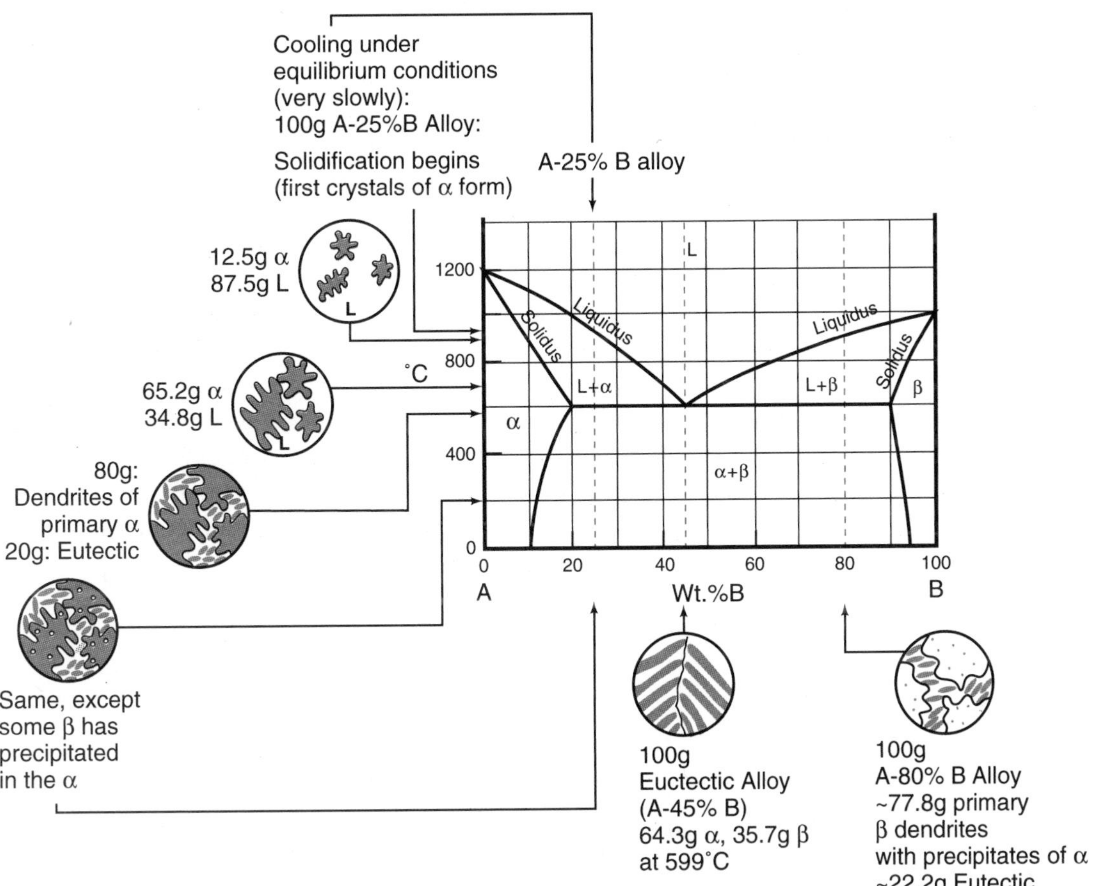

Fig. 7.7 Hypothetical A-B phase diagram, illustrating microstructures of various alloys.

Since the sum of the amounts of B in each phase equals 45g, the calculation is correct. This calculation follows the *lever rule*, so called because it is reminiscent of a lever balanced on a fulcrum (represented by the alloy composition):

α	← 25 →	Alloy	← 45 →	β
64.3g		100g		35.7g

That is,

$$\alpha \text{ fraction} = \frac{45}{25 + 45} = 45/70 = 0.643$$

$$\beta \text{ fraction} = \frac{25}{25 + 45} = 25/70 = 0.357$$

This procedure can be used to analyze the evolution of microstructure during the cooling of an alloy of A-25%B from the liquid state, as shown schematically in Fig. 7.7. Again, assume 100g of alloy. The alloy first enters the two-phase region when it cools below 920°C. Under equilibrium conditions (i.e., very slow cooling), crystals of α would nucleate in the liquid and would grow in the form of *dendrites,* meaning a branched structure. (Dendritic is from the Greek and means "tree-like.") The composition of this first-formed α would be 10%B, as given by drawing a tie line at 920°C.

The lever rule can be applied at lower temperatures, say 900 and 700°C, to follow the course of solidification.

At 900°C,

Composition of α = 11%B

Composition of liquid = 27%B

$$\text{Amount of } \alpha = \frac{27\text{-}25}{27\text{-}11} \text{ x } 100\text{g} = 12.5\text{g}$$

Amount of liquid = 87.5g

At 700°C,

Composition of α = 17%B

Composition of liquid = 40%B

$$\text{Amount of } \alpha = \frac{40\text{-}25}{40\text{-}17} \text{ x } 100\text{g} = 65.2\text{g}$$

Amount of liquid = 34.8g

It is apparent that the concentration of B in both the solid and liquid increases as solidification proceeds. This does not violate the conservation of matter, because the solid remains much lower in B than the initial liquid (i.e., the alloy as a whole). The solid and liquid compositions are seen to follow the lateral boundaries of the two-phase region, denoted as the *liquidus* and *solidus* lines, respectively, in Fig. 7.7. When the eutectic temperature, 600°C, is reached, the amount of liquid remaining has fallen to

$$\frac{25\text{-}20}{45\text{-}20}(100) = 20\text{g}$$

and the composition of this liquid has reached 45%B, which is the eutectic composition. This eutectic liquid at 600°C must then undergo the eutectic transformation into the two solid phases, α and β, simultaneously. Afterwards, the microstructure comprises 80g of primary α dendrites, formed above 600°C, and 20g of the eutectic mixture.

The total amount of α in the A-25%B alloy at this point includes the 80g of primary α and the α in the eutectic. The latter was previously calculated to be 64.3% of the total eutectic, which would mean that there is 0.643 x 20g = 12.9g of α in the eutectic, for a total of 92.9g of α in the alloy.

This calculation can be checked using a tie line in the two-phase region just below the eutectic temperature:

7430

$$\text{Amount of } \alpha \text{ in the alloy} = \frac{90\text{-}25}{90\text{-}20} \text{ x } 100\text{g} = 92.9\text{g}$$

Because the solvus lines slope outward below the eutectic temperature, the relative amounts of α and β at equilibrium must change as the temperature is further reduced. The primary α, which contained 20%B at the eutectic temperature, can
7440 hold only 12%B at 200°C, for example. Therefore, some β phase must precipitate in the dendrites of primary α, indicated schematically in Fig. 7.7.

The eutectic must also adjust itself somewhat. A eutectic alloy at 200°C would comprise

$$\text{Amount of } \alpha = \frac{94\text{-}45}{94\text{-}12} = 60\%$$

$$\text{Amount of } \beta = 40\%$$

This is in contrast with the 64.3%α, 35.7%β in the eutectic just below the eutectic temperature. Thus, the β regions in the eutectic mixture grow a bit at the expense of the neighboring α regions. This is accomplished by diffusion of A and B atoms so as to adjust the composition and amount of each phase.

So far the discussion has been concerned with a eutectic alloy and a hypoeutectic alloy, "hypo" meaning "less than." It remains only to consider a typical hypereutectic alloy, and the microstructure of one is shown schematically in Fig. 7.7. This A-80%B (or B-20%A) alloy would have

$$\frac{80\text{-}45}{90\text{-}45} = 77.8\% \text{ primary } \beta\text{, and } 22.2\% \text{ eutectic}$$ 7450

just below the eutectic temperature. Upon further cooling, some α would precipitate in the primary β, and the compositions and amounts of α and β in the eutectic would adjust themselves, as in the case of the hypoeutectic alloy.

The principles learned by consideration of the hypothetical eutectic alloy can now be put to use on a common alloy system used for soldering.

7.2.3 The Lead-Tin System (Soft Solder)

Alloys of lead and tin are used as solder for electronic equipment, plumbing, roofing, and other applications. (These alloys are not strong enough for holding the tubes of bicycle frames together; alloys for this purpose will be considered later.) The phase diagram for this system is shown in Fig. 7.8.

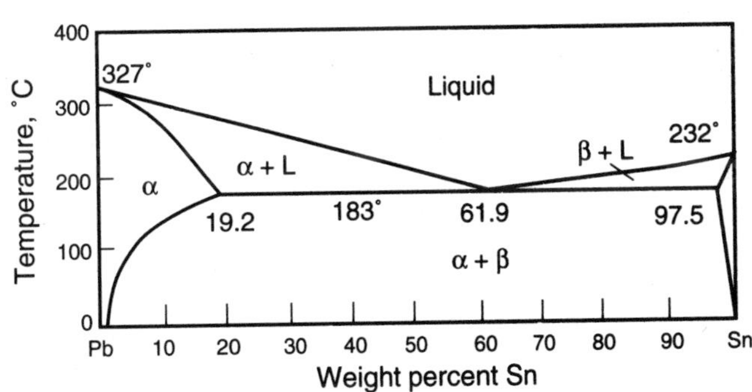

Fig. 7.8 The Pb-Sn phase diagram (From *Metals Handbook,* 8th ed., ASM, 1973, p. 330).

As in Figs. 7.6 and 7.7, this is a simple eutectic system; the addition of tin to lead lowers the melting temperature, as does the addition of lead to tin. The eutectic point is at 61.9% tin. This composition would be selected for soldering electronic equipment or copper tubing, because it requires the minimum temperature for melting, and it freezes at a constant temperature. The latter fact is illustrated schematically in the cooling curves shown in Fig. 7.9. (A cooling curve is determined by placing a thermocouple in a molten alloy and using it, in conjunction with a voltage-measuring device and a strip-chart recorder (cf. Section 2.6), to record the temperature *vs.* time as the alloy is allowed to cool to room temperature.)

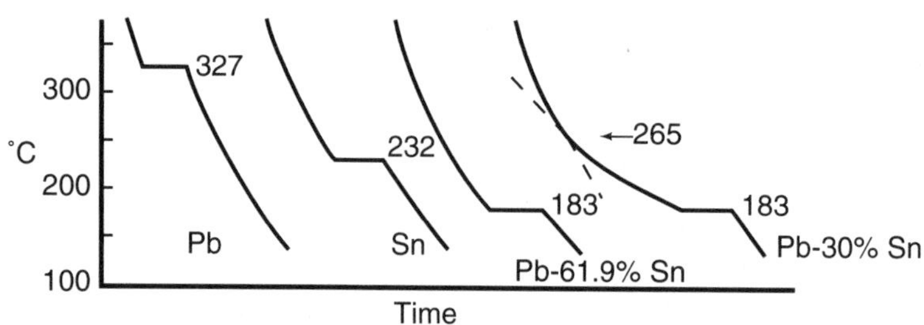

Fig. 7.9 A schematic set of cooling curves for the indicated compositions.

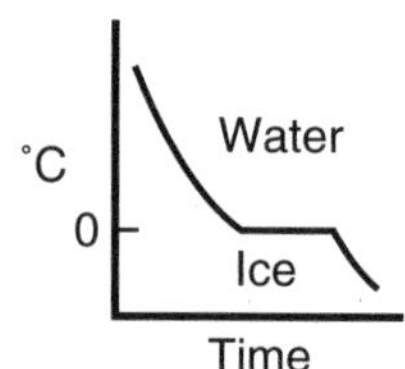

Three of the cooling curves in Fig. 7.9 have a similar shape. Each has a horizontal portion, above which one finds a smoothly varying cooling curve of a liquid, and below which is a smoothly varying curve for a solid material. This is the kind of cooling curve found for any pure substance, like water for example.

The solid-liquid equilibrium for water occurs at a fixed temperature: 0°C. When water is cooled to 0°C, even though heat continues to flow out, the temperature must remain constant from the time that ice begins to form until all of the liquid is gone. The cooling curves for lead and tin both follow this behavior, as does the one for the eutectic alloy.

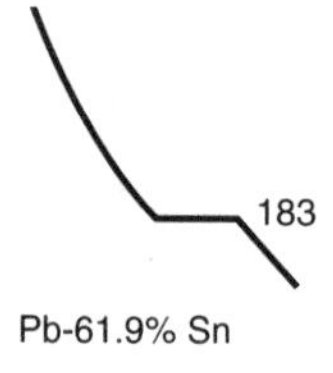

The microstructure of the solidified eutectic alloy is shown in Fig. 7.10. It consists of roughly plate-like, or lamellar, regions of the (dark-etching) Pb-rich phase, here called α, in a matrix of the light-etching, tin-rich β phase. This alloy was 100% liquid at just above 183°C. After the temperature of the liquid fell to 183°C, it remained constant during the liquid-to-solid transformation, even though heat continued to flow out of the container that held the alloy. The reason why the temperature did not fall during freezing is that the release of the latent heat of fusion was just sufficient to balance the heat loss from the container. The thermodynamic basis for this special behavior of pure elements and eutectic alloys will be discussed later, but it should be obvious why this freezing at constant temperature is ideal for electronics and copper tubing. It is necessary for the parts being soldered to be held in a fixed position until the solder is completely solidified, and one would like this to be finished as quickly as possible.

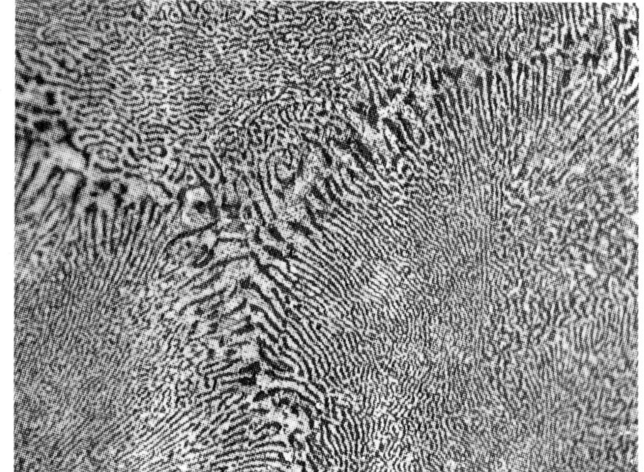

Fig. 7.10 Microstructure of the solidified eutectic alloy Pb-61.9%Sn comprising lamellae of α in a matrix of β.

A different kind of behavior is desired for solders used for roofing or filling the large joints in cast-iron waste pipes. Here, an extended range of freezing is useful, because it is necessary to work the solder into large gaps with hand tools, instead of having it flow in by capillary action. The cooling curve for the Pb-30%Sn alloy exhibits this desired behavior. It shows a decrease in slope at about 265°C, which corresponds to the release of the heat of fusion when the first solid begins to form. (This is, in fact, how the point on the liquidus line was determined experimentally.) Thus, the 30% tin alloy starts to freeze at 265°C, but it remains "mushy" down to 183°C, when the remaining liquid freezes at the eutectic temperature.

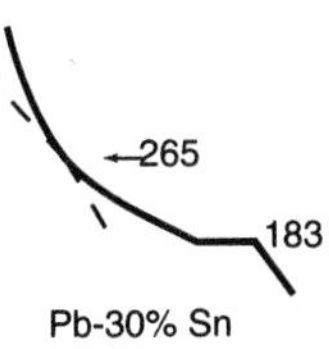

The cooling behavior and the resulting microstructure of the 30%Sn alloy is correlated with the phase diagram in Fig. 7.11. At 300°C the alloy is completely molten. As noted earlier, solidification starts at 265°C. Since the system has now entered a two-phase region, a tie line can be drawn at 265°C; this reveals that the composition of the first solid (α) that forms has about 10% Sn. When the temperature has fallen to 250°C, the amount of α has increased and the amount of liquid has decreased. The tie line at this temperature shows that the α should now contain about 12% Sn, and the liquid should contain about 37% tin. This means that, as solidification proceeds, the tin is being partitioned between the solid and liquid. That is, the freezing solid has much less tin than the original liquid, and the liquid becomes enriched in tin as the solid forms.

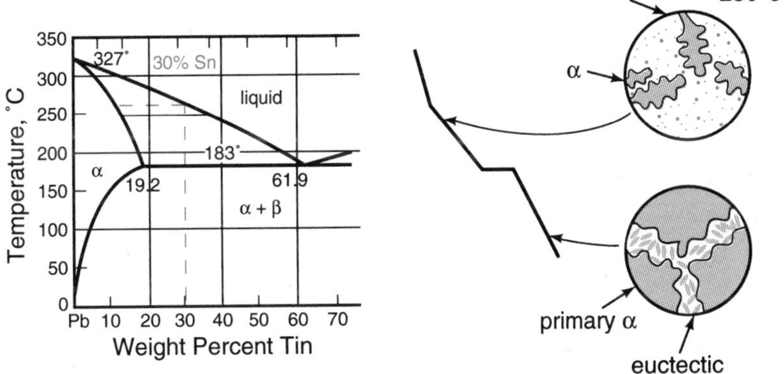

Fig. 7.11 The correlation of the phase diagram, the cooling curve, and the microstructures of the Pb-30%Sn alloy during cooling from the melt.

The relative amounts of solid and liquid in equilibrium at 250°C can be found by applying the lever rule:

$$\text{Relative amount of } \alpha \text{ at } 250°\text{C} = \frac{37\text{-}30}{37\text{-}12} = 28\%$$

$$\text{Relative amount of liquid at } 250°\text{C} = \frac{30\text{-}12}{37\text{-}12} = 72\%$$

When the temperature has fallen to 200°C, the relative amount of α has increased to (58-30)/(58-18) = 70%, because the α now contains 18% Sn and the liquid contains 58% Sn. Finally, when the temperature has reached 183°C, the composition of the liquid has reached 61.9%, which is the eutectic composition. This liquid must now solidify at a constant temperature into the two-phase solid mixture (cf. Fig. 7.10). After this has occurred, the microstructure can be described as having two *constituents.* One is *primary* α, or the α that solidified before the eutectic reaction, and the other is the two-phase eutectic. The lever rule is used to find the relative amounts of each as follows:

$$\text{Relative amount of primary } \alpha = \frac{61.9\text{-}30}{61.9\text{-}19.2} = 75\%$$

$$\text{Relative amount of eutectic constituent} = \frac{30\text{-}19.2}{61.9\text{-}19.2} = 25\%$$

The relative amount of α in the eutectic constituent can be found by treating the eutectic as a separate alloy having an overall composition of 61.9% Sn, as follows:

$$\text{Relative amount of } \alpha \text{ in the eutectic} = \frac{97.5\text{-}61.9}{97.5\text{-}19.2} = 45\%$$

The other 55% of the eutectic is, of course, β.

By making a large enough set of Pb-Sn alloys, one can use the method of cooling curves to trace out the complete liquidus curves for both hypoeutectic and hypereutectic alloys. It would also be found that, if the cooling rate is slow enough to maintain equilibrium conditions at each temperature, the eutectic reaction, signalled by the constant-temperature transformation at 183°C, is found only in the range 19.2% to 97.5%Sn. Therefore, a horizontal line is drawn between these compositions at this temperature (i.e., the eutectic temperature) as the lower boundary of the liquid+solid regions (the upper boundaries of which are the liquidus curves).

So far it has been explained how the two liquidus curves and the eutectic line are determined by the method of cooling curves. The solidus curves can be found in the same way. Figure 7.12 shows schematically how the cooling curve for a Pb-10%Sn alloy should look. Within the two-phase region the cooling rate is retarded by the emission of the heat of fusion by the increasing volume of solid. This produces the decrease in cooling rate at the liquidus temperature. The cooling rate becomes faster again when all the liquid is gone. Thus, the boundaries of both the liquid+α and the liquid+β regions can be determined by means of cooling curves. This method is called *thermal analysis.*

The two solid phases that form in the lead-tin system are called *terminal solid solutions,* which means that they are solid solutions based on each of the two pure components. Thus, the α phase is a solid solution based on FCC lead, and the β phase is a solid solution based on tin, which can have one of two crystal structures, tetragonal or diamond cubic, depending on whether the temperature is above or below 18°C, as explained in Appendix 7.1. The α and β phase fields can be interpreted in the following way: Lead has a solid solubility for tin that varies with temperature; the maximum solid solubility occurs at the eutectic temperature. At any temperature between 183°C and the melting point of Pb, any addition of Sn to the α phase beyond the composition indicated by the solidus line would result in the formation of a liquid phase in the formerly solid alloy. At any temperature below 183°C, excessive addition of tin to the α phase would result in the formation of the Sn-rich β phase, mixed in with the α.

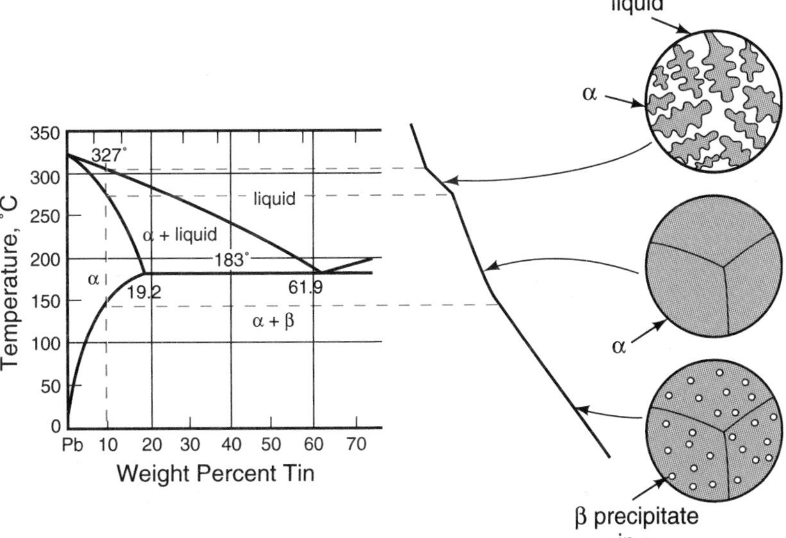

Fig. 7.12 The Pb-rich portion of the Pb-Sn phase diagram, showing the location of the 10%Sn alloy. A cooling curve for this alloy, showing the changes in slope at the liquidus and solidus temperatures, is correlated with representations of microstructures at several temperatures, assuming equilibrium conditions.

The extent of solid solubility of one element in another depends not only on the degree of chemical compatibility, but also on the sizes of the ion cores involved. For a given element, the size of the ion core actually varies, depending on what kinds of atoms surround it and what the crystal lattice is. However, one can get a rough idea from the closest spacing of the atoms in a crystal of the pure element. For lead, this is about 3.5Å, and for tin, it is either 3.0 or 2.8Å, depending on which crystal structure is considered (cf. Appendix 7.1). The point is that there is at least 14% difference in atomic size; this is near the limit beyond which solid solubility would be quite restricted. From the phase diagram, which shows a much larger solubility of tin in lead than *vice versa,* one might surmise that the size difference between the ion cores is less when the lattice is FCC than when the lattice is tetragonal or diamond cubic. However, the solubility difference could also be the result of chemical factors, such as different preferences for metallic *vs.* non-metallic bonding on the part of lead *vs.* tin.

If the 10% Sn alloy were cooled so slowly as to maintain equilibrium, the β phase would begin to precipitate in the solid α once the solvus line was crossed. This is represented schematically in Fig. 7.12 for the temperature of 100°C. In principle, the location of the solvus line could be determined by thermal analysis, because there is a heat of transformation associated with the transition from α to α+β. In practice, this heat effect is too small to be detected. More important, however, is the fact that solid-state transitions involving diffusion of atoms in a crystalline structure are always much slower than the transitions that involve diffusion in liquids. Therefore, the formation of β in α during cooling is likely to be kinetically retarded and thus not likely to occur at the equilibrium solvus temperature of a given alloy, even during very slow cooling. For this reason, the solvus is usually determined by heating specimens of a given composition to a series of temperatures in the vicinity of the expected transition, allowing each specimen to come to equilibrium at the temperature selected for it, and then quenching rapidly (e.g., in cold water) to "freeze in" the microstructure that existed at the selected equilibration temperature. The quenched specimens can then be examined metallographically or by x-ray analysis* to determine the temperature at which the β phase (formerly present) dissolves completely in the α. Obviously, a series of compositions would be needed to make a determination of the solvus line, and this method can only be carried out at temperatures high enough for the Sn atoms to diffuse out of the β phase in reasonable times. This makes the low-temperature portions of a solvus line very difficult to determine. The solvus of the β-phase field is, of course, determined in exactly the same way.

It should be clear that the choice of which component to put on the left in a phase diagram and which to put on the right is completely arbitrary, as is the choice of which phase to call α and which to call β. Thus, one must speak of α and β and hypo- and hyper eutectic only in the context of a particular representation of the phase diagram of an alloy system. One can find lead on the left in some handbooks of phase diagrams and tin on the left in others.

In principle, given the appropriate data, a phase diagram could be calculated using the laws of thermodynamics. One general rule is that between any two neighboring single-phase regions there must be a two-phase region comprising these two phases. The extent of this two-phase region may degenerate to a single point. For example, for a single component this occurs at the melting temperature, where the solid and liquid phases are in equilibrium. At a binary eutectic point, three phases are in equilibrium. More generally, the two-phase regions extend over substantial areas of the phase diagram, such as those that occur above and below the eutectic temperature in Pb-Sn alloys.

Example 7.1

Q. What is the latent heat of fusion, e.g., for the liquid-to-solid transformation of lead, in the context of thermodynamics?

A. The latent heat of fusion is the difference in enthalpy between the liquid and solid states, usually expressed on the basis of one mole of material (i.e., Avogadro's number, N_0, of atoms, or 6.02×10^{23} atoms). From the definition of enthalpy (cf. Section 6.1), H=E+pV, the change in enthalpy on freezing at a constant pressure would be given by

$$\Delta H = \Delta E + p\Delta V$$

The volume change would be only a few percent, so the $p\Delta V$ term at one atmosphere of pressure would be negligible. Therefore, the heat of fusion is essentially equal to the total binding energy of N_0 atoms in a crystal of the solid (cf. Fig. 2.7). This heat is released during freezing, and it must be put back into the solid in order to melt it.

---

* Because the β phase has a different crystal structure from the α phase, its x-ray diffraction pattern would show lines (i.e., diffracted beams) at angles different from those for the α phase.

Example 7.2

Q. (a) At what temperature does a Pb-40%Sn alloy begin to solidify upon cooling from the melt?

(b) How much solid is present (under equilibrium conditions) at 200°C?

(c) How much of the alloy is primary α at room temperature?

A. (a) From the phase diagram in Fig. 7.8, it can be seen that the liquidus line is crossed in a 40%Sn alloy at just below 250°C.

(b) The relative amount of α at 200°C is given by the lever rule as

$$\text{Relative amount of } \alpha \text{ at } 200°\text{C} = \frac{58\text{-}40}{58\text{-}18} = 45\%$$

(c) The total amount of primary α just below the eutectic temperature is given by

$$\text{Total primary } \alpha \text{ at } 182°\text{C} = \frac{61.9\text{-}40}{61.9\text{-}19.2} = 51\%$$

However, during cooling to room temperature, some β will precipitate in the α. The amount that should precipitate can be calculated as follows: Consider the primary α as a separate alloy with 19.2% Sn at 180°C. Upon cooling to room temperature, where the solid solubility of tin in lead is taken to be about 1%, and that of lead in tin to be zero, this alloy should have the following amount of β:

$$\text{Relative amount of } \beta = \frac{19.2\text{-}1}{100\text{-}1} = 18.4\%$$

Therefore, the remaining amount of primary α is given by

$$\text{Amount of primary } \alpha = \frac{100\text{-}18.4}{100} \times 51 = 41.6\% \text{ (of the total alloy)}$$

7.2.4 Microstructures of Hypoeutectic Lead-Tin Alloys

As noted earlier, solids tend to crystallize from the melt in the form of branched particles called dendrites. This is observable in transparent crystals, like succronitrile crystallizing in acetone, an example of which is shown in Fig. 7.13(a). Dendritic solidification can also be observed on surfaces of metal castings, as exemplified by Fig. 7.13(b). The primary phases (α or β) that form during solidification of Pb-Sn alloys would also follow this behavior. Therefore, the microstructures of as-cast alloys must be interpreted in this light. That is, the primary phase revealed in a metallographic section is a two-dimensional cut through a number of dendrites.

The reason for the development of this kind of solid/liquid interface in a hypoeutectic Pb-Sn alloy is that the α contains much less tin than the liquid from which it forms. Therefore, in order for the α to grow, tin must be transported away into the liquid by diffusion. If the α/liquid interface remained planar, the tin would tend to pile up along the interface and slow it down. The rate at which tin is transported away from the interface depends on the concentration gradient of the tin in the liquid alongside the solid/liquid interface. An example of such a concentration gradient is shown in Fig. 7.14(a) for the case of a 30%Sn alloy

solidifying at 250°C, where the tie line gives the solid and liquid compositions as 12 and 37%Sn, respectively (cf. Fig 7.11). (This fixes the tin concentrations on either side of the solid/liquid interface, where local equilibrium can almost always be assumed.) If a spike were to develop on the interface, the concentration gradient of tin at the tip of the spike would become much steeper, as shown in Fig. 7.14(b), and the diffusion of tin away from the tip would be correspondingly faster than from the planar interface.

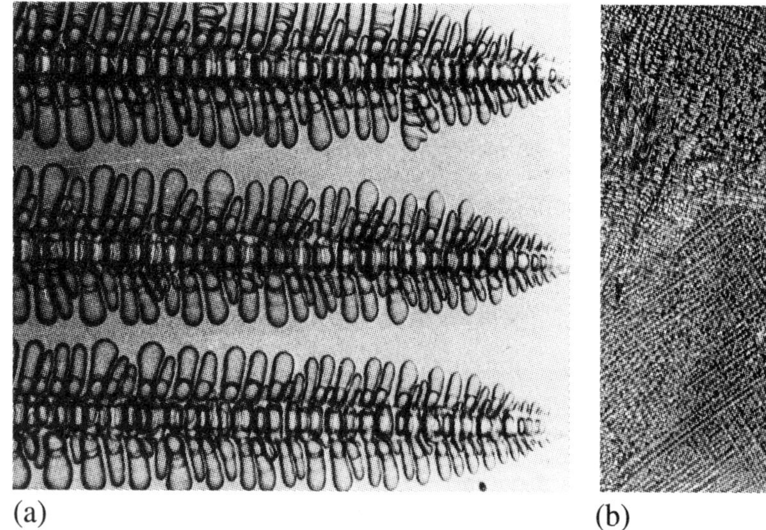

(a)

(b)

Fig. 7.13 (a) Dendrites formed during precipitation of succronitrile in acetone. (Prof. R. Trivedi, Iowa State Univ.) (b) Dendritic solidification observed on the surface of a Cu-Sn casting. (P. Villanueva, Univ. of Penn.)

In effect, at the tip of a spike, the tin can be rejected into a larger volume of liquid. Therefore, a spike can grow faster than the rate of advance of the planar interface, because the rate of advance is controlled by the rate of diffusion of tin in the liquid. As the spike thickens, it develops smaller spikes along its length for 7560 the same reason. (When a pure substance, like water, is supercooled, an analogous argument can be made in terms of the removal of the heat of fusion; here, the tip of the spike projects into a liquid that is cooler than along a planar solid/liquid interface. Therefore, heat flow out of the tip would be faster, and the tip would grow out ahead of the planar interface.)

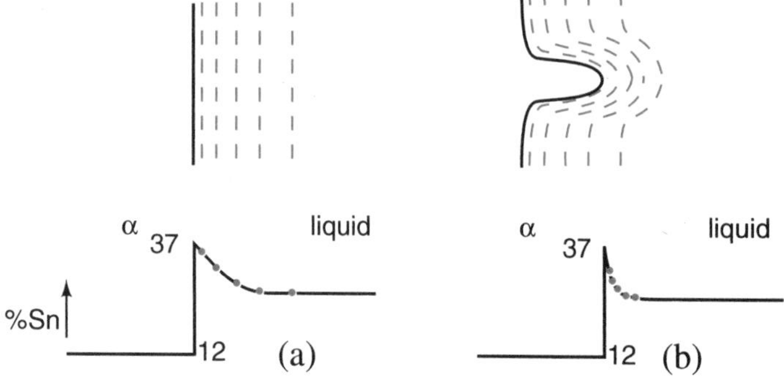

Fig. 7.14 (a) Schematic representation of the concentration gradient at a planar interface between solid α and the liquid in a Pb-30%Sn alloy freezing at 250°C. The dashed lines are lines of constant concentration and are an analog of a contour map. (b) The steeper concentration gradient at the tip of a spike (representing the beginning of a dendrite).

The microstructure of a slowly solidified Pb-30%Sn alloy is shown in Fig. 7.15. It shows sections of dendrites of primary α surrounded by the eutectic constituent. The primary α contains small particles of β that precipitated during cooling between 183°C and room temperature. The eutectic appears different from that formed in the eutectic alloy (cf. Fig. 7.10), although it is clearly a two-phase constituent. The eutectic in Fig. 7.15 appears to contain less α and more β than it should. The reason for this is the influence of the primary α. It can only be understood by first considering why the microstructure in the eutectic alloy in Fig. 7.10 is lamellar.

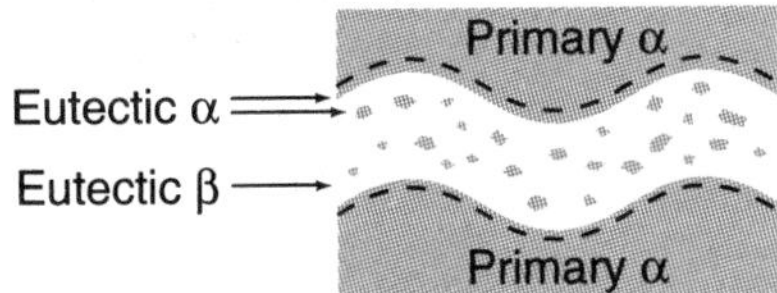

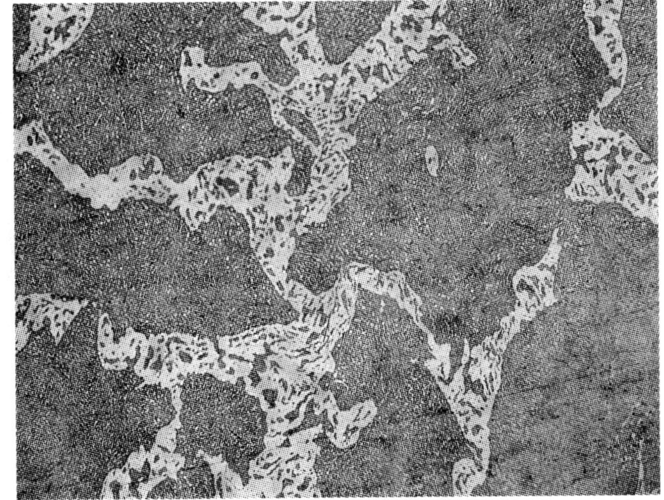

Fig. 7.15 Microstructure of a slowly solidified Pb-30%Sn alloy. The dark areas are primary α dendrites, which contain small particles of precipitated β. The dendrites are surrounded by the two-phase eutectic.

The key factor is that, in the eutectic reaction: liquid—>α+β, both solid phases must form simultaneously. This involves large mass transport in the liquid, because the α phase can hold only 19.2%Sn, and the β phase can hold only 2.5%Pb, whereas the liquid from which they form contains 61.9%Sn and 38.1%Pb. Thus, the simultaneous formation of α and β requires an enormous redistribution of Pb and Sn by diffusion in the liquid. If the alloy is losing heat at all rapidly, then the diffusion distance must be short. This is accomplished by the lamellar formation of α and β depicted schematically in Fig. 7.16, in which the redistribution of the Sn from the regions becoming α to those becoming β at the solid/liquid interface is indicated by the arrows. The flux of Pb atoms goes in the opposite directions. The same kind of short diffusion distance could be accomplished if the α phase took the form of needles instead of plates (lamellae). In the present case, plates are necessary owing to the large volume fraction of α in the eutectic.

α
β
α
β
α
β
α
β
Liquid

Fig. 7.16 Schematic representation of freezing of a lamellar Pb-Sn eutectic; the flux of Sn in the liquid is indicated by arrows; the flux of Pb is in the opposite directions.

Another important factor in the morphology of a eutectic microstructure is the direction of heat flow. Figure 7.16 is drawn with the assumption that the solid/liquid interface moves left to right, which means that heat flow is assumed to be unidirectional toward the left. The eutectic microstructure shown in Fig. 7.10 can be interpreted as the result of heat flow in the direction normal to the plane of the photomicrograph. That is, the solid/liquid interface can be imagined as moving toward the viewer and to be divided into cells, within each of which the α/β lamellae are aligned. Thus, the region of the microstructure illustrated in Fig. 7.10 shows the juncture of three of these cells.

Returning to Fig. 7.15, it is seen that the presence of primary α dendrites perturbs the normal eutectic solidification. The reason for this is two-fold. First, the advance of a solid/liquid interface during solidification of the interdendritic liquid cannot be unidirectional because of the convoluted shape of this liquid region. Second, because there is α already present, the liquid tends to phase-separate by "plating-out" some of the eutectic α as a thin layer on the primary α dendrites, while the remaining eutectic α and the eutectic β solidify in a somewhat disorganized manner farther away from the surfaces of the dendrites. (See inset, Fig. 7.15.) The plating-out of one phase of a eutectic on a pre-existing primary phase is known as *eutectic divorcement.*

The foregoing discussion of eutectic morphology should illustrate the fact that the phase diagram cannot be used to predict morphology. It only deals with the amounts and compositions of phases at equilibrium at a given temperature in a given alloy. This caveat cannot be stressed too strongly. It is easy to depart from equilibrium during solidification, because solid-state diffusion is necessary to maintain the equilibrium composition of a solid phase as temperature falls. This fact is illustrated very well in an alloy of Pb-10%Sn, in which one would not expect to find any eutectic microstructure, judging from the phase diagram (cf. Fig. 7.12). The microstructure of a cast sample of this alloy is shown in Fig. 7.17; there is a small amount of eutectic present, even though the last liquid should have disappeared well above 200°C. The explanation of this non-equilibrium solidification can be made with the aid of Fig. 7.18.

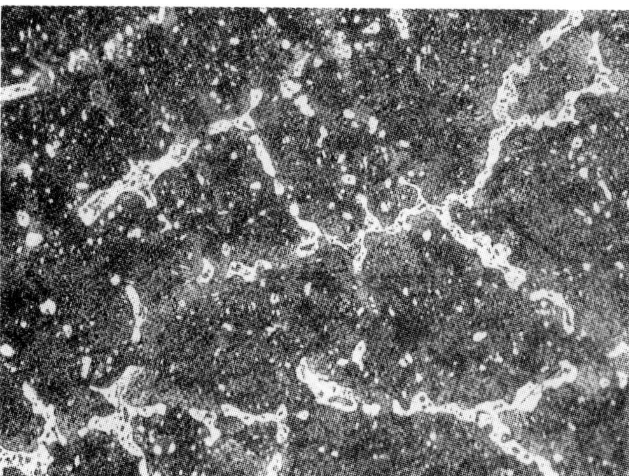

Fig. 7.17 The microstructure of a cast Pb-10%Sn alloy.

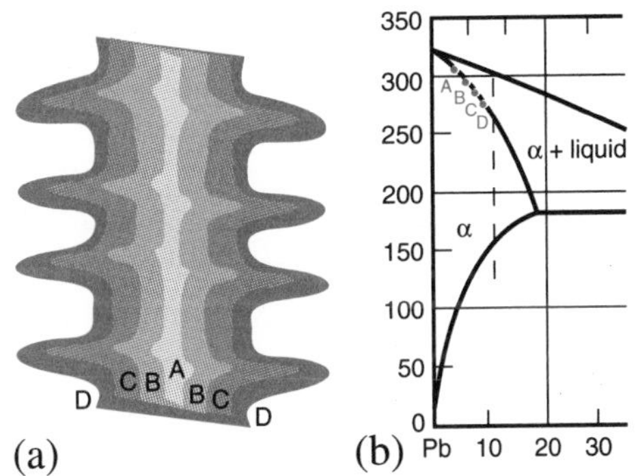

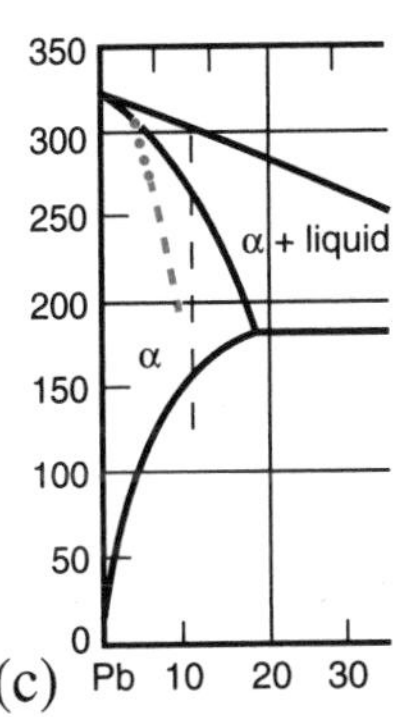

Fig. 7.18 (a) A portion of an α dendrite showing the positions of the solid/liquid interface at the temperatures indicated on the solidus curve in (b). (c) The non-equilibrium solidus, which represents the average composition of the α, resulting from the insufficiency in the time for diffusion in the solid α.

A portion of an α dendrite is shown schematically in Fig. 7.18(a), in which the shaded regions are meant to indicate the positions of the solid/liquid interface at four different temperatures. These temperatures are shown by the points on the solidus curve of the phase diagram shown in Fig. 7.18(b), which also correspond to the equilibrium α composition at each of these temperatures. It is obvious that, in order for the α dendrite to maintain the equilibrium composition as it cools, there must be time allowed for Sn to diffuse in from the surface to raise the Sn level in the core of the dendrite. If the time allowed during solidification is insufficient, then the average composition of the dendrite must be lower than the phase diagram would indicate at any given temperature below point A in Fig. 7.18(b). This would result in the *non-equilibrium solidus*, which is a plot of the average dendrite composition *vs.* temperature, shown in Fig. 7.18(c). The effect is that some liquid still remained at 183°C, and this underwent the eutectic reaction.

Essentially what has occurred is that the liquid remained too rich in Sn, because the dendrite grew without absorbing its full share of the Sn. This excess Sn concentration in the liquid continued to increase as more and more α formed; finally the temperature reached 183°C and there was still some liquid present, the Sn concentration of which had reached 61.9%Sn. The eutectic reaction was the inevitable result.

7.2.5 The Microstructure of a Hypereutectic Pb-Sn Alloy

All of the foregoing regarding a hypoeutectic alloy applies to a hypereutectic alloy. This follows from the fact that the designations are arbitrary; the phase diagram can be switched to its mirror image without loss of validity. Thus, little need be said further about the Sn-rich side of the Pb-Sn system. Most of it can be expressed by the microstructure of a cast Sn-10%Pb alloy, shown in Fig. 7.19.

The large white areas are the arms of primary β dendrites. Between the dendrite arms is a divorced eutectic in which the eutectic β has largely plated out on the β dendrites, leaving the α to form a coarse lamellar structure with the remaining β. This alloy would not be used for soldering, because tin is more expensive than lead, and because the volume change associated with the allotropic transformation in tin (cf. Appendix 7.1) could compromise the mechanical stability of an alloy with such large amount of tin.

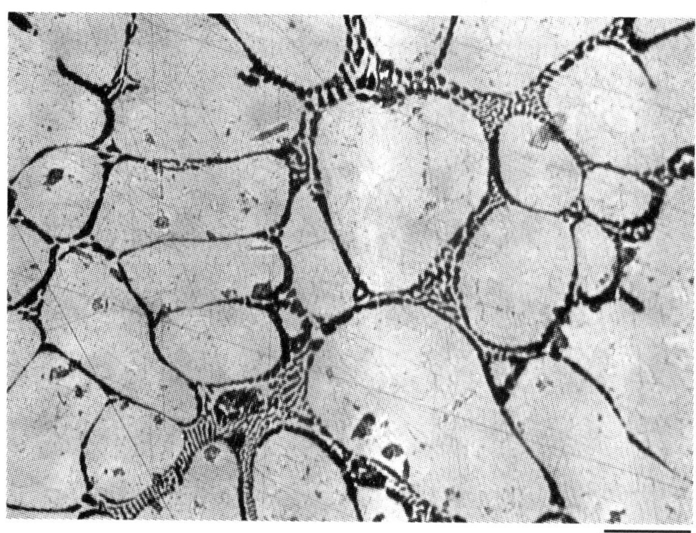

Fig. 7.19 Microstructure of a cast alloy of Pb-90%Sn showing dendrites of primary β and a divorced eutectic in which the eutectic β has separated from the eutectic α.

7.3 The Phase Rule

A proper phase diagram must be consistent with the laws of thermodynamics, as derived by J. Willard Gibbs. In particular it must obey the Gibbs *phase rule*, applicable to any system at equilibrium. The phase rule gives the number of thermodynamic variables (like temperature, pressure, and composition of each phase) that are not fixed in a system of C components and P phases existing together at equilibrium. This number of free variables is called *the number of degrees of freedom,* F, and the phase rule states that:

F=Degrees of freedom
C=No. of components
P=No. of phases

$$F = C - P + 2$$

For example, consider the two-phase equilibrium of ice and liquid water at 0°C, one atmosphere pressure. For this one-component system, the phase rule states that F = 1-2+2 = 1. This means that one variable, either temperature or pressure, can be varied while still maintaining the two-phase equilibrium. Thus, the freezing point is different from 0°C if the pressure is varied, but, for any given pressure, the freezing temperature is fixed. Both variables cannot be changed arbitrarily at the same time; otherwise, the system would depart from the two-phase equilibrium. (It would revert to a one-phase state.)

Since it is generally stipulated that pressure on an alloy will always be fixed at one atmosphere, one degree of freedom is used up *a priori*. Therefore, for most cases the phase rule can be recast to reflect the isobaric (constant pressure) case:

$$F = C - P + 1$$

As shown in more detail in Appendix 7.2, the phase rule comes directly from the definition of chemical equilibrium in a multi-phase system: that the composition of each phase remains constant. That is, there is no driving force for the transfer of any component from one phase to another. Such a driving force would be a difference in *chemical potential* between any two phases. This is analogous to a difference in electrical potential, which leads to the transfer of electrical charge in a conductor. Thus, the microstructure in Fig. 7.19, for example, shows the tin-rich β phase in equilibrium with the lead-rich α phase. "Equilibrium" means that there is no net flow of either element between the two phases, in spite of the large compositional difference between them. Therefore, the chemical potential of lead must be the same in each phase, and similarly for tin; this fact leads directly to the phase rule, as shown in Appendix 7.2. The F degrees of freedom in an alloy is nothing more than the number of free variables in the set of equations that express the fact that, at equilibrium, the chemical potential of each of the C components is equal in each of the P phases.

The constant-temperature portion of the cooling curves for the pure lead and pure tin, shown in Fig. 7.9, can be understood in exactly the same terms as would hold for the case of freezing of water: For the isobaric two-phase equilibrium at freezing in a one-component system, F = 1-2+1 = 0. Therefore, all variables are fixed, so the freezing of a pure substance must occur at a constant temperature.

The freezing of the eutectic alloy at the constant temperature 183°C occurs by the following reaction:

$$\text{Liquid} \longrightarrow \alpha + \beta$$

Therefore, at this temperature there is a three-phase equilibrium in this two-component system, and the phase rule states that F = 2-3+1 = 0. Again, freezing must occur at a constant temperature at the eutectic composition. Thus, the freezing of a eutectic at a constant temperature is a thermodynamic necessity, as long as the system is at equilibrium. It is possible to supercool a eutectic liquid and to make it freeze at some lower temperature, but the system is then far from equilibrium, and the phase rule does not apply.

7.4 Brazing Alloys

A common method for joining steel bicycle tubing employs *lugs,* illustrated in Fig. 7.20, to serve the same purpose as the copper fitting shown in Fig. 7.1. The stresses on a bicycle frame can be large, and Pb-Sn solder is too weak for this application, since room temperature is about two-thirds of the Pb-Sn eutectic temperature on the absolute scale. Hence, diffusion in Pb-Sn solder is rapid, and the solder would deform by *creep,* which is a time-dependent process of plastic flow involving self-diffusion (dislocation climb; cf. Fig. 5.8) occurring in metals at high temperatures (around 0.5 T_{MP} and above). Therefore, it is necessary to find an alloy that liquifies at a temperature much higher than 183°C.

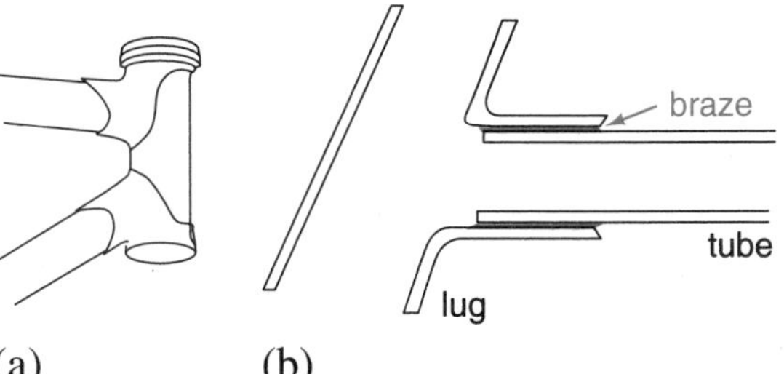

Fig. 7.20 (a) Lugged joints connecting the top tube and down tube with the head tube of a bicycle. (b) Schematic representation of the brazed joint between a lug and a tube.

One looks for an alloy for which room temperature is no higher than one-third the liquation temperature (in degrees Kelvin). Thus, the liquation temperature should be at least 900K, or about 625˚C. The alloy should also be readily available, preferably inexpensive, and able to form a low γ_{LS} with clean iron. There are essentially two families of alloys that are used for brazing steel frames; one is based on the silver-copper system and the other on copper-zinc. For hand-made lugged frames one can use either. The silver-rich alloys are based on the silver-copper eutectic system, the phase diagram of which is shown in Fig. 8.21(a). It is a simple eutectic and is essentially similar to the Pb-Sn system. The eutectic temperature of the binary alloy is 780˚C, and this can be lowered to around 670˚C by additions of zinc and tin, thereby creating a quaternary, instead of a binary, alloy.

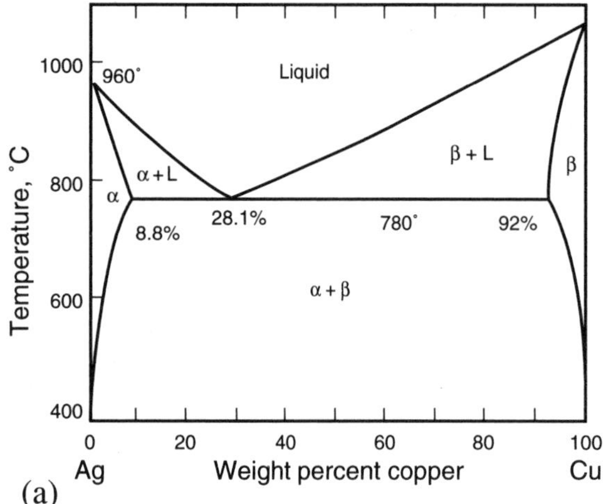

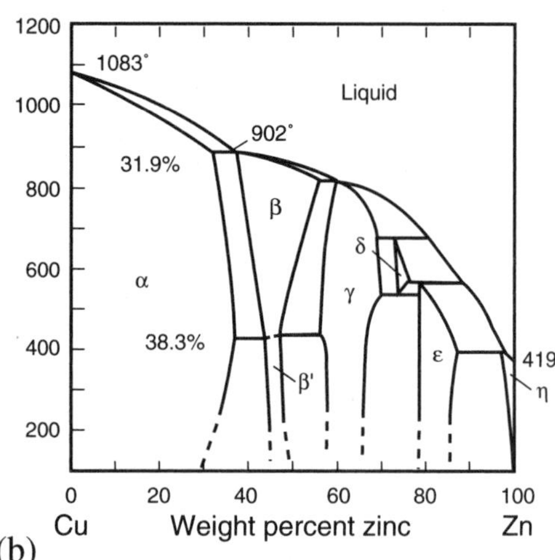

Fig. 7.21 (a) The Ag-Cu phase diagram. (b) The Cu-Zn phase diagram. (From M. Hansen and K. Anderko. *Constitution of Binary Alloys,* McGraw-Hill, N.Y. 1958, pp. 18 and 649, resp.)

The copper-zinc alloys are based on the alloy 60%Cu-40%Zn, sometimes called "Muntz" metal. The relevant part of the binary Cu-Zn phase diagram is shown in Fig. 8.21(b). This portion of the diagram shows what is called a peritectic reaction, in which there is a three-phase equilibrium at around 900°C. The reaction upon cooling is

$$\text{Liquid} + \alpha \longrightarrow \beta$$

The rest of the diagram is complicated and, fortunately, irrelevant. The important feature is that the 60-40 alloy must be heated above 900°C in order to liquify it. This liquation temperature is not changed much by the common additions of about one percent tin, iron, or nickel, so the steel tubes must be heated to a much higher temperature for brazing with the copper-zinc alloys than for the silver-based alloys.

An example of a brazed joint between a lug and a tube (both carbon steel) is shown in Fig. 7.22(a). Here, the steel is attacked by the etchant of nitric acid in alcohol, but the Cu-Zn brazing alloy is not. The width of this joint is 0.02mm, or 0.0008in.

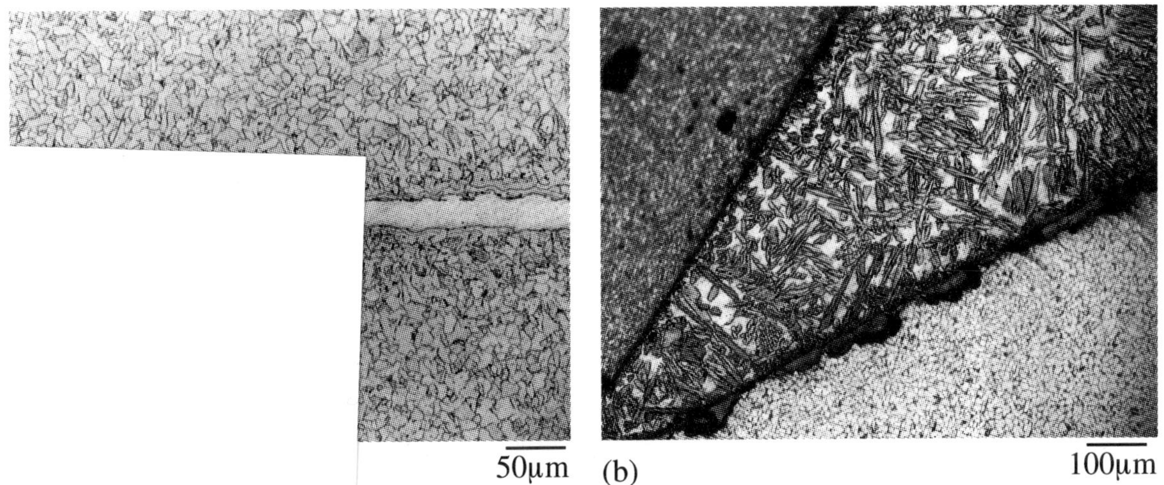

ən a lug and a tube, both made of carbon steel; etched
ə carbon steel. (b) Another brazed joint etched to reveal
0Zn brazing alloy.

hich the Cu-Zn alloy has been etched (using a
ıown in Fig. 7.22(b). The brazing alloy obviously
hly equal proportions; the matrix is the β phase, and
α. This microstructure can be rationalized with the
an be seen that the 60-40 alloy would first form the
that, when cooled below about 800°C, the α phase
appears that the α forms as plates having a crystal-
he β matrix.

y heating the joint area with an oxygen-acetylene
lure for lugged frames, which are produced in high-
e brazing. Here, the copper-zinc-based alloys are
is assembled and held together in a heat-resistant
alloy in the form of powdered metal or thin sheets
ən the framework is loaded into the brazing furnace
and allowed to reach temperature, the brazing alloy liquifies and spreads along the joint. In contrast with the localized heating during hand brazing, the heating during furnace brazing is obviously uniform over the entire frame.

Lugged construction can be used only when the tube diameters and the angles between the tubes correspond to a commercially available lug design. This is often not the case for frame-builders, and the traditional alternative has been to employ a process called *fillet brazing* or *braze welding*. For this, the copper-zinc alloys are always used, and this method is capable of producing strong and attractive joints. An example is shown in Fig. 7.23(a). In fillet brazing by hand, a torch is used to deposit the molten metal in the joint and to shape the fillet (pronounced *fill-it*) so that it has a smooth contour with large radii of curvature. The tubing is heated only locally, but for a much longer time than with the brazing of lugged joints.

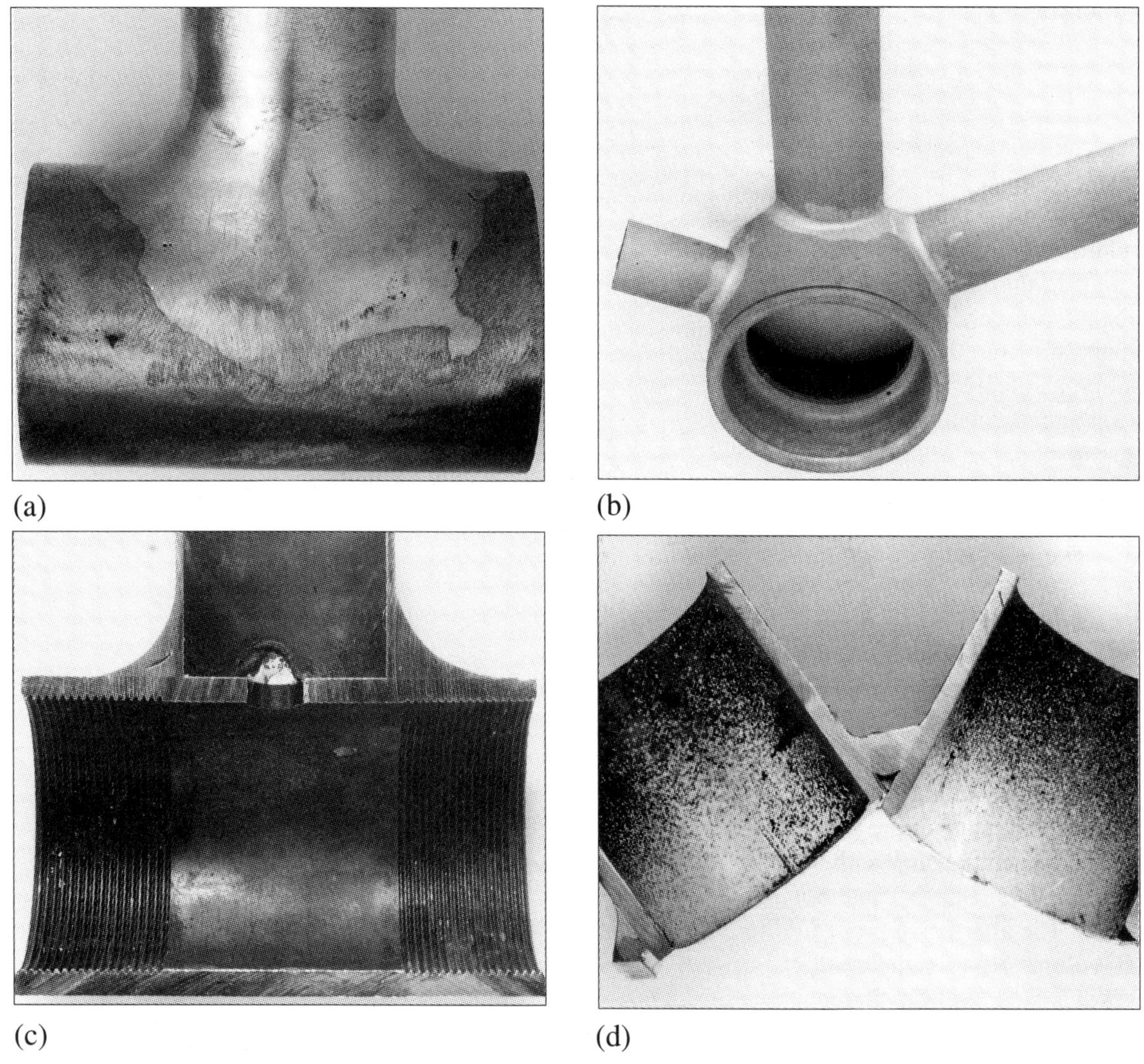

Fig. 7.23 Examples of joints made by fillet brazing. (a) A strong, hand-brazed joint with a large fillet. (b) A fillet-brazed bottom bracket with minimal fillets, resulting in a weak joint. (c) and (d) The cross-sections of these two joints.

There are commercially produced bicycles with fillet-brazed joints in which relatively small amounts of filler metal are applied, such as shown in Fig. 7.23(b). When a frame is painted, the nature of the joints is often not apparent. For the case shown in Fig. 7.23(b), when the paint was removed by sand-blasting, it was revealed that the bottom-bracket joints would have questionable resistance to fatigue failure, given the lack of cross-section in the joint.

Summary

Steel bicycle frames have traditionally been constructed from tubes joined by brazing, which is the high-temperature version of soldering, usually employing capillary action to draw a molten alloy into the crevice between the tube and a sleeve called a lug. This requires good wetting of the solid pieces by the liquid alloy, and for this the surfaces of the solid must be cleaned of oxide films. In addition, the process is made easier if the melting temperature of the liquid metal can be reduced significantly by alloying. The effects of alloying elements in this regard can be represented by the use of phase diagrams, which are essentially maps showing the equilibrium configurations of alloys as a function of composition and temperature. Simple eutectic phase diagrams are discussed in terms of (a) the experimental methods used to determine them, (b) the use of tie lines and the lever rule in determining the amounts and compositions of phases in two-phase regions, and (c) the microstructures that develop as a result of cooling from the liquid phase.

The reason for the formation of lamellar eutectics is given in terms of the need for a short diffusion distance during solute partitioning between the two phases. The reason for dendritic solidification is given in terms of the instability of a planar interface from which solute is being rejected during crystal growth. Solders made from lead-tin alloys are used as examples, and the silver-based and copper-zinc alloys used in bicycle construction are discussed.

The idea of a chemical potential as the driving force for mass flow is introduced, and the Gibbs phase rule is then derived in Appendix 7.2 from the condition that, at equilibrium, no net mass flow between coexisting phases can occur, meaning that the chemical potential of each component of an alloy must be the same in each of these coexisting phases.

Appendix 7.1 The Allotropic Transformation of Tin

Many pure elements undergo solid-state phase transformations, called *allotropic* transformations. Iron changes from BCC to FCC upon heating past 910°C. Tin undergoes a transformation from *diamond cubic* to *body-centered tetragonal* upon heating through 13°C; these structures are depicted in Fig. A7.1.1. Since tin is a Group IV element in the Periodic Table, like carbon, silicon, and germanium, it is not surprising that it can take on the crystal structure of diamond, as do silicon and germanium.

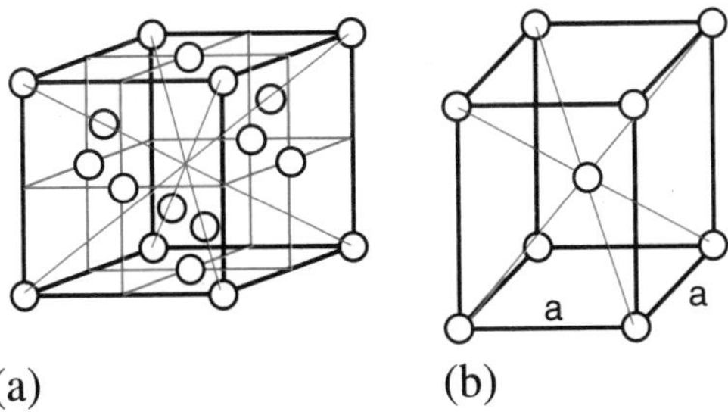

Fig. A7.1.1 The crystal structures of tin: (a) diamond cubic, (b) body-centered tetragonal.

In the diamond-cubic structure each atom has four neighbors, and each pair shares two electrons in covalent bonding, as in Fig. A7.1.2. In this way each atom can have a complete 8-electron outer shell, like an inert gas. This is a good example of how a bonding type can dictate the crystal structure. The Bravais lattice of the diamond cubic structure is FCC; however, there are two atoms associated with each lattice point in the diamond-cubic structure.

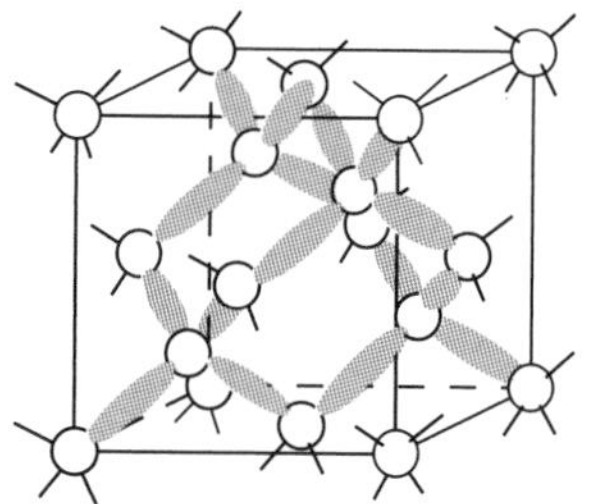

Fig. A7.1.2 Covalent bonds in a diamond-cubic crystal. (From L. H. Van Vlack, *Elements of Materials Science and Engineering,* 4th Ed., Addison-Wesley, Reading, MA, 1975, p. 37.)

Appendix 7.2 The Phase Rule

The phase rule is a simple equation that gives the number of fundamental variables that can be altered in value while maintaining the particular phase state, meaning an equilibrium of one phase, two phases, three phases, etc., in a system containing a known number of components. It is based on the general principle that the condition for equilibrium is the minimization of the Gibbs free energy, G, with respect to all relevant variables. It can be written

$$F = C - P + 2$$

where C is the number of components, P is the number of phases existing together in equilibrium, and F is the number of "degrees of freedom," meaning the number of unfixed variables.

Equilibrium means that no spontaneous changes occur in the system; the system is essentially changeless with time. A simple example is an ideal gas, which follows the law

$$pV = n\,RT$$

given in any elementary chemistry course, where p is the pressure, T the absolute temperature, n is the number of moles of the gas, V is the volume, and R is the gas constant. The *intensive* variables that determine the state of the gas are p and T; n and V are *extensive* parameters which depend on the amount of gas. Since in an ideal gas, $C = 1$ and $P = 1$, the number of degrees of freedom is 2. That means both temperature and pressure may be varied while still maintaining a one-phase equilibrium. It does not mean that p and T can be varied without limit. If T were reduced enough, or if p were increased enough, the gas would presumably condense. The phase rule only says that there can be some change in the two variables while still maintaining the gaseous state.

In an alloy with C components and P phases there is an additional factor relevant to the concept of equilibrium, and that concerns the possibility of net mass flow among the phases. By definition, equilibrium requires that all phases attain a steady state with regard to temperature, pressure, and composition; therefore, there can be no net mass flow between phases. In a system at equilibrium at constant p and T, a change in free energy in phase α resulting from the transfer of *dn* moles of component *i* from phase α to phase β would be offset exactly by an equal and opposite change in the free energy of phase β. The variation of free energy with n_i at constant p, T, and n_j, where n_j refers to all of the other components beside *i*, is defined as the *chemical potential*, μ_i

$$\mu_i = \left[\frac{\partial G}{\partial n_i}\right]_{p,T,n_j}$$

The chemical potential can be thought of as the driving force for mass flow, in the same way that a temperature gradient drives heat flow, and a gradient in electrical potential drives current flow. Thus, equilibrium requires that the chemical potential of each component be the same in all of the P phases. Only then will there be no mass flow. This means that for the ith component

P - 1 equations

$$\mu_i^\alpha = \mu_i^\beta = \mu_i^\gamma = \ldots = \mu_i^P$$

There is a similar set of P-1 independent equations for each of the C components; giving a total of C(P-1) equations.

C(P-1) equations:

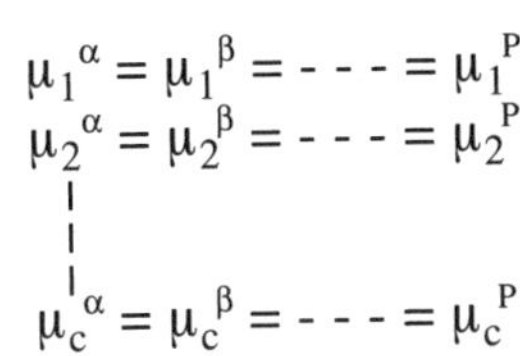

Now the composition of each phase can be specified by C-1 composition terms, since if the concentrations of all but one of the components is known, then that of the remaining one is given by subtracting the sum of the known concentrations from 100%. Therefore, in a system with P phases, there are P(C-1) independent concentration variables. If we ignore electrical, magnetic, surface, or other such influences, the only other relevant variables are temperature and pressure. Hence, the total number of variables that remains undetermined is

$$[P(C-1) + 2] - [C(P-1)] = C - P + 2$$

This is what is meant by the degrees of freedom, F. It is the number of variables that remain to be specified in order to define the state of a system completely. There is some freedom in the specification of these remaining variables. As noted in Section 7.3, it is common to give up a degree of freedom by fixing the pressure at one atmosphere, in which case the phase rule is written

$$F = C - P + 1$$

Glossary/Vocabulary - Chapter 7

Allotropic transformation — Many elements exist in several crystal structures, depending on temperature. The transformation from one to another is called allotropic. Iron transforms allotropically from BCC to FCC at 910°C. Titanium transforms from HCP to BCC at 883°C.

Brazing — Brazing is a technique for joining two solid pieces by melting a filler metal and letting it flow into the crevice between the two pieces. It is physically the same as soldering, but, technically, the process is called soldering only when the filler metal melts below 450° C. Brazing is a common method of joining the tubes of a steel bicycle frame. The most common filler metal is 60-40 Cu-Zn, or Muntz metal. It is necessary to remove any oxide layer from metal pieces and to use a flux to keep them clean in order that the filler metal wet the surfaces and flow between them under the influence of capillary action.

Capillary action — This is the flow of a fluid along a channel under the influence of surface tension. It is necessary that the fluid wet the surfaces in order for this to occur. This is what draws water into an absorbent tissue. It is also the process by which a filler metal is drawn into a crevice between metal pieces during brazing or soldering.

Chemical potential — The generalized driving force for chemical change in a material system is called the chemical potential. The basic driving force for mass flow is a gradient in chemical potential; this is often approximately proportional to a concentration gradient. However, if the chemical potential of a given element in each of two contiguous phases is the same, no mass flow will occur, even if the concentrations of this element are different in the two phases.

Component — The elements or compounds that are mixed in the various phases of a phase diagram are called the components of the phase diagram. A binary phase diagram has two components; a ternary phase diagram has three. The components of soft solder are lead and tin. The components of carbon steel are iron and carbon.

Contact angle — This is the angle between a solid surface and the tangent to a liquid drop drawn at the point of contact. A low contact angle denotes good wetting; a high contact angle poor wetting, as seen with a drop of liquid mercury on a floor.

Cooling curve — This is a plot of temperature *vs.* time for the cooling of a material, done in order to detect phase transformations that involve the release of heat, thereby causing a change in slope of the curve. Cooling curves are used to determine the freezing points of elements or compounds and the liquidus lines and eutectic temperatures in phase diagrams, like the Pb-Sn diagram.

Coring — See non-equilibrium solidification.

Dendrite — A dendrite is something shaped like a tree, i.e., something with branches. A solid often forms from a liquid or vapor in a dendritic configuration. A snowflake is dendritic. A dendritic configuration can often be distinguished in a metallographic sample of a cast metal.

Eutectic alloy — This is an alloy of a particular composition such that freezing occurs isothermally, and the liquid transforms simultaneously into two solid phases. A eutectic solder, Pb-61.0%Sn, is used whenever rapid solidification is desired, as in soldering electronic equipment.

Eutectic divorcement	This is the separation of phases during the solidification of a eutectic liquid in an off-eutectic alloy, during which the phase in the eutectic constituent that matches the primary phase tends to plate out on the primary phase. The reason for this is that it permits rapid solidification while reducing the total amount of interface formed, compared with a normal eutectic. In the Pb-Sn system, a hypoeutectic alloy appears to have a less-than-normal amount of the α-phase in the eutectic, particularly near the primary α dendrites, because the eutectic α has plated out on the primary α.
Eutectic reaction	This is the transformation of a liquid simultaneously into two solid phases, or vice versa. It occurs at a particular temperature, called the eutectic temperature, and the alloy composition at which this occurs is called the eutectic composition, or eutectic point. The two-phase aggregate formed by eutectic solidification is called the eutectic constituent. Eutectic is a Greek word meaning "easy melting." The lead-tin phase diagram is a simple eutectic diagram, the eutectic composition is at 61.9%Sn and the eutectic temperature is at 183°C.
Flux	This is a compound that can be melted by heat and that functions to dissolve oxides and other surface contaminants from metals during brazing/soldering or welding and to protect the hot metal surface from oxidizing. Examples of fluxes used in brazing and soldering are borax, boric acid, borates, fluorides, chlorides and rosin.
Hypereutectic alloy	This is an alloy with a composition to the right of the eutectic point. That is, it has a higher concentration of the right-hand component than the eutectic composition. In a simple eutectic diagram, a hypereutectic alloy would have primary β-phase, instead of primary α.
Hypoeutectic alloy	This is an alloy with a composition to the left of the eutectic composition, i.e., of a lower concentration of the component on the right-hand side of the diagram than the eutectic composition. A hypoeutectic solder has less than 61.9%Sn. The microstructure contains primary α and may also have some eutectic constituent.
Intermetallic compound	This is an intermediate phase in an alloy system, usually a binary alloy, in which the two components are present in a more-or-less fixed ratio; it has the stoichiometry of a chemical compound. It is usually an ordered phase, and the range of variation of the composition is usually small. The equilibrium second phase in the 6061 aluminum alloy, Mg_2Si, is an intermetallic compound. The β-phase in the Cu-Zn system would be considered an intermetallic compound only at lower temperatures, where it is ordered.
Lamellar	A micro-constituent, like a eutectic or eutectoid, that forms in a layered morphology is lamellar. That is, it comprises lamellae. Pearlite is a lamellar micro-constituent comprising lamellae of ferrite and cementite.
Lever rule	This is a scheme used to calculate the relative amounts of each phase in a two-phase region of a phase diagram at a particular temperature. The alloy composition is used as the fulcrum, and the tie line is the balancing beam. The lengths of the tie line on either side of the fulcrum are used to make the calculation. If the alloy composition falls 25% of the way along the tie line, going from left to right, then the alloy must have only 25% of the right-hand phase and 75% of the left-hand phase.

Liquidus line	A liquidus line is the boundary between a liquid and a liquid+solid region in a phase diagram. Solidification of a cooling liquid alloy begins after the temperature has fallen below the liquidus line.
Miscible	This means mixable at the atomic or molecular level. Liquids tend to be miscible; but there are many combinations that are not. Oil and water is a famous example. Copper and nickel are completely miscible in the solid state.
Muntz metal	This is the name given to the alloy 60%Cu+40%Zn. When cooled from the liquid it is a mixture of α and β brass. This is the most commonly used alloy for brazing of steel bicycle frames.
Non-equilibrium	This occurs more and more as the cooling rate is increased and as diffusion, particularly in the solid state, is not fast enough to maintain the phases at the compositions indicated in the phase diagram. When a Pb-10%Sn alloy is cooled, the primary α may not have time to absorb the proper amount of tin; that is, the interior of the dendrites would have less tin than the phase diagram indicates as the alloy cools. This dendrite is said to be cored. In this case, one finds some eutectic constituent in an alloy that should have none if it had been cooled under equilibrium conditions.
Peritectic reaction	This is the reaction: liquid + α —> β during freezing, and the reverse during melting. The name implies melting at a surface, and β grains melt by forming α + liquid at a surface or interface. The β phase in the Cu-Zn system forms peritectically
Phase rule	This is the rule devised by J. Willard Gibbs that gives the conditions required for chemical equilibrium in one or more phases. It is a relationship based on the relevant thermodynamic variables: temperature, pressure, and the composition of each phase. It gives the connection between the number of components C, the number of phases P that coexist at equilibrium, and the number of unspecified variables, or degrees of freedom, F. It states that F=C-P+2. In systems at atmospheric pressure, one degree of freedom is used up, since pressure is fixed. Therefore, F=C-P+1. For example, in eutectic solidification, F=2-3+1=0, which means that nothing may vary, and that the temperature and composition of all three phases are fixed.
Primary constituent	Also called a primary phase. This is the solid phase that forms first during freezing of an alloy. It usually forms as dendrites. During cooling of a hypoeutectic Pb-Sn solder, the α-phase forms as dendrites in the liquid. Both the α and the liquid become richer in tin as more α forms, and the liquid reaches the eutectic composition when the temperature has fallen to 183°C. This liquid then freezes eutectically, and the solidified alloy has two constituents: primary α and eutectic (α +β).
Soldering	Similar to brazing, except that the filler metal melts below 450°C.
Solid solubility	This is the saturation limit of a solid phase, or the maximum amount of solute that the phase can hold, at a particular temperature. It always varies with temperature, and it is often characterized in terms of the maximum solubility. The solid solubility of carbon in BCC iron varies from a few parts per million at room temperature to about 0.02% (by weight) at 727°C.

Solidus line The solidus line is the boundary between a solid and a solid+liquid region in a phase diagram. In the equilibrium solidification of an alloy, the alloy becomes completely solid once the temperature has fallen below the solidus line. The solidus is the locus of one end of a tie line in the solid+liquid region.

Solvus line This is the boundary between a solid phase and the adjacent two-phase (solid) region in a phase diagram. That is, it delineates the solid solubility of the relevant solute in that phase. In a solution treatment, the alloy must be heated to above the solvus line so that a single-phase region is reached.

Terminal solid solution This is a solid solution that terminates at one end of a phase diagram. That is, it comprises one of the constituents of the alloy as the solvent and therefore has the same crystal structure as this constituent. In the Pb-Sn system, both the α and β phases are terminal solid solutions.

Thermocouple This is a device consisting of a pair of dissimilar metal wires joined at one end and used to measure temperature. It operates by way of the thermoelectric effect, which is the tendency for electrons to flow from the hot (high-energy) end of a piece of wire down the temperature gradient to the cold end. A thermal emf is created when a circuit including dissimilar metals is set up. This emf is proportional to the difference in thermoelectric "power" between the two metals times the difference in temperature between the hot and cold end. To make a thermocouple, you weld the ends of the two wires together and use this joint as the hot end. The cold end is kept at a reference temperature, and the emf across the two wires is measured and converted to temperature using tables specific to each type of thermocouple, or is converted directly to temperature (using a special calibrated meter).

Tie line This is a horizontal line in a two-phase region of a phase diagram; it denotes a particular temperature. The end points denote the composition of each of the two phases. That is, the ends of a tie line denote the limits of solubility of each phase for the other. Thus, both phases in a two-phase region are saturated with respect to the other.

Wetting Wetting occurs when a fluid flows over a solid surface. Perfect wetting occurs when the contact angle between the fluid and the solid is zero. Wetting of a solid metal by a liquid metal is favored by increasing the solid/air interfacial energy and decreasing the liquid/solid interfacial energy. This is accomplished by cleaning the oxide off the metal surface.

X-ray analysis by diffraction This is the study of crystalline materials by the diffraction of x-rays, which can be used to determine the size and shape of the unit cell of a crystalline phase directly, and the location of atoms in the unit cell indirectly. The relative amounts of different phases can be determined approximately from the relative intensities of beams diffracted from each phase. An x-ray diffraction pattern from a Pb-Sn eutectic would show superimposed patterns from the α and β phases, respectively.

Exercises

7.1 Apply the phase rule to the Pb-30%Sn alloy in the two-phase region between 265°C and 183°C; explain the meaning of F=1. (Remember, pressure is fixed at 1atm.)

7.2 Calculate the amount of primary α phase in alloys of Pb-40%Sn and 60%Sn cooled to 182°C under equilibrium conditions.

7.3 What would happen if the microstructure shown in Fig. 7.10 were heated to 175°C and held there for a long time? Explain your answer.

7.4 Given below is the microstructure of a Ag-Cu alloy of unknown composition. Deduce what the composition is and explain your reasoning. (Hint: focus first on the eutectic constituent, and decide which phase is which, based on the phase diagram.) in Fig. 7.21(a).

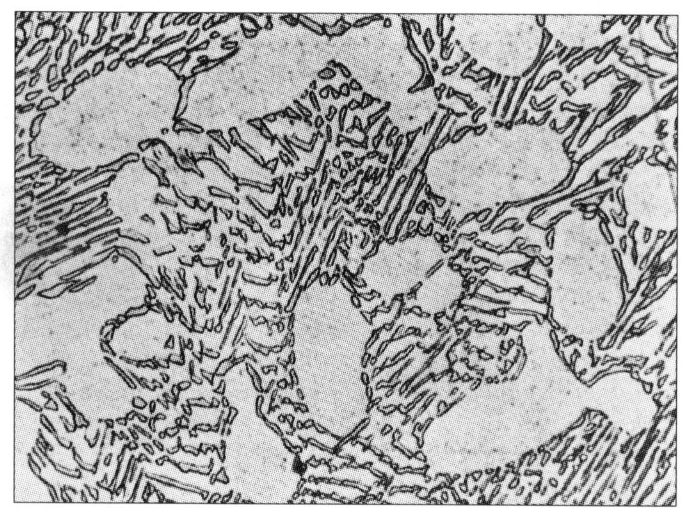

(Photomicrograph from R. E. Reed-Hill, *Physical Metallurgy Principles,* Van Nostrand, N. Y., 1973, p. 544.)

7.5 Sterling silver is Ag-7.5%Cu. Using the phase diagram in Fig. 7.21(a), tell what the microstructure would look like if the alloy were melted and cooled slowly under equilibrium conditions to room temperature, and what it would look like if it were cooled too rapidly for equilibrium to be achieved. Make sketches to illustrate your answer. (Review Fig. 7.18.)

7.6 The copper in sterling silver can provide solid-solution strengthening. Sterling silver equilibrated at 785°C and cooled rapidly is stronger and can be polished to a higher luster than if cooled slowly. Explain why.

7.7 Describe the changes that would occur in an alloy of Ag-70% Cu cooled from the liquid state to room temperature. Sketch the resulting microstructure and give the relative amount of each phase and each microstructural constituent (i.e., primary phase and eutectic). (Refer to Fig. 7.21(a) and review Fig. 7.7 and relevant text.)

7.8 Use the phase rule to calculate the number of degrees of freedom, F, for an alloy of Pb-20wt%Sn in the vicinity of 250°C and at 183°C. Explain the physical meaning of F in each case.

7.9 Consider a solid composed of one mole of A atoms and one mole of B atoms. What was the change in configurational entropy, compared with the pure A and B, that resulted from mixing the A and B? (Use Stirling's approximation.) Did the effect of the entropy *per se* cause an increase or decrease in the Gibbs free energy, G?

7.10[1] An alloy of Ge-50%Si is cooled very slowly from 1500°C. Using the phase diagram given below, please answer the following questions:

(a) At what temperature does freezing begin?
(b) At what temperature is freezing complete?
(c) At what temperature is the mixture half solid and half liquid?
(d) What is the composition of the first solid to form?
(e) What is the composition of the last liquid to freeze?
(f) What are the weight fractions of the two phases at 1250°C?
(g) What are the compositions of the two phases at 1250°C?
(h) What are the atomic fractions of Si and Ge in the alloy?

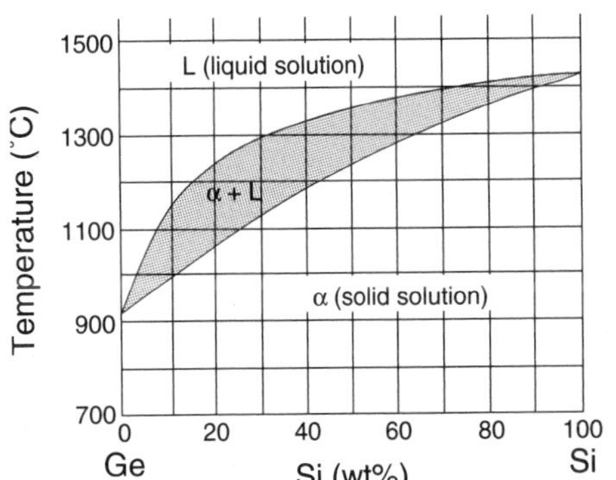

7.11 The crystal structure of silicon is diamond cubic (cf. Fig. A7.1.2). Deduce the crystal structure of germanium from the phase diagram above, and explain your answer.

[1]Contributed by Professor D. L. Callahan, Rice University.

8

PHASE TRANSFORMATIONS IN CARBON STEEL

In Fig. 5.20, the microstructure of a carbon steel spoke that was heated to 950°C and slowly cooled was shown. In Fig. 8.1, this microstructure is compared with that of the same kind of spoke cooled more rapidly from 950°C. The starting condition of the spoke before being wire drawn was somewhere in the range between these two conditions. The main objective of the present chapter is to understand the kinds of phase transformations that produce these microstructures, as well as the one that results when the steel is quenched rapidly, as into cold water, from such a temperature.

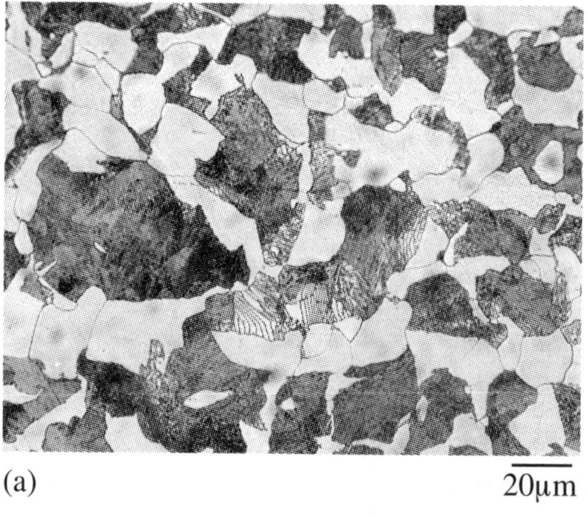

(a) 20μm

(b) 20μm

Fig. 8.1 Comparison of microstructures of a carbon steel spoke heated to 950°C and (a) furnace cooled or (b) air cooled.

8.1 The Iron-Carbon Phase Diagram

The microstructures comprise white-etching regions of a single phase, called *ferrite,* and grey-to-black-etching regions of a two-phase constituent, called *pearlite.* The pearlite will be shown to be analogous to the eutectic constituent found in the Pb-Sn system (cf. Fig. 7.10), and the ferrite is the analog of the primary phase that forms during cooling of a hypoeutectic alloy (cf. Fig. 7.15). To understand these microstructures, one needs not only the relevant phase diagram, but also another type of diagram that portrays kinetic information about the phase transformations. Kinetic diagrams are needed here, whereas they were not needed when discussing the liquid-to-solid transformation, because the transformations in steel occur in the solid state, in which diffusion rates are very slow compared with diffusion in the liquid state. As a result of the role of diffusion-controlled kinetics, it is possible to achieve a great variety of microstructures in steels. These microstructures have different properties. Therefore, to control the properties of a steel, one must have a clear understanding of how to control the microstructure. This starts with the phase diagram, shown in Fig. 8.2.

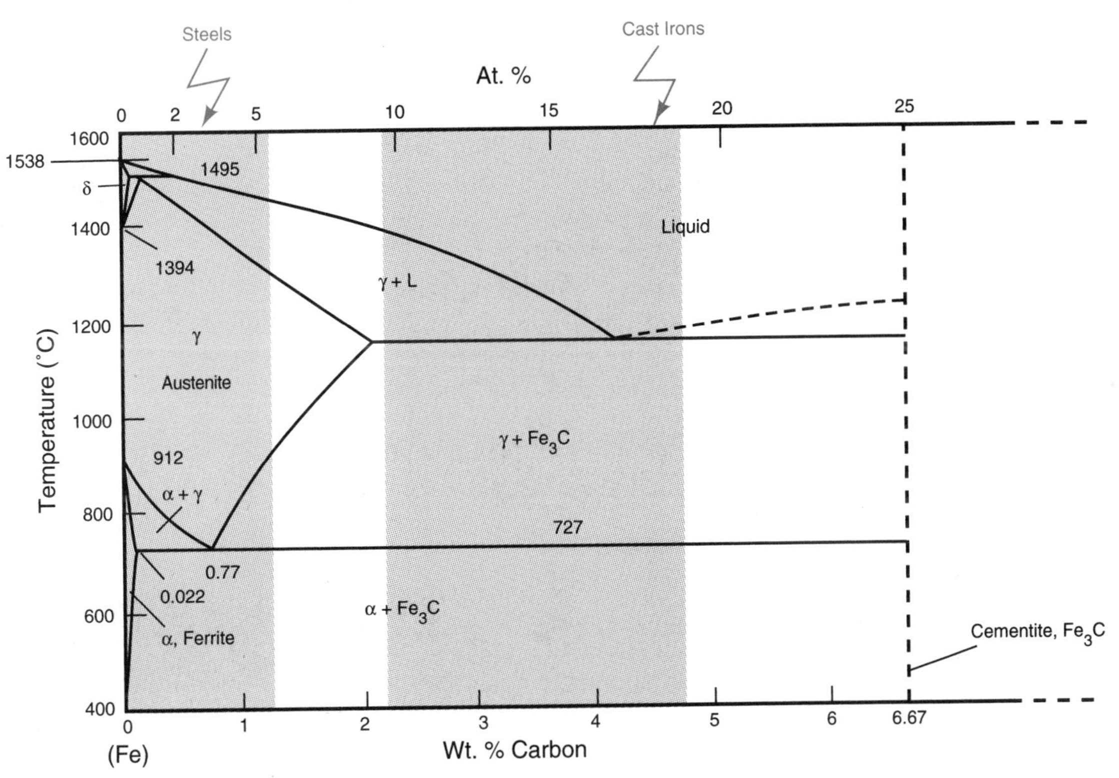

Fig. 8.2 The Fe-Fe_3C phase diagram. This is a metastable portion of the Fe-graphite system. The portions of the diagram relevant to steels and cast irons are indicated.

The iron-carbon phase diagram is of central importance to metallurgists, but only two regions of the diagram are widely used. One is relevant only to cast irons; this is the region that contains the eutectic reaction at 1148°C, where a relatively low-melting liquid freezes to the FCC γ phase plus graphite in the true equilibrium diagram.

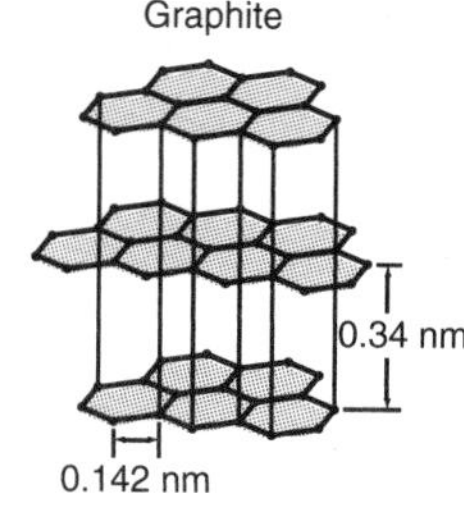

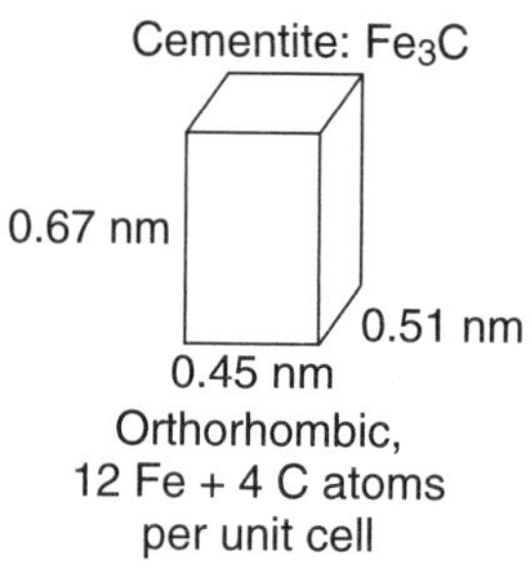

The crystal structure and bonding of graphite is very far from metallic. It consists of plates of connected, covalently bonded, six-carbon rings, with van der Waals bonding between the plates. Because of its non-metallic nature, graphite is rather difficult to nucleate in a solid metallic matrix. This is true in steels even when the carbon content is nearly 2%.

The difficulty of graphite nucleation results in the formation of the metastable Fe_3C phase *(cementite)* instead, especially in solid-state transformations. Although graphite can be made to form in high-carbon cast irons, it can only form in steels (<2%C) after heating for years at temperatures above 600°C. Thus, when dealing with most applications of steels, it is appropriate to work with the metastable Fe-Fe_3C diagram, shown in Fig. 8.2; this can be treated as an essentially stable system.

Cementite is an example of a metal carbide. As such, it is properly considered a ceramic in which the bonding is only partly metallic, the rest being mainly covalent. That is, some of the valence electrons are delocalized, as in metallic bonding, and the rest are shared between iron and carbon atoms. The crystal structure is dictated by the geometry that suits this kind of bond formation and by the necessity to fit together atoms of very different size.

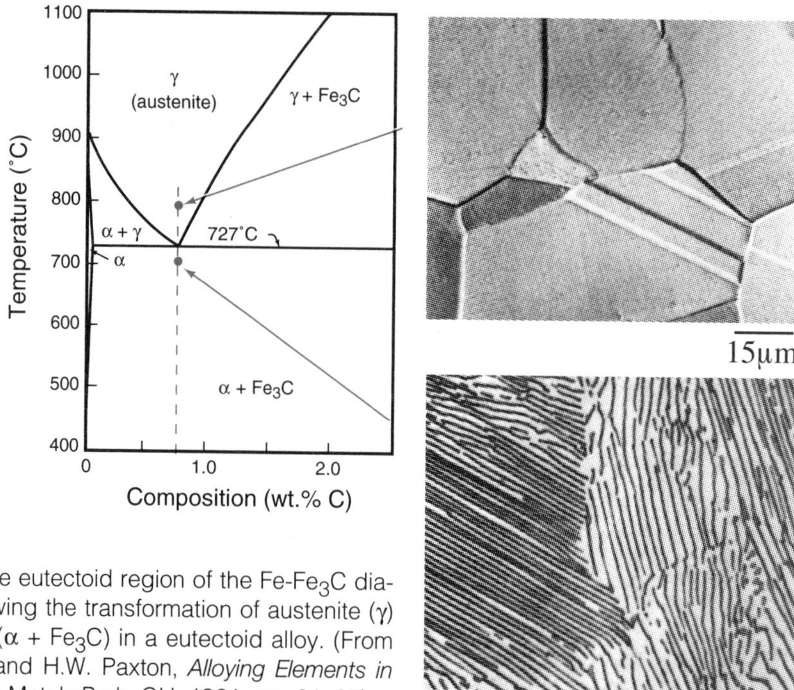

Fig. 8.3 The eutectoid region of the Fe-Fe_3C diagram, showing the transformation of austenite (γ) to pearlite (α + Fe_3C) in a eutectoid alloy. (From E.C. Bain and H.W. Paxton, *Alloying Elements in Steel,* ASM, Metals Park, OH, 1961, pp. 21, 27)

The part of the Fe-Fe_3C diagram of most interest is that containing the *eutectoid* reaction, shown isolated in Fig. 8.3. This is similar to a eutectic reaction, except that the single phase at the high temperature is a solid instead of a liquid. Thus, at 0.77%C the FCC γ phase, called *austenite,* transforms on cooling to BCC α, or ferrite, plus cementite. As in a eutectic alloy, the latter two phases are arranged in an intimate mixture, comprising alternating lamellae of ferrite and cementite. This is the constituent called pearlite.

8.2 Eutectoid Decomposition

The reason for the lamellar morphology of pearlite is exactly the same as explained in Fig. 7.16 for the formation of the Pb-Sn eutectic. During the decomposition of austenite, a large-scale redistribution of carbon must occur, because the ferrite can contain, at most, 0.02wt%C, and the cementite needs 6.7wt% (25at%)C. In order for these two phases to form in times on the scale of seconds or minutes, the diffusion distances must be short. This is achieved in a lamellar microstructure, as shown in Fig. 8.4, and the partitioning of the carbon can be carried out in the interface between the advancing pearlite colony and the parent austenite.

It must be emphasized that the phase diagram does not indicate that the austenite should decompose into pearlite. It only indicates that ferrite and cementite should form. Thus, the lamellar morphology is dictated by kinetic, rather than thermodynamic, considerations. Moreover, the only way to produce pearlite is to cause austenite to decompose in a certain range of rates.

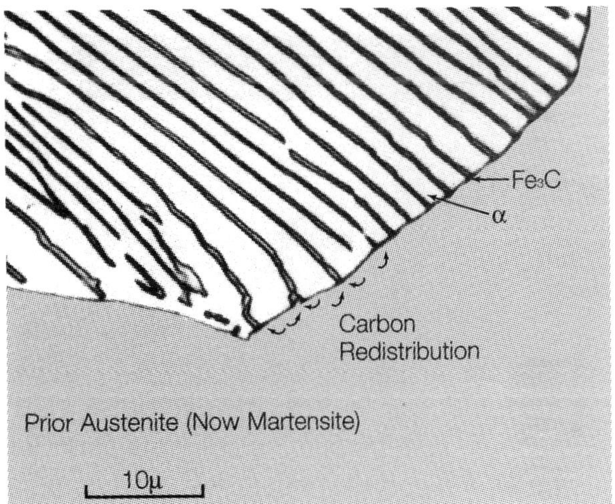

Fig. 8.4 Part of a pearlite colony growing into austenite. The edge-wise growth of the alternating plates of α and Fe_3C provides a mechanism of rapid transformation, since only short-range diffusion of carbon is required. (From P.G. Shewmon, *Transformations in Metals,* McGraw-Hill, N.Y. 1969, p. 227.)

8.2.1 Isothermal Transformation

The decomposition of austenite was first studied in a systematic way by isothermal transformation of specimens that were quenched from the austenite region to some temperature below the eutectoid temperature, held for a time, and then quenched rapidly to room temperature. The process is illustrated in Fig. 8.5.

Fig. 8.5 Schematic representation of the experimental procedure used to carry out the partial transformation illustrated in Fig. 8.6.

The microstructure formed by the partial isothermal transformation of a eutectoid steel (~0.8%C) is shown in Fig. 8.6. The pearlite nucleated at the austenite grain boundaries and then grew in nodules into the austenite grains. When the transformation was interrupted, the remaining austenite transformed to martensite. (This involves a diffusionless process that is so rapid it cannot be suppressed.)

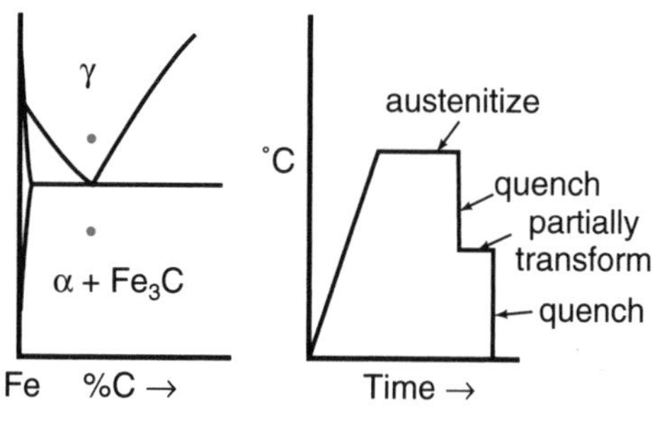

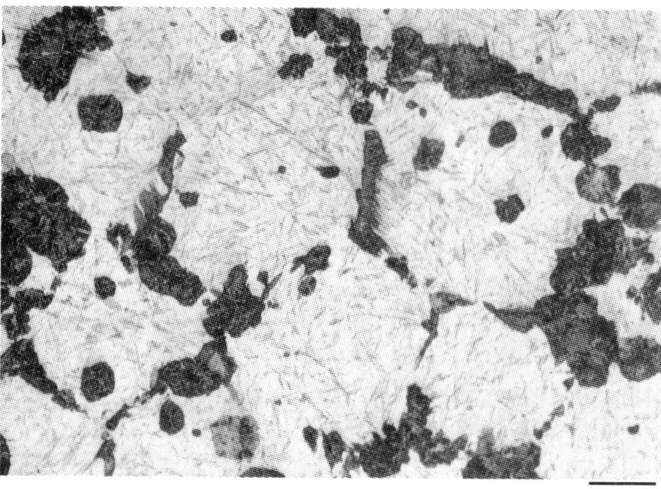
100μm

Fig. 8.6 The formation of nodules of pearlite at austenite grain boundaries during cooling of a eutectoid steel; the transformation was interrupted by quenching. The heat treatment employed is shown schematically, in conjunction with the phase diagram. (Photomicrograph by E. Anderson, Univ. of Penn.)

When the eutectoid transformation is compared with the freezing of a eutectic alloy, it is apparent that equilibrium conditions are not maintained in the steel. Otherwise, there would be a cooling curve with an isothermal portion, reflecting the three-phase equilibrium at the eutectoid temperature, as shown for the Pb-Sn eutectic in Fig. 7.9. The reason the eutectoid decomposition occurs far from equilibrium is that the driving force for this transformation is smaller than that driving the eutectic solidification.

The driving force for the eutectoid decomposition is simply the difference between the free energy of the austenite phase and that of the α+Fe_3C mixture. This free energy difference can be written

$$\Delta G = G_{\alpha+Fe_3C} - G_\gamma$$

and can be understood from a schematic plot of free energy *vs.* temperature, which can be assumed to be linear over a restricted range of temperature. Since G=H-TS,
8240 the free energy of both the austenite and the α+Fe_3C mixture must decrease with increasing temperature, as in Fig. 8.7. The curves must cross at 727°C, where all three phases are in equilibrium. Above 727°C, austenite is stable; therefore, the austenite free-energy curve lies below the one for α+Fe_3C. The reverse is true below 727°C. The vertical distance between the two curves at any temperature is

the driving force for the transformation from one condition to the other. Thus, it is apparent that the driving force for the $\gamma \longrightarrow \alpha$+$Fe_3C$ transformation is zero at 727°C, and it increases continuously as the temperature falls below 727°C.

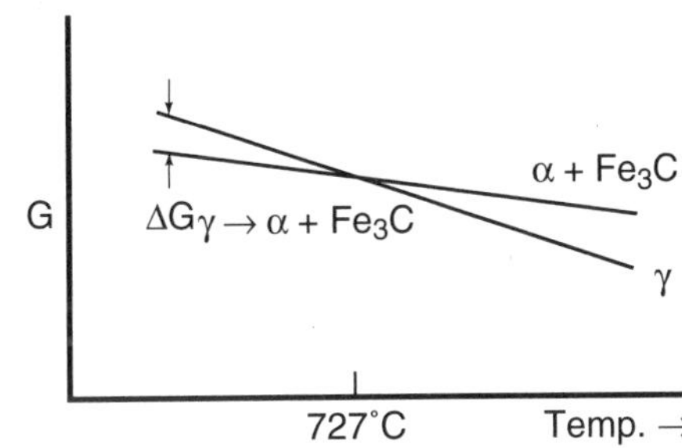

Fig. 8.7 Schematic representation of the free energy *vs.* temperature for austenite and α+Fe_3C, showing the equilibrium at 727°C and the increasing driving force (ΔG) for austenite decomposition below that temperature.

Because the initial and final states are both solids, the scale of the free-energy change for a eutectoid decomposition is much smaller than for eutectic solidification in which the initial state is a liquid with weak bonding between atoms, and the final state is solid with strong bonding between atoms. Thus, the austenite must be undercooled in order to produce pearlite, because the pearlite is a rather high-energy configuration of α+Fe_3C. This is a result of the large amount of area of α/Fe_3C interface, and a concomitant large interfacial energy. That is, the ΔG must be increased by undercooling to "pay for" the energy needed to form the large amount of α/Fe_3C interface in the pearlite. (The ΔG is energy released in the transformation, and the interfacial energy is consumed.) The fact that the transformation product is not in its minimum-energy configuration attests to the importance of the kinetic factors in the formation of pearlite.

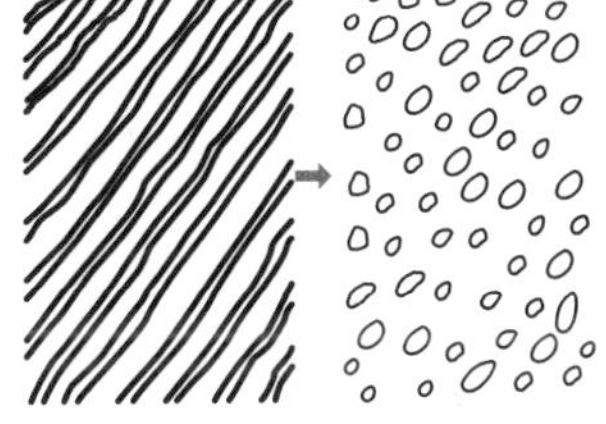

If the transformation depicted in Fig. 8.6 had been allowed to go to completion, and if the steel had then been held at this high temperature for a long time, the lamellar pearlite would have gradually broken up into globules of Fe_3C in a matrix of α by a process called *spheroidization.* The total amount of interfacial energy would continue to fall as coarsening of the particles of cementite occurred.

The decomposition of austenite in a eutectoid steel (i.e., 0.77%C) is a classical substitution reaction in which one constituent substitutes completely for another. In that respect, it is similar to the recrystallization of a cold-worked metal; both cases involve only short-range diffusion at the interface between the old and the new constituents. As in any substitution reaction involving nucleation and growth of the new constituent, the kinetics can be described by an S-shaped curve, in which, after some incubation time, the rate of transformation goes through a maximum. After that, the rate decreases, because the untransformed volume is depleted, and the transformed regions impinge on one another.

As already seen in Fig. 5.6, the kinetics of this kind of transformation can be expressed as a series of "S-curves" at different transformation temperatures. The S-curve portrays the fraction transformed as a function of time at a constant transformation temperature. To determine such a set of curves for a eutectoid steel, one follows the procedure illustrated in Fig. 8.5, austenitizing a series of specimens and transferring them, one at a time, into a hot-salt bath at the selected transformation temperature. Each specimen is then held for a different time at the transformation temperature before the transformation is arrested by quenching the specimen to room temperature. The amount of transformation can then be assessed by metallographic examination, as done for Fig. 8.6. This process is repeated for different transformation temperatures. The results would appear as shown in Fig. 8.8.

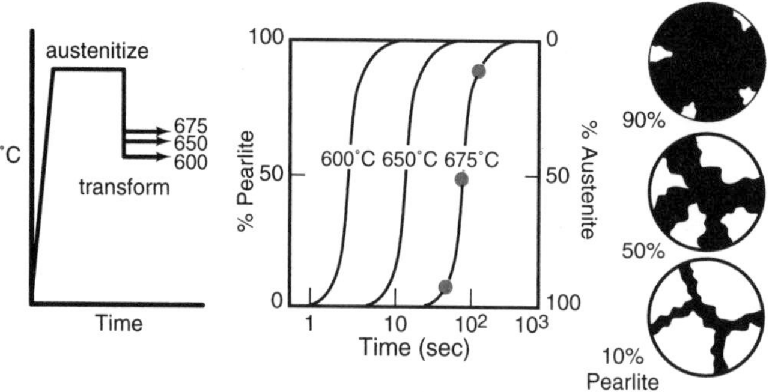

Fig. 8.8 S-curves showing how, in a eutectoid steel, the volume transformed from austenite to pearlite changes with time at different temperatures. The corresponding heat treatments and microstructural changes are also illustrated.

It would be found that the rate of transformation reaches a maximum at a particular temperature. The overall transformation kinetics can be expressed as a set of "C-curves," constructed from a series of S-curves, as shown in Fig. 8.9. The S-curve for a given transformation temperature provides, for example, the times for the beginning, the mid-point, and the end-point of pearlite formation.

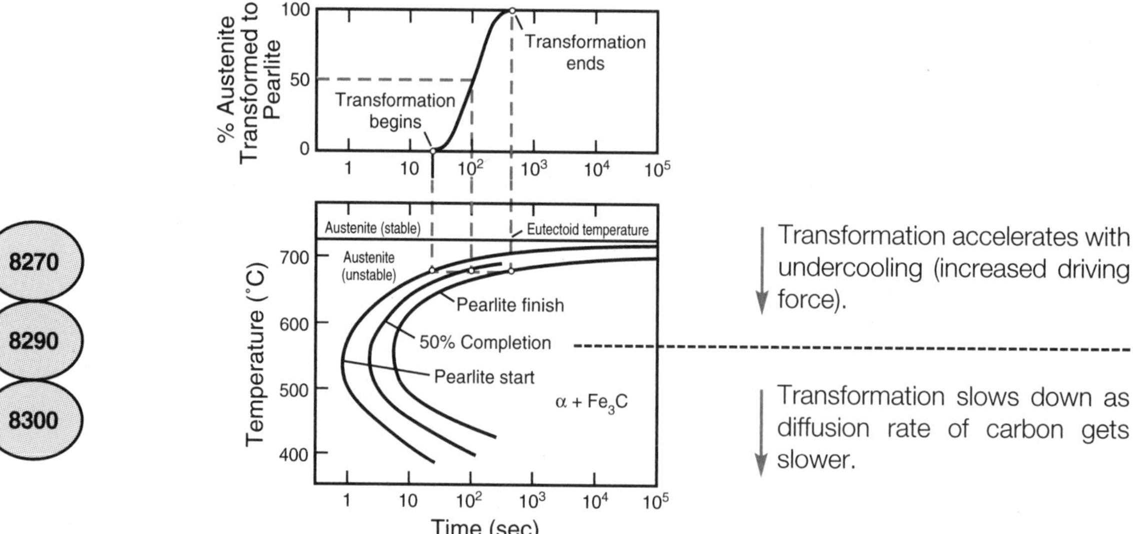

Fig. 8.9 The S-curve is used to construct the C-curve, as shown. A specimen quenched to 680°C and held for about 100 seconds would show 50% pearlite when quenched to room temperature. (Adapted from *Atlas of Isothermal Transformation and Continuous Transformation Diagrams,* Amer. Soc. for Metals, Metals Park, Ohio, 1977, p. 28.)

It can be seen from Fig. 8.9 that the rate of transformation goes through a maximum at around 550°C, referred to as the "nose" of the C-curve. The rate decreases as the transformation temperature is raised above the nose, because the thermodynamic driving force for the γ-to-pearlite transformation falls to zero as the temperature approaches 727°C. The rate also decreases as the temperature is lowered below the nose of the C-curve, owing to the temperature dependence of the rate of diffusion of carbon (cf. Fig. 8.4). That is, at low temperatures there is plenty of driving force, but here the transformation rate is controlled by the rate of carbon diffusion. Above the nose, the diffusion rate is rapid enough, and the driving force is rate-controlling.

When a eutectoid steel is transformed below the nose of the C-curve, the transformation product is still α+Fe_3C, but it is not called pearlite, because the lamellar microstructure cannot form at such low temperatures. Instead, a very fine microstructure is formed that comprises plate-like ferrite with cementite particles either surrounding or embedded in the ferrite plates, depending on whether it forms just below the nose or at even lower temperatures. This two-phase constituent is known as *bainite,* and its microstructure is so fine that an electron microscope is required to analyze it.

upper bainite

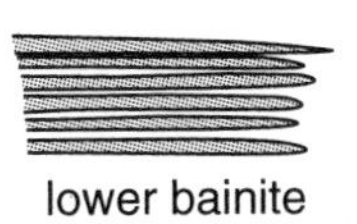

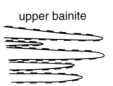

lower bainite

The C-curve is part of an *isothermal transformation* diagram, or IT diagram. It is useful for the study of transformation kinetics aimed at a fundamental understanding of the process. However, such a diagram should not be used directly for the heat treatment of steel. For a heat treatment consisting of austenitizing and cooling, one needs information about the kinetics of transformations occuring over a range of temperatures during continuous cooling.

8.2.2 Transformation during Cooling

A *continuous-cooling-transformation* (CT) diagram can be constructed from measurements of length changes in a small-diameter cylidrical specimen that is transformed from austenite at various cooling rates. These measurements are carried out in a dilatometer, shown schematically in Fig. 8.10(a). The specimen is heated by the surrounding furnace into the austenite region, and its temperature is measured continuously by a thermocouple. It is then allowed to cool at different rates, either by controlling the falling temperature of the furnace or by use of a cooling gas. A quartz rod resting on top of the specimen transfers the length changes to some type of displacement transducer, represented schematically as a dial guage. The millivolt readings from the thermocouple and the transducer are fed to the x and y terminals of an x-y recorder. Since the transformation γ-to-α involves a volume expansion (BCC α is not close packed), the dilatometer can detect the beginning and the end of the formation of ferrite and pearlite (which is mostly ferrite). An example of the type of curve that is obtained is shown in Fig. 8.10(b).

The time/temperature combinations for the beginning and end of the transformation found on curves for different cooling rates are plotted as points on a transformation diagram, as shown by the solid curves shown in Fig. 8.11. By comparing the CT diagram with the IT diagram (dashed curves), it can be seen that the nose of the CT diagram occurs at a lower temperature and at a longer time than that of the IT diagram.

(a)

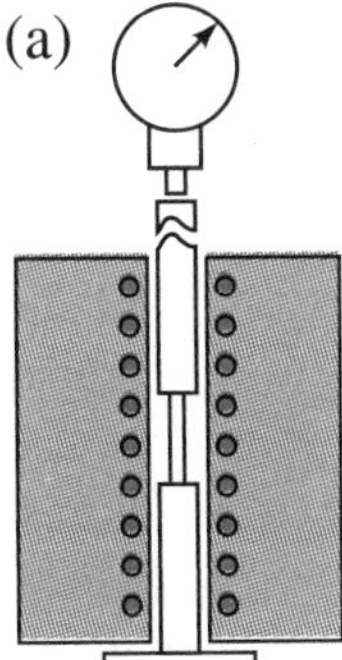

Fig. 8.10(a) Dial gauge dilatometer (b) dilation during cooling through the decomposition of austenite into pearlite.

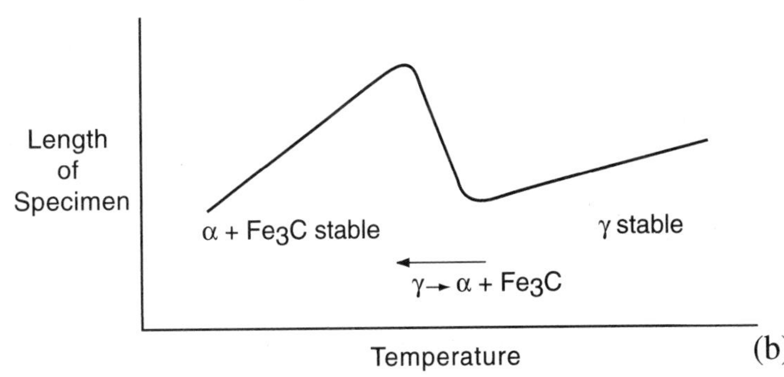

(b)

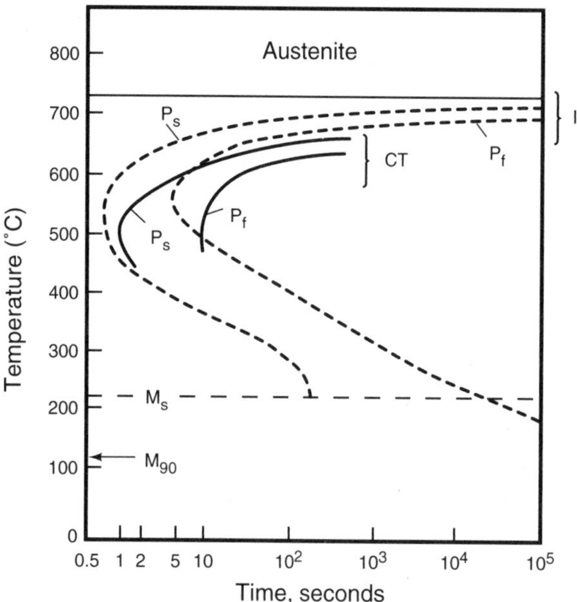

Fig. 8.11 Comparison of the isothermal and continuous-cooling-transformation diagrams for a eutectoid steel. (See sect. 8.4.1 for explanation of M_S and M_{90}(From *Atlas of Isothermal Transformation and Transformation Diagrams,* ASM, 1977, p. 28)

Example 8.1

Q. What are the relative amounts of ferrite and cementite in the pearlite of a slowly cooled eutectoid steel?

A. This can be found by use of Fig. 8.2 and the lever rule, as follows:

$$\text{Relative amount of } \alpha = \frac{6.67\text{-}0.77}{6.67\text{-}0.02} = 88.7\%$$

$$\text{Relative amount of } Fe_3C = \frac{0.77\text{-}0.02}{6.67\text{-}0.02} = 11.3\%$$

Example 8.2

Q. Using the IT diagram in Fig. 8.9, find the time necessary for the formation of 50% pearlite in a eutectoid steel by isothermal transformation at 600°C, and compare the expected appearance of that pearlite with pearlite formed in a similar way at 650°C. Consult Fig. 8.4 to visualize the growth of pearlite into austenite.

A. The time to reach 50% pearlite at 600°C is found from the time axis of Fig. 8.9 to be just under 5 seconds, compared with about 12 seconds at 650°C.

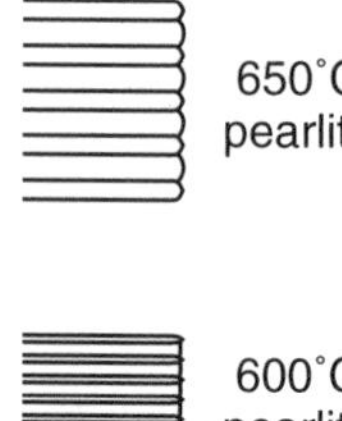

Since the growth of pearlite requires diffusive partitioning of carbon at the advancing lamellar front, and since the transformation proceeds more rapidly at 600 than at 650°C (even though the diffusivity of carbon is lower at 600°C) the diffusion distance at 600°C must be shorter than at 650°C. The conclusion is that the pearlite formed at the lower temperature must be finer; i.e., the lamellae must be closer together. (The finer pearlite would appear darker when etched, because the grooves formed at the α/Fe_3C interfaces would tend to overlap to a greater degree.)

8.3 Transformations in a Hypoeutectoid Steel

8.3.1 The "Equilibrium" Condition

The microstructure of the furnace-cooled carbon-steel spoke in Fig. 8.1(a) can now be evaluated. The sample was austenitized at 950°C and slowly cooled. The microstructure comprises roughly equal amounts of pearlite and ferrite. The first question is: What is the carbon content? This can be answered by first considering how the microstructure was formed and then using the lever rule. The ferrite is the *proeutectoid* phase. That is, it formed before the eutectoid transformation, and is analogous to the primary constituent that forms before the eutectic in the solidification of an alloy like a hypoeutectic Pb-Sn solder (cf. Fig. 7.15). The ferrite is stable as soon as the temperature falls below the boundary between the γ and γ+α phase fields; this is analogous to the liquidus line in a eutectic diagram. As the temperature falls, more ferrite forms, and the carbon content of the remaining austenite increases toward 0.77%. That is, as ferrite forms, carbon must diffuse away from it into the surrounding austenite.

After the maximum amount of proeutectoid ferrite has formed, the remaining austenite decomposes eutectoidally. If the microstructure is roughly 50% proeutectoid ferrite, then the carbon content of the steel must be about halfway between 0.02 and 0.77%. That means the spokes must have been made from steel with about 0.4%C. A metallurgist would then guess that a 1040 steel had been used. The 10 refers to a "plain-carbon" steel, meaning nominally unalloyed, and the 40 means 0.4%C. (Any low-alloy steel is designated by the first two digits, which refer to the specific alloy elements present; the last two digits refer to the carbon content in this AISI/SAE system of steel designation.*)

In actual fact, a plain-carbon steel does have elements other than iron and carbon that are added on purpose. For example, manganese is added at levels usually below 1% to scavenge sulfur, which is a deleterious impurity. In this way the sulfur is collected into manganese-sulfide inclusions, which are less deleterious, depending on their size, shape, and quantity. A bit of silicon or aluminum may also be added to the molten steel for purposes of tying up oxygen and nitrogen. Again, this would produce less-deleterious "dirt" in the form of oxides and nitrides. However, the amounts of these other elements are low enough to ignore when using the phase diagram; hence the designation "plain-carbon" steel.

8.3.2 Isothermal Transformation

The isothermal transformation kinetics of a 1040 steel can be represented by the IT diagram in Fig. 8.12, which also indicates the relationship to the phase diagram and the evolution of microstructures at temperatures above and below the eutectoid temperature. The application of this diagram can be described as follows: Let three specimens of a carbon-steel spoke be austenitized at 850°C and rapidly cooled to 750°C, then held for 2, 10, and 300 seconds, respectively. These isothermal holds are terminated by a rapid quench to room temperature. The schematic microstructures indicate that the steel was still fully austenitic after two seconds, but that after 10 seconds ferrite had begun to form at the austenite grain boundaries. The fact that carbon is rejected from the transformed regions is represented in the figure by speckles along the ferrite/austenitelarge as

* AISI = American Iron and Steel Institute; SAE = Society of Automotive Engineers

boundaries. After 300 seconds, the steel had essentially come to equilibrium, with about 40% ferrite and 60% austenite, as can be checked by using the lever rule in the two-phase region of the phase diagram. (A tie line can be drawn at 750°C, and the end points would be found at about 0.01 and 0.65%C; the overall alloy composition is, of course, 0.4%C.)

Alternatively, a transformation temperature of 675°C could be chosen. Let five specimens be austenitized, cooled rapidly to 675°C, and held for the fol-
8370 lowing times, respectively: 0.5, 1, 2, 6, and 60 seconds. The microstructures at these times would be the following:

0.5 sec	The specimen is still fully austenitic.
1 sec	Ferrite has begun to form at austenite grain boundaries; carbon is being expelled into the surrounding austenite.
2 sec	The formation of proeutectoid ferrite is almost complete; the carbon content of the remaining austenite is approaching the eutectoid concentration (0.77%).
6 sec	Pearlite begins to form where the carbon concentration is high.
60 sec	Transformation is complete; microstructure is like Fig 8.1(a).

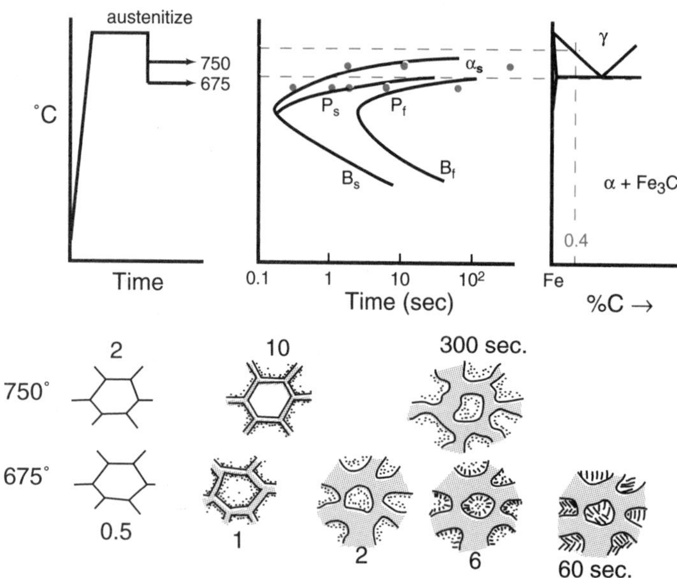

Fig. 8.12 The IT diagram for a 1040 steel, shown in relation to the phase diagram. The evolution of microstructure during isothermal holds at 750°C and 675°C is shown schematically.

The major difference from the IT diagram for a eutectoid steel (Fig. 8.9) is that the formation of proeutectoid ferrite must be accounted for. The ferrite nucleates on the austenite grain boundaries and grows into the austenite grains at a rate determined by the rate of diffusion of carbon away from the interface. That is, the carbon "piles up" in the austenite ahead of the advancing ferrite, and the ferrite cannot advance at a rate faster than that allowed by the diffusion of carbon down the resulting concentration gradient. This carbon pileup is represented by the speckles alongside the ferrite in the microstructures shown in Fig. 8.12 and is depicted schematically in Fig. 8.13 for ferrite forming at temperature T_1.

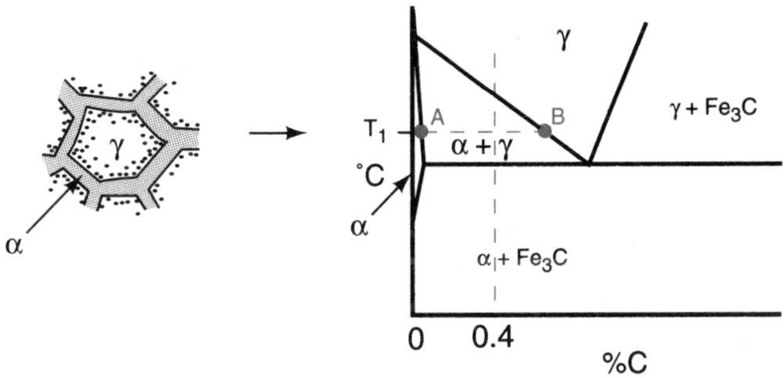

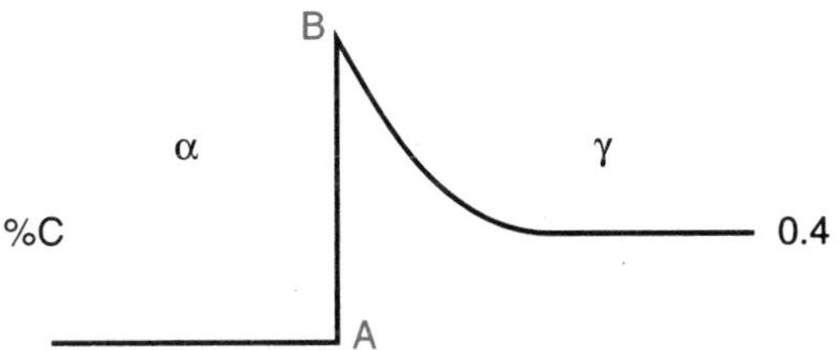

Fig. 8.13 Schematic representation of the piling-up of carbon in the austenite ahead of an advancing ferrite region at temperature T_1. The carbon must diffuse away (down the concentration gradient) in order that the ferrite can grow, since the ferrite can hold no more carbon than A%. The austenite in equilibrium with ferrite (i.e., at the interface) must contain B%, according to the phase diagram.

Note that the relevant diffusion distance for the formation of proeutectoid ferrite is much larger than for the formation of pearlite (cf. Fig. 8.4), since all the diffusion during pearlite growth takes place at the pearlite/austenite interface. Thus, pearlite can grow much more rapidly than large, "blocky" regions of ferrite.

The formation of proeutectoid ferrite is governed by its own C-curve. Since this ferrite forms prior to the pearlite, its C-curve lies at shorter times. Also, instead of having an asymptotic relationship with the eutectoid temperature, the ferrite-start curve has an asymptotic relationship with the temperature above which ferrite is unstable, i.e., about 800°C for a 1040 steel.

8.3.3 Transformations during Cooling of a 1040 Steel

The CT diagram for a 1040 steel is shown in Fig. 8.14. Again, it differs from the CT diagram for the eutectoid (1080) steel in that the curve for the start of the formation of proeutectoid ferrite must be shown. Note, also, that the nose of the CT diagram for the 1040 steel occurs at a shorter time than for the 1080 steel (Fig. 8.11). This is a manifestation of the fact that the transformation from γ to α+Fe_3C is retarded by an increase in the carbon content.

Fig. 8.14 The continuous-cooling-transformation diagram for a 1040 steel. (Adapted from C. F. zurLippe and J. D. Grozier, in *Atlas of Isothermal Transformation and Continuous Transformation Diagrams*, ASM, 1977, p.

The reason for the different appearance of the furnace-cooled and air-cooled spokes (Fig. 8.1) can be explained with the aid of the CT diagram in Fig. 8.14. Two cooling curves, representing air cooling and furnace cooling, respectively, are plotted on the CT diagram. For the case of air cooling, the time period available for the formation of proeutectoid ferrite (before the pearlite reaction starts) is only on the order of 10 seconds long. However, for the case of furnace cooling, the time for this transformation extends over several hundred seconds. Therefore, it is quite reasonable that in the furnace-cooled spoke the formation of proeutectoid ferrite has gone to completion, whereas, in the air-cooled spoke, the transformation was obviously interrupted soon after it had begun.

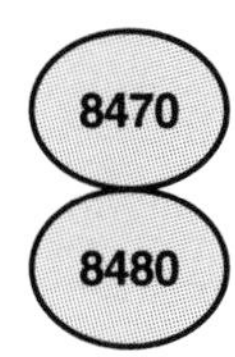

In addition to the fact that the formation of proeutectoid ferrite did not go to completion in the air-cooled spoke, one other feature of this microstructure deserves special mention. That is the extensions of ferrite plates jutting out from the blocky ferrite that formed along the austenite grain boundaries.

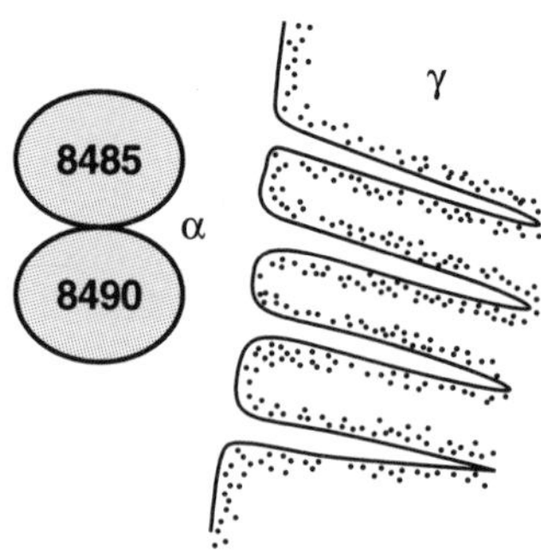

These ferrite side-plates are called *Widmanstätten* ferrite, after the man who first reported such a structure in meteorites. They form for the same reason that dendritic arms form at an advancing planar interface during solidification (cf. Fig. 7.14). An advancing plate of ferrite can reject carbon from its tip much more rapidly than from a flat interface, because the concentration gradient at the tip is much steeper. (The diffusion distance at the tip is about equal to the radius of curvature of the tip.) Thus, when ferrite is made to form quickly and at relatively low temperatures (cf. Fig. 8.1b), the planar interface becomes unstable, and what starts out as blocky ferrite switches to a plate-like growth mode.

If the cooling rate is such that the temperature gets too low for pearlite to form, then, as mentioned earlier, the two-phase decomposition product takes on the bainitic morphology. This can be viewed as the natural extension of Widmanstätten-ferrite formation. The only real difference between the two is that bainite has fine particles of cementite embedded in, or along, the ferrite plates.

Finally, it should be noted that, since the proper amount of proeutectoid ferrite did not form during air cooling of the 1040 steel spoke, the austenite that finally transformed to pearlite, or pearlite plus bainite, could not have had the proper amount of carbon (0.77%). Obviously, this was no impediment to the formation of the two-phase constituents. This emphasizes the point that, under nonequilibrium conditions, the phase diagram cannot be relied upon to give the compositions of the various constituents.

8.3.4 Processing of Spokes

In the manufacture of carbon steel spokes the starting condition was probably not the furnace-cooled, or "annealed," condition, because furnace cooling after austenitization is slow and, therefore, expensive. Rather, the air-cooled or "normalized" condition was probably used. The 1040 steel wire, which contained almost 7% cementite in the form of fine pearlite, was cold-drawn to the desired diameter. Cementite is normally a non-plastic, brittle material; however, it can be deformed plastically during cold drawing, because the drawing die imposes large radial pressures on the wire, opposing the tendency to brittle fracture or hole formation. (Decades ago Bridgman showed that one could even deform marble plastically, if sufficient hydrostatic pressure were imposed along with an applied tensile stress.)

Thus, during cold drawing, both the ferrite and cementite are plastically deformed to very large strains so that both phases become strung-out in the drawing direction (cf. Fig. 5.17). In the cold-drawn condition, in addition to being strengthened by the presence of a very high dislocation density, the 1040 steel has a component of strengthening by what might be called the "composite" effect. Here, a softer material (e.g., ferrite) is intimately bonded to a dispersed material (e.g., pearlite) that is harder and stiffer. The cementite carries more of the load than would an equivalent volume fraction of the ferrite. This composite effect is employed in many new "engineered" structural materials, including fiber-strengthened polymeric materials, which will be discussed in Chapters 13 and 14 in the context of bicycle frames and tires.

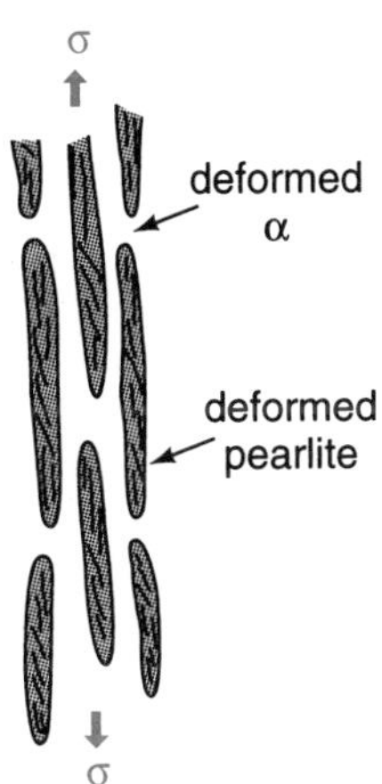

Example 8.3

Q. In Fig. 8.14 the cooling curve for the air cooling exhibits a decrease in slope following the beginning of the formation of ferrite. Explain.

A. The decrease in slope arises from the release of the heat of transformation ($\gamma \rightarrow \alpha$), and the phenomenon is the same as the change in slope that occurs when a liquid alloy cools past the liquidus temperature (cf. Fig. 7.9). In the case of the transformation in steel, the effect is called *recalescence.* (Heat effects are used in *thermal analysis,* which is an alternative method for determination of CT diagrams; it requires small specimens, sensitive measurement of temperature *vs.* time, and carefully controlled cooling rates.)

8.4 The Martensite Transformation

It has been pointed out that austenite that has not transformed *via* a diffusion-controlled transformation (e.g., to ferrite or pearlite) will transform in a diffusionless manner to martensite when quenched to room temperature. This new phase is not shown on the phase diagram, because it is not an equilibrium phase; it is only metastable. However, it is the desired phase for hardening of steel, because the hardness of martensite can be very high, depending on carbon content. This property is used to great advantage in components subject to wear, which is dealt with in the next chapter. For the present, only the nature of the martensite transformation will be described.

8.4.1 Hardening of Steel

Steel is hardened by heating it into the austenite region of the phase diagram and quenching, usually in water or oil, as shown schematically in Fig. 8.15. The purpose of the rapid cooling is to avoid the formation of ferrite or pearlite, which are relatively soft constituents. If the steel is cooled rapidly enough to temperatures where diffusion is slow, then the unstable austenite must transform martensitically.

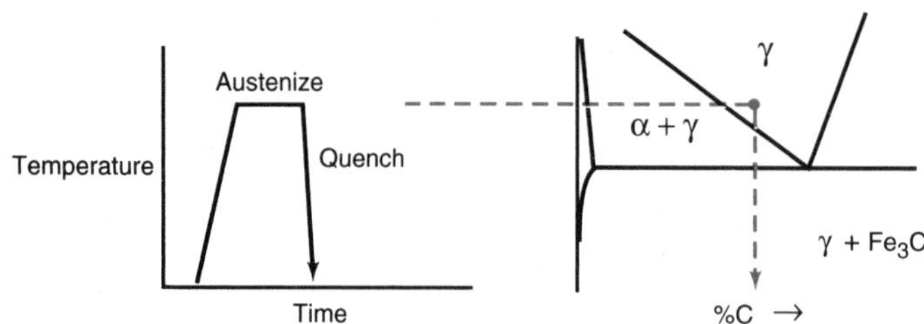

Fig. 8.15 Heat treatment required to harden a 1060 steel, i.e., to transform it to martensite.

In a martensitic transformation, no diffusion occurs. That is, the compositions of the parent phase and the product are identical; there is no partitioning of solute during the transformation. A martensitic transformation takes place by rapid shearing of the parent crystal lattice into the lattice of the new phase. This occurs by the propagation of special kinds of dislocations along the advancing interface of the new phase, which usually forms as plates having a special crystallographic relationship (called a *habit* relationship) to the parent phase. The shearing from the parent FCC crystal to the new martensite crystal is complicated and can be viewed as comprising a homogeneous primary shear, similar to that in crystallographic *twinning* (see Appendix 9.1), and a nonhomogeneous secondary shear caused by dislocations and twins on the submicroscopic scale. Figure 8.16 shows schematically what this would look like in a grain of austenite. The reason for the lens-like shape of the martensite plate is that this minimizes the strain energy induced in both the martensite and in the parent phase by virtue of the difference in specific volume between the two phases. (Austenite is close-packed; martensite is not and therefore has a greater specific volume.)

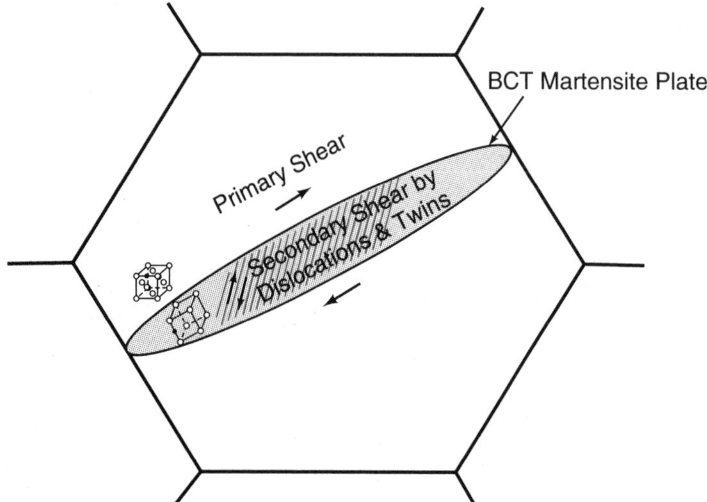

Fig. 8.16 Schematic representation of a martensite plate formed in a grain of austenite.

Note that the high density of defects in the martensite plate (from the secondary shear) means that the martensite comes with some strain hardening already built in. The interaction between these defects and carbon atoms (trapped in solid solution during the quench) is of major importance in the high hardness possible in iron-carbon martensite.

The special feature of Fe-C alloys that makes the martensite transformation a hardening process is that austenite can dissolve rather large amounts of carbon, but ferrite dissolves only a very small amount. The difference in the maximum carbon solubility in the two phases is two orders of magnitude (0.02 *vs.* 2.0%). This means that, when austenite containing a fair amount of carbon is quenched, the carbon is trapped in a crystal structure that is trying to shear into BCC ferrite. The result is a *body-centered tetragonal* (BCT) crystal structure, which can 8500
be viewed as a BCC crystal distorted along one axis, as shown in Fig. 8.17.

The tetragonal distortion is the result of the trapped carbon, which, as described in Section 6.2, occupies octahedral sites. A dilute solution of carbon in α iron causes only local tetragonal distortion (cf. Fig. 6.3), but in a concentrated solution there is an overall distortion of the lattice into a tetragonal crystal structure. This has two lattice parameters, instead of one, and the volume of the unit cell is $a{\cdot}a{\cdot}c$, rather than a^3. X-ray measurements of Fe-C martensites of varying carbon contents have shown that, as carbon content is decreased, the c parameter decreases and the a parameter increases, so that they converge to the lattice parameter of BCC iron at zero carbon content. That is, when carbon-free γ-iron is quenched and made to transform martensitically, the product is BCC.

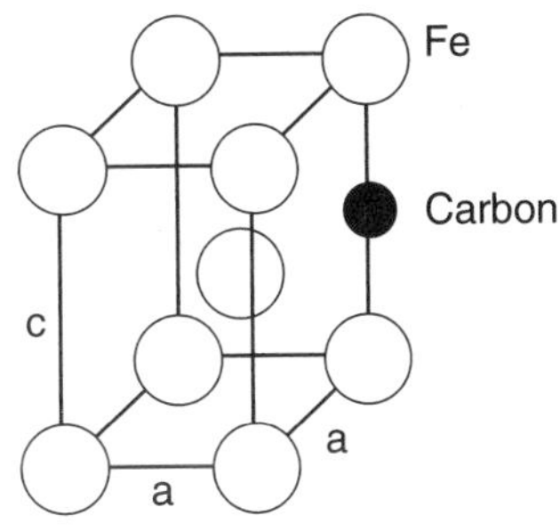

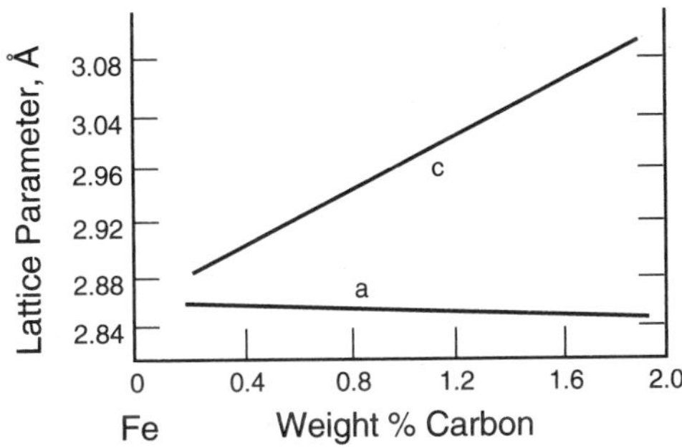

Fig. 8.17 (a) Unit cell of BCT iron-carbon martensite and (b) the effect of carbon concentration on the lattice parameters. Note that at 0% carbon $c = a = 2.86$ Å, the lattice constant for BCC α-iron. (From E.C. Bain and H. W. Paxton, *Alloying Elements in Steel,* ASM, Metals Park, OH, 1961, p. 36.)

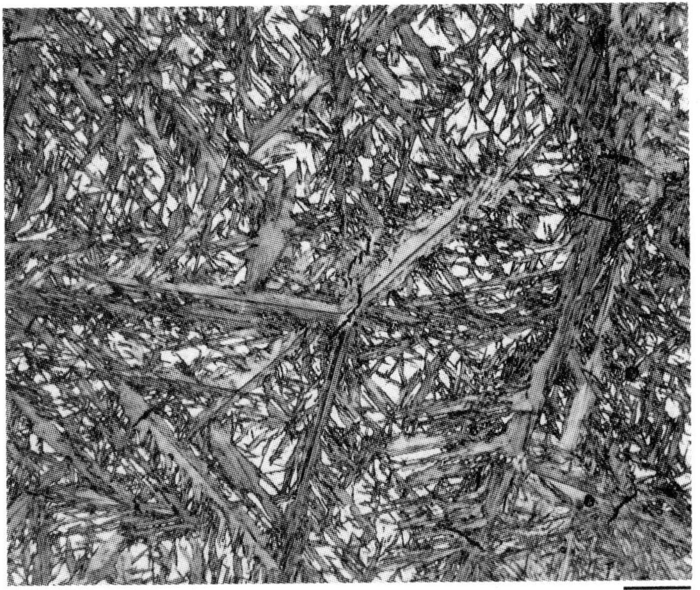

Fig. 8.18 Martensite plates in a partly transformed 1.4% steel. The white background is retained austenite. The martensite is slightly tempered at 160°C. (From A. R. Marder and G. W. Ruyak, Bethlehem Steel Corp.)

In a partially transformed, high-carbon steel the martensite plates can be made to stand out against the white background of retained austenite, as in Fig. 8.18, by *tempering,* which involves the precipitation of Fe_3C from the supersaturated (i.e., unstable) martensite. When tempering is carried to completion, the product is BCC ferrite with finely distributed carbide particles. In the early stages of tempering, the carbides are submicroscopic, but they cause a polished surface to become roughened by the etching process. Therefore, the incident light is scattered randomly, and the martensite plates appear dark.

The reason this steel transformed only partially when quenched to room temperature can be explained as follows: An Fe-C martensite is not only a metastable phase; it is also highly distorted by the supersaturation of carbon. Therefore, a large driving force is necessary for its formation. This driving force is provided by undercooling the austenite to a very large degree (quickly enough to avoid ferrite and pearlite, of course). The amount of martensite that forms depends on the degree of undercooling. The first martensite plates form at the *martensite-start* temperature, or M_s. Progressively more plates form as the temperature is reduced below the M_s. The reason still more driving force is needed is that there is a spectrum of potential nucleation sites for the plates, and only those requiring the least driving force are activated at the M_s.

The temperature at which the martensitic transformation is essentially complete is called the *martensite-finish* temperature, or M_f. (The transformation is never totally completed by a cooling treatment, because it is impossible to form new plates once the untransformed volume falls to a very low level; thus, any quenched steel would have at least a few volume percent of retained austenite, which could be seen only with the aid of an electron microscope.)

Because the martensitic transformation is diffusionless, it cannot be represented by a C-curve on a transformation diagram, in the manner of ferrite, pearlite, and bainite. That is, the amount of martensite formed depends on the temperature reached during cooling, not on the amount of time spent at any given temperature. Thus, the existence of the martensite transformation can be indicated on a transformation diagram only by the temperature at which it begins and the fractions of martensite that form at temperatures below the M_s.

8510 It has been seen from the phase diagram in Fig. 8.2 that carbon is an austenite stabilizer; that is, an increase in carbon content expands the temperature range over which austenite is stable. Also, the amount of distortion in a martensite plate is a function of the amount of carbon trapped in it. This increases the driving force (i.e., undercooling) needed to drive the transformation. Therefore, the M_s temperature decreases as the carbon content increases, as shown in Fig. 8.19. So does the M_f temperature. When the carbon content is higher than about 1%, the M_f is far enough below room temperature that the retained austenite (which etches white) is easily seen in an optical microscope (Fig. 8.18).

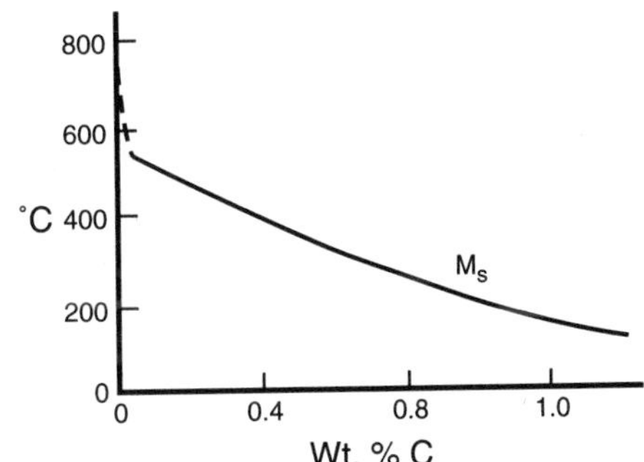

Fig. 8.19 The decrease in the M_S temperature with increasing carbon content in Fe-C alloys. (From *Principles of Heat Treatment of Steel*, G. Krauss, ASM, 1980, p. 52)

Example 8.4

Q. In Fe-C martensite the BCT crystal structure is the result of the entrapment of carbon atoms in one of the three sets of octahedral sites depicted in Example 6.3. Let the z sites be the ones occupied in a martensite plate in a 0.43%C steel; calculate the fraction of possible sites occupied by carbon.

A. Converting 0.43%C to atomic percent (approximately $56/12 \cdot 0.43 = 2$at%), we find that there is about one carbon atom for every 50 iron atoms in the steel. Like a BCC crystal, a BCT crystal has two iron atoms and one z-type octahedral site per unit cell (4 z edges, each shared by 4 unit cells). Therefore, there are 25 possible z-type octahedral sites for every 50 iron atoms. Thus, in the martensite plate in the 0.43%C steel, only one octahedral site in 25 is occupied by a carbon atom. Obviously, the influence of carbon in iron must be very large for such a low site occupancy to change the crystal structure.

Summary

The various microstructures developed by heat treatment of a carbon steel spoke can be understood by use of a portion of the Fe-Fe_3C phase diagram. This portion contains the solid-state analog of a eutectic reaction, called a eutectoid reaction, in which a high-temperature solid phase decomposes upon cooling into two other solid phases. In this case the FCC (austenite) γ-phase transforms to pearlite, comprising a lamellar mixture of BCC (ferrite) α-phase and Fe_3C (cementite). Because the driving force for this reaction is smaller than for the eutectic reaction (i.e., the ΔG is smaller), and because solid-state diffusion is much slower than diffusion in a liquid, the eutectoid decomposition is comparatively sluggish. For this reason it is necessary to use transformation diagrams (or time-temperature-transformation-TTT diagrams) to display the kinetics of transformation of steels of various compositions. The isothermal-transformation diagram is useful to gain an understanding of a transformation, but a continuous-transformation diagram is more useful for purposes of heat treatment. With the CT diagram for the 1040 carbon steel spoke one can readily understand the difference in the microstructures of a slowly cooled *vs.* an air-cooled spoke (after austenitization). The C-curve shape of a transformation diagram can be understood by considering the effect of undercooling on the thermodynamic driving force and the countervailing effect on the rate of diffusion. Finally, the diffusionless transformation of austenite to martensite upon quenching so rapidly as to suppress the diffusion-controlled formation of ferrite and cementite was considered, along with the effect of the carbon content on the degree of tetragonality of martensite and the M_s temperature.

Glossary/Vocabulary - Chapter 8

Bainite — This is a plate-like aggregate of ferrite+cementite that forms when austenite is cooled too rapidly to form pearlite, but not rapidly enough to form martensite. If the carbide particles are on the periphery of the plates, it is called upper bainite, and if they are within the plates, it is called lower bainite. A bainite is essentially as hard as a tempered martensite that has a similar carbide distribution. Bainite has attributes of both Widmanstättin ferrite (in that it is plate-like) and pearlite (in that it is a ferrite/cementite aggregate).

Body-centered tetragonal, BCT — This is one of the 14 Bravais lattices. It is, in effect, a BCC lattice that is stretched along one axis, so that there are two lattice parameters, instead of one. Martensite that contains carbon is BCT, because the carbon trapped during quenching distorts what would otherwise be a BCC crystal (i.e., ferrite).

C-curve — This is a representation of data from a study of the kinetics of a phase transformation, usually a set of isothermal transformations. Temperature is plotted on the vertical axis, and the time to reach a specific stage of the transformation (e.g., 1%, 50%, 99% complete) is plotted on the horizontal axis. The C shape comes from the small amount of driving force (i.e., undercooling) at high temperatures and slow diffusion at low temperatures. The "nose" of the curve depicts the maximum rate (shortest times), where the constraint of diffusion begins to assert itself. The best-known C-curves are the isothermal (IT) diagrams for carbon and low-alloy steels.

Cast iron — This is a high-carbon Fe-C alloy in which the eutectic reaction at 1147°C is important. The term covers the carbon range from >2% to about 5% (by weight). In grey cast iron, the eutectic reaction produces austenite+graphite, and the room-temperature microstructure is a mixture of either ferrite+graphite or ferrite+graphite+cementite. In white cast iron, the eutectic reaction produces austenite+cementite, and graphite is absent from the room-temperature microstructure, except when it is produced by heating below the eutectoid temperature.

Cold drawing (metals) — This is a method of producing tubes and wires. It starts with a rod that is drawn through a series of cylindrical dies, which reduce the diameter and strain harden the material. In the case of tube drawing, the starting rod is first pierced, and a mandrel is inserted in order to define the inner diameter. For a large overall reduction in diameter, annealing stages must be used; otherwise, the strain hardening would get so large as to preclude drawing. However, the final state is left in the cold-worked, i.e., strain-hardened, condition. Bicycle spokes are always used in the as-cold-drawn condition.

Continuous-transformation (CT) diagram — This is a representation of data from a study of the kinetics of a phase transformation during continuous cooling from the initial temperature. It can be determined by thermal analysis or by interrupting the cooling by quenching of specimens at different stages and analyzing them metallographically. These are commonly associated with plain-carbon and low-alloy steels.

Dilatometer	This is a device for monitoring changes in dimensions of a specimen as it is heated or cooled. It is used to study transformations that involve volumetric changes. The austenite-to-ferrite transformation in steels can be studied easily by dilatometry, because of the expansion associated with the formation of non-close-packed ferrite in close-packed austenite.
Eutectoid reaction	This resembles the eutectic reaction, except that it involves a solid phase transforming to two (new) solid phases, rather than starting with a liquid phase. The classical example is the decomposition of austenite in Fe-C alloys to form pearlite, ferrite+cementite, the eutectoid constituent in carbon steels.
Eutectoid steel	This is an Fe-C alloy with about 0.8% carbon (0.77% to be exact). Its SAE/AISI designation is 1080. A eutectoid steel is completely pearlitic after being cooled (not quenched) from austenite.
Habit relationship	In phase transformations that produce plate-like new phases, the new phase is often related crystallographically to the parent phase. That is, some planes and directions in the new phase tend to be parallel to some planes and directions in the parent phase. Such a plane in the parent phase is called a habit plane. When a plate of Widmanstätten ferrite forms, a {110} plane of the ferrite tends to be parallel to a {111} plane of the parent austenite, and the close-packed directions tend to line up as well.
Isothermal-transformation (IT) diagram	See C-curve.
Martensite	This is the product of a diffusionless transformation that occurs when a steel is quenched rapidly from the austenite region of the phase diagram to below the martensite-start temperature. It is a single metastable phase, the crystal structure of which is BCT, with the lattice parameters depending on the carbon content. The hardness of martensite increases with the carbon content. A steel is hardened by austenitizing and quenching to form martensite.
M_f temperature	This is the temperature at which a martensitic transformation during cooling is essentially complete.
M_s temperature	This is the temperature at which a martensitic transformation begins during cooling.
Normalized steel	To normalize a steel means to heat it into the austenite region and air-cool it. This produces a reasonably soft microstructure of ferrite+cementite, and it is faster than a full anneal. The pearlite in a normalized steel is considerably finer (and harder) than in a fully annealed, i.e. furnace-cooled, steel.

Orthorhombic	This is subset of the 14 Bravais lattices in which the unit cell is a rectangular prism. That is, all the angles are 90 degrees and all three edges are of unequal length. There are four types: simple, base-centered, body-centered, and face-centered. Cementite (Fe_3C) is orthorhombic. Polyethylene crystallizes with a body-centered orthorhombic unit cell.
Plain-carbon steel	This is a steel that contains essentially only iron and carbon. Small amounts of manganese are added to scavenge residual sulfur, and small amounts of aluminum and/or silicon may be added to scavenge oxygen and nitrogen. Anything else is a residual impurity. The AISI/SAE designation for a plain-carbon steel starts with 10, with the following digits giving the carbon content in fractions of a percent. For example, a 1040 steel is a plain-carbon steel with 0.40wt% carbon.
Proeutectoid ferrite	This is the ferrite that forms in steel being cooled from austenite before the eutectoid transformation occurs. The proeutectoid ferrite forms along the prior austenite grain boundaries, because they supply a built-in interface for the nucleation of the new phase.
Recalescence	This is the release of heat that accompanies the austenite-to-ferrite transformation. It is often accompanied by a visibile brightening of the dull-red steel. Recalescence can be observed as a change in slope of a cooling curve.
Retained austenite	This is the untransformed austenite that remains after a steel is quenched to form martensite. In steels with carbon contents below about 1%, it can only be observed by transmission electron microscopy or x-ray analysis. In a component that needs great dimensional stability, like a bearing, retained austenite must be eliminated by transformation; otherwise, the component can be distorted after it is put in service when the transformation finally occurs at long times.
Spheroidization	This is a diffusion-controlled process by which a pearlitic, bainitic, or martensitic steel is converted to spheroidal carbides (in a ferritic matrix). The driving force is the reduction in total interfacial energy of the carbide/ferrite interface. It progresses by the diffusion of carbon from small to large particles, or from regions of interface having large curvature to regions of small curvature. In the case of martensitic or bainitic steels, spheroidization may be considered as the most advanced stage of tempering.
Thermal analysis	This is the analysis of changes that occur in a material during heating or cooling. Various transitions occur with release or absorption of heat, and these can be detected by monitoring the temperature of the specimen. The determination of cooling curves during the solidification of an alloy is an example of thermal analysis.
Undercooling	This means cooling a material below the temperature at which its high-temperature state becomes unstable. Liquid water cooled below 0°C would be undercooled, because ice is then the stable phase. A eutectoid steel cooled below 727°C is undercooled. So is any supersaturated solid solution.

Widmanstätten ferrite — This is the kind of proeutectoid ferrite that forms during fairly rapid cooling from austenite, as opposed to the blocky ferrite that forms during slower cooling. The planar interface of blocky ferrite becomes unstable, and plates of ferrite begin to project from it. The plates can grow rapidly at their tips, because of the short diffusion distance there, which permits rapid diffusion of carbon away from the growing plate. The breakdown of the planar interface here is analogous to that which leads to dendritic solidification in a liquid. Widmanstätten ferrite was first discovered in meteorites by Dr. Widmanstätten.

Exercises

8.1 Explain why the proeutectoid ferrite in Fig. 8.1(b) appears to lie in a cellular network.

8.2 Given a 1030 steel being cooled very slowly from the austenite region:

(a) At what temperature can ferrite first start to form?

(b) Give the relative amount and the composition of each phase present at 750°C, assuming equilibrium conditions.

(c) Give the relative amount of each phase and of each microstructural constituent present at 725°C, again assuming equilibrium.

8.3 Using Fig. 8.4, estimate the volume fraction of Fe_3C in pearlite. Using the approximation that ferrite and Fe_3C have the same density (i.e., volume fraction equals weight fraction), compare your estimate with the value calculated from the phase diagram with the lever rule.

8.4 A eutectoid steel is austenitized at 800°C and quenched rapidly to 625°C, where it is held for isothermal transformation. Using Fig. 8.9, give the time (approximately) to form 75% pearlite. What would the other 25% be? What would the latter be if the steel were quenched rapidly to room temperature at this time?

8.5 A one-inch diameter bar of 1080 steel is austenitized and quenched so that the microstructure at room temperature contains martensite, bainite, and pearlite.

(a) Sketch the cross-section of the bar and indicate on it where you would expect to find the largest fraction of each of these three constituents.

(b) Name the phases present in the quenched bar.

8.6 A 1090 steel is austenitized at 850°C and very slowly cooled.

(a) At what temperature could a new phase first appear? What is this phase?

(b) Sketch the microstructure you would expect to find at room temperature, and give the relative amount of each constituent.

8.7 If a 1080 steel were quenched to martensite and then tempered for a long time at, say, 650°C, the microstructure would comprise spheroids of Fe_3C in a matrix of ferrite. How could this microstructure be converted to pearlite?

8.8 What experiments would you use to develop a heat treatment for a 1040 carbon steel spoke that would result in a microstructure resembling that of a slowly cooled 1060 steel. (An approximation giving the principles employed is sufficient.)

8.9 Devise a heat treatment of a 1040 carbon-steel spoke that would produce about 50% ferrite and 50% martensite.

8.10 The growth rate of pearlite remains essentially constant as the growth pro-
[illegible] wth rate of proeutectoid ferrite slows down as
[illegible] n.

9

FRICTION AND WEAR; HARD MATERIALS

The efficient use of human power is obviously crucial to the success of the bicycle. Minimization of energy wasted on friction is just as important as the minimization of weight. Smoothness of operation and sureness of mechanical connections are part of this picture, and these require the minimization of wear. Friction and adhesive wear are closely related, and the remedies for friction and wear are similar, so the two phenomena can be discussed in the same context. From the materials standpoint, the ideal approach would be two smooth, hard components separated by a film that can withstand a large pressure but has almost no resistance to shear.

9.1 Friction

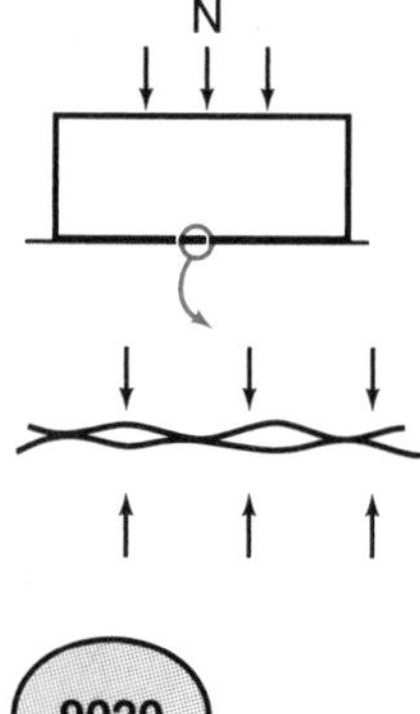

The root cause of friction and adhesive wear of metallic components, like bicycle chains and bearings, is the fact that metal surfaces are never smooth and inert; rather, they are rough and chemically active. This means that mating surfaces make contact at their respective asperities; it also means that chemical bonding can occur if there is metal-to-metal contact, because of the nature of metallic bonding.

When metal atoms are isolated from each other, as in a vapor, their valence electrons occupy discrete energy levels, each of which can hold only two electrons, according to the Pauli Exclusion Principle. When these electrons become constrained in a small volume in the crystalline state, a large number of energy levels is required, and these levels are squeezed so closely together that they form a quasi continuum, referred to as an *energy band.* The formation of such a band is illustrated schematically in Fig. 9.1.

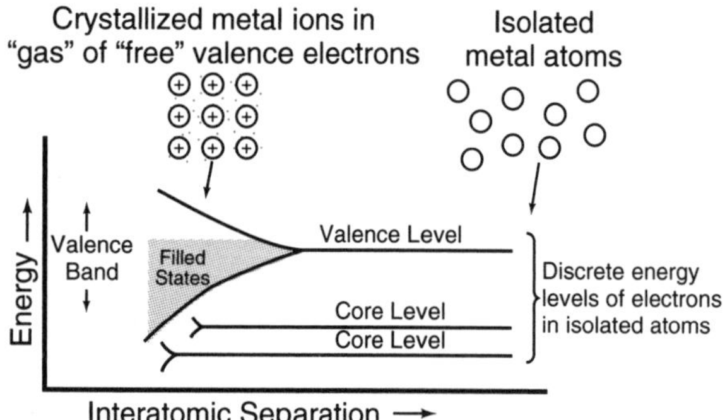

Fig. 9.1 Schematic illustration of the formation of an energy band from a discrete electron-energy level of isolated metal atoms when these atoms are condensed into a crystal. A valence band is shown here to be partly filled; i.e., only a fraction of the available energy states is occupied with valence electrons.

The configuration of an energy band is such that it is asymmetric with respect to the original valence level of isolated atoms. That is, the bottom of the energy band extends farther below the original valence level than the top of the band does above it. This means that, even if the valence band were filled in the crystalline state, the average level of the valence electrons would be below that in the isolated-atom state. This reduction in the average energy of the valence electrons resulting from band formation is the source of the binding energy that causes the crystallization to occur (below the freezing point).

When clean metal surfaces are brought into close proximity, the electrons in the valence band on one side of the interface co-mingle with those on the other side, forming a metallic bond in the same way as occurs during crystallization. This "cold welding" process occurs easily when metal surfaces are rubbed together in a vacuum, where the oxide that covers most metallic surfaces is unable to re-form. This problem can also occur at normal atmospheric pressure, albeit less readily. It is known as "seizing" when it occurs between the components of a machine. On the microscopic scale, it is the predominant mechanism behind friction and adhesive wear of metallic components.

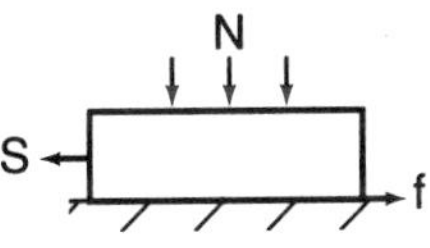

When two metal surfaces are pressed together by a large force normal to the boundary plane, flattening of the surface asperities can occur by means of plastic deformation. The flattening increases the contact area in the interface and, thus, the area over which cold welding can occur. This is why the frictional force between two sliding objects increases with the normal force acting across the contact surface. The frictional force is defined as the force that opposes the relative sliding of two solids subjected to both a normal force, N, and a shearing force, S. Experiments have shown that the frictional force, f, is proportional to N through the coefficient of friction, μ. The μ for the beginning of motion, static friction, is generally greater than for sliding friction, because there is more cold welding at the beginning of sliding.

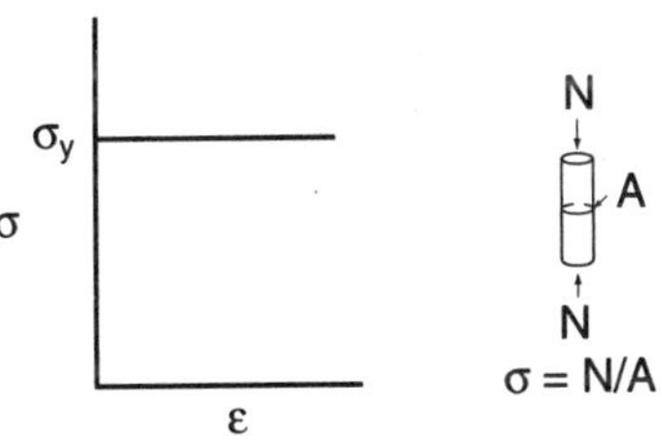

This relationship can be understood in a general way if strain hardening is ignored and the solids are approximated as "perfectly plastic," meaning that the stress-strain curve is horizontal after yielding occurs (in compression) at $N/A = \sigma_y$. Thus, the contact area, A, increases with N according to

$$N = \sigma_y A$$

where σ_y is the tensile yield stress.

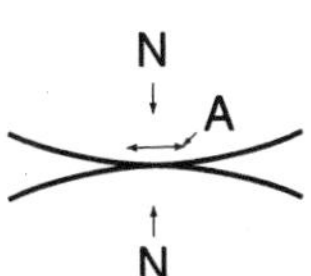

If bonding occurs across the boundary, then sliding requires the shearing of the metallic bridges. This requires a shear stress of at least $\sigma_y/2$, which, from Schmid's law (cf. Section 2.5), would be the yield stress in pure shear. Thus, the frictional force can be approximated by:

$$f = (\sigma_y/2)A$$

Substituting $\sigma_y = N/A$ gives $f = \mu N$, with $\mu = 0.5$.

This model is too simplistic; it assumes that cold welding occurs along the whole contact area. However, it is reasonable to expect that the amount of cold welding would increase with deformation of the asperities (i.e., with N), since this deformation would help to break up the oxide layers and other barriers that inhibit cold welding. Thus, in general, in order to reduce μ, one or more of the following must be done:

1. Reduce the deformation of the asperities; i.e., harden the mating solids.
2. Reduce the cold welding; i.e., reduce metal-to-metal contact.
3. Create a boundary region that is weak in shear.

9.2 Wear

The shearing of metallic bridges just described produces *adhesive wear*. When the cold-welded asperities are subjected to large local plastic deformation, they are strain hardened for some distance back from the original interface, as shown schematically in Fig. 9.2(a). Thus, when plastic shearing of this metallic bridge takes place, it tends to occur not on the original interface but in the softer metal some distance away, as in Fig. 9.2(b). This results in transfer of metal from one side of the interface to the other, producing adhesive wear of the side that lost the metal. Further shear of the type shown in Fig. 9.2(c) produces debris in the form of bits of hardened metal sheared from rubbing surfaces. Subsequent oxidation can lead to hard metal-oxide particles. When such particles are pushed along the surfaces ahead of other sliding asperities, microscopic grooves are cut in the surface. This is the mechanism of *abrasive wear.*

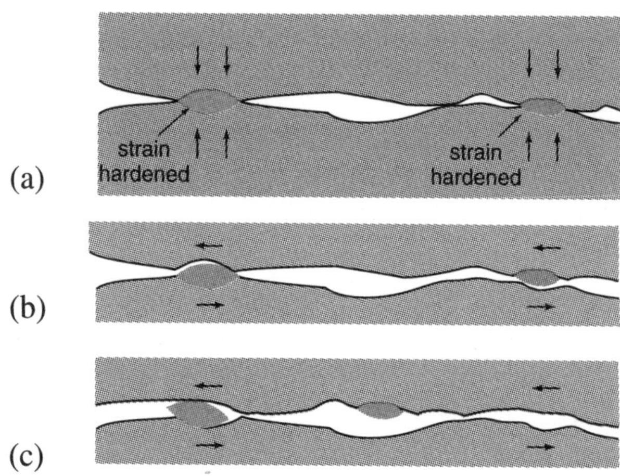

Fig. 9.2 Mechanism of adhesive wear, involving cold welding followed by shearing of the metal bridges.

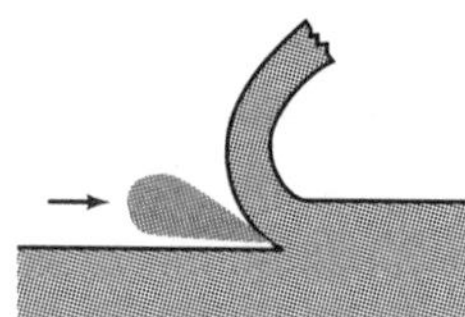

Abrasive wear is akin to metal removal in a machining process, but on the microscale. It involves plowing furrows in the surface of a metal when a particle is pushed along the surface. It occurs by means of plastic deformation so large that the material is completely sheared away.

To reduce abrasive wear one must:

1. Eliminate hard particles (e.g., dirt) as much as possible.
2. Separate the surfaces by creating an interfacial layer that is thicker than the size of the hard particles and is weak in shear.

Applying these principles to the chain and bearings of a bicycle, one would want to make the mating surfaces as hard as possible, thereby reducing the flattening of the asperities, and to use lubricants to create an interfacial layer that would prevent cold welding and would be weak in shear. Another possible alternative is to consider the use of ceramic components. Not only are ceramics much more difficult to deform plastically than metals, but their surfaces are less reactive. Thus, cold welding is less likely.

9.3 Lubrication

Regardless of the material used, a primary resource to combat friction and wear is lubrication. The functions of a good lubricant should already be clear from the foregoing discussion of friction and wear. There are essentially two types of lubrication: *boundary lubrication,* which operates at low sliding velocities to provide a layer of material weak in shear that prevents metallic contact, and *hydrodynamic lubrication,* which serves the same function and gives a much lower coefficient of friction at high velocities.

A common boundary lubricant is an oxide film that prevents cold welding between metallic components. The absence of such a film on surfaces cleaned (e.g., by ion bombardment) in ultra-high vacuum (e.g., outer space) leads to cold welding; this is a problem encountered in space technology.

An oxide film can be removed by mechanical abrasion. When this happens, the result is the production of debris that can lead to rapid abrasive wear. Therefore, oxide films are not generally considered appropriate for lubrication. Sulfides would be much better, because they tend to be soft, particularly in shear, and sulfur adsorbs strongly on most metallic surfaces. Molybdenum disulfide is a well-known solid lubricant, because it forms platelike crystals that slide past each other easily. In this respect it is similar to graphite, having only van der Waals forces between the crystal planes (cf. Section 8.1).

A more common type of boundary lubricant employs chain-like organic molecules, one end of which has a chemical group that bonds strongly to a metal surface. The molecular coatings act somewhat like the bristles on a brush on each opposing surface and thereby tend to prevent metal-to-metal contact. Although strong (covalent) bonds exist within the molecules, the intermolecular forces are of the weak van der Waals type. Hence, the molecular films are weak in shear.

When the relative motion between metallic components occurs at high speeds, hydrodynamic lubrication can occur. 9150
This relies on the principle that it is difficult to squeeze out all of a fluid trapped between two solids under pressure. A classical example is a shaft turning in a bearing ring containing oil.* Generally, some force presses the shaft against one side of the ring. As the shaft turns, oil is dragged into the wedge-like space between the shaft and ring, as shown in Fig. 9.3(a). Ideally, the shaft is supported fully on this film, which may be under very high pressure.

In this case, all the shear occurs in the oil film, and the value of μ may be as low as 0.001. The actual value depends on the viscosity, η, of the oil, the relative velocity, v, of the components, and the pressure, p, as shown in Fig. 9.3(b). In special cases of extremely high speeds, pressurized air can be used; examples are high-speed dental drills and gyroscopes.

* Another example is the hydroplaning of an automobile on a wet road.

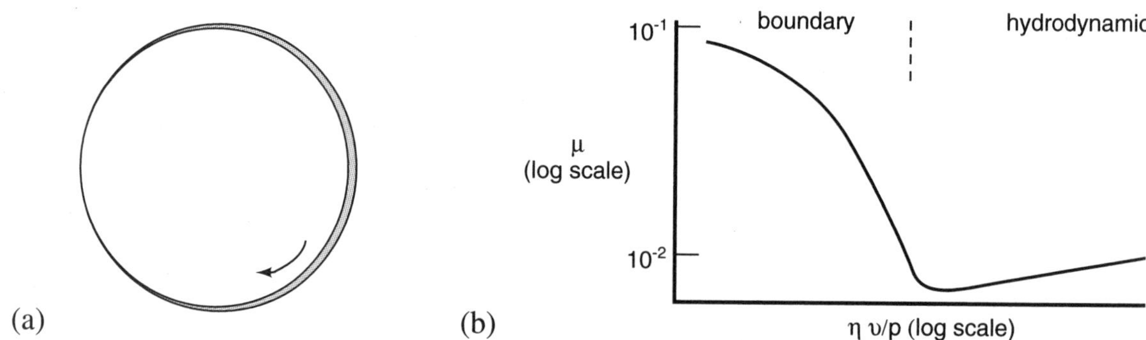

Fig. 9.3 (a) Schematic illustration of trapping of a viscous oil between a rotating shaft and the support ring; the shaft rides on a pressurized film of oil. (b) Dependance of μ on the viscosity of, and pressure on, the oil film and the relative velocity of the moving parts in the boundary and hydrodynamic regions.

For the wheel bearings of a bicycle, the lubricant should provide adequate boundary lubrication at low speeds and good hydrodynamic lubrication at high speeds. Thus, the chain-like organic molecules must bond at one end to the metal, and the chains must be long enough to provide sufficient viscosity to resist the high pressures and form a thick-enough boundary film. However, the viscosity must not be raised so much as to increase the coefficient of friction to unacceptable levels. The lubricant should be resistant to oxidation and breakdown at high temperatures and, of course, be noncorrosive. The art and science of formulating lubricants include not only the configuration of the organic molecules, but also the additives that impart these other characteristics.

A much more demanding set of requirements is found in modern automobile engines. Here, the lubricant must be formulated to withstand the extreme pressures of high-compression engines, to provide a detergent action to remove combustion products, and to have a relatively constant viscosity over a fairly large temperature range. Thus, an engine oil must not be so viscous as to prevent starting in the dead of winter, but it must still protect the engine from wear at high speeds in the summer. Compared to this, lubrication of a bicycle is fairly straightforward.

9.4 The Use of Hardened-Steel Components

In present day technology, the "materials fix" used to combat friction and wear in the bearings and chain of a bicycle is to make them of hardened steel. A steel commonly used in bicycle bearings is designated 52100, which means it contains 1.45% chromium and 1% carbon. The high carbon content is used to provide a microstructure of hard plate-like martensite in which are embedded small particles of carbide, as illustrated by Fig. 9.4. This microstructure can be obtained by austenitizing a hypereutectoid steel somewhat above the eutectoid temperature (where high-carbon austenite and residual (spheroidal) carbides would be formed) and quenching to room temperature. Several precautions are needed in the heat treatment of this kind of steel; they are discussed in Section 9.4.4.

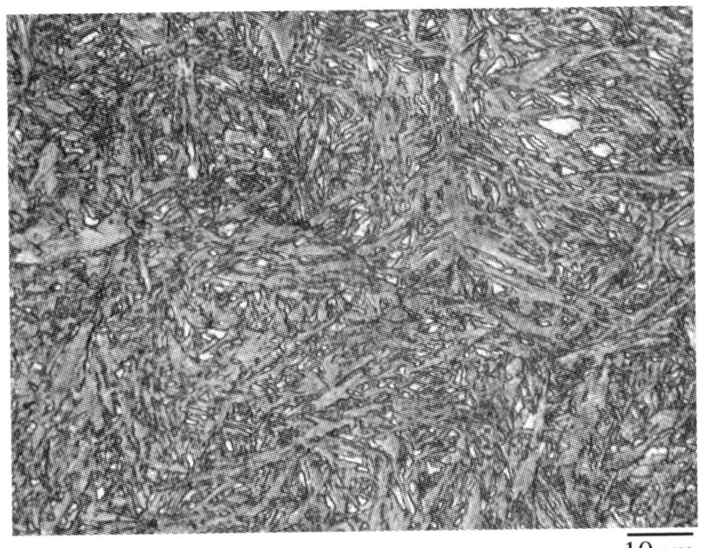

Fig. 9.4 Microstructure of a 52100 steel bearing.

9.4.1 The Hardness of Martensite

The shearing process that transforms austenite to martensite in Fe-C alloys is complicated on the atomic scale. Part of the shearing occurs by the creation and glide of slip dislocations or by the formation of twins on a very fine scale. (Twinning is explained in Appendix 9.1.) Accomplishment of the martensitic transformation partly by slip predominates in low-carbon martensites, whereas this occurs mainly by twinning in high-carbon steels. In either case, the martensite has a very high defect concentration as soon as it is formed, and the interaction of the trapped carbon with these defects is the primary source of the hardening phenomenon. The hardness of martensite increases sharply with the carbon concentration, as shown in Fig. 9.5. The effect of carbon is so great that the hardness of martensite can be considered to be a function of only the carbon content.

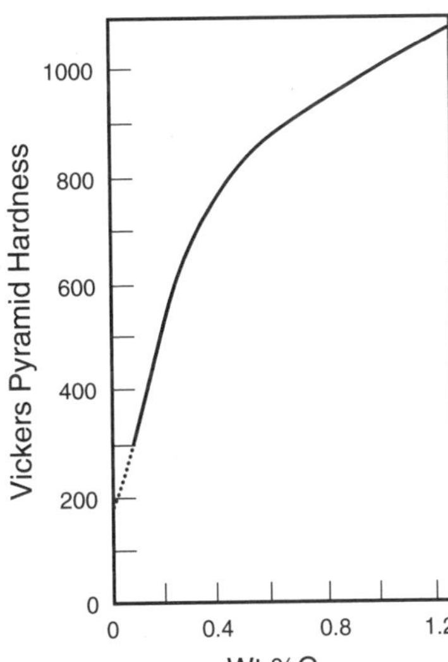

Fig. 9.5 The hardness of martensite depends only on the carbon content. (From E. C. Bain and H. W. Paxton, *Alloying Elements in Steel,* ASM, Metals Park, OH, 1961, p. 3.)

9.4.2 Hardenability of Steel

The hardening of small components, such as bicycle chains and bearings, is fairly straightforward, because, for a carbon content above about 0.4%, it is easy to cool a small component quickly enough to form martensite. However, a component with a thick cross-section would present a problem, because the cooling rate in the interior would be considerably slower than at the surface. Hence, the interior could transform to the unwanted soft products, ferrite and pearlite. For such cases the diffusion-controlled decomposition of γ must be retarded by the addition of alloy elements. Some elements, like manganese and nickel, stabilize the austenite phase and thereby lower the driving force for the $\gamma \rightarrow \alpha$ transforma-
9200 tion, allowing it to occur at lower temperatures where martensite or bainite is favored. Other elements, like chromium, molybdenum, and vanadium, are strongly attracted to carbon atoms and interfere with the diffusion of carbon in austenite. This would be expected to retard a diffusion-controlled reaction. These
9205 alloying elements are said to impart *hardenability* to a steel. This does not mean that they increase the hardness of the martensite, but rather that they enhance the tendency to form martensite (or bainite) during quenching. A comparison of the CT diagrams of a 1040 steel and a 4340 steel (which contains about 1.7%Ni, 0.7%Cr, and 0.3%Mo) is shown in Fig. 9.6. The latter can be transformed to martensite or bainite with a rather slow cooling rate, compared to the 1040 steel.

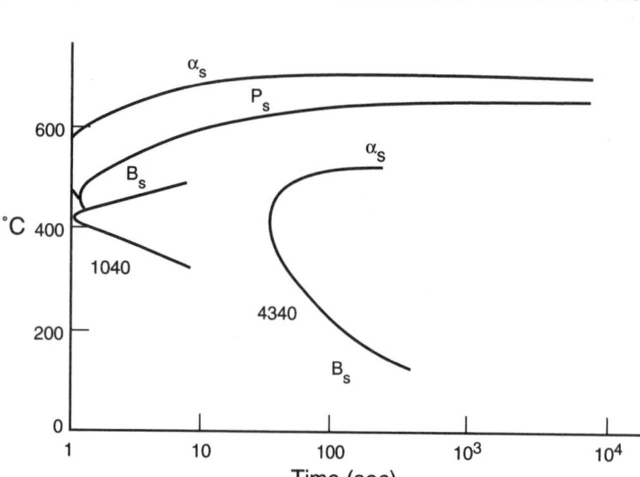

Fig. 9.6 Comparison of the CT diagrams for a 1040 and a 4340 steel.

The standard way of measuring the hardenability of a steel is the Jominy end-quench method. This employs a specimen called a Jominy bar, cooled one-dimensionally in a special fixture, which is illustrated in Fig. 9.7(a). In this procedure a bar is austenitized, and then is quickly transferred from the austenizing furnace to a quenching fixture. Here, a stream of water of a specified temperature flows from a nozzle of specified diameter so that it reaches a specified height above the nozzle. Most of the heat flow out of the bar occurs at the bottom face, against which the water is directed. Comparatively little heat loss occurs by radiation from the sides of the bar.

The one-dimensional cooling is allowed to continue until the whole bar is cooled essentially to room temperature. A flat surface is created by grinding the bar longitudinally, and hardness measurements are made at intervals along the bar starting at the quenched end. A comparison between a 1040 steel and a 4340 steel is made in terms of the Jominy hardness curves in Fig. 9.7(b). The alloy elements obviously make a very large difference in the hardenability of a 0.4%C steel.

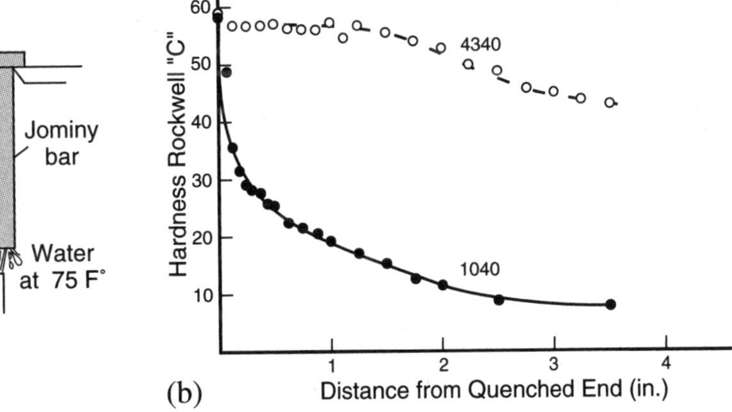

Fig. 9.7(a) Schematic illustration of a Jominy end-quench test used to produce essentially one-dimensional cooling of an austenized steel bar. (b) Comparison of Jominy hardness curves of a 1040 and a 4340 steel, showing the much greater hardenability of the latter.

9.4.3 Tempering of Steel

The hardness of a quenched steel brings with it a tendency toward brittleness. Therefore, one usually sacrifices some of the hardness to gain toughness, which is the reason for tempering a hardened steel. This is illustrated schematically in Fig. 9.8. The extent of tempering is selected to fit the application. For example, knife blades are made from high carbon steel and are only lightly tempered (i.e., tempered at a relatively low temperature), since hardness is much more important than toughness in this application. However, bicycle chains are complex in geometry and are subjected to complicated stresses, so toughness is important. Therefore, steels with lower carbon content are used, and tempering is carried out at somewhat higher temperatures.

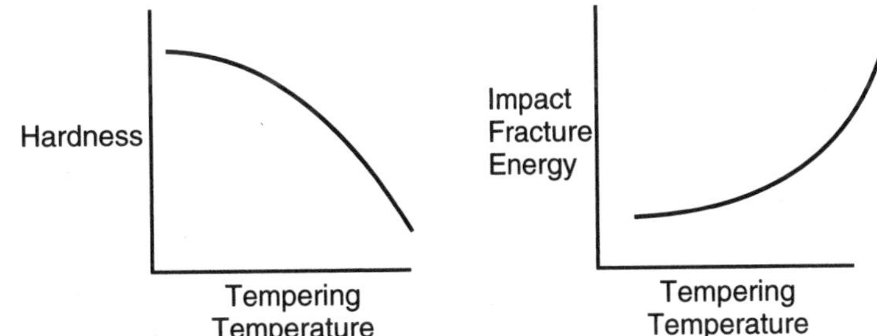

Fig. 9.8 Idealized representation of variation of hardness and toughness during tempering.

The martensite in lower-carbon steels is lath-like, rather than plate-like, and this makes the microstructure fine and complex. Observation by transmission electron microscopy is necessary to clarify it. An example is shown in Fig. 9.9.

Tempering occurs in stages. First, a transition carbide having a hexagonal crystal structure forms, and the martensite becomes somewhat less tetragonal. Then, cementite forms and the martensite becomes still less tetragonal. At higer temperatures or longer times, the cementite particles coarsen (driven by the minimization of interfacial energy) and the matrix becomes BCC.

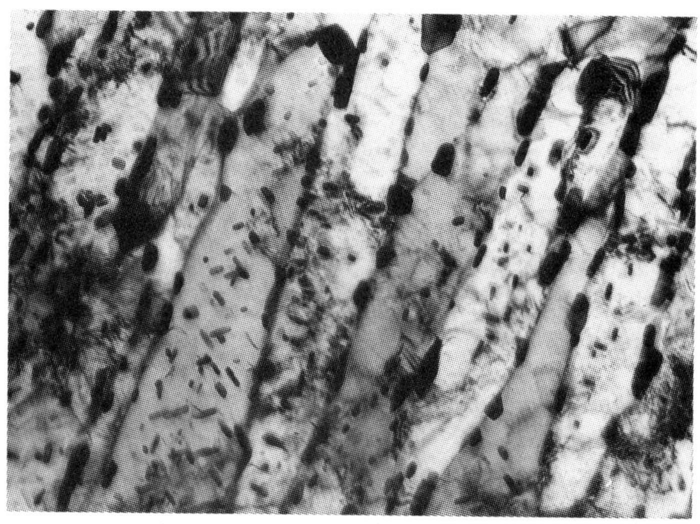

Fig. 9.9 A 4130 steel (0.55Cr, 0.2Mo) water quenched from 900°C and tempered for 1h at 650°C. (Courtesy F. Woldow and Prof. George Krauss, Colorado Schoo of Mines.)

In an alloy steel, when the temperature is high enough for the diffusion of substitutional solutes, alloy carbides can form. In the case of chromium, these can be M_7C_3 or $M_{23}C_6$, where M is either chromium or iron. These form initially in a fine distribution. Since they act as effective barriers to dislocation motion, they provide some additional hardening, superimposed on the softening due to coarsening of cementite. This is generally called *precipitation hardening,* but in alloy steels it is called *secondary hardening.* The secondary hardening produced by chromium and molybdenum is illustrated in Fig. 9.10. It is important not only in bearings, but also in cutting tools such as drill bits. In the latter case, the secondary hardening (utilizing Cr, Mo, W, and V) retards softening, and therefore wear, during high-speed metal cutting.

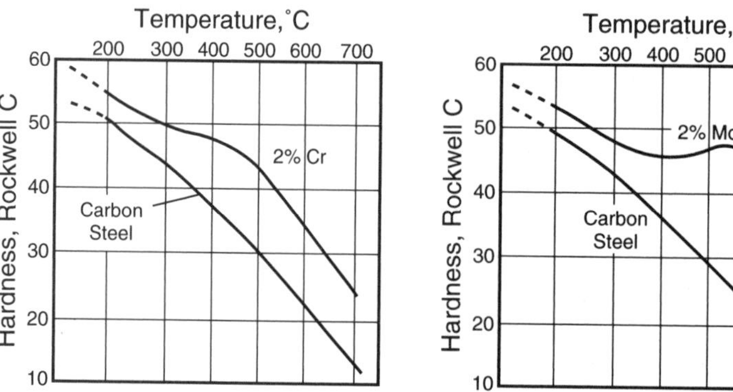

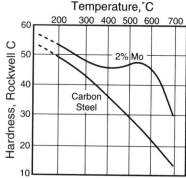

Fig. 9.10 Illustration of secondary hardening in 0.35%C steel caused by formation of chromium and molybdenum carbides. (From E.C. Bain and H. W. Paxton, *Alloying Elements in Steel,* ASM, Metals Park, OH, 1961, pp. 197 and 200)

The fact that chromium and molybdenum form fine-scale, stable carbides is why Cr-Mo steels are used for lightweight bicycle tubing, as will be discussed in the next chapter. The steel in Fig. 9.9 is a bicycle-tubing alloy. The coarse, inter-lath carbides are probably M_3C, and the fine intra-lath ones are probably alloy carbides.

9.4.4 Heat Treatment of Steels

When applied to steels, the term "heat treatment" generally means "hardening," which involves austenitizing, quenching, and tempering. In addition to achieving the desired final hardness, one wants to avoid two potential pitfalls: Cracking or distortion can result from quenching, and dimensional instability can result from retained austenite. Cracking or distortion is caused by the large temperature gradients between the inside and outside of an object that accompany rapid cooling. These thermal gradients mean that the volume changes from thermal contraction or a phase transformation occur nonuniformly, and the inevitable result is the buildup of stresses, called *thermal stresses,* between the inside and the outside of a rapidly cooled object.

Consider the effect of thermal contraction alone. When a hot cylinder is quenched, the outside contracts and thus squeezes the inside, which responds by deforming plastically (because its strength is relatively low at the high temperature). By the time the inside starts its thermal contraction, the outside is already cold and hard. Hence, the inside is constrained from contracting fully. The residual stress pattern, therefore, is tension on the inside and compression on the outside.

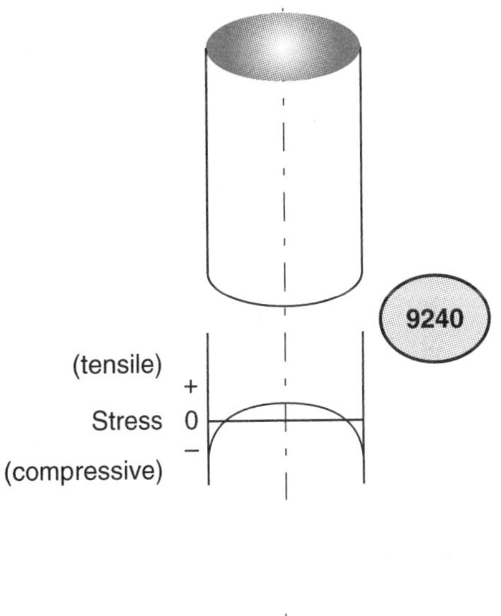

9240

If there is a defect of sufficient magnitude on the inside, the tensile stress could cause the object to crack. If the geometry of the object were more complicated, i.e., if the cross-section were not uniform and the object lacked simple symmetry, then the thermal stresses could cause distortion by plastic deformation.

Alternatively, consider the effect of a dilational phase transformation, like that of close-packed austenite to non-close-packed martensite. The same reasoning would lead to the conclusion that the residual stress pattern would be compression on the inside and tension on the outside. Here, a defect in the outside region could grow into a crack. This becomes more probable as the carbon content is increased, because the toughness of martensite decreases as hardness (i.e., carbon content) increases.

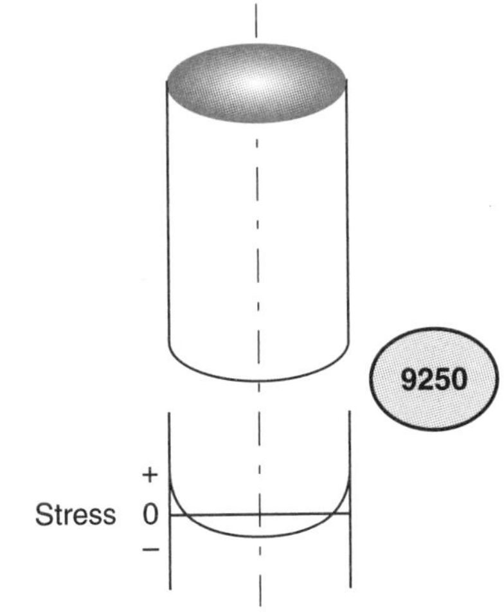

9250

Now, consider the effects of increasing the carbon content of a steel. As pointed out in Section 8.4, the M_s and M_f temperatures fall as the carbon content increases. This means that, in a high-carbon steel, the volume changes due to the martensitic transformation take place at low temperatures. For this reason, the associated stresses are less likely to be relieved by plastic flow. The combination of the low transformation temperatures and the high hardness of the martensite makes cracking during a water quench a distinct possibility when the carbon content is greater than about 0.3%, depending on the size of the object.

The way to prevent quench cracking and distortion is to use a slower quench. For example, oil, or even hot oil, is often used instead of water. This usually calls for more hardenability than is found in carbon steels, so alloy steels must be used, except with thin cross-sections. This is one reason a chromium steel like 52100 (1.45%Cr, 1.00%C) is used for bicycle bearings.

The problem of dimensional stability is related to the amount of retained austenite (e.g., cf. Fig. 8.18), which is increased by high carbon contents (i.e., low M_s and M_f). If a steel with retained austenite is allowed to sit at or above room temperature for a long time, some of the austenite could begin to transform isothermally to bainite. This could occur because the lower part of the C-curve for the bainite transformation (cf. Fig. 8.11) continues to have meaning, regardless of the fact that most of the steel has transformed martensitically. Since the γ-to-bainite transformation is dilational, such a transformation could produce dimensional distortion (or even cracking if the hardness is high enough) after a component, like a bearing, is machined to high-precision tolerances.

To prevent this distortion, two measures can be employed. One is to cool a quenched high-carbon steel to cryogenic temperatures (like 77K, using liquid nitrogen) immediately after the quench, in order to approach or to get below the M_f. The other is to temper the steel at temperatures high enough to transform the retained austenite to bainite during the tempering treatment. In this case it is desirable to have chromium or other carbide-formers in the steel, to retard softening during tempering (cf. Fig. 9.10). This is another reason for using 52100 steel for bearings.

Bicycle chains are made of thin-walled parts. Since thin high-carbon components have sufficient hardenability to be oil-quenched, alloy steels are not needed here. The normal approach is to use the minimum carbon content needed to give the desired hardness, since the toughness of steels of equivalent hardness is inversely related to carbon content. (Remember that hardness is controlled by the tempering treatment, as well as by the carbon content of martensite.) Figure 9.11 shows the microstructure of a pin from a chain. It comprises a mixture of bainite and tempered martensite. From the standpoint of mechanical behavior, these two constituents can be considered more or less equivalent.

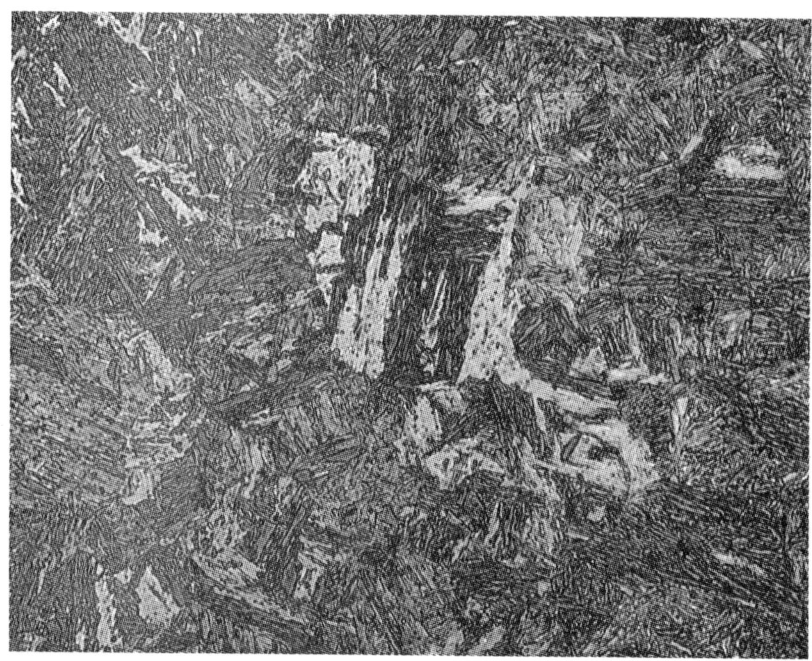

Fig. 9.11 Microstructure of the pin from a bicycle chain, consisting of bainite and tempered martensite.

Example 9.1

Q. Assume that a highly alloyed steel, when hardened by quenching to room temperature, has 10% retained austenite. Calculate the volume expansion that would occur if this austenite later transformed to a ferrite-like phase (i.e., martensite or bainite).

A. FCC austenite has a packing density of 0.74, while that of ferrite is 0.68 (cf. Example 1.3). Therefore, a $\gamma \rightarrow \alpha$ transition would involve a volume expansion, $\Delta V/V$ = (0.74-0.68)/0.74 = 8%. In a steel with 10% retained austenite, the expansion would be 0.1 x 8% = 0.8%, which would be intolerable in a precisely manufactured component, like a bearing set. A $\Delta V/V$ of 0.008 would translate approximately to a linear strain, $\Delta l/l$, of 0.003 (since $\Delta V/V \approx 3\Delta l/l$, if second-order terms and higher are ignored in the expression $\Delta V/V = [(1+\Delta l)^3 - 1]/1$). Such a transformation would obviously produce a very large residual stress in the component.

9.4.5 Surface Hardening

The simplest and cheapest method to improve wear resistance would be to use a high-carbon steel in the quenched-and-lightly-tempered condition. This is appropriate for the bearings, which are loaded mainly in compression. Here, the brittleness of high-carbon martensite is not a problem. However, the chain obviously cannot be made from a brittle material.

One possible approach for the chain would be to use a low-carbon steel for the components and then to create a high-carbon surface by *case hardening*. This can be done by *carburization,* which involves heating the steel in an atmosphere that deposits carbon on the surface in the temperature range where austenite is stable (because austenite has a high solubility for carbon). For example, one could use either a $CH_4 + H_2$ or a $CO + CO_2$ atmosphere. These produce carbon according to:

$$CH_4 \longrightarrow C + 2H_2 \quad \text{or} \quad 2CO \longrightarrow C + CO_2$$

The carbon then diffuses into the steel, and the high-carbon surface region gives a hard, wear-resistant case supported by a lower-carbon, and therefore tough, core. The process and its effects are illustrated in Fig. 9.12.

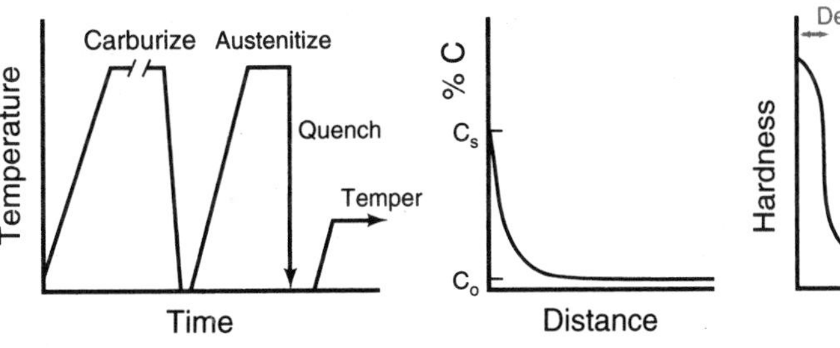

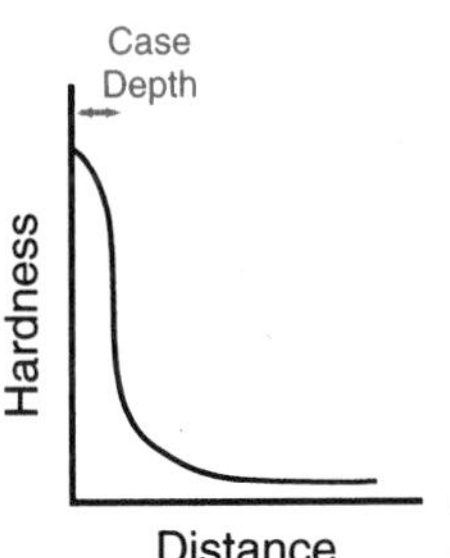

Fig. 9.12 Thermal cycle and resulting carbon and hardness profiles in case hardening by carburizing.

The case thickness should be sufficient to give the desired wear resistance without being so great as to allow large cracks to form, since the latter could lead to fracture of the component. Since hardness and toughness are inversely related (cf. Fig. 9.8), a hard case would tend to be brittle and the softer core would tend
9280 to be tough. Surface hardening allows the surface to be hard and wear-resistant without having low toughness throughout the component. That is, the tough core can act as a crack-arrestor, if a crack should happen to occur in the case. The subject of cracks will be addressed in the next section.

The case depth would obviously increase with the temperature and time of carburization, and it is necessary to be able to predict and control this process. For this one must understand something about diffusion in solids.

The analysis of diffusion is exactly analogous to the analysis of heat flow; the same equations are used. It is also analogous to the flow of electric current in a conductor. In all three cases the flow of something is proportional to a driving force. The latter can be a gradient in mass concentration, or temperature, or electrical potential. For mass flow, the constant of proportionality is the *diffusion coefficient* (also called the *diffusivity*). This is analogous to the thermal conductivity or electrical conductivity. The fundamental driving force for mass flow is actually the gradient in chemical potential; however, in many cases this is approximately equivalent to the concentration gradient.)

Thus, for diffusion one can write:

$$\text{Mass flux} = \text{J (mass/unit area/unit time)} = \text{constant} \cdot dC/dx,$$

where C is the concentration (mass/unit volume) and x is the distance along which diffusion occurs. For simplicity, flow in only one dimension is assumed, but the extension to three dimensions is straightforward.

9290 The preceding expression is known as *Fick's first law* and is normally written as:

$$J = -D\, dC/dx$$

where D is the diffusion coefficient. Note that $J>0$ when $dC/dx<0$.

To predict the case depth in surface hardening of steel by carburization, it is necessary to determine how much carbon accumulates in a given region during some diffusion time, Δt. That is, the rate of accumulation of carbon, ΔC/Δt, in some region of thickness, Δx, must be calculated. For this a simple mass balance is used: The accumulation in the region Δx in time Δt equals the flux in, J_1, minus the flux out, J_2. That is, ΔC x volume = $(J_1 - J_2)$ x area x time

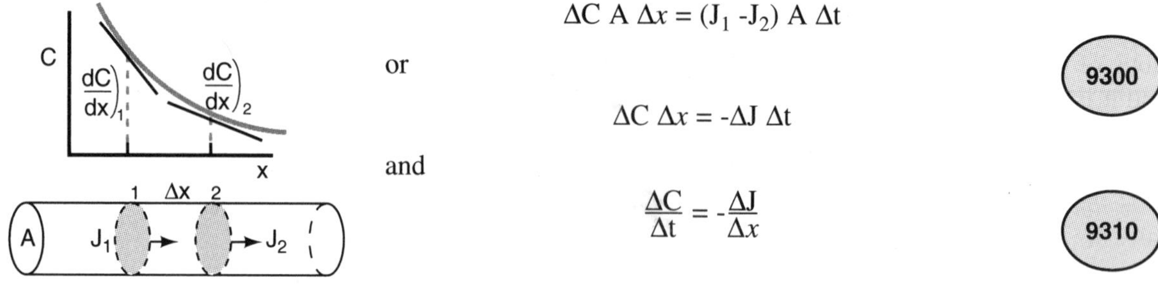

$$\Delta C\, A\, \Delta x = (J_1 - J_2)\, A\, \Delta t$$

or 9300

$$\Delta C\, \Delta x = -\Delta J\, \Delta t$$

and

$$\frac{\Delta C}{\Delta t} = -\frac{\Delta J}{\Delta x}$$ 9310

If the Δx become infinitesimal, this can be written in differential form:

$$dC/dt = -dJ/dx \quad \text{or} \quad dC/dt = d/dx(D\ dC/dx)$$

This becomes

$$dC/dt = D\ d^2C/dx^2$$

for the case where D does not depend on C, which is an approximation often made for ease of calculation. This diffusion equation is known as *Fick's second law* and is applied whenever one wishes to calculate C as a function of t and x.

To solve this second-order differential equation, the boundary conditions must be established. For example, in carburization, at time t = 0, the bulk concentration is C_o. At all times the surface concentration is C_s and at t = ∞ the bulk concentration becomes C_s. Solutions for the diffusion equation for various sets of boundary conditions are available, mainly from studies of heat flow. For one-dimensional carburization when C_s is fixed, the solution for the concentration at any value of x, C_x, at time t is

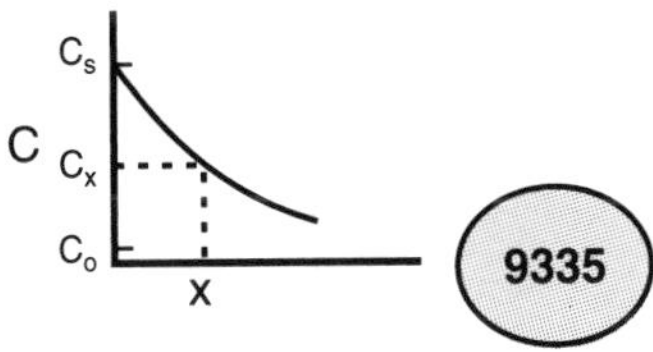

$$\frac{C_x - C_o}{C_s - C_o} = 1 - \mathrm{erf}\left(\frac{x}{2\sqrt{Dt}}\right)$$

The error function, erf, is used in the statistics of random processes, and its appearance in this solution to the diffusion equation emphasizes the fact that the dispersion of carbon in the solid comes by way of random jumping of carbon atoms among interstices in the crystal lattice. Values of the error function are given in Table 9.1.

Table 9.1 erf z for various values of z

z	erf (z)	z	erf (z)	z	erf (z)
0	0	0.55	0.5633	1.3	0.9340
0.025	0.0282	0.60	0.6039	1.4	0.9523
0.05	0.0564	0.65	0.6420	1.5	0.9661
0.10	0.1125	0.70	0.6778	1.6	0.9763
0.15	0.1680	0.75	0.7112	1.7	0.9838
0.20	0.2227	0.80	0.7421	1.8	0.9891
0.25	0.2763	0.85	0.7707	1.9	0.9928
0.30	0.3286	0.90	0.7970	2.0	0.9953
0.35	0.3794	0.95	0.8209	2.2	0.9981
0.40	0.4284	1.0	0.8427	2.4	0.9993
0.45	0.4755	1.1	0.8802	2.6	0.9998
0.50	0.5205	1.2	0.9103	2.8	0.9999

Note that z, the argument of erf z, is a dimensionless quantity. Thus, $\sqrt{Dt}$ has the dimensions of distance. (D has the dimensions m^2/sec or cm^2/sec in compilations of data.) The quantity $\sqrt{Dt}$ is, therefore, a characteristic diffusion length, and it is often used as a rough estimate of the length scale over which diffusion has occurred during time t for a given value of D.

In order to calculate the depth of carburization, one must know the value of D at the temperature of interest. Values of D have been determined experimentally for various systems. They are tabulated according to the known exponential dependence of D on temperature, T, expressed in degrees Kelvin:

$$D = D_o \exp - (Q/RT)$$

where Q is the *activation energy* and R is the gas constant (cf. Section 6.3.1). When Q is given in cal/mole, then R is ≈ 2cal/mole-K. Values of D_o and Q for several systems are given in Table 9.2.

Table 9.2 Selected Values of D_o and Q

System	D_o(cm²/sec)	Q(kcal/mole)
C in α-Fe	6.2×10^{-3}	19.2
C in γ-Fe	0.1	32.4
Ni in Ni	1.3	66.8
Nb in Nb	12	105

The carburization process is considerably more expensive than ordinary heat treatment because of the specialized equipment and skills as well as the time and energy required. If case hardening were used for the components of bicycle chains, the cost of the chains would be beyond the reach of most customers. The alternative is simply to use a medium-carbon steel and to temper (after austenitizing and quenching) to a hardness that corresponds to a toughness sufficient for the application. This requires that some wear resistance be sacrificed. The economic question is whether it is cheaper to replace periodically the worn chains made of conventionally heat-treated steel or to pay the initially higher cost of case-hardened chain, which would have much longer life. The nature of the product and the market have decided in favor of the former. This means that lubrication and cleanliness are doubly important in the lives of chains.

Although carburization is not used for chains, it is routinely used for the freewheel cogs. Surface hardening is needed here to provide reasonable wear life for the gear teeth.

Example 9.2

Q. Referring to Fig. 9.12, it is desired to carburize a 1010 steel to a case depth of 0.2mm (0.008in), defined as the distance below the surface at which the hardness (and, therefore, the carbon content in a quenched steel) is halfway between the value at the surface and the value in the relatively soft core. Calculate the time needed for this at 925°C in an H_2/CH_4 mixture that can saturate the surface with carbon.

A. Assume that the surface is flat enough so a one-dimensional diffusion analysis is sufficient. A solution is required to Fick's second law:

$$dC/dt = D\, d^2C/dx^2$$

where C is the carbon concentration (which is a function of distance from the surface, *x*) t is time, and D is the diffusivity of carbon in iron at the appropriate temperature. The solution, given in Section 9.4.5, is

$$\frac{C_x - C_0}{C_s - C_0} = 1 - \text{erf}\left(\frac{x}{2\sqrt{Dt}}\right)$$

where C_x is the carbon concentration at any point x (here taken to be 0.2mm); C_0 is the initial carbon concentration in the steel (0.1%); C_s is the carbon concentration at the surface, and erf is the error function (Table 9.1).

If the surface is saturated at 925°C, then from the phase diagram (cf. Fig. 8.2) the carbon content of the austenite at the surface, C_S, is 1.25%. The desired carbon concentration at x = 0.2mm is then (1.25 - 0.1)/2 + 0.1 = 0.675%. That is,

$$\frac{C_x - C_0}{C_s - C_0} = 0.5$$

and the error function can be written

$$\text{erf } z = 1 - 0.5 = 0.5$$

Entering this value in Table 9.1 and interpolating, z is found to be 0.477. Thus,

$$\frac{x}{2\sqrt{Dt}} = 0.477$$

For x = 0.02cm,

$$\sqrt{Dt} = \frac{0.02}{2(0.477)}$$

A value is now required for D. Consulting the data in Table 9.2, $D = D_0 \exp\text{-}(Q/RT)$ for T = 925+273=1198K can be written

$$D = 0.1 \exp - \frac{32400}{2 \cdot 1198} = 1.3 \times 10^{-7} \text{cm}^2/\text{sec}$$

The required time is then obtained from

$$1.3 \times 10^{-7}\ t = \left(\frac{0.01}{0.477}\right)^2$$

giving t = 3380 sec = 56 minutes.

9.5 Cracks in Solids

Case hardening is used when it is desirable to have a very hard, wear resistant surface without the danger of brittle fracture of the whole component. Whether or not a crack will propagate in a given material is the subject of fracture mechanics. The tendency for crack propagation depends on four factors:

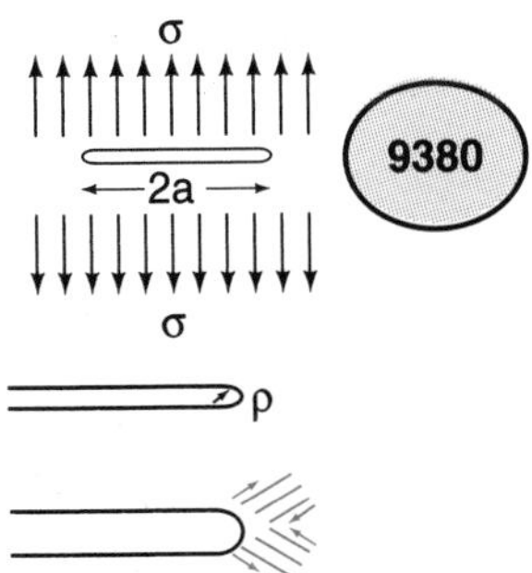

1. The component of stress acting normal to the plane of the crack, σ.
2. The square root of the crack length, $\sqrt{2a}$.
3. The sharpness of the crack, or the radius of curvature at the crack tip, ρ.
4. The inherent toughness of the material, which means the ability of the material to deform plastically so as to cause the crack tip to become more blunt.

The question of whether or not a crack propagates must depend on the value of the stress at the crack tip. It can be shown from the theory of elasticity that, for an elliptical crack in a plate subjected to a tensile stress, σ, the maximum stress (at the crack tip) is given by

$$\sigma_{max} = \sigma\left(1 + 2\sqrt{\frac{a}{\rho}}\right)$$

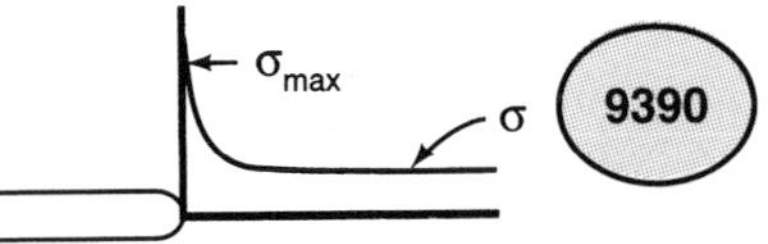

For example, for a circular hole, $a=\rho$, and the stress-concentration factor is 3. That is,

$$\sigma_{max} = 3\sigma$$

9400 Thus, the stress-concentration factor increases directly with the length of the crack and inversely with the radius at its tip. Since plastic flow would make the radius larger, it must decrease the stress-concentration factor.

The science of fracture mechanics was developed from the theory and experiments of Griffith, who studied the fracture of glass, choosing it as an ideal model material. In linear elastic fracture mechanics, the stress at a crack tip is characterized by a parameter called the *stress-intensity factor,* K, given by

$$K = Y\sigma\sqrt{a}$$

where Y is a geometrical constant. The basic premise is that a crack will begin to extend in an unstable manner when the stress-intensity factor reaches a critical value, K_c, which is a property of the material. A tough material is one with a high K_c.

In an elastic material (like glass) in which plastic flow does not occur, K_c can be related to Young's modulus and to the energy to create new surface in the material. This was done by Griffith, and the theory is outlined in approximate fashion in Appendix 9.2.

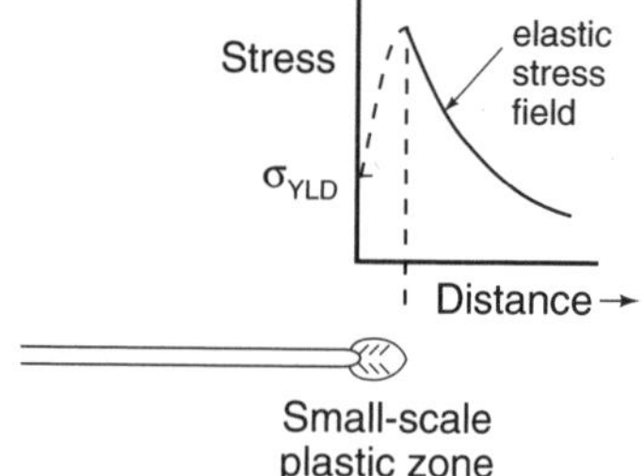

This approach applies to metallic materials under conditions in which plasticity is confined to a small region around the crack tip. In this case the *small-scale-yielding approximation* is used. Here, it is assumed that whatever occurs at the crack tip depends on the elastic stress field outside the plastic region, and that the latter is very small, compared to the length of the crack.

Since K is a parameter that describes the elastic stress field, it must also control the events in the plastic region. Therefore, although K_c for a metallic material cannot be related directly to known material properties, it can be measured by experiment and then used as an empirical material parameter. The small-scale-yielding approximation can be used either when the yield stress of the material is high, or when the applied stress is low (i.e., K is small). The latter case, for example, is used to deal with the propagation of fatigue cracks, even in ductile materials.

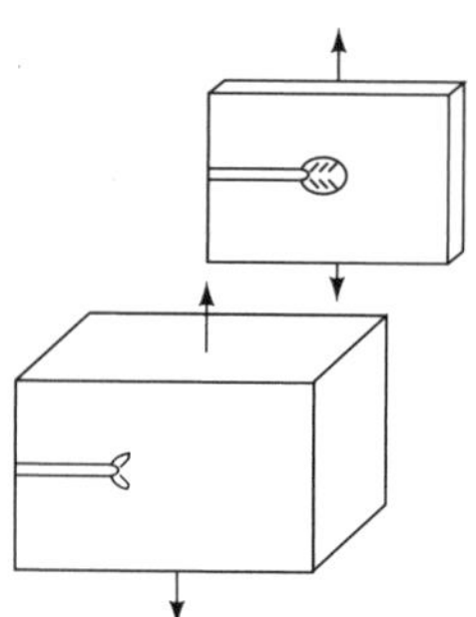

The amount of plasticity at a crack tip depends on the thickness of the cracked body. For a thin sheet, in which stress components normal to the plane of the sheet can be set equal to zero (the condition called *plane stress*), the plastic zone would be larger than in a thick plate, in which strain components normal to the plate can be ignored (the condition of *plane strain*).

The condition of plane strain is used as a reference condition in fracture mechanics. Thus, one can measure the K_c for a material under plane-strain conditions and treat the result as a material constant, to be applied in any case in which the geometrical factor, Y, can be calculated. The critical value of K_c in plane strain is called the *plane-strain fracture toughness,* designated K_{Ic}, and values are tabulated for various high-strength materials, as a function of the yield stress, for example. In a case-hardened steel, the K_{Ic} of the case would be very low, but that of the core would be much higher. If the case thickness is small enough, there is little likelihood that a crack in the case could propagate into the core in an unstable manner and cause the component to fracture.

9.6 The Use of Ceramics for Bearings

Ceramics are generally based on solid oxides, carbides, nitrides, or borides, and they have certain properties that make them attractive for use as bearings for bicycles. These are:

1. High hardness
2. Non-reactive surfaces
3. Low weight

The high hardness means that surface asperities are not easily flattened, and it is difficult to gouge the surface by plastic deformation. Low surface reactivity means that cold welding is difficult. Both these factors favor low friction and long wear. Low weight is a self-evident advantage on a bicycle and results from the fact that ceramics are composed mainly of elements with low atomic weights. Ceramic bearings have been developed for engines designed to run at high temperatures, where the high-temperature strength and chemical inertness of ceramics, compared to metals, are of great advantage. However, now that they are available, their possible use on bicycles may be envisioned for the future.

The main disadvantage of ceramics is their very low toughness, which is a direct result of their great resistance to plastic flow (i.e., high hardness). The high stresses that can occur at the tips of crack-like flaws cannot be relieved readily by dislocation motion. Thus, flaws provide the sites for the initiation of brittle fracture, which occurs when the stress intensity at some flaw reaches the critical value. The energy needed to propagate a crack is small, again because little energy is dissipated by dislocation motion at the crack tip. Thus, the challenge in making structural ceramic components is to eliminate flaws. However, since bearings are loaded in compression, a low toughness is tolerable.

The properties of ceramics stem directly from their structure and bonding. The bonding is usually ionic or covalent. That is, one or more valence electrons are either transferred from one element to another or are shared between the two elements. In many cases, the bonding is actually a combination of the two. That is, a valence electron can be viewed as spending part of its time attached to one element (which is then the anion) and the rest of its time being shared equally between the two reacting elements. In any case, the bonding is very different from that in a metal.

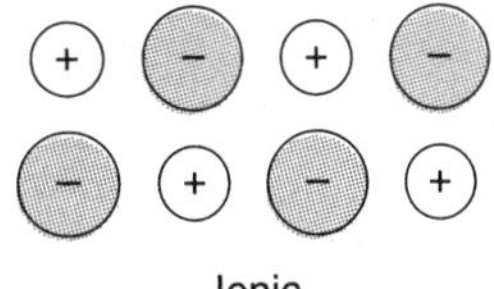

Ionic

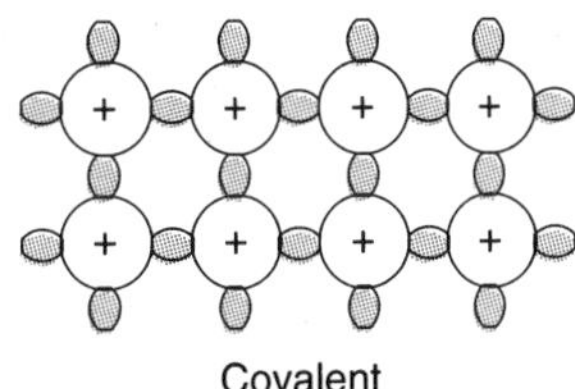

Covalent

This difference in bonding means that ceramics do not tend to cold weld as metals do when surfaces are rubbed together. There is no sea of free electrons at the surface to merge with the electron sea of a mating surface. The atoms on covalently bonded ceramic surfaces tend to rearrange themselves to minimize the number of "dangling bonds." Ionically bonded ceramics tend to adsorb molecules from the environment to saturate the surface bonds.

9.6.1 Crystal Structures

Ceramics may be crystalline, amorphous (i.e., glassy) or mixtures of the two. The crystal structures are more complex than those found in metals for several reasons, including the following:

1. A ceramic is usually composed of more than one element.
2. The elements are present in a definite ratio, dictated by the necessity for overall charge neutrality in an ionic solid or by the number of possible covalent bonds.
3. In an ionic solid, ions of one sign may be nearest neighbors only of ions of the other sign; the number of nearest neighbors depends on the relative sizes of the ions, because ions are not allowed to overlap. In a covalent solid the bonds must have specific lengths and directions.

Examples of the crystal structures of some important ceramics are shown in Fig. 9.13. Magnesia, MgO, and alumina, Al_2O_3, are mainly ionic. The former has the same crystal structure as rocksalt (NaCl). Silicon carbide is covalent and has a crystal structure similar to diamond or silicon. (Both the rocksalt and diamond cubic structures are FCC, with two atoms (or ions) associated with each lattice site.) In a covalent solid the number of neighbors of any given atom often follow the so-called 8-N rule. The total number of electrons in the shared-electron bonds around any given atom is then eight, the number needed for an inert-gas-type full "outer shell." If an element has a valence of N, it needs 8-N neighbors to complete its outer shell. Since both silicon and carbon have a valence of four, silicon carbide crystallizes in the diamond-cubic structure, as do silicon and carbon themselves. In this structure each atom has four neighbors.

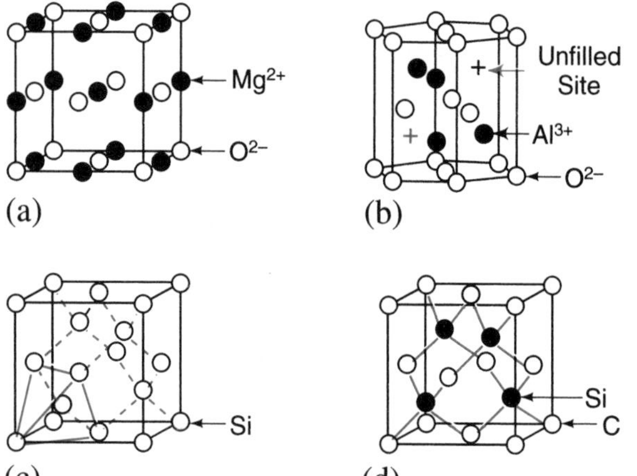

Fig. 9.13 Crystal structures of (a) MgO, the rocksalt structure, (b) Al_2O_3, (c) silicon, the diamond-cubic structure, and (d) silicon carbide. (Adapted from M.F. Ashley and D.R.H. Jones, *Engineering Materials 2,* Pergamon Press, Oxford, 1986, pp. 154, 156)

9.6.2 Dislocation Motion and Ductility

Dislocations exist in crystalline ceramics, as they do in metals. However, the nature of the bonding in ceramics makes dislocation motion difficult, except at high fractions of the melting temperature, where the thermal energy is often sufficient to overcome barriers to dislocation glide. In metals, bonding is more or less non-directional, so the angular relationships between atoms in a crystal may usually be distorted without large expenditures of energy. In addition, all the ions in the valence-electron "gas" are of like sign, so the number of possible slip systems is not constrained in the same way as in ionic crystals. Figure 9.14 shows schematically that shear on certain planes in an ionic crystal would bring ions with like charge into first-neighbor proximity (like the horizontal shear in Fig. 9.14b). This would meet with very high resistance, and slip of this type would not occur except at quite high temperatures.

Glide on the diagonal plane in the ionic crystal would occur with less difficulty, which means that single crystals of the appropriate orientation can deform at reasonably low stresses. However, in polycrystalline materials, in order for the constituent grains to remain bonded together, it is necessary that several slip systems operate in each grain, since each grain of a grain pair tends to deform on its own planes of maximum shear stress. This means that neighboring grains are forced either to take on complex changes in shape or to come apart along the grain boundaries. In the most general case, each grain would need to have five independent slip systems available. For FCC metals, this is not a problem, because there are 12 possible slip systems, and 8 of these are independent (cf. Chap. 4). However, in an FCC ionic crystal with the rocksalt structure, for example, certain of these slip systems are forbidden because of the like-charge-overlap problem depicted in Fig. 9.14(b). This difficulty leads to very limited ductility (and toughness) in ionic polycrystals.

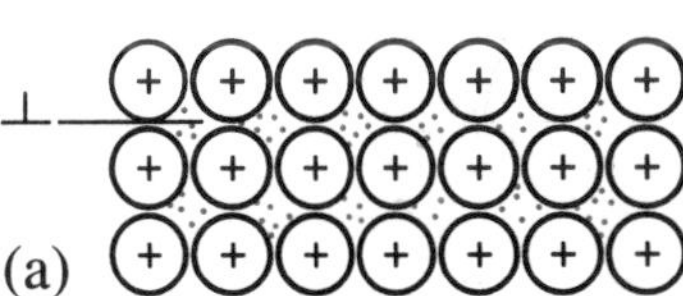

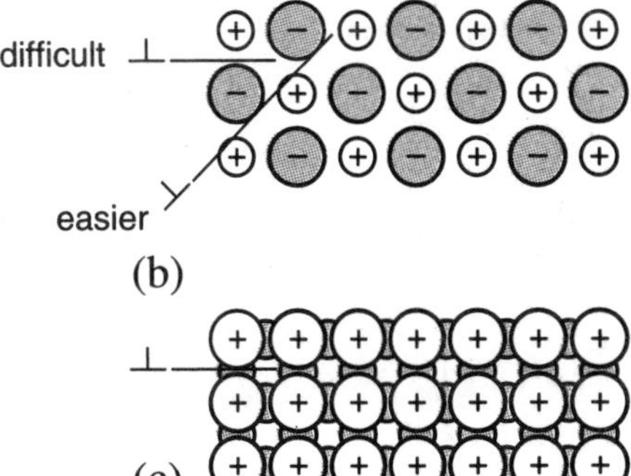

Fig. 9.14 Schematic illustration of dislocation glide in crystals with three types of bonding, showing that glide is relatively unconstrained in (a) metals compared with (b) ionic crystals or (c) covalent crystals. (Adapted from Ashby and Jones, loc. cit., p. 164)

With covalent ceramics, even with single crystals, ductility is limited by the fact that dislocation glide must necessarily break strong localized bonds. This is so difficult that covalently bonded crystals are essentially elastic solids up to about half the absolute melting temperature. That is, dislocation glide requires so much energy at lower temperatures that the necessary applied stresses would be well above those needed to propagate the flaws that inevitably exist (cf. Appendix 9.2). (For example, there are bound to be submicroscopic cracks on the surfaces from contacts with other solids. Even light contact forces generate large stresses, if the contact area is very small.)

9575 9.6.3 Forming of Ceramics, Sintering

Metals are normally produced by processes that begin with melting in a container made of ceramics. This option is not available to most ceramics, because their melting temperatures are so high no material can contain them. In addition, even when a solid ceramic block is produced, it cannot be formed into useful shapes by deformation processing, as metals can, owing to the high hardness and minimal ductility. However, these problems were solved by our ancestors long before the techniques for metal production were worked out. It is known that primitive cultures that had not advanced to the use of metals had nevertheless become quite adept at making a variety of ceramic objects. This technology was also well advanced in western societies long before the industrial revolution, as can be illustrated by consideration of the teacup.

The making of a teacup begins with molding of clay, which is a mix of sheet-like units of a metal silicate and water. The metal silicate may be viewed as an "alloy" of one or more metal oxides, like MgO, CaO, or Al_2O_3, and silicon dioxide, SiO_2.

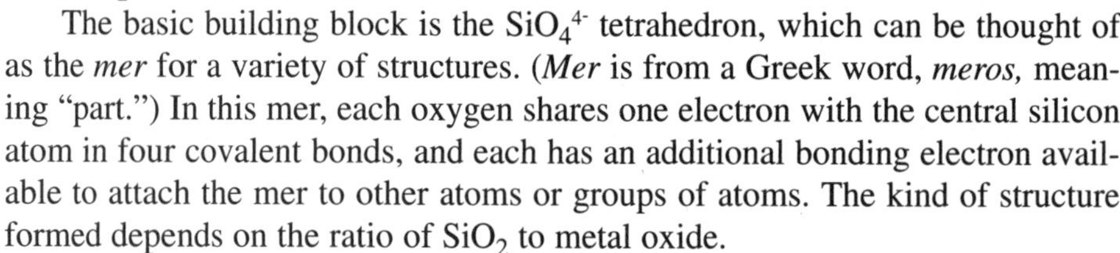

The basic building block is the SiO_4^{4-} tetrahedron, which can be thought of as the *mer* for a variety of structures. (*Mer* is from a Greek word, *meros,* meaning "part.") In this mer, each oxygen shares one electron with the central silicon atom in four covalent bonds, and each has an additional bonding electron available to attach the mer to other atoms or groups of atoms. The kind of structure formed depends on the ratio of SiO_2 to metal oxide.

$Si_2O_7^{6-}$

The simplest kinds of silicate structures utilize SiO_4^{4-} mers or *dimers* of $Si_2O_7^{6-}$ surrounded by metal ions. For example, forsterite, Mg_2SiO_4, is a silicate in which each SiO_4^{4-} tetrahedron is surrounded by four Mg^{2+} ions, which form bridges to adjacent tetrahedra. That is, each Mg^{2+} ion has contributed one electron to an oxygen in each of two SiO_4^{4-} tetrahedra.

If the MgO:SiO_2 ratio is a bit higher than 2:1, the structure becomes chainlike, as shown in Fig. 9.15, in which chains of SiO_4^{4-} tetrahedra are held together along their length by metal ions. The oxygens forming the connecting links between tetrahedra are called *bridging oxygens.*

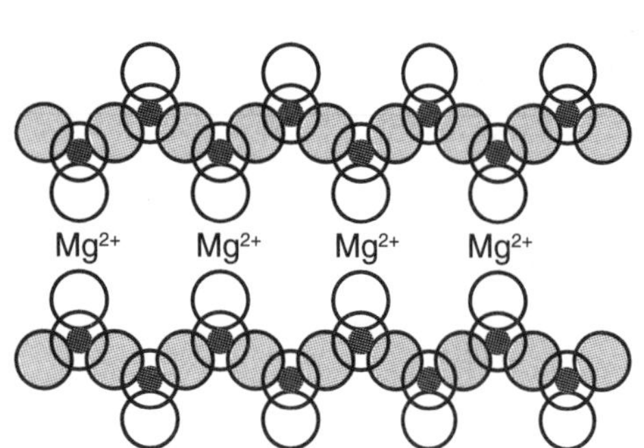

Fig. 9.15 The structure of $MgSiO_3$, a chain-like silicate. The bridging oxygens are shaded; the remaining oxygens carry a -1 charge and can bond with metal ions.

At still higher metal-oxide:SiO_2 ratios, the structures become sheet-like. As illustrated in Fig. 9.16, the oxygens at three corners of each tetrahedron are bridging oxygens, and the remaining oxygen is left to form bonds with other ions, particularly metal ions. The bridging oxygens on the lower side of the sheet each have two silicons as neighbors; therefore, they cannot form any more primary bonds. However, the sheets are polarized, with the side having the bridging oxygens appearing negative and the side with the metal ions appearing positive. Hence, adjacent sheets can form secondary bonds, especially with water, which is a polar molecule.

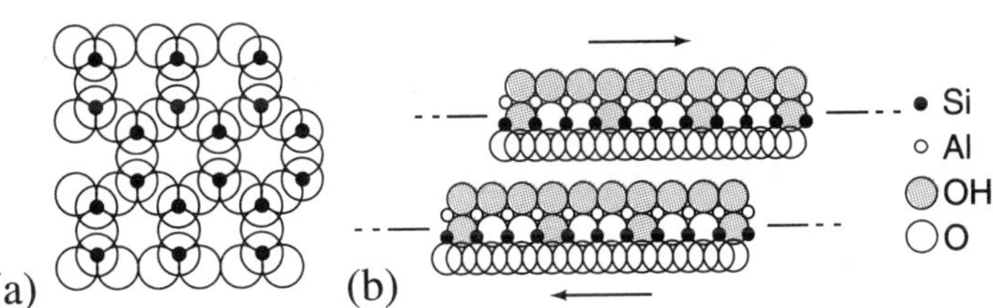

Fig. 9.16 (a) A sheet-like silicate; this structure is found in clay and mica. (b) Schematic illustration of shearing between sheets of clay lubricated with adsorbed water molecules, making the clay highly plastic for easy molding. (From L. H. Van Vlack, *Elements of Materials Science,* 2nd ed., Addison-Wesley, Reading, Mass., 1964, p. 229.)

The secondary bonds between sheets are weak, so the sheets may be easily cleaved apart, as with mica, for example, or sheared, when clay is molded. Thus, in making a teacup, clay comprising sheet-like silicates containing adsorbed water is molded into the desired shape and then heated *(fired)* in a kiln to drive off the excess water. This causes some of the silicate to form a disorderly three-dimensional network, i.e., a glass, in which nearly all the oxygens are bridging oxygens. The glass is fluid at the firing temperature. Upon cooling, the glassy phase becomes rigid and acts to bond the crystalline particles together, as illustrated in Fig. 9.17. This process is an example of *liquid-phase sintering,* the glass phase being a liquid at the firing temperature.

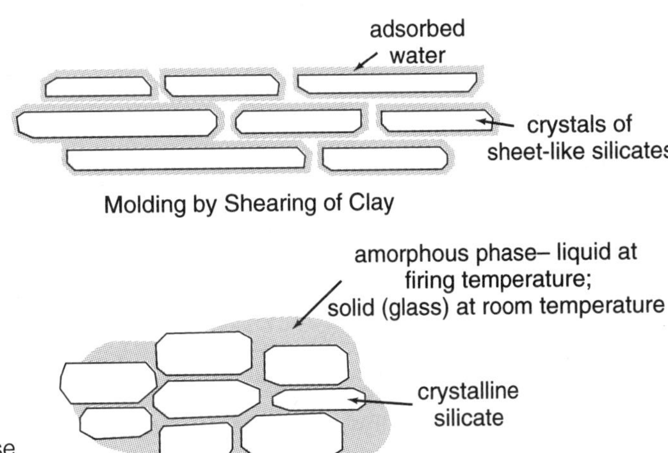

Fig. 9.17 Schematic illustration of liquid-phase sintering during making of pottery.

The sintering of glass spheres by heating them to a temperature at which the glass becomes viscous is illustrated in Fig. 9.18. Capillary action causes the glass at the sphere surfaces to flow to reduce the sharp angles formed along the points of contact.

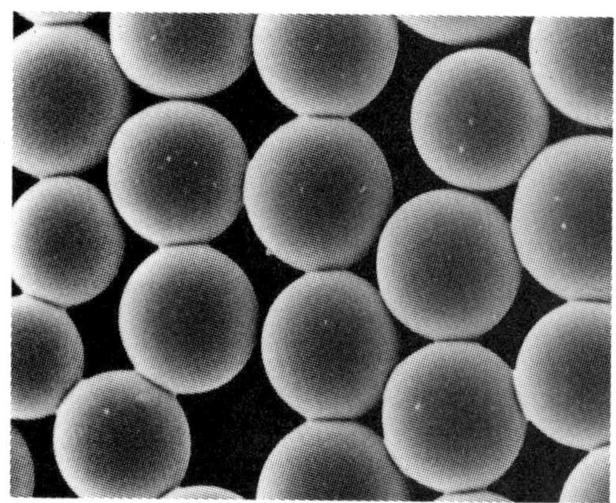

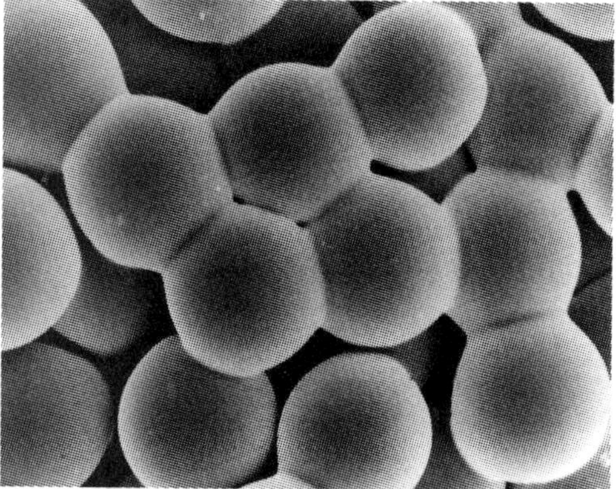

Fig. 9.18 The sintering of glass spheres by heating into the temperature range at which viscous flow can occur. (Courtesy of J. Zhao and M. P. Harmer, Lehigh University.)

Sintering can occur in crystalline solids by diffusion at temperatures above half the absolute melting point; in this case it is called *solid-state sintering*. It can be illustrated by Fig. 9. 19(a) to (c), which shows how two spherical particles can slowly merge by diffusion of atoms along the interface between them into the cusp at the periphery of the contact region. The driving force for this diffusion is, again, capillarity. The solid-vapor surface energy is higher than the grain-boundary energy, and the approach to equilibrium would require that the contact angles increase to the equilibrium value, governed by the balance of interfacial tensions, as shown in Fig. 9.19(d) and (e).

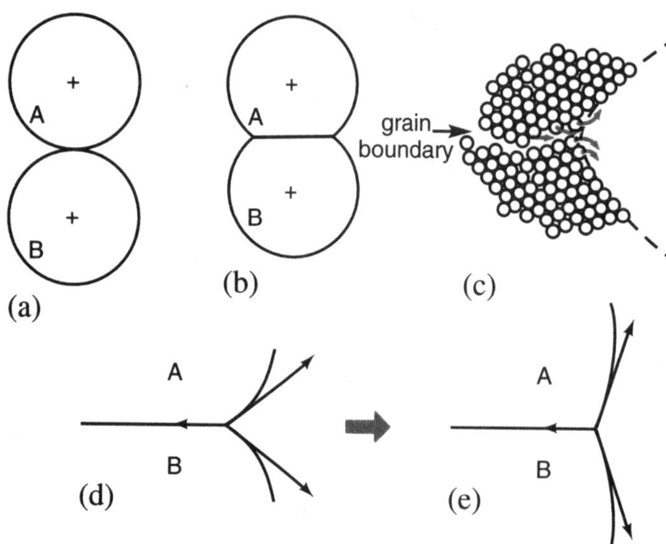

Fig. 9.19. (a) Two spheres in contact before sintering begins. (b) The formation of a solid neck between them as the result of diffusion along the grain boundary that separates them, as shown in (c). (d) The imbalance of interfacial tensions at the periphery of the contact area during the sintering process. (e) The equilibrium balance of interfacial tensions, which would represent the end-point of sintering of this pair of particles.

9600 If sintering were carried out long enough, one could reach 100 percent density. In practice, the process is often stopped short of complete densification, and there is a residue of porosity. As long as the residual pores lie along grain boundaries, as shown in Fig. 9.20(a), they could, in principle, be eliminated, because the grain boundaries are paths of relatively rapid diffusion. However, if grain growth occurs and leaves the pores isolated within grains, as shown in Fig. 9.20(b), then it would be impossible to eliminate them in any reasonable time, owing to the slowness of lattice diffusion.

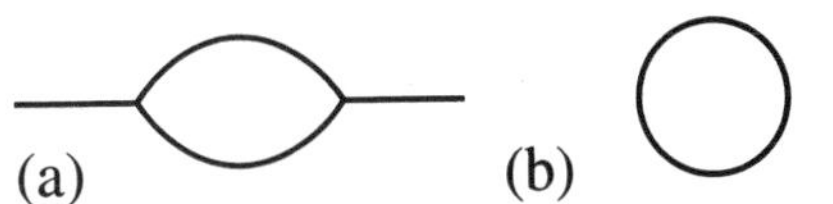

Fig. 9.20 (a) A residual void along a grain boundary, and (b) the same void after grain growth has caused the migrating boundary to leave it behind. Note the equilibrium shape in each case.

9.6.4 Silicon Nitride Bearings

After several decades of development, bearings have been fabricated from silicon nitride, Si_3N_4, a covalently bonded ceramic that occurs in two types, or *polymorphs,* called α and β. The β phase is the stable phase at elevated temperatures. The crystal structures of the two phases are closely related, as shown in Fig. 9.21. Both are made of SiN_4^{8-} tetrahedra arranged in two basic patterns. In this structure, each nitrogen forms bonds with three silicons, in contrast with a silica glass in which each oxygen bonds to two silicons. This is a consequence of the fact that oxygen is in group VI of the periodic table, and nitrogen is in group V.

Fig. 9.21 Models of the crystal structures of the two polymorphs of Si_3N_4.

Commercially, Si_3N_4 is made in two forms. One is almost pure silicon nitride, mostly α-phase, but it contains 10 to 30% porosity and is suitable mainly for low-stress applications at high temperatures, where its high creep strength and good resistance to thermal shock can be utilized to advantage. The process by which it is made starts with fine silicon powder (<5μm) that is then heated in nitrogen gas close to the melting point of silicon (1410°C) . The basic reaction is

$$3\ Si + 2\ N_2\ (g) \longrightarrow Si_3N_4$$

The reaction takes only a few hours. This may appear surprising, since the silicon powder starts out with a thin coating of SiO_2 , which under certain conditions acts as a reaction barrier. Also, one might expect that a coating of Si_3N_4

would form around the silicon particles and slow the reaction. However, it is now believed that the reaction is not direct, as shown above, but rather involves the transport of silicon through a vapor phase from the solid silicon particles to
9640 α-Si_3N_4 nucleated elsewhere. The main carrier gas is probably SiO, although the vapor phase would also contain SiO_2 at this high temperature. The important reactions are the following:

$$Si + SiO_2\ (g) \longrightarrow 2\ SiO\ (g)$$

$$2Si + O_2 \longrightarrow 2SiO\ (g)$$

$$Si + H_2O\ (g) \longrightarrow SiO\ (g) + H_2$$

The reaction that produces the silicon nitride would then be

$$3SiO\ (g) + 2N_2 \longrightarrow Si_3N_4 + 3/2\ O_2$$

One notable feature of this reaction is that there is almost no overall volume change between the initial silicon powder and the final silicon nitride powder, which has a very fine grain size (<1μm). The volume difference between the two powders is taken up by the porosity. Another remarkable aspect is the rather high strength of the intergranular bonding in the α-Si_3N_4. The fracture stresses measured in four-point bending are in the range 100 to 300 MPa, which is impressive in a brittle solid with such high porosity. It has not yet proved possible to make fully dense, essentially pure α-Si_3N_4. However, if this were accomplished, the material would have a very attractive combination of toughness, high-temperature strength, and thermal-shock resistance.

Pure α-Si_3N_4 would not be suitable for bearings, because the high porosity would give inadequate fracture toughness; the bearings would crumble into powder when loaded in compression. However, a fully dense solid based on Si_3N_4 can be made by liquid-phase sintering. In this process, one starts with α-Si_3N_4 powder and adds some mixture of oxides that, when combined with the ever-present SiO_2, gives a eutectic temperature in the desired range. Examples of oxides used for this purpose are Al_2O_3, MgO, and Y_2O_3. The process not only results in a dense product, but also replaces the α-Si_3N_4 with the β phase.

A remarkable feature of β-Si_3N_4 is its capacity to accommodate large amounts of Al_2O_3 and AlN (or Al_3O_3N) in solid solution. Such a solid solution is called a β-SiAlON. In the sintering process, the α-Si_3N_4 dissolves in the eutectic liquid and is transported to particles of β-Si_3N_4, where it reprecipitates as rods of β-SiAlON. The process is illustrated schematically in Fig. 9.22.

The densification process is sometimes assisted by application of a compressive stress during sintering. If the compression is uniaxial, it is called *hot-pressing;* if it is hydrostatic, the process is called *hot-isostatic-pressing,* or *HIP*ing. In
9660 the latter case, the powder is encapsulated (for example, in a thin-walled stainless-steel can) and the pressure is applied by a gas, such as argon, in the sintering reaction chamber. Silicon nitride bearings can be machined from pieces cut from hot-pressed plate, but this is very expensive. A more promising approach for commercial applications would be the use of near-net-shape HIPed pre-forms.

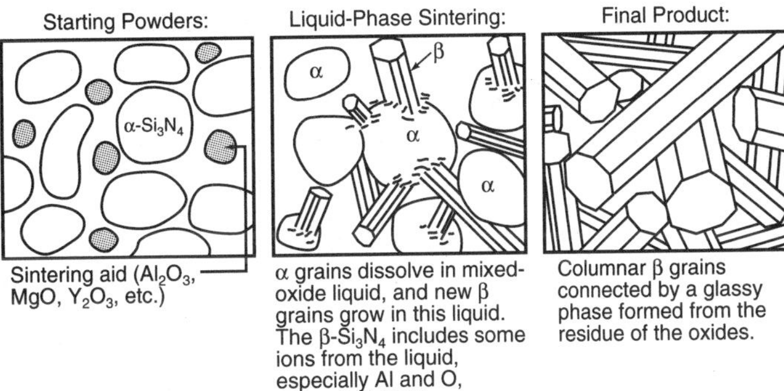
Starting Powders:
Liquid-Phase Sintering:
Final Product:
α-Si3N4
α
β
α
α
Sintering aid (Al2O3, MgO, Y2O3, etc.)
α grains dissolve in mixed-oxide liquid, and new β grains grow in this liquid. The β-Si3N4 includes some ions from the liquid, especially Al and O, giving β-SiAlON.
Columnar β grains connected by a glassy phase formed from the residue of the oxides.

Fig. 9.22 Schematic illustration of the solution-precipitation model for the liquid-phase sintering of Si_3N_4. (After G. Ziegler, *Materials Science Forum,* vol. 47, 1989, p. 162.)

In the ideal process, all of the liquid phase would be taken up in the formation of the SiAlON, and the resulting product would be a fully dense polycrystalline solid. This has not yet been achieved, and all sintered Si_3N_4 is found to have some glassy phase between the β-SiAlON grains. It is found in virtually all grain boundaries. For certain special, low-energy boundaries, and in boundaries along which the oxides are completely consumed in the SiAlON reaction, the glassy phase is confined to three-grain junctions. The two cases are illustrated schematically in Fig. 9.23. The wetting criterion depends on whether the grain boundary energy γ_{ss} is greater than or less than twice the solid/liquid interfacial energy γ_{sl}. An example of the intergranular glassy phase is shown in Fig. 9.24.

Since the density of Si_3N_4 bearings is less than half that of steel, their use in bicycles would afford a small weight saving, in addition to longer wear-life.

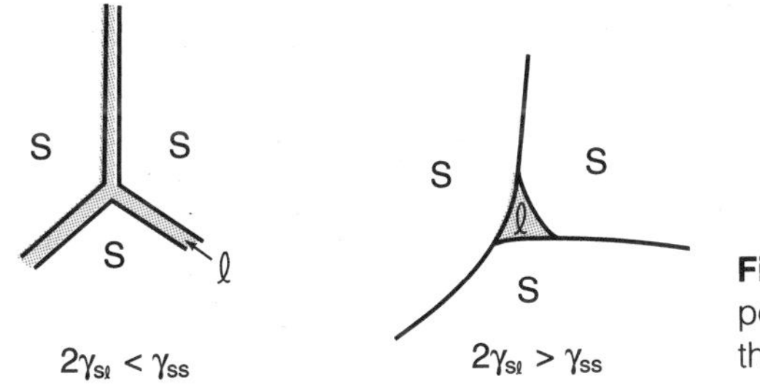
S
S
S
ℓ
$2\gamma_{s\ell} < \gamma_{ss}$
S
S
ℓ
S
$2\gamma_{s\ell} > \gamma_{ss}$

Fig. 9.23 Schematic illustration of two possible morphologies of glassy phase in the β-SiAlON grain boundaries.

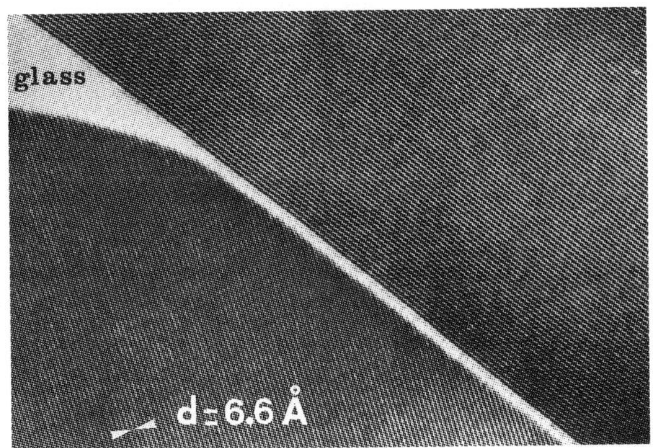
glass
d=6.6 Å

Fig. 9.24 Example of the intergranular glassy phase in a β-SiAlON. (From J. Y. Laval and A. Thorel, *Materials Science Forum,* vol. 47, 1989, p. 143.)

The elongated grains in the β-SiAlON give rise to what is called "R-curve" behavior. This occurs when stable crack extension occurs in a fracture toughness specimen, so that the crack extends under a rising load. That is, the resistance to crack extension, R, increases as the crack extends, as shown in Fig. 9.25. The R is given by the value of the instantaneous stress intensity, $K = K_R$.

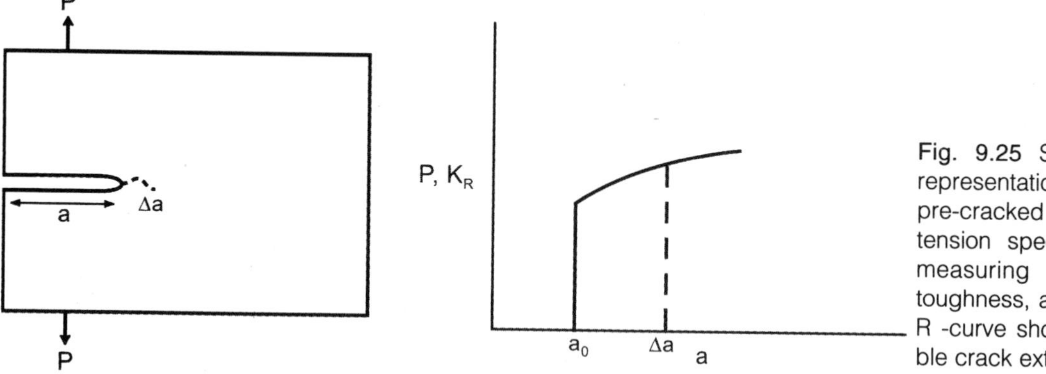

Fig. 9.25 Schematic representation of (a) a pre-cracked compact-tension specimen for measuring fracture toughness, and (b) an R -curve showing stable crack extension.

This R-curve behavior in β-SiAlON occurs when the glassy phase between the elongated grains fails and the grains are pulled out of the matrix, similar to what occurs in the CFRP discussed in Section 13.4. The friction between the pulling grains and the matrix is what provides the resistance to crack extension. Thus, paradoxically, it is the weakness of the boundaries of the elongated grains that gives rise to the apparent increase in fracture toughness as the crack extends. (Similar behavior can be found in ductile metals, in which crack extension occurs by void formation (i.e., rupture) ahead of a pre-crack. Here, the stretching ligaments between the voids are the analogs of the pulling grains.)

It must be noted, however, that this resistance to crack extension involves irreversible damage accumulation ahead of the pre-crack. Thus, a specimen loaded to some point on the R-curve and then unloaded is in a condition inferior to its starting condition. This is in contrast to the case of a metal that undergoes only strain hardening ahead of a crack in a specimen that is loaded and then unloaded.

Although the glassy phase has the beneficial effect of allowing R-curve behavior, its presence gives rise to creep deformation when the material is stressed at temperatures above the glass-transition temperature. Thus, the usefulness of the β-SiAlON at elevated temperatures is thereby limited. This is an important consideration, because many of the applications contemplated for this material involve elevated temperatures.

Summary

The nature of friction and wear was discussed in reference to the chain and bearings of a bicycle, as were the principles of lubrication. The need for hard materials for these applications was made obvious. In this context, the hardening, tempering, and hardenabilty of steel were considered, along with the problem of residual stresses from quenching. The subject of diffusion in a concentration gradient was discussed in relation to the case hardening of steel components by carburizing, in which a hard, wear-resistant surface is combined with a softer, tough core. The reason a thin case is desired was explained through the use of fracture mechanics, by which it was shown that the tendency of a crack in the brittle case to propagate through the component depends on the square root of the crack length (i.e., the case thickness). A ceramic is an alternative type of hard material for bearings. After a general discussion of the structures and behavior of ceramics and their production by liquid-phase or solid-state sintering, the case of silicon-nitride bearings was considered, including the reaction of nitrogen and silicon to form porous α-Si_3N_4 and then the liquid-phase sintering with added oxides to form β-SiAlON, an example of crystalline grains held together by a glassy phase.

Appendix 9.1 Twinning in Crystals

Twins are a special kind of defect in crystals, in which the lattice points on either side of the "twinning plane" have a mirror-image relationship. They can be the result of growth faults during recrystallization, or they can form as a result of a shear stress during plastic deformation or a martensitic phase transformation. The most commonly observed twins are the growth-fault type, called *annealing twins* in FCC metals, as shown in stainless steel in Fig. A9.1.1. They are characterized by straight, low-energy boundaries that enclose regions showing an etching response different from the surrounding grain. The deformed brass depicted in Fig. 2.10 shows annealing twins being crossed by slip lines; note the orientation of the slip planes within a twin compared to those in the matrix.

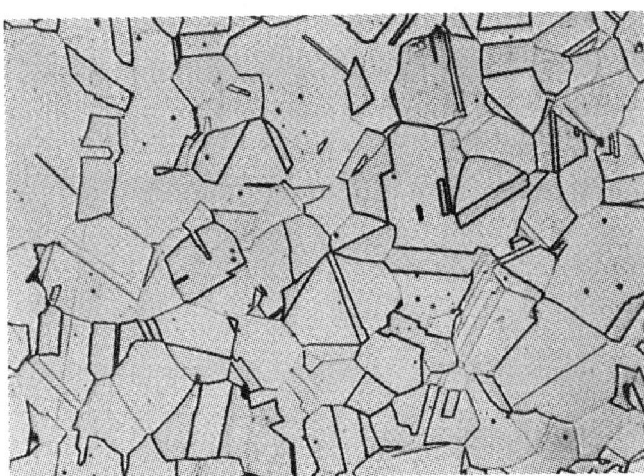

Fig. A9.1.1 Annealing twins in a recrystallized stainless steel spoke.

An annealing twin forms in an FCC crystal when a fault occurs in the stacking of close-packed planes. Referring to Fig. 3.7, a layer of atoms could form on B sites, instead of A sites, during a recrystallization anneal. After that, the normal ABC-type (i.e., CBA) stacking could proceed, and the crystal, except at the stacking fault, would remain FCC. Later on, another stacking fault could reverse the stacking to the original ABC. The region between the two faults is called an annealing twin and is of the type ABCA<u>BCB</u>ACBA.....CB<u>ACA</u>BCABC. Figure A9.1.2 shows the atomic arrangements in a six-layer twin of that type. Within the twinned region, the atoms are in mirror-image positions with respect to those outside, hence the name "twin." The straight boundaries of the annealing twins are thus {111} planes.

Since the stacking at these boundaries is not FCC (i.e., the stacking is ABA-type, instead of ABC-type), the atoms there are in a state of somewhat higher energy, but this *stacking-fault energy* is always much lower than the average grain boundary energy, because the two parts of the crystal are completely coherent. Only the second-neighbor positions are wrong.

The ABABAB... type of close-packed-plane stacking produces a crystal structure called hexagonal close packed (HCP), models of which are shown in Fig. A9.1.3. A number of metals, such as zinc, magnesium, cadmium, and berylium, crystallize in the HCP structure. It is striking that such a seemingly minor difference in stacking can change the symmetry of a crystal from cubic to hexagonal.

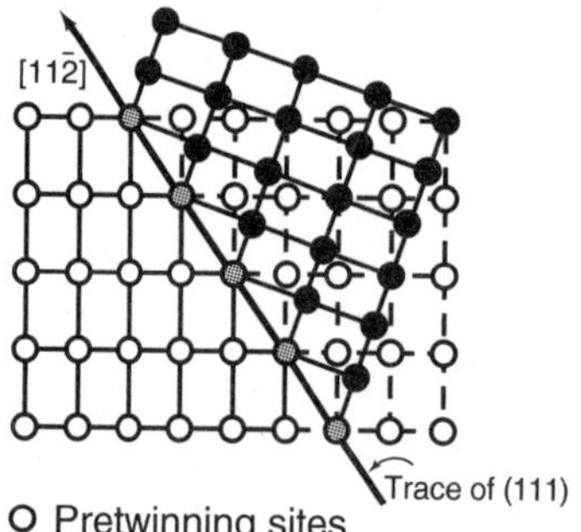

Fig. A9.1.2 Atom positions in a twin in an FCC crystal.

Examination of Fig. A9.1.2 shows that a shear stress in the [11$\bar{2}$] direction on the (111) plane could produce the kind of shear that could create a twin. This would be a coherent shear, meaning that all the atom movements are coupled and follow a strict pattern, and the atomic displacements in each plane are smaller than would occur in slip. However, a large overall shear strain can be produced, since the atoms move on every plane. Twins that form in response to a shear stress are called *deformation twins.*

The formation of a deformation twin is in some ways similar to the formation of a martensite plate in response to a shear stress, as occurs on a sub-microscopic scale in heavily deformed austenitic (FCC) stainless steel (cf. the strain markings in Fig. 3.3).

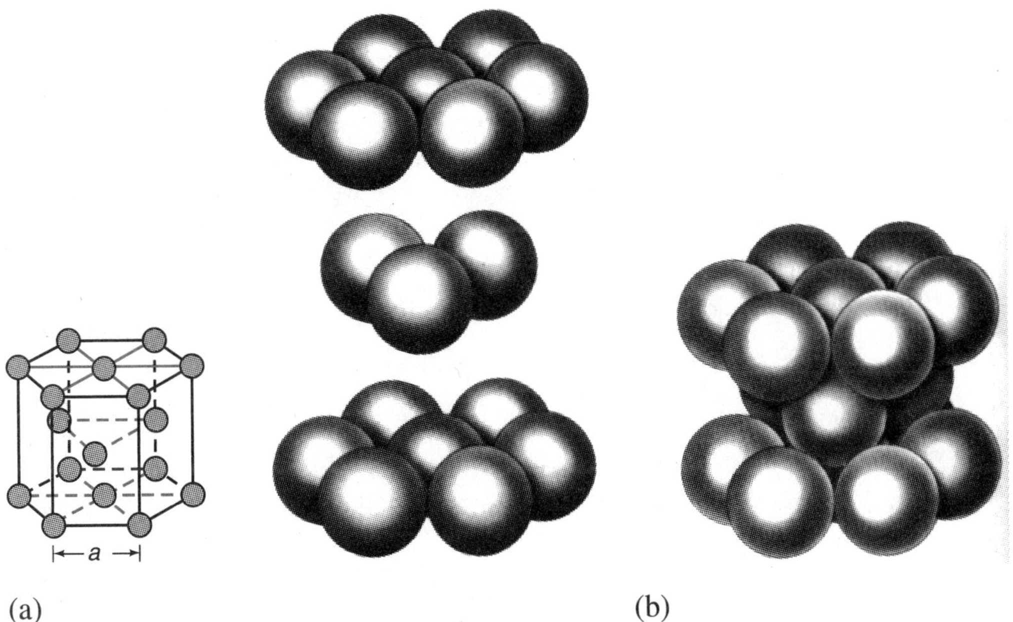

(a) (b)

Fig. A9.1.3 Models of an HCP crystal: (a) a ball-and-stick model, showing the hexagonal symmetry and (b) a hard-sphere model, showing how the atoms pack together. (From A.G. Guy, *Elements of Physical Metallurgy,* Addison-Wesley, Reading, Mass., 1959, p. 82)

Appendix 9.2 Linear-Elastic Fracture Mechanics

The goal of fracture mechanics is to specify the conditions under which a body of a given geometry containing a crack-like flaw will fracture. It is most easily applicable to bodies that do not undergo large-scale plastic deformation before fracture, and in this case one employs the stress-intensity factor, K, defined by

$$K = Y \sigma \sqrt{c}$$

where Y is a geometry-dependent constant, σ is the stress far from the crack (i.e., the tensile stress normal to the crack plane), and 2c is the crack length (i.e., the dimension along the direction in which crack propagation would occur). The importance of K lies in the fact that the tensile stress in the region of the tip of a crack is proportional to K. The stress-intensity factor can be used as a fracture criterion in any material that can fracture by extension of a crack when a critical value of the tensile stress is reached. This kind of fracture can be called stress-controlled fracture. (Materials with high toughness tend to fail by *rupture,* meaning that they come apart as the result of the growth and coalescence of damage (i.e., voids) produced during plastic deformation. Rupture can be considered strain-controlled fracture. In this case, K is not a good fracture criterion, and another kind of fracture mechanics must be employed.)

If one were to know the critical value of K necessary for crack extension for a given geometry, material, and loading condition (e.g., temperature), one could use this value, K_{CRIT}, in one of two ways:

1. If the size of the worst flaw is known, the critical stress for fracture can be calculated

$$\sigma_{CRIT} = \frac{K_{CRIT}}{Y\sqrt{c}}$$

2. If the service stress, σ, is specified, the size of the largest tolerable flaw can be calculated

$$c_{MAX} = \left(\frac{K_{CRIT}}{Y\sigma}\right)^2$$

The value of K_{CRIT} is always obtained from experiment, and under certain conditions it can be treated as a material constant.

This kind of analysis stems from the work of A. A. Griffith in the years around 1920, culminating in the now-famous Griffith equation, which relates the fracture stress to the crack length in an elastic solid. (In an elastic solid, no plastic deformation occurs; an example is silica-based glass at room temperature, e.g., ordinary window glass. This was the material used by Griffith to check his theory.)

To derive the Griffith equation in an approximate way, consider a semi-infinite plate of unit thickness loaded to a fixed displacement by a stress σ. The strain energy per unit volume is given by

9410 $$SE/vol. = 1/2\sigma\varepsilon = \sigma^2/2E$$

Imagine that a crack of length 2c forms in the center of the plate shown in Fig. A9.2.1; strain energy is released in the region around the crack.

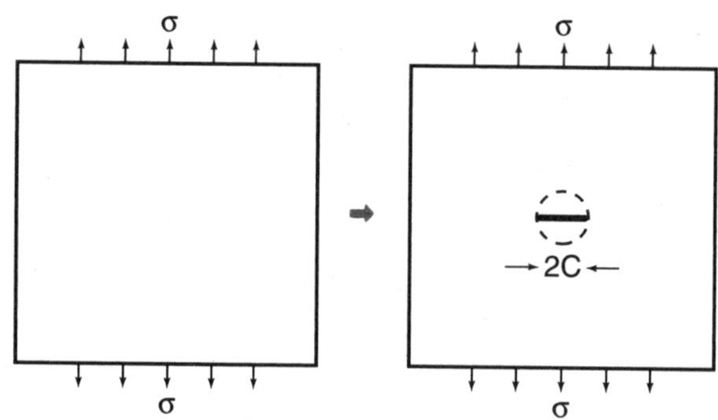

Fig. A9.2.1 Semi-infinite thin plate in which a Griffith crack is formed.

For a first approximation, let the volume in which strain energy is released be πc^2 times unity (the thickness). The total strain energy released is then

9430 $$\text{Total strain energy} = -\left(\frac{\sigma^2}{2E}\right)\pi c^2$$

This energy can offset the energy needed to create the two new surfaces along the crack. This is given by

$$\text{Surface energy} = 2\gamma\, 2c\, 1 = 4c\gamma$$

where γ is this surface energy per unit area.

The total energy change is given by

$$E = \frac{-\pi\sigma^2 c^2}{2E} + 4c\gamma$$

At equilibrium

$$\frac{dE}{dc} = 0 = \frac{-\pi\sigma^2 c}{E} + 4\gamma$$

or

$$\sigma = \sqrt{\frac{4E\gamma}{\pi c}}$$

This is very close to the actual relationship (obtained by a much more complicated derivation). It gives the length of a crack (2c) that is just stable for a given applied stress, σ. At a slightly higher stress the crack would become unstable, as shown schematically in Fig. A9.2.2.

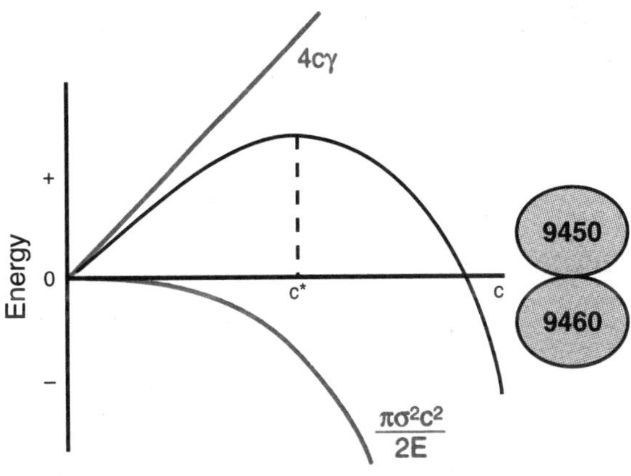

9450

9460

Fig. A9.2.2 For a stress σ, the crack becomes unstable at $c = c^*$, found from maximizing the combination of the energy released and the surface energy required.

The actual Griffith equation for a thin, brittle plate is

$$\sigma = \sqrt{\frac{2E\gamma}{\pi c}}$$

and it can be re-arranged to give K_{CRIT}:

$$K_{CRIT} = \sigma\sqrt{\frac{\pi c}{2}} = \sqrt{E\gamma} \quad \text{(note: here } Y = \sqrt{\frac{\pi}{2}}\text{)}$$ 9470

In this case K_{CRIT} is a material constant, since both E and γ are material constants.

In metallic materials in which plastic deformation would occur at the crack tip during crack extension, the actual work of fracture must include the "plastic work," along with γ. Here, K_{CRIT} must be determined by testing of cracked specimens.

This kind of analysis can be used for high-strength materials, in which plastic flow is confined to the crack-tip region. For example, it can be used for hardened steels, and particularly for a carburized surface layer on steel.

Glossary/Vocabulary - Chapter 9

8-N rule	This is a rule of thumb for determining the number of neighboring atoms in a covalently bonded crystal. If N is the valence of any particular atom, that atom needs 8-N neighbors sharing electrons in order for it to have the full complement of eight valence electrons in its bonding configuration. Diamond and silicon, each having atoms of valence four, need a coordination number of four (i.e., four bonding neighbors) to satisfy the 8-N rule. Si_3N_4 would have four N atoms around each Si and three Si atoms around each N.
Abrasive wear	This is the loss of material from a surface by the gouging-out of channels by hard particles lying between two surfaces being sheared past one another. The particles can be foreign (dirt) or they can be generated by the debris left from adhesive wear.
Adhesive wear	This is closely related to the primary cause of friction, and it involves the transfer of material from one surface to another when the surfaces are being sheared past one another while a force is applied normal to the interface. It is caused by cold welding across the touching asperities on the respective surfaces. The normal force acts to flatten the asperities and to increase the contact area over which cold welding can occur.
Annealing twins	Twinning can occur as a growth fault during recrystallization, in which case it is called an annealing twin. Because zinc lowers the stacking-fault energy of copper, annealing twins are abundant in brass. They are also abundant in austenitic stainless steel. They are not common in aluminum, which has a high stacking-fault energy.
Boundary lubrication	This occurs when a solid or semi-solid material lies in an interface and reduces the resistance to shear between the interfaces. A grease made of polymer chains, one end of which bonds to one or the other surface, can be an effective boundary lubricant.
Bridging oxygens	These are oxygen atoms that form links between metal atoms in various solids. Following the 8-N rule, each oxygen can bond covalently to two metal atoms. The oxygen atoms in a structure made of SiO^{4-} tetrahedra are bridging oxygens between Si atoms.
Brittleness	Brittleness is the opposite of toughness. It denotes the ease of crack propagation in a material. It is often associated with high strength, because of the difficulty of crack-tip plasticity in a high-strength material. A brittle material does not absorb much energy in a fracture test. Glassy materials are brittle, because crack-tip plasticity is essentially absent. As-quenched martensitic steel with even moderately high carbon content is normally rather brittle.

Carburization	This is a surface hardening, or case hardening, treatment carried out by heating a steel in an atmosphere of H_2/CH_4 or CO/CO_2, that deposits carbon on the surface. Inward diffusion of carbon raises the carbon content of the surface regions so that high-carbon martensite is formed when the steel is quenched. Gear teeth, such as the cogs on a bicycle freewheel, are often case hardened by carburizing.
Case hardening	This is the general term for hardening of the outside surfaces of a steel component by introducing extra amounts of carbon and/or nitrogen by diffusion at an elevated temperature, either to cause high-carbon martensite to form upon quenching, or to form a fine dispersion of alloy nitrides (like AlN), and thereby to make the surface harder and more resistant to wear.
Cation	This is a positively charged ion (that would be attracted to a cathode). It is normally an ionized metal. Sodium is the cation in NaCl.
Ceramic	A ceramic is a non-metallic, inorganic (i.e., not based on carbon) solid that may be either crystalline or amorphous (i.e., glassy), and that comprises more than one element, usually in a stoichiometric compound. Carbides, oxides, and nitrides are common crystalline ceramics. Glassy silicates are examples of amorphous ceramics.
Coefficient of friction	The frictional force that opposes sliding of a body is given by the coefficient of friction times the force on the body acting normal to the sliding surface. The coefficient of friction depends on the nature of the sliding surfaces and on the presence of any substance that could act as a lubricant.
Cold welding	This is the formation of a chemical bond between touching clean surfaces that inhibits relative shear between the surfaces and that leads to "seizing" of the two surfaces. This is a problem mainly when two clean metallic surfaces come into contact, because of the ease of formation of the metallic bond.
Covalent bonding	When two or more atoms share their valence electrons in a localized region, a covalent bond is formed. Carbon or silicon in the diamond-cubic structure are bonded covalently. The internal bonding in a water molecule is covalent.
Deformation twinning	Twinning can occur in response to a shear stress, as well as by a growth fault during recrystallization. A deformation twin is thus a special kind of shear band that is an alternative form of plastic deformation to a slip band, in which planes shear by a coordinated motion of atoms over a distance of less than the Burgers vector of a slip dislocation. Deformation twinning is favored by low deformation temperatures or high strain rates, mainly because these tend to inhibit dislocation mobility. Martensite plates in high-carbon steels contain deformation twins.
Diffusion coefficient (diffusivity)	This is a constant, D, for a particular diffusing element in a particular material that relates the diffusive flux to the concentration gradient at a given temperature: Flux, J, = -D dC/dx, for one-dimensional mass flow. D increases exponentially with temperature, and is often dependent on the local concentration, C, of the diffusing species, although that dependence is rarely known and is usually ignored. D is the analog of electrical conductivity and thermal conductivity. This flux equation is called Fick's first law. For carbon diffusing in iron, D is much higher in ferrite than in austenite at a given temperature, because ferrite is not close packed, whereas austenite is.

Dimer	This is two mers together in one unit. A silica dimer is two SiO_4^{4-} tetrahedra joined together to give $Si_2O_7^{6-}$.
Fick's second law	This is the differential equation that gives the rate of build-up of concentration of a diffusing element with time at a particular location in a material. This rate of build-up is given by the diffusion coefficient times the second derivative of the concentration gradient: $dC/dt = D\ d^2C/dx^2$. This equation has the same form as the one that gives the rate of temperature change during heat flow. It can be solved for any set of initial and boundary conditions. Many solutions are available in books on heat flow.
Fracture mechanics	This is the science that aims to understand the conditions for extension of a crack in terms of the stresses applied to the solid and the geometry of the crack, as well as the properties of the material (Young's modulus and fracture toughness). The aim is to calculate the critical stress for fracture, given the crack size, or the critical crack size for unstable propagation, given the expected applied stress. Linear elastic fracture mechanics is applied to elastic materials or to elastic-plastic materials with a high yield strength. So-called post-yield fracture mechanics is applied to lower-strength materials in which extensive plastic flow occurs at a crack tip before crack growth.
Frictional force	Friction is the resistance against the shear of one surface over another. It is caused mainly by actual bonding between the two surfaces, as in cold welding of metals, and secondarily by mechanical interference of asperities on one surface with those of another. The frictional force is parallel to planes that are being sheared past one another. It is equal to the coefficient of friction times the force acting normal to the shearing surfaces.
Griffith equation	This is the first fracture criterion ever derived from first principles, and it forms the foundation of fracture mechanics. Griffith derived from an energy balance the stress necessary to extend a crack in an elastic solid, according to: $\sigma=\sqrt{2E\gamma/\pi c}$, where E is the Young's modulus of the material, γ is its surface energy, and c is half the crack length. Griffith verified this equation by doing experiments on thin glass bulbs containing cracks, the length of which he measured beforehand. He also measured the surface energy of the glass in the fluid state.
Hardenability	This is the capacity of a steel to be transformed to martensite, instead of the diffusion-controlled transformation products, ferrite and cementite. It must be defined for a particular specimen geometry and size in order to define a reference cooling rate. The Jominy end-quench specimen is commonly used for this. Hardenability is increased by adding alloy elements to a steel. 4340 steel is highly hardenable and has Ni, Cr, and Mo as alloy elements. 4130 steel, commonly used for bicycle frames, has Cr and Mo and less carbon and is not as hardenable.
Hardening of steel	Steel is hardened by heat treating it to form martensite or bainite. First, it is austenitized (by heating into the austenite region of the phase diagram), and then it is quenched rapidly enough to suppress the diffusion-controlled transformation to ferrite and cementite as much as possible. Martensite is formed at relatively low temperatures in a diffusionless process. Its hardness depends on dislocation pinning by carbon and increases in proportion to the carbon content. Components that need to be wear resistant, like bearings and bicycle chains, are made of hardened steel, as are tools such as chisels, knives, and axes.

Hexagonal close-packed (HCP) This is a crystal structure that comprises the stacking of close-packed planes in an ABABAB.. stacking sequence, as opposed to the ABCABC.. sequence found in FCC crystals. It is, of course, close packed. Examples of HCP metals include Zn, Cd, Be, Ti (below 883°C), and Mg.

Hot isostatic pressing (HIP) Sometimes sintering is carried out under a compressive stress, in which case it is called hot pressing. If the applied stress is hydrostatic pressure, it is called hot-isostatic pressing, or HIPing. HIPing is often used to produce shapes that are close to the final one desired. This would be the solid-state analog of casting.

Hydrodynamic lubrication This occurs when one surface shearing over another rides on a fluid film. The coefficient of friction in this case can be very low. A shaft turning in a journal and riding on a film of oil is a common example. So is the phenomenon of "hydroplaning," which occurs when an automobile on a wet road reaches a critical speed, at which the tires lose contact with the road and are supported by a film of water.

Ionic crystal This is a crystal comprising an ordered array of positive and negative ions such that there is an overall neutral charge. Each ion is surrounded by ions of the opposite sign; the attractive force between the neighboring ions follows Coulomb's law. The positive ions, called cations, are normally smaller than the negative ions, called anions. Table salt, NaCl, is the classical example.

Jominy bar This is a test bar used for study of the kinetics of phase transformations and for characterizing the hardenability of steels. It is one inch in diameter and four inches long, and it is water cooled at one end after being austenitized and placed rapidly in a special holder over a vertical stream of water of a specified temperature and flow rate. Every point along this one-dimensionally cooled specimen has a known cooling rate. The Jominy test was originally developed to characterize hardenability. Each steel has an expected range of Jominy curves for its allowable range of composition; these are plots of hardness vs. position along the bar, starting at the quenched end.

Lubricant This is a substance placed between contacting solids to keep the surfaces of the solids from coming into contact with each other and to provide an intervening layer that is weak in shear. That is, a lubricant is intended to reduce sliding friction. The most common lubricants are oils or greases made of paraffin chains.

Mer Mer is a Greek work meaning "part." It is used in the context of a polymer, meaning a large molecule made of many repeated mers.

Metallic bonding Simple metals may be considered as an array of positive ions embedded in a sea of delocalized, or "free," electrons. The energies of these electrons range over an energy band, in contrast to the discrete energy levels occupied by these electrons in isolated atoms. The attractive force arises from the fact that the mean energy level in the filled energy band of the crystal is lower than the level that the electrons would have in isolated atoms. Classical examples of simple metals are Cu, Ag, and Au.

Molybdenum disulfide This is a compound, MoS_2, that has a sheet-like crystal structure, behaving much like graphite in that it is easily sheared parallel to the sheets. It is a good lubricant, useful for sliding surfaces subject to high pressures across the surfaces.

Monomer	This is a molecule that when joined together with other molecules forms a polymer. The molecules may be all the same, or they may include more than one type.
Pauli exclusion principle	This states that any given energy state can contain only two electrons, and these must have opposite spin. This is the basis for the hierarchy of discrete energy states in atoms and for the formation of energy bands in solids (in which discrete energy levels are separated by very small energy gaps).
Perfectly plastic material	This is an approximation of plastic behavior of a material in which strain hardening is assumed not to exist. That is, the stress-strain curve is assumed to be horizontal after yielding occurs. This is done to simplify calculations related to plasticity. Low-carbon steels actually do have a horizontal portion of the stress-strain curve just after yielding, as do many linear polymers, so the approximation has some connection to reality in a few materials.
Plane strain	This is a state of stress in which all components of strain lie in a plane. In a thick plate with a crack passing through it, the crack-tip region in the center of the plate is often in plane strain, because of the constraint exerted by the material away from the crack, preventing the material at the crack tip from contracting under a tensile stress. This state of stress minimizes the extent of plastic flow near the crack tip.
Plane-strain fracture toughness, K_{Ic}	This is the critical stress-intensity factor for the onset of fracture in a cracked specimen thick enough to be essentially in plane strain. It is used as a reference parameter to characterize fracture toughness; values are tabulated for different materials at various strength levels. K_{Ic} increases as yield strength decreases, because more energy is dissipated by plastic flow. In fracture mechanics, K_{Ic} is proportional to the square root of Young's modulus times a parameter G, which is the analog of surface energy in an elastic specimen and includes plastic work.
Plane stress	This is the state of stress in a thin membrane, in which all the stress components must lie in the plane of the membrane. That is, the membrane is too thin to have any stress components normal to its plane (since the surfaces are assumed not to have any force components acting normal to them). A point on the surface of a balloon under internal pressure is in a state of plane stress.
Precipitation hardening	This is strengthening of an alloy by the formation of a finely dispersed second phase. The alloy is solution treated and quenched, then aged at a temperature in the two-phase region. The strengthening precipitate is generally a metastable phase. Maximum hardening occurs when the spacing of the precipitates is a minimum and dislocations are forced to cut through the precipitates.
Reaction bonding	This is a process by which a chemical reaction not only produces a new material, but also binds it together in a solid. β-Si_3N_4 is produced by reacting α- Si_3N_4 with oxides such as MgO, Al_2O_3 and Y_2O_3 at a high temperature at which the oxides are molten. Some aluminum and oxygen dissolve in the Si_3N_4, converting it to β-SiAlON, which is a solid solution of these elements in β-Si_3N_4. When cooled to room temperature, the residual oxides form a glassy phase that acts as a bonding agent between the grains of β-SiAlON.

Residual stress This is an internal stress in a solid that is caused by some process that deforms the solid in a non-uniform way. The most common types of residual stress are thermal stresses and those that result from external forces that cause non-uniform plastic deformation. If a beam is bent so much that the regions far from the neutral axis are plastically deformed, then the region that was in tension will have a residual compressive stress after the beam is unloaded, and vice versa. This arises from the fact that a plastically deformed region does not return to its original dimensions when it is unloaded, so the residual stresses can be viewed as a result of the beam's trying to become straight again.

Quench cracking This is the cracking that can occur in the surface regions of a steel that is austenitized and quenched to form martensite. It comes from the fact that the transformation from austenite to martensite is expansive, because martensite is non-close-packed, whereas austenite is close packed. The martensite forms first on the surface and later in the interior; it is the latter that puts the surface in tension at low temperatures, and this tensile stress can produce cracks. The tendency for quench cracking increases with the carbon content of the steel. As the carbon content is increased, the M_s temperature decreases, meaning that the internal expansion takes place at lower temperatures, at which stress relaxation by plastic flow is less likely, and also the hardness of the surface martensite is higher, again making plastic relaxation more difficult.

Secondary hardening This is a special kind of precipitation hardening found in alloy steels containing strong-carbide forming elements like Mo, W, V, etc. These carbides form at high tempering temperatures and remain very fine, because their growth requires the diffusion of substitutional alloy elements. A well-known example is "high-speed" steel used for drill bits. They will cut metal at high speeds (therefore, high temperatures) for a relatively long time without softening.

Silicon nitride, Si_3N_4 This is a stoichiometric compound that can be sintered to make solid objects that are very hard and resistant to high temperatures. It exists in two polymorphs, α and β. Modified β-Si_3N_4 is used for bearings, particularly for high-temperature applications.

Sintering This is a method for turning a powder into a solid without melting it. It is used for particles of materials with high melting temperatures that are difficult to melt. Solid-state sintering is carried out by heating a powder to a temperature at which surface and interface diffusion is rapid. The forces of surface energy drive diffusion along the boundaries between particles, filling the voids. In liquid-phase sintering, some material is added that liquifies at the sintering temperature, and the mass transport takes place in the liquid phase. Powdered metals are usually densified by solid-state sintering. One can approach full density as long as the grain boundaries do not migrate away from the residual pores. Silicon nitride is densified by the effect of added oxides, which form a liquid phase out of which the β-Si_3N_4 grows as the α-Si_3N_4 dissolves, and the residual oxide forms a glass that helps bind the new β-Si_3N_4 grains together.

Small-scale-yielding approximation For the case of a crack in a high-strength material, one often assumes that the plastic zone around the crack tip is very small, so that the stress field near the tip can be approximated by the elastic solution, using the stress-concentration factor. This assumption is implicit in the use of linear-elastic fracture mechanics. That is, the use of plane-strain fracture toughness, K_{Ic}, implies the small-scale-yielding approximation.

Stacking-fault energy A stacking fault is a two-dimensional crystal defect that comprises a mis-registry of two planes of atoms. Because this is not the minimum-energy configuration, there is an excess energy per unit area associated with such a defect. A stacking fault in an FCC crystal consists of one plane of atoms that is not in the ABCABC.. stacking sequence, but rather in a ABCBACBA.. sequence. This comprises, in effect, three layers of HCP-type stacking.

Stress intensity factor This parameter has units of stress times the square root of crack length, and it is used to calculate the elastic stress field in the vicinity of a crack. Nominally, $K=Y\sigma\sqrt{a}$, where a is the crack length, and σ is the applied stress away from the crack. Y must be calculated from the geometry of the crack; values of Y are tabulated in handbooks for many kinds of cracks. The various components of the stress field at a point near the crack tip are proportional to $K/\sqrt{r}$ times $f(\theta)$, where r, θ are the coordinates of the point with respect to the crack tip. In the Griffith equation for a crack in a thin plate, $K=\sqrt{\pi c/2}$, or $Y=\sqrt{\pi/2}$.

Tempering This is the heat treatment of a steel that has been austenitized and quenched to form martensite. It involves heating in the ferrite+carbide region of the phase diagram (i.e., below the eutectoid temperature) to promote the decomposition of the metastable matensite. It is done to improve toughness at the sacrifice of some hardness. Tempering proceeds in stages that include the formation of a metastable carbide, the transformation of any retained austenite (to ferrite+carbide), the formation of cementite, and finally the formation of alloy carbides in the case of an alloy steel. These stages occur in shorter times as the tempering temperature is raised.

Exercises

9.1 Two traditional approaches to minimizing friction and wear are to use hardened-steel components or hardened steel in conjunction with a copper-based alloy containing dispersed particles of a low-melting-point metal, like lead, such that the steel slides relative to the leaded alloy. Explain the principles behind each approach.

9.2 Explain the distinction between the concepts of hardness and hardenability.

9.3 The hardenability curves in Fig. 9.7 both start at essentially the same hardness; explain why. Describe the expected microstructure at a distance of two inches from the quenched end in each steel.

9.4 So-called high-speed steels are used for cutting tools, such as drill bits used to drill holes in metals. The name refers to the fact that the bits resist softening even when driven at high speeds. These steels normally contain chromium and molybdenum; use Fig. 9.10 to explain the principles involved.

9.5 Referring to Example 9.2, calculate the carburizing time for a temperature of 850°C.

9.6 A crystalline powder can be densified by either solid-state sintering, which involves only the powder, or by liquid-phase sintering, which involves the addition of a "sintering agent." The latter is a material that liquifies at the sintering temperature. Describe the mechanism of densification in each case, and describe the expected microstructural evolution as the sintering time approaches infinity.

9.7 Explain why the void in Fig. 9.20(a) is drawn as lenticular, whereas the one in Fig. 9.20(b) is drawn as spherical.

9.8 Referring to Fig. A 9.1.2, draw a cubic unit cell showing the $[11\bar{2}]$ direction lying in the (111) plane.

10

PRECIPITATION HARDENING

Wheel rims must have high strength to support the spoke tension and to resist impacts on rough roads. However, a low mass is essential, because the rims turn at high speeds with a large radius of rotation, and the gyroscopic effect must be minimized, especially in the front wheel, which must be easy to turn while steering.

Most current high-quality wheel rims are made from precipitation-hardened aluminum alloys, which have a high strength-to-mass ratio. These alloys originated from an accidental discovery in 1906 by a German metallurgist, Alfred Wilm, who was trying to find an aluminum alloy that could be hardened by quenching, in the manner of steel. He found that an Al-Cu-Mn-Mg alloy, although not hard immediately after a quench, did harden during aging at room temperature. When Al-based-alloy phase diagrams were investigated, it was realized that the hardening phenomenon was related to the precipitation of a second phase from a supersaturated solid solution. For example, the Al-Cu diagram on the aluminum-rich end, shown in Fig. 10.1, is a simple eutectic between the aluminum-based FCC α phase and the intermetallic compound, $CuAl_2$, denoted as the θ phase. The details of the precipitation reaction, even in this simple system, remained obscure for decades, as did the explanation of its profound strengthening effect.

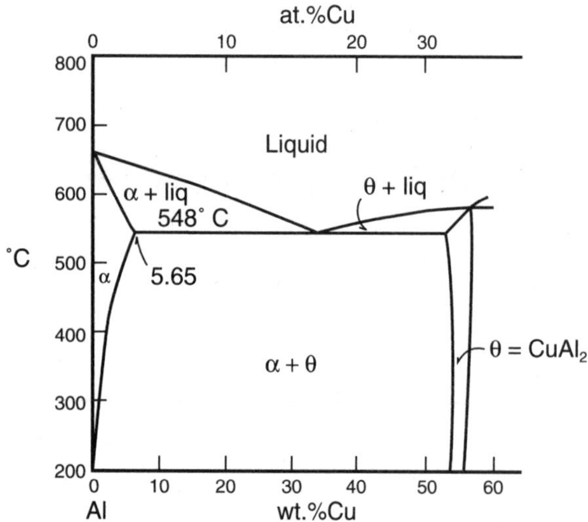

Fig. 10.1 The Al-rich end of the Al-Cu phase diagram, i.e., the Al-$CuAl_2$ diagram. (Adapted from *Metals Handbook,* ASM, 1948, p. 1158.)

10.1 Mechanism of Precipitation Hardening

Precipitation hardening involves the formation of a dense array of strong obstacles to the motion of dislocations. One might think that this is essentially similar to solid solution hardening in a concentrated solid solution; however, this is not the case. In solid solution hardening the resistance to dislocation motion arises only from the elastic interaction between the individual solute atoms and the dislocations. In precipitation hardening the dislocations have to contend with either clusters of solute atoms or fine particles of a second phase with a crystal structure different from the matrix phase.

To achieve the maximum effect, the array of obstacles must be so dense that 10030
the dislocations are forced to cut through them in order to glide. The shearing of a particle by dislocation glide is shown schematically in Fig. 10.2, drawn with the assumption that a slip plane in the particle lines up with one in the matrix (which is not necessarily true). Each dislocation shears the particle by an amount equal to the Burgers vector of the dislocation.

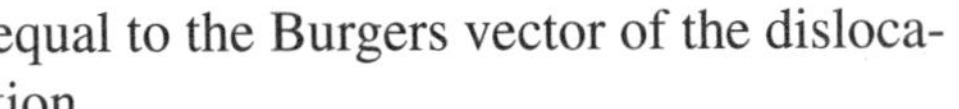

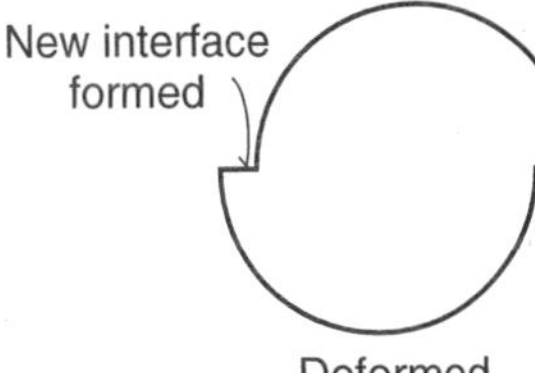

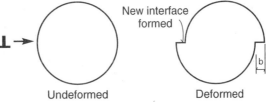

Fig. 10.2 Schematic illustration of the shearing of a particle by a dislocation gliding in the matrix.

An example of particles in an aluminum-lithium alloy that are sheared by the passage of dislocations through them is shown in Fig. 10.3. In this transmission electron micrograph the particles are made to appear white in a black background by using the dark-field technique, in which a diffracted electron beam from a particle is used to form the image on the screen (rather than using the direct beam, which gives the usual bright field image). In Fig. 10.3 the particles have a crystal structure different from the matrix; therefore, they diffract the electron beam at a Bragg angle different from that of the matrix. Thus, the matrix appears dark. However, the particles are all monocrystalline, and they all bear the same crystallographic orientation relationship with the matrix. Hence, they are all imaged together, i.e., with one diffracted beam.

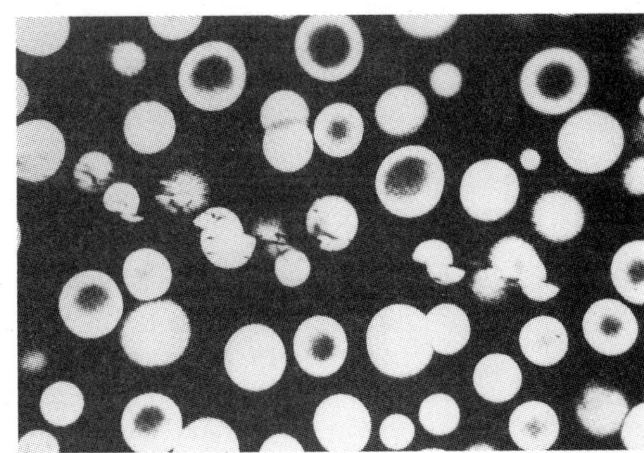

Fig. 10.3 Illustration of particles in an Al-Li alloy that have been sheared by the passage of a number of dislocations. In this case the particles have a crystal structure different from the matrix, and they all "light up" in dark-field illumination, because they all have the same orientation with respect to the matrix. (Dark-field transmission electron micrograph courtesy of Prof. David Williams, Lehigh University.)

Precipitation hardening can be a potent strengthening mechanism in crystalline solids, because particles can present a formidable barrier to the motion of dislocations. The origins of this barrier effect will be described below.

Not all alloys containing an array of dispersed particles are strong. The degree of strengthening depends mainly on the spacing of the particles. The hardening effect is relatively small if the particles are spaced far enough apart that dislocations can bow out in loops between them. If this were to happen, the particles could be bypassed, in the manner depicted schematically in Fig. 10.4, which was originally conceived by Orowan.

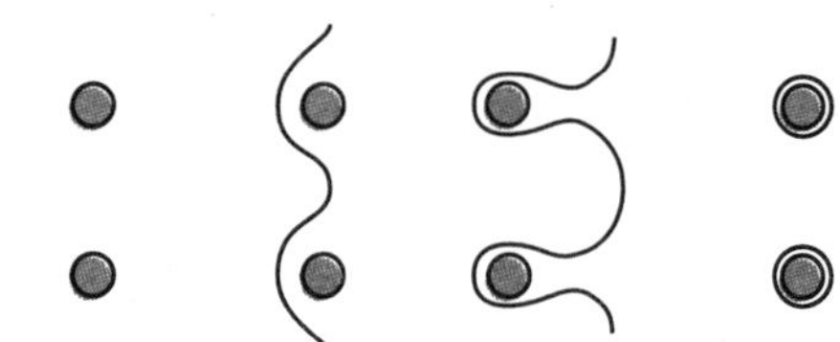

Fig. 10.4 Bypassing of particles by a dislocation that forms a loop by bowing out between the particles. This requires a shear stress of approximately 2Gb/L, where L is the interparticle spacing; it is known as the *Orowan mechanism.*

As shown in Section 4.5.2, the force to form a loop between pinning points (provided by hard particles) is inversely proportional to the particle spacing. Thus, for maximum hardening the spacing should be such that the shear stress necessary to form a loop is greater than that needed to cut through the particle. The volume fraction of particles should, of course, be as large as possible; that is, at a given (fine) spacing, the particles should be as large as possible.

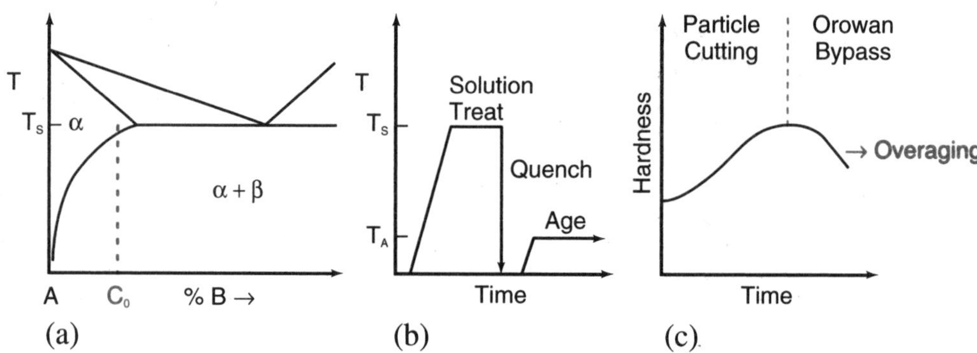

Fig. 10.5 (a) A portion of the phase diagram for a hypothetical alloy that exhibits precipitation hardening. (b) The heat treatment used to produce this hardening. (c) The resulting hardening curve, showing the change in hardness during aging.

The essential features of precipitation hardening can be described with reference to a hypothetical alloy, a partial phase diagram for which is shown in Fig. 10.5(a). The alloy composition is denoted by C_0, and the equilibrium precipitate would be the β phase. The heat treatment for precipitation hardening is shown schematically in Fig. 10.5(b). The alloy is first heated into the single-phase α region (temperature T_S) and quenched rapidly to retain a supersaturated solid solution at room temperature. This is called a *solution treatment.* Next, the solution-treated alloy is aged by heating at some temperature, T_A, in the two-phase region.

A representation of a typical hardening curve is shown in Fig.10.5(c). The solution-treated α is somewhat harder than the annealed condition (i.e., slowly cooled from the α region) because of solid-solution strengthening. The hardness increases further with time at temperature T_A and passes through a maximum, after which *over-aging* (caused by coarsening of the precipitate) occurs and the hardness decreases.

Example 10.1

Q. The particles in Fig. 10.3 were obviously too densely spaced for dislocations to bow around them by the Orowan process (shown in Fig. 10.4). Remembering that the particles exist in a thin foil on the order of 0.1μm in thickness, estimate the shear stress needed for the Orowan process to occur. The lattice parameter of aluminum (FCC) is $4.05\text{x}10^{-10}$m, and the shear modulus is given by G=E/2(1+ν), where ν, Poisson's ratio, is 0.34.

A. The average particle spacing appears to be approximately 0.2μm. The result of Section 4.5.2 is that the shear stress, τ, to bow out a loop is Gb/r. Taking r to be half the particle spacing, L, τ is 2Gb/L. Table 2.1 gives E for aluminum as 69GPa; therefore, G= 69/2(1+0.34)=25.7GPa. The Burgers vector, b, is the lattice parameter multiplied by $\sqrt{2}/2$; therefore, the shear stress for the Orowan process is given by

$$\tau = \frac{2 \cdot 25.7\text{x}10^{9}\text{N/m}^2 \cdot 4.05\text{x}10^{-10}\text{m}\sqrt{2}/2}{0.2\text{x}10^{-6}\text{m}} = 73.5\text{MPa}$$

10.2 Requirements for Precipitation Hardening

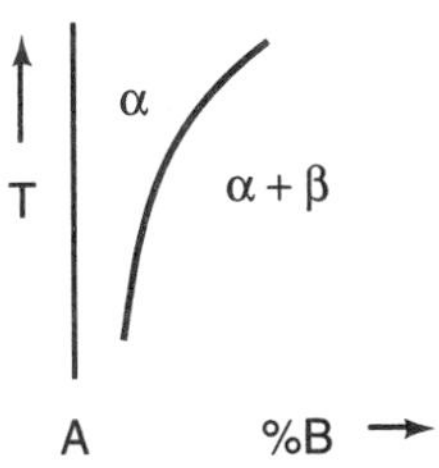

The primary requirement for precipitation hardening is that the alloy system in question must contain a single-phase field that gets narrower as the temperature is decreased. For example, in Fig. 10.5(a) the α-phase exhibits a decreasing solubility of the solute element B (or, equivalently, of the second phase, β) as the temperature drops. This is obviously necessary for a solution treatment to be carried out.

Another requirement is that it must be possible during the aging process to form a precipitate on a very fine scale so that dislocation loops cannot form between the particles, as in Fig. 10.4. The distribution must be so fine that the particles are cut by dislocations gliding in the matrix, as in Fig. 10.2. This is a difficult requirement to meet, because an alloy with a fine-scale precipitate contains a very large total area of particle/matrix interface. That means the content of interfacial energy in the system would be large, unless the particle/matrix interface has an especially low energy. The role of interfacial energy is discussed in more detail in the next section, but here it should be noted that relatively few alloys are known to meet this requirement.

The final requirement is simply that the precipitate that forms must present a significant barrier to the passage of a dislocation. This can occur for any of several reasons, described in Appendix 10.1.

10.3 Principles of Precipitation

The driving force for precipitation is the difference in free energy (per unit volume of alloy) between the supersaturated condition and the condition after precipitation. This free-energy difference is denoted ΔG_V, and it is exactly analogous to the driving force for the decomposition of austenite in steel, as depicted in Fig. 8.7. 

Thus, ΔG_V times the volume of a precipitate particle is used to express the energy change that drives the formation of a particle. Since this energy is released in the transformation, it is written as a negative term. This is needed to offset the increase in energy that occurs when the interface is formed between the new particle and the matrix. This positive energy term is given by the interfacial energy per unit area of interface, γ, times the area of the interface. Thus, for a spherical particle the total change in free energy is given by

$$\Delta G = - \Delta G_V \, 4/3 \, \pi \, r^3 + \gamma \, 4 \, \pi \, r^2$$

10150 where $4/3 \, \pi \, r^3$ and $4 \, \pi \, r^2$ are the volume and area, respectively, of a sphere. The two opposing energy terms are plotted as a function of particle radius in Fig. 10.6(a), and the resultant, found by summing these two, is plotted in Fig. 10.6(b). Note that when r is small the positive term dominates, but when r is large the negative term dominates. Thus, for small values of r, the formation of a small particle would cause an increase in free energy because of the large surface-to-volume ratio.

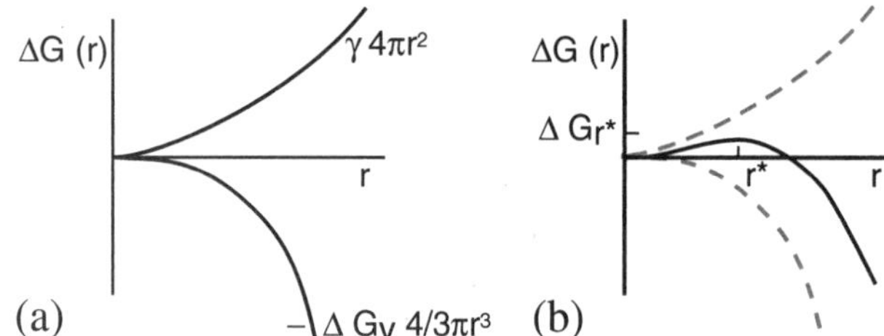

Fig. 10.6 (a) Variation of the volume-energy term and the surface-energy term with the size of a precipitate particle. (b) The resultant total energy change, found by summing the curves in (a).

These ideas can be applied directly to the formation of a water droplet in a supersaturated vapor. The ΔG_V is the difference in free energy per unit volume between the supersaturated vapor and liquid water. One can imagine that, at some instant, a number of water molecules spontaneously collide in the vapor to form a small cluster. The question is whether this cluster will grow into a droplet (by the addition of more molecules) or whether it will re-evaporate. That is, is the cluster stable or unstable? The answer depends on the size of the cluster, 

because a process will continue spontaneously only if it leads to a reduction in free energy (since equilibrium is characterized by a minimum in the free energy).

The criterion for stability of a particle can be understood by reference to Fig. 10.6(b) and specifically to the particle size r*, at which the curve of total free energy change passes through a maximum. If the cluster is smaller than r*, then it is unstable, because the only way to decrease the free energy is for the cluster to shrink. A cluster with r > r* would be stable and would grow spontaneously into a water droplet. A cluster of the critical size, with r = r*, could go either way. The value of r* is found by taking the first derivative of the expression for the total free-energy change and setting it equal to zero (to locate the maximum of the curve):

$$\left(\frac{d\Delta G}{dr}\right)_{r=r^*} = 0 = -\Delta G_V\, 4\,\pi\, r^2 + \gamma\, 8\,\pi\, r$$ 10180

This gives

$$r^* = \frac{2\gamma}{\Delta G_V}$$

From this argument it can be seen that the minimum stable size of a particle can be reduced by having either a small γ or a large ΔG_V.

The same principle applies to precipitation from solid solution. In order to have a fine precipitate, the particle/matrix interfacial energy must be small, and the driving force for precipitation must be large. The driving force ΔG_V increases with undercooling, i.e., cooling below the temperature at which the α phase is no longer stable (which is the $\alpha/\alpha+\beta$ phase boundary), while the interfacial energy γ is approximately independent of temperature. Therefore, fine precipitates are normally characteristic of low aging temperatures. 10185

The process just described is called *homogeneous nucleation,* which means that the nucleation of stable particles occurs homogeneously throughout the volume of the supersaturated matrix. This can be difficult in the case of the formation of clouds from supersaturated water vapor. The γ of the liquid/vapor interface is large, because the structure of the two phases is so different, and undercooling may not be sufficient to overcome this. Then, we have to rely on *heterogeneous nucleation* for cloud formation. This involves the formation of water droplets on existing particles, usually some kind of suspended dust. The dust provides a substrate upon which a water droplet can form in the shape of a spherical cap, as shown in Fig. 10.7. The substrate must form a low-energy interface with a water droplet, thereby giving rise to a low contact angle θ between the water and the substrate. It is apparent that such a droplet having the critical radius r* contains far fewer molecules than does an isolated spherical droplet having the same radius (cf. Fig. 10.7). Therefore, the probability that a critical nucleus can form from a simultaneous collision of water molecules is much higher if an appropriate substrate is available for heterogeneous nucleation.

(a)

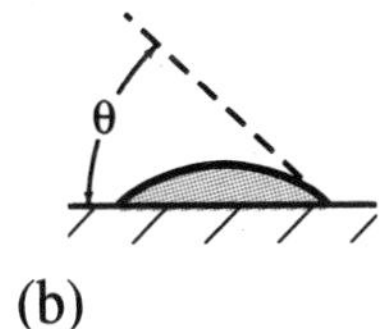

(b)

Fig 10.7 (a) A spherical drop having the critical radius r*. (b) A droplet having the same radius of curvature formed on a substrate on which it spreads into a spherical cap having a contact angle θ.

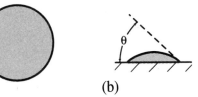

In precipitation from solid solution, the most effective substrate for heterogeneous nucleation is a grain boundary. Thus, a high-γ precipitate is likely to form first along grain boundaries, particularly if the undercooling is not large. Heterogeneous nucleation can also occur along dislocations within the grains. This precipitate would be distributed on a scale too coarse to produce significant hardening. This is what occurs in alloy systems in which a low-γ precipitate cannot form. For precipitation hardening to occur, homogeneous nucleation is essential. Therefore, the alloy system must allow the formation of a low-γ precipitate (usually a metastable precursor to the equilibrium second phase).

10.4 Factors that Control γ

The existence of interfacial energy arises from two factors; one is structural and the other is compositional. In solid-state precipitation, if the crystal structure of the new particle is different from that of the matrix phase, as shown schematically in Fig. 10.8, then the atoms along the interface are not completely surrounded by the structure in which their free energy is minimized. For example, the atoms in the β phase (Fig. 10.8) are at their lowest free energy when they are within the β crystal structure. The atoms along the interface are only partly in the β phase; some of their nearest neighbors are in positions characteristic of the α phase. Therefore, they are in a higher energy state than the atoms in the interior of the β phase. This extra energy (per unit area of interface) is the structural component of γ.

Similarly, when the composition of the particle is different from that of the matrix, as it usually is, the atoms bordering each phase are not completely surrounded by the composition that minimizes their free energy. For example, the β phase in Fig. 10.8 is an ordered array in which each A atom is surrounded by a B atom, and *vice versa.* The atoms in the interface do not have nearest neighbors that are all of the opposite type. Therefore, their energy is greater than that of atoms deeper in the β phase. This extra energy (per unit area of interface) is the compositional, or chemical, component of γ. In metallic alloys the structural component of γ tends to be larger than the compositional component.

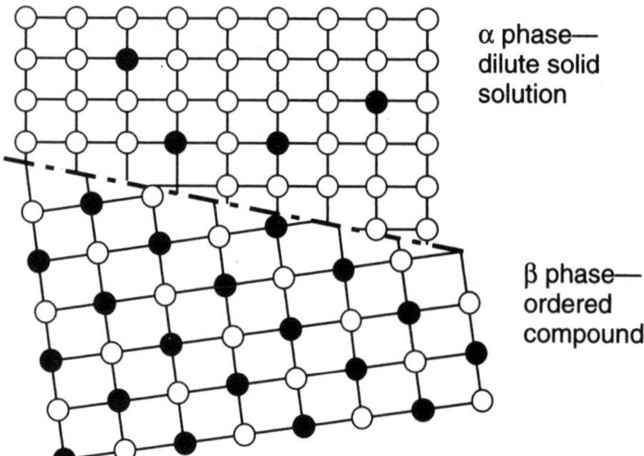

Fig. 10.8 Schematic representation of the interface between a β precipitate and an α matrix.

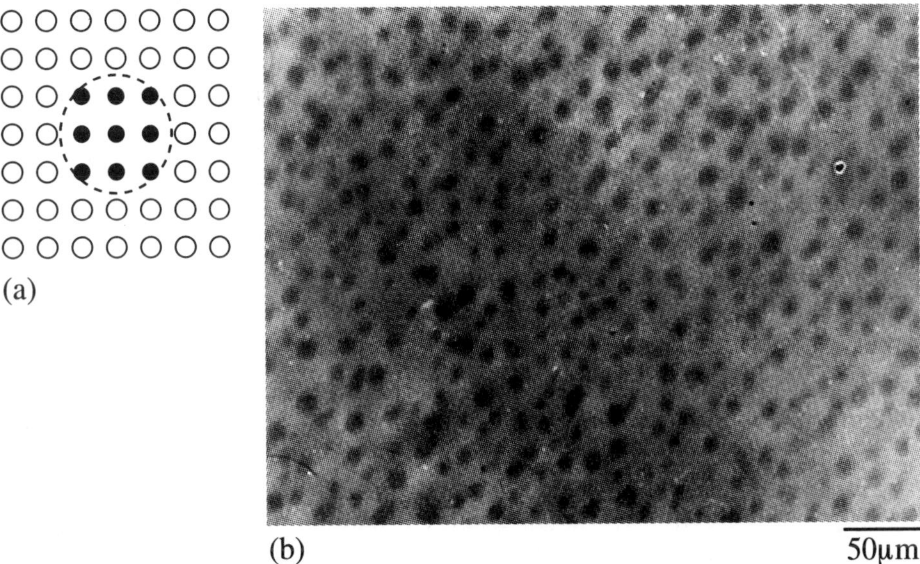

Fig. 10.9 (a) Schematic representation of a spherical particle having the same crystal structure as the matrix. (b) Example of such particles, called G-P zones, in an Al-Ag alloy. (From R.B Nicholson, G. Thomas, and J. Nutting, *J. Inst. of Metals,* vol. 87, (1958-59), p. 431.)

The minimum γ in a metallic alloy would be found in the kind of particle represented schematically in Fig. 10.9(a). Here, the two elements are of nearly equal atomic size, and the particle retains the same crystal structure as the matrix. Hence, only a chemical component of γ exists. This occurs in an Al-Ag alloy, as illustrated in Fig. 10.9(b). These particles are not the equilibrium second phase, which is the compound Ag_2Al, indicated by the phase diagram in Fig. 10.10. Thus, when the particles form, the free energy of the system has not reached its minimum value; therefore, these precipitates are metastable. (This means there is still a driving force for the formation of Ag_2Al.) The metastable precipitates shown in Fig. 10.9 are known as Guinier-Preston zones, or G-P zones, after the discoverers of this phenomenon. The G-P zones are responsible for the first stage of precipitation hardening in the Al-Ag alloy.

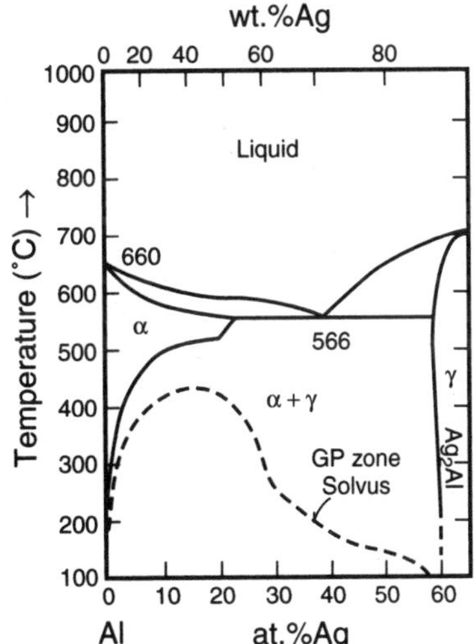

Fig. 10.10 Portion of the Al-Ag phase diagram. (After R. Baur and V. Gerold, *Zeitschrift für Metallkunde,* vol. 52, (1961), p. 671.)

The Al-Cu system also forms G-P zones, but they are plate-like, instead of spherical, as shown schematically in Fig. 10.11, because the copper atoms are substantially smaller than the aluminum atoms of the matrix. This gives rise to the kind of lattice strain shown in Fig. 10.11, and this strain is minimized when the particles form as platelets a few atom layers thick. (The strain-energy effect here overcomes the tendency to form spheres, which minimize the surface-to-volume ratio and, thus, the interfacial area.) The strain energy associated with the Al-Cu G-P zones is an energy-per-unit-volume and is, of course, a positive term. Its effect is to subtract from the ΔG_V and thus to lower the net driving force for precipitation. Therefore, the formation of these G-P zones requires a particularly large degree of undercooling.

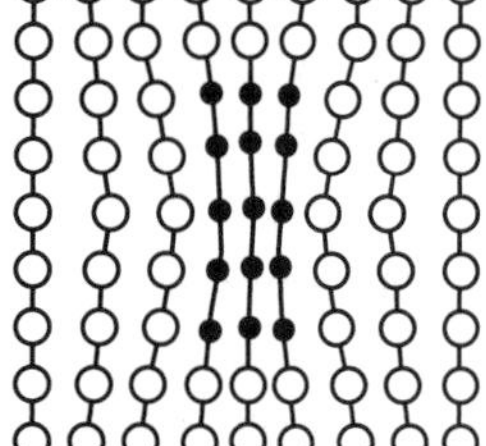

Fig. 10.11 Schematic representation of a G-P zone in an Al-Cu alloy.

Precipitation from solid solution can involve the formation of more than one metastable phase. For example, in the Al-Cu system the precipitation sequence can involve two additional metastable phases after the formation of G-P zones. The next precipitate to form after the G-P zones is called θ". Its crystal structure, as shown in Fig. 10.12, is such that it matches up with the α matrix without strain along two of the crystal axes, and it can be strained to match up along the third axis.

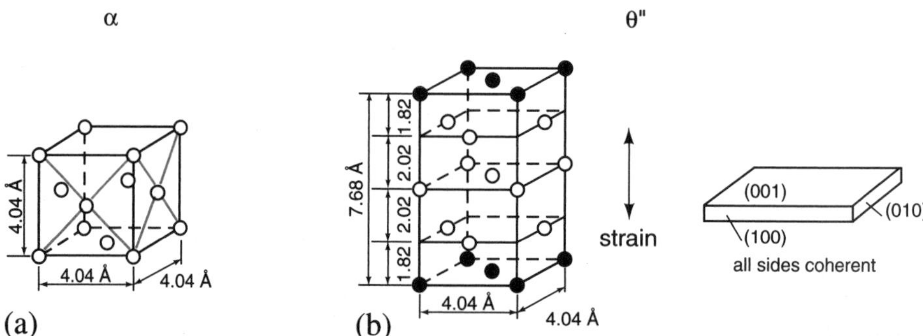

Fig. 10.12 Comparison of the crystal structures of the (a) α and (b) θ" phases in the Al-Cu system. (From D. A. Porter and K. E. Easterling, *Phase Transformations in Metals and Alloys,* Van Nostrand Rheinhold (UK), 1981, p. 297; reproduced by permission.)

When this matching occurs, the particle is said to be *coherent* with the matrix. If the volume of the θ" particle becomes too large, the total strain energy becomes excessive, and the particle then becomes *semi-coherent,* meaning that the mismatch is accommodated by the formation of a periodic array of edge dislocations along the interface. A coherent and a semi-coherent interface are compared schematically in Fig. 10.13. If the crystal structure of the particle is so different from the matrix that no matching is possible, as in Fig. 10.8, it is said to be *incoherent* with the matrix; in this case the structural component of γ is a maximum.

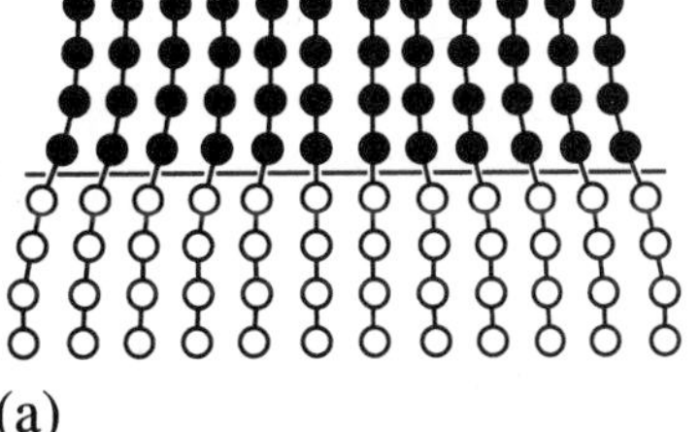
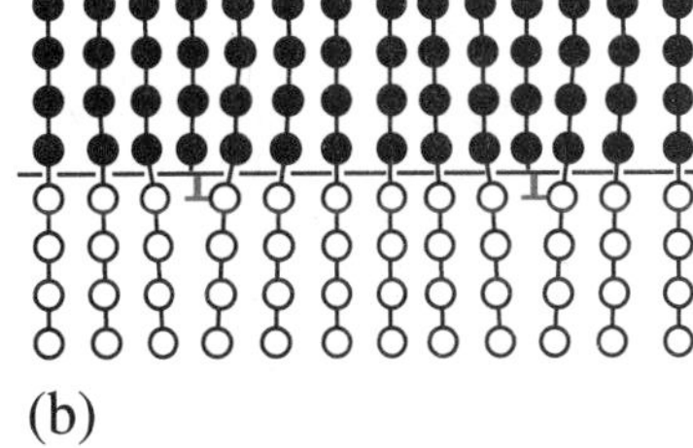

(a) (b)

Fig. 10.13 Schematic comparison of (a) coherent and (b) semi-coherent interfaces. (From Porter and Easterling, loc. cit., pp. 144 and 145.)

Example 10.2

Q. Where would the solvus line lie for one of the metastable Al-Cu precipitates, compared with the equilibrium solvus shown in the phase diagram in Fig. 10.1?

A. Since the θ phase would eventually form in an alloy quenched from α and aged in the α+θ region, the degree of supersaturation in the quenched α must be larger for the θ phase than for any other precipitate. Therefore, the solvus line for a metastable precipitate must lie to the right of the $\alpha/\alpha+\theta$ solvus shown in Fig. 10.1, and, with the sequence of metastable precipitates found in Al-Cu, the less stable the precipitate is, the farther to the right must its solvus be.

Example 10.3

Q. Calculate the maximum possible volume fraction of precipitate in an Al-4%Cu alloy, assuming that the densities of α and all the precipitates are equal.

A. The equilibrium θ precipitate would have the largest volume fraction, because its solvus curve is farthest to the left in the phase diagram of Fig. 10.1. It would contain 52wt%Cu. If the aging temperature were lower than about 250°C, the equilibrium α could be assumed to contain no copper. Therefore, the lever rule would give the weight fraction of θ equal to 4/52 = 0.077. Thus, if the densities of α and θ were the same, the volume fraction of θ would be 7.7%.

Example 10.4

Q. What would be the difference in interfacial energy between the coherent and semi-coherent interfaces shown in Fig.10.13?

A. The difference would lie in the dislocations. It would be a Gb^2-type term per unit length of dislocation for every dislocation in the interface.

10.5 Stages of Precipitation Hardening

The height of the maximum in the $\Delta G(r)$ curve in Fig. 10.6(b), denoted ΔG^*, represents an energy barrier to the nucleation of a stable particle. The probability that such a particle will nucleate depends exponentially upon ΔG^*, since the rate of nucleation is given by an expression of the form

$$\text{Rate} \propto \exp - (\Delta G^*/RT)$$

10250

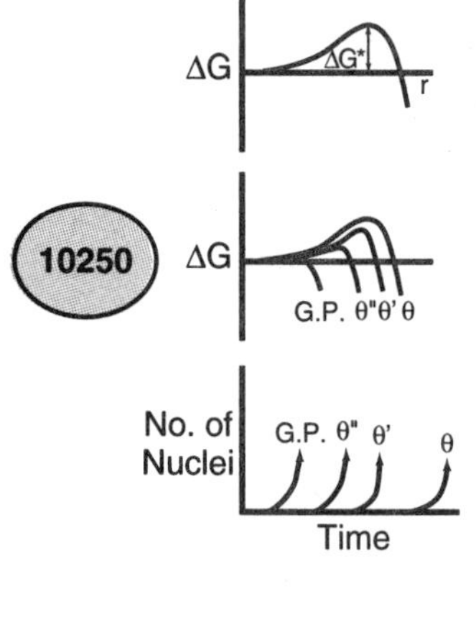

In the aluminum-based alloys discussed here, the G-P zones have the smallest γ, and at large undercooling ΔG_v is large; therefore, ΔG^* is small, and the rate of nucleation is large. Hence, at large undercooling, G-P zones form first. In an Al-Cu alloy the θ" phase has the next largest ΔG^*, and is the next to form.

When the θ" forms, the G-P zones begin to dissolve in order to supply copper atoms to the new, more stable precipitate. Later, another metastable phase, called θ', forms; it has a semi-coherent relationship with the matrix, which is why its ΔG^* is larger than for θ" (i.e., its γ value is larger because of the interface dislocations). When the θ' forms, the θ" begins to dissolve. Finally, the stable θ phase, which has the largest ΔG^*, will form if aging is carried out long enough.

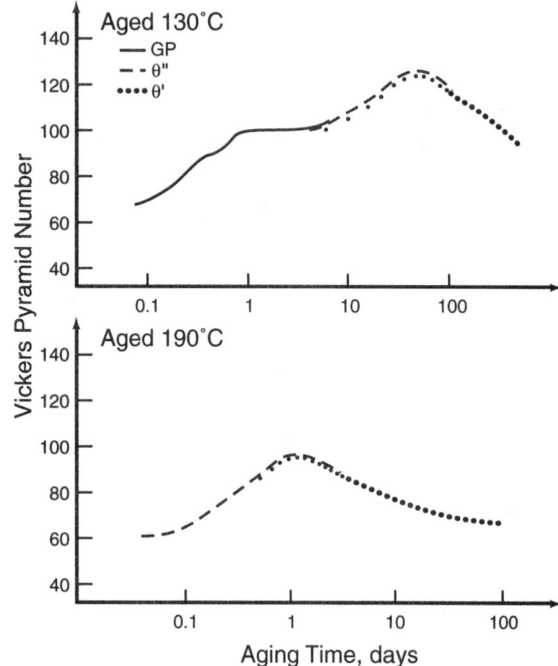

Fig. 10.14 Stages of hardening in Al-4%Cu at two temperatures. (From J. M. Silcock, T. J. Heal, and H. K. Hardy, *J. Inst. of Metals,* vol. 82, 1953-54, p. 239.)

The sequence of precipitation is reflected in the hardening curve (i.e., hardness *vs.* aging time). If precipitation occurs in stages, then hardness increases in corresponding stages. An example from an Al-Cu alloy is shown in Fig. 10.14. From the curve for aging at 130°C one can conclude that the resistance to cutting by dislocations is stronger for the θ" particles than for the G-P zones, since the hardening peak is higher for the θ". Because the θ' has a larger γ than θ", it has a larger r^*. That means it forms on a coarser scale, and, after the θ" has dissolved, the hardness starts to decrease, because the dislocations can begin to loop around the θ' particles (cf. Fig. 10.14 for aging at 190°C).

Overaging (meaning a decrease in hardness with continued aging) is caused by the continued coarsening of precipitate particles, making it increasingly easy for dislocations to loop around them. (For a given volume fraction of precipitate, larger particles means fewer particles, therefore a greater spacing between particles.) The coarsening is driven by the tendency to minimize the total amount of particle/matrix interfacial energy in a way analogous to grain growth, except that coarsening requires diffusion of solute from small particles to large particles. This coarsening is exactly analogous to the coarsening of cementite in steel, as discussed in Section 5.6.2. The rate of coarsening depends on the diffusivity of the solute, and therefore on temperature, and on the magnitude of the driving force, which is the particle/matrix interfacial energy.

10.6 Fabrication of Wheel Rims

Wheel rims have quite complicated cross sections, as shown in Fig. 10.15. Manufacturers wish to achieve maximum stiffness with minimum mass, but it is also necessary to provide high strength to hold the bead of a tire that is inflated to a pressure of 100 psi or more. These cross sections are achieved in an economical way by *extrusion,* which is the process by which one gets toothpaste from a tube. This is a highly developed art in the aluminum-fabrication industry. Many high-volume components (e.g., storm-window frames) are made that way.

In the extrusion of an age-hardenable aluminum alloy, a billet of the alloy is heated to a soft condition and then placed in a die held in a large hydraulic press. The die has a hole in one end corresponding to the desired shape. The ram of the press then forces the alloy to flow through the die.

The resulting extrusion is cut to the desired lengths and heat treated by solution treatment, quenching into cold water, and aging as needed. It can be bent into a circle and joined by adhesive bonding, with the aid of thin metal splines that hold the ends together, in order to complete the wheel rim.

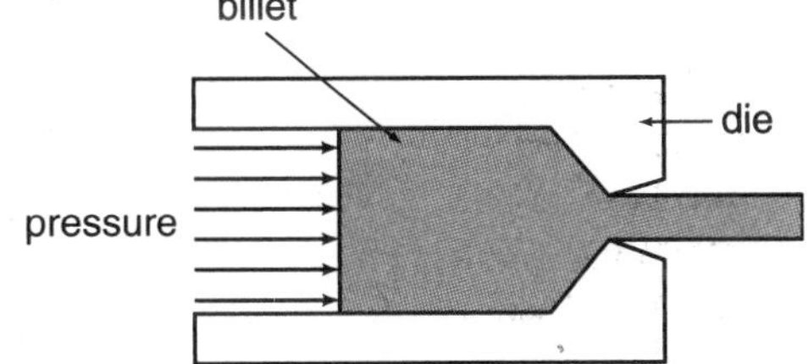

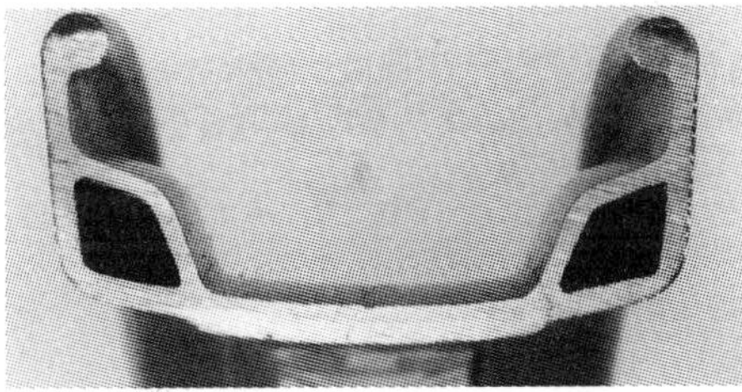

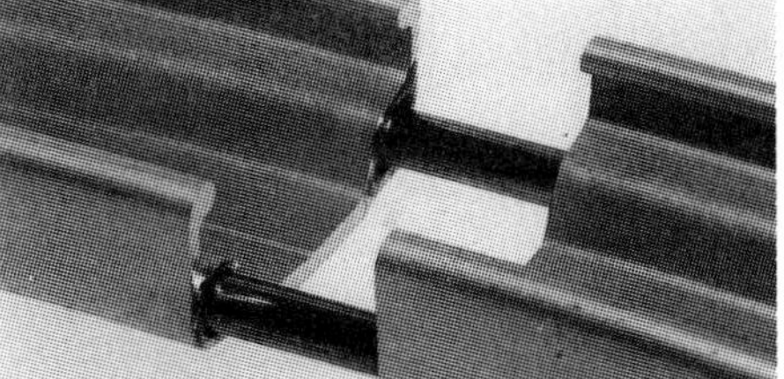

Fig. 10.15 Example of the cross-section of a wheel rim and the method of closing the circular rim with splines. (Courtesy of Sun Metal Products.)

For components like wheel rims and frame tubes, one uses wrought aluminum alloys, which are designated by a four-digit code followed by a so-called "temper" designation. The latter indicates the state of heat treatment and/or cold work of the material. Some of the commonly used temper designations and their meanings are given in Table 10.1

Table 10.1 Some Temper Designations for Aluminum Alloys

Designation	Meaning
O	Annealed; i.e., slowly cooled from a high temperature.
H	Strain hardened to some degree (indicated by some following digits).
T3	Solution treated (i.e., quenched from the all-α region of the phase diagram), then cold-worked and aged at room temperature.
T4	Solution treated and naturally aged (i.e., at room temperature).
T6	Solution treated and aged at some elevated temperature (so-called "artificially" aged) to maximum hardness.

Commercially-pure aluminum (99.0%Al) is designated 1100. Age-hardenable alloys based on Al-4%Cu are in the 2000 series; those based on Al-Mg are in the 5000 series; those in the 6000 series contain Mg and Si and, sometimes, Cu and/or Cr. The alloys in the 7000 series are based on the Al-Zn-Mg ternary system and often contain small amounts of Mn, Cu, and/or Cr; they are capable of reaching the highest strength.

The current alloy of choice for use in bicycles is 6061 T6; its composition and properties are compared with two other common age-hardenable alloys in Table 10.2. It can be seen that the 6061 T6 does not reach strengths as high as the other two more heavily alloyed compositions. The reason for its selection is that it combines adequate strength with good formability, weldability, and corrosion resistance.

Table 10.2 Compositions and Properties of Some Age-Hardenable Aluminum Alloys

Designation	Composition (wt%)						Mechanical Properties (T6)		
	Cu	Mg	Si	Zn	Mn	Cr	Yld. Str. (MPa)	UTS (MPa)	elong (%)
2014	4.4	0.4	0.8	-	0.8	-	420	490	13
6061	0.25	1.0	0.6	-	-	0.25	280	320	12
7075	1.5	2.5	-	5.5	-	0.3	510	580	11

The 6061 alloy can be approximated as an Al-1.0%Mg-0.6%Si alloy, and the equilibrium condition below about 500°C would consist of the α phase (FCC aluminum with some magnesium and silicon in solid solution) plus the compound Mg_2Si. Normally, for a ternary alloy one must represent the phase diagram by a stack of triangular planes, one for each temperature of interest, of the type shown in Fig. 10.16(a). However, in the Al-Mg-Si case, one can simplify this by using the quasi-binary phase diagram, Al-Mg_2Si, as shown in Fig. 10.16(b).

The commercial alloy 6061 is solution treated at about 530°C and quenched in cold water. It is then aged 6 to 10 hours at 175 to 180°C to give the T6 condition. This treatment will give a very dense, fine, metastable, rod-like precipitate, the composition and crystal structure of which are still a subject of some debate. The precipitate in a model alloy that approximates 6061 is shown in Fig. 10.17.

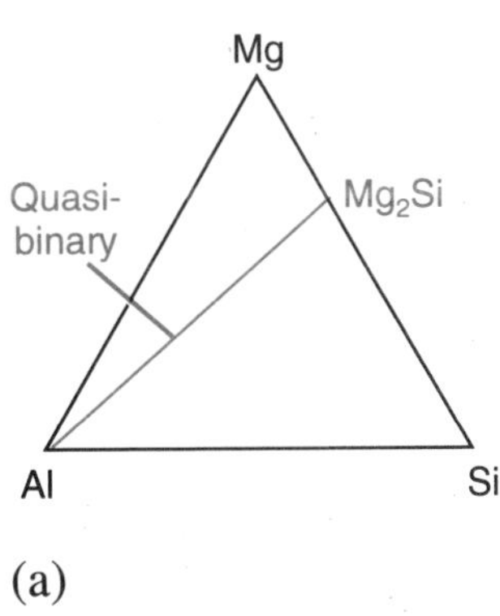

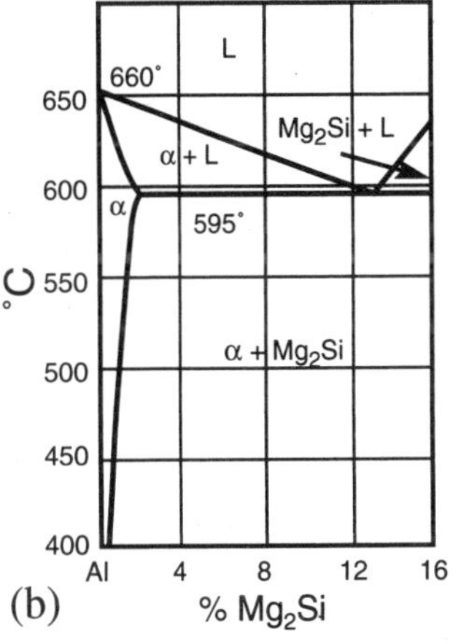

Fig. 10.16 (a) An isothermal plane of the three-dimensional ternary Al-Mg-Si phase diagram. (b) Part of the quasi-binary phase diagram Al-Mg_2Si. (From *ASM Metals Handbook,* 1948 ed., p. 1246.)

Fig. 10.17 Rod-like precipitate in Al-Mg-Si alloy aged for 8h at 190°C. Courtesy of Dr. Byung-Ki Cheong and Prof. David Laughlin, Carnegie Mellon Univ.

Summary

Precipitation-hardened aluminum alloys are important for wheel rims as well as for tubing for frames. Through precipitation hardening, the yield strength of aluminum can be raised by more than a factor of ten without a significant change in density. This requires the formation of a finely dispersed precipitate on the size scale of 50 to 100 atom diameters. The spacing of the precipitate must be so small that dislocations are forced to cut through the particles, rather than bypassing them by bowing out in loops. The fineness of the precipitate necessarily means that the total amount of precipitate/matrix interfacial area is very large. The formation of such a precipitate requires a combination of a large thermodynamic driving force (i.e., a large ΔG_V from undercooling) and a minimal value for the interfacial energy. The latter usually means that the precipitate must be a special metastable phase, rather than the equilibrium phase one would expect from a supersaturated solid solution, since the interfacial energy of the latter is generally large. This requirement puts a severe limitation on the number of alloys systems for which precipitation hardening is possible. The principles discussed here are applied to the 6061 alloy employed for bicycle components, which is strengthened by a metastable phase related to the compound Mg_2Si.

Appendix 10.1 Strengthening Effects of Precipitate Particles

There are several possible reasons why particles would be difficult for a dislocation to cut through. One obvious reason is depicted in Fig. 10.2; it involves the increased amount of particle/matrix interface that results from the shearing of the particle by the dislocation. Since this interface formation requires a certain energy per unit area, the applied stress must do extra work to achieve it.

Another possibility is that the resistance to dislocation motion inside the particle may be greater than that in the surrounding matrix. One would say that the particle presents a greater lattice friction to dislocation motion. Often a precipitate will have a more complicated crystal structure than the simple metal matrix. For example, the particle may be ordered; that is, it may have different types of atoms in specific lattice sites. When one dislocation passes through an ordered structure, it disrupts this order on the slip plane; the order is not restored until a succeeding dislocation comes along. This is depicted in Fig. A10.1.1.

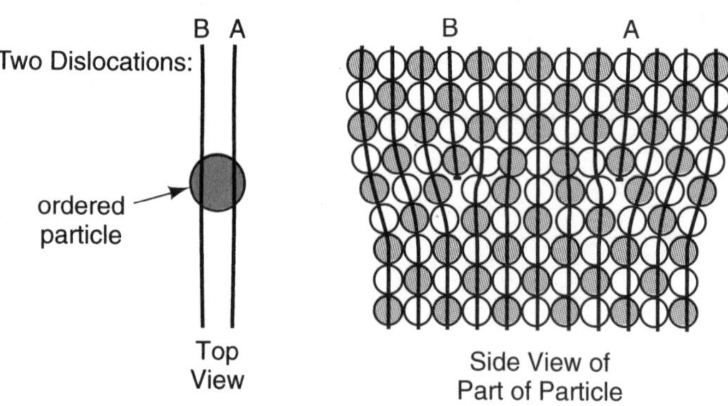

Fig. A10.1.1 Disruption of order by passage of a dislocation through an ordered particle; in the ordered structure, unlike nearest-neighbor atoms are preferred. Dislocation A creates like nearest-neighbors on the glide plane; this planar defect is eliminated by dislocation B, which follows along behind A.

All crystals present some amount of lattice friction to the motion of dislocations. This may be visualized in terms of the variation in the dislocation-core energy as the dislocation moves from one position of minimum energy to the next, as indicated schematically in Fig. A10.1.2. The slope of the energy *vs.* distance curve represents a force (work = force times distance; d(work)/d(distance) = force), and that force must be overcome by the applied shear stress; hence, the lattice-friction stress, sometimes known as the Peierls stress, after Rudolph Peierls, who first calculated it for a simple crystal structure. In soft FCC metals, like aluminum and copper, this friction stress is small, which is why they are ductile at all temperatures. In BCC transition metals, like iron, it is large for screw dislocations, and screws achieve high mobility only at temperatures well above absolute zero, as discussed in Appendix 6.1. In ordered phases the friction stress can be high as a consequence of the wrong nearest-neighbor pairs created by dislocation motion. This is only one of the possible sources of increased lattice friction that may be found in a precipitate.

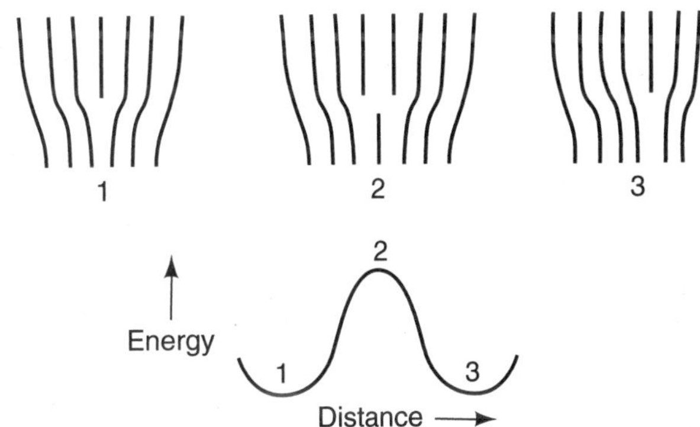

Fig. A10.1.2. Schematic depiction of variation in the energy of a dislocation core as the dislocation moves from one lattice position to the next.

Another possible source of resistance to dislocation motion is a difference in shear modulus between the particle and the matrix. Since the energy of a dislocation is proportional to Gb^2, a dislocation would naturally tend to avoid regions of high G and to be attracted to regions of low G. Thus, a particle with a G different from that of the matrix would interfere with dislocation motion by either repelling the dislocations or attracting them.

Finally, some precipitate particles or atomic clusters can set up an elastic strain field because they contain solute atoms of a different size than the matrix, or because they are constrained to take on the same lattice spacing as the matrix. One example is the Al-Cu G-P zone shown in Fig. 10.11; another is the precipitate in the Al-Mg-Si alloy shown in Fig. 10.17. The elastic strain field around each particle gives rise to the special diffraction contrast in which the region on either side of the rod-shaped particles appears dark.

Glossary/Vocabulary - Chapter 10

6061-T6 aluminum alloy This is a precipitation-hardenable alloy that contains Mg and Si as the main elements that form the strengthening precipitate. T6 is a temper designation that means solution treated and aged at a temperature above room temperature. This is the common alloy used for rims of bicycle wheels and other high-strength bicycle components like tubes from frames.

Compositional component of γ γ being the interfacial energy between a particle of a second phase and the matrix, the compositional component of γ is that part of the interfacial energy that comes from the fact that atoms in the interface are not completely surrounded by atoms of the right type for either of the two adjacent phases. This is the minor component of the interfacial energy, compared with the structural component.

Coherent interface This is an interface between two phases in which there is complete registry of atomic planes from one phase to the other. Therefore, the interface has no structural component to the interfacial energy. This occurs most commonly with small particles of a metastable precipitate. Often a coherent precipitate particle must have a significant amount of lattice strain in order to maintain this coherency. When the particle grows, the lattice strain energy finally becomes too large, and the coherency is lost.

Critical radius Assuming a spherical shape of a new phase forming in a supersaturated parent phase, this is the radius of the smallest particle of the new phase that is stable and can grow. A particle of smaller radius would be unstable and would spontaneously shrink and disappear. For the formation of a liquid drop in a supersaturated vapor, one can easily derive an expression for the critical radius in terms of the volume free energy released when the new phase forms, ΔG_V, and the energy of the new interface, γ: r^* is given by $2\gamma/\Delta G_V$.

Dark-field technique This is a technique used in transmission electron microscopy when it is desired to enhance the visibility of a second phase that is present in small amounts. A diffracted beam from that phase is used to form the image on the screen. The surrounding material, which has a different crystal structure, remains dark, because all the diffracted beams from that phase are blocked by the aperture diaphragm. The spherical shapes of the precipitate in an Al-Li alloy are revealed nicely by the dark-field technique.

ΔG^* This is the energy barrier to the nucleation of a second phase from a supersaturated solid solution. It is the height of the maximum in the plot of ΔG vs. r, the particle radius. The rate of formation of stable nuclei of the new phase increases exponentially as ΔG decreases.

Extrusion This is a process of metal forming in which a billet is heated and pressed through a die by a ram. It is the same process by which pasta is made or toothpaste is squeezed from a tube. Long lengths of aluminum alloys that have complex cross sections, like the rims of bicycle wheels, are normally extruded.

Guinier-Preston (G-P) zones	These are very small clusters of atoms found in supersaturated solid solutions in the early stages of aging. They are a metastable precurser to the formation of later stages of precipitation (stable or metastable) and they usually give some amount of precipitation hardening. In solution-treated and quenched Al-Cu alloys, G-P zones form at early times at low aging temperatures and consist of platelets of Cu atoms one to three atom layers thick and less than 100 atoms in diameter.
Heterogeneous nucleation	This is the nucleation of a second phase in a supersaturated parent phase not randomly, but on structural defects that act to lower the energy barrier for this nucleation, often by providing an existing interface on which the new phase can form. Much less undercooling is required for heterogeneous nucleation than for homogeneous nucleation. Cloud seeding to produce rainfall (using AgI crystals) works by providing a substrate on which ice can form, leading to heterogeneous nucleation of rain drops.
Homogeneous nucleation	This means the nucleation of a second phase in a supersaturated parent phase at random locations throughout the parent phase, without regard for the presence of any structural defects that could enhance the nucleation rate. The formation of G-P zones in a supersaturated alloy occurs by homogeneous nucleation. Homogeneous nucleation is generally a prerequisite for precipitation hardening.
Incoherent interface	An interface between two phases that has no registry between atom planes in each phase is called incoherent. This has the highest level of the structural component of the interfacial energy. Most equilibrium second phases that form ultimately in the process of aging a supersaturated solid solution are incoherent.
Interfacial energy	This is the excess energy associated with atoms or molecules in the interface between two phases or two crystals of the same phase by virtue of the fact that these atoms or molecules are not in their minimum-energy configuration. See also grain boundary energy. When one of the two adjoining phases is a vapor or vacuum, we use the term surface energy.
Metastable	This means a system that is stable against only very small perturbations, but not larger ones. It is a kind of temporary stability that lasts only until sufficient energy is available to provide the activation toward a more stable condition. A brick standing on a table on its smallest face is metastable; it would fall over if the table were shaken vigorously enough. Many precipitates that form in supersaturated alloys are metastable; in time, they are replaced by more-stable phases.
Ordered precipitate	A multi-component crystal in which each atom type occupies a specific type of site in the unit cell is said to be ordered, or to possess long-range order. This is common in stoichiometric chemical compounds, and it also occurs in concentrated solid solutions in metallic alloys.

Orowan mechanism	This is a way that dislocations can pass through an array of dispersed particles of a second phase without having to cut through the particles. If the particles are far enough apart, the dislocation can bow out to form a loop between a pair of particles, and this loop can expand until it hits other loops forming between adjacent pairs. When these loops touch, dislocation annihilation takes place, because the touching segments are of opposite sign. The result is a complete dislocation line and a residual loop left around each particle. When a precipitation-hardened alloy is overaged, the particles become so coarse and widely spaced that the Orowan mechanism can take place. The alloy is then past the state of maximum hardness.
Overaging	This is an aging treatment for precipitation hardening carried out for too long a time, so that particle coarsening permits the Orowan mechanism to take place. The alloy is then past the condition of maximum hardness. A 6061 T6 aluminum alloy heated to 200°C would overage in a few hours.
Semi-coherent interface	When a coherent interface breaks down, it usually becomes semi-coherent, meaning that the lattice mismatch between two phases is taken up by dislocations lying in the interface (with their Burgers vector parallel to the interface) in a regularly spaced array.
Solid-solution hardening	Strengthening a metal by the addition of an alloying element in solid solution; it may be either substitutional or interstitial. Solute atoms are generally either too large or too small for their sites in a crystal lattice: therefore, they strain the lattice and set up a stress field centered on themselves. These stress fields can interact with the stress field of a dislocation, either attractively or repulsively. In either case, dislocation motion is impeded, and the effect is an increase in the resistance to plastic deformation, i.e., hardening. Most alloys are hardened this way. Examples are zinc or tin in copper to make brass or bronze. Titanium tubes for bicycles are strengthened by aluminum and vanadium.
Solution treatment	This is a heat treatment comprising the heating of an alloy into a single-phase region of the phase diagram so that any second phase present would be dissolved. This is the first step in precipitation hardening. For example, a 6061-aluminum alloy is first solution treated before being aged to precipitate the hardening phase.
Structural component of γ	γ being the interfacial energy between a particle of a second phase and the matrix, the structural component of γ is that part of the interfacial energy that comes from the fact that atoms in the interface are not completely surrounded by atoms that occupy the "right" positions for one crystal structure or the other. This is the major component of the interfacial energy; it is a maximum in an inchoherent interface.
Supersaturated solid solution	This is a solid solution that contains more solute than the solubility limit would permit at equilibrium at that particular temperature. It is produced by a solution treatment at an elevated temperature (at which all the solute is soluble), followed by rapid cooling to trap all the solute in solid solution. A supersaturated solid solution is the starting point for the aging treatment that produces precipitation hardening. When the aluminum alloy 6061 is solution treated, a supersaturated solid solution of magnesium and silicon in aluminum is formed.

Temper designation

Precipitation-hardenable aluminum alloys are given temper designations to indicate their condition with regard to hardening. Condition O means annealed (not solution treated) and is the softest condition. T4 means solution treated and aged at room temperature, and T6 means solution treated and aged at some elevated temperature.

Exercises

10.1 What kind of solvus line is needed for precipitation hardening? Explain your answer.

10.2 What other important characteristics must an alloy system have in order to exhibit precipitation hardening? Explain your answer.

10.3 Explain how the precipitates in a 6061 aluminum alloy might resist being cut by dislocations.

10.4 Show the similarities and differences between the response to heat treatment of a Cr-Mo alloy steel (quenching and tempering) and of an Al-Cu alloy (precipitation hardening). Use schematic plots wherever appropriate and explain what takes place in each alloy.

10.5 The skins of most commercial airplanes are fabricated from panels of precipitation-hardened aluminum-based alloys. However, these alloys cannot be used for many supersonic military aircraft; these require skins of stainless steel or titanium alloys, which results in a weight penalty. Explain why aluminum-based alloys cannot be used, considering the fact that supersonic flight entails aerodynamic heating by collisions of the aircraft with gas molecules in the air.

10.6 Copper with 2% beryllium is a precipitation-hardening alloy; the Cu-rich end of the phase diagram is given here. Describe the experiments you would do to devise the heat treatment that gives the maximum hardness in this alloy. (Keep it as simple as possible.)

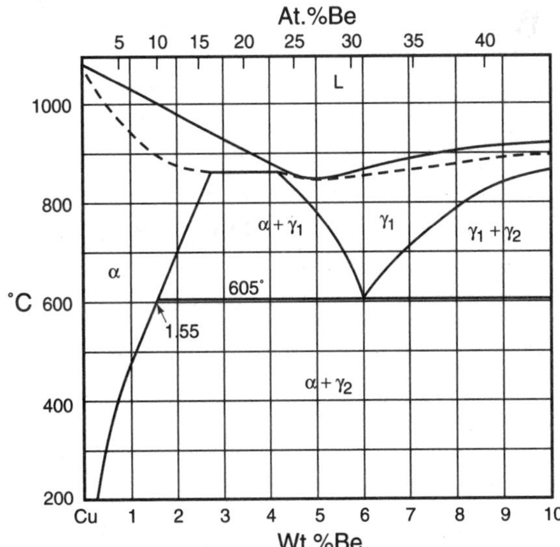

Metals Handbook, 8th ed., ASM, 1973, p. 271.

11

THE BICYCLE FRAME

The classical design of the bicycle frame, which is more than a century old, is shown in Fig. 11.1. The rear section is a triangle, and the front section is nearly a triangle, so together they form an almost-perfect truss. In addition to the yield strength, the other important design parameters are the weight and the stiffness. The yield strength is a function only of the material chosen, but the weight and stiffness are functions of both the material and the tube geometry. That is, both the density and the elastic modulus of the material and the diameter and the wall thickness of the tubes act together to produce the final weight and stiffness of the frame. A small amount of beam theory is necessary for one to calculate the stiffness of a tube and the maximum stress in a tube subjected to bending; this is reviewed in Appendix 11.1. The reason why bending is more important than tensile loading is reviewed in Appendix 11.2. We will use the formulae for the moment of inertia of a tube and the maximum stress in bending in conjunction with considerations of the properties of several alloys to see how these are combined in frame design.

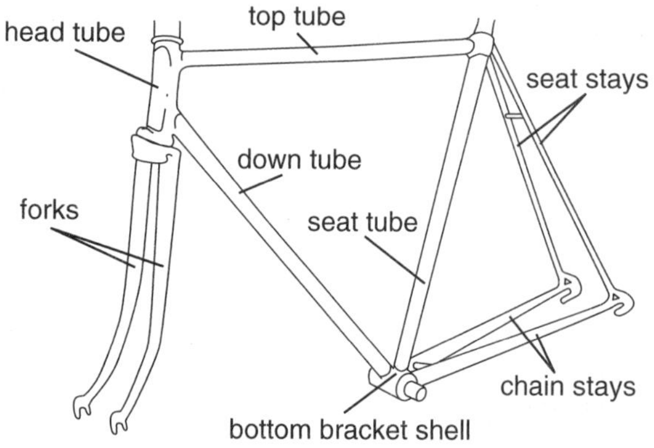

Fig 11.1 The complete frame of a conventional diamond-frame bicycle.

11.1 Alloys for Bicycle Frames; General Considerations

The earliest bicycles were made of wood or wood reinforced with somewhat primitive steel, as illustrated in Fig. 11.2(a). One of the most successful kinds of wood for this purpose was bamboo; an example is shown in Fig. 11.2(b). Aside from the cost of the handwork, the major problem in the development of wood-frame bicycles was joining the individual pieces into a structural framework. This has remained a challenge for all subsequent materials. Ironically, bicycle technology has begun to return to fiber-reinforced materials, of which wood was the prototype. However, for most of the past century the dominant materials have been metallic, primarily steel.

During the century following the 1870s, steel was the dominant material for bicycle frames, and bicycle evolution essentially ceased for the last two-thirds of that period. However, just as aviation technology was an offspring of the bicycle in the early twentieth century, in the 1970s the bicycle became the beneficiary of developments in aerospace technology, particularly with regard to materials. This is nowhere more evident than in frames. Today, there are frames fabricated from high-strength aluminum and titanium alloys and graphite-fiber reinforced polymers. The availability of these materials and the expertise to process them has come directly from the aerospace field, which, in a sense, is now repaying its technological debt. In the rest of this chapter the application of metallic alloys to frame building is examined.

(a)

(b)

Fig. 11.2. (a) A pre-World-War I wooden bicycle frame with steel-reinforced joints. (Courtesy of *Cycling Weekly,* IPC Magazines, London.) (b) A 19th-century frame made of bamboo. (from A. Sharp Bicycles and Tricycles, An Elementary Treatise on their Design and Construction, Longmans, Green, London, 1896. Reprinted by MIT Press, Cambridge, MA, 1979, p. 287.)

The first consideration for a frame is that, under any foreseeable conditions, it should never be loaded above the yield strength of the material at any location on the frame. That is, the yield strength must be high enough that the behavior is always elastic. The next consideration is that the frame have enough elastic stiffness that it does not distort excessively during hard riding. The most critical regions in this regard are, first, the juncture of the front fork and the head tube and, second, the area of the bottom bracket, where the seat tube, down tube, and chain stays meet and where the forces on the pedal crank are supported.

Some elastic deflection in the plane of the frame is desirable for rider comfort. If the frame were absolutely rigid, every road bump would deliver a shock. The desirable amount of in-plane deflection depends on where the rider is in the spectrum between world-class racer and weekend recreational rider. Whatever the application, every rider values the minimization of weight. Thus, a premium is placed on low density materials with high strength and adequate stiffness. This is the reason for the introduction of light alloys for frames. A comparison of the relevant properties of these light alloys with traditional carbon steel and Cr-Mo alloy steel is made in Table 11.1.

Table 11.1 Comparison of the Properties of Metallic Frame Materials.

Material	Young's Modulus, E (GPa)	Density, ρ (g/cm^3)	0.2% Yield Stress, σ_{yld} (MPa)	E/ρ	σ_{yld}/ρ
Carbon steel	210	7.8	240	26.9	30
Cr-Mo steel	210	7.8	665	26.9	85
6061-T6 Al	70	2.7	260	25.9	95
Ti-3Al-2.5V	110	4.5	700	24.4	156

Note that the aluminum alloy has about one-third the density of the steel but only about one-third the stiffness, so the stiffness-to-density ratio is about the same for each. The titanium alloy is intermediate in both properties, and, again, the ratio is about the same. However, if the materials are compared on the basis of yield strength, the titanium alloy is somewhat stronger than the Cr-Mo steel, and the strength-to-density ratio is almost twice as large. The aluminum alloy is considerably weaker than the titanium alloy and the Cr-Mo steel, but its strength-to-density ratio is still greater than steel. The carbon steel compares very badly with the other alloys in strength-to-density ratio.

For performance of bicycle tubing, however, tube geometry is as important as material properties. As shown in Appendix 11.1, for a tube of outer and inner diameters D and d, the maximum stress for a given bending moment, M, is

$$\sigma_{max} = \frac{M\,D}{2\,I}$$

where I, the moment of inertia, is

$$I = \frac{\pi}{64}(D^4 - d^4)$$

Therefore, a low yield strength in the material can be compensated for by an increase in tube diameter and/or thickness.

The use of alternatives to steel must be based on some set of design criteria that include yield strength, weight, and the stiffness of the frame as a whole. The stiffness of a tube can be characterized by the curvature, $\frac{1}{r}$ imposed by a given bending moment according to

$$\frac{1}{r} = \frac{M}{E \cdot I}$$

and the weight can be characterized by the mass per unit length of tube, given by

$$\text{Mass per unit length} = \text{density x area} = \text{density x } \frac{\pi}{4}(D^2 - d^2)$$

Therefore, flexing of tubes can be reduced by increasing their moment of inertia by increasing tube diameter and/or thickness, but this is done at the expense of lightness. With the use of a given wall thickness of a low-stiffness material like aluminum, the moment of inertia increases as D^4, but the weight increases only as D^2.

A number of specimen frames are compared in Table 11.2 with regard to tube geometries and three measures of performance: mass per unit length, curvature produced by a bending moment of 100 N-m (885 in-lb), and the maximum stress at this bending moment, expressed as a fraction of the yield stress of the tube material.

Table 11.2 Characteristics of Typical Bike Frames

Material		D (OD) (in)	d (ID) (in)	Wall Thickness (in)	Moment of Inertia $\pi/64\,(D^4\text{-}d^4)$ in^4	cm^4	Weight/ Unit Length g/m	Curvature for a Given Bending Moment $1/r = M/EI$ mm/100N-m	Max. Stress for a Given Bending Moment $\sigma_m = \frac{MD}{2I}$ MPa/100N-m	$\%\sigma_{YLD}$
Road Bikes										
Carbon steel		1.130	1.030	0.050	0.025	1.041	860	48	138	58
Cr-Mo steel		1.133	1.060	0.036	0.018	0.750	601	67	190	29
6061-T6 Al		1.134	1.020	0.056	0.027	1.124	332	127	128	50
Mountain Bikes										
6061-T6 Al	top tube	1.50	1.40	0.05	0.06	2.50	397	57	76	30
A	down tube	2.00	1.87	0.06	0.185	7.70	688	19	32	12
	seat tube	1.25	1.05	0.10	0.06	2.50	629	57	63	25
6061-T6 Al	top tube	1.375	1.213	0.081	0.069	2.87	575	49	61	24
B	down tube	1.575	1.413	0.081	0.106	4.41	662	32	45	18
	seat tube	1.375	1.213	0.081	0.069	2.87	575	49	61	24
Ti-3Al-2.5V	top tube	1.25	1.16	0.045	0.034	1.41	549	64	45	18
	down tube	1.25	1.16	0.045	0.034	1.41	549	64	45	18
	seat tube	1.25	1.16	0.045	0.034	1.41	549	64	45	18

11.2 Comparisons of Steel, Aluminum-Alloy, and Titanium-Alloy Frames

11.2.1 Road Bikes

The Cr-Mo steel can be used as a standard for comparison. It can be seen that the carbon steel tubing is about 40% heavier, and the σ_{max}/σ_y for a given bending moment would be 50% higher than for alloy steel. The carbon steel tubing is stiffer, however; this is a result of the greater wall thickness, which is necessary to compensate for its low yield strength. Thus, the alloy-steel tubing is lighter and more resistant to fatigue cracking (owing to the higher strength) but is less stiff than the carbon steel.

These steel tubes were from road bikes, also known as racing-type bikes. They are intended to be light in weight and to be ridden over smooth surfaces. A 6061-T6 aluminum alloy tube from the same type of bicycle is also listed in Table 11.2. It has the same outer diameter as the steel tubes, and its wall thickness is about the same as the carbon steel tube. However, owing to the low density of aluminum, its weight is only 55% of the alloy steel tube. Because its yield strength is higher than the carbon steel, the maximum stress for a given bending moment would fall in between that for the alloy steel and carbon steel. Aside from its lightness, a rider would also feel the greater flexibility of the aluminum frame, because tube curvature caused by any given bending moment would be almost twice that found in the alloy steel tubing.

11.2.2 Mountain Bikes

A mountain bike is meant for riding over rough terrain; therefore, it must withstand larger impact forces than a road bike. The design goal should be to minimize σ_{max}/σ_y for a given bending moment without sacrificing lightness or optimum stiffness. The solution is to use tubing with a large diameter but with about the same wall thickness used for road bikes. However, manufacturers have applied this solution in different ways, as indicated in Table 11.2. One of the two Al-alloy frames has much fatter tubing than the other, but in both, the down tube has the maximum diameter, with the top tube and seat tube having the same smaller diameter in one, but different diameters in the other. The two frames have more or less the same characteristics in terms of maximum stress and weight, but they may have noticeable differences in riding character as a result of different combinations of tube stiffness.

The Ti-alloy tubing is superior to the Al-alloy tubes in terms of maximum stress and is similar to them in weight and stiffness. It might also be noted that the diameter of these tubes is much closer to those found in a road bike than the diameters of the Al-alloys; this is possible as a result of the greater strength and elastic modulus of titanium compared to aluminum.

The values for yield strength given in Table 11.2 are those for tubing, *per se*. However, these values cannot be applied in the vicinity of joints made by thermal processes, i.e., brazing or welding, because of the softening effects of the heat. The remainder of this chapter will be focussed on the microstructure of each metallic material (which is the source of the yield strength) and on the effects of thermal joining processes on microstructure and strength.

The alternative joining process is adhesive bonding, which employs an epoxy adhesive and a component at each joint that serves to define the joint angles and to form the space containing the adhesive. (In the use of such components, brazed and bonded joints are similar.) Bonded joints require only low temperatures for curing, and these do not affect the strengths even of aluminum alloys. However, bonded joints are a relatively recent innovation in frame building, and experience with joint durability is still being evaluated. Bonded joints will be discussed in Chapter 13.

11.3 Steel Frames

Several factors led to the dominance of steel for building bicycle frames. The rapid development and spread of large-scale steel making and the growth of the machine-tool industry that followed enabled the production of steel tubes. The development of alloy steels enabled the achievement of high strength in tubes joined by brazing. Moreover, steel has a high Young's modulus in comparison to its potential metallic competitors and can be strengthened by several processes, including the fine ferrite/carbide microstructures obtainable from the decomposition of alloyed austenite. The challenge has been to achieve or maintain high strength at the joints of frames assembled by brazing or welding.

11.3.1 Effects of Brazing on Steel Tubing

The most economical material for a bicycle frame would be thin-walled, cold-drawn carbon-steel tubing, if the tubing could be joined together without heating. The strength achieved by strain hardening of the mostly ferritic steel would permit the tubing wall to be thin, achieving lightness, and the high modulus would allow great leeway in tube design to achieve the desired frame stiffness. This is actually achievable as a result of recent developments in adhesives. However, at present, brazing is still generally used for frames joined with lugs. Even with silver-based brazing alloys, this requires heating the tubing in the vicinity of 700°C, which would recrystallize, and thereby soften, a cold-drawn tube. If a Cu-Zn brazing alloy were used, the steel would be completely transformed to austenite, because, as the phase diagram in Fig. 7.21(b) indicates, the 60Cu-40Zn alloy has a liquidus above 900°C.

The conclusion is that carbon steel tubes cannot be permanently strengthened by cold work if they are to be used in a brazed frame. After furnace brazing, the microstructure of the tubing would be in the normalized (austenitized and air-cooled) condition. In order to achieve the required strength, the wall-thickness of the carbon steel tubes must be greater than that of strain-hardened tubing. This means that a carbon-steel frame must be heavier than one made from thin-walled tubing.

A lightweight, brazed steel frame can be made from thin-walled tubing if an appropriate alloy steel is used. A steel commonly chosen contains chromium and molybdenum as the major alloy elements, along with about 0.3 to 0.4% carbon. These two alloy elements are BCC transition metals, and one of their effects in iron is to stabilize the BCC α phase. The result is an increase in the eutectoid temperature and a decrease in the carbon content at which the eutectoid reaction occurs, as illustrated schematically in Fig. 11.3. Thus, for a given carbon content, a slowly cooled Cr-Mo steel should have more of the eutectoid microstructure than would a plain-carbon steel.

An even more important property of these alloy elements is that they form carbides that are significantly more stable than Fe_3C; this is especially true for molybdenum. This effect has already been noted with regard to the phenomenon of secondary hardening during tempering, as illustrated in Fig. 9.10. As pointed out in Section 9.4.3, this is the result of the formation of fine carbides at elevated temperatures (i.e., where the diffusion of the substitutional alloy elements can occur).

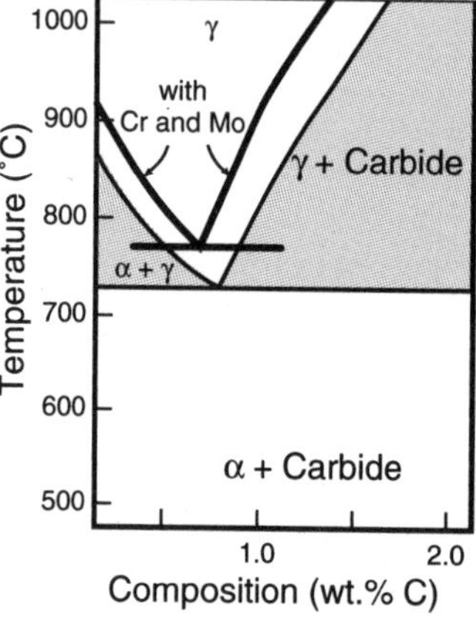

Fig. 11.3 Schematic illustration of the effect of the addition of ferrite-stabilizers, like chromium and molybdenum, on the eutectoid region of the iron-carbon diagram.

Another property of these elements, especially molybdenum, is that they have a strong affinity for carbon in solid solution in iron. The effect is, first, to retard the kinetics of the transformation of austenite to ferrite-plus-carbide (i.e., both elements increase hardenability) and, second, to alter the morphology of the eutectoid transformation product from lamellar pearlite to a much finer distribution of globular carbides in a ferrite matrix.

The result of these changes can be seen by comparing the microstructures of the seat stays from a lightweight, alloy-steel frame and a heavyweight low-carbon-steel frame, both of which had been assembled by furnace brazing, as shown in Fig. 11.4. The brazing alloy was Cu-Zn, which had to be heated above 900°C to be liquified; thus, the tubes would have been austenitized during brazing. When the fixture holding the frame was removed from the furnace and allowed to cool in air, the alloy steel, Fig. 11.4(b), began to transform by forming Widmanstätten ferrite and blocky ferrite on a very fine scale. Then the remaining austenite transformed eutectoidally to a ferrite-plus-carbide mixture, which is the analog of pearlite in this alloy steel. (Some of this two-phase constituent may be bainite, but the microstructure is too fine to be sure.) In any case, this fine two-phase constituent comprises 70 to 80% of the microstructure and is responsible for the high strength, compared to what would be found in a plain carbon steel with the same carbon content. (Figure 8.1(b) shows an air-cooled 1040 steel, which has 0.4% carbon, instead of the 0.3% in the 4130 alloy steel shown in Fig 11.4(b), but it still provides a useful comparison.)

In contrast, the low-carbon steel shown in Fig. 11.4(a) consists almost entirely of ferrite, with only a very small amount of pearlite. Thus, the carbon steel has the same ferritic matrix as the alloy steel, but without the dispersed carbides. The fact that it has only about half the strength of the alloy steel necessitates a greater wall thickness, as shown by the comparison of cross sections of the tubes in Fig. 11.4.

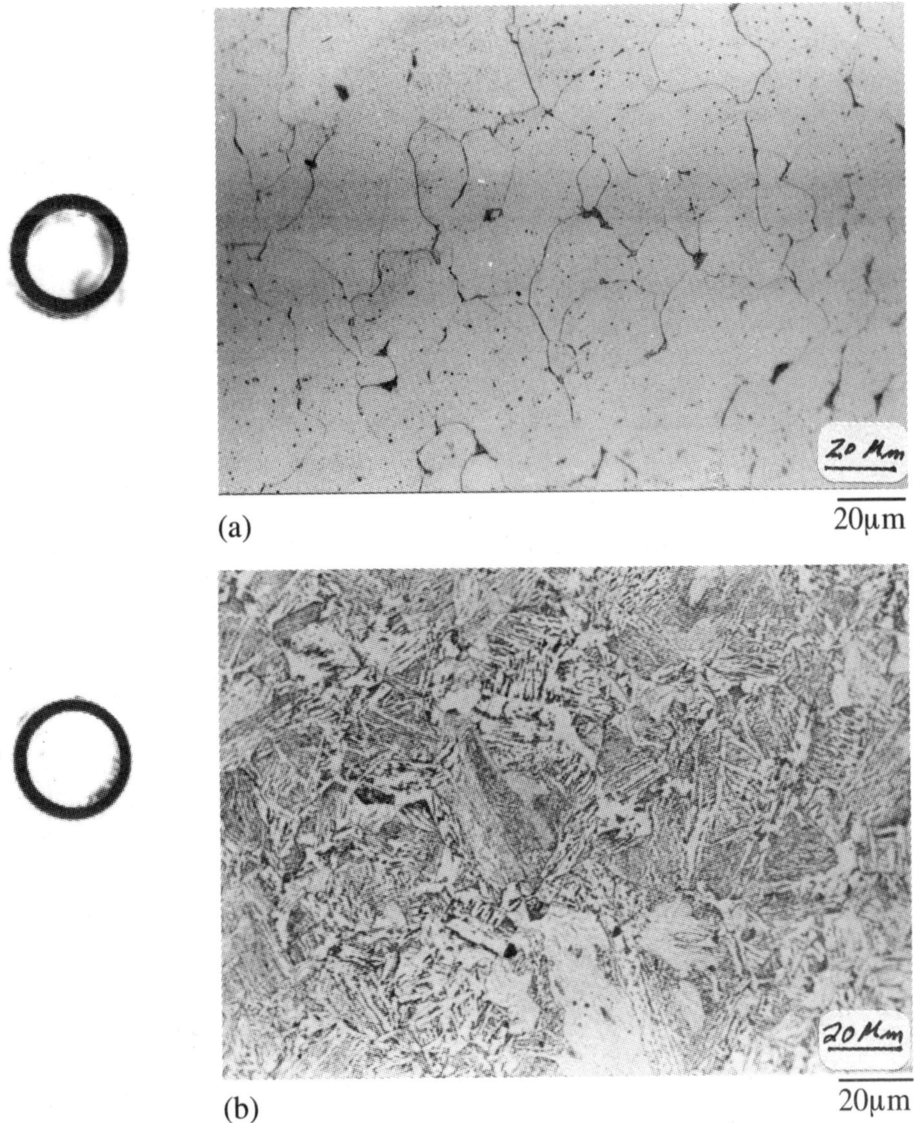

Fig. 11.4 Comparison of microstructures of the seat stay from (a) a heavy carbon steel frame, and (b) a lightweight alloy steel frame, with the cross-section of each stay shown alongside each microstructure.

Figure 11.5 shows load vs. elongation curves obtained from tensile specimens of tubes from the same two bicycles. Note that load, not stress, is plotted here, and the geometry of the tensile specimens cut from the frame was the same, except for the greater wall thickness of the carbon-steel tube. It is remarkable that, even though the alloy steel tube had a thinner wall than the carbon steel, it still carried about 50% more load before necking occurred. This means that the design thickness of the alloy steel tube was determined not by its yield strength, which is much more than adequate, but by the requirements for elastic stiffness of the frame.

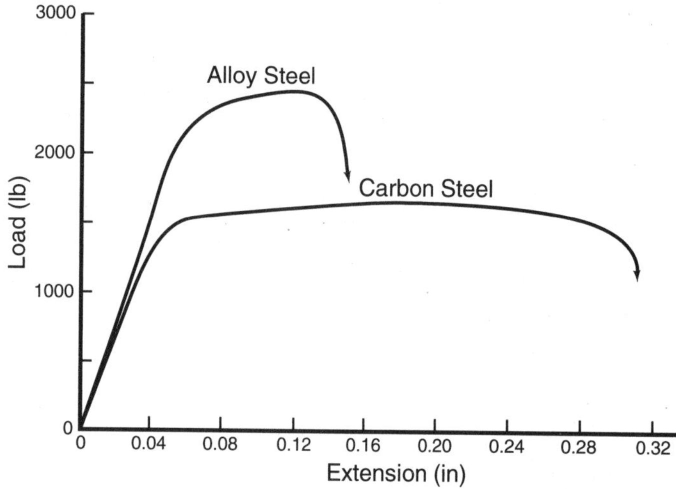

Fig. 11.5 Comparison of the load *vs.* extension curves of an alloy-steel tube and a carbon-steel tube from the same bicycle manufacturer.

11.3.2 Lugs; the Fabrication of Complex Shapes

The function of a lug is to hold the tubes at a particular angle and to provide a precisely dimensioned channel along which liquid brazing alloy can spread. In order to minimize weight, the lug should have a thin wall, and the joint area should be kept to a minimum, consistent with obtaining a sufficiently strong joint. Examples of two kinds of lugs are shown in Fig. 11.6. The arms of the lugs are designed to provide a large joint area where needed to resist the loading of the frame at that location. For example, in the top-tube-to-head-tube lugs shown in Fig. 11.6, the joint must resist the bending forces in the plane of the frame. Hence, there is more joint area at the top and bottom of the top tube and at the front and rear of the head tube (in Fig. 11.6b) than at the sides of these tubes.

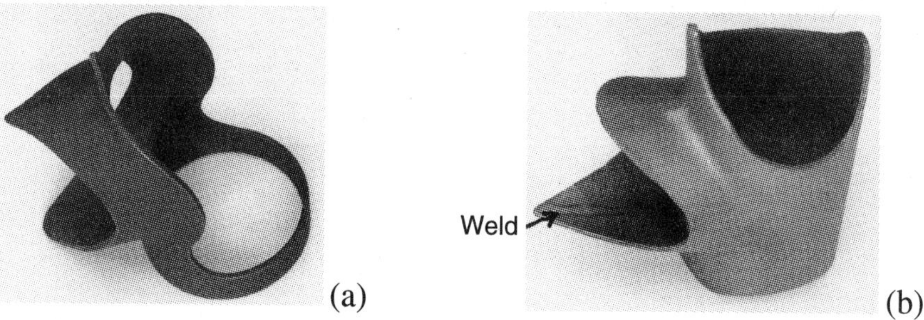

Fig. 11.6 Examples of top-tube-to-head-tube lugs: (a) investment cast, (b) fabricated from sheet.

One common method of producing a lug is the process of *investment casting,* also known as the lost-wax process. This process has been used to make artifacts dating to the time of the pharaohs. The first step is to make a replica of the desired article out of wax, which can be carved and molded easily at room temperature. Next, the wax replica is invested, or encased, in a ceramic mold by repeatedly coating it with a slurry, or paste, of a ceramic powder mixed with water, allowing each coat to dry before applying the next. In actual production, a kind of tree of wax replicas, connected by branches of wax, is constructed before the investment process. The tree is connected to the outside of the large ceramic mold by a larger wax branch. The mold is then heated in a furnace to densify it by sintering (cf. Section 9.6.3), i.e., to make it a solid ceramic with a minimum of porosity.

During the firing of the mold, the wax is vaporized, therefore "lost," leaving cavities into which molten metal may be poured. The mold may be heated before the casting is poured to allow the hot metal to flow throughout all the branches before solidifying. When the mold is cool, it is broken apart, and the cast pieces are cut from the tree. Usually only a minimum of finishing is needed, for example by grinding to remove excess metal, before the part is ready for use. The special art required is the knowledge of how to allow for the shrinkage of the mold during firing and of the metal during solidification to produce lugs of the desired dimensions (e.g., with the required clearances between the lugs and the tubes).

Any metal casting will contain some unavoidable amount of porosity from two sources. First, most materials contract upon solidification. When a liquid freezes, as most do, by the nucleation and growth of solid dendrites (cf. Section 7.2.4), the spaces between the dendritic arms contain the last liquid to freeze. Because of the contraction, there will not be enough liquid to fill these interdendritic spaces with solid; the result is so-called shrinkage porosity.

The other source of porosity is the evolution of gases, mainly oxygen and nitrogen, which are more soluble in liquid metals than in solid. The same phenomenon occurs when water freezes; thus, the porosity due to formation of gas bubbles can be seen in ice cubes. An example of the porosity found in an investment-cast lug is shown in Fig. 11.7. This low-carbon steel lug also contains a dispersion of fine particles; these are inadvertent impurity inclusions arising, most probably, from the entrainment of ceramic particles in the liquid metal as it flowed into the mold.

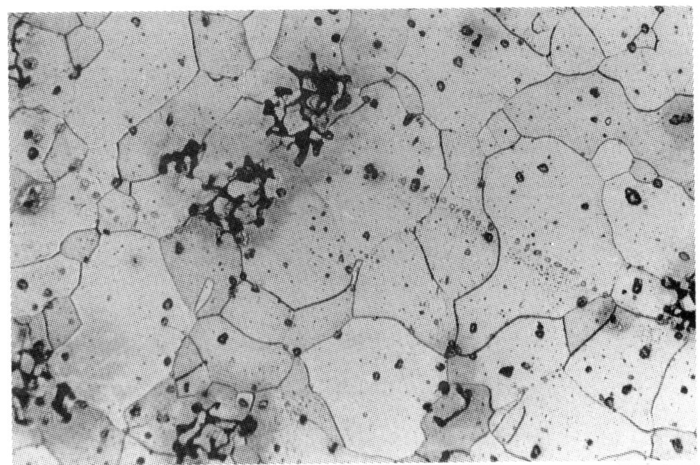

Fig. 11.7 Example of the porosity in an investment-cast low-carbon steel lug.

In bicycle lugs the casting porosity is generally not a problem, since the solidified brazing alloy is likely to have even larger cavities, due mainly to insufficient flow of the alloy to fill the space entirely, and in any case the brazing alloy is probably softer than the steel. However, in general, one must be aware that castings contain some degree of porosity and may also have coarse grain sizes if they solidify slowly. Thus, a casting is often not as strong as a wrought object made of the same material. A wrought object is something that is mechanically shaped, for example by rolling or forging, after the material was initially produced (usually by solidification). During high-temperature deformation processes, the porosity initially present in a cast ingot is removed by pressure-welding.

The second method of producing a bicycle lug is to shape it out of sheet and to use welding to close it into the final form. An example is shown in Fig. 11.6(b). Here, a low-carbon steel sheet produced by cold-rolling, i.e., a wrought product, was press-formed in a die to a shape that could then be curled and welded into the form of a lug. This is obviously a faster process than investment casting, and it produces a stronger and thinner lug, but it involves the use of large expensive capital equipment and is only employed when a sufficiently large number of lugs of the same design are to be made.

11.3.3 Fabrication of Steel Frames by Welding

An alternative method of assembling lugless steel frames is welding by the tungsten inert gas (TIG) process. This was used originally for mountain bikes, which have non-standard tube sizes and angles, but it is now being applied more generally. The fundamental difference between welding and brazing is that the pieces to be joined by welding do not remain solid. They are fused along the joint, together with a filler metal.

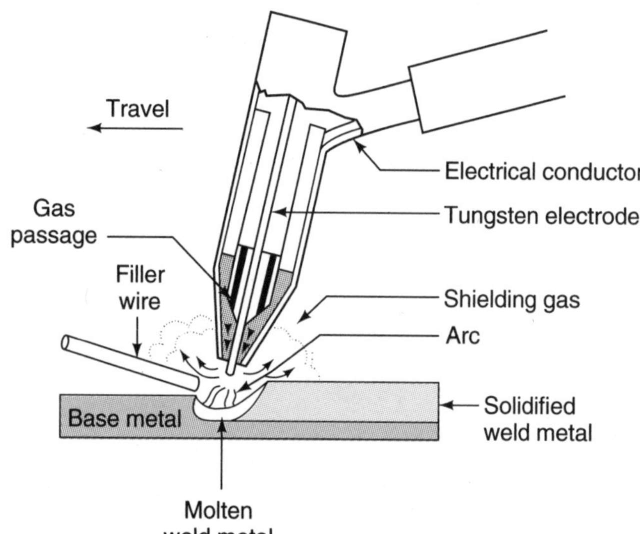

Fig. 11.8 Schematic illustration of a TIG welding gun in operation. (From S. Kalpakjian, *Manufacturing Engineering and Technology,* Addison-Wesley, 1989, p. 829.)

In the TIG process, which is simply a special variant of arc welding, an electric arc is struck between the tungsten electrode in the welding "gun" and the article to be welded. An arc is a high-temperature plasma of ionized gases, generated when two conductors with a large voltage difference are brought near each other. The voltage difference is created by an electrical generator attached to the tungsten electrode, shown in Fig. 11.8, while the "work," e.g., bicycle frame, is grounded. The gun is also connected by a hose to a container of argon or helium gas; this gas is blown over the joint to prevent oxidation of the weld pool. Filler metal is added to the joint by a separate wire, also shown schematically in Fig. 11.8. The process allows precisely located and controlled welding, and the heat-affected zone, the HAZ, can be kept quite small by using a small gun and carefully controlled heat input.

Weld joints at the head tube of an alloy steel mountain bike are shown in Fig. 11.9, along with the results of microhardness measurements in the vicinity of the joints. (Microhardness tests are carried out by using a small diamond-pyramid indenter attatched to a special microscope.) There are two important features of these joints. The first is that the weld metal and HAZ are both harder than the tubes themselves. The reason for this is evident from the microstructures shown in Fig. 11.9.

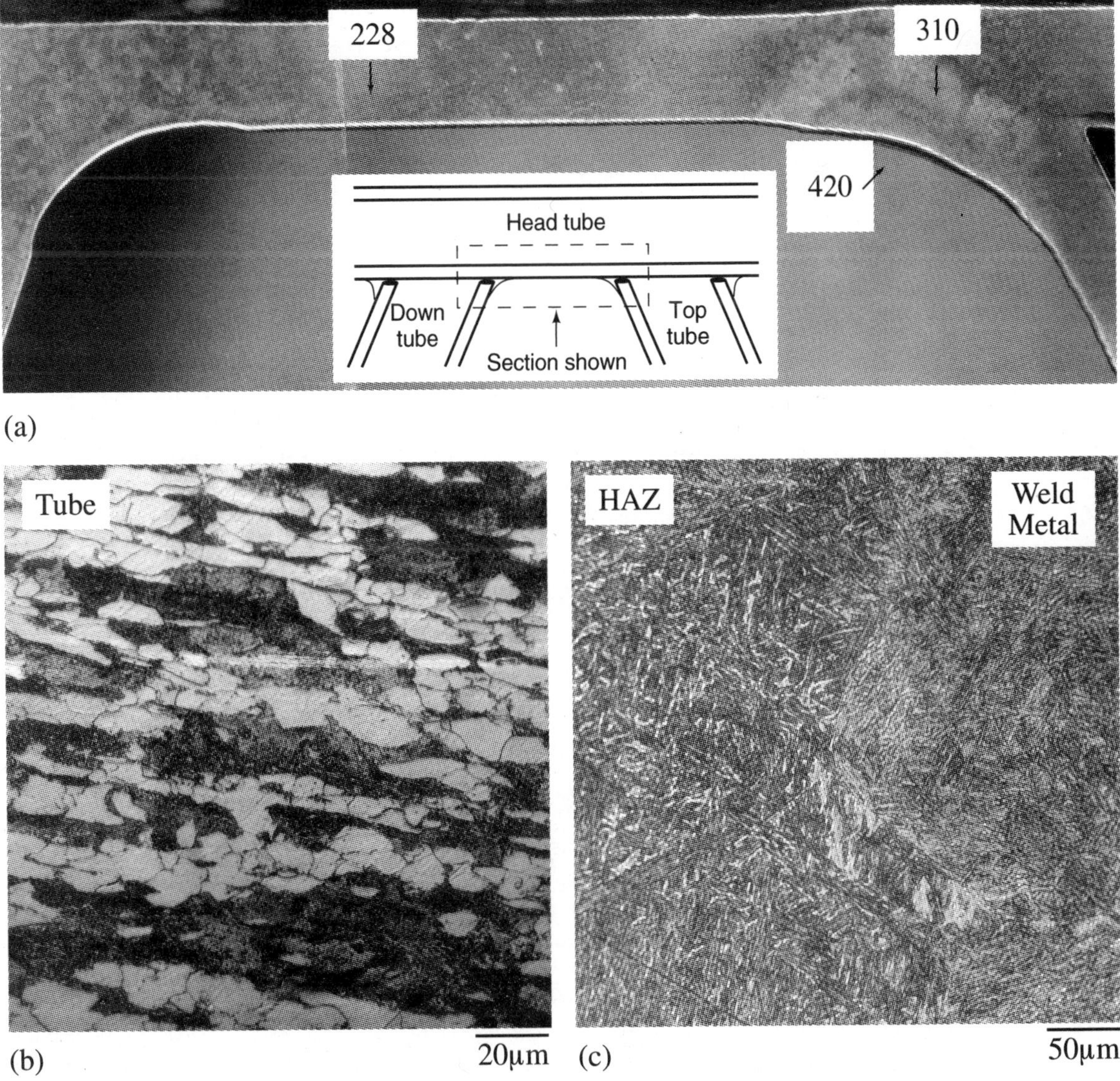

Fig. 11.9 (a) Weld joints between the head tube and the top and down tubes of an alloy steel mountain bike, showing microhardness values at various locations and the microstructures of (b) the original tube as well as (c) the juncture of the weld metal and heat-affected zone.

The tubes exhibit a banded microstructure, (Fig. 11.9(b)) characteristic of a hot-worked alloy steel in which microsegregation of the alloy elements (Mn, Cr, and Mo) took place during solidification of the original ingot. The microstructure comprises alternating bands of ferrite and high-carbon (alloy-rich) bainite mixed with quasi-pearlite. (The eutectoid decomposition product in a Cr-Mo steel is not lamellar pearlite, but rather a mixture of ferrite and rod-like or globular carbides as shown in Fig. 11.4b.)

In contrast, the weld metal is fully bainitic. The bainite was formed during rapid cooling from the austenite, which had formed during solidification. The cooling was rapid because a small volume of molten metal was surrounded by the cold metal of the tubes, which conducted heat away quickly. The HAZ is also fully bainitic, but the bainite was formed from austenite of a much smaller grain size than in the weld metal, because it had not reached such a high temperature in the austenitic phase field. The boundary region between the HAZ and the weld metal is also shown in Fig. 11.9.

The second important feature is the "lack-of-penetration" type of defect in the inside of both weld joints; one is shown at higher magnification in Fig.11.10(a). This type of defect arises when the fusion zone has not penetrated completely through a joint. In this particular case, only a portion of the original gap between the two pieces of tubing was actually closed by fusion. When the joint was made, a weld bead was deposited alongside the joint, forming a bridge between the two pieces of tubing, as shown schematically in Fig. 11.10(b) and (c). This is a common type of defect in a butt joint, and it acts as a stress concentrator in the joint. It can lead to premature fatigue fracture, for example. In this case, the problem arises from poor welding technique; the amount of energy input to the joint was insufficient to fuse the joint all the way through.

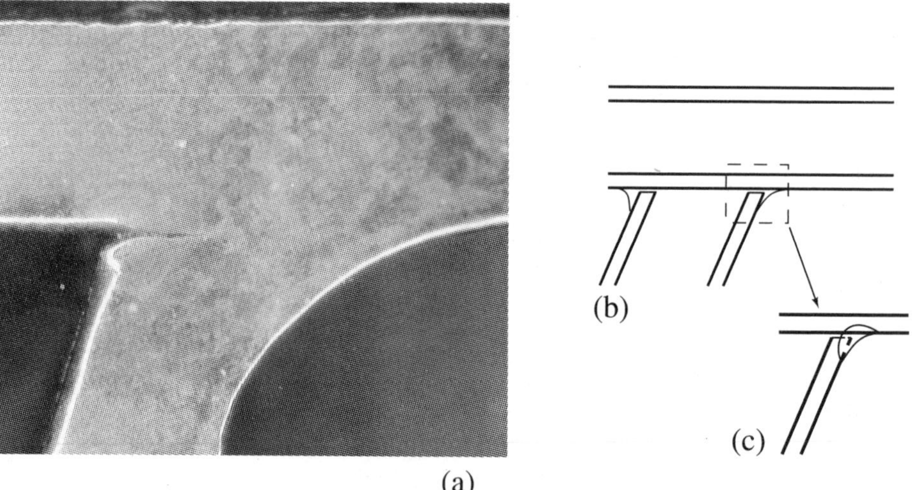

Fig. 11.10 (a) A lack-of-penetration defect in the interior of the joints shown in Fig. 11.9. (b) and (c) A schematic representation of how that joint was made.

With thin-walled tubing, it is not a trivial matter to get the energy input just right, and particular skill is required of the welder. In this situation, it is advisable to weld test pieces occasionally, so that they can be sectioned and checked to ensure that the welding technique is producing full-penetration welds. Alternatively, the joints can be subjected to non-destructive testing, using radiography, for example. This adds expense to the manufacturing process, but it would lessen the probability of a joint failure.

The insidious aspect of this type of defect is that it is on the inside of the tube and is, therefore, invisible to the user of the bike. The elimination of such defects is important in bicycle parts that are highly stressed in bending, such as around bottom brackets and in the joints of the head tube. The latter is particularly important in mountain bike frames, which, by virtue of their elongated-diamond design, are subject to large bending moments at the head tube, particularly when ridden over rough terrain.

11.3.4 Butted Tubing

To compensate for the softening during heating of the joints of hand-brazed or welded frames, the wall thickness of the end-sections of the tubes can be left larger in the tube-drawing process, as shown in Fig. 11.11. Such tubes are called butted tubes. To make them requires the use of a special mandrel, which is a solid cylindrical tool placed inside the tube during final drawing through the dies. This is obviously more expensive than making tubes with uniform wall thickness. It is often used to save weight on high-priced bikes joined by brazing.

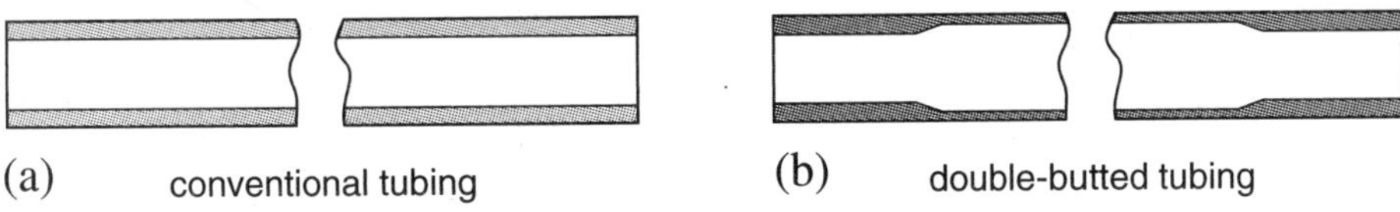

Fig. 11.11 A schematic comparison of (a) conventional and (b) double-butted tubing.

Butted tubing is unnecessary for furnace-brazed bicycles, since the effects of heat are uniform over the entire frame. It is also unnecessary for frames to be joined by adhesive bonding, where only low-temperature heating is used to cure the adhesive. In this relatively new method of bicycle construction, a lightweight steel frame can be made using unbutted alloy-steel tubing assembled by bonding the tubes to lugs with an epoxy adhesive. Weight savings come from the elimination of the butted ends and the brazing alloy and sometimes from the substitution of aluminum for steel lugs. The nature of adhesives for this purpose will be covered in Chap. 13.

11.4 Joining of Light-Metal Frames

11.4.1 Al-Alloy Frames

The aluminum alloy of choice for frames is 6061 T6. As indicated in Chap. 10, the strengthening of the alloy is achieved by a solution treatment followed by water quenching and an aging treatment above room temperature. The tubing can be joined by either adhesive bonding or welding. In welding of tubing that was precipitation-hardened prior to welding, the heat-affected zones alongside the fusion zone of a weld would be over-aged, i.e., softened. Of course, the weld metal would also be soft, since it would be in the as-cast condition, but this weakness could be offset by a large volume of weld metal, so that the cross-section through the weld metal is larger than the thickness of the tube. The softened HAZ has no such simple remedy, and the frame designer must keep the extent of this region small by limiting energy input during the welding process.

One of the weld joints in mountain bike B (Table 11.2) was sectioned and polished metallographically so that the hardness at various points in the joint region could be measured. The joint is shown in Fig. 11.12(a), and the distribution of hardness values is shown in Fig. 11.12(b). The diamond-pyramid hardness (DPH) in the weld metal averages 73, whereas the hardness of the tubing far from the joint exceeds 150. The HAZ extends quite far from the weld metal, due to the large thermal conductivity of the aluminum alloy and the fact that overaging occurs rapidly in this material at a few hundred degrees centigrade. Thus, contrary to the case of the weld joint in the alloy steel, the joint in a welded Al-alloy frame is much softer than the tubing, and the soft HAZ is quite extensive. This must be considered by the designer when specifying the diameter and wall thickness of the tubing.

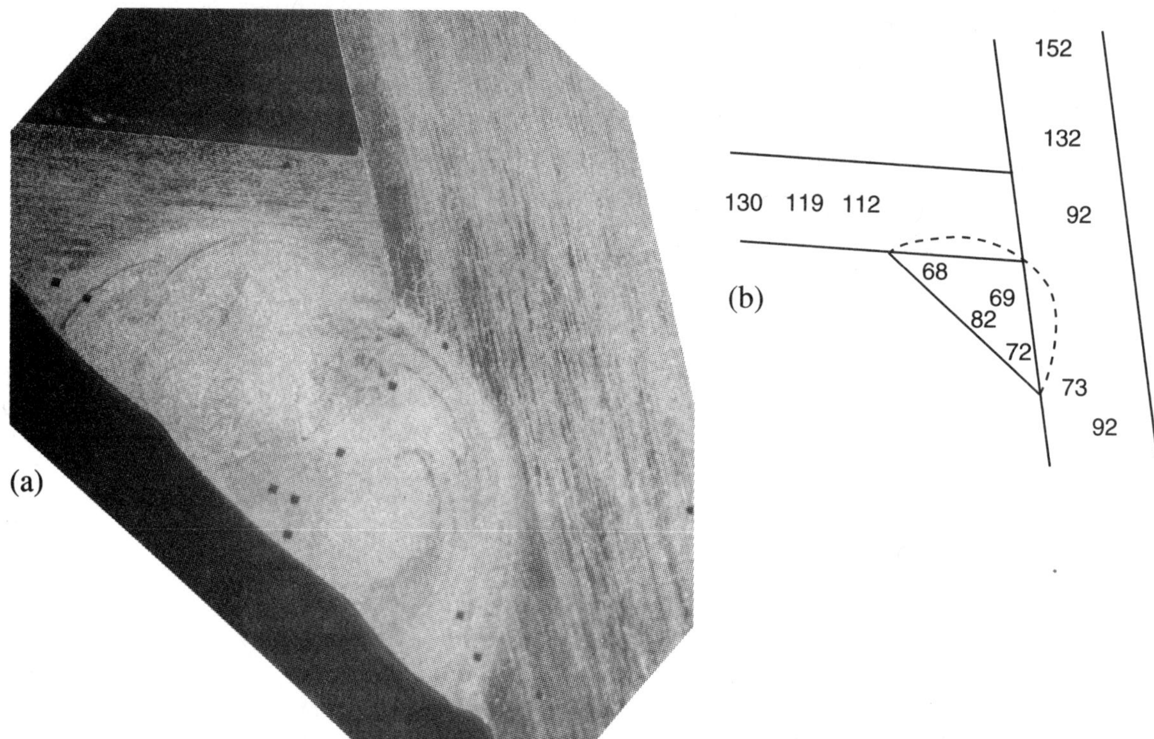

Fig. 11.12 (a) Cross-section of welded joint between the top tube and head tube of mountain bike B (cf. Table 11.2). (b) Diamond-pyramid hardness at various points in the joint region, determined by microhardness tests.

One way to eliminate the softened HAZ is to heat-treat the entire frame after welding is completed. Since this would involve rapid quenching from the solution-treatment temperature, it carries the strong possibility of distortion of the frame as a result of thermal stresses (cf. Section 9.4.4). The frame would have to be constrained in a rigid fixture during heat treatment, adding significantly to the manufacturing cost. The aging treatment applied after quenching would presumably relieve much of the residual stresses due to quenching.

It can be seen in Fig. 11.12, and more clearly in Fig. 11.13, that the joint in this mountain bike suffers from the same kind of lack-of-penetration defect that afflicts the steel joint in Fig. 11.10. This crack-like flaw in the unwelded section of the joint could lead to fatigue failure through the joint, particularly in such a soft region. This defect occurs on the inside of a tube, where it is invisible.

Fig. 11.13 The juncture of the lower side of the top tube and the head tube depicted in Fig. 11.12(a), showing the crack-like defect from the almost complete lack of penetration of the weld metal into this juncture. This is the result of an inadequate amount of energy delivered by the welding gun.

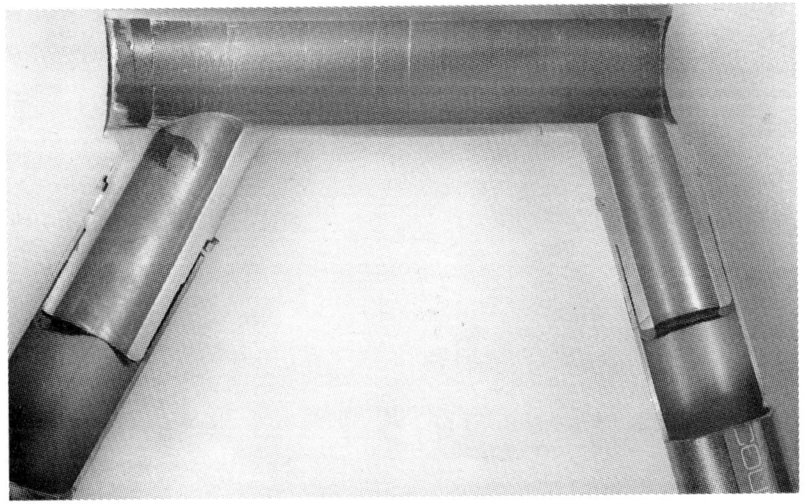

Fig. 11.14 Cross-section of joints between the top and down tubes and the head tube of the aluminum-alloy road bike listed in Table 11.2, showing the use of epoxy adhesive for the bonding of the joints.

The softening associated with welding of aluminum-alloy tubes can be avoided by using adhesive bonding. The Al-alloy road-bike tubing listed in Table 11.2 was joined together in that manner. The joints of the top tube and down tube to the head tube are shown in the sectioned frame in Fig. 11.14. This kind of head tube with tubular arms can be fabricated either by casting or by forging and machining. The heat-treated tubes are simply pressed over the arms, which have ridges to keep the tube-to-arm spacing uniform, and the epoxy adhesive (applied to the arms before assembly) is cured.

The cured epoxy is a glassy network polymer (see Chap. 13) and, as such, is a brittle material. That means that a bonded joint does not have the "give" that is found in a brazed joint; a brazing alloy can deform plastically if a joint is overstressed, but the epoxy cannot deform plastically without cracking. For this reason, it is imperative that the bonded joints be designed to carry all conceivable loads without plastic deformation.

11.4.2 Titanium Alloy Frames

Titanium alloys present a different set of challenges to a frame builder, primarily because titanium is a highly reactive metal. It forms a very stable oxide, carbide, and nitride, and it readily absorbs oxygen, carbon, and nitrogen in solid solution. It is not practical to heat-treat titanium in air, because the surface layers become hardened and embrittled by the uptake of these interstitial impurities. Thus, vacuum heat treatment is necessary for titanium and its alloys.

The attractiveness of titanium alloys for certain applications, in spite of the high processing costs, is that they are less dense than alloy steels, while having comparable strengths, and they can be highly resistant to chemical attack, as long as the surface is passivated by the TiO_2 film. In addition, they have melting temperatures higher than that of iron. As a result, titanium alloys have found applications in the aerospace and chemical industries.

Titanium undergoes an allotropic transformation from HCP to BCC at 883°C (analogous to the α-to-γ transformation in iron at 910°C), as indicated in Fig. 11.15. It is common to formulate titanium alloys by adding at least two elements, one of that dissolves preferentially in, and stabilizes, the α (HCP) phase and
11360 another that dissolves in the β (BCC) phase. In this way one can get a two-phase alloy at room temperature with solid-solution strengthening in each phase. If the two-phase mixture can be produced on a fine scale, the effect is analogous to refinement of grain size, and this can produce substantial additional strengthening.

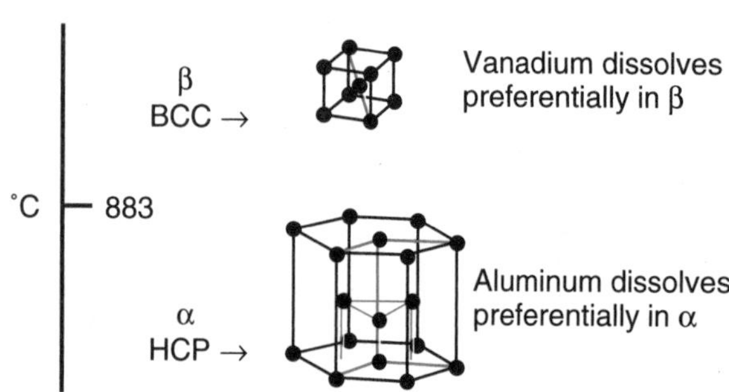

Fig. 11.15 Schematic representation of the allotropic transformation in titanium at 883°C, indicating the preferences of the alloying elements aluminum and vanadium for the respective phases.

The fact that aluminum is an α-stabilizer and vanadium is a β-stabilizer is reflected in the respective phase diagrams, as shown in Fig. 11.16. For either alloy element, it can be expected that, because of the β-to-α transformation, one can heat a titanium alloy into the all-β region and then produce a variety of microstructures by varying the cooling rate to room temperature. This will be illustrated for the case of the Ti-3%Al-2.5%V alloy used for bicycle tubing.

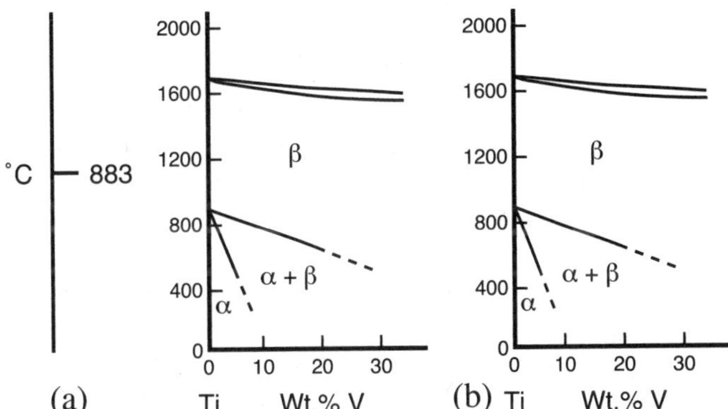

Fig. 11.16 (a) Titanium-rich side of the titanium-aluminum phase diagram and (b) the titanium-vanadium phase diagram.

The most common high-strength titanium alloy is Ti-6Al-4V, in which one can produce a fine microstructure having a high volume fraction of β in α, with large solid-solution strengthening in each phase. This alloy is not ideal for bicycle tubing, however, because it strain hardens so rapidly that tube drawing would require frequent anneals in a vacuum and would be quite expensive. Hot working is also impractical, since it would have to be done in a protective environment.

Seamless tubing is produced for aerospace applications, usually from the Ti-3Al-2.5V alloy, which has only half the solid-solution strengthening and much less β at room temperature than the Ti-6Al-4V alloy. The availability of this tubing is the main reason for its selection for bicycle frames, but the properties of this alloy make it well-suited for frames, as evidenced by Tables 11.1 and 11.2. The high strength is made possible by the combination of: (a) solid-solution hardening of α by aluminum and of β by vanadium, (b) the fineness of the microstructure, achieved by heat treatment, and (c) the strain hardening from the tube-drawing process.

In order to interpret the microstructures found in the bicycle, it is necessary first to examine the relatively simple microstructure obtained by slowly cooling the alloy from the all-β region, shown in Fig. 11.17(a). The alloy was heated to 1000°C, and this produced a rather coarse-grained β. When the alloy was cooled below the β/α+β phase boundary, plates of α formed along certain crystallographic planes in the β grains. This is Widmanstätten α, and it is analogous to the Widmanstätten ferrite formed in carbon steels (cf. Section 8.3.3).

The images in Figs. 12.17 and 12.18 were obtained with a scanning electron microscope (cf. Fig. 13.26). In these figures the α phase appears dark, and the β phase, which stands out on the etched surface, appears white.

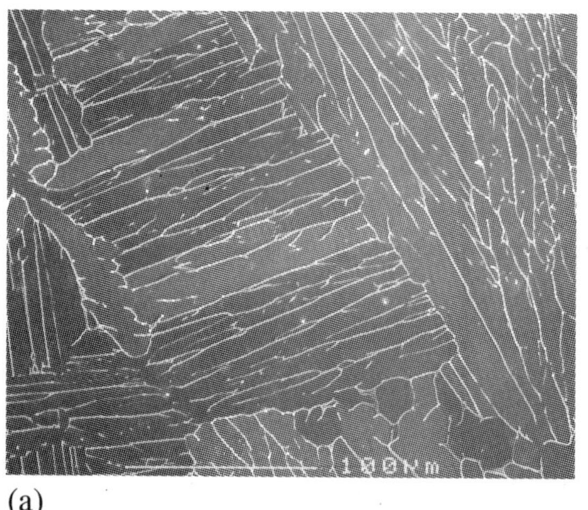

(a)

(b)

Fig. 11.17 (a) Microstructure of Ti-3Al-2.5V furnace-cooled from 1000°C, showing Widmanstätten α with residual β between the α plates. (b) Same alloy air-cooled from 1000°C; the α is now in very thin plates. Scanning electron micrographs using secondary electrons; courtesy John Marcon and Jeff Pfaendtner, Univ. of Penn.

As the α formed, the vanadium, which had been in solid solution in the β (along with the aluminum), was rejected into the remaining β, since the vanadium is more soluble in β than in α. Thus, the rate of formation of the α was controlled by the rate of outward diffusion of vanadium (a substitutional solute) in the same way that the formation of Widmanstätten ferrite is controlled by the diffusion of carbon into the surrounding austenite. The reason for the plate-like morphology of the α is that the rejected vanadium "piles-up" along the flat faces of the α and slows the rate of motion of that α/β boundary, whereas the rate of motion of the tip of the plate is much less affected by this piling-up.

The final condition is a microstructure consisting almost of entirely Widmanstätten α, with residual β in the spaces between the α plates. The fineness of this microstructure, even in the furnace-cooled condition, is the direct result of the slowness of diffusion of vanadium in the β phase.

An even finer microstructure is formed by air-cooling from the β region, as shown in Fig. 11.16(b). Here again the α has formed in very thin plates, which are the analog of bainite in steel. The strength of the air-cooled alloy is higher than that of the furnace-cooled because of the finer microstructure.

The microstructure of the cold-drawn tubing is shown in Fig. 11.18(a) and (b). It comprises flattened α grains elongated in the drawing direction. The microstructures of weld metal and the adjacent HAZ are shown in Figs. 11.18(c) and (d), respectively. Both are characteristic of an alloy cooled from the β region rather quickly, as seen from a comparison with Fig. 11.17(b). Although the weld metal and HAZ are not strain hardened, the microstructure is still quite fine; this produces a high strength in the joint. The effect of welding on the joint strength can be judged from the microhardness measurements shown in Table 11.3.

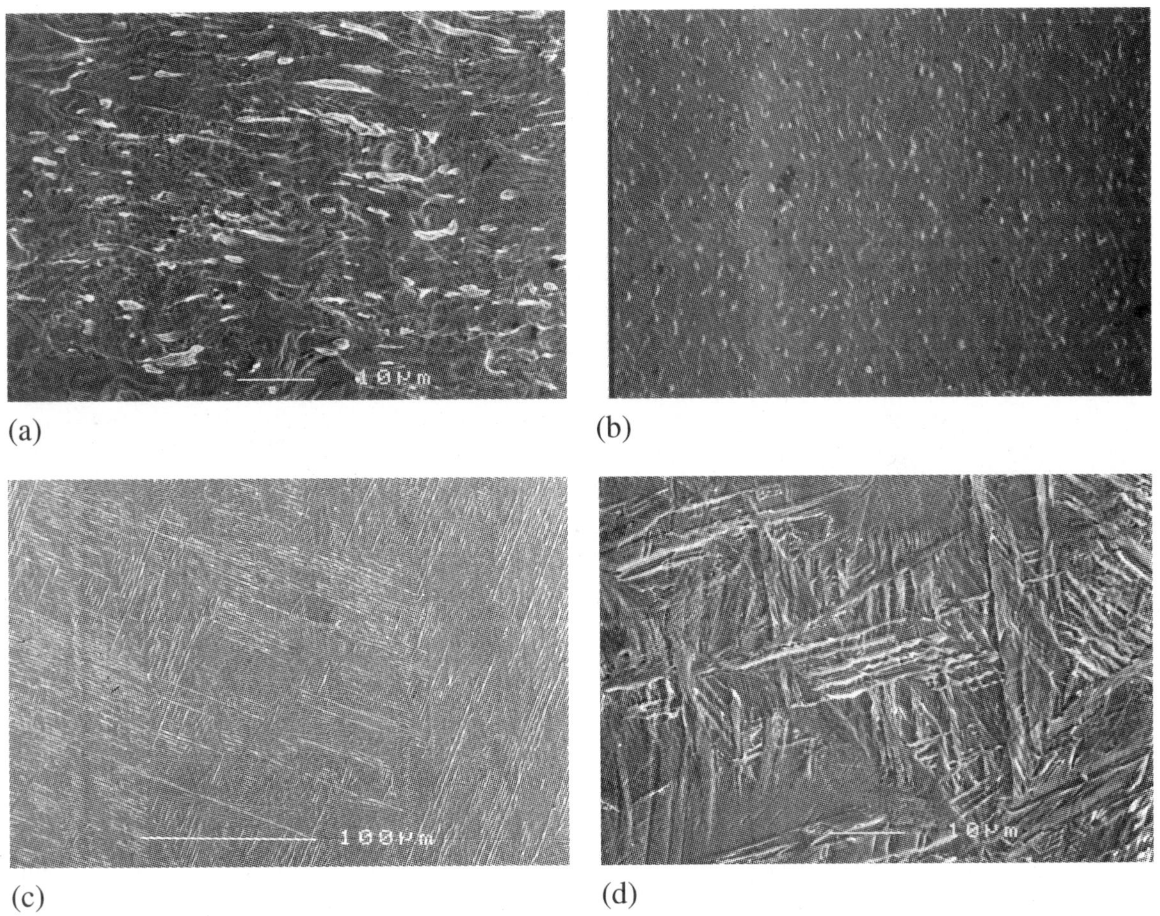

(a) (b) (c) (d)

Fig. 11.18 Microstructures of tube and weld joint in Ti-3Al-2.5V bicycle frame. (a) Longitudinal section of as-drawn tube. (b) Transverse section of as-drawn tube. (c) Weld metal. (d) HAZ. SEMs by Marcon and Pfaendtner, Univ. of Penn.

Table 11.3 Microhardness Values at the Weld Joint in the Ti-Alloy Frame

Location	Average Hardness (DPH)
Base metal (tube)	250
HAZ	215
Weld metal	214

It is apparent that the HAZ and weld metal have about 85% of the hardness of the cold-drawn tube. Thus, strain hardening accounts for only a minor fraction of the strength of the tubing, and the loss of this hardening from the heat of welding is not a major concern.

It must be realized that the titanium-alloy frames are assembled by welding under a protective blanket of argon gas. The inside of the tubing also needs to be filled with argon to prevent uptake of the interstitial impurities oxygen, nitrogen, hydrogen and carbon from the air. If this is not done, the weld metal and HAZ can be embrittled. In effect, the interstitials pin dislocations to the extent that the resultant strengthening produces a large loss of ductility.

Because the surface of the titanium alloy is passivated by an extremely thin layer of titanium oxide, it is impervious to atmospheric corrosion. Therefore, the frame can be left unpainted, with its distinctive dull-grey metallic sheen. This appearance is one of the factors that make titanium-alloy bikes attractive to many people. However, owing to the high manufacturing costs, it is unlikely that welded all-titanium-alloy frames will ever be used for mass-market bicycle production.

11.4.3 Hybrid Frames

Except for welded all-steel frames, virtually all frames are constructed from combinations of materials. For example, because of the critical need for high strength and toughness in the front fork, many non-steel frames are made with steel front forks. (In principle, a titanium alloy could be used, but the material is not yet available commercially in the required shape.) One can also find frames made from Cr-Mo steel tubing adhesively bonded to aluminum-alloy joint fittings, such as head tubes. This trend is likely to continue. For example, frames with titanium-alloy tubing could be made much less expensively by use of adhesive bonding to aluminum-alloy or stainless steel fittings. The evaluation of such frames is still generally made in a subjective manner by a wide variety of riders. Progress in this field would probably be accelerated by the development of a systematic testing protocol to provide quantitative determinations of some critical features of frame behavior.

Summary

In a bicycle frame the most important stresses come from bending moments. These occur where the front section joins the head tube, at the bottom bracket, and in the chain stays. The moment of inertia of the components, as well as the elastic modulus, yield strength, and density, are the factors that must be integrated for proper design.

Most bicycle frames are made from metallic materials, as opposed to carbon-fiber-reinforced polymers (discussed in Chap. 13). The three common alloy types, steel, aluminum, and titanium, all have the same stiffness/density ratio, but vary widely with respect to strength/density ratio and response to brazing or welding. The traditional manner of assembly of tubes into frames is brazing, which is applicable only to steels, owing to the stability of the oxide films on the other two alloy types. Most brazing employs lugs, which are either investment-cast steel or fabricated from formed and welded sheet steel. Inexpensive (heavy) brazed frames are made from steel with a carbon content of about 0.1% or less. Lightweight steel frames are made from Cr-Mo steel with about 0.3% carbon. The microstructure of this alloy steel comprises mainly the eutectoid-decomposition product, which is a fairly fine dispersion of carbide particles in ferrite, even in furnace-brazed frames (which are air-cooled from the austenite region).

TIG welding is now a common joining method for alloy steel frames, particularly in mountain bikes, and this technique can work very well, because the weld metal and HAZ have a bainitic microstructure, due to the high hardenability of the Cr-Mo steel. However, the potential for welding defects stemming from lack of full penetration of the fusion zone through the joint must be recognized.

The same potential exists for welded frames of other alloys, of course, but welded aluminum frames suffer from the presence of very soft weld metal and an HAZ softened by overaging. The HAZ is also large, due to the high thermal conductivity of aluminum.

The titanium alloy used for bicycle frames is Ti-3%Al-2.5%V; it was originally developed for aircraft hydraulic lines and is therefore available as tubing. Welding must be done in an inert environment, including the insides of the tubes, but the weld metal and HAZ have about 85% of the strength of the cold-worked tubing, due to a fine two-phase microstructure in which each phase has substantial solid-solution strengthening.

In the future, it can be expected that an increasing proportion of frames will be assembled by means of adhesive bonding, in which an epoxy adhesive is used in conjunction with either internal or external lug-like fittings. This, of course, eliminates all problems associated with heating, such as annealing or overaging.

Appendix 11.1 The Ideal Case: Pure Bending

Stresses in bent beams are usually calculated with reference to the ideal case of pure bending, which means that no shearing forces exist in the beam, only a bending moment. This can be achieved by symmetrical four-point loading, as shown in Fig. A11.1.1(a). Here, the central portion of the beam (between the inner loading points) is in pure bending, since the shearing forces balance out to zero in that portion. (Prove this for Exercise 11.3 at the end of the chapter.)

It is obvious that the bottom surface of the beam is compressed and the top is extended in the longitudinal direction. Therefore, a plane perpendicular to the longitudinal axis, i.e., the x axis, would experience a tensile stress on its upper part and a compressive stress on its lower part, as indicated schematically by the arrows.

(a)

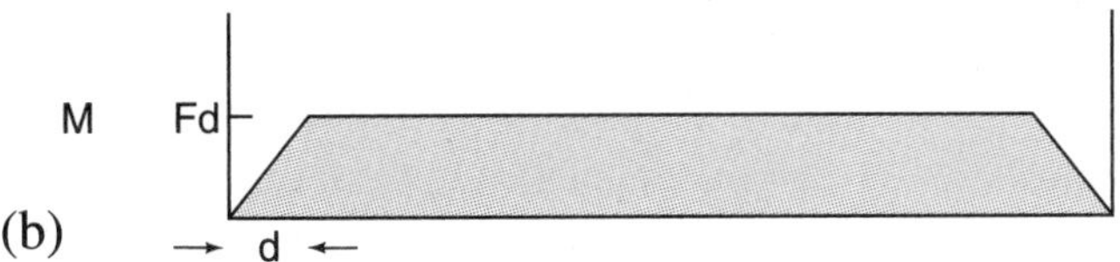

Fig. A11.1.1 (a) A beam loaded in symmetrical four-point bending. The central portion has no shearing forces and is therefore in pure bending. (b) The bending-moment diagram, showing the constant moment in the central portion.

The resulting deformation is exhibited in the grid inscribed on the rubber beam shown in Fig. A11.1.2(a). Clearly, the normal stress on a plane transverse to the long axis of the beam must pass through zero somewhere between the top and bottom surfaces. Since the beam is assumed to be isotropic and homogeneous and the loading symmetrical, the point of zero stress (and strain) must be at the center of the beam. This defines the *neutral axis* of the beam, which is actually a planar surface the area of which remains unchanged when the beam is bent. The neutral axis is the x axis in Fig. A11.1.1.

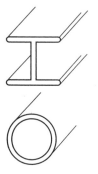

An obvious fact about the beam in Figs. A11.1.1 and A11.1.2 is that the deformation, and thus the stress, increases with the distance from the neutral axis. In other words, most of the load is carried by the outer portions of the beam. Therefore, if one wishes to design a beam with a given weight per unit length, i.e., with a given amount of material, one should try to concentrate this material as far from the neutral axis as possible. Two beam geometries that accomplish this are the I-beam and the cylindrical tube. The former is used when the beam is to be loaded in only one direction; the latter, being symmetrical, can be loaded in any transverse direction or even twisted about its axis. This is why bicycles are made from tubes.

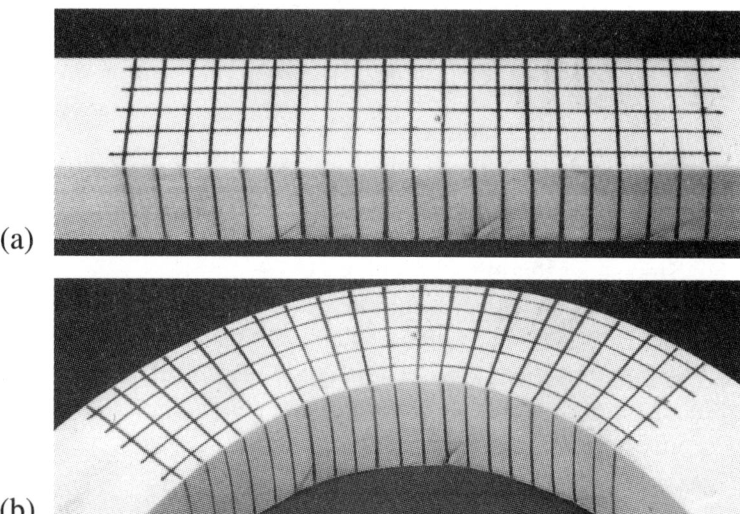

Fig. A11.1.2 Indication of the nature of the deformation of a grid inscribed on a rubber beam (a) before and (b) after pure bending.

From the appearance of the grid in Fig. A11.1.2 it is apparent that, in an isotropic, homogeneous beam in pure bending, planes that are perpendicular to the longitudinal axis before bending remain planar and perpendicular to this axis after bending. Moreover, the longitudinal displacements in the beam, indicated by the spreading-apart of the planes in the upper portion and the squeezing-together in the lower portion, are clearly linearly related to y, the distance from the neutral axis. This means that the displacement per unit length, i.e., the strain, can be written as

$$\varepsilon = C\,y$$

where C is a constant. Thus, Hooke's law ($\sigma = E\varepsilon$) can be written as

$$\sigma = E\,C\,y$$

where σ is the longitudinal stress (acting on any transverse plane), and E is Young's modulus.

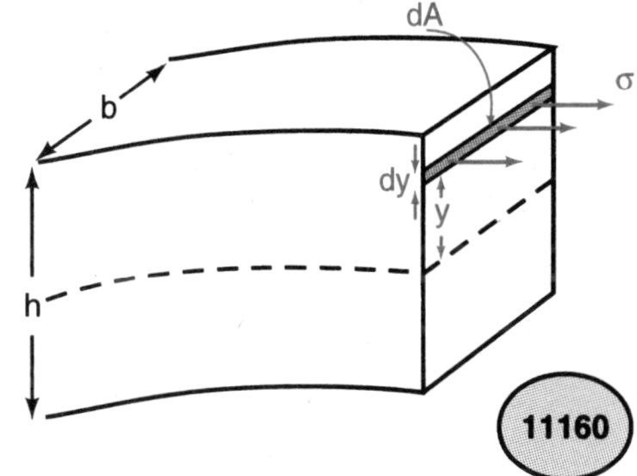

The value of σ at any y can be related to the bending moment, M, (force times moment arm) in the following way. Consider an element of area dA of the cross-section of a bent beam; let this element of area be a distance y from the neutral axis. The longitudinal force on this element is σdA, where dA is bdy.

Therefore, the corresponding contribution to the bending moment, dM, is

$$dM = \sigma\, b\, y\, dy$$ 11160

Remember that the force on this element is due to the stress in the part of the beam to the right of the cut acting on the part of the beam to the left of the cut. Since the stress is tensile in the upper half of the beam, the force acts to the right, and the moment on this element is clockwise. Below the neutral surface, the stress is compressive; therefore, the force is negative (i.e., acts to the left), but, since y is negative, the moment is still clockwise. To sum up the moments on all elements of the area, integrate over all values of y (i.e., from $y = -h/2$ to $y = h/2$). 11170
Thus,

$$M = \int_{-h/2}^{h/2} \sigma\, b\, y\, dy$$

and, substituting $\sigma = CEy$,

$$M = E\,C \int_{-h/2}^{h/2} b\, y^2\, dy$$

with C and E placed in front of the integral sign, since they are never functions of y. If the beam is not rectangular, b is a function of y.

The integral is known as the *second moment of area* of this plane, or, more commonly, as the *moment of inertia* of this beam. It is designated as I; thus, one 11180
can write the total moment as

$$M = C\,E\,I.$$

where

$$I = \int_{-h/2}^{h/2} b\, y^2\, dy$$

The constant C can now be evaluated with reference to Fig. A11.1.3, which depicts a beam of original length l_0 bent by an angle θ so that the radius of curvature of the neutral axis is r.

Since r is the distance from the center of curvature to the neutral axis (where $y = 0$), one can write

$$l_0 = r\,\theta$$ 11190

where θ is the angle (in radians) subtended by the curved beam. (Remember that the length of an arc is given by the radius of curvature times the angle subtended in radians; this is the definition of a radian.)

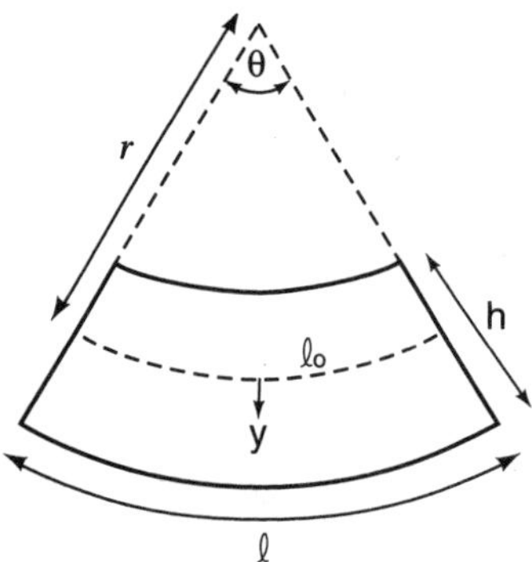

Fig. A11.1.3 A beam in pure bending; the radius of curvature is r. ($r >> h$.)

Now, for any other value of y, there will exist a longitudinal strain that is defined as

$$\varepsilon = \frac{\Delta l}{l_0}$$

where $\Delta l = (l - l_0)$ is the change in length of the beam at some value of y.

Therefore, the tensile strain (below the neutral axis) can be written as

$$\varepsilon = \frac{(r + y)\,\theta - r\,\theta}{r\,\theta} = \frac{y}{r}$$

Since the constant C is defined by $\varepsilon = Cy$,

$$C = \frac{1}{r}$$

and this quantity is known as the *curvature* of the beam.

This value for C can now be substituted in the expression for the moment,

M=CEI to give:

$$\frac{1}{r} = \frac{M}{E\,I}$$

Because the stress, σ, is equal to $C\,E\,y = \frac{M}{E\,I} \cdot Ey$, it can be written as

$$\sigma = \frac{M\,y}{I}$$

and the maximum stress in the beam is, therefore,

$$\sigma_{max} = \frac{M\,h}{2\,I}$$

Thus, the maximum stress increases with M and with the height of the beam, h, as one would expect, and it is inversely proportional to I.

A11.1.1 Moments of Inertia

The general expression for the moment of area of a beam of width b (the dimension parallel to the axis of bending) is

$$I = \int_{y_{min}}^{y_{max}} b(y)\, y^2\, dy$$

where y is the distance from the neutral axis, as shown in the generalized cross-section in Fig. A11.1.4(a). Note that, in general, b is a function of y; i.e., $b = b(y)$.

For a rectangular cross-section, Fig. A11.1.4(b), b is a constant and can be moved in front of the integral sign. The integral can then be evaluated (to within a constant) as

$$\int y^2\,dy = \frac{y^3}{3}$$

11220

Thus, since $y_{min} = -h/2$ and $y_{max} = h/2$, the moment of inertia is

$$I = b\left[\left(\frac{y^3}{3}\right)_{y=h/2} - \left(\frac{y^3}{3}\right)_{y=-h/2}\right]$$

or

$$I = b\left[\frac{h^3}{24} - \frac{-h^3}{24}\right] = \frac{bh^3}{12}$$

This means that I increases very rapidly with h. Therefore, for a beam that contains a given amount of material, one can get the most out of this material by making h as large as possible, as this makes the maximum stress for a given M as small as possible. This is the principle of the I-beam.

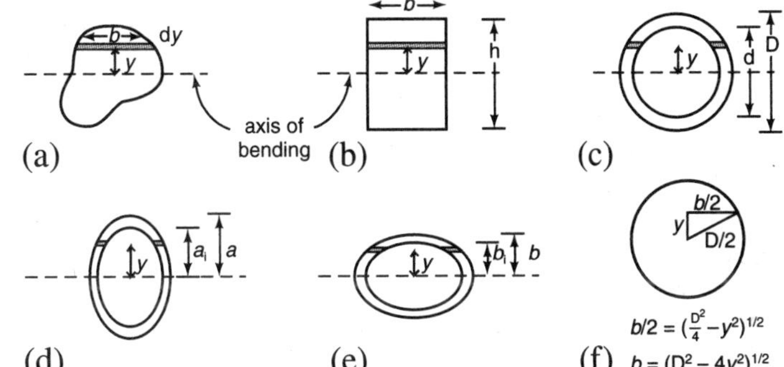

Fig. A11.1.4 Various cross sections of beams showing an area element in each at a distance y from the neutral axis.

For a cylindrical tube, as shown in Fig. A11.1.4(c), the moment of inertia is found by first solving for I for a circular cross-section of diameter D equal to the outer diameter of the tube and then subtracting the I for a circular cross-section of diameter d equal to the inner diameter. For the value of b, which obviously varies with y, the relationship shown in Fig. A11.1.4(f) is used. The I for the circular beam is given by

$$I = \int_{-D/2}^{D/2} (D^2 - 4y^2)^{1/2}\, y^2\, dy = \frac{\pi D^4}{64}$$

Therefore, for the circular tube

$$I = \frac{\pi}{64}(D^4 - d^4)$$

A similar procedure is used for the elliptical tube shown in Figs. A11.1.4(d) and (e). The I for a solid elliptical beam bent around its minor axis (Fig. A11.1.4d) would be given by

$$I = \frac{\pi}{4} a^3 \cdot b$$

Therefore, for the elliptical tube bent about its minor axis

$$I = \frac{\pi}{4} (a^3 \cdot b - a_i^3 b_i)$$

and about its major axis

$$I = \frac{\pi}{4} (ab^3 - a_i b_i^3)$$

Appendix 11.2 - Bending *vs.* Axial Loading

It was pointed out earlier that the normal stresses (tensile or compressive) developed in bending are usually significantly higher than those developed in axial loading. This can be demonstrated quantitatively with the aid of Fig. A11.2.1, which shows a bar being loaded in uniaxial tension and as a cantilever beam.

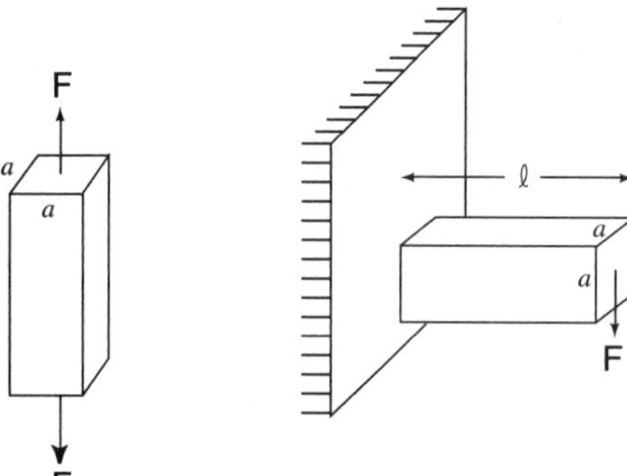

Fig. A11.2.1 A bar of length *l* and cross-section *a* x *a* loaded (a) in uniaxial tension and (b) as a cantilever beam.

The bar has a square cross-section, *a* on a side, with a cross-sectional area of a^2. The stress in the tensile specimen due to the axial force F is given by

$$\sigma = \frac{F}{a^2}$$

The maximum tensile stress in the same bar loaded in bending is given in Section A11.1 by

$$\sigma_{max} = \frac{M_{max}\, y_{max}}{I}$$

The maximum bending moment occurs where the cantilever is attached to its mounting and is given by $F \cdot l$. The value of y_{max} is $a/2$, and the moment of inertia is found from the value for a rectangular beam as follows:

$$I = \frac{b\,h^3}{12} = \frac{a^4}{12}$$

Thus, the maximum stress is given by

$$\sigma_{max} = F \bullet l \bullet \frac{a}{2} \bullet \frac{12}{a^4} = \frac{6Fl}{a^3} = \frac{6l}{a}\left(\frac{F}{a^2}\right)$$

Thus, the tensile stress is a factor of $6l/a$ higher than for the case of uniaxial loading. Since *l* is usually much larger than *a*, this factor can be very large.

Appendix 11.3 - Buckling of a Thin Strut under Axial Compression

A thin strut, like a spoke, cannot be loaded axially in compression to any substantial load without danger of buckling. It is common experience that any slender body loaded by compressive forces at its ends can easily suffer the elastic instability known as buckling. The reason for this can be seen from Fig. A11.3.1. As the axial force F is gradually increased from zero, the strut is initially straight and stable, as shown in (a). However, if the strut becomes even slightly curved, as shown in (b), the sections AB and BC become levers that exert a bending moment on the strut. The maximum moment occurs at point B and is equal to y_0F. A further increase in F would cause more bending, leading to elastic collapse of the strut. The slenderness of the strut allows small strains to produce a large overall change in shape. One can determine the force at which a strut (having length l and moment of inertia I) becomes curved and, thus, on its way to instability.

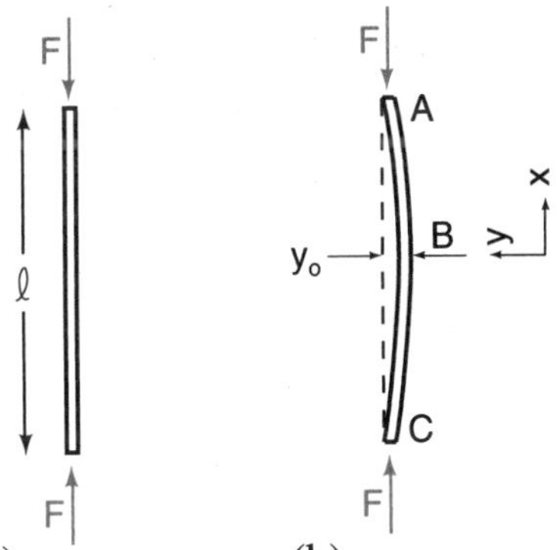

Fig. A11.3.1 A thin strut loaded in axial compression (a) while still stable and (b) just as buckling has commenced.

The relationship between the bending moment and the radius of curvature of a beam is given by

$$\frac{M}{EI} = \frac{1}{r}$$

In the present case, M at any point y along the strut is given by $M = F \cdot y$. Therefore,

$$\frac{1}{r} = \frac{F\,y}{EI}$$

In terms of the coordinate system shown in Fig. A11.3.1, the equation representing the curved strut, approximating it as a curve in the x,y plane, can be written as

$$\frac{d^2y}{dx^2} = -\frac{1}{r}$$

Therefore, one can construct a differential equation with a known solution as follows:

$$\frac{d^2y}{dx^2} + \alpha^2 y = 0$$

where α is defined as

$$\alpha^2 = \frac{F}{EI}$$

The general solution to this differential equation is

$$y = m \sin \alpha x + n \cos \alpha x$$

where m and n are arbitrary constants. This is the equation for the curved strut.

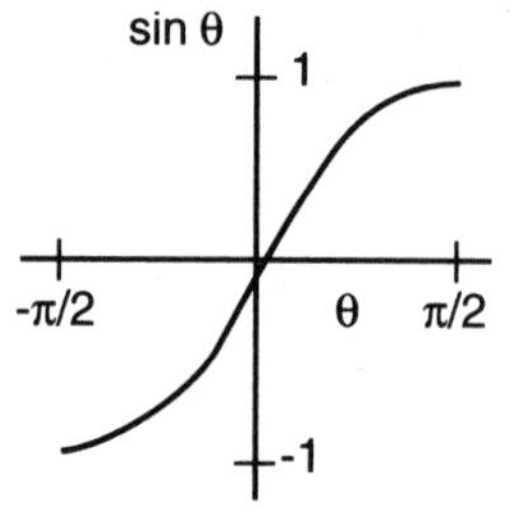

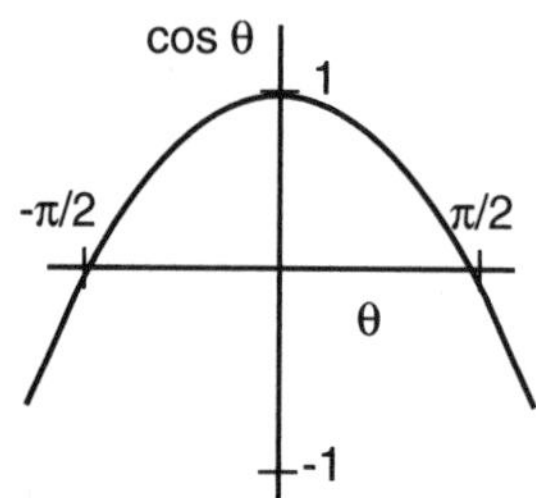

Fig. A11.3.2 Plots of sin θ and cos θ *vs.* θ.

Now if one examines the shapes of the sine and cosine functions, as shown in Fig. A11.3.2, it is obvious that the cosine function is consistent with the shape of the strut, while the sine function is not. Therefore, the constant m is set equal to zero and $n = y_0$, and the equation for the shape of the strut becomes

$$y = y_0 \cos \alpha x$$

It is also clear that $y = 0$ at $x = l/2$ or at $x = -l/2$. Thus,

$$y_0 \cos \alpha l/2 = 0$$

which means, if y_0 is to be finite, $\alpha l/2 = \pi/2$, or $\alpha l = \pi$. Therefore, from the definition of α,

$$\frac{F}{EI} = \frac{\pi^2}{l^2}$$

or, finally

$$F = \frac{\pi^2 EI}{l^2}$$

This gives the critical force to start buckling (i.e., to have a curved strut that satisfies the equation $y = y_0 \cos \alpha x$). Obviously, F decreases greatly as l increases and as the strut becomes thinner in the direction perpendicular to the axis of bending (i.e., as I decreases). This expression would give the critical force for the buckling of a bicycle spoke if the spoke were loaded as shown in Fig. A11.3.1(a), i.e., with both ends pin-jointed.

Glossary/Vocabulary - Chapter 11

α-stabilizer This is an alloy element that increases the temperature range of stability of the α-phase in an alloy. That is, in the relevant phase diagram, the α-phase field expands as the concentration of the α-stabilizer increases. Carbon is an α-stabilizer in Fe-based alloys. Aluminum is an α-stabilizer in Ti-based alloys.

Adhesive bonding This is a method of joining components in a structure by means of an adhesive, usually an epoxy. A large surface area must be used, because the strength of the adhesive is not large. Bicycle frames are put together by this technique, which employs lug-like arrangements, much like brazed joints, to provide the large bonding-surface area.

Alloy steel This is a steel containing alloy elements such as nickel, chromium, molybdenum, vanadium, etc. Alloy elements are added to increase hardenability or resistance to softening during tempering.

Anodizing of aluminum This is the forming of a thicker-than-usual coating of aluminum oxide on an aluminum component, by making the aluminum act as the anode in what is essentially a corrosion process. The coating is often porous and can be dyed various colors in the anodizing bath. It can also be sealed by treating it so that the pores are filled. These coatings can be use for decoration, for wear protection, and for reduction of sliding friction.

Arc welding The is a kind of welding in which the pieces to be fused and the filler metal are melted by the heat of an electric arc, formed by a large voltage difference between the work (i.e., the pieces) and either the filler metal (a rod or wire) or an electrode (as in the TIG process). An alternative type of welding is done in the flame of a gas torch. Arc welding is generally faster, cheaper, and easier to control.

β-stabilizer This is an alloy element that increases the temperature range of stability of the β-phase in an alloy. That is, the β-phase field expands as the concentration of the β-stabilizer increases. Vanadium is a β-stabilizer in Ti-based alloys.

Bending-moment The amount of bending in a stressed body depends not only on the applied forces, but also on the spacing of the forces. A bending moment about some reference point is a force multiplied by the distance between that point and the point of application of the force. This distance is called the moment arm. A 3-foot stick bent (centrally) across the knee with a force of 20 lb at each end experiences a maximum bending moment (at the center) of 20 x 1.5 = 30 ft-lb.

Bonded joints This is another name for joints made by adhesive bonding.

Buckling A long, thin rod when loaded by a force at the end and parallel to the long axis of the rod, if sufficiently large, would cause the rod to begin to bend and then to collapse in bending. This is called buckling. A bicycle spoke set vertically on a table and compressed from the upper end would buckle when the compressive force becomes large enough.

Butted tubing	Butting of tubes means altering the tube-drawing process to leave the ends of the tubes thicker than the central portions. (Tubes butted on both ends are called double-butted.) This is done by use of a special mandrel, which is a bar inserted into a tube during tube-drawing to prevent the tube from collapsing under the pressure of the die. This is done on expensive bike frames to minimize weight while still leaving enough thickness at the joints to compensate for any softening during hand-brazing or welding.
Casting	This is a process that involves the melting of a metal or alloy and pouring the molten metal into a mold in which it solidifies, taking the shape of the mold. The casting so produced may have essentially the desired final shape of some component or object, or it may have a simple shape suitable for further processing, usually by large-scale deformation. In the latter case, the casting is called an ingot.
Cr-Mo steel	This is a common alloy steel. The chromium and molybdenum give it both hardenability and resistance to softening during tempering. 4130 is the steel used for so-called "chromoly" bicycle frames. It contains about 1%Cr and about 0.2%Mo.
Curvature of a beam	The curvature or a beam is the inverse of the radius of curvature. For a beam in pure bending, the curvature is given by M/EI, where M is the bending moment, E is Young's modulus, and I is the moment of inertia.
Furnace brazing	This is the process in which a bicycle frame is assembled with tubes and lugs, with the brazing alloy placed in each lug joint in the form of solid foil, and the assembly fixed in a jig to hold everything in the proper configuration. The whole jigged assembly is then placed in a furnace to allow the brazing alloy to melt and flow along the joints, and then it is removed and cooled. Virtually all brazed steel frames that are not hand brazed are made this way.
Heat-affected zone, HAZ	This is the region next to the weld metal in a welded joint, a region that has been brought to a high temperature, but not fused. It is a region that undergoes all of the microstructural changes associated with heating, such as grain growth, coarsening of precipitates, recrystallization, etc. The HAZ of a weld joint in an aluminum bicycle frame is large because of the high thermal conductivity of aluminum, and it is softened by overaging.
Investment casting	This is a technique for casting objects of complex shape. It involves making a wax replica of the object, encasing the wax in a ceramic mold that is built up gradually by applying layers of wet powder, firing the mold to densify (sinter) it and to burn off the wax, and finally pouring in the molten metal for the casting. (The word invest in this case means to encase.) This is a common method for fabrication of the lugs used to assemble the tubes of bicycle frames.
Lack-of-penetration defect	This is a common type of welding defect caused by the failure of the welder to achieve fusion all the way through a joint. The problem is that it serves as a built-in stress concentrator, which can be a site of early fatigue failure. It is not easy to weld thin-wall tubing, as in bicycle frames, that is, to apply just enough power to fuse the whole joint without burning away the tube wall.
Low-alloy steel	This is a steel having less than about five weight percent of alloy elements in total. Common alloy elements are chromium, nickel, molybdenum, and vanadium. Manganese is also a common alloy element, but it is virtually always added, even to plain-carbon steel.

Lug This is the device used to hold bicycle tubes at the appropriate angles at joints in a frame and to help form the crevice into which liquid metal flows during brazing. Lugs have complicated geometries and are fabricated by investment casting or by welding of formed sheet.

Microhardness test This is a hardness test made with a very small indenter and a light load, measured in grams, making an indentation so small that a microscope must be used to measure its size. The most common indenter is a diamond pyramid, giving the diamond-pyramid hardness, DPH. This technique is used to measure hardness that varies on the microscopic scale, as in the carburized layer of a case-hardened steel.

Moment of inertia This is the second moment of area of the cross section of a beam with respect to its neutral axis. Because a bent beam carries most of the stress in sections away from the neutral axis, the moment of inertia is a measure of the capacity of a beam to resist bending. It is designated by the letter I. The moment of inertia of a rectangular beam of width b and height h is $bh^3/12$.

Neutral axis This is the plane running through a bent beam from end to end on which there is no stress. It is the plane where the transition from tension to compression occurs.

Porosity This is the general name given to internal voids in a solid. These can be residual voids left over from incomplete sintering, or they can be the result of gas evolution or shrinkage during solidification from the liquid state.

Radiography This is a type of non-destructive testing that is essentially similar to a medical x-ray examination. X-rays, or gamma rays from a cobalt-60 source, are passed through a solid object and then onto a piece of x-ray film. The shadowgraph-like image can reveal regions of lower density than the rest of the solid. Thus, internal flaws like voids or cracks can be detected.

Ti-3%Al-2.5%V This is a less-highly alloyed version of the Ti-6Al-4V alloy, which is one of the most commonly used Ti alloys. It is much easier to process into tubing than the 6-4 alloy. At room temperature it is mostly α, Al being an α stabilizer, with residual β. The latter is stabilized by V. This alloy was originally developed for the hydraulic lines on airplanes because of its high strength-to-weight ratio. It is also excellent for the tubes on expensive bicycle frames.

Ti-6%Al-4%V This is a Ti alloy having both α and β phases present at room temperature. It is considerably stronger than the Ti-3Al-2.5V alloy, but is not easily processed into tubing. This alloy is readily available in plate form, and it is used for the dropouts on bicycle frames made of the Ti-3Al-2.5V alloy.

TIG welding Welding is a method of joining of metals that involves fusion (i.e., melting) of the two pieces, often with the addition of a filler metal, which is also fused. Aluminum and steel bicycle frames are often joined by TIG welding. TIG means tungsten-inert gas; the tungsten tip is used to strike the arc, and the filler metal is a wire that feeds through the welding device. The weld pool is shielded by inert gas that is blown through the device to prevent oxidation.

Weld metal This is the region of a weld joint that has been fused. It is normally a mixture of the base metal and the filler metal. The weld metal has the microstructure of a casting, but it is cooled fairly rapidly by the surrounding cold base metal.

Exercises

11.1 Discuss the advisability of fabricating the front-fork tubes from a lightweight, high-strength, but brittle, material.

11.2 The cross-section of the rim of a particular design of bicycle wheel is shown here; give the rationale for this rim design from what you now know about bending of beams.

11.3 Prove that the beam shown in Fig. A11.1.1 has no shear stresses in the portion between the inner two loading points.

11.4 In an alloy that solidifies dendritically in a casting (or a weld or a braze), explain where in the microstructure the shrinkage and gas porosity will be found and why.

11.5 Suppose you are preparing an investment casting pattern out of wax for a tubular shape, such as one leg of a lug. The ceramic to be placed around the wax is known to undergo a volume shrinkage of 10% when fired. If the finished dimensions of the lug are to be 1.1in ID and 1.2in OD, what should the dimensions of the wax pattern be?

11.6 Assume that the eutectoid composition of a 4140 (Cr-Mo) steel is reduced from 0.77% to 0.65% by the alloy elements, how much proeutectoid ferrite and how much eutectoid constituent would be expected in an austenitized and slowly cooled sample?

11.7 If a titanium-alloy road bike were to be made with tubing of the same OD as the Cr-Mo steel bike (cf. Table 11.2), and if it were to have the same tube stiffness (i.e., the same EI product), how would the two types of tubing compare on the basis of weight per unit length?

11.8 Compare the three types of high-performance tubing: 6061 aluminum alloy, Ti-2.5Al-2V, and Cr-Mo steel, with regard to the strengthening mechanisms employed, describing how they work and the effect of welding on the tube strength.

11.9 Explain how it is possible to make a bicycle tube lighter by using an aluminum or titanium alloy while maintaining the same or greater stiffness as with steel, even though the ratio of the Young's modulus to density is virtually the same for all three alloys.

12

POLYMERIC MATERIALS

12.1 Characteristics of Polymers

Polymers have been used in bicycles in the form of rubber tires for a century. More recent applications include adhesives and fiber-reinforced materials for frames, wheels, and other components. Linear polymers represent a class of materials entirely different from the metallic and ceramic materials considered so far in that they are long-chain molecules made of repeated units called *mers*. In metals and crystalline ceramics, individual atoms or ions can move about independently and take part in a variety of reactions. The properties of these aggregates of atoms or ions can be considered three-dimensionally, since one type of bonding predominates in each material, and it is essentially uniform in all directions.

Polymers, on the other hand, exhibit a much wider range of structures and properties. At one extreme, they can be similar in structure to a glassy ceramic, like an oxide glass, in which atoms are connected in a three-dimensional network of covalent bonds. At the other extreme, they can exist as long-chain, linear molecules with a strong, covalently bonded backbone. The chains are highly flexible and, at sufficiently high temperatures, can writhe about like snakes. In fact, one useful conceptual model of a linear polymer in the amorphous state is that of a collection of earthworms, as shown in Fig. 12.1. In an actual linear polymer there is relatively weak (i.e., secondary) bonding between chains, depending on the interchain spacing; this type of bonding is discussed in Appendix 12.1. If the temperature of the polymer becomes low enough, the wriggling of the chains practically ceases, and the secondary bonds then give the polymer the character of a three-dimensional solid.

Fig. 12.1 A collection of tangled earthworms, serving as a model for a linear polymer at a temperature where viscous flow is possible. (Photograph of *Lumbricus rubellus* by Runk/Schoenberger; from Grant Heilman, reproduced with permission.)

Rubber used for tires is made from one of several possible linear polymers that are subjected to a special treatment, called *vulcanization,* which converts the viscous, amorphous mass into a rubbery material. To understand the structure and properties of a rubber, it is first necessary to understand the characteristics of linear polymers in general.

The most important characteristic of a linear polymer is the flexibility of the long-chain molecule. The simplest such molecule has a backbone of singly-
12010 bonded carbon atoms, as shown in Fig. 12.2(a). In addition to the two bonds per carbon that constitute the backbone, each carbon bonds to two other atoms, or groups of atoms, that attach themselves to the backbone. However, it is the character of the single carbon-carbon covalent bond that gives the backbone its flexibility. The only constraints on this bond are its fixed length and the fixed angle between neighboring carbon bonds. This allows a bond to rotate and take any position along the conic surface that preserves this angular relationship, as shown in Fig. 12.2(b). At sufficiently high temperatures the chains are free to become coiled and kinked to such an extent that they comprise an amorphous glob, like the "can of worms" depicted in Fig. 12.1.

12025

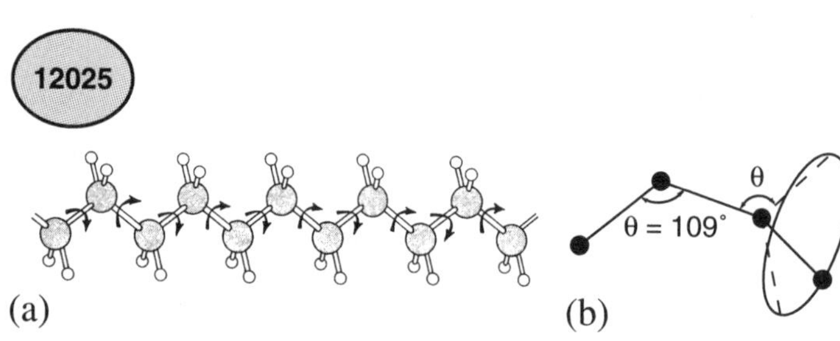

Fig. 12.2 (a) A linear polymer with the simplest possible backbone, a singly-bonded carbon chain. (b) The freedom of rotation in a single carbon-carbon bond. (Adapted from N. G. McCrum, C. P. Buckley, and C. B. Bucknall, *Principles of Polymer Engineering,* Oxford University Press, 1988, pp. 50 and 51; reprinted by permission of Oxford University Press.)

When the temperature is relatively high, the chains have a high kinetic energy and can wriggle about rather freely. Entropy tends to be maximized by the randomness of the chain configurations. The usual way to describe this is the path of a "random walk," which would be characterized by a large number of steps, all of the same length, but of completely random directions in space. That is, each step has an equal probability of being in any possible direction. Because of the easy motion of the chains, they can slide past each other readily, and the polymeric mass acts as a viscous fluid. The viscosity decreases, i.e., the ease of flow increases, as temperature increases.

Another important characteristic of a linear polymer is the length of the chains. The lengths are generally not all the same, but are distributed about some average. At any given temperature, viscosity increases as average chain length increases, because the chains are more likely to get tangled as they become longer. (The increase in viscosity with chain length is not linear; it becomes increasingly steep as length increases.) A classical example is the paraffin, or n-alkane (C_nH_{2n+2}), family of molecules in which each of the lateral carbon bonds is occupied by a hydrogen atom, as shown in Fig. 12.3. Methane, CH_4, is a gas at room temperature, but decane, $C_{10}H_{22}$, is an oily liquid (i.e., a paraffin oil). When the chain length is increased to $C_{36}H_{74}$, for example, the material has become a paraffin *wax.* When the average chain length is of the order 10^2 to 10^4 carbon bonds, the material is called *polyethylene.* In this condition, there are so many entanglements along each molecule that the material behaves like a solid at room temperature. That is, it is able to support a shear stress without significant viscous flow.

(a) a paraffin (b) polyethylene

Fig. 12.3 The molecular structure of (a) a paraffin and (b) of polyethylene.

Although polyethylene acts like a solid at room temperature, it becomes a viscous liquid when heated; the increasing thermal energy allows increasing amounts of chain wriggling. If it is cooled back to room temperature, it again acts like a solid. This is called *thermoplastic* behavior. It is one of the characteristics that gives many polymers their great commercial value, because the temperatures at which large-scale flow occurs are generally much lower than the liquation temperatures of metallic alloys having equivalent strength. Thus, many articles of commerce are fabricated from thermoplastics by means of *injection molding,* in which the fluid polymer is forced into a die cavity and allowed to cool, producing a "plastic" part having the desired, often very intricate, shape.

A simple linear polymer, like polyethylene, does not usually assume a homogeneous, amorphous configuration upon cooling. Wherever possible, regions of neighboring chains tend to align themselves so that interchain spacing is minimized and the secondary bonds can exert maximum influence. These regions take on a three-dimensional long-range order and become, therefore, crystalline. The crystalline regions are mechanically strong in the direction parallel to the chain axes, because their strong backbones are aligned and because the secondary bonding inhibits sliding between chains. The crystalline regions of a partly crystalline polymer are more dense than the amorphous regions because of the tighter packing of the chains.

The character of a long-chain polymer changes if the chains become branched during the polymerization process. Branches, depicted schematically in Fig. 12.4 using polyethylene as an example, can vary in length, depending on the conditions of polymer synthesis. Since they interrupt the periodicity of aligned chains, branches retard the tendency toward crystallization. Thus, one would want to minimize branching when making high-density polyethylene milk containers, for example. Because branching also inhibits sliding between chains, it imparts strength to an amorphous polymer, and for this reason branching is sometimes designed into a polymerization process.

Fig. 12.4 Schematic representation of branching of a polyethylene molecule.

A further step up in complexity occurs when covalently bonded links are formed between neighboring chains by single atoms or short segments of chains. In the extreme, a three-dimensional network can be formed. This can be envisioned as a giant three-dimensional supermolecule, as illustrated schematically in Fig. 12.5. It does not soften or melt when heated, since it is held together tightly by covalent bonds. Because it does not flow and change shape when heated, a network polymer is called a *thermoset.* If it is heated excessively, it decomposes as the covalent bonds are broken chemically; e.g., by oxidation.

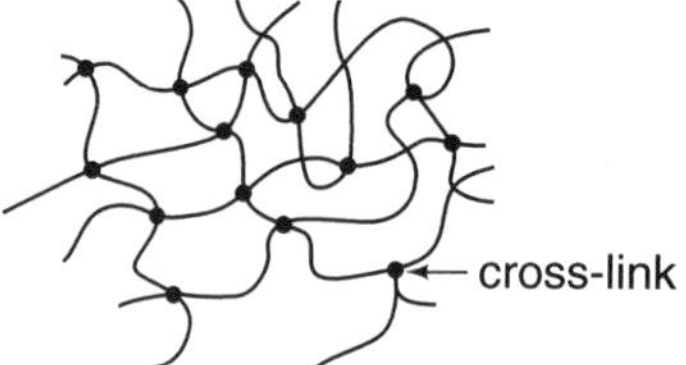

Fig. 12.5 Schematic representation of a network polymer, a thermoset.

An intermediate architecture is found in an elastomer, which is the technical name for a material that shows rubber-like elasticity. Here, a polymer that is initially linear is treated to introduce cross-links by the formation of occasional bridges between chains. These consist of atoms or small molecules that form covalent bonds on adjacent parts of chains, as shown in Fig. 12.6. An elastomer is analogous to a network polymer with a relatively low density of cross-links. When an elastomer is in the relaxed state, the chain segments between the cross-links tend to be curled-up and kinked in a random arrangement. However, they can be straightened out when a stress is applied, so that overall extensions of several hundred percent are possible. Upon release of the stress, the elastomer springs back to its initial shape. A rubber band is the most common example.

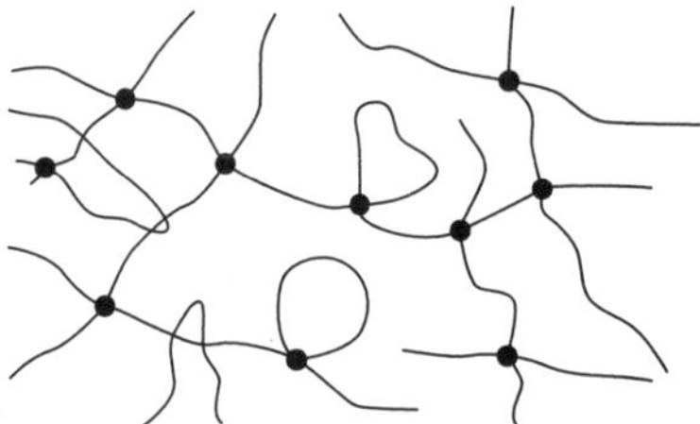

Fig. 12.6 Schematic representation of an elastomer.

The presence of covalent cross-links prevents melting when an elastomer is heated. If the temperature becomes too high, only decomposition occurs. Thus, an elastomer is intermediate in behavior between a thermoplastic and a thermoset. It might be noted that the covalent cross-links present a formidable obstacle to the recycling of rubber tires. So far no viable procedure has been worked out to break the cross-links selectively, leaving the main chains intact. If such a process were to be discovered, it would have major commercial significance.

One of the goals in this chapter and the next two is to understand the structure, properties and behavior of fiber-reinforced composite materials. Tires are examples of such a composite, having an elastomeric (rubber) matrix. The distinguishing characteristic of elastomeric behavior is the enormous amount of recoverable strain, as illustrated in Fig. 12.7.

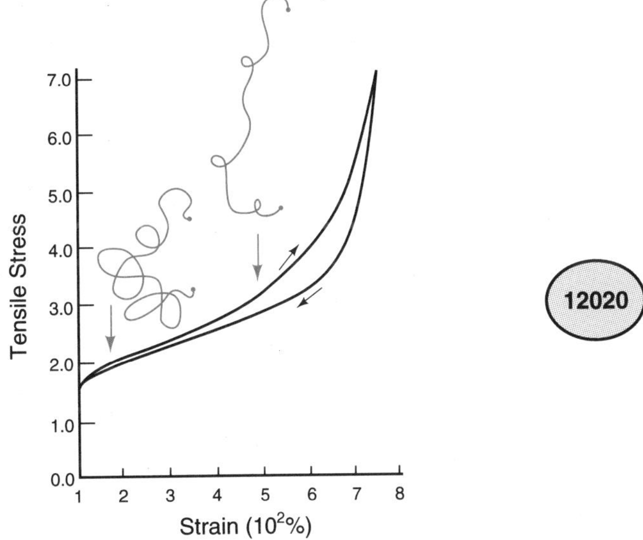

12020

Fig. 12.7 Sress-strain behavior of a lightly cross-linked natural rubber at 50°C showing hysteresis during a full loading cycle. (Adapted from L. H. Sperling, *Introduction to Physical Polymer Science,* Wiley, New York, 1996, pp. 305 and 306. Reprinted by permission of John Wiley & Sons, Inc.)

The unloading part of a stress-strain curve of an elastomer does not follow the loading curve exactly. This effect is known as *hysteresis,* and the extent of it depends on the amount of crystallization that occurs in the rubber when it is stretched. (The crystallization occurs in regions where the stretched chains become aligned enough for the secondary bonds to promote the formation of crystallites; these crystallites "melt" again when the stretching force is relaxed.) To understand elastomeric behavior, it is best to begin by considering the simplest linear polymer, the thermoplastic polyethylene.

12.2 Polyethylene

12.2.1 Molecular Structure

As shown in Fig. 12.3, polyethylene, PE, is simply a carbon chain with two hydrogens attached to each carbon. The basic unit is the C_2H_4 mer, as illustrated in Fig. 12.8(b).

(a) H H / C=C / H H (b) [H H / –C–C– / H H]

Fig. 12.8 Structure of (a) the ethylene monomer and (b) the polyethylene mer.

Polyethylene is made by polymerizing ethylene, C_2H_4, which has a double bond between the carbons (Fig. 12.8a). This is accomplished by reacting a large amount of ethylene with a small amount of an "initiator," which breaks the double bond in the ethylene to form a mer. An example of an initiator for PE is hydrogen peroxide, which can act as two H-O molecules, each of which has an unpaired electron. Such a molecule is called a *free radical.* The free radical reacts with a monomer, and another free radical is formed. This reacts with another mer, and so on to form a chain molecule, as illustrated in Fig. 12.9.

```
                             H H                 H H
                             | |                 | |
H2O2 ——> 2H–O •     H–O • +  C=C  ——>   H–O–C–C •
                             | |                 | |
                             H H                 H H
```

• = unpaired electron

```
       H H          H H                  H   H   H   H
       | |          | |                  |   |   |   |
H–O–C–C •    +    C=C     ——>     H–O–C – C – C – C •
       | |          | |                  |   |   |   |
       H H          H H                  H   H   H   H
```

Fig. 12.9 Action of hydrogen peroxide as the initiator in free-radical polymerization of PE.

This process, called *addition polymerization,* repeats itself until the growing chain runs into an initiator, as illustrated in Fig. 12.10, or to the end of another growing chain.

```
     ┌ H H ┐
     │ | | │
H–O ─┤ C–C ├─ O–H
     │ | | │
     └ H H ┘n
```

Fig. 12.10 An n-mer chain of PE terminated by an OH group.

The termination of a chain is a statistical event. Therefore, addition polymerization results in a distribution of chain lengths. The physical and chemical behavior depend very much on both the average chain length (i.e., the molecular weight of the average chain) and the spread in the values of chain length. The distribution of chain lengths can be characterized, for example, in terms of the number-average molecular weight of the population of chains. This is defined by taking n_i as the number of molecules with a molecular weight M_i and writing the number-average molecular weight as

n_i — M_i

$$\overline{M}_N = \frac{\Sigma\, n_i M_i}{\Sigma\, n_i}$$

One also speaks of the *number-average degree of polymerization,* N, given by

$$N = \overline{M}_N / M_0$$

where M_0 is the molecular weight of one mer, which is 28 in the case of PE.

12.2.2 Crystallization

Most liquids tend to crystallize when cooled past the melting point. With polymers, the length, variability in length, and flexibility (and entanglement) of the molecules makes crystallization much more difficult than in the case of atomic solids, like metals, or solids comprising small molecules. In addition, the reliance on secondary (e.g., van der Waals) forces to bind the molecules together means that the melting point would be rather low, and at low temperatures the molecular mobility, needed for crystallization, is also low (i.e., the viscosity is high). Despite these facts, the simplicity of the PE molecule allows it to crystallize, at least partially, unless the liquid is quenched very rapidly. The unit cell is orthorhombic, as shown in Fig. 12.11, and the crystals are formed by the folding of the chains to create a sheave with a thickness equal to the fold length, as indicated in Fig. 12.12(a).

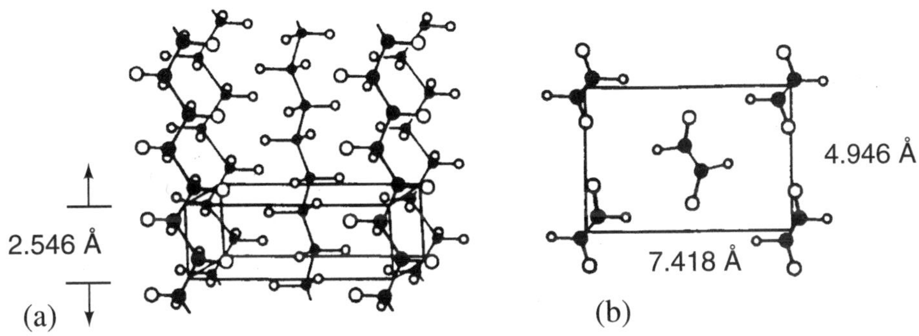

Fig. 12.11 Crystal structure of orthorhombic polyethylene; (a) unit cell, (b) projection of the unit cell along the chain direction. (From *Introduction to Polymers,* R. J. Young, Chapman and Hall, London, 1981, p. 159.)

When liquid PE is cooled fairly slowly, crystallization occurs by the growth of crystalline lamellae in three dimensions outward from a nucleation point to form "spherulites" (cf. Fig. 12.12a). If the cooling is slow enough, the spherulites grow until they contact one another, much in the manner of crystallization of a metal. If there is any material left between the spherulites, it remains amorphous. The spherulites themselves are not fully crystalline, because the lamellae are separated by the parts of molecules that were not incorporated in the folded-chain crystalline lamellae. Some of these act as tie-molecules between adjacent lamellae, because they have an end embedded in each. The gross morphology of the spherulites can be observed in thin sections shaved from a bulk specimen with a special knife, called a microtome, or by crystallization of a film of PE or a similar polymer on a microscope slide. For illumination in the optical microscope one uses transmitted polarized light, as was done to obtain Fig. 12.12(b).

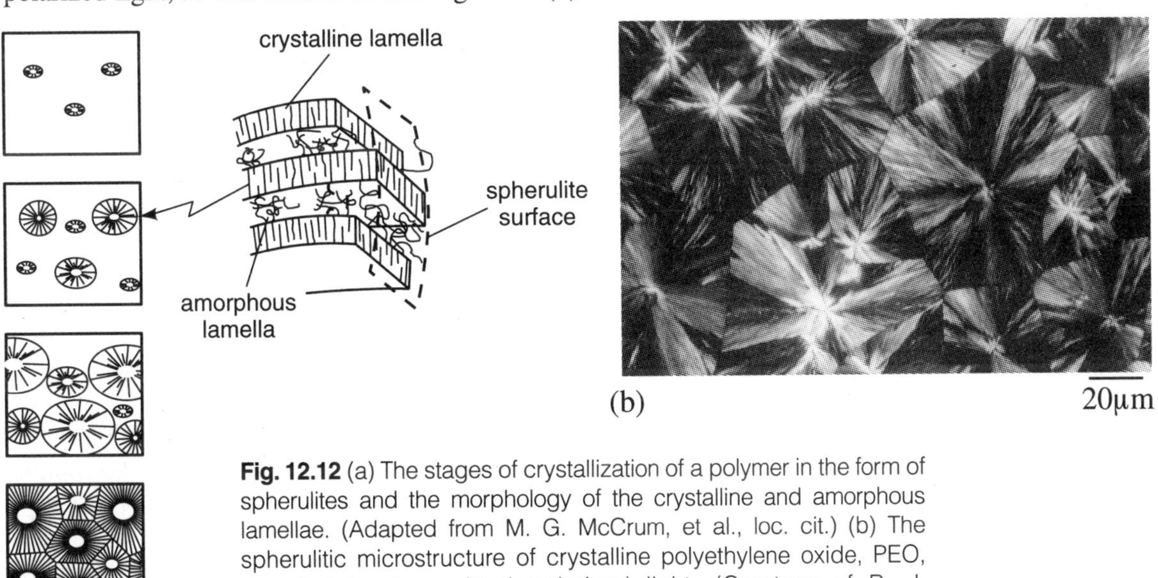

Fig. 12.12 (a) The stages of crystallization of a polymer in the form of spherulites and the morphology of the crystalline and amorphous lamellae. (Adapted from M. G. McCrum, et al., loc. cit.) (b) The spherulitic microstructure of crystalline polyethylene oxide, PEO, revealed by transmitted polarized light. (Courtesy of R. J. Composto, Univ. of Penn.)

The properties of polyethylene depend on the degree of crystallinity, as shown in Table 12.1. Thus, high-density PE (or HDPE) is two to three times stronger than normal low-density PE (or LDPE). That is, the increase in the degree of crystallinity is the analog of a strengthening mechanism in a metallic alloy. The strengthening comes from the fact that in the crystalline regions the molecular chains are aligned and packed tightly together. The covalently bonded backbone of the chains is extremely strong. That is, a very large force is required to stretch the length of a carbon-carbon bond or to change the bond angle from 109°. Therefore, the crystalline regions act like hard inclusions in the amorphous matrix, in which inter-chain sliding and chain straightening can occur. The overall strength of the material obviously would increase with the percent crystallinity.

Table 12.1 Comparison of Properties of Low-Density and High-Density PE.

	Low-Density PE	High-Density PE
Crystallinity, %	~ 65	~95
Density, g/cm³	0.92 - 0.93	0.95 - 0.96
Tensile Strength, MPa	6 - 18	20 - 38
Tensile Modulus, GPa	~ 0.2	~ 1.0

12.2.3 The Glass Transition

As with any liquid, the process of crystallization of a linear polymer can be followed by observing the volumetric change during cooling. The melting temperature T_M of a polymer can be determined from the discontinuous decrease in

volume that accompanies crystallization, as shown in Fig.12.13(a).

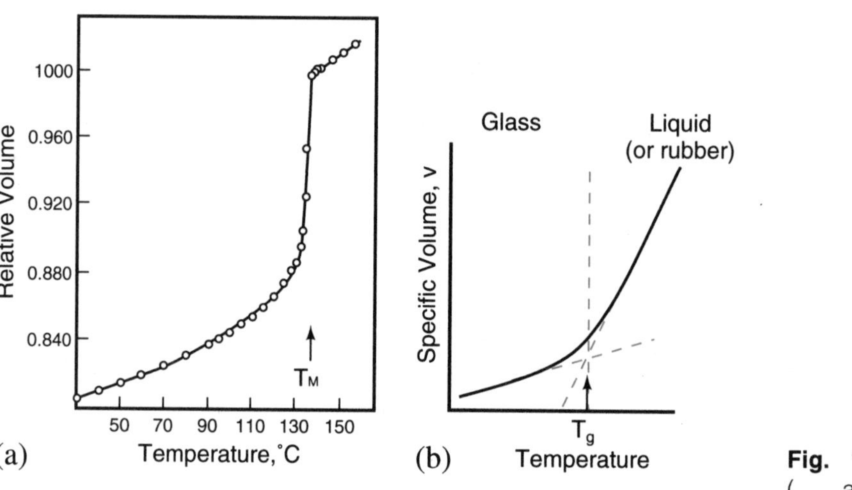

Fig. 12.13 (a) Discontinuous decrease in volume that accompanies crystallization when polyethylene is cooled through the melting temperature. (From L. Mandelkern, *Chem Revs,* vol. 56, 1956, p. 911, reproduced with pemission of the American Chemical Society.) (b) Schematic representation of the variation of the specific volume upon cooling through the glass transition.

A linear polymer usually fails to crystallize completely when cooled below T_M, because the chains are tangled in the melt, and there is not enough mobility in the chains to allow them to reorganize completely into crystalline nuclei and for the nuclei to grow as complete crystals. The tendency to crystallize depends on the viscosity of the polymer at T_M, and this depends on the architecture of the chains. (The simpler the chain, the lower the viscosity at T_M.) In the supercooled amorphous regions that fail to crystallize, a different kind of transition occurs. This is the *glass transition,* and it is considered to occur at a temperature, T_g, defined by extrapolation of the two branches of the curve depicting thermal contraction above and below the transition range, as shown in Fig 12.13(b). Molecular motion involving the backbone of a chain (as opposed to oscillation of side groups) essentially ceases below the glass transition. Therefore, the coefficient of thermal contraction or expansion in the glassy state is smaller than in the supercooled-liquid state above T_g. Heating a glassy (amorphous) linear polymer above the glass transition effectively "melts" the secondary bonds between molecules.

In contrast with this behavior of an amorphous polymer, a crystalline region in a polymer undergoes the classical melting transition, just like a metal. This is because the chains in a polymer crystal are aligned close together, and the chain spacing is uniform, as opposed to the spectrum of chain spacings found in an amorphous polymer. Therefore, all of the secondary bonds give way at the same temperature, instead of over a range of temperatures. This temperature is significantly higher than that at which melting begins in the amorphous regions, where the chain spacing is, on average, greater. A partly crystalline polymer becomes rigid gradually as temperature is reduced, as depicted in the low-temperature branch of the curve in Fig. 12.13(a).

Example 12.1

Q. What structural features are necessary for a polymer to be a thermoplastic?

A. The polymer must be a linear polymer or a branched linear polymer and must have a flexible backbone. That is, the bonds along the backbone must be able to rotate so the chain can coil and uncoil.

12.3 Viscoelasticity

The glass transition in a thermoplastic polymer is somewhat analogous to a ductile-brittle transition in a metallic material. Below T_g plastic deformation is essentially nonexistent, and the material can be cracked in a brittle manner. A common example is a polystyrene drinking cup, which is glassy at room temperature, and for which T_g is around 100°C. Above T_g, the polymer can deform plastically; i.e., it is a "plastic." However, the fundamental difference between such a thermoplastic and a completely crystalline material, like a metal, is that the deformation of the thermoplastic is time dependent. (In metals this only occurs at temperatures where self-diffusion is rapid.) The time dependence arises from the fact that the amorphous regions are really part of a supercooled viscous liquid. The plastic deformation occurs by the translation of one part of a molecule past another, and this requires molecular mobility, which is thermally activated. That is, the rate depends exponentially on temperature.

A polymer above T_g behaves like a mixture of two kinds of materials. One
12140 is an elastic material in which reversible deformation occurs by bond bending. It
follows Hooke's law (strain is proportional to stress) and can be modeled as a
spring with a certain spring constant, as in Fig. 12.14(a). The other is a viscous
material, following Newton's law of viscosity, which states that strain rate is proportional to stress; it deforms by disentanglement of the chains. A viscous mate-
12150 rial can be modeled by a dashpot, which is a piston-and-fluid arrangement of the
type used to control the rate of closing of a door, as shown in Fig. 12.14(b). Here,
the proportionality constant η is the *viscosity.*

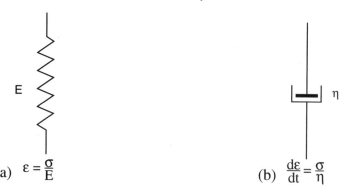

Fig. 12.14 (a) The spring model of an elastic region in a polymer. (b) The dashpot model of a viscous region.

In principle, a viscoelastic polymer can be modeled as some combination of springs and dashpots in order to devise a mathematical description of its deformation behavior. Some simple versions of such models are depicted in Fig. 12.15. They are too simple to mimic the behavior of a real polymer, but they are useful for discussion of some aspects of time-dependent polymer deformation.

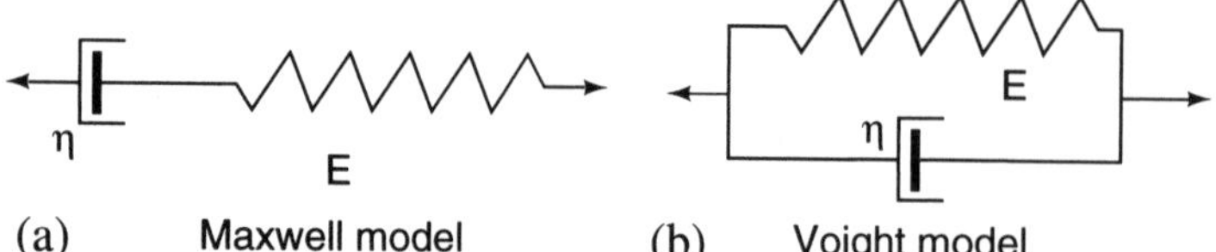

Fig. 12.15 Some simple models for viscoelastic behavior.

To illustrate the use of such a model, consider the effect of a sudden force applied to a Maxwell solid (a spring and dashpot in series). The spring would extend immediately, but the dashpot would at first not respond at all. If the force were applied for only a very short time and then removed, the solid would seem to be completely elastic. This is the behavior of Silly Putty® when it is bounced on the floor like a rubber ball. On the other hand, if a ball of Silly Putty is allowed to rest on a surface for a long time, it will eventually flatten out under its own weight. Here, the force is small, and the elastic deformation is negligible, but, given enough time, the viscous flow can be appreciable, even with a small force. This, again, would correspond to the behavior of a Maxwell solid.

Two important aspects of polymer deformation are creep and *stress relaxation,* which are illustrated in Fig. 12.16. To illustrate creep one can choose a Voight model (a spring and dashpot in parallel) and hang on it a constant load. Initially there is no extension, because the dashpot does not respond quickly. However, extension does occur with passage of time, as shown in Fig. 12.16(a), until the spring is fully extended to the amount allowed by Hooke's law.

To illustrate stress relaxation, the Maxwell model is better. Here, the polymer is pulled to a certain extension, and the pulling grips are fixed in place. Initially, only the spring responds, and the stress has the value indicated by Hooke's law. However, as the dashpot responds with time, the extension is accommodated by viscous flow and the spring relaxes, as shown in Fig. 12.16(b). The time-dependent deformation of a real polymer is much more complicated and depends not only on the viscosity (which varies exponentially with temperature), but also on the details of the molecular architecture and the microstructure of the polymer.

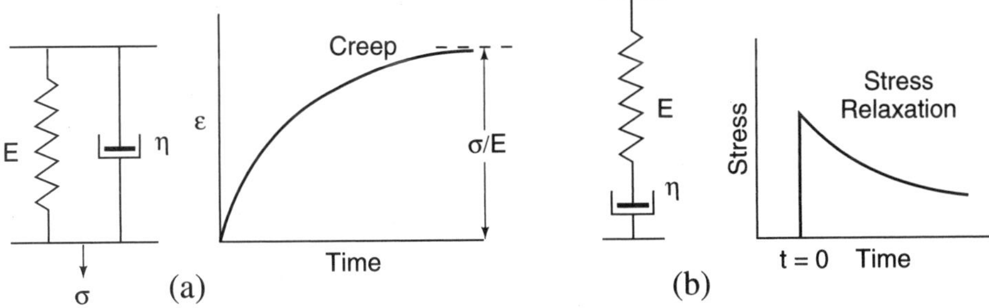

Fig. 12.16 Schematic illustration of (a) creep and (b) stress relaxation in a polymer.

Just as the elastic response to an applied stress in a metal or ceramic can be characterized by Young's modulus, the response of a polymer is characterized by the *viscoelastic modulus.* This is defined to take stress-relaxation into account; it is the stress corresponding to a given strain after a specified time of loading, e.g., 10 seconds. The viscoelastic modulus must be strongly dependent on temperature, since it involves viscous flow, This can be illustrated by the behavior of amorphous polystyrene. Polystyrene, the mer of which is shown in Fig. 12.17(a), is an example of another *vinyl* polymer, which refers to the family of mers in which at least three of the side groups of the carbon pair are hydrogen. Because the mer contains a benzene ring, polystyrene is also an example of an aromatic (i.e., smelly) hydrocarbon. (Polyethylene is also a vinyl; here, the fourth side group happens to be hydrogen.) Some other types of simple linear polymers, vinyl and otherwise, are described in Appendix 12.2. The dependence of the viscoelastic modulus of polystyrene is depicted in Fig. 12.17(b).

It can be seen that the behavior of the polystyrene varies enormously over a rather small temperature range. As already noted, the glass-transition temperature is around 100°C, so it is glassy at room temperature. Thus, a polystyrene drinking "glass," when squeezed too much, cracks in a brittle manner. However, in the vicinity of T_g the viscoelastic modulus falls by several orders of magnitude, and upon heating the behavior changes rapidly from glassy to "leathery" to rubbery before viscous flow begins.

(a)

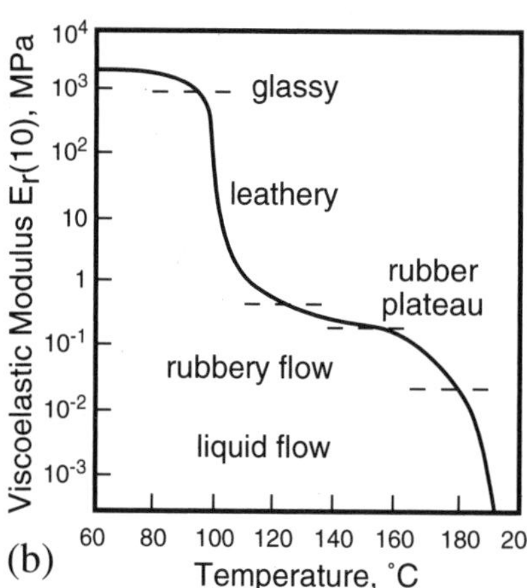

(b)

Fig. 12.17 (a) The polystyrene mer; (b) the dependence of the viscoelastic modulus (for 10-second relaxation) on temperature for amorphous polystyrene. (From A. V. Tobolsky, *Properties and Structure of Polymers,* Wiley, 1960, p. 73. Reprinted by permission of John Wiley & Sons, Inc.)

As with polyethylene, certain kinds of polystyrene can be produced with a high volume fraction in the crystalline state. In this case, the viscoelastic modulus falls by a much smaller amount at T_g, reflecting the small volume fraction of amorphous polymer, but it falls precipitously at T_M. This behavior is illustrated by the top curve in Fig. 12.18.

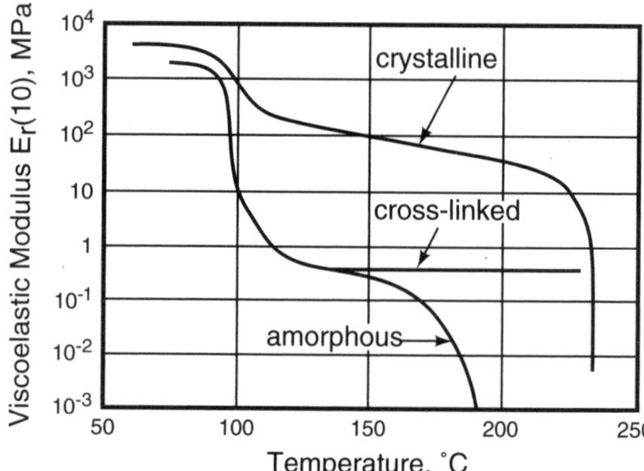

Fig. 12.18 Temperature dependence of the viscoelastic modulus of polystyrene in the amorphous, crystalline and cross-linked states. (From A. V. Tobolsky, *Properties and Structure of Polymers,* Wiley, 1960, p. 75. Reprinted by permission of John Wiley & Sons, Inc.)

Whether or not polystyrene can crystallize depends on the *tacticity* of the chains, as described in Appendix 12.2. If the large (benzene-ring) side group is always on the same position for every mer in each chain, then the polystyrene is called *isotactic.* This kind of polystyrene can crystallize, although the large aromatic-ring acts as a retardant. However, if the large side group is located randomly in the mers in any chain, the polystyrene is *atactic,* and crystallization can never occur because long-range order is impossible in a polymer in which the chains themselves are disordered.

The regions labelled "leathery" and "rubbery" between the glassy and liquid states in Fig. 12.17 represent behavior that is controlled by entanglements in and between chains. The entanglements act as temporary barriers to the translation of one part of a chain past another. The duration of the blockages depends on the kinetic energy in the chains, therefore on the temperature. Thus, the transition from glass to liquid is retarded and is spread over a range of temperatures. The extent of this range, particularly of the rubbery plateau, increases with the average length of the chains.

The effect of some cross-linking in amorphous polystyrene is shown in Fig. 12.18. Here, covalent bridges are formed between linear chains, and these prevent the chains from sliding past each other after they have uncoiled. Thus, the transition to viscous flow is prevented. Instead, the rubbery region is extended, and the polystyrene becomes an elastomer; i.e., it is capable of being stretched by large amounts without permanent deformation. This is the kind of behavior found in rubber.

12.4 Rubber

The rubber used in tires can be made by the addition polymerization of monomers called conjugated dienes. Important examples are *isoprene, chloroprene,* and *butadiene,* the structures of which are given in Fig. 12.19. Note that in each case the central bond is a single carbon-carbon bond and that the two carbons are free to rotate 360° about this bond axis. However, there can be no rotation about the axes of the double bonds.

$CH_2{=}C(CH_3){-}CH{=}CH_2$ (isoprene) $CH_2{=}C(Cl){-}CH{=}CH_2$ (chloroprene) $CH_2{=}CH{-}CH{=}CH_2$ (butadiene)

Fig. 12.19 Structures of isoprene, chloroprene, and butadiene monomers.

When these monomers polymerize, the double bonds at each end become single bonds, and the single bond in the center becomes a double bond. The doubly bonded central carbon atoms are then no longer free to rotate about the bond axis. Thus, there are two possible configurations that each mer can assume, as shown in Fig. 12.20, and this configuration becomes locked in during polymerization. In each case, two *isomers* are shown. The two have the same chemical composition, but the structure of the mers differs in an important way. That is, the two central side groups can be either on the same side or on opposite sides of the central carbon atoms. These two cases are called *cis* and *trans,* respectively.

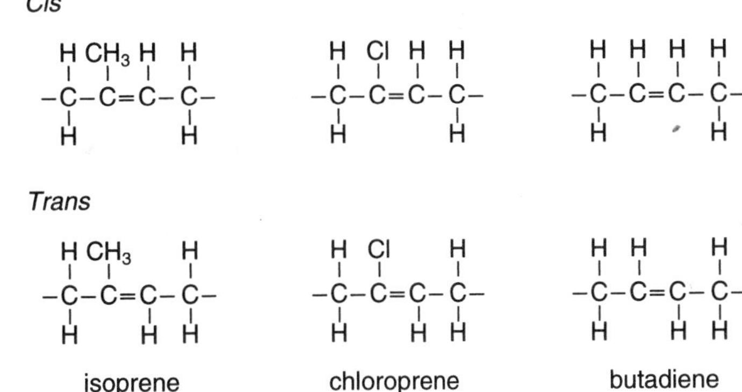

Fig. 12.20 The two isomeric forms, *cis* and *trans,* of the mers that can form from each of the monomers shown in Fig. 12.19.

Taking polyisoprene as an example, an alternative representation of the isomers that conveys the contrast more clearly is given in Fig. 12.21, along with the resulting configurations of the two polymer chains.

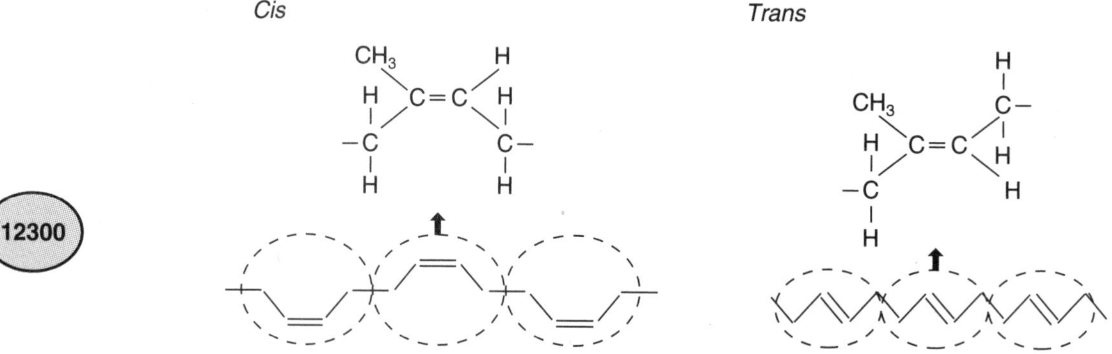

Fig. 12.21 The cis and trans mers of polyisoprene and the configuration of the polymer chains formed from each.

The substance known as natural rubber is the cis form of polyisoprene. It is obtained from the the *Hevea Brasiliensis* tree as a *latex,* meaning a suspension of polymer molecules in water, and it can also be made synthetically. The trans form of polyisoprene is called *gutta percha.* It is found in the latex of a different family of tropical trees, and its properties are quite different from the cis form. The more compact conformation of the chains of the trans form (Fig. 12.21) allows it to crystallize more readily, as indicated by the higher melting temperature:

	T_g (°C)	T_M (°C)
cis	-73	28
trans	-58	74

The cis form has a much lower percent crystallinity at room temperature, due to its less compact chain configuration. Because crystalline regions do not participate in elastomeric behavior (which involves uncoiling and recoiling of chains), the trans form with its greater crystalline content does not produce a good elastomer.

Raw natural rubber, i.e., cis-polyisoprene, is not elastomeric, because there is nothing to prevent the chains from flowing past one another interminably when the chains are uncoiled by stretching. That is, the raw rubber would behave like soft taffy when stretched. Elastomeric behavior can be imparted to the rubber by vulcanization, which means reacting the rubber with sulfur mixed in with the hot liquid cis-polyisoprene. The sulfur breaks double bonds in adjacent chains and forms a sulfur bridge cross-linking the two chains, as shown in Fig. 12.22.

The stiffness, or "hardness," of the rubber depends on the amount of sulfur mixed in; i.e., on the density of cross-links. Hence, the properties of the rubber can be varied over a wide range, as indicated by Fig. 12.23, which shows the effect of the degree of vulcanization on the viscoelastic modulus.

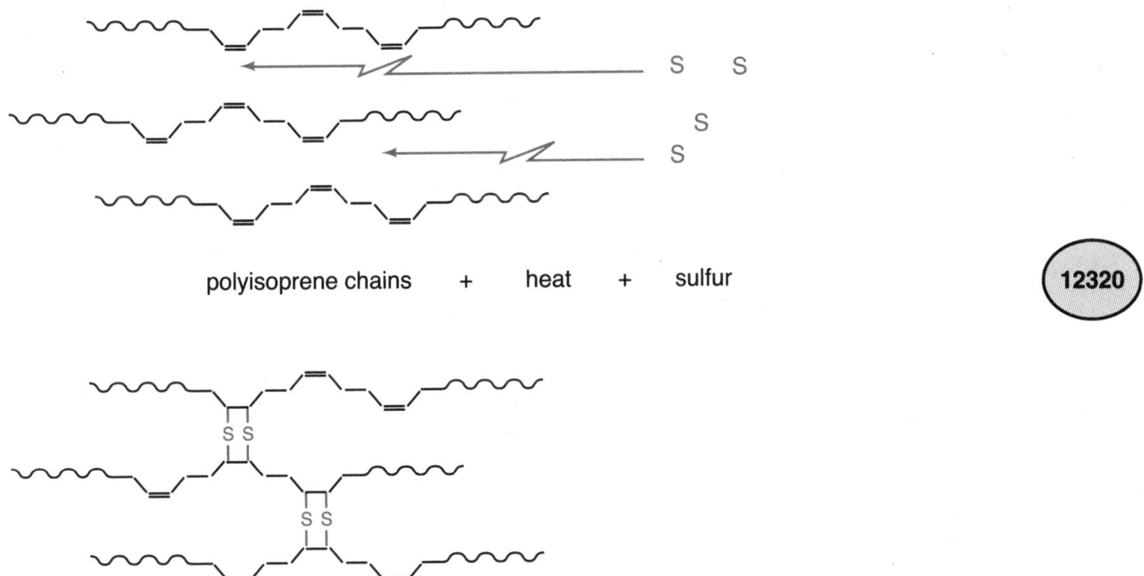

12320

Fig. 12.22 Location of sulfur in a vulcanized rubber.

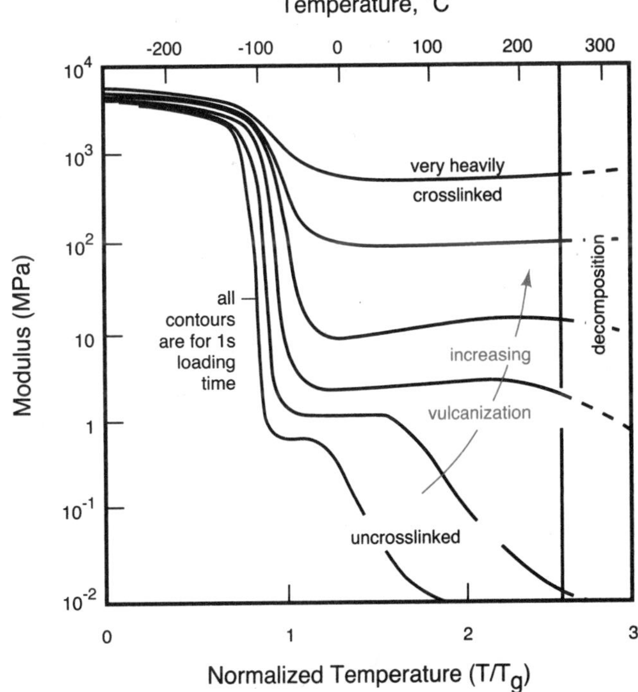

Fig. 12.23 Influence of increased cross-linking by sulfur (increasing vulcanization) on the temperature dependence of the viscoelastic modulus of polyisoprene. (From M.F. Ashby and D.R.H. Jones, *Engineering Materials, Vol. 2,* Pergamon Press, Oxford, 1986, p. 227.)

Since oxygen is in the same periodic group as sulfur, it can also cross-link, and thus harden, polyisoprene. This is the cause of the hardening and surface cracking in aged rubber tires. The process is hastened by the presence of ozone, a more reactive form of oxygen, and also ultra-violet (UV) radiation (e.g., sunlight), which activates the breaking of the double bond of the O_2 molecules.

12330

The unique behavior of rubber makes it an excellent shock absorber. It deforms extensively and easily, but not permanently. Thus, it can absorb a great deal of energy and then release it in a controlled way. Its elastomeric behavior can be tailored to various requirements by adjusting the degree of cross-linking, i.e., the amount of sulfur mixed in with the rubber (cf. Fig. 12.23).

In addition to polyisoprene, synthetic rubbers can be made by having hydrogen or chlorine in the place of the methyl group, which gives polybutadiene or polychloroprene, respectively (cf. Fig. 12.19). Tires are often made of copolymers of polystyrene and polybutadiene, in which the two mers are distributed randomly along the chains. This is the analog of a solid solution in a metallic alloy.

An elastomeric rubber can be extended elastically by several hundred percent. This stretching occurs mainly by uncoiling of the chains, which remain interconnected by the cross-links. Since there is not much bending or stretching of covalent bonds (except at very high strains), there is not much change in the
12270 bond energy (i.e., enthalpy). Therefore, the increase in free energy when an elastomer is stretched an amount ΔX by force F comes from the decrease in entropy as the chains become more nearly aligned. Thus, the work done in stretching an elastomer can be expressed as:

$$F \Delta X = \Delta G = -T \Delta S \qquad (\Delta H \text{ is small})$$

Therefore, the restoring force at constant temperature is proportional to the change in entropy with extension, ΔX:

$$F_T \propto \frac{-\Delta S}{\Delta X}$$

As the temperature increases, the restoring force for a given ΔX, or TΔS, obviously increases, which is why the viscoelastic modulus increases with temperature in the region of rubber elasticity (cf. Figs. 12.18 and 12.23).

When natural rubber is stretched sufficiently, the chains become so aligned that a significant degree of crystallization occurs. This can be demonstrated by x-ray diffraction, as shown in Fig. 12.24, or by detecting the heat of crystallization.

One can detect the release of this heat by wetting the lips and quickly stretching a rubber band held between the lips; that is, the rubber band is felt to warm up. If the rubber band is allowed to relax quickly, the melting of the crystalline regions is accompanied by an input of heat from the lips; that is, the rubber band is felt to become cool.

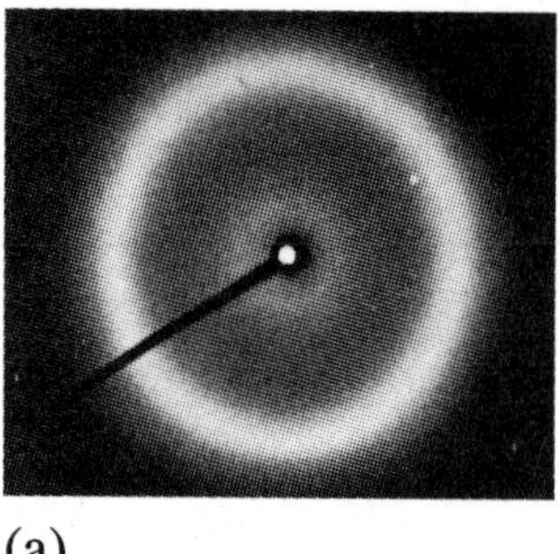
(a)

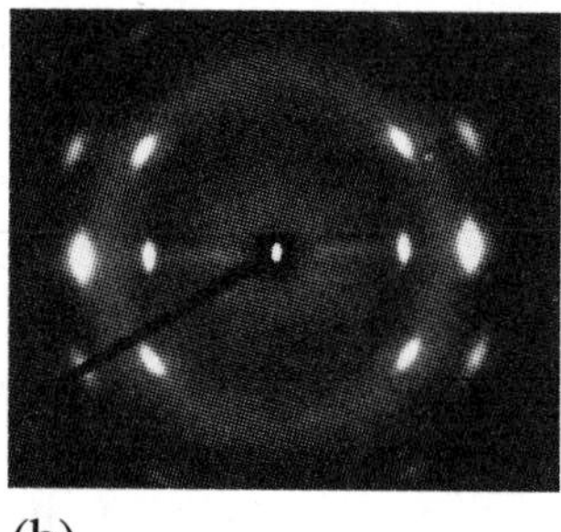
(b)

Fig. 12.24 X-ray (Laue) patterns of polyisoprene in (a) the relaxed (i.e., amorphous) condition and (b) the stretched (crystalline) condition (from S.D. Gehman, *Chem. Revs.*, vol. 26, 1940, p. 203.)

Exercise 12.2

Q. Can a thermoset be melted so that it can be reshaped?

A. No. Once the chemical reaction to form a thermoset component has taken place, the primary covalent bonds are very difficult to break. Thermosets show a weaker glass transition than thermoplastics; the modulus change at T_g decreases as the density of cross links increases.

Summary

Tires are fiber-reinforced composites in which the matrix is an elastomeric rubber based on a cross-linked linear polymer like polyisoprene. The subject of linear polymers is introduced by consideration of the simplest one, polyethylene. The flexibility of chains, by virtue of easy rotation around single C-C bonds, allows coiling and tangling of chains. This increases entropy at the expense of raising enthalpy. The latter can be reduced by crystallization, which is relatively easy in PE, due to the simplicity of its mer. The structure of highly crystalline PE comprises spherulites consisting of crystalline and amorphous components, the spherulites being arranged in a way analogous to the microstructure of a polycrystalline metal. The amorphous component undergoes a glass transition upon cooling, involving "melting" of van der Waals bonds over a small range of temperature, whereas the crystalline component undergoes a classical melting-crystallization transition at a specific temperature.

Polymers are viscoelastic above their glass-transition temperature, and their mechanical behavior must be defined in terms of the viscoelastic modulus, which is time dependent. The glass transition can be observed in a plot of the viscoelastic modulus (on a log scale) *vs.* the temperature. The location of this transition depends on the molecular architecture. Thus, the T_g for PE is about -130°C, whereas for polystyrene, with its large aromatic side group, it is about 100°C.

Polymer chains that contain double bonds can be cross-linked; a classic example is the vulcanization of rubber with sulfur. Cross-linking can convert a linear polymer to an elastomer, which exhibits a rising viscoelastic modulus with increasing temperature over an extended temperature range (above T_g). This behavior arises from the inhibition of the sliding of chains past one another; they can only uncoil and recoil as a tensile stress is applied and relaxed. Thus, the restoring force in a stretched elastomer is the entropy increase associated with recoiling.

The extreme versatility of polymeric materials arises from the great variety of polymer architecture and possibilities for polymer mixing, as well as factors such as branching, cross-linking, and different degrees of crystallization.

Appendix 12.1 Secondary Bonds

In addition to the strong, primary bonding types, i.e., metallic, ionic, and covalent, there exists a much weaker type of secondary bonding, called Van der Waals bonding, which is electrostatic in origin. Such bonding arises whenever the center of negative charge in an atom or molecule does not coincide with the center of positive charge. In such a case an electric dipole is formed, and bonding occurs between the negative end of one dipole and the positive end of the next. This bonding is not only relatively weak, but it acts over a much shorter range than does a primary bond. The energy of the Coulombic field around a dipole falls off as $1/r^6$, in contrast with that around a single charge, which falls off as $1/r$.

There are two classes of van der Waals bonds. The first arises from fluctuating dipoles, and is best exemplified by the inert gases. The magnitude and direction of the dipole of a given atom fluctuates with time as the center of charge of the electrons fluctuates. The dipole of one atom can, at any instant, induce a dipole in an adjacent atom, allowing an electrostatic interaction to build up among neighbors, if atomic vibrations due to thermal energy are minimized. The strength of such bonding necessarily increases with the number of electrons, as illustrated by the melting and boiling points of inert gases in Table A12.1.1.

Table A12.1.1 Melting and Boiling Points of Some Atomic and Molecular Gases

Gas	Number of Electrons	M.P. (K)	B.P. (K)
He	2	1.6	4.2
Ne	10	24	27
Ar	18	84	87
H_2	2	14	20
O_2	16	54	90

Similar effects can occur in molecules, like H_2 and O_2 (cf. Table A12.1.1), but the description is more complex because of the nature of the electron clouds and the relative motion of the nuclei in each molecule.

The second class of Van der Waals bonding arises from permanent dipoles. An example, depicted schematically in Fig. A12.1.1, is the water molecule, which has a fairly large dipole moment and, of course, much higher melting and boiling points than the molecules in Table A12.1.1.

Van der Waals bonding accounts for the weak cohesion between polymer chains and atomic planes in crystals like graphite, in which all the primary bonds lie in the planes. Such bonding is the reason for the excellent lubricating property of graphite and other materials with a similar layered structure.

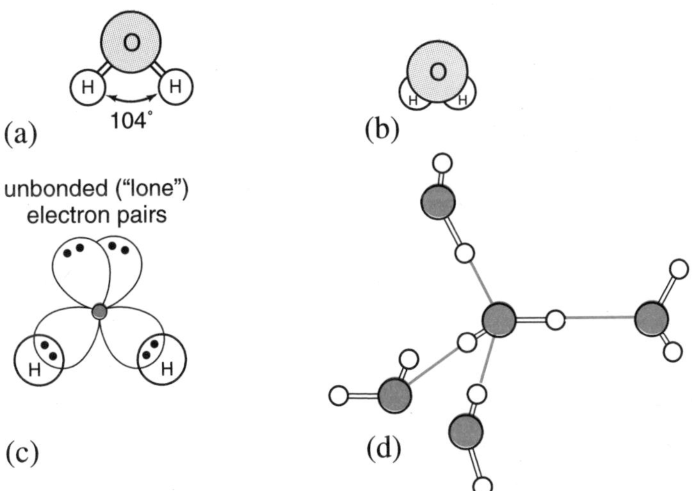

Fig. A12.1.1 Schematic representation of water molecule (a) in a ball-and-stick model, (b) in a space-filling model, and (c) showing the molecular orbitals of the oxygen, pointing to the corners of a tetrahedron, giving rise to a highly polar molecule. (d) Bonding between water molecules; the lone pairs of the oxygens of one molecule are attracted to the hydrogens of others.

Appendix 12.2 Architecture of Some Simple Polymers

Polyethylene is the simplest of the vinyl-type polymers. In the other vinyls, shown in Fig. A12.2.1, one of the hydrogens is replaced by another element or chemical group, such as chlorine in polyvinyl chloride (PVC), a methyl group in polypropylene, or a benzene ring in polystyrene. If all the hydrogens are replaced by fluorine, the result is polytetrafluoroethylene (PTFE). In polymethyl methacrylate (PMMA), a *vinylidene,* two of the hydrogens are replaced, one by a methyl group and the other by an acetate group. All of these linear polymers are thermoplastic, meaning that they soften upon heating.

Vinyls:

Polyethylene (-130)
(e.g., milk containers)

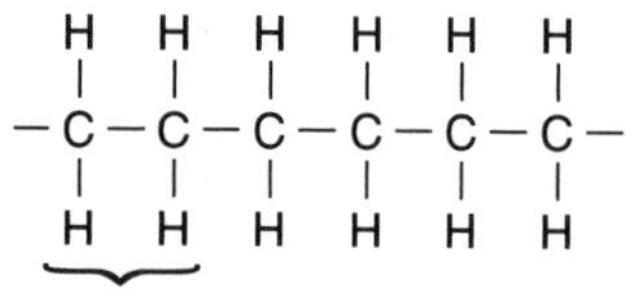

```
  H   H   H   H   H   H
  |   |   |   |   |   |
- C - C - C - C - C - C -
  |   |   |   |   |   |
  H   H   H   H   H   H
```

Polypropylene (-14)
(e.g., sports clothing, ropes)

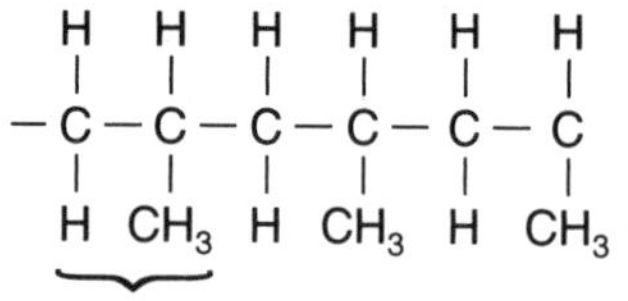

```
  H   H    H   H    H   H
  |   |    |   |    |   |
- C - C  - C - C  - C - C
  |   |    |   |    |   |
  H   CH3  H   CH3  H   CH3
```

Polyvinyl chloride (87)
(e.g., PVC pipes and hoses)

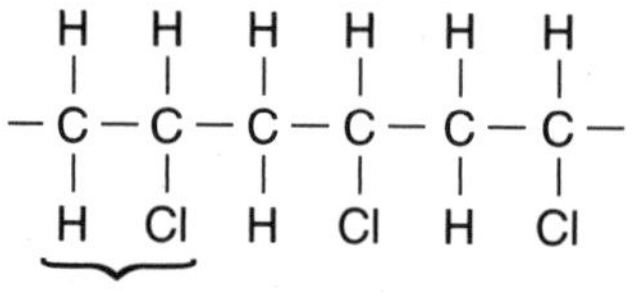

```
  H   H   H   H   H   H
  |   |   |   |   |   |
- C - C - C - C - C - C -
  |   |   |   |   |   |
  H   Cl  H   Cl  H   Cl
```

Polystyrene (100)
(e.g., "glass" or foam drinking cups)

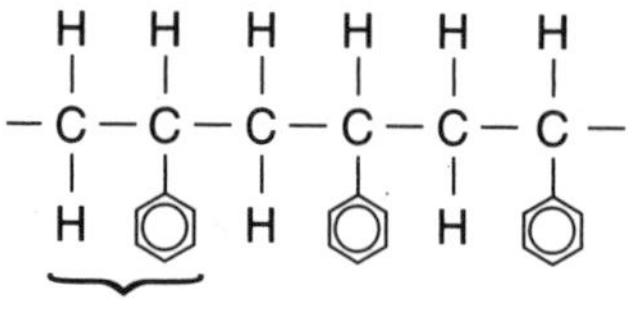

```
  H   H   H   H   H   H
  |   |   |   |   |   |
- C - C - C - C - C - C -
  |   |   |   |   |   |
  H   ⌬   H   ⌬   H   ⌬
```

Others:

Polytetrafluoroethylene (-90)
(e.g., Teflon®)

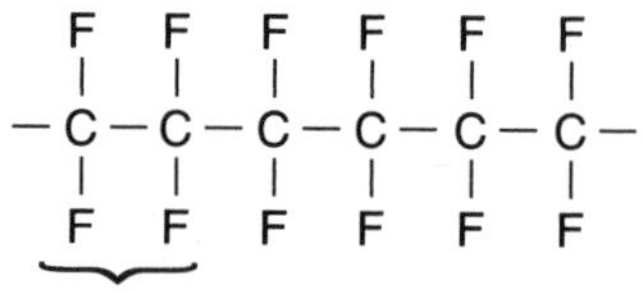

```
  F   F   F   F   F   F
  |   |   |   |   |   |
- C - C - C - C - C - C -
  |   |   |   |   |   |
  F   F   F   F   F   F
```

Polymethyl Methacrylate (105)
(e.g., Plexiglas®, Lucite®)

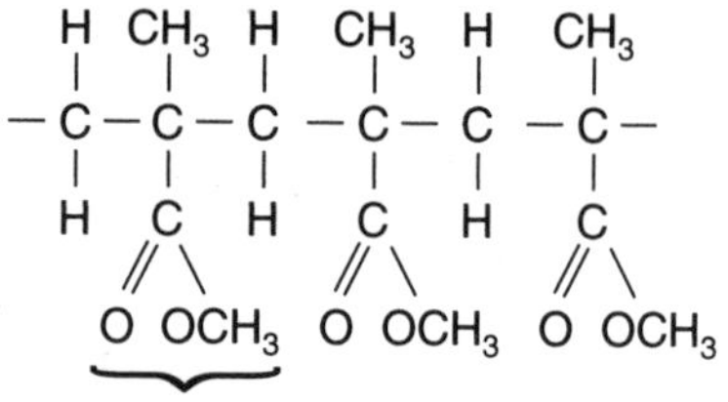

```
  H  CH3   H  CH3   H  CH3
  |   |    |   |    |   |
- C - C  - C - C  - C - C -
  |   |    |   |    |   |
  H   C    H   C    H   C
     // \     // \     // \
    O  OCH3  O  OCH3  O  OCH3
```

One Mer

Fig. A12.2.1 Examples of some simple polymers, with T_g (in °C) shown.

As the mer becomes more complicated, crystallization becomes more difficult, and as the side groups become larger, molecular motion becomes more difficult and T_g rises.

Linear polymers with side groups may form in several configurations, the properties of which may be quite different; these are shown in Fig. A12.2.2. If the side groups are all on the same side of the chain, it is called *isotactic.* If they alternate from side to side in a regular way, it is *syndiotactic,* but if they are arranged randomly, it is *atactic.* The first two can crystallize, but the third cannot. Atactic polymers generally have poor mechanical properties, and until recently it has not been possible to produce consistently syndiotactic polymers. Therefore, most commercial polymers are isotactic.

The tacticity, as well as the extent of branching and the distribution of molecular weights, depends on the manufacturing process, which varies from one producer to another. Because of that, generic materials properties given in handbooks are not very precise, and the data supplied by each manufacturer must be used for design purposes.

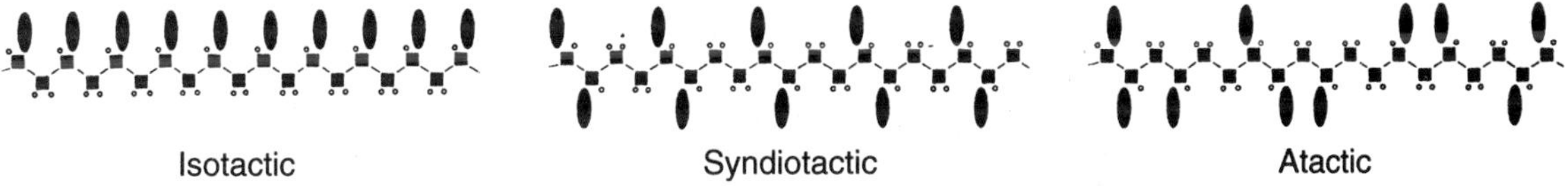

Fig. A12.2.2 Schematic representation of three configurations of a vinyl-type polymer formed from a monomer of the type CH_2=CHR. (From M.F. Ashby and D.H.R. Jones, *Engineering Materials, Vol. 2,* Pergamon Press, Oxford, 1986, p. 212.)

Glossary/Vocabulary - Chapter 12

Addition polymerization	This is a polymerization process in which chains grow by the addition of mers to the chain end. Polyethylene is made by the reaction of a free radical on the end of a chain interacting with a doubly bonded ethylene monomer molecule, breaking the double bond and adding the mer to the chain.
Atactic	See tacticity.
Benzene ring	This is a six-carbon ring with a hydrogen bonded to each carbon and with double bonds alternating around the ring. Compounds with such a ring are called aromatic because of their noxious odor. The double bonds can be considered to oscillate with adjacent single bonds, so that there is on average 1.5 bonds per carbon pair.
Branched polymer	Branching means the formation of short chains as side groups on a long-chain linear polymer; this occurs during the polymerization process. Polyethylene used for high-strength applications, like gas mains, is made branched. The branches inhibit deformation by making it more difficult for chains to slide past each other.

Butadiene	A conjugated diene used as the monomer for polybutadiene, which is a synthetic rubber. It has the formula CH_2=CH-CH=CH_2. It resembles isoprene, the monomer of natural rubber, except that the second C has H as its side group, rather than CH_3 as in isoprene.
Chloroprene	A conjugated diene used as a monomer for polychloroprene, a synthetic rubber. The side group of the second carbon is Cl, rather than CH_3 as in isoprene.
cis-Polyisoprene	A polymer that can form in different configurations of the mer is said to form different isomers. Polyisoprene, polybutadiene, and chloroprene can exist in the cis or trans isomeric form, depending on whether the side-group and the hydrogen on either side of the double bond are on the same side of the monomer (cis) or on opposites sides (trans).
Conjugated diene	Dienes are alkenes that contain two carbon-carbon double bonds. Double bonds that alternate with single bonds are said to be conjugated.
Creep	This is time-dependent plastic deformation. In crystals it occurs by way of thermally activated dislocation motion or by a diffusive process. In polymers it occurs by viscous flow; that is, by sliding of molecules past one another. It is important for metallic materials operating in the vicinity of half the absolute melting temperature or above. In polymers it can occur above the glass-transition temperature.
Cross linking	A cross link is a strong bridge formed by covalent bonding between two polymer molecules. The classical example is the vulcanization of rubber, in which sulfur atoms break double bonds in adjacent chains of, for example, cis polyisoprene, and themselves act as cross-links.
Dashpot	This is a device used to model viscous, or time-dependent, mechanical behavior. It comprises a cylinder with a piston, the motion of which is controlled by the flow of a fluid through a restricted orifice. Automobile shock absorbers are dashpots.
Degree of polymerization	This is a measure of the average length of a polymer chain in polymeric material. The number average degree of polymerization is given by the number-average molecular weight of a chain divided by the molecular weight of one mer.
Elastomer	This means a rubber-like material; i.e., one that can be stretched elastically by very large amounts compared to other elastic materials. Whereas metals deform elastically by much less than one percent, elastomers can be deformed by several hundred percent. Elastomeric behavior, or rubber elasticity, is highly non-linear, in contrast with normal elasticity (e.g., of metals), which is linear in most observable cases and becomes only slightly non-linear only in special circumstances where large elastic strains are possible.
Entanglement	The chains of a linear polymer are normally coiled and kinked as a result of the ease of rotation around single bonds and the tendency of entropy to be maximized. This inhibits the sliding of chains past one another, because the chains become mutually entangled, like long pieces of rope left lying in a disorganized lump. This is the primary cause of viscosity in a fluid linear polymer and of strength in a "solid" linear polymer (above the glass-transition temperature).

Free radical	This is an unpaired, or un-bonded, electron sticking out of a molecule, ready to take part in, or initiate, a chemical reaction. That is, it is highly chemically active. Hydrogen peroxide, H_2O_2, can be viewed as two H-O molecules, each with a free radical consisting of an unpaired oxygen electron.
Glass transition	This is the transition from a fluid to a glass that occurs in a material that becomes rigid, but does not crystallize, upon cooling. The temperature representing the approximate mid-point of this gradual process is called the glass-transition temperature, T_g. Amorphous linear polymers undergo a glass transition at a temperature that depends on the complexity of the polymer molecule.
Gutta percha	This is trans polyisoprene, as opposed to cis polyisoprene. It comes from a different type of tree from the one that produces natural rubber. Because of its molecular configuration, it has a greater tendency to crystallize than does cis polyisoprene. This prevents it from becoming very elastomeric when cross-linked. Gutta percha can be used as the core of golf balls, and in dentistry it is used to close the root canal of a tooth from which the root has been extracted.
High-density polyethylene, HDPE	This is polyethylene with about 95% crystallinity. It has two-to-three times the strength and about five times the stiffness of low-density polyethylene. This is used for containers, like milk containers, where strength is more important than great flexibility.
Hysteresis	This refers to the dissipation of energy in a process that, although cyclic, does not follow the same path in each half-cycle. The totally reversed stress-strain curve of an elastomer forms a loop, the area of which represents the energy dissipated as heat.
Injection molding	This is a process of forming objects out of thermoplastics by pouring the liquid polymer into a chamber and then squirting it (by moving a piston) into a cavity that has the shape of the object to be formed. Parts made from polyethylene are often injection molded, for example.
Isotactic	See tacticity.
Linear polymer	A polymer is made up of repeated molecular units called mers that are connected by covalent bonds. The dominant structural feature of most common polymers is chains of carbon atoms connected by single or double bonds. Linear polymers are long-chain molecules that can have many thousands of repeated mers. Network polymers represent the other extreme in which the structure is essentially one rigid giant molecule. Polyethylene is the simplest linear polymer, comprising a chain of C_2H_2 units. Natural rubber is a linear polymer, polyisoprene, that is cross-linked by sulfur atoms during vulcanization.
Low-density polyethylene	This is polyethylene with only about 65% crystallinity. Squeeze bottles, meant to be highly flexible, rather than very strong, are made of low-density PE.
Maxwell solid	This is a model of a viscoelastic material in which a spring and a dashpot are connected in series. The behavior of the material is characterized by the stiffness of the spring (represented by a Young's modulus) and the viscosity of the dashpot. This model is useful for describing stress relaxation in a viscoelastic material.

Network polymer	This is a three-dimensional amorphous material made up of a structural groups interconnected by covalent bonds. It is, in effect one giant molecule, and it is normally made by reacting two molecular compounds, producing what is called a thermoset. The first commercial polymer, Bakelite, is a network polymer. Technically, silica glass could be considered an inorganic network polymer.
Paraffin	This is a family of molecules, called n-alkanes, of the general formula C_nH_{2n+2}. As n increases, the properties of a paraffin range from an oil, to a grease, to a wax, to a polymeric solid, polyethylene.
Polyethylene, PE	This is a linear polymer made of repetitions of the mer C_2H_4. Because of its simplicity, polyethylene crystallizes readily to a high degree when cooled from the liquid state. The remaining part is amorphous. Milk containers are made from high-density (i.e., highly crystalline) PE.
Polymerization	This is the process of making a long-chain linear polymer or a network polymer by reacting one or more monomers so as to connect them by covalent bonds. Polyethylene is made by simple addition polymerization, in which the end of a growing polymer chain simply converts a doubly bonded C_2H_6 monomer to a $-C_2H_4-$ mer and adds it to the chain.
Polymethylmethacrylate, PMMA	This is a vinylidene polymer, because two of the possible four hydrogens along the singly bonded carbon chain are replaced by other side-groups. In this case, they are a methyl group and an acetate group. Commercially this is known as Plexiglass™ or Lucite™ (or Perspex™ in Britain).
Polytetraflouroethylene, PTFE	This is Teflon™, and it resembles polyethylene, except all the hydrogens are replaced by flourines. This is the non-stick coating used for many applications, like fry pans.
Polystyrene	This is a vinyl polymer in which the side-group is a benzene ring. Because of the large side-group, the glass-transition temperature is over 100°C. Thus, polystryene is used for plastic drinking "glasses," for example.
Polyvinylchloride, PVC	This is a vinyl polymer in one of the hydrogens of PE is replaced by chlorine. This is the main component of plastic pipes for household plumbing.
Random walk	A bug that hops in random directions on a table, but always with the same length of hop, executes a two-dimensional random walk. A vacancy in a crystal hopping from one lattice site to another in the process of self-diffusion executes a random walk. The distance it travels from a given point in n hops is given by $\sqrt{n}$. This is also the average distance between the two ends of a linear polymer molecule made up of n mers. (The distance is measured in units of the size of one mer.)
Spherulitic crystallization	In general, a spherulite is anything that forms in the shape of a little sphere. Many polymers crystallize in the form of spherulites, in which the crystallization starts at a central point and proceeds along lamellae that grow radially from the center like the petals of a chrysanthemum. (In between the lamellae is an amorphous array of un-crystallized chains.

Stress relaxation This is the process of gradual decrease of stresses that arise from a deformation after which the overall dimensions of the component remain fixed. If a polymer is stretched rapidly and the ends then fixed, the stress in the polymer will gradually relax as viscous flow occurs. If a bicycle frame is welded, there are residual stresses (thermal stresses) in the vicinity of the welds; these can be relaxed by creep if the frame is heated.

Syndiotactic See tacticity.

Tacticity This indicates how the side-group is arranged from mer to mer on a vinyl polymer. If it is in the same position (always on the same side of the chain), the polymer is isotactic. If it alternates from side to side from mer to mer, it is syndiotactic. If it is arranged randomly, it is atactic. The first two can crystallize, the first more readily than the second, but the third obviously cannot.

Thermoplastic This is a linear polymer that can become fluid upon heating. That is, it is not significantly cross-linked or highly branched, so the molecules can flow past one another, given enough thermal activation. Thermoplastics are readily formed by injection molding. They become rigid if cooled below their glass transition temperature.

trans-Polyisoprene See gutta percha.

Vinyl polymer This is a linear polymer with three hydrogens plus a fourth side-group bonded to a singly bonded carbon chain. Polyethylene is a vinyl polymer in which the fourth side-group is hydrogen. In polyvinylchloride it is chlorine.

Viscoelastic modulus This is a time-dependent elastic modulus defined in a stress-relaxation test. The stress after a specific relaxation time is divided by the displacement used to impose the stress. It is necessary to use this kind of modulus for a viscoelastic material. A plot of the viscoelastic modulus *vs.* temperature for a linear polymer shows the transition from glassy to leathery to rubbery to fluid behavior.

Viscoelasticity This refers to a mixture of elastic behavior, in which all strains are recoverable upon unloading, and viscous behavior, in which the shear-strain rate is proportional to shear stress and in which strains are not recoverable. That is, there is a mixture of time-dependent and time-independent behavior. Polyethylene that is partly crystalline and partly amorphous shows viscoelastic behavior above its T_g. The crystalline part is elastic and the amorphous part viscous. Silly Putty® is elastic when stressed very rapidly and viscous when allowed to deform over time.

Voight solid This is a model of a material that uses a spring and a dashpot in parallel, rather than in series like the Maxwell model. This model can be used to demonstrate creep in a solid that exhibits time-dependent mechanical behavior.

Vulcanization This is the name given by Charles Goodyear to the process he invented to cross-link cis polyisoprene (natural rubber) by heating it in contact with sulfur. The sulfur breaks the double bonds of adjacent polymer chains and forms covalent bonds linking the two chains. This prevents the chains from sliding past one another after they are straightened by an applied stress. The degree of vulcanization is controlled by the amount of sulfur mixed in with the polymer. The properties can range from gooey to almost rigid.

Exercises

12.1 Calculate the molecular weight of a single mer of polystyrene.

12.2 If a sample of polystyrene has a (number-average) degree of polymerization of 27,000, what is the number-average molecular weight?

12.3 Given that the length of a C-C single bond is 1.54 Å (= 1.54×10^{-8}cm), what is the maximum possible length of an average molecule in problem 12.2? (Remember what the carbon chain (molecular backbone) looks like.)

12.4 A copolymer is one made up of two different mers. An example is poly (butadiene-styrene). The different mers may form some pattern in each molecule, or they may appear at random along each molecular chain. (a) For the case of regular alternation of single (different) mers, sketch the repeating unit in a chain of this copolymer. (b) If the number-average molecular weight of this copolymer is 2.5×10^6 g/mole, what is the degree of polymerization?

12.5 Consider the creep curve in Fig. 12.16(a). After the system has been allowed to equilibrate under the imposed stress σ, i.e., to reach a strain of σ/E, let the stress suddenly be removed. Draw the entire strain *vs.* time curve from the initial application of stress to the final equilibration after the stress has been removed.

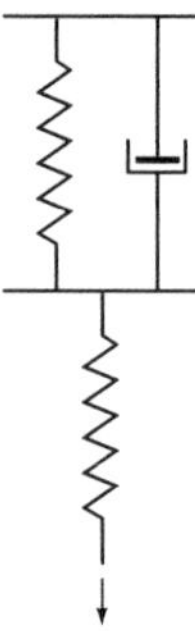

12.6 Perform the same exercise for the combination of springs and dashpots shown at left, and relate the curves to the effect of carbon redistribution in a stressed crystal of BCC iron (cf. Example 6.3.).

12.7 For polyisoprene with a degree of polymerization N, what is the minimum number of sulfur atoms needed to vulcanize the polyisoprene to saturation? Describe the expected mechanical behavior of this material.

12.8 Consider a strap of vulcanized rubber suitable for use in a tire that would exhibit an elongation (before fracture) of about 300%. A weight is hung from one end of the strap, the other end of which is attached to a horizontal beam. The extension caused by the weight is 30%. If the strap were warmed with a hot blower, would it get longer or shorter? Explain your reasoning.

12.9 Compare the behavior of the heated rubber strap in Problem 12.8 with the behavior one would find with a metal strap, and explain the difference.

13

COMPOSITE MATERIALS: RIGID MATRIX

Composites are multi-phase materials, the phases being combined to produce a behavior superior to that of any one of them acting independently. Tires are a good example of a composite in which fibers are used for reinforcement. If a tire were produced without fibers, it would expand like a balloon upon being inflated. The fibers are necessary for the tire to sustain the internal pressure. That is, the stress in the wall of the tire is carried mainly by the fibers. However, a tire obviously could not be made from fibers alone. The rubber is necessary to seal in the air and to give the tire its shock-absorbing properties. Thus, both the fibers and rubber matrix play essential roles in tire performance. The fibers have a high strength and a relatively high elastic modulus, which enable them to carry the stress due to the internal pressure. The rubber matrix has a much lower strength and stiffness, which enable it to deform elastomerically and absorb road shocks in concert with the enclosed high-pressure air.

Composites have been encountered before, in the form of pearlitic steel, and everyone is familiar with natural composite materials in the form of wood, especially bamboo, a composite of cellulose fibers in a matrix of lignin, and bone, a composite of collagen fibers in a matrix of apatite crystals. Most fiber-reinforced composites used as structural materials are like tires or wood; they have strong, high-modulus fibers in a softer, ductile, low-modulus matrix. However, some are like bone, having a brittle matrix. A common example of the latter is reinforced concrete, in which the brittle concrete matrix is strengthened by strong, high-modulus steel rods. (It may be noted that this idea is far from new; pueblo-dwelling Native Americans have been using straw to reinforce mud bricks and plaster for many centuries, and gypsum-based plaster has been reinforced with horsehair for perhaps as long a time.)

Bicycles are making increased use of fiber-reinforced, polymer-matrix composites for frames and wheels. The object is to produce a high-strength lightweight structure, with stiffness tailored to fit the application. The light weight comes from the fact that only elements with low atomic weight are used, and the high strength comes from the strong covalent bonding along the backbone of the fibers. Bicycle manufacturers have also recently employed metal-matrix composites, in which, for example, an aluminum alloy is strengthened by a dispersion of ceramic fibers or particles, such as silicon carbide or aluminum oxide, which have high strength and stiffness.

13.1 Principles of Fiber Reinforcement

A rope is a material consisting completely of fibers, with no matrix. The main strands may be continuous, running end to end, but these strands are often made up of shorter, fine, discontinuous fibers. For tensile strength the strands rely not only on the strength of each fiber, but also on the friction between the fine fibers, which prevents their slipping past one another and coming apart. A rope has extremely anisotropic tensile behavior: It is strong in tension along its axis, but very weak in transverse tension. Only the friction arising from the braiding of the main strands keeps them from separating. In addition, a rope has no resistance to compression or bending (excluding steel-wire ropes). The reason is the very small moment of inertia of the constituent fibers, as can be understood from the simple beam theory of Chapter 11, which showed that the curvature of a cylindrical beam subjected to a bending moment, M, is given by

$$\frac{1}{\rho} = \frac{M}{EI}, \text{ where } I = \frac{\pi D^4}{64}$$

Because the fiber normally has a very small diameter, D, I is very small, and a small M can produce a large curvature, as indicated schematically in Fig. 13.1(a), even if the fiber has a large elastic modulus, E.

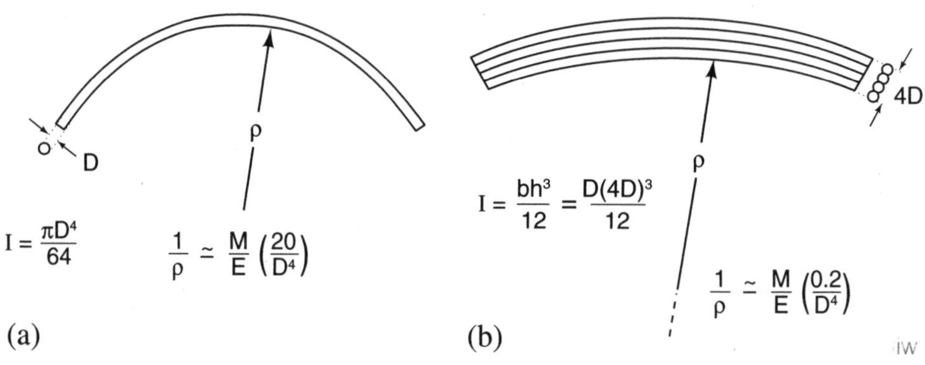

Fig. 13.1 (a) A single fiber with diameter D and elastic modulus E bent by a moment M. (b) A stack of four such fibers bonded together and loaded by the same bending moment.

How, then, is it possible, for example, to employ a bundle of parallel, fine glass fibers to make a pole for pole-vaulting? The answer is that one must glue the fibers together to increase I. The principle is illustrated by Fig. 13.1(b), in which a stack of four bonded fibers comprises a rectangular beam of cross-section Dx4D. (It is assumed that the composite is constrained to lie in a plane.) Due to the increase in I, the curvature for a given M and E is reduced by a factor of 100 by combining the four fibers. The essential factor, however, is that the glue must be strong enough to keep the fibers from sliding past one another. That is, they must all be forced to bend together. If the bond between the fibers does not have enough shear strength, then they could bend independently, and the composite effect would be lost. It is not difficult to achieve a high shear strength between fibers, because the surface area of a fiber is large. Thus, even for a large shearing force, the shear stress in the interface would be small.

In actual practice, of course, the fibers are laid up in two lateral dimensions, not just one, and the bonding agent forms a matrix that completely encases the fibers, as shown schematically in Fig. 13.2(a). The matrix of a vaulting pole is a polymer, and it has a Young's modulus that is much smaller than the modulus of the glass fibers. Therefore, the modulus of the composite must be some kind of average between the moduli of the matrix and the fibers.

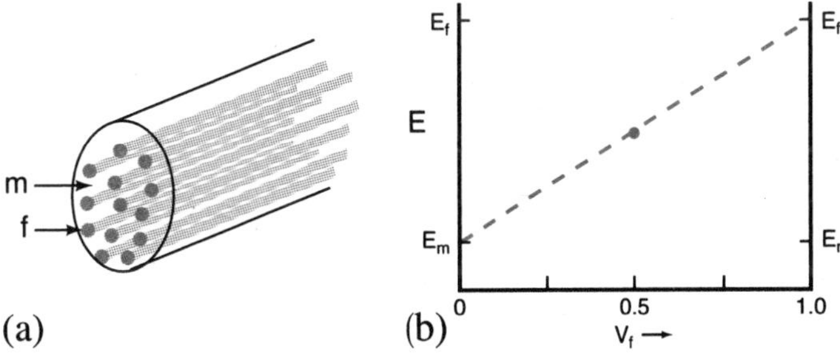

Fig. 13.2 (a) A composite of fibers (f) and a matrix (m) in which the volume fraction of fibers is 0.5. (b) The linear relationship between the elastic modulus of the composite and the volume fraction of fibers, depending on the moduli of the fibers and the matrix, respectively.

Intuitively, one would expect that, for such a composite stressed in simple tension along its length, the modulus of the composite would depend on the volume fraction of fiber *vs.* that of the matrix. If the pole were made entirely of the matrix polymer, the modulus, E_m, would be low. If it were entirely glass, the modulus, E_f, would be high, but the pole would be too brittle to use. If the volume fraction of fibers, V_f, were, say, 50%, one would guess that the modulus of the composite, E_c, would lie halfway between the two, as shown in Fig. 13.2(b). This guess would be exactly correct, as shown by the argument in the following section.

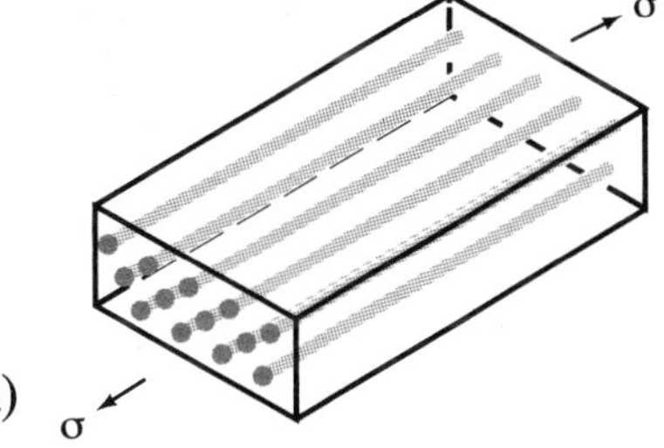

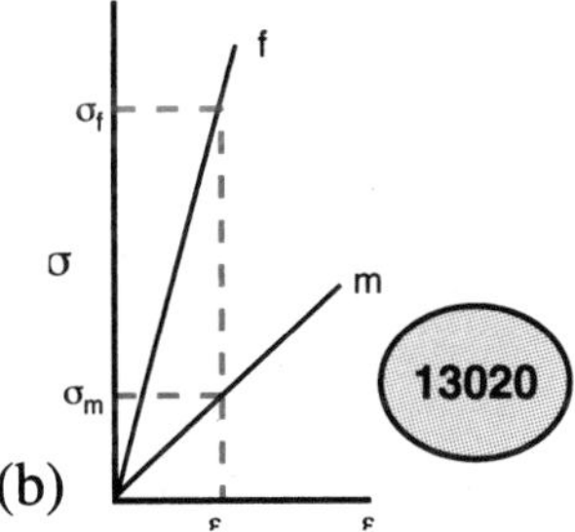

Fig. 13.3 (a) A parallel-fiber composite with continuous fibers stressed along the direction of the fibers. (b) The stress-strain curves of the matrix and of the fiber, tested in isolation.

13.1.1 Longitudinally Stressed Fibers in a Continuous-Fiber Composite

As long as the fibers cannot slide relative to the matrix, and, thus, to one another, the tensile strain in the fibers and the matrix must be the same in the longitudinally stressed composite shown in Fig. 13.3(a). Therefore, if only elastic behavior is considered, the stress in a fiber and in the matrix would depend on the strain in the composite (according to Hooke's law), and, due to its higher modulus, the stress in a fiber would necessarily be higher than in the matrix, as indicated schematically in Fig. 13.3(b).

In any composite stressed in a direction parallel to the fibers, the total force on the composite must be the sum of the forces on each component:

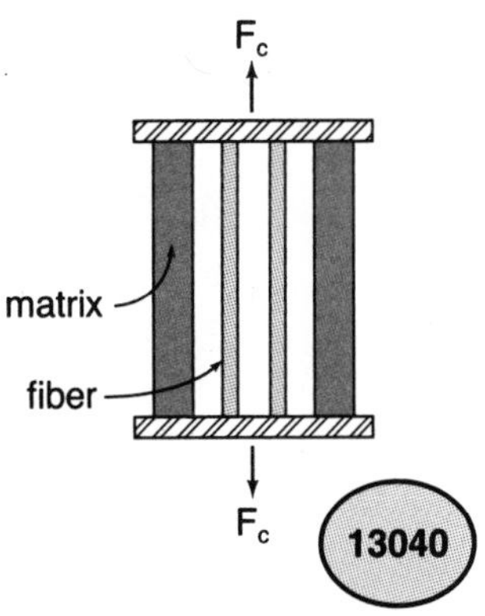

$$F_c = F_f + F_m$$

For a unit area of composite, taking the force to be stress times area, A, this can be written

$$\sigma_c = \sigma_f A_f + \sigma_m A_m$$

where A_f and A_m are the respective area fractions. Since for parallel phases, the area fraction is the same as the volume fraction, V, and since $V_f = 1 - V_m$,

$$\sigma_c = \sigma_f V_f + \sigma_m (1 - V_f)$$

or, from Hooke's law,

$$\varepsilon_c E_c = \varepsilon_f E_f V_f + \varepsilon_m E_m (1 - V_f)$$

Because all the strains are equal and can be cancelled out,

$$E_c = E_f V_f + E_m (1 - V_f)$$

which gives the linear "rule of mixtures" shown in Fig. 13.2(b).

Thus, the elastic properties of a composite can be tailored to fit the application. For example, the "spring" imparted by a vaulting pole can be adjusted to fit the weight of the athlete by varying the volume fraction of fibers, and/or by varying the modulus of the polymer matrix (i.e., by varying the degree of polymerization, the amount of cross-linking, etc.). The stiffness of the wall of a tire can be controlled in a similar manner.

It should be noted that in a fiberglass composite, the polymer matrix also plays the important role of protecting the surfaces of the glass fibers against damage. Glass, being a brittle material, is sensitive to the presence of very small surface flaws, which can act as Griffith cracks (cf. Appendix 9.2). Such cracks can be caused by surface contact between fibers or with another solid. Another function of a relatively tough matrix is to act as a crack-arrestor in the event that a fiber breaks. When the crack reaches the matrix, it can either blunt by forming a void, or it can be deflected into a direction parallel to the stress by traveling along the fiber/matrix interface, which is often relatively weak in tension. These possibilities are illustrated in Fig. 13.4.

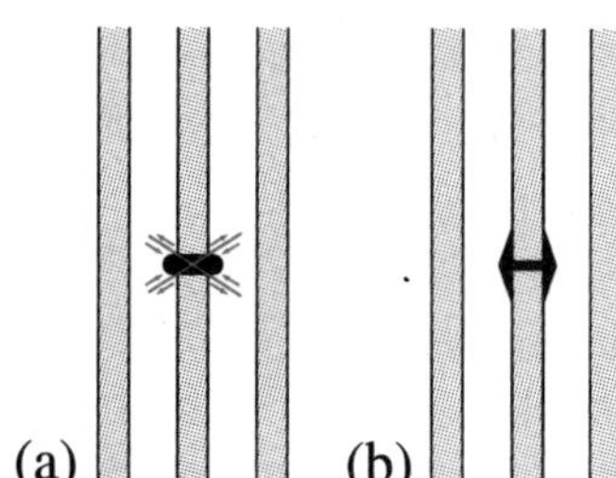

Fig. 13.4 Mechanisms of crack arrest by a tough matrix when a fiber breaks: (a) blunting, and (b) deflection into the fiber/matrix interface.

13.1.2 Transversely Stressed Fibers

As in the case of a rope, a composite can be weak in the direction perpendicular to the fibers. Thus, it is common experience for a piece of wood to be split easily along the direction of the "grain." In the case of transverse loading, Fig. 13.5, the matrix and the fibers are loaded in series, each element transmitting the full load to the next. Therefore, the forces must be equal in the matrix and the fibers. For continuous fibers, the fibers and the matrix can be considered geometrically similar. Hence, the force per unit area, or stress, rather than the strain, must be equal in each:

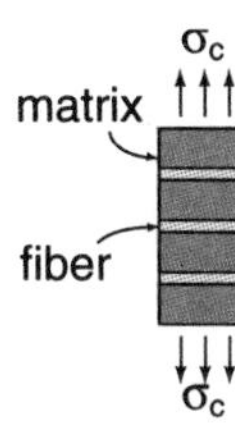

$$\sigma_c = \sigma_f = \sigma_m$$

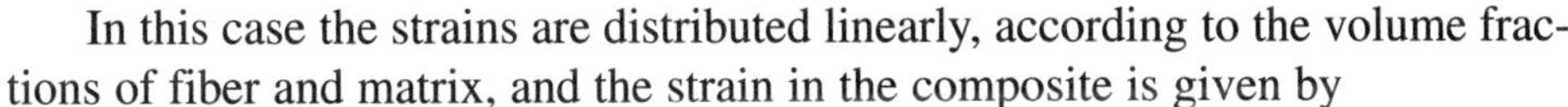

In this case the strains are distributed linearly, according to the volume fractions of fiber and matrix, and the strain in the composite is given by

$$\varepsilon_c = \varepsilon_f V_f + \varepsilon_m (1 - V_f)$$

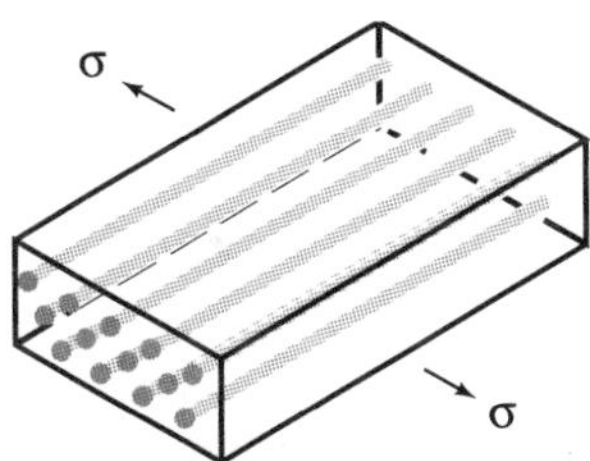

Fig. 13.5 A transversely loaded composite.

Using Hooke's law and setting the stress in the composite, fibers, and matrix equal to σ, this can be written as

$$\frac{\sigma}{E_c} = \frac{\sigma}{E_f} V_f + \frac{\sigma}{E_m} (1 - V_f)$$

which, upon dividing through by σ gives

$$\frac{1}{E_c} = \frac{V_f}{E_f} + \frac{1 - V_f}{E_m}$$

or, rearranged,

$$E_c = \frac{E_f E_m}{E_f (1 - V_f) + E_m V_f}$$

The expression for the modulus of the longitudinally stressed continuous fibers gives an upper bound for the modulus of any composite, and the expression for the transversely stressed continuous fibers is a lower bound for the modulus of any type of composite. For example, a composite with short (discontinuous) fibers, even if not aligned, would have a modulus between the two bounds. These upper and lower bounds for the Young's modulus of a composite are plotted as a function of the volume fraction of the reinforcing phase, whether fibers or particles, in Fig. 13.6.

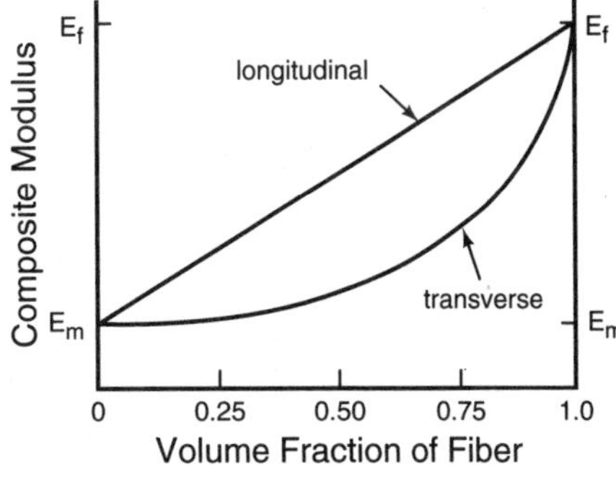

Fig. 13.6 Upper and lower bounds for the elastic modulus of composites as a function of volume fraction of the reinforcing phase.

The modulus is the most important mechanical property of a composite loaded in the elastic region (below the yield stress). The spacing between the upper and lower bounds gives some idea of how much the elastic modulus of a material strengthened by a set of parallel fibers can vary with the direction of loading. This anisotropy cannot always be tolerated. For example, when wide sheets of wood are required in a structure, one normally specifies plywood, in which thin layers of wood are stacked and glued so that each successive layer has its grain oriented at 90° to that of its neighbors. Here, one gets effective stiffening in two directions in the plane. (It is not isotropic in the plane, however; the modulus goes through minima at 45° to the fiber directions. To make such a material isotropic in the plane, the fibers would have to be aligned randomly; this would give a modulus somewhere in between the two bounds.)

13.1.3 Discontinuous Fibers

Sometimes, materials are strengthened by aligned but discontinuous fibers, as shown schematically in Fig. 13.7(a). Here, the reinforcement is less effective than in the continuous-fiber case, because the fibers are not uniformly loaded; the ends of the fibers carry less stress than the middle portions. This can be understood by examining what happens near the ends of a fiber. For this, consider an isolated fiber embedded in a matrix with a much lower elastic modulus.

13110 As shown in Fig. 13.7(b), for a given applied stress the elastic strain in the matrix beyond the ends of the fiber is relatively large. However, the matrix strain along the central region of the fiber is much smaller, being equal to that in the fiber itself. (In the central region the situation is the same as in a composite with continuous fibers.) Over a certain distance from each end of the fiber there is a transition from the higher to the lower value of tensile strain in the matrix. As is evident from the figure, this variation in tensile strain creates a shear strain and stress in the matrix. The shear stress acts on cylindrical surfaces in the matrix that lie parallel to the axis of the fiber. The most important of these surfaces is the fiber/matrix interface. To get the maximum reinforcement from the fibers, this interface must be strong enough that debonding does not occur.

13120 As indicated in Fig. 13.7(c), the shear stress in the fiber/matrix interface acts over a region at each end of the fiber and serves the same function as the grips on a tensile specimen in a tensile test. That is, it serves to load the fiber in tension by transfering load from the matrix to the fiber. This load is given by $2\tau(x)\pi rx$, where r is the radius of the fiber and x is the length along the fiber measured from its end. The shear stress $\tau(x)$ falls from a maximum at the fiber end, where the strain mismatch between fiber and matrix is largest, to zero at the point along the fiber where this mismatch disappears.

The interfacial shear stress at the fiber ends must be balanced by the tensile stress, $\sigma(x)$, in the fiber. As the shear stress decreases to zero, the tensile stress builds up to a constant value in the central region, as shown in Fig. 13.7(c). The region of tensile stress buildup is called the *transfer length.* Over this length the fiber is carrying less of the load than would a continuous fiber, and this represents a loss of reinforcement efficiency. The effect is negligible for fibers with a long aspect ratio (i.e., length/diameter), but it becomes important as the aspect ratio decreases. Thus, significant reinforcement is lost in the case of short fibers.

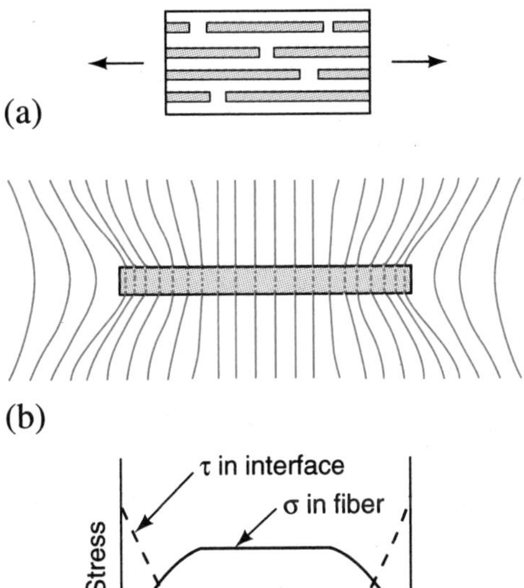

Fig. 13.7 (a) Schematic representation of a portion of a composite strengthened by discontinuous fibers. (b) Displacements in and near a discontinuous fiber. (c) Schematic plot of the tensile stress in the fiber and the shear stress in the fiber/matrix interface as a function of distance from the fiber ends.

It should be obvious that, if the fibers are replaced by elongated particles, the stress in the particle may never reach the maximum possible value. For this reason, particles are not very efficient in raising the elastic modulus. The composite modulus for short fibers and for particles is generally near the lower bound in Fig. 13.6.

13.1.4 Composite Behavior

Although the principles of fiber strengthening described above apply equally to tires and bicycle frames, these two structures are at opposite ends of a spectrum of mechanical behavior. In tires the matrix is highly viscoelastic. In frames, the matrix should have minimal viscoelasticity to avoid energy dissipation during the cyclic loading associated with pedaling. (Tires, of course, are required to dissipate large amounts of energy from road shocks.) Thus, while yielding and fracture are not a consideration with regard to tires, they are for frames. The matrix materials used for frames are glassy, brittle network polymers. Therefore, if the composite is loaded so much that fibers begin to break, then brittle fracture of the composite can occur.

Composites in which the matrix is capable of some plastic flow can have high toughness. This is because a crack that forms in a fiber would not propagate easily into a tough matrix, as indicated schematically in Fig. 13.4. Fracture of the composite would occur after a sufficient number of fibers have broken, but much energy would be absorbed by the separation of the fracture faces because of the frictional forces associated with fiber-pullout. This behavior is found in glass-fiber-reinforced composites like vaulting poles and fishing rods. The energy dissipated through viscoelastic deformation is of less concern in these items than in bicycle frames and tennis rackets.

13.2 Fibers For Reinforcement

13.2.1 Organically Based Fibers

Fibers have been used to reinforce tires for many decades. The first fibers used in tires were cotton, which is essentially cellulose, a natural polymer for which the formula is shown in Fig. 13.8. This is the fiber that strengthens plants, including woods. Later, the first fiber produced (partly) by man was introduced in the form of *rayon,* obtained by replacing one or more of the OH groups on cellulose fibers by the acetate group, also shown in Fig. 13.8. Depending on the number of OH groups replaced, a mono-, di-, or tri-acetate mer is produced. These mers can be found mixed in a rayon fiber. Rayon can exhibit stronger inter-fiber secondary bonding than cotton does, due to the larger polarity of the acetate group compared with the OH group. To make rayon fibers out of cellulose triacetate, water can be used as a plasticizer for the purpose of drawing fibers from the liquid. It would be removed by heat after the fiber is drawn.

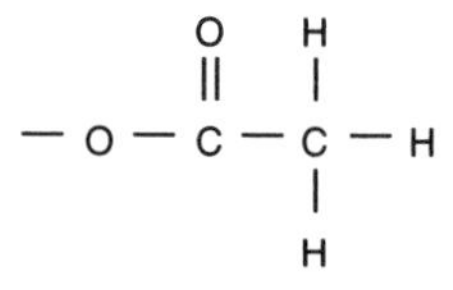

acetate group

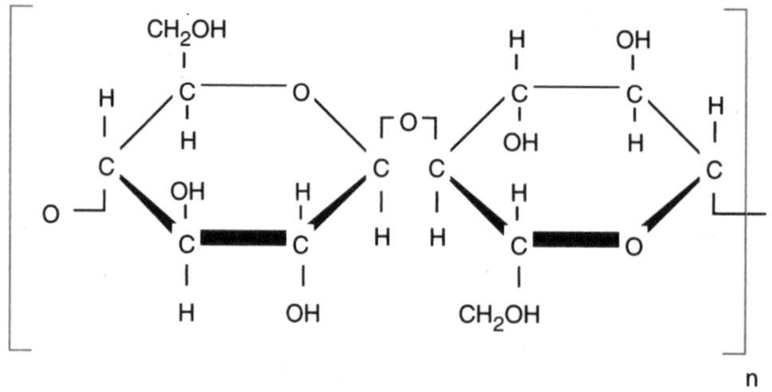

Fig. 13.8 The molecular structure of cellulose, showing the OH groups that act as reaction sites for acetate groups in the manufacture of cellulose acetate (rayon).

The first completely man-made fiber was *nylon,* invented by Wallace Carothers of the DuPont company and commercialized in 1939. Nylon is a polyamide and comprises, in effect, short paraffin-type chains connected by amide groups, which have the form

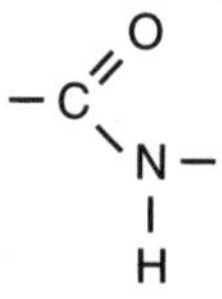

$$-\mathrm{C}(=\mathrm{O})-\mathrm{N}(\mathrm{H})-$$

as shown in Fig. 13.9. It is made by a *condensation reaction* in which two different molecules react to give a long-chain polymer plus a by-product. In the production of nylon 6.6, one reactant, adipic acid, has an OH on each end, and the other, hexamethylene diamine, has a hydrogen at each end. When these react, the by-product is water. The mer of this polymer can be viewed as having two parts, each with six carbons; hence the designation 6.6.

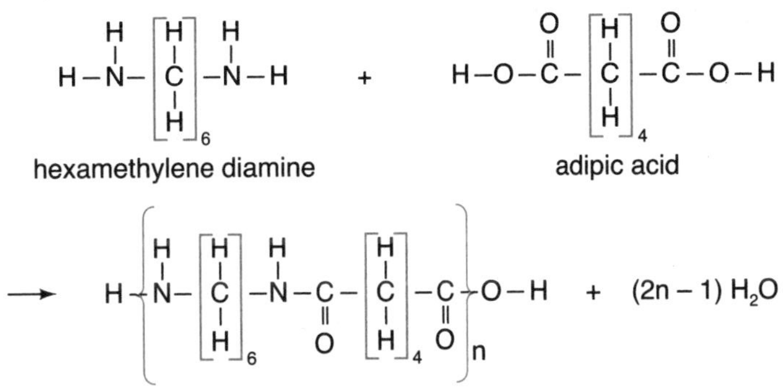

$$\text{H}_2\text{N}-[\text{CH}_2]_6-\text{NH}_2 \;(\text{hexamethylene diamine}) + \text{HO}-\overset{\text{O}}{\overset{\|}{\text{C}}}-[\text{CH}_2]_4-\overset{\text{O}}{\overset{\|}{\text{C}}}-\text{OH} \;(\text{adipic acid})$$

$$\longrightarrow \text{H}\left(-\text{NH}-[\text{CH}_2]_6-\text{NH}-\overset{\text{O}}{\overset{\|}{\text{C}}}-[\text{CH}_2]_4-\overset{\text{O}}{\overset{\|}{\text{C}}}-\right)_n\text{O}-\text{H} + (2n-1)\,\text{H}_2\text{O}$$

Fig. 13.9 The reaction that produces nylon 6.6.

To make nylon fibers, the polymer is heated to the liquid state and forced through a spinnerette, which is a plate with a myriad of small holes. The fibers are partly crystalline as they exit the holes in this extrusion-type process. After this they are extended (cold drawn) to increase the molecular alignment and the degree of crystallization, as shown schematically in Fig. 13.10. In this state further extension of the fiber is resisted almost entirely by the strong covalent bonds along the backbone of the molecular chain. The Young's modulus of nylon, for example, is of the order of 3 GPa (3000 MPa); this can be compared, for example, to that of an average tire rubber, which is less than 100 MPa.

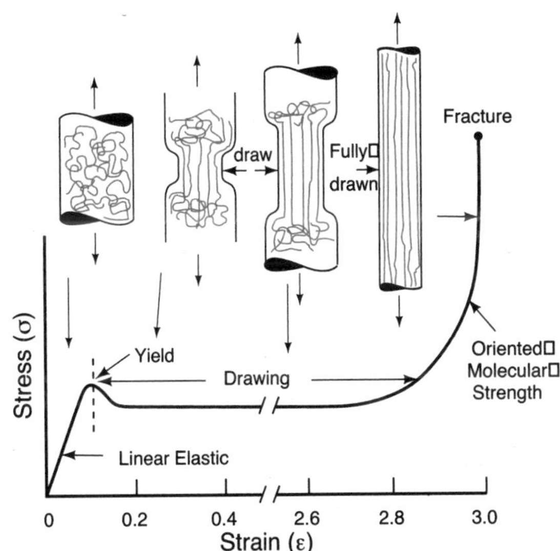

Fig. 13.10 Schematic illustration of cold-drawing of a linear polymer. (From M.F. Ashby and D.R.H. Jones, loc. cit., p. 229.)

The architecture of a nylon molecule, particularly with regard to the absence of a large side-group, is almost as simple as that of polyethylene. For that reason it crystallizes readily, and the van der Waals bonding between the closely spaced chains is strong. In addition, the molecule can form two hydrogen bonds per mer, as indicated in Fig. 13.11. The high strength of a nylon fiber arises from these two features, both of which make sliding between chains relatively difficult.

Nylon was originally developed for fabrics, and this is still its primary application, although it is also widely used for ropes and single-strand applications like fishing lines. It found widespread application as automobile tire cord for a number of years.

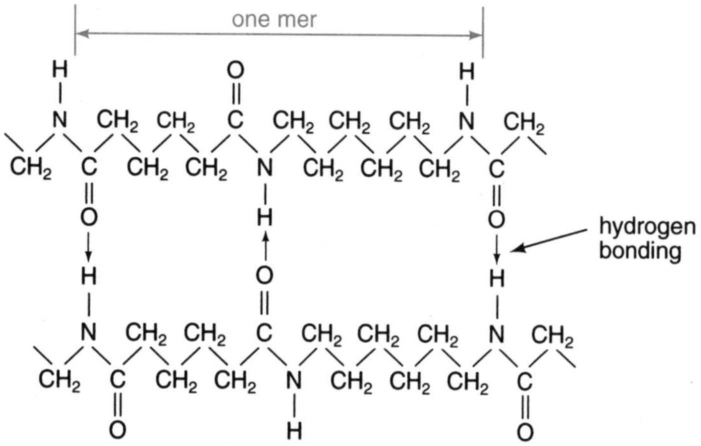

Fig. 13.11 Structure of crystalline nylon 6.6.

Another high-strength organic fiber, developed originally for tire cord by DuPont, has the trade name *Kevlar®*. It is an aromatic polyamide with the chemical formula shown in Fig. 13.12(a). It is produced by extrusion, stretching, and drawing, so that the molecules line up in planar sheets, as shown in Fig. 13.12(b). The aromatic rings result in a fairly rigid chain, and again there is the opportunity for two hydrogen bonds per mer. In the fiber the sheets are stacked in radial lamellae, as shown in Fig. 13.12(c). The tensile modulus is about 130 GPa, or more than forty times that of nylon. This is a direct result of the greater stiffness of the six-carbon aromatic ring, compared with a simple carbon chain. Although not commercially successful as tire cord, Kevlar has found many applications in high-performance composite materials.

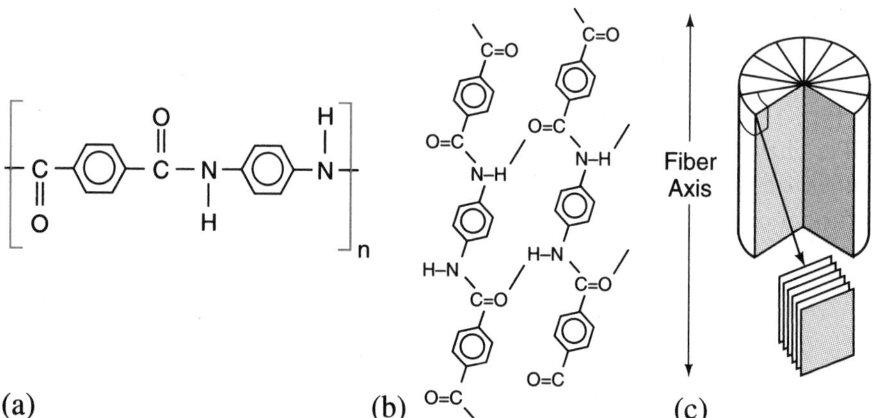

Fig. 13.12 (a) The mer of poly(p-phenylene terephthalamide) molecules. (b) The interchain hydrogen bonding which occurs when these molecules are aligned. (c) Schematic representation of the supramolecular structure of Kevlar® aromatic polyamide fibers depicting the radially arranged sheets. (After D. Tanner, J.A. Fitzgerald, and B. R. Phillips, *Verlag Chemie,* 1989.)

The stiffest fibers available for reinforcement of composites are made from graphitization of molecules of a polymer precursor. Their structure is based on layers of the hexagonal arrays of carbon atoms characteristic of graphite, as shown in Fig. 13.13(a). A graphite crystal would consist of such planes stacked in an ABAB... sequence and would have a calculated modulus of 910 GPa in an *a* direction. In a carbon fiber, the layers are stacked less regularly into small semi-crystalline units, which are, in turn, aligned with the fiber axis, but in a very complex structure, shown schematically in Fig. 13.13(b).

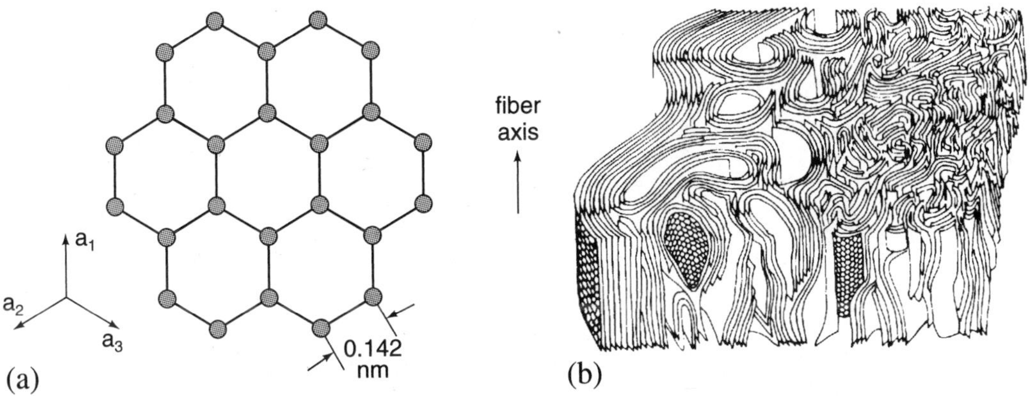

Fig. 13.13 (a) Arrangement of carbon atoms in a layer plane of graphite. (b) Schematic representation of a graphite fiber. (a) From D. Hull, *An Introduction to Composite Materials*, Cambridge University Press, 1981, pp. 9 and 10. Reprinted with permission of Cambridge University Press. (b) From S.C. Bennett, PhD.Thesis, Univ. of Leeds, 1976.

Graphite fibers can be made, for example, from polyacrylonitrile, PAN, shown in Fig. 13.14(a), by stretching the polymer and heating it in oxygen to cause the nitrile groups (-C≡N) to interact to produce the chain of rings shown in Fig. 13.14(b). Further processing then produces the graphite structure.

Carbon fiber can be processed into two types, with tensile moduli of 390 GPa (Type I) or 250 GPa (Type II). Type I has the lower tensile strength: 2.2 *vs.* 2.7 GPa. The tensile strengths of the carbon fibers are clearly limited by the voids and other irregularities in the fiber structure. This could presumably be improved with further development.

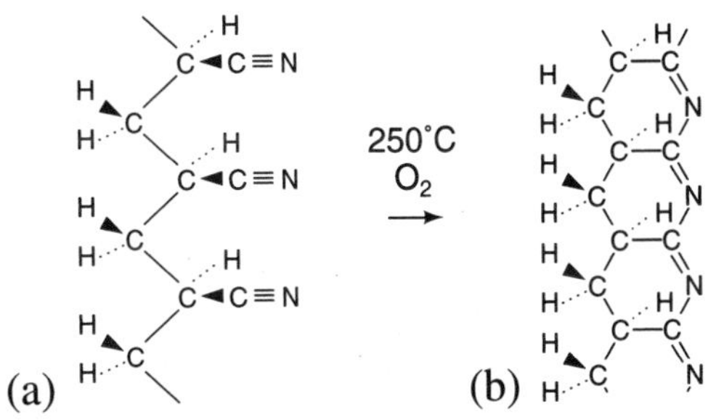

(a) 250°C O_2 → (b)

Fig. 13.14 (a) Structure of PAN. (b) Product of first stage of reaction in the formation of a carbon fiber. (From D. Hull, loc. cit. p. 12; reprinted with permission of Cambridge University Press.)

At present, carbon fibers are too expensive to be used as tire cord, but they are the primary reinforcement in composite bicycle frames, as will be discussed below, as well as for sports equipment and military aircraft.

It is instructive to compare the stiffness of four kinds of organically based fibers, as in Table 13.1, and to consider the reasons for the differences from one fiber to the next. The simplest fiber is polyethylene, which has a backbone of aligned chains of singly bonded carbon atoms. Because the chains have only hydrogen atoms as side-groups, each chain has a very small cross section. Therefore, they can be packed together at a very high density, and the large number of chains per unit area of cross section of the fiber results in a very high modulus.

Table 13.1 Comparison of the Elastic Moduli of Four Fibers

Fiber	Polyethylene	Nylon 6.6	Kevlar	Carbon
Elastic Modulus (GPa)	>3*	3	130	250 or 390
Structure	Carbon chains, small cross section	Carbon chains, lateral hydrogen bonds	Chains of carbon rings, lateral hydrogen bonds	Sheets of interlocked carbon rings

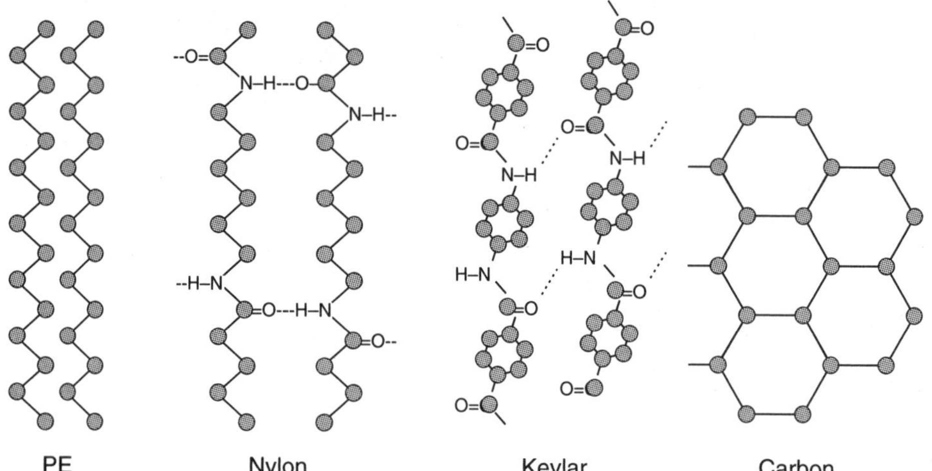

The chain structure of nylon 6.6 is not too different from that of polyethylene, but the effective cross section of each chain is larger, due to the size of the amide groups. However, these groups provide the sites for hydrogen bonding between chains, and this retards the tendency for sliding between chains. This effect is responsible for the high modulus of nylon fibers.

The Kevlar fiber structure has chains of hexagonal rings of carbon, which are considerably stiffer than a simple linear carbon chain, and these rings are bonded laterally by hydrogen bonds. Therefore, it is not surprising that the modulus of Kevlar is much higher than that of nylon.

Finally, the carbon fibers are also composed of six-carbon rings, but these rings are interlocked in a two-dimensional array, which is, of course, much more effective than the hydrogen bonding of Kevlar. Therefore, carbon fibers have the highest modulus of all.

* The modulus of polyethylene can reach 170 GPa in the case of *SPECTRA®* fibers, which are made from PE chains with extremely high molecular weights and are drawn to a high degree of crystallinity.

13.2.2 Inorganically Based Fibers

Most present-day automotive tires are reinforced with inorganic fibers, either glass or steel. Silica-based glass can be drawn into fibers from the molten state. The building block of such a glass is the SiO_4^{4-} tetrahedron (as noted in Section 9.6.3), with the silicon covalently bonded to four neighboring oxygens, each oxygen sharing two silicon atoms, as shown in Fig. 13.15(a). The three-dimensional network (Fig. 13.15(b)) formed by pure silica makes a strongly bonded glass that has a low coefficient of thermal expansion and is, therefore, highly resistant to thermal shock. However, it is also extremely viscous at high temperatures; hence, it is difficult to work into shapes and virtually impossible to draw into fibers. Silica glasses are made less viscous (and less resistant to thermal shock) by the addition of other oxides, which act to break up the silica network and are called network modifiers. An example of such an additive is Na_2O. A sodium ion can bond to only one oxygen (which is also covalently bonded to a silicon), and this does not form a bridge to a neighboring SiO_4^{4-} tetrahedron, as shown in Fig. 13.15(c).

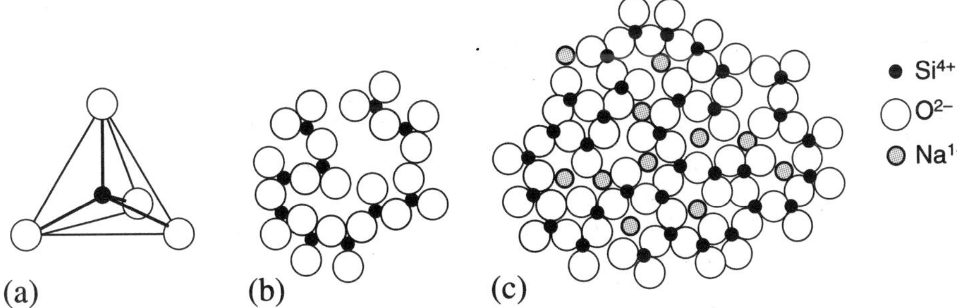

Fig. 13.15 (a) The SiO_4^{4-} tetrahedron. (b) Schematic representation of SiO_2 glass in which only three of the four tetrahedral oxygens are shown. (c) Network modification by the addition of Na_2O.

Viscosity decreases with the amount of network-modifying oxides added to the silica, making it possible to adjust the trade-off between workability and thermal shock resistance to fit the application. An indication of the range of viscosity possible in silica glasses is given in Fig. 13.16.

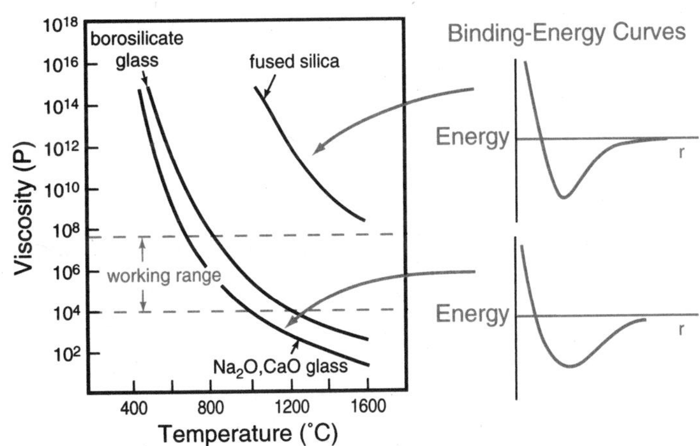

Fig. 13.16 . Effect of network modification on viscosity. (Adapted from E.B. Shand, *Modern Materials,* Vol. 6, Academic Press, N. Y., 1968, p. 262.)

Obviously, workability is of paramount importance for making glass fibers; hence, they normally contain only about 55% silica. The fibers are made by heating the glass in a platinum container with holes in it through which the fibers are drawn. The glass is a Newtonian-viscous fluid, meaning that it obeys Newton's law of viscous flow in which the rate of shear strain, $d\gamma/dt$, is proportional to the shear stress, τ.

$$d\gamma/dt = \tau/\eta \qquad \eta = \text{viscosity}$$

This also means that the tensile strain rate in a fiber being drawn is proportional to the tensile stress, σ.

$$\frac{d\varepsilon}{dt} \propto \sigma$$

or

$$\frac{dA}{Adt} \propto \frac{P}{A}$$

Therefore, the rate of reduction of area A, is proportional to the load, P.

$$\frac{dA}{dt} \propto P$$

The result is that the rate of thinning of the fiber, dA/dt, must be constant along the length of the fiber, since P is constant along the length. That is, the fiber can be drawn as much as desired without the formation of a neck, contrary to the case of a metallic wire (for which Newton's law does not hold, even when the wire is hot).

Glass fibers have an elastic modulus of about 70 GPa, compared with about 3 GPa for nylon, for example, but they are quite fragile. A freshly-drawn fiber is free of surface flaws, and in this state its fracture strength approaches the ideal value of about E/10. However, even slight contact with another solid can induce surface cracks due to the high stresses generated by even light loads when the contact area is very small. A surface crack can extend when the tensile stress reaches the value given by the Griffith equation. (See Appendix 9.2.)

Freshly drawn glass fibers are coated with *size* (an organic film) to protect their surfaces, but are further protected when embedded in a polymer. As noted earlier, this is one of the main functions of the matrix in a fiber-reinforced composite material: to protect the fibers from surface damage.

Wires made from eutectoid steel are also used in tire construction. For bicycles, they are used along the two beads that fit against the rim in a clincher-type
13250 tire, shown in Fig. 13.17(a), but they are also used for casing reinforcement in automobile tires. The wire-drawing process is the same as used to make piano wire and is called *patenting*. It involves a succession of drawing dies separated by baths of molten lead. The wire is drawn through a die and then passed into a lead bath so that it is heated above the eutectoid temperature and transformed to austenite. It passes into a second lead bath held at a temperature below 560°C, in which the wire transforms to fine pearlite. It is then cold drawn. The process may be repeated several times, and results in a microstructure in which cementite lamellae a few nanometers thick and spaced as closely as 40 nm are aligned with the wire axis, as shown in Fig. 13.17(b). The tensile strength can be as high as

1.5 GPa, and the Young's modulus is over 200 GPa. It is one of the strongest metallic materials available commercially and is surprisingly ductile, having a typical reduction in area of about 20%.

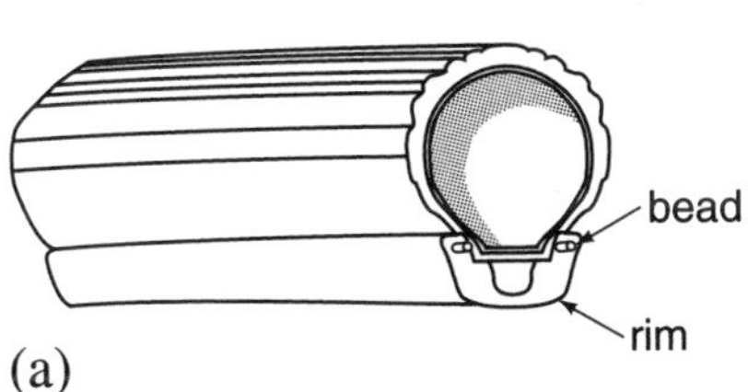

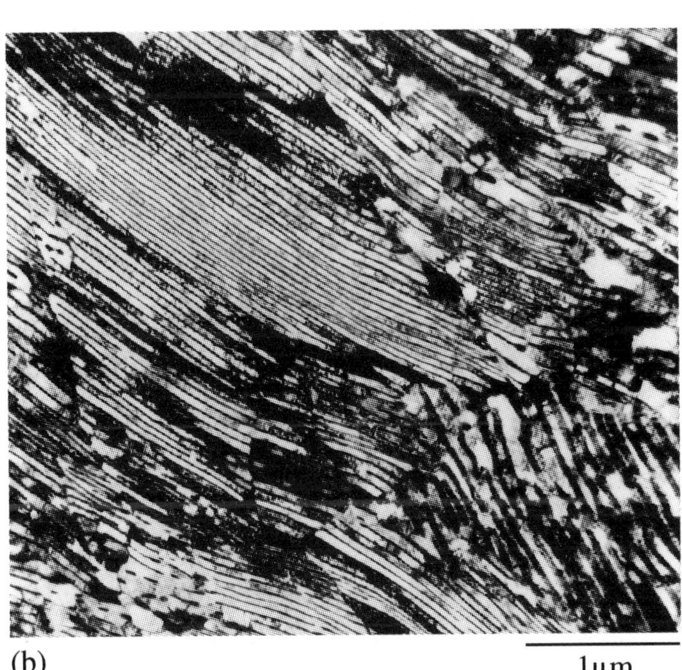

Fig. 13.17 (a) Steel wires are embedded in the rubber to hold the tire bead onto the wheel rim. (b) Section of cold-drawn wire of pearlitic steel (transmission electron micrograph, 20,000X). (G. Langford, *Metall. Trans. A,* vol. 8A, 1977, p. 861.)

A comparison of the stress-strain curves of the stiffest reinforcing fibers is made in Fig. 13.18. It is apparent that patented steel wire competes very well with carbon and Kevlar on the basis of elastic modulus. It is much more dense, however, and is not a viable choice where weight saving is important.

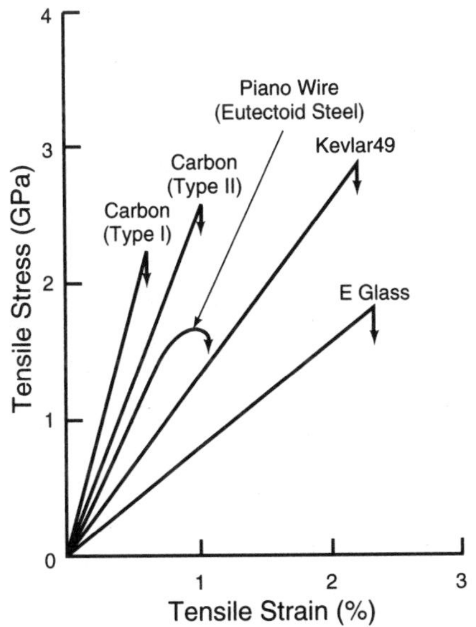

Composition of E Glass	
SiO_2	52.4
Al_2O_3, Fe_2O_3	14.4
CaO	17.2
MgO	4.6
Na_2O, K_2O	0.8
Ba_2O_3	10.6

Fig. 13.18 Comparison of the stress-strain curves of several high-strength fibers. (Adapted from D. Hull, *An Introduction to Composite Materials*, Cambridge University Press, 1981. Reprinted with permission of Cambridge University Press. , p. 15.)

13.3 Network Polymers for Composites and Adhesives

13.3.1 Formation of Network Polymers

Network polymers are used in bicycle construction both as adhesives and as the matrix materials in fiber-strengthened composites. The most common are epoxy resins. These applications require a material with enough fluidity to fill the spaces between fibers, or between parts to be adhesively bonded, that will cure into a stiff solid. Ideally, the solid would exhibit essentially no viscous behavior. That is, creep and stress relaxation are undesirable in this application. This can be achieved by forming a three-dimensional network with a very large number of links between the basic structural units. In this way the units are prevented from sliding past each other, and the solid becomes essentially one giant molecule. It is then a glassy material. Elastic deformation can occur only by distortion of the molecular cage. It can deform plastically by shear (which involves breaking of covalent bonds) only when loaded to high stresses in compression. The yield stress is so high that, when loaded in tension, the material would crack before yielding. Thus, such a network polymer would have a low fracture toughness.

The first commercially successful network polymers were the phenolic resins called Bakelite, invented by Leo Baekeland in 1907. The basic network-forming reaction employs formaldehyde, H_2CO, to link together molecules of phenol, which are mainly benzene rings and which can form links at up to three sites around the ring, as shown in Fig. 13.19. (Note that the H atoms lie at three types of sites in the phenol molecule, considering the symmetry with respect to the OH group.) This illustrates a general requirement for the formation of a network: The primary molecular building block must be multifunctional; that is, it must have more than two reaction sites per molecule. (A molecule having only two reaction sites would produce a linear polymer, rather than a network.)

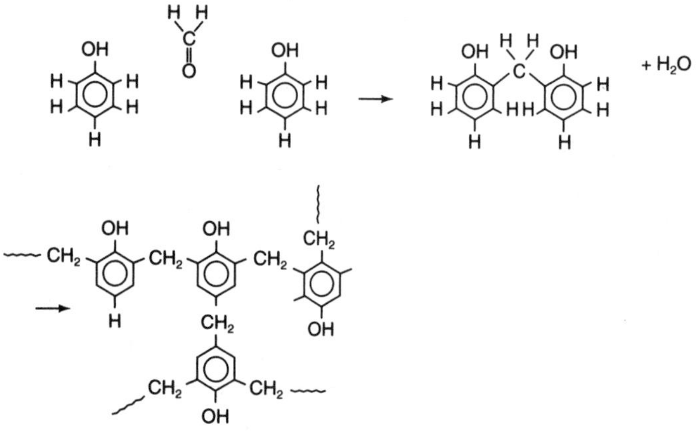

Fig. 13.19 Phenol-formaldehyde reaction. The phenol (C_6H_5OH) contributes hydrogen, and the formaldehyde (CH_2O) contributes oxygen to produce water as a by-product. The rings are joined by a CH_2 bridge. When this occurs in three dimensions, a network polymer is formed.

Epoxy resins are much more complicated chemically, but also much more versatile. To produce an epoxy resin one starts by forming a prepolymer by reacting epichlorohydrin and bisphenol A in an aqueous alkaline environment, as shown in Fig. 13.20. The former contains an epoxy group, which has the configuration

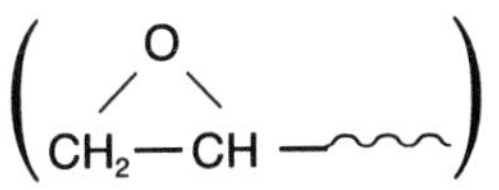

$$\left(\overset{\displaystyle O}{CH_2{-}CH}{-}\sim\!\sim\right)$$

and this provides the key factor in the later network formation. In order to have this group at both ends of the chain of the prepolymer, excess epichlorohydrin is used. The sodium hydroxide is needed to neutralize the HCl that forms as a by-product of this condensation reaction.

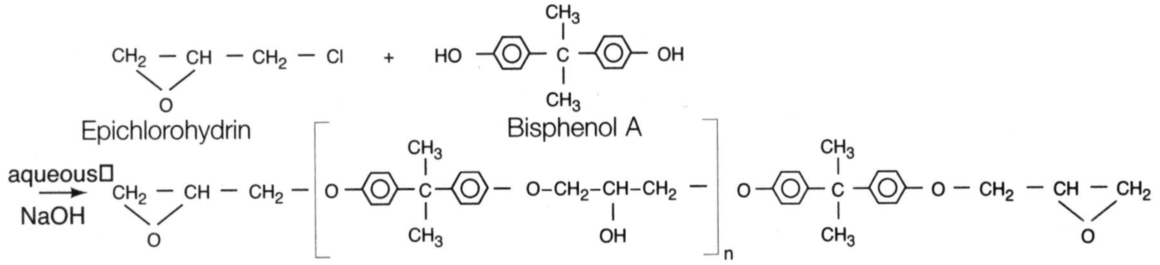

$CH_2-CH-CH_2-Cl$ (Epichlorohydrin) + $HO-C_6H_4-C(CH_3)_2-C_6H_4-OH$ (Bisphenol A)

$\xrightarrow{\text{aqueous NaOH}}$ $CH_2-CH-CH_2-\left[O-C_6H_4-C(CH_3)_2-C_6H_4-O-CH_2-CH(OH)-CH_2-\right]_n O-C_6H_4-C(CH_3)_2-C_6H_4-O-CH_2-CH-CH_2$ (terminal epoxy rings)

Fig. 13.20 Reaction of epichlorohydrin and bisphenol A to form the epoxy prepolymer.

This prepolymer can be produced as a solid (which may then be ground into a powder) or as a viscous fluid, depending on the degree of polymerization. The network is formed by reacting the prepolymer with a multifunctional curing agent that reacts with the terminal epoxy groups, as shown in Fig. 13.21.

13290

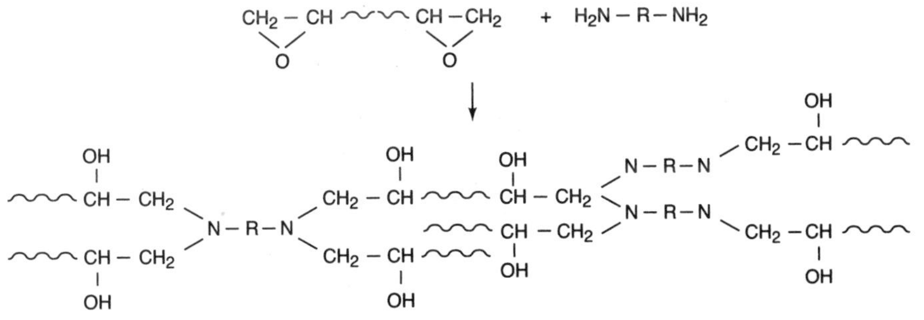

$CH_2-CH\sim\sim CH-CH_2$ (epoxy rings at both ends) + $H_2N-R-NH_2$

↓

$\sim\sim CH(OH)-CH_2-N(-CH_2-CH(OH)\sim\sim)-R-N(-CH_2-CH(OH)\sim\sim)_2$ … (crosslinked network of N–R–N links joined through $CH_2-CH(OH)$ groups)

Fig. 13.21 Formation of an epoxy resin by reacting the prepolymer with a diamine.

Because an epoxy prepolymer molecule may have an extended length, and because the network of the epoxy resin is formed by tying together only the ends of these molecules, the resin may exhibit a glass transition, in contrast with the behavior of a network polymer like Bakelite. However, room temperature is normally below the T_g of epoxies, so they are classified as brittle materials.

13.3.2 Adhesive Bonding

With regard to adhesive bonding with an epoxy resin, it is essential that intimate molecular contact be made between the resin and the substrate so that bonding forces are established between the atoms or ions on the substrate and the molecules of the resin. These bonding forces are usually of a secondary nature. Typical bond energies are compared in Table 13.2. Calculations of bond strengths in the case of the weakest secondary bonds, i.e., dispersion forces (due to induced dipoles arising from internal electron movements, apart from any permanent dipole moments), indicate that they would be higher than the bond strengths observed experimentally. It appears, therefore, that actual bond strengths are controlled by factors such as voids or other kinds of defects in the joint, or the action of stress raisers, or the failure to achieve intimate contact, rather than by the type of the molecular-level bonding achieved.

Table 13.2 Bond Types and Typical Bond Energies. (From A. J. Kinloch, *Adhesion and Adhesives,* Chapman and Hall, New York, 1987, p. 79.)

Bond Type		Bond Energy (kJ/mol)
Primary		
	Ionic	600 - 1000
	Covalent	60 - 700
	Metallic	110 - 350
Secondary - Hydrogen		
	Hydrogen bonds involving fluorine	Up to 40
	Hydrogen bonds not involving fluorine	10 - 25
Secondary - van der Waals		
	Permanent dipole-dipole interactions	4 - 20
	Dipole-induced dipole interactions	<2
	Dispersion (London) forces	0.08 - 40

For intimate contact the resin should wet the surface; that is, the contact angle should be zero (cf. Fig. 7.2). When it is not zero, pressure is required to force the resin to spread over the surfaces of the joint. The surface of the substrate may be roughened to provide increased area for bonding. (This also increases the fracture energy of the joint by increasing the amount of plastic or viscoelastic deformation accompanying the propagation of a crack along the joint.) The roughening may be done by a chemical process, like anodizing of aluminum, or by mechanical abrasion. A benefit of the latter is that it removes weak surface films like oil, grease and wax. However, surface roughening increases the contact angle, and thus it can complicate the achievement of intimate contact between the resin and substrate. In the case of an anodized surface, polymer molecules can actually diffuse into the surface pores by the process of *reptation* (i.e., snake-like penetration of the voids by the long-chain molecules), assuming wetting occurs or sufficient pressure is applied to the joint. This can give a very strong bond.

The design of an adhesive joint is important to its strength. It should avoid peeling-type forces, aiming rather for shear or compressive loading. In a proper joint the stresses are well distributed, and good resistance to fatigue failure can be achieved.

There are two types of epoxy resin in common use. In one, often referred to as a two-part adhesive, the curing agent is added to the prepolymer at the time of use, and the reaction occurs at ambient temperature. In the other, the curing agent is mixed with the prepolymer by the manufacturer, and the mixture must be heated for the curing reaction to occur. In either case, the curing reaction is designed to occur with no by-product; that is, it is not a condensation reaction.

13.4 Carbon-Fiber Reinforced Composites

13.4.1 Case Study of a Hybrid Composite Frame

A bicycle frame made from carbon-fiber reinforced plastic (CFRP) can have a Young's modulus comparable to metallic tubing, superior yield strength, and a much lower weight. This is still a relatively new engineering material, however, and the techniques for applying it to bicycles are still being developed. An example is a frame made of CFRP tubes, joined with components of cast aluminum alloy, as shown in Fig. 13.22(a).

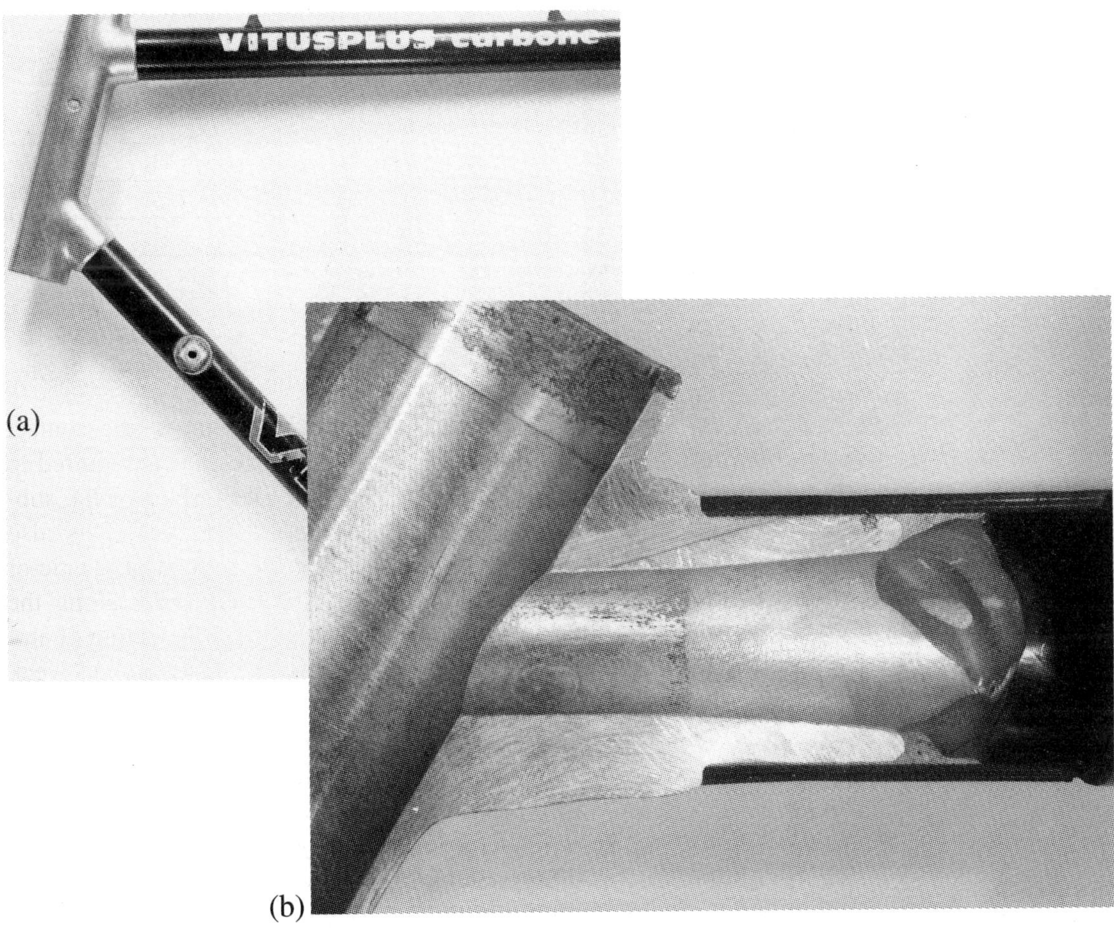

Fig. 13.22 (a) Part of a frame made from CFRP tubes joined to a cast-aluminum-alloy head tube. (b) The epoxy-adhesive joint between the CFRP tube and the head tube.

As shown in Fig. 13.22(b), the CFRP tube is attached to a protrusion on the aluminum-alloy head tube by means of an epoxy adhesive, as was done with the aluminum frame shown in Fig. 11.14. The potential problem with this design is that the abrupt change in cross-section of the frame at the joint produces a large localized change in stiffness of the frame. Such a discontinuity tends to act as a point of stress concentration; therefore, it is a point where a fracture could occur.

The microstructures of the three materials at the joint are shown in Fig. 13.23. The casting is a hypoeutectic Al-Si alloy, shown at higher magnification in Fig. 13.24(a). The α-Al dendrites make up about one-fifth of the microstructure, indicating that the alloy composition is about 10.5% silicon, as can be deduced by application of the lever rule to the Al-Si phase diagram shown in Fig.
13320 13.24(b). This type of alloy is commonly used for cast components of bicycles, such as pedal cranks, handlebar stems, etc.

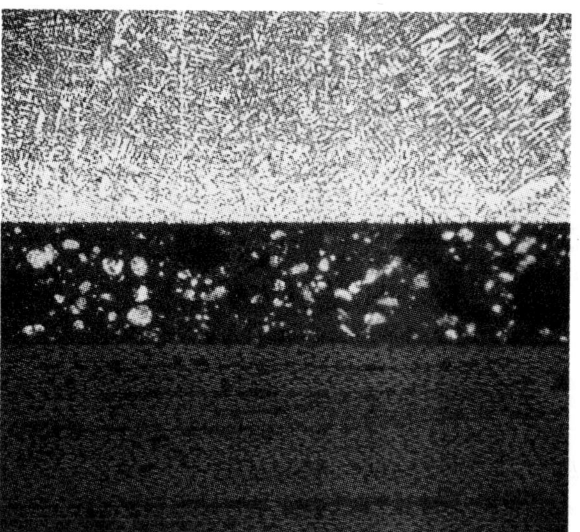

← Al alloy

← Epoxy

← CFRP

Fig. 13.23 Microstructures of the three materials across the joint shown in Fig. 13.22: the cast aluminum alloy, the epoxy adhesive, and the CFRP tube.

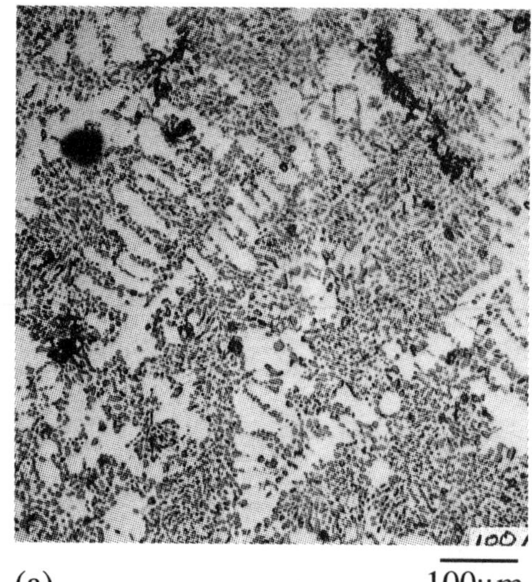

(a) 100μm

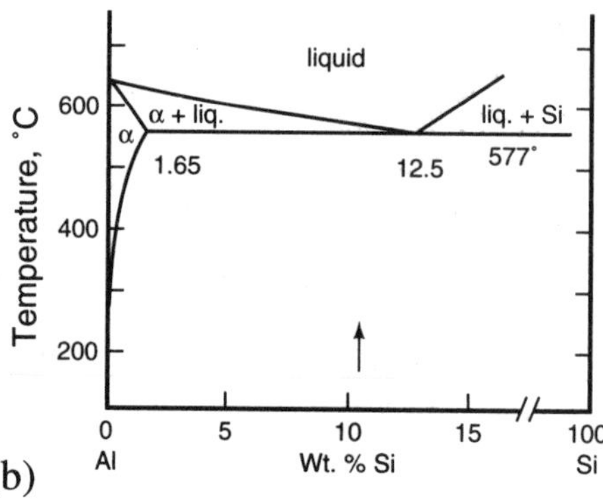

(b)

Fig. 13.24 (a) The aluminum alloy at a higher magnification and (b) the Al-Si phase diagram, the arrow showing the probable composition of the alloy.

The epoxy used for the adhesive contains particles that appear to be metallic. It was hypothesized that the particles are from an aluminum powder added to the epoxy to act as an inexpensive stiffener. This can be confirmed by an examination of the microstructure of the epoxy in a scanning-electron microscope (SEM) equipped with an energy-dispersive x-ray detector. The scanning-electron image of the epoxy and the x-ray map of this area, made with the characteristic x-rays emitted by aluminum, are shown in Fig. 13.25.

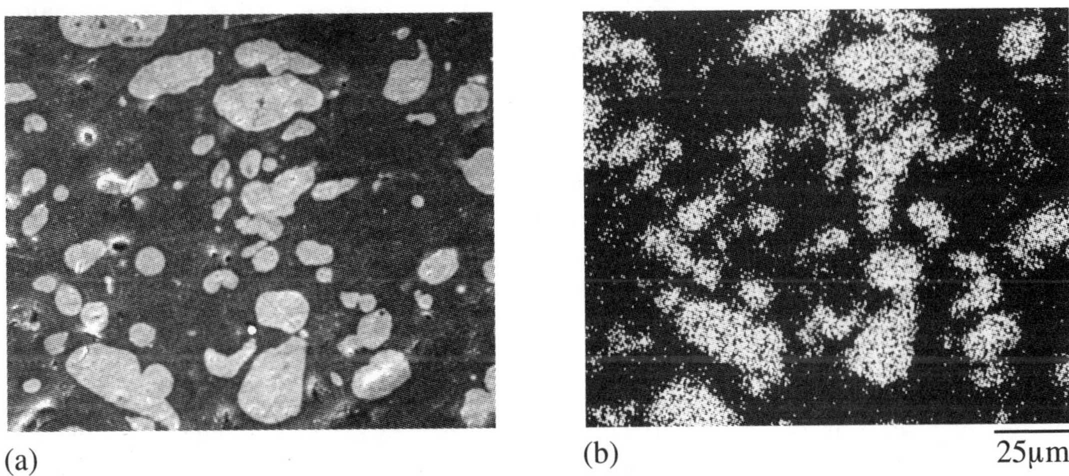

Fig. 13.25 (a) Scanning-electron image of the epoxy, showing the dispersed particles assumed to be aluminum. (b) Map made with x-rays having a wave-length characteristic of emission by aluminum, confirming that assumption. (Courtesy of Deborah Ricketts, Univ. of Penn.)

As shown in Fig. 13.26, a scanning electron microscope bears a great similarity to the transmission electron microscope shown in Fig. 4.15(a). The principal difference is the addition of deflection coils, similar to those used on a TV picture tube, which enable the electron beam to be scanned across the specimen. An image of the surface can be formed by collecting the back-scattered electrons in a detector and sending the signal from the detector to a cathode-ray tube (CRT), the beam of which is synchronized with the scanning electron beam. This is how the image in Fig. 13.25(a) was formed. The aluminum particles scatter more electrons than the surrounding epoxy, which is made of elements with lower atomic numbers than aluminum; hence, the signal from the particles is stronger, and they appear lighter than the epoxy matrix.

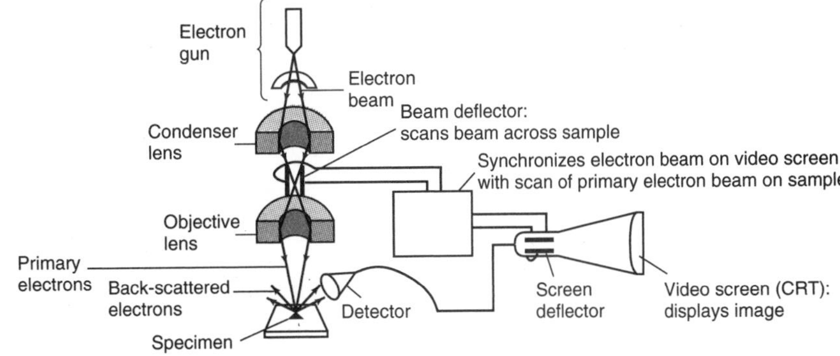

Fig. 13.26 Schematic representation of a scanning electron microscope.

The scanning electron beam knocks electrons out of their customary energy levels in the atoms near the surface of the specimen. This gives rise to the emission of x-rays as the excited electrons fall back to their former energy levels. Since each element emits its own characteristic x-ray spectrum, the x-rays emitted by the specimen can be used for chemical analysis of the surface regions. For this purpose the SEM must be equipped with an x-ray detector, the signal from which can be displayed on a CRT that is synchronized with the scanning electron beam.

Because it was suspected *a priori* that the particles were aluminum, the x-ray detector was tuned to an aluminum x-ray peak, and the signal was used to form the image on the CRT. The x-ray map thus formed, Fig. 13.25(b), shows a one-to-one correspondence between the particles in Fig. 13.25(a) and the regions emitting characteristic aluminum x-rays. Thus, the particles are aluminum-rich.

As shown in Table 2.1, the Young's modulus of aluminum is more than ten times that of an epoxy resin. Therefore, the addition of aluminum particles stiffens the epoxy to some extent. However, this is much less effective than stiffening by fibers; the modulus would be fairly close to the lower bound in Fig. 13.6. Nonetheless, the properties of the epoxy are improved somewhat by the addition of this "filler," which is actually less expensive than the epoxy. This works well as long as the epoxy bonds well to the particles. In the present case this is not a problem, since one of the two components being joined by the epoxy is, in fact, aluminum.

The epoxy contains a substantial amount of porosity, which is probably the result of air entrained when the epoxy was mixed. It may also have come from gases evolved during curing, if this was done at an elevated temperature. The epoxy adhesive appears to be bonded well to the epoxy matrix of the CFRP, as might be expected; no seam can be seen in the microscope. On the other side of the joint, the epoxy follows the contours of surface roughness of the aluminum casting, which gives a kind of mechanical locking along that interface.

The microstructure of the CFRP tubing is shown at low and high magnifications in Fig. 13.27. It is apparent that the tube was made in about 20 layers, with the carbon fibers in different orientations in the various layers. In the section cut transverse to the longitudinal direction, Fig. 13.27(a) and (b), a good deal of porosity can be seen between the layers where the bonding between them was incomplete. This is probably not a serious defect, since there is only a stress across these interfaces when the tube is twisted.

The layers were probably made from tape in which the carbon fibers were held in a partially cured epoxy. The layers of tape were probably laid up on a cylindrical form, called a mandrel, and the completed tube was then cured, probably at an elevated temperature. In some of the layers the fibers run along the longitudinal direction, since their cross-sections are circular in Fig. 13.27(b). The diameter of the fibers can be estimated to be about 6μm. The layers in which the fibers exhibit an elliptical cross-section are obviously ones in which the tape was wound in a helix around the mandrel. The longitudinal fibers are meant to resist bending of the tube, and the helically wound fibers are meant to resist twisting.

The layers in which the tape runs longitudinally can be seen more clearly in Fig. 13.27(c), where these layers comprise fiber sections that are very long ellipses. (They would be infinitely long if the fibers were straight and the plane of the section were exactly parallel to the fiber axis.) It can be seen that in this tube, which was the down tube, the longitudinal fibers are in the first six layers, counting from the inside diameter (bottom of Fig. 13.27c), and in the twelfth and thirteenth layers. Presumably, this tube design was based on a stress analysis for this particular tube and the expected loads to be applied.

Note that this tube could not be analyzed using the beam theory outlined in Chapter 11 because it is not uniform. That is, the elastic modulus varies from layer to layer due to the different fiber orientations. This is one of the great advantages of using fiber-reinforced composites; the properties can be tailored to fit the requirements within the cross-section of the component itself.

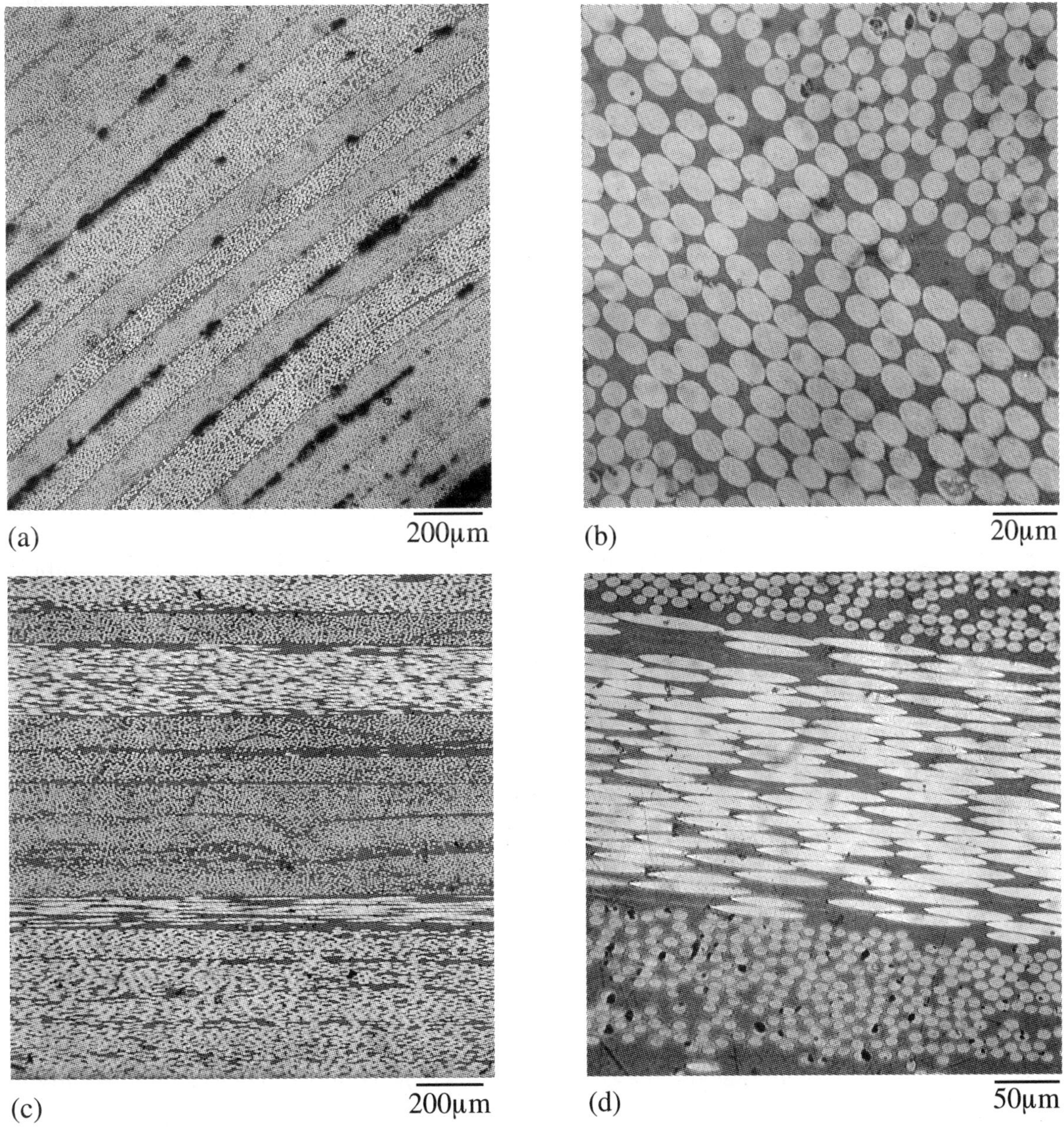

Fig. 13.27 (a) and (b) transverse section of the CFRP down tube shown in Fig. 14.22. (c) and (d) longitudinal section of the same tube.

The tensile behavior of the CFRP tube can be demonstrated by the stress-strain curve shown in Fig. 13.28(a). It is apparent that the tube is completely brittle; it failed in tension without any detectable plastic deformation. Thus, although the CFRP is stiff and light, it has almost no capacity to absorb energy when it fractures, as a metallic material would. A portion of the fracture surface of the CFRP as observed in the scanning electron microscope is shown in Fig. 13.28(b)*. The main feature is the protrusion of broken fibers above the fracture surface of the epoxy. This means that the fibers broke while embedded in the epoxy and were then pulled out of the matrix. This fiber-pullout phenomenon is a common feature of the fracture of composites, and provides a mechanism for some energy dissipation during fracture and makes a contribution to the fracture toughness of a composite material.

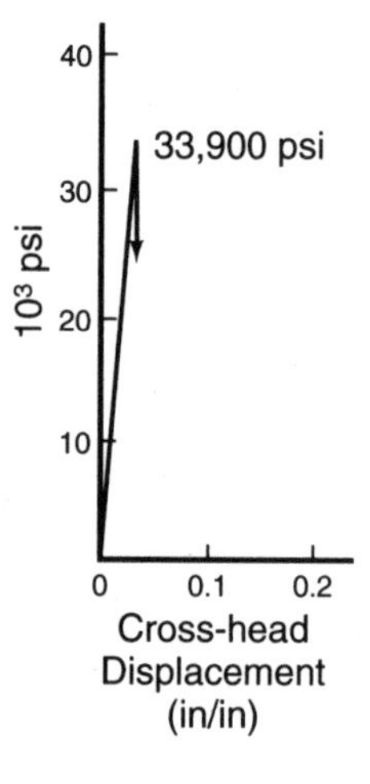

(a)

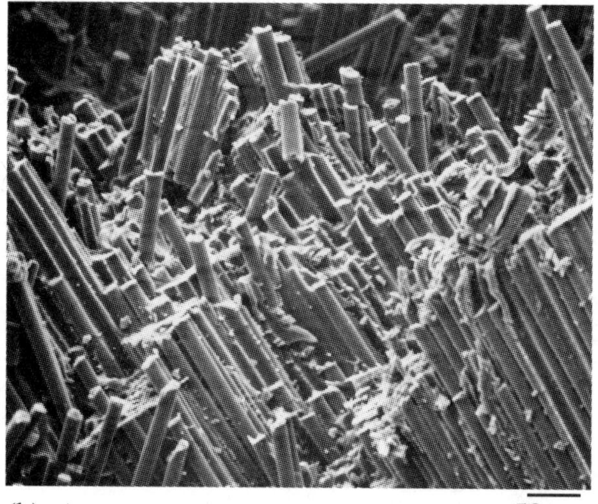

(b) 50μm

Fig. 13.28 (a) Stress-strain curve of CFRP tube shown in Fig. 13.22. (b) Scanning-electron micrograph of the fracture surface, showing the results of fiber pullout.

Brittle behavior is an unavoidable feature of the CFRP. It is necessary that the polymer matrix be glassy; otherwise, the flexing of the tubing during use would dissipate energy. That is, the bicycle would have a "spongy" feel to a rider. Because the polymer matrix is not viscoelastic, it cannot act as a microcrack arrestor when the fibers start to break. The result is that the CFRP used for bicycle tubing is inherently brittle (as opposed to fishing rods or vaulting poles, which are intended to be flexible). Because of this behavior, it can be risky to make a component like the front fork of a bicycle out of CFRP. Front forks can receive large, sudden loads, and a brittle failure here would obviously threaten rider safety.

13.4.2 Monocoque Frames

A logical next step after CFRP tubes bonded to metal connecting pieces was to construct a one-piece frame using a continuously wound carbon-fiber tape impregnated with partially cured epoxy, with metal reinforcement at critical places. The first commercial-scale bicycle of this kind was the Kestrel, an example of which is shown in Fig. 13.29. Except for the elongated cross-section of the members, the frame has essentially the same shape as a conventional road bike.

* This image was formed by *secondary* electrons emitted from the specimen, rather than back-scattered electrons as used in Fig. 13.25

Fig. 13.29 A monocoque CFRP frame by Kestrel.

A radically different frame design, permitted by use of the monocoque CFRP approach, was the Zipp frame shown in Fig. 13.30. The rear section has the shape of a boomerang, and the seat is cantilevered over the back wheel by a CFRP bar that acts somewhat as a shock absorber. Obviously, one must have complete confidence in the fracture resistance of this bar, because a failure here would be disasterous for the rider.

Fig. 13.30 The Zipp CFRP frame with cantilevered seat.

Perhaps the most famous monocoque bike is the one developed by Lotus of England for the 1992 Olympic Games in Barcelona, based on an original 1982 design by Mike Burrows. On this bike, shown in Fig. 13.31, a new world record was set in the 4000m pursuit race by gold medalist Chris Boardman of England. The frame has an air-foil cross section, and the wheels are held by axles cantilevered from the frame and monoblade front section, respectively. The monocoque was formed from carbon-fiber cloth impregnated with epoxy resin over a polyurethane foam core with Kevlar inserts. The steering column was titanium, and the chainset, pedals, and rear sprocket were made from titanium and steel. The stress analysis needed for the optimization of the geometry was done by the finite-element method. In this technique the frame and wheels are modeled by a mesh of elements of known strength and stiffness, each of which bears its part of the total load. When a load is applied to the frame or wheel in the computer model, the stress on any element can be calculated by the computer program, and this reveals the necessary carbon-fiber configuration at that location. This is a good example of how modern engineering design can be coupled with the custom tailoring of a material to give the required properties at every point in a structure.

Fig. 13.31 The Lotus monocoque pursuit racing bike.

13.4.3 Composite Wheels

In support of the adage that there is nothing new under the sun, one can find in the book by Archibald Sharp (1896) the picture that is reproduced here as Fig. 13.32. It shows both a disc wheel on the rear and an aerodynamically configured four-spoke wheel on the front of an early diamond-frame bicycle. Thus, what are taken today as recent innovations had actually been introduced within a few years of the development of the modern diamond frame. The disc wheel is intended to reduce the aerodynamic drag caused by spokes. It is suitable as a rear wheel, but would produce difficulties in steering if placed on the front, because the center of aerodynamic pressure would be forward of the steering axis. This would create unwanted torque, especially in strong cross winds. Therefore, a more open design is needed for the front wheel. It can be seen that a disc wheel and a three-spoke aerodynamic wheel were used in the Zipp and Lotus bikes (Figs. 13.30 and 13.31).

Fig. 13.32 A rendering of an early bicycle with a rear disc wheel and an open-spoke wheel in the front. (A. Sharp, 1896, loc. cit. p. 352.)

Another version of the open-spoked wheel was introduced by the DuPont Company in 1990 and is shown in Fig. 13.33(a). Its design utilized wind-tunnel experiments to minimize drag on the spokes and rim, arriving at the shapes shown in Fig. 13.33(b). The rim acts both as the leading edge and the trailing edge of an airfoil as the wheel rotates. The fact that the wheel has about 50% open area gives it good steering characteristics and stability in cross winds. The wind-tunnel experiments showed that this design had the lowest drag of any wheel tested and only about one-third the drag of a conventional 36-spoke wheel and one-half of that of a 24-spoke wheel.

The wheel is fabricated from CFRP fabric impregnated with epoxy resin. The number, orientation, and packing density of the carbon filaments required to give the wheel the desired stiffness and strength, especially when loaded between the spokes, was determined by computer modeling using the finite-element method. The type of mesh used is shown in Fig. 13.33(c).

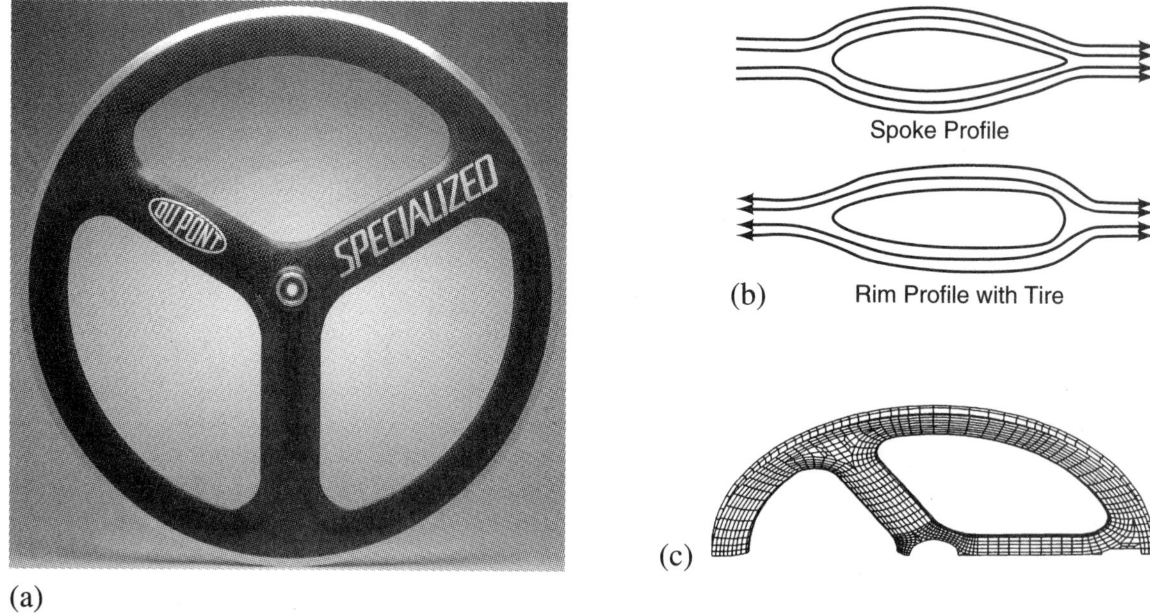

Fig. 13.33 (a) The DuPont composite wheel. (b) The profiles of the spokes and rim as optimized to minimize drag. (c) Mesh used for finite-element model of the wheel. (M. W. Hopkins et al., 35th Intnl. SAMPE Symposium, April, 1990.)

Summary

In a fiber-reinforced (FR) composite material such as a rubber tire or bicycle frame, the function of the fibers is to carry the load. This is achieved by employing a fiber with an elastic modulus greater than that of the matrix. The main function of the matrix is to deform and, by so doing, to transfer load to the fibers.

The stiffness of a FR composite depends on the orientation of the fibers relative to the stress. Thus, when stress is applied along the fiber direction, the modulus of the composite follows a rule of mixtures in which the modulus increases linearly with the volume fraction of fibers. When stress is applied at right angles to the fibers, the modulus of the composite depends mainly on that of the matrix until the volume fraction of fibers is well in excess of 50%. When the fibers are not continuous, the load transfer occurs over a certain distance at each end of a fiber, and this means that the efficiency of stiffening of the composite by the fibers is significantly reduced from the continuous-fiber case.

The first fibers used for tires were completely natural, namely cotton. Later, a partially man-made fiber was invented; this was rayon, or cellulose acetate. The first completely man-made fiber was nylon, which is made by a condensation reaction, as opposed to the addition polymerization used to make PE. Nylon has a backbone of single covalent bonds, almost the same as PE, but it also has hydrogen bonds, which retard interchain sliding more effectively than the van der Waals bonds between PE chains. A more recent invention was Kevlar, which is a polyamide like nylon (and therefore has interchain hydrogen bonds), but which has aromatic rings along the chains that give the chains considerably more stiffness than the single covalent bonds of PE and nylon. The ultimate in stiffness is found in fibers made from graphitized polymers. Here, the aromatic rings extend in two dimensions, and the chain-like structure is almost completely converted to one of irregularly interleaved sheets.

A common reinforcing fiber is silica-based glass. This is a three-dimensional amorphous structure in which covalently bonded and linked SiO_4^{4-} tetrahedra are mixed with network modifiers in sufficient quantity to allow fiber drawing at reasonably low temperatures. The drawing is done simply by pulling on the fibers (above T_g), which works by virtue of the Newtonian-viscous nature of molten glass. Another inorganic fiber used in tires is patented eutectoid steel, or "piano wire." This can compete with graphite fibers in terms of stiffness and strength, but not density.

The opposite end of the spectrum from a thermoplastic linear polymer is a thermosetting network polymer, the prototype of which was Bakelite, or phenol formaldehyde. Toward the latter end of this spectrum are the highly cross-linked polymers used for adhesives and as the matrix for fiber-reinforced components of very high stiffness, such as CFRP bicycle tubes. Epoxies are the most common example. They employ a prepolymerization by a condensation reaction and then a multifunctional curing agent that ties the ends of the prepolymer chains together into a three-dimensional network. The T_g and the extent of viscoelastic behavior depend on the lengths of the chains of the prepolymer.

Part of a bicycle frame fabricated from CFRP tubes adhesively bonded to aluminum-alloy fittings was dissected and examined metallographically, including the use of an SEM with x-ray analysis. A tensile test of a specimen cut from a tube illustrated the low toughness of this material. The use of CFRP to make monocoque frames and wheels was illustrated by means of recently developed products.

Glossary/Vocabulary - Chapter 13

Anisotropic — A body is anisotropic with respect to some property if the value of that property depends on the direction along which that property is measured. A fiber-reinforced fishing rod is anisotropic with respect to most properties. For example, it is stiffer in the axial direction than in the transverse direction.

Aspect ratio — This is the ratio of length to diameter of a fiber. In a fiber-reinforced composite with discontinuous fibers, the larger the aspect ratio the smaller is the fraction of the total length occupied by the transfer length, thus the greater the efficiency of the fiber reinforcement.

Bakelite — This is the commercial name for the network polymer phenol formaldehyde. It is a three-dimensional network of aromatic rings connected by CH_2 bridges. Bakelite is made by a condensation reaction by mixing phenol, C_6H_5OH, and formaldehyde, CH_2O, from which water is a by-product. The incompletely polymerized compound can be ground up and later compacted with pressure and heat to complete the reaction and produce its final solid shape.

Carbon fiber This is a high-strength, high-modulus fiber made from a graphitized polymer. It comprises essentially highly defective long sheets of graphite parallel to the fiber axis. The common types are either high-strength (2.7 GPa) with a modulus of about 250 GPa or lower strength (2.2 GPa) with a modulus of about 390 GPa.

Cellulose This is the natural fiber found in plants, including wood. Wood fibers reacted with acetate compounds produce cellulose acetate, of which rayon is an example. This was one of the first commercially produced polymers.

Carbon-fiber reinforced plastic, CFRP This is a composite material in which graphitized carbon fibers are embedded in a polymer matrix, often an epoxy resin. The volume fraction of fibers can be on the order of 2/3, in which case the elastic modulus in the fiber direction can be about 25% higher than that of steel, if a high-modulus fiber is used.

Cold-drawing of a linear polymer This is a process for making fibers out of a linear polymer. A pre-fiber is pulled from the melt and then pulled again while cold so that the coiled molecules are straightened and aligned. This occurs inhomogeneously, starting in a kind of neck and propagating along the pre-fiber. Nylon fibers are made by this process. The process can be demonstrated by pulling on the polyethylene rings used to package beverage cans in six-packs.

Composite elastic modulus This is the overall elastic modulus of a composite material. It is a function of the shape, orientation, volume fraction, and modulus of the reinforcing phase and of the modulus and volume fraction of the matrix phase. For a fiber-reinforced composite with continuous fibers, the composite modulus in the direction of the fibers follows a rule of mixtures. That is, it is a linear sum of the modulus times the volume fraction of each phase.

Condensation polymerization This is a method of polymerization in which two reacting species produce a mer with at least two functional groups that can bond to other such mers to form a chain or a network. Nylon is a linear polymer produced by a condensation reaction between hexamethylene diamine and adipic acid. Bakelite is a network polymer made by a condensation reaction between phenol and formaldehyde.

Crack arrest A crack in a brittle material can be arrested if it runs into a phase that is tougher (i.e., less brittle). The driving force for crack propagation is the release of elastic strain energy (created by the applied stress). When the crack runs into the tougher material, strain energy is dissipated by plastic deformation of this material at the crack tip. Then, if there is insufficient energy to continue to drive the crack, it stops.

Curing agent This is the reagent that is used to bind the pre-polymer molecules of an epoxy into a three-dimensional network. It must be able to form bonds at more than two sites, otherwise it would only be capable of forming a chain. A diamine, $H_2N\text{-}R\text{-}NH_2$, can bind to the ends of four pre-polymer chains, one at each of the hydrogen sites.

Discontinuous fibers See transfer length and aspect ratio.

Drawing of glass fibers Fibers can be drawn from molten glass by merely pulling on the stream of viscous glass that comes through the plate-with-holes called a spinnerette. The cross section of the viscous stream decreases uniformly; that is, necking does not occur, because the glass obeys Newton's law of viscous flow. The freshly drawn cold fiber has a strength approaching the theoretical strength of glass (~E/10, ~ 7.6GPa), because it contains no surface flaws. Once the fiber is contacted by another solid body, however, the strength drops precipitously to the value given by the Griffith equation, because tiny surface cracks are generated by the contact stress, which can be very high, given the very small area of contact.

Energy-dispersive x-ray analysis This is often done in a scanning electron microscope using a device that can discriminate among the components of an emitted x-ray beam as a function of the energy of the photons. When converted to wavelength, the results can be displayed as peaks of various intensities (proportional to the number of photons) as a function of wavelength. It can also be used to make an "x-ray map" of the various phases in a material. The particles of aluminum in a filled epoxy adhesive can be revealed by making an image with the x-rays having the wavelength characteristic of aluminum (K_α).

Epoxy adhesives An epoxy adhesive is a network polymer made by reacting a prepolymer that contains the epoxy group (a ring of -O-CH_2-CH-) at each end with a multifunctional molecule that can bond to at least four ends of prepolymer molecules. Epoxies are used for adhesive bonding of tubes in bicycle frames and for the matrix of carbon-fiber-reinforced-polymer (CFRP) composite materials.

Fiber pull-out When a fiber-reinforced composite material fractures, the fibers often are broken not in the ultimate plane of the fracture but in locations removed from it. In this case, the crack surfaces are bridged by unbroken segments of fiber that must be pulled out of the matrix as the crack opens. This is an energy-absorbing process that contributes to the toughness of the composite, because work must be done against the resistance to shear in the fiber/matrix interface.

Fiber-reinforced composite This is a composite material that usually comprises a compliant matrix in which are embedded stiffer fibers. The function of the fibers is to carry the load, and the matrix holds the fibers together and transfers load to them. A tire is an example of a fiber-reinforced composite.

Finite-element method This is a method for calculating the stresses and strains in various parts of a complicated structure under external loads. The structure is modeled by a mesh of small linear elements of specified stiffness. A computer program is used to solve for the stress in each element. This method is necessary for the design of the fiber orientations in various locations of a monocoque structure like a bicycle frame or wheel.

Kevlar This is a linear polymer used to make high-strength, high modulus fibers. It is a polyamide, poly(p-phenylene terephthalamide). The chains are essentially benzene rings connected by amide groups. The chains are bonded to each other in the form of sheets by hydrogen bonds, and the sheets lie parallel to the axis of the fiber.

Network modifiers These are metal oxides that, when mixed with molten silica, break up the network of SiO_4^- tetrahedra, so that the viscosity is reduced. This is done to make forming of complex shapes easier at moderate temperatures. Commonly used oxides for this purpose are CaO, MgO, Na_2O, K_2O, BaO, Al_2O_3, and Fe_2O_3.

Newtonian viscosity This is time-dependent deformation behavior in which the material follows Newton's law in which strain rate is proportional to stress, with the proportionality constant equal to $1/\eta$, where η is the viscosity. Most fluids follow this law. Amorphous linear polymers are assumed to follow it also.

Nylon This was the first completely man-made fiber. It is a polyamide, and it essentially comprises short paraffin segments between amide groups, [O=C-N-H]. Nylon fibers are highly crystalline and are made by cold-drawing of partly crystalline pre-fibers pulled from the melt.

Patenting of steel This is a process for making ultra-high-strength wire from a eutectoid steel. It involves successive stages of austenitizing, transforming to fine pearlite in a lead bath, and cold drawing. The result is a composite of ferrite and cementite in which the cementite lamellae have a thickness on the order of nanometers and are spaced tens of nanometers apart. This is used for tire cord and for piano wire.

Polyacrilonitrile, PAN This is a vinyl polymer with the fourth side-group as a nitrile group [-C≡N]. PAN is used as a precursor for the production of carbon fibers.

Polyamide This is a polymer the mer of which contains the amide group, [O=C-N-H]. Nylon is a polyamide; so is Kevlar.

Pre-impregnated tape, "prepreg" This is a tape made of a woven fiber, like graphitized carbon or Kevlar, impregnated with uncured epoxy that, when heated, will cure into a rigid fiber-reinforced solid. Such a tape can be wrapped, in layers if desired, around a pre-form like polystryene foam, to make a monocoque structure, such as a bicycle frame. It could also be wrapped around a removable mandrel to make tubes for conventional bicycle frames in which the tubes are connected by adhesive bonding to special fittings, like metal lugs.

Reptation This is the process by which diffusion occurs in a linear polymer. The long-chain molecules migrate by a snake-like motion through the tangle of neighboring chains. By this process, welding can take place between two polymeric components that are brought into contact and heated. Chains on each side of the joint reptate across the interface into the other polymer.

Rule of mixtures Applied to a composite material, this means that a property of the composite is the sum over all phases of the corresponding property of each phase times the volume fraction of that phase. In a composite strengthened by continuous parallel fibers, the modulus of the composite in the direction of the fibers follows the rule of mixtures: $E_c=E_fV_f+E_mV_m$, where m and f refer to matrix and fibers, respectively.

Scanning-electron microscope, SEM This is an electron microscope used to examine the surface of specimens too thick for transmission electron microscopy. The surface is imaged by electrons scattered or emitted from the surface when it is swept by an electron beam, much the same as the sweeping of the beam in a TV picture tube. The SEM is the primary tool for the examination of fracture surfaces.

Silica glass This is an inorganic glass based on SiO_2. Pure silica glass is just fused and vitrified quartz. Most silica-based glasses contain one or more metal oxides, known as network modifiers, added to decrease the viscosity above the glass-transition temperature and thereby make the glass easier to work into shapes at convenient temperatures.

Spinnerette This is a plate with many small holes through which can be forced a viscous fluid, like a polymer or a silica-based glass, to make the precursors of fibers. The precursors to nylon fibers are made by forcing the polymer melt through the holes of a spinnerette.

Transfer length In a fiber-reinforced composite with discontinuous fibers loaded parallel to the fibers, where the matrix (having a lower elastic modulus) tends to deform more than the fibers, load is transferred from the matrix to the fibers because the two are bonded together. In the central portion of a fiber, the displacements in the fiber and the matrix are the same, but at the ends of a fiber the displacements are not the same, thereby creating a shear stress in the fiber/matrix interface. This shear stress diminishes to zero over the transfer length, and over this length the tensile stress in the fiber rises from zero to its maximum value. Over the transfer length, the fiber is not carrying as much of the load of which it is capable. Thus, a composite with discontinuous fibers is less efficient in its use of the fibers than is one with continuous fibers.

Exercises

13.1 A fiber-reinforced composite consists of continuous, parallel strands of glass fiber (E = 70 GPa) embedded in a polyester resin (E = 4.0 GPa). The fibers occupy 65% of the total volume. Calculate the elastic modulus of the composite.

(a) in the direction parallel to the fibers, and

(b) in the direction perpendicular to the fibers.

13.2 A fiber composite is to be made from Kevlar polyamide fibers (E = 130 GPa) in an epoxy matrix (E = 5 GPa). (a) What volume fraction of Kevlar fibers is needed to make the longitudinal modulus of the composite equal to 45 GPa? (b) What volume fraction of fibers would be needed if one substituted for the Kevlar either Type-I or Type-II carbon fibers? (Use Table 2.1.)

13.3 Calculate the curvature in a cylindrical bundle of 100 fibers bonded together, instead of the four-fiber bundle shown in Fig. 13.1. Do the same for 1000 fibers in the bundle.

13.4 With regard to the choice of matrix for a fiber-composite, compare the expected crack-arresting capabilities of a glassy thermoset *vs.* a cross-linked linear polymer above its glass-transition temperature. What are the advantages and disadvantages of each type of matrix?

13.5 Why, in a composite strengthened by discontinuous parallel fibers, should the fiber length be made as long as possible?

13.6 Use Fig. 13.16 to explain why Pyrex®, a borosilicate glass, is used to make kitchenware that can be transferred from the refrigerator to the stove without breaking, as opposed to pure silica, which would have the ultimate thermal-shock resistance, or soda-lime glass, which would have the ultimate workability. Include an explanation of what is meant by thermal shock and workability, and how and why these are changed according to the composition of the glass. Which kind of silica-based glass is used for making fibers, and why?

13.7 (a) Explain why a multifunctional polymer molecule is needed to make a network polymer. (b) There is an important difference between the reaction used to make Bakelite and that used for curing of an epoxy resin (not in making the prepolymer). What is it and why would it be important for some applications?

13.8 Explain the important factors in the functioning of an adhesive.

13.9 Using Fig. 13.27 as an example, describe the considerations that a bicycle designer would use in specifying how the layers of so-called pre-preg tape (carbon fibers in partially cured epoxy) are to be laid-up in the manufacture of a bicycle tube.

14

COMPLEX MULTISCALE COMPOSITES: TIRES

As experience has shown, the tires of cars and trucks are critical components from the standpoint of safety, as well as being important for fuel economy and performance of the vehicle. Modern vehicle tires are highly sophisticated and complex composite-material systems. They consist of an elastomeric matrix reinforced on the macroscale by various types of fibers and on the nanoscale by graphitic particles of carbon black and/or silica and other reinforcing fillers. The matrix is formed from a combination of natural and synthetic rubbers, mostly polydienes. At the end of the manufacturing cycle, the matrix is cross linked with sulfur by vulcanization.

The properties and performance depend sensitively on the kind of rubber selected for the tread. In particular, different choices have to be made depending on whether one wants to maximize tread wear or driving performance. The technology continues to evolve, and opportunities exist for new developments in materials engineering.

Tires have to serve a number of functions. Referring to the numbered arrows in Fig. 14.1, they must:

1. carry the load of the vehicle,
2. provide cushioning and damping,
3. transmit torque for accelerating and braking,
4. provide a cornering force (lateral force on turns),
5. generate a steering response, and
6. have low rolling resistance.

In addition, tires have to resist abrasion, generate minimum noise and vibration, be durable over their life span, and be dimensionally stable.

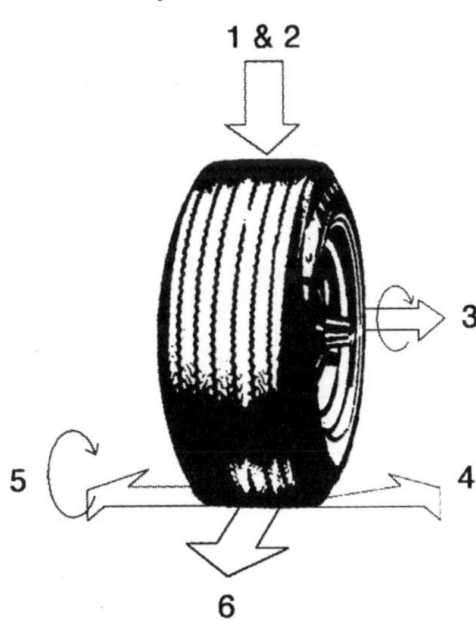

Fig. 14.1 Forces and torques applied to a tire.

14.1 Tire Construction

Tires can be made in two configurations; the older technology is bias ply and the newer is radial ply. These are illustrated in Fig. 14.2. In bias-ply tires the cord runs at an angle of 25 to 40° to the centerline of the tire.

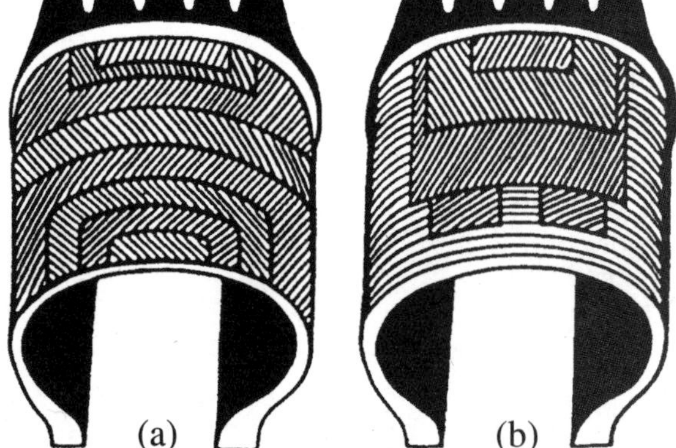

Fig. 14.2 (a) Bias-ply *vs* (b) radial-ply construction of tires. (From T. L. Ford and F. S. Charles, *Basic Compounding and Processing of Rubber,* H. Long ed., ACS Rubber Division 1985)

The important components of a radial tire are illustrated in Fig. 14.3. The tread has to provide wear resistance, traction, wet-skid response, good cornering, and minimal generation of heat. This is achieved by blending combinations of natural rubber (NR), polybutadiene (PBD), and styrene-butadiene rubber (SBR) along with carbon black or silica, oils, vulcanizing agents, and stabilizers.

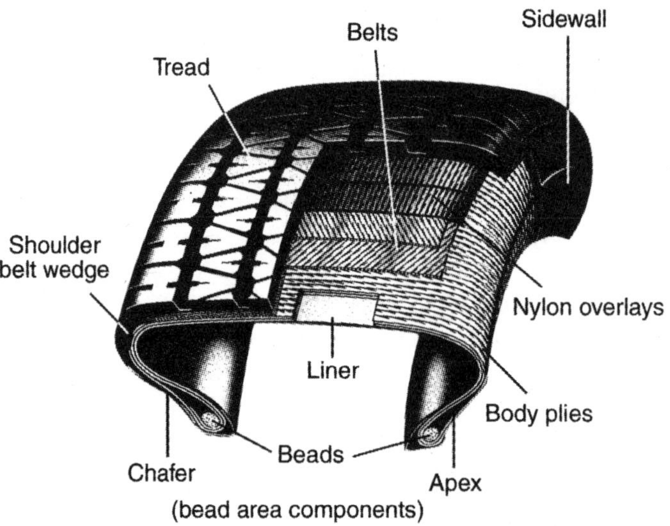

Fig. 14.3 Components of an automobile tire. (Reprinted from F. J. Kovac and M. B. Rodgers, *Science and Technology of Rubber.* 2nd ed, J. E. Mark, B. Erman, and F. R. Eirich eds., Academic Press, 1994, with permission from Elsevier.)

The **belts** are layers of (usually) steel wire that run circumferentially beneath the tread. They stiffen the casing and protect the underlying ply cords from road hazzards. They also help to resist wear and damage and improve handling response.

Cords are made by twisting filaments of either steel or textile into a yarn, and then twisting two or more yarns to form the string-like cord.

The **plies** are the primary reinforcement of the casing. They are usually textile cords extending from bead to bead, with a turn-up around the beads.

The **beads** are loops of steel-wire cord that anchor the plies and lock the tire onto the rim.

The **tread base** is a rubber compound designed to give good adhesion to the belt and to help in heat dissipation and in giving low rolling resistance.

The **nylon overlays** around the belt are there to resist expansion of the tire from centrifugal force at high speeds.

The **sidewalls** protect the casing and help to support the tread; they also exert major control of the ride characteristics of the vehicle/tire combination.

The **liner** is a butyl-type rubber that covers the inside of the tire body and contains the compressed air.

The bead-area components are the **apex**, which fills the bead/ply region, and the **chafer**, which protects the bead wires.

Finally, the **shoulder belt wedge** comprises high-adhesive rubber compounds in the shoulder region between the belts and the casing. It is there to improve tread-wear resistance and durability.

Example 14.1

Q. Belts are necessary for radial-ply tires, but not for bias-ply tires. Explain why.

A. The angled cords in the bias-ply tire would resist circumferential forces, as from braking or acceleration, but the radial-ply cords would not. Therefore, belts are needed in the latter.

14.2 Reinforcement Materials

As indicated in Fig. 14.4, the first tire cords were made from cotton, the use of which did not disappear completely until almost 1960. Rayon started to be used around 1940, and its use lasted until after 1980. Nylon started around 1950 and is still widely used. Polyester started in the 1960s, followed by fiberglass, steel, and aramids (like Kevlar.) The principal fibers today are polyester, nylon, and steel. Except for polyester, these fibers have already been discussed in the previous chapter, so we will add only a consideration of polyesters here.

14030 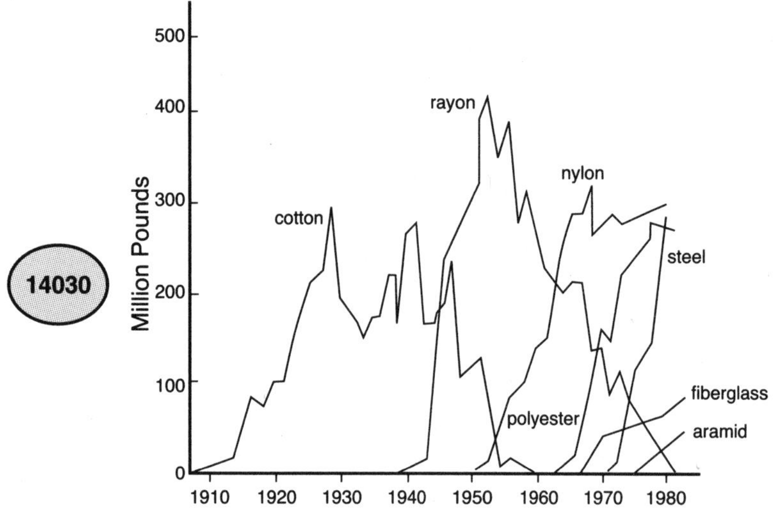

Fiber	Modulus (grams per denier - gpd)*
Cotton	70
Rayon	120
Nylon	50
Polyester	80
Fiberglass	260
Steel	280
Aramid	500

Fig. 14.4 Trends in tire-cord usage. (From R.J. Dill & H. Long, *Basic Compounding and Processing of Rubber,* H. Long ed., ACS Rubber Division 1985)

An ester is an organic compound that is the product of the reaction of an acid and an alcohol. It has the general form

14040

$$R_1 - O - \overset{\overset{\large O}{\|}}{C} - R_2$$

The OH^- of the alcohol forms water with the H^+ of the acid, and the organic radical of the alcohol combines with the rest of the acid. A polyester can be formed by the reaction of a difunctional acid with a difunctional alcohol, leading to a molecule that is also difunctional. Therefore, it can continue to react with the original reactants. One of the most important polyesters is poly(ethylene terephthalate), which is the product of the reaction between ethylene glycol (an alcohol, since it has an OH group) and terephthalic acid.

14050

$$HO-\underset{H}{\overset{H}{C}}-\underset{H}{\overset{H}{C}}-OH \qquad HO-\overset{\overset{O}{\|}}{C}-C_6H_4-\overset{\overset{O}{\|}}{C}-OH \qquad \left[O-\underset{H}{\overset{H}{C}}-\underset{H}{\overset{H}{C}}-O-\overset{\overset{O}{\|}}{C}-C_6H_4-\overset{\overset{O}{\|}}{C}\right]$$

ethylene glycol — terephthalic acid — polyethylene terephthalate (PET)

This is a condensation-type polymerization with water as a by-product. The chain can grow from either end in a step-wise mode, because the ends can react with either of the two monomer reactants. PET is widely applied in textile fibers, sheets, bottles, etc. Some familiar trade names are Mylar films and Dacron fibers.

PET became preferable to nylon in tire cord mainly because it is more resistant to so-called "flat-spotting." The early nylon-corded tires would develop flat

* A denier is a linear-density unit used for textiles and is defined as the mass in grams per 9000 meters in length. Thus, it depends on the density and diameter of the fiber. Therefore, the modulus in gpd is also dependent on these factors. To get the specific cross-section area of a fiber in cm^2, divide the denier number by $9x10^5$ times the fiber density in g/cm^3. One gpd in MPa is approximately 88.32 times the density.

spots because, when stopped for an extended period of time, the cords in the foot print would cool faster (because that part of the tire is in contact with the ground) than the cords in the rest of the tire. The latter would therefore stretch by viscous flow a bit more than the faster-cooling cords in the foot print. This would produce an annoying thumping of the tires when the vehicle was run again, and this would last until the flat spot became rounded as it got hotter than the rest of the tire during running. The reason why PET is more resistant to flat-spotting is that its glass-transition temperature is about 80°C, as opposed to 50°C for nylon.

14.3 Tire Cord

14.3.1 Textile-Fiber Cord

14060

A tire cord is essentially a very thin rope. As noted earlier, it starts with filaments of a fiber, and these are bundled together to form a basic tire yarn (BTY). Two or more of these BTYs are then twisted together to form a cord yarn, as shown in Fig. 14.5(a) by a process called cabling, as shown in Fig. 14.5(b). In the cabling process, the inner yarn comes from a supply pot that does not rotate, and the outer yarn is pulled off a supply package on a rotating creel. The twists give durability and fatigue resistance. Three-ply cords, that is, having three strands of cord yarn, have the best durability.

To make a sheet of a tire ply, the cords are woven into a fabric by the use of small crossing threads called picks, as shown in Fig. 14.6. The fabric is then infiltrated with an adhesive that provides bonding to the rubber matrix and stabilizes the fabric. The adhesive is bonded to the fibers by molecular penetration of the filaments and by chemical reactions. It is obviously important to get maximum coverage of the fibers by the adhesive.

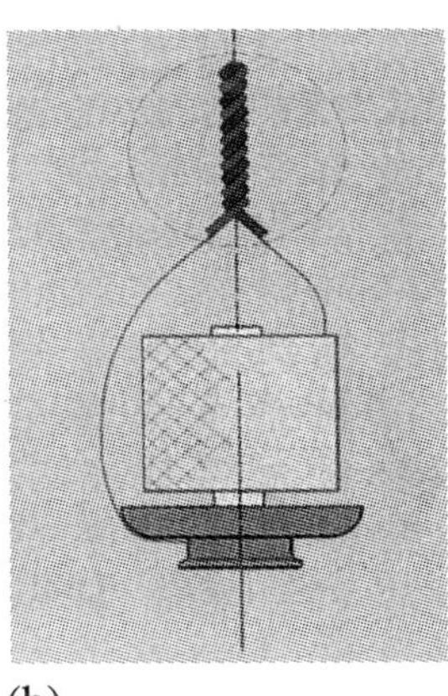

(a) (b)

Fig. 14.5 (a) Two BTYs twisted to form a cord yarn. (b) Principle of cabling. (From T. Gries and W. Mrose, Chemical Fibers International, vol 51, supplement, August, 2001, p. 56-58; courtesy of Zimmer AG)

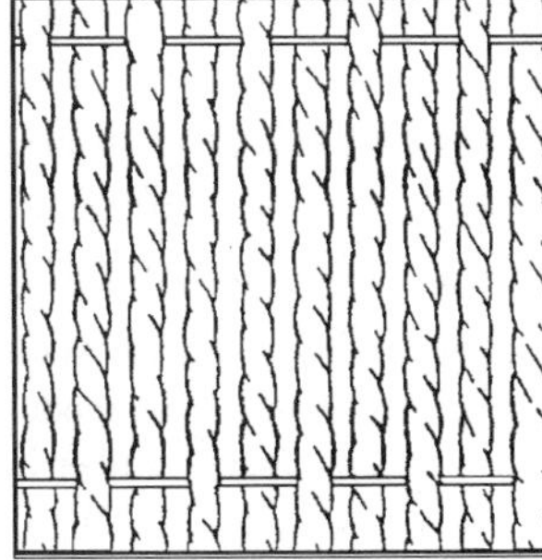

Fig. 14.6 Construction of fabric from polyamide cord. (From R.J. Dill & H. Long, *Basic Compounding and Processing of Rubber,* H. Long ed., ACS Rubber Division 1985)

14.3.2 Steel-Wire Cord

The filaments are brass-plated steel wires drawn to a diameter in the range 0.15 to 0.40 mm; the wires are typically 1065 steel. An example of a steel cord is shown in Fig. 14.7. Here, four twisted filaments are made into strands, and six strands are twisted around a seventh to give a cord. A single-filament wrapper wire helps keep the strands together.

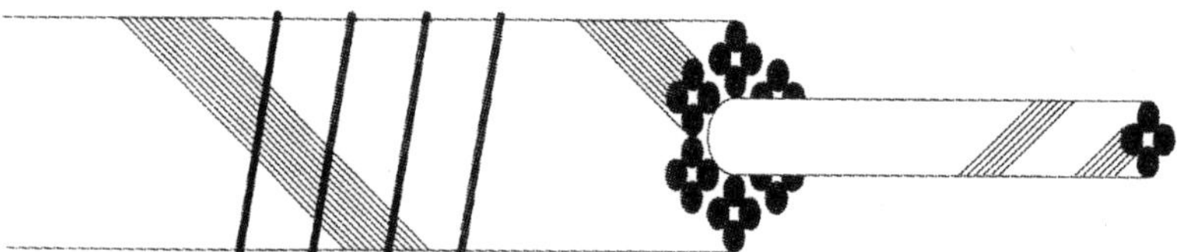

Fig. 14.7 Construction of steel-wire cord. (Reprinted from F. J. Kovac and M. B. Rodgers, *Science and Technology of Rubber.* 2nd ed, J. E. Mark, B. Erman, and F. R. Eirich eds., Academic Press, 1994, with permission from Elsevier.)

The function of the brass plating is to provide bonding of the rubber matrix to the steel wires. This is accomplished by the growth of copper sulfide crystals from the wire surface into the surrounding rubber, employing some of the sulfur in the vulcanizing chemicals. The film is porous, so that the rubber molecules can become entangled in it.

14.4 The Rubber Matrix

The main components of the rubber compound are:

1. the polymer network,
2. the filler or reinforcing system,
3. the stabilizing system, and
4. the vulcanizing system.

The polymers used are four types: natural rubber (NR), polybutadiene (PBD), styrene butadiene (SBD), and butyl rubber. The filler in tires is generally carbon black. The stabilizer system is meant to retard oxidation, which degrades the rubber. The polymer network will be considered first, and the other three components will be considered in the later discussion of rubber compounding. Most of the rubber used in modern radial tires is natural rubber (cf. Chapter 12), obtained mainly from plantations in Southeast Asia. According to Barbin and Rodgers (Ref. 1, p. 420), the benefits of using natural rubber for tires as opposed to synthetic rubber include improved green strength (i.e., prior to vulcanization), better adhesion between components, better tear strength, lower operating temperatures, and lower rolling resistance, thus better fuel economy. However, synthetic rubbers employ important materials technologies, and they will be the main topic of discussion here.

14.4.1 Polymerization of Dienes

The commercial production of rubber for tires requires a process that has a sufficiently high rate and high yield and from which the molecular weight is sufficiently high for the desired mechanical properties. The process of free-radical addition, or chain-growth, polymerization, as illustrated previously in Fig. 12.9, is not used for polymerization of a bulk diene or one that is dissolved in a solvent. The reason why bulk or solution polymerization is inappropriate is that the rate constant for chain termination k_t in dienes is too high relative to that for chain propagation k_p. This can be seen by comparing the rate constants of butadiene with those of a vinyl polymer, as seen in Table 14.1. The rate constant for chain propagation in a vinyl polymer, like polystyrene, for example, is two orders of magnitude larger than the rate constant for chain termination. Therefore, long chains of PS can be formed. However, for butadiene, the probability that a growing chain adds another monomer is about the same as the probability that the chain is terminated. Therefore, a high-molecular-weight butadiene polymer cannot be achieved by this method.

Table 14.1 Propagation and Termination Rate Constants (l/mole-sec.) (Ref. 1)

Monomer	k_p	k_t
Styrene	176	3.6
Butadiene	100	≈100

Taking another diene as an example, the polymerization of bulk isoprene at 85°C is very slow and has a low yield of rubber, as opposed to an oil made of short polyisoprene chains. This is shown by the data in Table 14.2. Also, the molecular weight of the rubber that does form is too low by at least an order of magnitude. Raising the temperature speeds up the process, but this degrades the yield and the molecular weight even more.

Table 14.2 Bulk Polymerization of Isoprene. (Ref. 1)

Temperature (°C)	Time (hr)	Yield: (%)Oil	Yield: (%)Rubber	MW of the Rubber
85	100	7.9	16.3	4600
85	900	—	35.3	5700
145	12.5	54.7	15.6	4000

14.4.2 Emulsion Polymerization

One process used to make polydienes employs an emulsion of the monomer in water, along with a surfactant (e.g., a soap) and a free-radical initiator. The monomer is only slightly soluble in water. The system can be portrayed schematically as in Fig. 14.8.

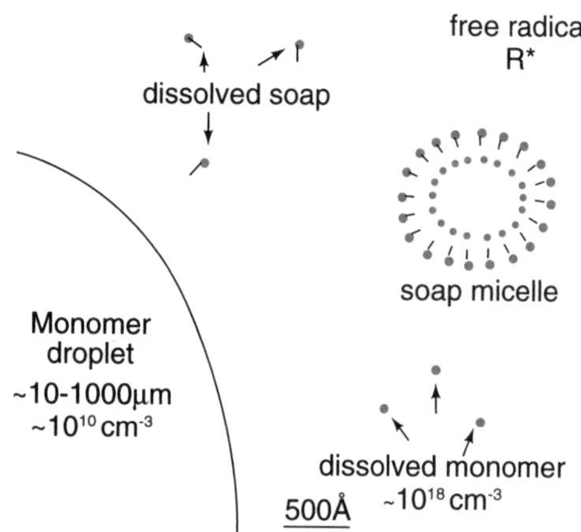

Fig. 14.8 Components of an emulsion polymerization system comprising monomer droplets, dissolved monomer and soap molecules, inactive soap micelles containing monomer, and active soap micelles in which polymerization is occurring.

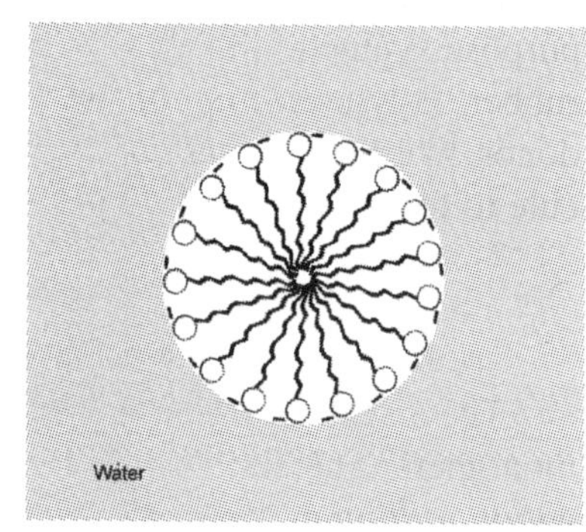

Ordinary soap is a mixture of salts of long-chain fatty acids (carboxylic acids), having the form $RCOO^-Na^+$, and thus each molecule has a non-polar end and a polar end. The polar end is soluble in water, but the non-polar end is not. Therefore, the soap molecules do not float around individually in water, but rather clump together in units called micelles. This allows the hydrophobic non-polar ends to be shielded from the water. The micelles remain isolated because of the mutual repulsion of the similar charges on their surfaces that result from the negatively charged carboxylate groups that cover these surfaces.

Initially, in emulsion polymerization, the monomer is located mostly in large droplets in the emulsion, with a small amount in solution in the water. Some

monomer is concentrated inside each of a large number of soap micelles. The polymerization process gets started when an initiator radical enters a micelle. Each soap micelle then grows into a particle containing polymer and unreacted monomer, and the particle is coated with soap molecules that serve to stabilize it and isolate it from other polymer particles. The polymer molecule continues to grow as more monomer molecules penetrate the soap film. It keeps growing until another radical diffuses

into the particle and meets the advancing end of the chain. Therefore, the chain length is controlled by the rate at which radicals enter the soap-enclosed particle.

As the polymer particles grow, more and more of the dissolved soap molecules are used up to cover the increasing surface area of the particles. The particles break up when there is not enough soap left to cover the surfaces. The higher the concentration of soap in the water, the longer the soap-enclosed particles can endure. This leads to more and smaller particles of latex (the name given to polymer particles in water).

Because the growing chains are isolated in the latex particles, they cannot terminate each other. Chain termination can occur only when a second free radical enters the soap-enclosed particle. Therefore, this process gives a fast rate of polymerization and a higher molecular weight than would occur in a homogeneous system, like free-radical polymerization of a diene in bulk or from solution.

Emulsion polymerization can produce chains of excessively high molecular weight. The problem is that cross-linking reactions can occur during the polymerization of diene-based polymers. If the molecular weight gets too high, this can cause the formation of an insoluble gel, which inhibits further processing. To prevent this, a small amount of a regulator, like a thiol* with a weak H-S bond is added to the mix. The end of a growing chain can attack this bond, with the result that the chain is terminated by the hydrogen atom. A new chain is then started by the action of the rest of the thiol as an initiator. By adding the right amount of the thiol, the chain length can be controlled, and the rubber then remains amenable to processing.

14.4.3 Anionic Polymerization

A chain-growth type of polymerization that is used for dienes in solution is anionic polymerization. It is also used for polymerization of the main general-purpose synthetic rubber used in tires, which is a copolymer: styrene-butadiene rubber. Polymerization of butadiene in solution can be initiated by an electron donor, like metallic sodium, which can transfer an electron to a monomer molecule to form what can be called an anion radical, as shown below

$$(CH_2 = CH - CH = CH_2) + Na \rightarrow (CH_2 = CH - CH - CH_2)^{\circ}\ Na^+$$

The negatively charged anion radical can then propagate by addition of monomers. The end of the chain remains an active center for continued propagation as long as there are not impurities present that could terminate the chain. Thus, the polymer chain has a "living" end, and the propagation proceeds as shown below.

$$\sim\!\sim\!\sim CH_2 - CH = CH - CH_2^{\circ}\ Na^+ + (CH_2 = CH - CH = CH_2)$$
$$\longrightarrow \sim\!\sim\!\sim\!\sim\!\sim\!\sim\!\sim CH - CH = CH - CH_2^{\circ}\ Na^+$$

The sodium counter ion stays with the negatively charged end of the active center and protects it from being terminated by meeting another chain. In this process all the chains start to grow at essentially the same time, so the polymer tends to be mono-disperse; that is, the distribution of chain lengths is quite narrow. The details of the polymerization reaction depend on the nature of the initiator, the monomer, and the solvent, and on the presence of impurities.

14.4.4 Styrene Butadiene Rubber

Styrene-butadiene rubber, or SBR, can be made either by emulsion polymerization or by anionic polymerization. Initially, it was made by emulsion polymerization at 50°C. Later, polymerization at 5°C was found to give a more uniform molecular-weight distribution and less tendency for gel formation due to cross linking.

Emulsion polymerization of butadiene by itself gives a mix of chain microstructures. At 5°C there is about 13% cis-1,4, about 70% trans-1,4, and the balance is vinyl-1,2. The terminology 1,4 means that the chain bonds involve the first and fourth carbon atoms of the mer; 1,2 means the first and second. Thus, the bonds in polybutadiene are situated as shown in Fig. 14.9.

* Thiols are analogous to alcohols; they contain the SH group, which is the analog of the OH group of an alcohol.

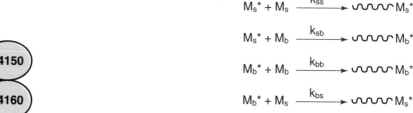

cis-1,4	trans-1,4	vinyl-1,2
$T_g(K) = 171$	215	269

Fig. 14.9 The various configurations of polybutatiene and the values of the glass-transition temperature.

Example 14.2

Q. Why are dienes used to make rubbers?

A. The double bonds serve as sites for cross-linking during vulcanization.

In co-polymerization of SBR, the composition of a growing chain depends on the rates at which each of the two monomers joins the end of the chain. These rates depend, in turn, on which of the two mers lies at the end of the chain as it encounters the next monomer. So there are four possible reactions, each with its own rate constant:

$$M_s^* + M_s \xrightarrow{k_{ss}} \sim\sim\sim M_s^*$$

$$M_s^* + M_b \xrightarrow{k_{sb}} \sim\sim\sim M_b^*$$

$$M_b^* + M_b \xrightarrow{k_{bb}} \sim\sim\sim M_b^*$$

$$M_b^* + M_s \xrightarrow{k_{bs}} \sim\sim\sim M_s^*$$

M_s = styrene monomer, M_b = butadiene monomer, * = radical at end of chain

One can define a monomer reactivity ratio for both monomers: for styrene, $r_s = k_{ss}/k_{sb}$ and for butadiene, $r_b = k_{bb}/k_{bs}$. This ratio defines the relative reactivity of a growing chain end with its "own" monomer versus the "other" monomer.

It turns out that in SBR polymerization r_s is 0.5, and r_b is 1.6. This means that butadiene would enter the chain at about three times the rate of styrene, if they had equal concentrations at the beginning. In any case, the chain becomes more concentrated in styrene as it grows. If the styrene concentration gets too high, the rubbery qualities are lost. For example, with an initial ratio of butadiene to styrene of 75/25, the chain ends at 60% conversion are about 23wt% styrene, and the overall concentration is about 20wt%. At 90% conversion the chain ends reach more than 36wt% styrene. For tires, emulsion polymerization of SBR is

stopped at around 65% conversion, and the unconverted monomer is then recycled.

In recent times, SBR for tires has been made by anionic polymerization. The considerations of reaction constants and reactivity ratios given above for emulsion polymerization still apply, but the values would be different for anionic polymerization, depending on the initiator and solvent used.

14.4.5 Butyl Rubber.

Butyl rubber is highly impermeable to air and it shows very little absorption of water. This makes butyl rubber ideal for the lining of tubeless tires. Other applications include engine and radiator hoses in autos and insulation on high-voltage electrical cables. Butyl rubber is a copolymer of isobutylene and isoprene in a ratio of about 50:1.

$$
\sim 50\ \begin{array}{cc} H & CH_3 \\ | & | \\ C & = C \\ | & | \\ H & CH_3 \end{array}
\quad + \quad
\begin{array}{cccc} H & & & H \\ | & & & | \\ C = & C - & C = & C \\ | & | & | & | \\ H & CH_2 & H & H \end{array}
\longrightarrow
$$

Isobutene Isoprene

$$
\left[\begin{array}{cc} H & CH_3 \\ | & | \\ -C & = C- \\ | & | \\ H & CH_3 \end{array}\right]
\left[\begin{array}{cccc} H & & & H \\ | & & & | \\ -C = & C - & C = & C- \\ | & | & | & | \\ H & CH_2 & H & H \end{array}\right]
$$

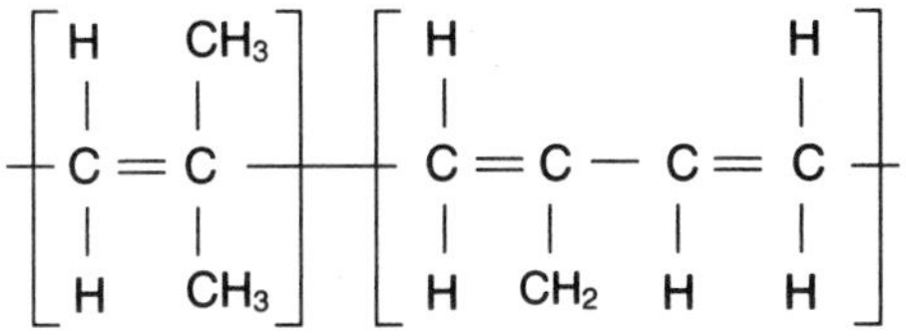

Butyl

The role of the isoprene is to provide the double bond needed for vulcanizaton. The process used is cationic polymerization, which is one of the mechanisms of chain-growth polymerization. For butyl rubber, the process is carried out at around -100°C using aluminum chloride $AlCl_3$ in solution with methyl chloride CH_3Cl. The cation is Al^{3+}. The chain growth proceeds as follows:

$$\sim\sim\sim -(CH_2 - CH = CH - CH_2)^- Al^{3+} + (CH_2 = CH - CH = CH_2) \longrightarrow$$

14190

Example 14.3

Q. How can one rationalize the low permeability of butyl rubber to oxygen and its resistance to the absorption of water?

A. Butyl rubber is mostly polyisobutylene, which is made up of compact, non-polar, symmetrical mers. Its chains should pack tightly, with a fairly high T_g, so there should not be much free volume for the diffusion of oxygen or water molecules. The solubility of these polar molecules should also be low in polyisobutylene, because of its non-polarity.

14.5 Rubber Compounding

Compounding is the technical name given to the addition of modifiers to a rubber in order to optimize its properties. The modifiers include the filler, the stabilizing system, and the vulcanizing system. These are added to the basic polymer system.

The main polymers used in tires are NR, SBR, PBD, and butyl rubber (BR). Blends of NR and PBD are used in treads and side walls to optimize tear strength, rolling resistance, heat build-up, and adhesion between different components of the tire. SBR is added to treads to improve wet-skid resistance and improve traction.

The most important parameter that determines the performance of the polymers used for tires is the glass-transition temperature, T_g. Some important effects are:

Property	Favored by
Abrasion resistance	low T_g
Traction and wet grip	high T_g

The value of T_g can be adjusted through several factors. One is the configuration of the butadiene, which can take three forms: cis, trans, or vinyl, as we have already seen in Fig. 14.9. The value of T_g depends on the configuration, ranging upward from around 171K as trans and vinyl are mixed with pure cis (Fig. 14.9). The T_g can be raised by increasing the content of styrene in SBR or by increasing the content of vinyl-1,2 butadiene units. The styrene is twice as effective as the vinyl in this regard.

Obviously, one cannot maximize all properties in the same rubber, and trade-offs are necessary according to the objectives for any particular tire. For example, high mileage (long life) and maximum traction are generally incompatible.

The unique properties of an elastomer depend on the presence of carbon-carbon double bonds, but these also make the elastomer susceptible to degradation by oxidation, which is promoted by oxygen, ozone, heat, light, and dynamic loading. The amount of sulfur in the vulcanization system is also a factor. Low-sulfur systems, which favor monosulfidic crosslinks, have better heat and oxidation resistance but poorer fatigue resistance, whereas high-sulfur systems produce polysulfidic crosslinks, which are thermally less stable and are more easily oxidized. However, the latter have better fatigue resistance. Oxidation occurs by both the breakdown of polysulfide to monosulfide cross links and chain scission.

Ultraviolet light promotes oxidation at the exposed surface of tires by the formation of free radicals that set up an autocatalytic chain reaction. The results are the breakdown of polysulfide to monosulfide cross links and chain scission, which softens the rubber and decreases its resistance to abrasion. This is retarded to some degree by the presence of carbon black. However, long-time exposure to UV light in the presence of heat and moisture can lead to craze cracking of the surface, and this in turn can lead to abrasive loss from the surface and also to fatigue failure.

Because tire manufactures generally employ high-sulfur vulcanization systems, stabilizers, especially anti-ozonants, are particularly important. One class that is commonly used is para-phenylenediamines (PPDs), which have the following general structure:

$$R - NH - C_6H_4 - NH - R'$$

Large molecules are best, because they are less volatile and they migrate less in the rubber during service.

14.6 Reinforcement of Rubber by Nanoscale Particles

14.6.1 Carbon Black

Carbon black is a nanoscale particulate filler that consists of aggregates of nodular particles. Part of one aggregate cluster is shown in Fig. 14.10(a), and the overall appearance of a number of clusters is shown in Fig. 14.10(b).

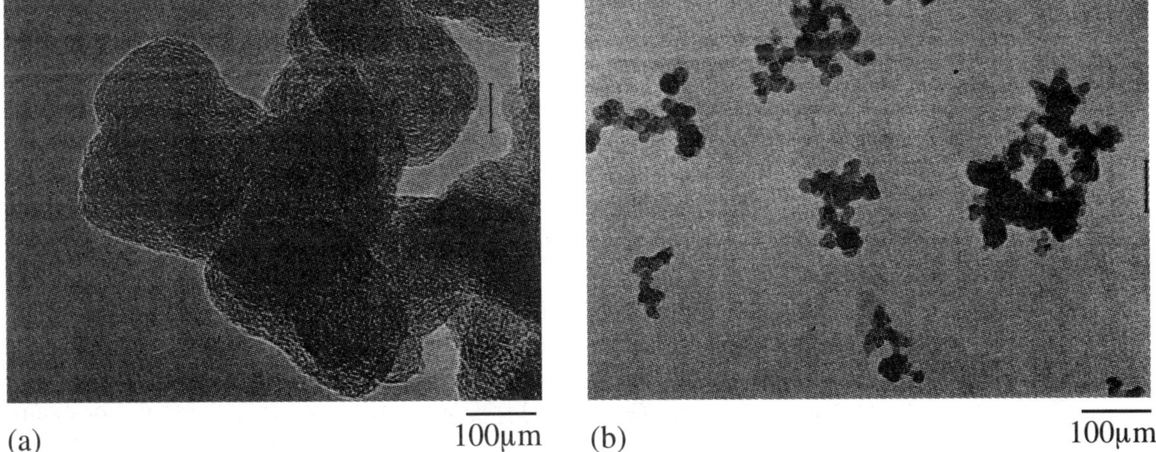

Fig. 14.10 (a) Part of a cluster of nodular carbon-black particles. (b) Aggregate clusters of carbon black. (Reprinted from A. I. Medalia and G. Kraus, *Science and Technology of Rubber*. 2nd ed, J. E. Mark, B. Erman, and F. R. Eirich eds., Academic Press, 1994, with permission from Elsevier.

Each particle consists of a nodule made up of quasi-graphitic layers arranged concentrically around a hollow interior. The most important characteristics of a sample of carbon black are the surface area of each particle and the bulkiness of the average cluster of particles. Because the particles are so small, their surface area is on the order of several hundred m^2/cm^3, and this is important because the polymer chains of the rubber tend to form chemical bonds with the particles by interacting with the particle surface. In the field of rubber technology, the bulkiness of a cluster is referred to as its "structure," so a black with high structure means that the clusters of particles are large. The particles of a cluster are strongly bonded to each other, so each cluster represents a strong, low-density inclusion in the polymer matrix.

The reason for using particulate reinforcement is that it greatly improves the mechanical behavior of rubber. Figure 14.11 shows schematically the effect of the concentration of carbon black on the properties of tires. PHR means parts per hundred rubber; e.g., a PHR of 50 means 50g of black per 100g of rubber.

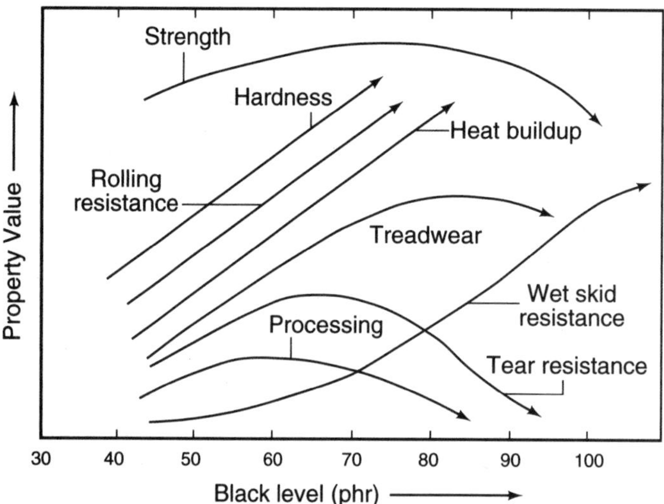

Fig. 14.11 Effects of amount of carbon black on properties of compounded rubber in tires. (Reprinted from W. W. Barbin and M. B. Rogers, *Science and Technology of Rubber.* 2nd ed, J. E. Mark, B. Erman, and F. R. Eirich eds., Academic Press, 1994, with permission from Elsevier.)

Most of the carbon black used for tires is made by incomplete combustion of either gas or oil in an excess of air to make a turbulent flow of hot gases, into which is sprayed a feedstock like residual oil. This forms a hot smoke of clusters, such as depicted in Fig. 14.10(b), and the smoke is then quenched in water. The product is called furnace black, and the surfaces of the particles are neutral or alkaline, with a low oxygen content.

The mixing of the carbon black into the rubber is a critical step in tire-making technology, because the goal is to retain high structure (which gives low tread wear) and to get as random and homogeneous a dispersion of the clusters as possible. The main problem to be overcome is achieving the desired dispersion of the clusters, which is impeded by the fact that the bonding of the chains to the particles tends to cement the clusters together. Thus, it is difficult to disperse low-structure, high-surface-area blacks. On the other hand, high-structure blacks are incorporated more slowly, but are dispersed more easily. After the dispersion is completed, the chains that are bonded to particles of black have a reduced mobility, but the chains are long enough and there are enough un-bonded chains that the glass transition temperature of the mix is increased by only a few degrees.

The chemical bonding of the rubber molecular chains to the surfaces of the carbon black is crucial to the strength of a vulcanized rubber. This is shown by the schematic stress-strain curves of Fig. 14.12.

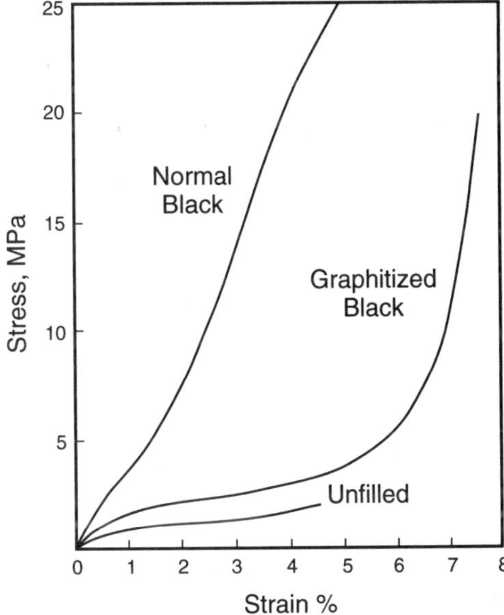

Fig. 14.12 Schematic stress-strain curves of vulcanized rubber. (Reprinted from A. I. Medalia and G. Kraus, *Science and Technology of Rubber.* 2nd ed, J. E. Mark, B. Erman, and F. R. Eirich eds., Academic Press, 1994, with permission from Elsevier.)

The lowest curve is for an unfilled rubber, and the highest curve is for a rubber reinforced with carbon black in the normal way. The intermediate curve represents a rubber filled with a carbon black that has been heated to a high temperature to promote graphitization prior to being mixed with the rubber. The graphitization has saturated most of the bonding sites on the surfaces of the carbon particles, leaving them nearly inert with respect to interaction with the rubber chains. This gives poor adhesion between the rubber and the surfaces of the carbon black.

In the normally filled rubber, with good interfacial bonding (the highest curve), the strain in the rubber regions that are not near the carbon clusters is larger than the strain in the unfilled rubber (lowest curve). This is because the clusters are essentially rigid, so they do not share in the deformation. Essentially, a filled rubber is a composite of high-modulus inclusions dispersed in a low-modulus matrix, as discussed in Chapter 13.

The wear resistance of a tire tread generally increases as the amount of filler is increased (cf. Fig. 14.11), but the details depend on the severity of the wear; i.e., on the nature of the surface on which the tire is rotated. If the surface has a lot of sharp asperities that give abrasive wear, the wear resistance decreases beyond a certain level of hardness of the rubber, i.e., amount of reinforcement.

14.6.2 Silica and Silicates

Silica is used as a nanoscale particulate filler in tires to improve tear strength and to reduce heat buildup in service. It also improves wet traction, because it is more hydrophilic than carbon black. Silica can be almost as effective in reinforcement as carbon black if it is used in conjunction with silane coupling agents to bond the silica particles to the rubber polymer molecules. One limitation is that silica is hydroscopic, and hydration of the surfaces of silica particles reduces the reinforcing effect of the particles. Therefore, dry storage of the silica is required.

An example of a silane coupling agent is bis(3-triethoxisilylpropyl)tetrasulfane (TESPT), and the resulting surface composition of the particles before compounding is

```
Si —¦— O                  OC2H5
           >  Si  <
Si —¦— O                  (CH2)3 — S — S
                                        |
Si —¦— O                  (CH2)3 — S — S
           >  Si  <
Si —¦— O                  OC2H5
```

Similar considerations hold for the various silicates that can be used by particulate reinforcement of rubber. These include calcium silicates, aluminum silicates (e.g., kaolin clay), magnesium silicates (e.g. talc), and sodium aluminum silicates.

14.7 Vulcanization

Natural rubber is gummy and deforms permanently when a stress is applied. As described in the Chapter 12, rubber is turned into an elastomer by the process of vulcanization, in which cross links between chains are formed by mixing the heated rubber with sulfur. In the case of tires, long rubber molecules with molecular weights ranging from 1 to 5 x 10^5 are converted into segments with molecular weights of 4 to 10 x 10^4 between cross links. Since vulcanized rubber cannot flow under stress, all processing like rolling, extruding, and molding has to be done before the vulcanizing reaction occurs.

Vulcanization makes rubber stronger, tougher, and more elastomeric, and it improves fatigue life and reduces heat generation from cyclic loading. The property changes are shown schematically in Fig. 14.13. These curves are the result of empirical testing. The maxima in tear strength, fatigue life, toughness, and tensile strength are a reflection of the general tendency in materials for cracking resistance to decrease as hardness increases beyond a certain level.

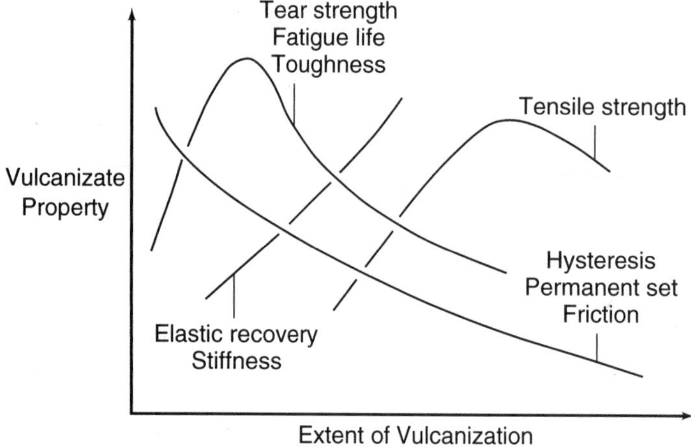

Fig. 14.13 Schematic variation of properties of rubber as a function of the extent of vulcanization. (Reprinted from A. Y. Coran, *Science and Technology of Rubber.* 2nd ed, J. E. Mark, B. Erman, and F. R. Eirich eds., Academic Press, 1994, with permission from Elsevier.)

In tire making, the molding process has to be complete before vulcanization occurs. Premature vulcanization is called "scorch." Scorch resistance is characterized by the time for cross-linking to begin at some particular temperature, as shown schematically in Fig. 14.14. The objective in tire making is to delay cross-linking until all the molding and shaping is complete and then to have vulcanization occur rapidly and saturate at a pre-determined, controllable level.

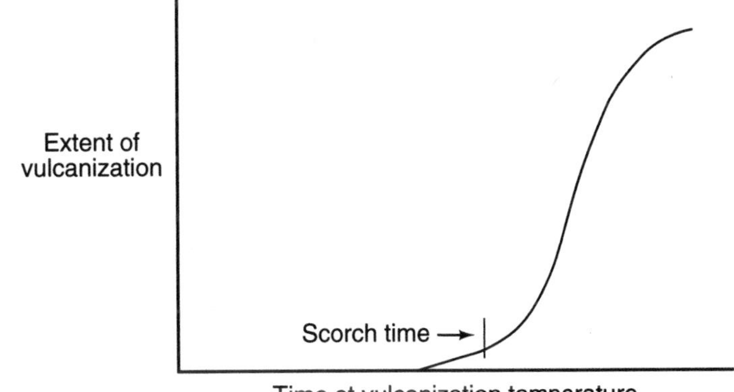

Fig. 14.14 Schematic representation of the kinetics of vulcanization showing how the scorch time is defined. (After A. Y. Coran, *Science and Technology of Rubber.* 2nd ed, J. E. Mark, B. Erman, and F. R. Eirich eds., Academic Press, 1994.)

The process of vulcanization of NR with sulfur that was developed by
Charles Goodyear in 1841 was very slow and it had a short scorch time, as shown
in Fig. 14.15. The process had to be accelerated to make it a more widespread
commercial process, and this was first achieved in 1906 by the addition of ani- 14280
lene to the sulfur (Fig. 14.15). Because anilene is toxic, it was soon replaced by
thiocarbanilide.

Because the molding of tires takes time, it was necessary to develop ways to
delay the start of vulcanization, that is, to increase the scorch time. This was
achieved first in the 1920's by the addition of 2-mercaptobenzothiazole (MBT). 14290
The process was later improved by the use of other complex sulfur-bearing
organic molecules to inhibit premature vulcanization even more effectively. The
progress in this regard is illustrated in Fig. 14.16.

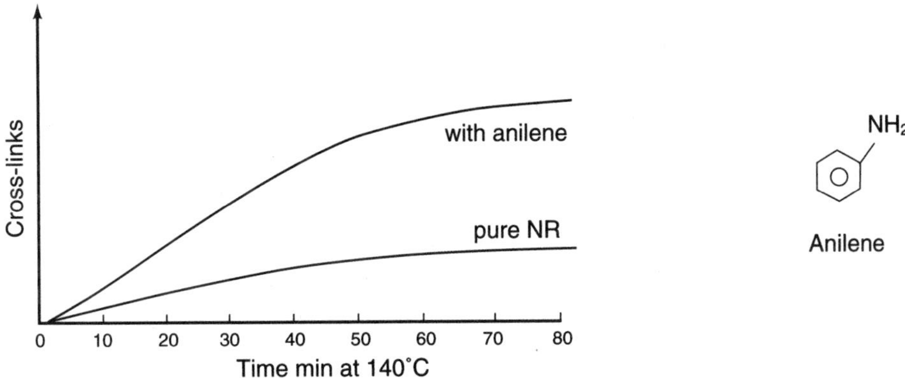

Anilene

Fig. 14.15 Rate of vulcanization of natural rubber by sulfur alone (lower curve) and the effect of addition of aniline. (After A. Y. Coran, *Science and Technology of Rubber. 2nd ed,* J. E. Mark, B. Erman, and F. R. Eirich eds., Academic Press, 1994.)

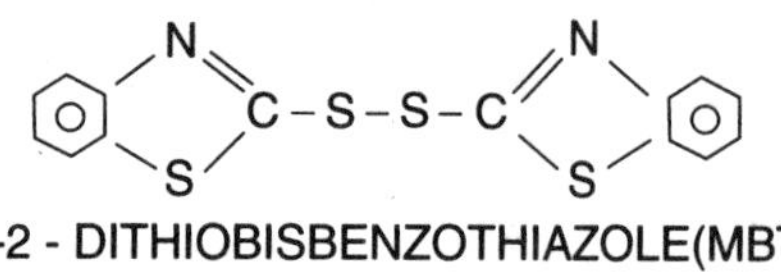

(A)

2-2 - DITHIOBISBENZOTHIAZOLE(MBTS)

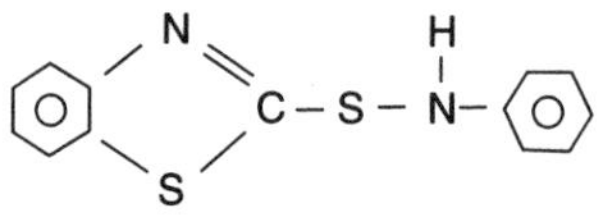

(B)

BENZOTHIAZOLESULFENAMIDE(BTSNHR)

(C)

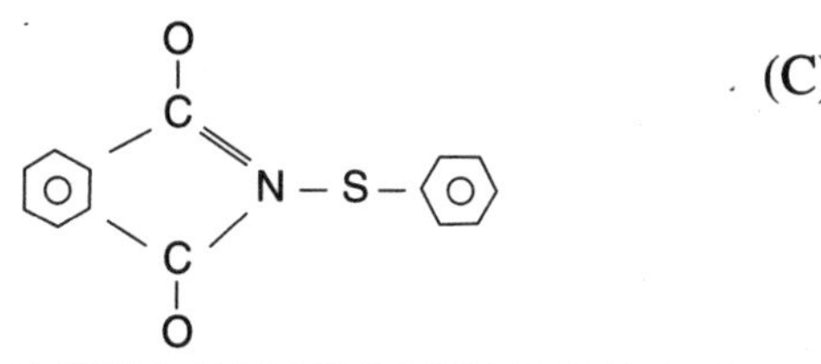

N-(CYCLOHEXYLTHIO)PHTALIMIDE(CTP)

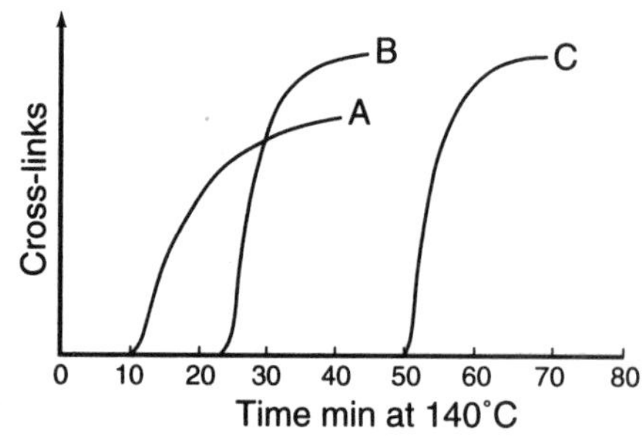

Fig. 14.16 Modification of vulcanization kinetics over time by use of MBTS in 1925 (curve A), BTSNHR in 1937 (curve B), and the addition of CTP to BTSNHR in 1968 (Curve C). (Reprinted from A. Y. Coran, *Science and Technology of Rubber.* 2nd ed, J. E. Mark, B. Erman, and F. R. Eirich eds., Academic Press, 1994, with permission from Elsevier.)

14.8 Rubber Processing

14.8.1 Mixing.

The first step in processing is to combine the ingredients of the rubber in an intimate mixture. This is done in a mixing chamber with counter-rotating rotors, as shown in Fig. 14.17. The ingredients are forced into the chamber from the top by means of a ram, and the mixed compound is removed through a door at the bottom. The mixture is kneaded and circulated in the chamber by the wings on the rotors until the desired degree of uniformity is achieved.

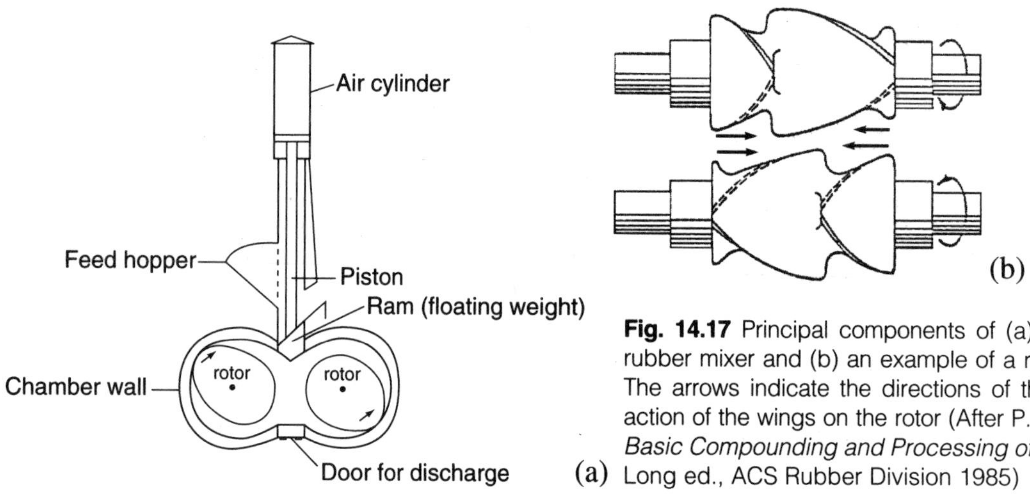

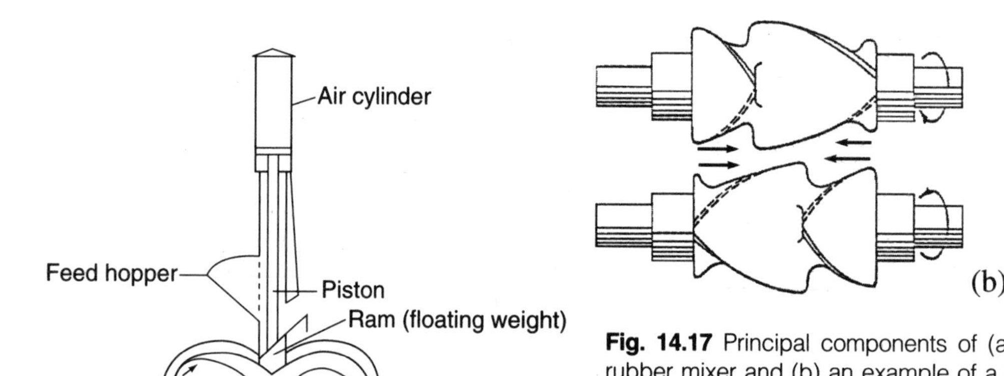

Fig. 14.17 Principal components of (a) an internal rubber mixer and (b) an example of a rotor design. The arrows indicate the directions of the pumping action of the wings on the rotor (After P.S. Johnson, *Basic Compounding and Processing of Rubber,* H. Long ed., ACS Rubber Division 1985)

The polymer is put into the chamber first, and its molecular weight is reduced by chain scission; this is done at temperatures up to around 180°C. After that, plasticizers, some carbon black, and oils are added. After further mixing, the rest of the carbon black is added, along with the stabilizing system (anti-oxidants). The final addition is the components of the vulcanization system. After the mixing is complete, the compound can be rolled into sheet and water cooled, or pelletized and air-cooled. 14343

14.8.2 Extrusion.

The as-mixed ("green") compound is formed by extrusion in a screw-type machine into shapes that are appropriate for later forming into a tread, a sidewall, or an apex, for example. There are two types of extruder: hot feed and cold feed. In the hot-feed system, as shown in Fig. 14.18, the compound is heated in a rolling mill and then fed into the barrel of the extruder. The compound passes from the feed zone into the compression zone, where it is heated further by shear. Then, it passes into the metering zone, where it is heated more to reduce its viscosity further, and then finally into the die that forms the desired shape.

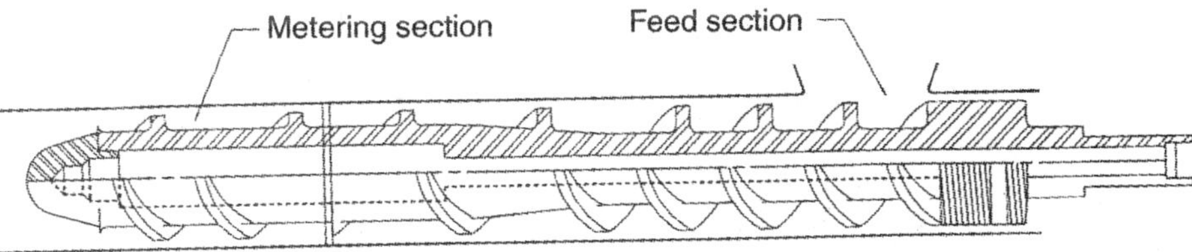

Fig. 14.18 A hot-feed extruder. (Reprinted from F. J. Kovac and M. B. Rodgers, *Science and Technology of Rubber.* 2nd ed, J. E. Mark, B. Erman, and F. R. Elrich eds., Academic Press, 1994, with permission from Elsevier.)

A cold-feed extruder differs mainly in that it is much longer, because of the need to heat the compound by shear in the extruder. This eliminates the need for the warm-up rolling mill, but it requires more extensive temperature sensing as well as computer control to achieve the desired temperature and pressure profiles in the extruder.

14.8.3 Calendering.

In this part of the process, fabric or steel cord is coated with rubber compound by means of a set of rolls that rotate in opposite directions, as shown in Fig. 14.19. Mating pairs of rolls can rotate at the same speed or different speeds; the latter case is used to heat the compound by shear so as to force it into the crevices of the cord. The clearance between the rolls can be adjusted to achieve the desired thickness of compound.

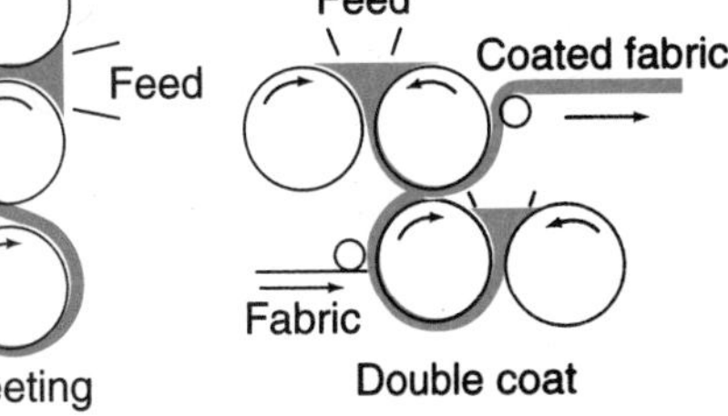

Fig. 14.19 Calendering operations. (After W. A. Allee, *Basic Compounding and Processing of Rubber,* H. Long ed., ACS Rubber Division 1985)

14.9 Tire Molding

Tires are manufactured in a special kind of press by the process of bladder molding. The layers of materials are laid up in the press in their final configuration and then pressed against the walls of a mold by means of an inflated bladder that fills the inside of the tire. The mold surfaces are heated to about 180°C, and they have inscribed on them the patterns of the treads and the writing that goes on the sidewall. The bladder is pressurized by steam, so the tire to be cured is heated from both sides. The process is shown schematically in Fig. 14.20 for
14360 the case of a segmented mold. The sidewall segments close first, and then the tread segment. Then the bladder is inflated against the inside of the uncured tire. The cure time is on the order of a quarter-hour. After the tire is cured, the bladder is pushed downward by a piston into the bladder well, and the tire is removed robotically from the opened mold. The segments of the mold open up to facilitate this step.

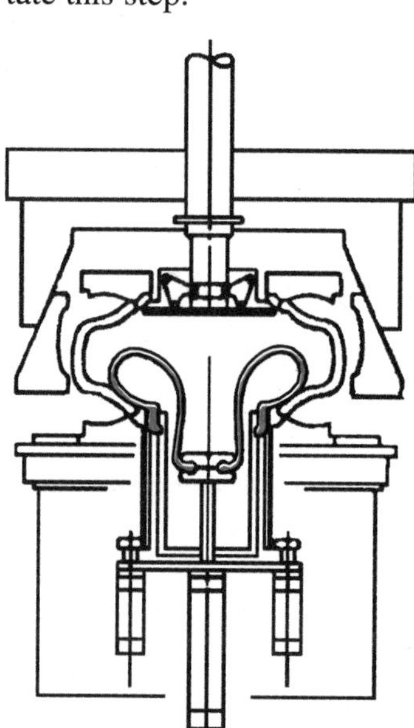

Fig. 14.20. Curing press with a segmented mold (After J. G. Sommer, *Basic Compounding and Processing of Rubber,* H. Long ed., ACS Rubber Division 1985)

14.10 Failure of Tires in Service

A tire is obviously subject to tread wear, so tires have to be replace periodically. This does not constitute failure of the tire. Also, some tires are damaged by what the industry calls road hazards. That means the tread gets punctured by an object on the road, or the sidewall gets damaged by contact with something like a sharp curb, for example. In the present context road hazards are excluded, and tire failure means the deflation of a tire because some aspect of its structural integrity is lost. This can happen suddenly and without prior warning.

A failure can occur by the separation of the steel belts that lie just under the tread. If this debonding occurs, the tread is likely to pop off the tire. The adhesive that is supposed to bond the belts together and to the tire body is, of course, a rubber compound. It has to have the right composition and be mixed and cured properly. Also, the surface of the steel has to have the proper brass plating and to be free of things that could interfere with the bond, like a thick oxide film, or even rust. In other words, there are several ways that the process could go wrong, including even the relative humidity in the tire-making plant. There appears to be no way to test each tire as it is made for the integrity of these bonds. Quality control only involves the periodic destructive test of a tire coming off the production line to see if the bonds are strong enough in a particular batch of tires.

Aside from the tire itself, the other factors that affect the probability of tire failure are the loads on the tires and the temperature of the tires. Particular attention to heat buildup in tires is required in regions with warm climates. In many cases a tire that has failed was probably under-inflated, which would make it flex more while rolling and thus tend to make it overheat. Of course, this would be more important as the driving speed is increased, especially if the vehicle is heavily loaded.

The consequences of tire failure are a function of the vehicle, particularly the center of gravity. The higher the center of gravity, the more likely is a rollover when a tire fails.

14.11 Triblock Copolymers by Anionic Polymerization

An important type of material not yet used in tires, but widely used in shoes 14370
and sports equipment, is the triblock copolymer, ABA, made from styrene and a diene, like butadiene, where the A refers to polystyrene, PS, and the B to polybutadiene, PBD. The PS and the PBD are mutually incompatible, so they aggregate into two separate phases. The room temperature structure of such a material having roughly 30% PS (in terms of the total molecular weight of each chain) comprises glassy regions of PS surrounded by chains of PBD, as shown schematically in Fig. 14.21. The special feature of this two-phase structure is that the segments of PS and PBD are covalently bonded to each other, so the two polymers cannot separate completely. Rather, the PS segregates in what become the glassy regions, but these are still covalently bonded to chains in the surrounding PBD matrix.

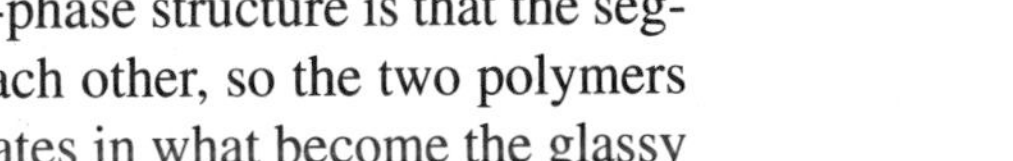

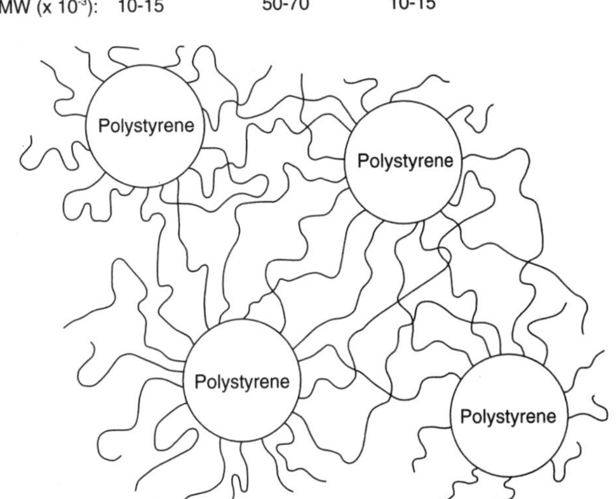

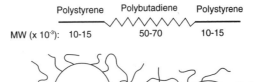

Fig. 14.21 Schematic representation of structure of thermoplastic elastomer made from an ABA triblock copolymer of PS and PBD (Reprinted from R. P. Quirk and M. M. Morton, *Science and Technology of Rubber*. 2nd ed, J. E. Mark, B. Erman, and F. R. Eirich eds., Academic Press, 1994, with permission from Elsevier.)

This material behaves like a thermoplastic elastomer. It can be melted and molded into shapes like a thermoplastic, but it behaves like an elastomer when it is cooled, because the domains of PS act like crosslinks. The result is a polymer of high tensile strength and good toughness, because the PS domains can absorb energy by deforming at high stresses. The strength increases with the concentration of PS, as shown in Fig. 14.22.

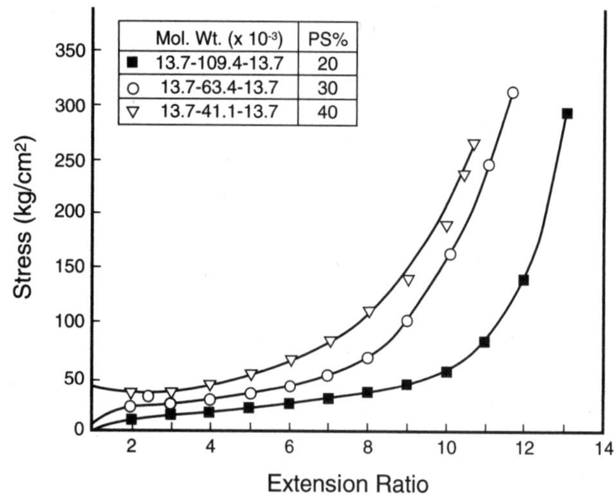

Fig. 14.22 Tensile behavior of styrene-isoprene-styrene triblock copolymers as a function of the percent of PS. (Reprinted from R. P. Quirk and M. M. Morton, *Science and Technology of Rubber.* 2nd ed, J. E. Mark, B. Erman, and F. R. Eirich eds., Academic Press, 1994, with permission from Elsevier.)

This kind of triblock copolymer is made by anionic polymerization. The basic reaction can be illustrated schematically with an initiator containing lithium acting on styrene, as follows

$$A^{-}\ Li^{+} + m\ [STYRENE] \rightarrow A - [PS]_{m}\ Li^{+}$$

In this reaction, a mix of the initiator and styrene monomer leads to chains of polystyrene having a remarkably narrow distribution of chain lengths, and each chain ends with a $C^{-}Li^{+}$ ion pair. The polymerization stops when the monomer is all consumed, but it would recommence if more monomer were added. The chains can be designated PSLi.

A diblock copolymer can be made by adding butadiene monomer instead of styrene, because the "living" ends of the chains would just go on as before, as shown here:

$$+ m\ [BUTADIENE] \rightarrow A - [PS]_{m} - [PBD]_{m}\ Li^{+}$$

The result would be PS-PBDLi. The triblock copolymer is made by shifting back to the styrene monomer after the butadiene is consumed.

$$+ m\ [STYRENE] \rightarrow A\text{-}[PS]_{m} - [PBD]_{m} - [PS]_{m}\ Li^{+}$$

The reaction can finally be terminated by adding an appropriate reagent, having, say, a hydroxyl group, ROH. The result can be written as PS-PBD-PS. The degree of polymerization in each phase is simply given by the monomer/initiator ratio, because the chains get started at nearly the same time, and they all have more or less the same access to the monomer molecules. This is what gives the narrow distributions of molecular weight.

The microstructure of an ABA triblock copolymer can be varied by increasing the content of the A phase. It would go from isolated ordered spheres of A, such as shown in Fig. 14.23, to rods, then lamellae, and finally to an interconnected two-phase aggregate. Obviously, the mechanical behavior would vary with the microstructure. 14380

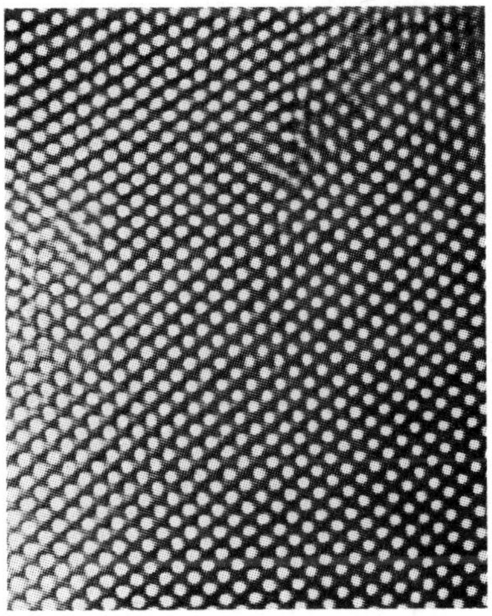

Fig. 14.23 Transmission electron micrograph of a thin film of a styrene-isoprene-styrene block copolymer. (MW 16,200-75,600-16200) x100,000. (Reprinted from R. P. Quirk and M. M. Morton, *Science and Technology of Rubber*. 2nd ed, J. E. Mark, B. Erman, and F. R. Eirich eds., Academic Press, 1994, with permission from Elsevier.)

References

1. *Science and Technology of Rubber, 2nd ed,* J. E. Mark, B. Erman, and F. R. Eirich eds., Academic Press, 1994.
2. *Basic Compounding and Processing of Rubber,* H. Long ed., ACS Rubber Division, 1985.
3. *Heavy Duty Truck Tire Engineering,* T. L. Ford and F. S. Charles, 34th L. Ray Buckendale Lecture, SAE, 1988.
4. *Polyamide Tire Cord Technology,* T. Gries and W Mrose, Chemical Fibers International, Aug. 2001, P. 55.
5. *Mechanics of Pneumatic Tires, 2nd ed.,* S. K. Clark, ed., U. S. Govt. Printing Office.

Summary

Tires are polymer-based composites in which the strengthening elements range from the macroscale (e.g., fibers) down to the nanoscale (e.g., carbon black). They are complex material systems that are designed to provide a wide range of properties, which depend on the nature of the polymer mix. Natural rubber (cis-polyisoprene) is used extensively, as is the copolymer styrene butadiene rubber (SBR). Several types of polymerization reactions are employed, including emulsion polymerization, anionic polymerization, and cationic polymerization. The most important single property of the polymers used in tires is the glass-transition temperature.

The nanoscale fillers, carbon black and silica, are crucial strengthening particles in tire rubber. They are analogous to the strengthening particles in precipitation-hardened metallic alloys. The mechanical properties of the rubbers depend mainly on the amount of filler and on the degree of cross-linking during vulcanization. The vulcanization process has been developed to a very high degree such that the cross-linking can be delayed until tire molding is complete, and it then occurs rapidly so as to permit a high production rate. This has been achieved by the use of complex sulfur-containing molecules that are mixed in with the rubber.

Glossary/Vocabulary - Chapter 14

Accelerated vulcanization	Increasing the rate of cross-linking of rubber molecules by adding an organic accelerator to the mix of rubber and sulfur. The process works in steps: first, monomeric polysulfides, then, polymeric polysulfides, then cross-linked rubber.
Anionic polymerization	A form of free-radical chain-growth polymerization in which the initiator contains an anion. PBD can be made by using an initiator that contains a sodium ion.
Beads	Loops of steel wire that anchor the plies and lock the tire onto the wheel. They are made from patented wires of high-carbon steel.
Belts	Layers of textile or steel wire that run circumferentially beneath the tread. They stiffen the casing and protect the ply cords from road hazards.
Butyl rubber	A copolymer of isobutylene and isoprene in a ratio of about 50:1. It is impermeable to air and is used as the liner for tubeless tires.
Calendering	A rolling process used to put a rubber coating on textile or steel cord. The rolls rotate in opposing directions, sometimes at different speeds.
Carbon black	A nanoscale filler for rubber comprising clusters of hollow, quasi-graphitic particles. The rubber molecules bond to the surfaces of the particles. It is an essential strengthening mechanism in tires.
Cationic polymerization	A form of chain-growth polymerization in which the initiator contains a cation. It is used in the making of butyl rubber.
Compounding	The addition of modifiers to the basic polymer system of rubber to improve its properties. These include the filler, stabilizers, and vulcanizing systems.
Copolymer	A polymer made by mixing two different monomers. One can have a random mix of the mers along the chain, or the mers can be segregated into blocks to make a block copolymer.
Emulsion polymerization	A process used to make polydienes in which the almost-insoluble monomer molecules are dispersed in an emulsion in water. The polymerization reaction occurs inside micelles formed with the aid of soap molecules.
Filament	A strand of fiber that is twisted with other filaments to make a yarn. Strands of yarn are then twisted in the opposite sense to make a cord.
Incorporation	The penetration of rubber chains into the voids of the clusters of carbon black. This occurs during mixing in a high-shear mixer.
Latex	An aqueous suspension of a hydrocarbon polymer that occurs naturally or is made synthetically. In emulsion polymerization, the particles formed from the micelles are suspended as a latex.
Liner	The layer of butyl rubber that lines the inside of a tubeless tire. Butyl rubber is impervious to air, and it does not absorb water.
Micelle	An aggregate of large molecules, e.g., soaps or surfactants, that comprises an electrically charged colloidal particle. A micelle can form a molecular container that has a hydrophobic end on the inside and a hydrophilic end on the outside.
Mixing of rubber	The process of blending the components of a tire before rolling or extrusion and molding. The sequence of adding the components is: polymer, plasticizer, carbon black, oils, more carbon black, vulcanizing system.

Modifier	Components added to rubber polymers during compounding to optimize the properties. For tires these include: the filler, stabilizers, and the vulcanizing system.
Natural rubber	A polymer that comes from the Havae Braziliensis tree in the form of a latex. The polymer is cis-polyisoprene. It can be cross-linked with sulfur to make a common elastomer.
PBD	Abbreviation for polybutadiene. Butadiene is copolymerized with styrene to make SBR.
PET	Abbreviation for poly(ethylene terephthalate). It is used for Mylar film and Dacron fibers. This is a polyester formed by condensation polymerization of ethylene glycol and terephthalic acid.
Plasticizer	An organic compound added to a polymeric material to facilitate processing and/or to increase the flexibility and toughness of the final product. It replaces polymer-polymer bonds with polymer-plasticizer bonds and thereby aids the movement of polymer-chain segments past each other.
Plies	The textile or steel cords that wrap around the tire body and extend from bead to bead. They are the primary fiber-reinforcement of the casing. The wrap can be either radial or on a bias.
Polybutadiene	A synthetic thermoplastic polymer made by polymerizing 1,3-butadiene. The cis-isomer is similar to natural rubber. It is used in tire treads because of its resistance to cracking, abrasion, and heat build-up.
Polydiene	A polymer comprising a carbon backbone having every third bond being a double bond. Common examples are NR and PBD.
Polyester	A polymer chain made by the reaction of a difunctional alcohol with a difunctional acid. This is a condensation polymerization with water as a by-product.
Polyethylene terephthalate	See PET.
Reactivity ratio	The ratio of the reaction constants for the addition of one or the other monomer molecule to the end of a growing chain of a copolymer. This is a function of the identity of the last molecule on the growing chain.
Regulator	A compound added during emulsion polymerization to prevent chains from becoming too long. If the chains become too long, there is a tendency for cross-linking and concomitant gel formation.
SBD	Abbreviation for styrene butadiene. See SBR.
SBR	Abbreviation for styrene butadiene rubber. This copolymer is the main general purpose synthetic rubber used in tires.
Scorch	The term used for premature vulcanization of rubber. Scorch interferes with the tire-molding process.
Solution polymerization	The polymerization of monomer molecules contained in a solution. This is analogous to bulk polymerization; only the concentration of the monomer varies.
Stabilizer	A compound added to rubber to retard environmental degradation. The greatest problem is reaction with oxygen or ozone, which can cause chain scission and the breakdown of the polysulfide cross-links.

Structure of carbon black The bulkiness of the clusters of carbon black in rubber. High structure means large clusters. Higher structure translates to greater wear resistance, all other things being equal.

Surfactant A molecule that tends to segregate to the surface of a solution and lower the surface tension. This includes detergents, wetting agents, and emulsifiers. Soap is a surfactant because soap molecules have a hydrophobic end and a hydrophilic end.

Styrene-butadiene rubber See SBR.

Thermoplastic elastomer A polymer that can be melted and molded like a thermoplastic, but acts like an elastomer when it is cooled. An example is the PS-PBD-PS triblock copolymer. (The PBD is not vulcanized.)

Thiol An organic compound that resembles an alcohol, but with the oxygen of the hydroxyl group replaced by sulfur. Thiols are used as regulators in emulsion polymerization to keep chains from growing too long and forming an insoluble gel.

Tire cord The fibers that provide reinforcement in tires. They are used to make both the plies and the belts.

Triblock copolymer A block copolymer in which each chain has the configuration ABA. This is made by adding monomer of B to chains of A with "living" ends, and then monomer of A again to the living ends of AB chains.

Yarn A fiber made by twisting filaments together. Strands of yarn can be twisted in the opposite sense to make tire cord. The cord can be woven into a fabric.

Exercises

14.1 Why is a tire a good example to use when explaining the principles of fiber reinforcement of a composite material?

14.2 What is a diene? What is a conjugated diene?

14.3 In free-radical-initiated polymerization of dienes in bulk or in solution, the rate constant for chain termination is too high. How does emulsion polymerization get around this problem? How does anionic polymerization get around it?

14.4 How do we know that chemical bonding between rubber and carbon black is important for the properties of tires?

14.5 Why is it physically reasonable that a low T_g would be good for abrasion resistance and a high T_g would be good for traction and wet grip?

14.6 How can the T_g be varied in the synthetic rubbers used in tires?

14.7 How and why would you expect the mechanical properties to compare between a diblock copolymer and a triblock copolymer made of PS and PBD as in Fig. 14.21?

15

FLEXIBLE CONNECTIVE TISSUE

In keeping with the overall plan of this book, in which the bicycle and related components are used as the conceptual framework for learning about structural materials, we consider here the leg of the rider. The leg is a kind of an analog of an engine: fuel, oxygen, and electrical signals are the inputs, and mechanical work is the output. The materials to be considered are bone, cartilage, ligaments, muscles, and tendons. There are many similarities to materials already covered, but a fundamental difference comes from the fact that they are living materials. In addition, they have unique characteristics that we have not encountered before: They are self-assembling composite materials. For the most part they are filamentary, and in the flexible tissues their largest component is water. Their mechanical properties are intimately related to their microstructures, and they add a new dimension to the study of materials science from which engineers can take some valuable lessons.

We will focus on the knee, which is the largest joint in the body and the joint most subject to injury and repair. Some of the relevant parts of the knee are shown in Fig. 15.1. As shown schematically in Fig. 15.2, the knee is encased in a capsule made of fibrous tissue that develops with the periosteum, the membrane that surrounds the bones. The inside surface of the capsule is lined with the synovial membrane, or synovium. This is vascular connective tissue, laid up in folds, and its inner surface is lined with synovial cells. The capsule normally contains only a small amount of synovial fluid, the primary purpose of which is lubrication of the joint. This is a viscous, yellowish-white fluid that resembles egg white, which is where the name comes from. (The Latin word ovum means egg.)

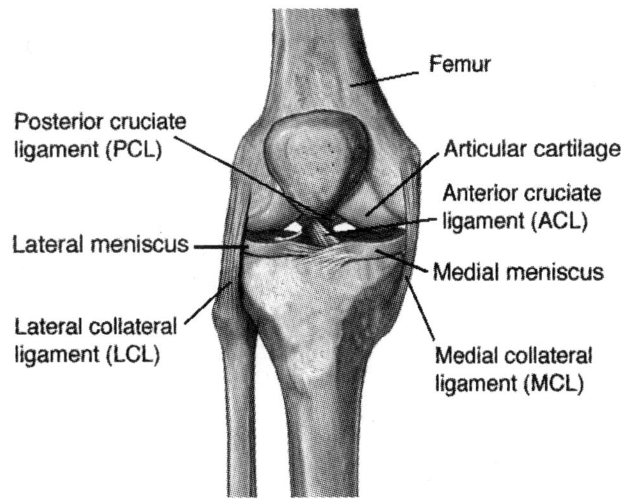

Fig. 15.1 The important components of the knee joint. (Copyright © 2004 Nucleus Medical Art. All rights reserved. www.nucleusinc.com.)

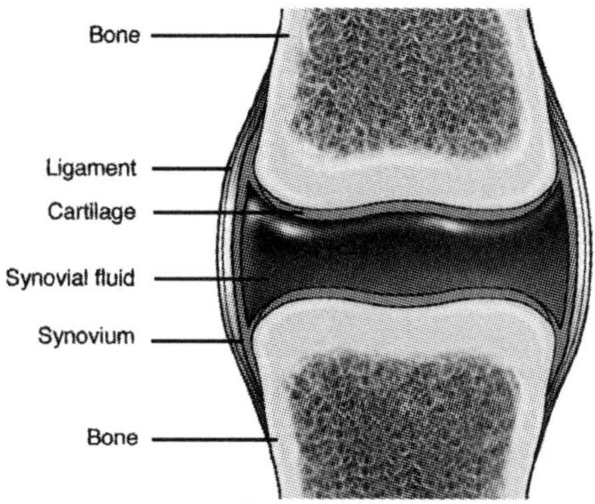

Fig. 15.2 Schematic representation of a synovial joint. (Copyright © 2004 Nucleus Medical Art. All rights reserved. www.nucleusinc.com.)

The synovial fluid comprises principally blood plasma and hyaluronic acid, which is a long-chain disaccharide polymer that is synthesized by the synovial cells. This fluid provides hydrodynamic lubrication that is enhanced by the special properties of the fluid. First, it is thixotropic, meaning that its viscosity decreases as the velocity gradient increases. Secondly, the fluid acts like a gel under rapid loading, and so it resists being squeezed out under sudden compression.

15.1 Cartilage

Cartilage in general is a tough, elastic, almost colorless structural material found in vertebrates. There are three general types: First, hyaline cartilage, which is pearly bluish in color. It comprises the fetal skeleton, which later calcifies to form bone, and, along with the ribs, forms the wall of the thorax; it also forms the friction-reducing material in joints. Second, white fibrous cartilage, which forms the discs of the spine. Third, elastic cartilage, which is found in the ear, nose, and tubes like the trachea and larynx. Here, we will be concerned with articular* cartilage, the hyaline cartilage that forms a layer over the ends of certain bones and lubricates joints in conjunction with the synovial fluid.

15.1.1 Microstructure of Articular Cartilage

Articular cartilage is made up of an extracellular matrix (ECM), upon which the mechanical properties depend, and in which are scattered the cells called chondrocyctes, the function of which is to produce the ECM. The microstructure of articular cartilage is depicted in Fig. 15.3, and a schematic representation of the components is shown in Fig. 15.4.

Cartilage
Bone

Fig. 15.3 Hyaline cartilage that covers the end (epiphysis) of a long bone are chondrocytes distributed in an extracellular matrix. (From Michael H. Ross, Gordon I. Kaye, and Wojciech Pawlina, *Histology, a Text and Atlas,* Lippincott, Williams & Wilkins, 1995.)

*Articular means having to do with joints.

15.1.2 Collagen

The main structural element of cartilage is Type-II collagen fibril, which is a protein, i.e., a polypeptide, a long-chain polymer having a molecular weight of over 10,000. Collagen is the most abundant protein in mammals and is thus one of the most important of all organic materials. In addition to cartilage, collagen is also the principal structural element of tendon, ligament, and bone, and in the latter it forms the scaffold on which calcification occurs.

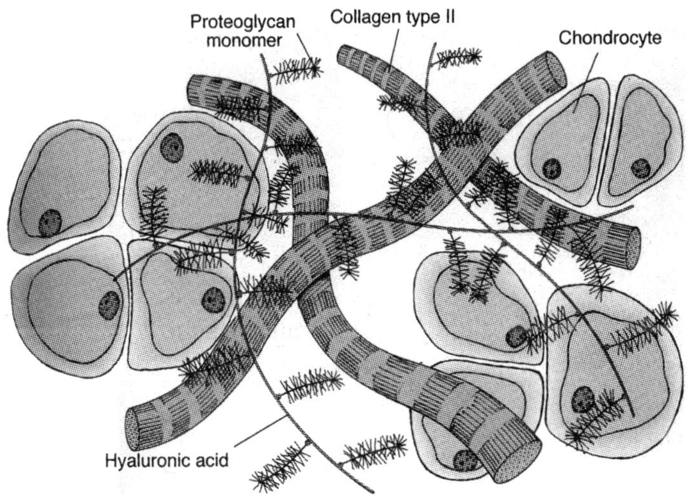

Fig. 15.4 Schematic representation of the structure of hyaline cartilage, showing the chondrocytes and the polymeric components of the extracellular matrix (called ground substance - see Section 15.1.4). (From Michael H. Ross, Gordon I. Kaye, and Wojciech Pawlina, *Histology, a Text and Atlas,* Lippincott, Williams & Wilkins, 1995.)

A polypeptide is formed from the reaction of the amino group and the carboxyl group of an amino acid, as shown by the example in Fig. 15.5. The peptide bond is the same as an amide bond, so a polypeptide is also a polyamide.

$$^{+}H_3N-CH(R_1)-COO^{-} + {}^{+}H_3N-CH(R_2)-COO^{-} \longleftrightarrow {}^{+}H_3N-CH(R_1)-C(=O)-NH-CH(R_2)-COO^{-}$$

Fig. 15.5 The formation of a peptide bond in the polymerization reaction of two amino acids.

Greek Alpha

α-Carbon: $^{+}H_3N-CH-COO^{-}$

Proteins are polymers of α-amino acids, so called because the amine group is attached to the carbon next to the carboxyl group, which is known as the α-carbon. There are twenty α-amino acids in all, and they are distinguished by the particular side group R that is attached to the basic unit. Examples of the α-amino acids found in collagen are shown in Fig. 15.6. The smallest and simplest amino acid is glycine, which plays a critical role in the structure of collagen fibers.

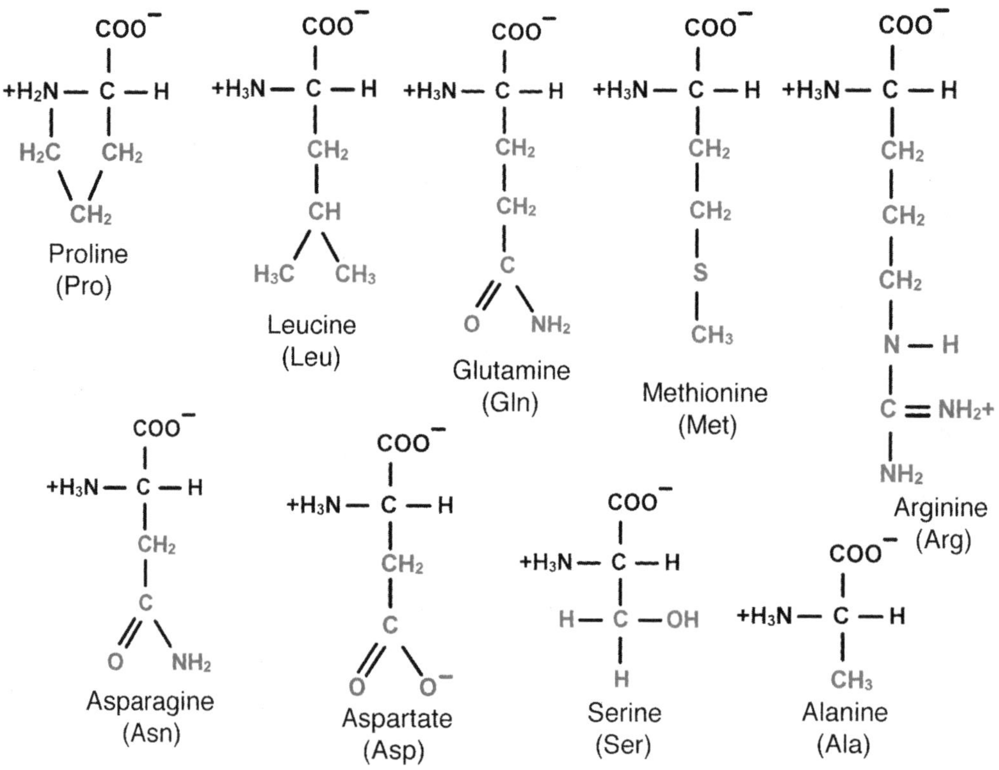

Proline (Pro)
Leucine (Leu)
Glutamine (Gln)
Methionine (Met)
Arginine (Arg)
Asparagine (Asn)
Aspartate (Asp)
Serine (Ser)
Alanine (Ala)

Fig. 15.6 Examples of the α-amino acids found in collagen.

Polypeptide chains always have a positively charged amino group on one end and a negatively charged carboxyl group at the other. Each amino acid unit in the chain is called a residue; an example is shown in Fig. 15.7.

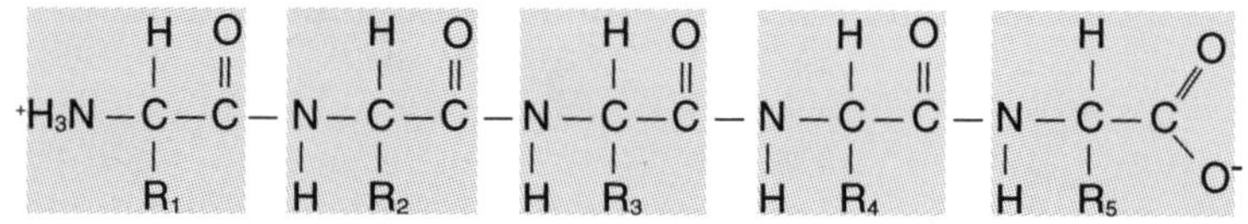

Fig. 15.7 Schematic representation of the units called residues in a polypeptide chain.

The peptide group is rigid and planar because the double bond does not actually stay on the C-O pair, but oscillates between that and the C-N pair. Thus, neither bond allows rotation. However, the other C-N and C-C bonds are pure single bonds, and they do allow rotation.

15080 The polypeptide chains in collagen are in the form of a right-handed helix called an α-helix. This is a rod-like structure that has a backbone consisting of a repetition of two carbons and one nitrogen, as shown in Fig. 15.8(a). The entire chain is shown in Fig. 15.8(b), in which the dashed lines denote the hydrogen bonds that stabilize the helix. These hydrogen bonds link the CO group of each residue to the NH group that lies four residues further down the chain. The side groups lie on the outside of the chain, as indicated in Fig. 15.8(c), because the inside of the helix has no room for them.

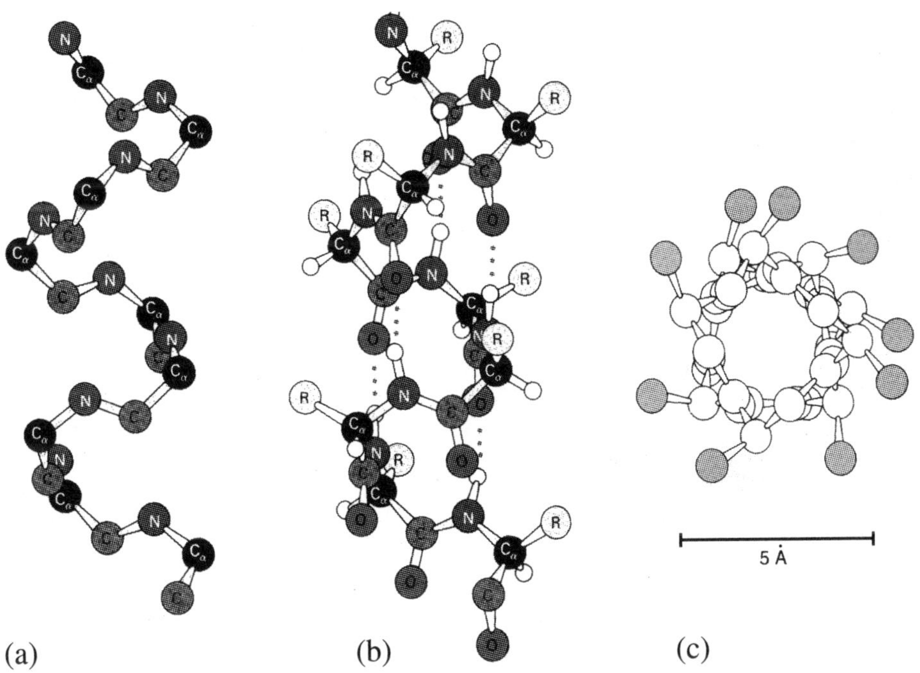

Fig. 15.8 (a) Model of a right-handed α-helix, showing only the backbone made up of a nitrogen, an α-carbon, and a carboxyl carbon. (b) The entire helix, showing the hydrogen bonds (dotted) between the NH and CO groups; these stabilize the helix.(c) A cross-sectional view of the helix, showing the side chains on the outside; the size of the inner free space is exaggerated. (From Lubert Stryer, Biochemistry, 3rd ed. © 1975, 1981, 1988 by Lubert Stryer. Used with permission of W. H. Freeman and Co.)

The building blocks of a collagen fibril are molecules comprising triple-helical chains of tropocollagen that are 300 nm long and 1.5 nm in diameter. The Type-II collagen in cartilage is composed of three identical chains laid up in a staggered array, as shown in Fig. 15.9.

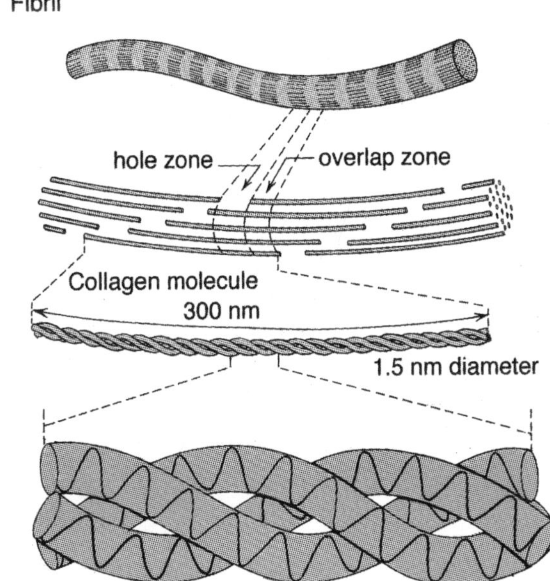

Fig. 15.9 Diagram showing how a Type-II collagen fibril is made up of staggered collagen molecules, which are triple-helix chains of tropocollagen. (Adapted from Michael H. Ross, Gordon I. Kaye, and Wojciech Pawlina, *Histology, a Text and Atlas,* Lippincott, Williams & Wilkins, 1995.)

The staggered-chain arrangement shown in Fig. 15.9 can be revealed by staining a specimen of a fibril with a heavy-metal ion. These ions can only fit into the gaps between the ends of the molecules, and this gives rise to the striations that can be seen in a transmission electron micrograph.

In mature collagen fibril there are cross-links between the amino-terminated region of one molecule and the carboxyl-terminated region of a molecule in an adjacent row, as shown in Fig. 15.10. These cross-links add to the strength and elastic modulus of the fibrils.

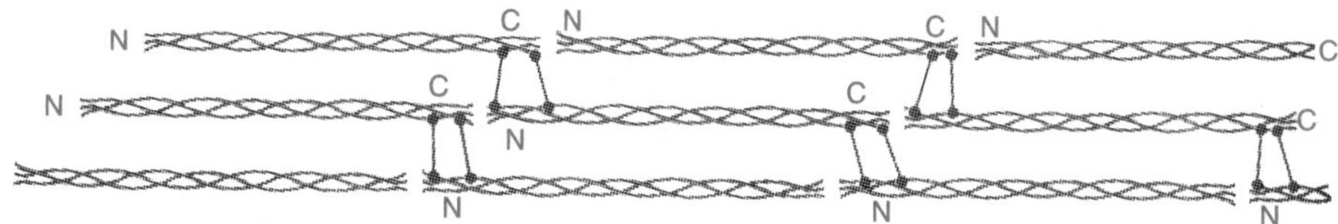

Fig. 15.10 Location of cross-links between adjacent tropocollagen molecules in a collagen fibril. (From Lubert Stryer, Biochemistry, 3rd ed. © 1975, 1981, 1988 by Lubert Stryer. Used with permission of W. H. Freeman and Co.)

The collagen molecules are unusual proteins in that they contain a large amount of glycine, the smallest of the amino acids. In fact, every third residue in the tropocollagen chain must be glycine, because this is the only one that can fit in the interior of the helix. The fact that there are three residues per turn requires that every third one be glycine. An example of the kinds of amino-acid sequences found in tropocollagen chains is shown in Fig. 15.11.

-Gly–Pro–Met–Gly–Pro–Ser–Gly–Pro–Arg-
-Gly–Leu–Hyp–Gly–Pro–Hyp–Gly–Ala–Hyp-
-Gly–Pro–Gln–Gly–Phe–Gln–Gly–Pro–Hyp-
-Gly–Glu–Hyp–Gly–Glu–Hyp–Gly–Ala–Ser-
-Gly–Pro–Met–Gly–Pro–Arg–Gly–Pro–Hyp-
-Gly–Pro–Hyp–Gly–Lys–Asn–Gly–Asp–Asp-

Fig. 15.11 A example of the amino acid sequences in tropocollagen chains. (Adapted from Lubert Stryer, *Biochemistry,* 3rd ed. © 1975, 1981, 1988 by Lubert Stryer. Used with permission of W. H. Freeman and Co.)

In addition to the unusual amount of glycine, tropocollagen molecules also contain more proline than in most other proteins, as well as two amino acids rarely found in proteins: 4-hydroxyproline and 5-hydroxylisine. The hydroxylation of proline has been found to be an important stabilizing factor in the triple-helical rods.

15.1.3 Zones of Articular Cartilage

Articular cartilage can be characterized in terms of zones, as illustrated by Fig. 15.12. Below the articular surface is the superficial tangential zone (STZ) in which the collagen fibrils are aligned tangentially with the surface. Below that is the middle zone, which comprises roughly half the thickness and in which the collagen fibrils are randomly arrayed and less densely packed. The last third is the dense zone, in which the fibrils are aligned normal to the underlying bone. Just below the dense zone, the cartilage is calcified and is united with the subchondral* bone.

*Chondral means having to do with cartilage.

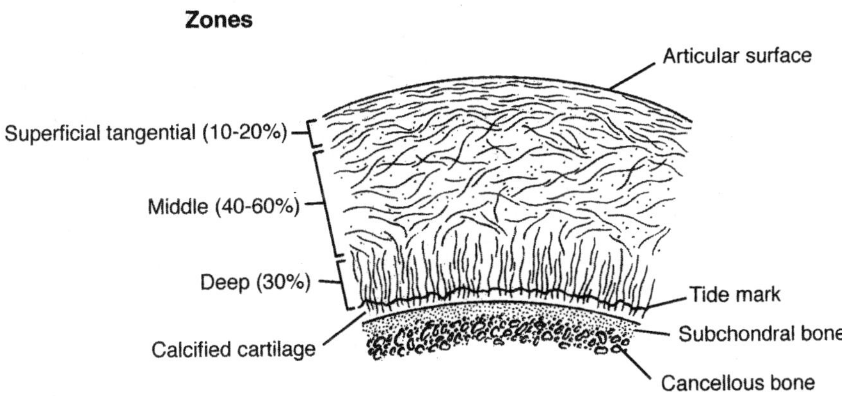

Fig. 15.12 Schematic representation of the zones of articular cartilage and the arrangement of the collagen fibrils in these zones. (Adapted from V.C. Mow, C.S. Proctor, M.A. Kelly in *Basic Biomechanics of the Musculoskeletal System, 2nd ed.,* M. Nordin and V.H. Frankel eds, Lea and Febiger, Philadelphia, 1989, pp 31 - 57.)

15.1.4 Ground Substance

In the ECM, the collagen fibrils are embedded in an amorphous, viscous, transparent material known as ground substance. It behaves like a semi-fluid gel, because it is a combination of a water-based fluid and a large, somewhat inflexible network of proteoglycan molecules (cf. Fig. 15.1). These consist of a protein chain to which are covalently bonded side chains of disaccharides called glycosaminoglycans (GAGs) arrayed in a brush-like structure, as shown in Fig 15.13. The proteoglycan molecules are attached by means of link proteins to long chains of hyaluronic acid. The GAG chains are acidic (i.e., negatively charged), because they contain hydroxyl, carboxyl, and sulfate side groups. In hyaline cartilage the GAGs are keratan sulfate and chondroitin sulfate (cf. Fig. 15.13).

The collagen and the proteoglycans are not homogeneously distributed in articular cartilage. In the STZ the collagen concentration is high and the proteoglycan concentration is low. The reverse is true in the large middle zone. The principal function of the collagen is to provide tensile strength to the cartilage and to contain and immobilize the proteoglycans. The local proteoglycan concentration is particularly high around the chondrocyctes. These cells synthesize both the collagen and the proteoglycans. Also contained in the ECM are other types of smaller collagens, which will not concern us here.

By far the major component of cartilage is water. The concentration of water ranges from about 80% in the STZ to about 65% in the deep zone. In the STZ, the tangential arrangement of the collagen and the high concentration of water both serve to give a low resistance to shear stresses. This keeps the velocity gradient in the synovial fluid low so that its high viscosity is maintained. In the rest of the cartilage, the water serves to give compressive strength to the cartilage as well as to contain and transport important ionic and molecular species. The compressive strength comes from the fact that the permeability of the collagen/proteoglycan network is very low. That is, a large pressure gradient causes only a very slow flow of the fluid, which is constrained in the interstices of the network. The reason for the constraint is that, first, the interstices are small and, second, that the network is very hydrophilic. The polar groups along the proteoglycan chains are caused by the ionization of carboxyl and sulfate groups to COO^- and SO_3^-. These polar groups make it possible for the chains to trap and hold water molecules. At the same time, the electrostatic repulsion from the polar groups exerts a swelling force on the polymeric network, and this acts to make room for the interstitial water. Another factor that promotes swelling is the osmotic pressure due to the counter ions, Na^+, Ca^{2+}, and K^+, which are necessary to balance the charges of the polar groups. These factors all work together to establish the low degree of permeability of the network to water.

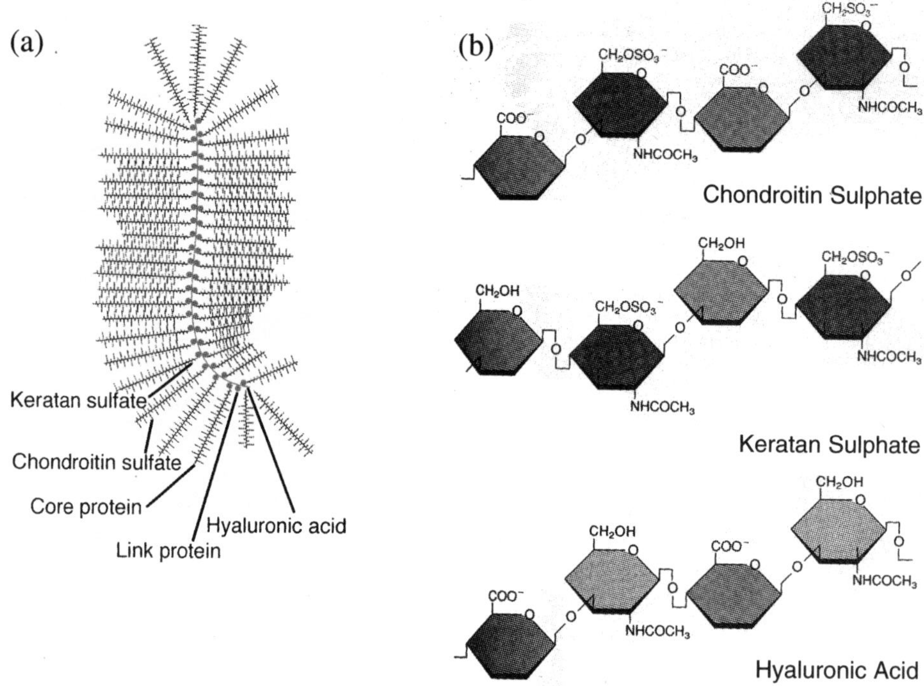

Fig. 15.13 (a) Schematic representation of a proteoglycan aggregate. (b) The repeating structures of the GAGs in this proteoglycan. Acidic side groups shown bold. ((From *Biochemistry, 2nd ed.* by Christopher K. Matthews and K. E. Van Holde. Copyright © 1996 by the Benjamin/Cummings Publishing Company, Inc. Reprinted by permission of Pearson Education, Inc.)

15.1.5 Mechanical Behavior of Cartilage

Articular cartilage is a viscoelastic material. This comes from the friction between sliding polymer chains and from the time-dependent flow of the intermolecular water-based fluid under compressive forces. Thus, when specimens of cartilage are tested, they are found to undergo creep deformation. For example, when cartilage is loaded in compression, the fluid slowly exudes from the network, and the network becomes compacted, as illustrated schematically in Fig.
15150 15.14. A constant-displacement type of loading would produce stress relaxation at a rate dependent on the intermolecular friction and the flow of the interstitial fluid. These factors are also responsible for the energy dissipation that occurs during cyclic loading of the cartilage.

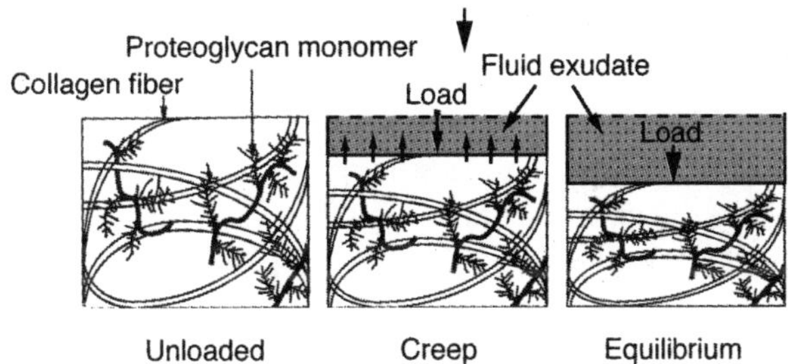

Fig. 15.14 Schematic representation of the effect of a constant load on articular cartilage. In effect, the load is supported by the fluid matrix in a manner similar to that by the air in a tire with a slow leak. (From H. J. Mankin, V. C. Mow, J. A. Buckwalter, J. P. Iannotti, and A. Ratcliffe, in *Orthopaedic Basic Science,* Amer. Acad. Of Orthopaedic Surgeons, 1994.)

The STZ has a high tensile modulus (~50MPa) by virtue of the highly aligned collagen fibrils. The modulus decreases toward ~5MPa down through the middle and deep zones, because of the random arrangement of collagen in the middle zone and arrangement perpendicular to the bone in the deep zone (cf. Fig. 15.12).

When the cartilage is compressed, the attachment to the subchondral bone constrains the lateral expansion, and this can lead to large shear stresses in the interface. If the compression is large enough, this can cause the cartilage to separate from the bone.

Even though it has no blood supply, cartilage is metabolically active to some degree. Nutrients and oxygen are thought to diffuse in from the synovial fluid to the chondrocytes.

It has been found that both the loading of joints and their motion are necessary to maintain the normal structure and properties of cartilage. If a joint is immobilized without any applied load for an extended period of time, the balance between synthesis and degradation of tissue is shifted. This leads to a decrease in the proteoglycan content, an increase in the water content, and cell death, which tends to transform the cartilage into just a collection of collagen fibrils. Moderate running, for example, has been found to increase the proteoglycan content, leading to an increase in stiffness of the tissue. This is thought to be stimulated by increased flow of water and ions in the polymer network and by deformation of the chondrocytes.

15.1.6 Injury in Cartilage

Unlike most body tissues, damage to cartilage is not repairable after an injury. The lack of a blood supply means that there can be no analog to the formation of scar tissue, and the normal response to injury does not operate. There are no cells present that can synthesize the ECM in mature cartilage, because by maturity the division and proliferation of chondrocytes has virtually stopped. Also, the size and quality of the proteoglycans synthesized by the chondrocytes diminishes with age. After an injury, some proliferation of chondrocytes occurs, but there is no migration of cells to the site of the injury, because they are too tightly bound in the polymer matrix.

If an injury penetrates to the subchondral bone, which does have a blood supply, the wound then has access to growth factors and undifferentiated cells. These can repair the bone damage, but the new cartilage that forms tends to be fibrous. The small amount of hyaline cartilage that forms does not persist. The result is a tissue that lacks stiffness and that has a high permeability for water. It is therefore less durable than normal cartilage, and it tends to deteriorate as a result of normal activities.

15.2 The Meniscus

The menisci are two cup-like pads of tissue that are attached to the plateau at the top of the tibia. The function of the menisci is to help to stabilize the knee joint. They distribute the load of the chondryles (knobs) of the femur on the tibial plateau, and they act to attenuate the shock waves that come from walking and running. They also are part of the lubrication system of the joint. As shown in Fig. 15.15, their outer borders are attached to the ligaments in the joint, and their inner borders taper down to a thin edge.

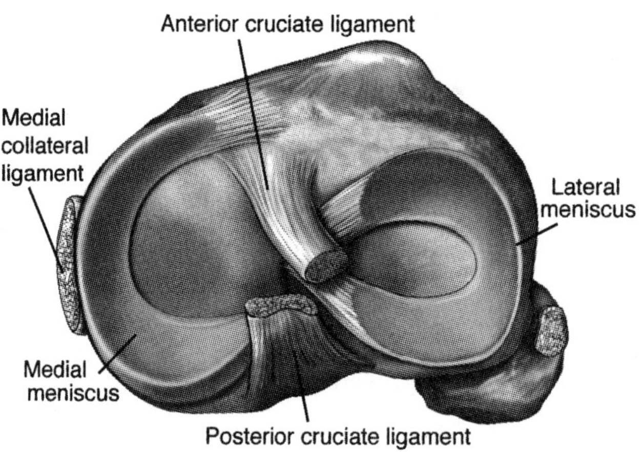

Fig. 15.15 The medial and lateral menisci that lie on the plateau of the tibia in the knee joint. (Copyright © 2004 Nucleus Medical Art. All rights reserved. www.nucleusinc.com.)

15.2.1 Microstructure of the Meniscus

The menisci are somewhat analogous to cartilage; they are referred to as fibrocartilaginous. The dominant type of collagen is Type I, rather than Type II as in hyaline cartilage. (In Type-I collagen, which is found in bone, skin, ligament and tendon, two of the polypeptide chains are identical and the other is slightly different.)

The proteoglycan content of the meniscus is only about 10% of that of hyaline cartilage, and the GAG population is somewhat different. However, the structure is similar to that of hyaline cartilage, and adhesive glycoproteins are present to bind the polymer network together. Like hyaline cartilage, the menisci are about 75% water. They contain a mix of chondrocytes and fibroblasts (cells that make collagen). The collagen fibrils in the menisci are oriented horizontally in the middle and deep zones, and there are shorter fibrils oriented radially, mostly in the surface layer.

15.2.2 Mechanical Behavior of the Meniscus

The arrangements of the collagen fibrils serve to resist the large tensile stresses that occur when a compressive load is applied. These tensile stresses arise because a compressive load would act to extrude the menisci out of the joint, if they were not tied down by the attachments to the tibia and the ligaments. The circumferential and radial collagen fibrils also resist this extrusion effect. As in hyaline cartilage, the polymer network has a low permeability for fluid, and this allows the fluid to carry the compressive load.

The meniscus is a viscoelastic material, and it can undergo the same kind of creep and stress relaxation as hyaline cartilage. Because of the alignment of the collagen fibrils, the meniscus is anisotropic with regard to stiffness and strength. The non-uniform distribution of the collagen makes the mechanical properties also non-uniform. The tensile strength has been found to vary from below 100 MPa to around 300 MPa, depending on the location.

15.2.3 Injury to the Meniscus

Injury to the menisci, usually the medial meniscus, is common in sports that involve sudden twisting forces on the knee joint, as in soccer, track and field, and downhill skiing. The injuries manifest themselves as tears of various types. Most of each meniscus is not vascular, so these tears are resistant to healing, as is the case with articular cartilage.

In contrast with articular cartilage, however, some of the meniscus is vascular. The femoral artery, which goes down the back of the leg, has branches at the knee called genicular arteries. These are branched further into a network on the periphery of the meniscus, and they penetrate into 10 to 30% of the width. Another genicular artery feeds the regions near the anterior and posterior ends of the pads, called the horns. These latter regions also contain nerve endings. Thus, repair of injuries is possible in these vascular regions. Unfortunately, most injuries tend to occur in the avascular regions.

15.3 Tendon

Tendon is a fibrous connective tissue that connects muscle to bone. For the knee joint, we can use the example of the quadriceps and patella tendons, shown in Fig. 15.16. This is an unusual arrangement in that it contains the patella bone, which lies within the body of the overall tendon. The overall tendon connects part of the quadriceps muscle to the tibia.

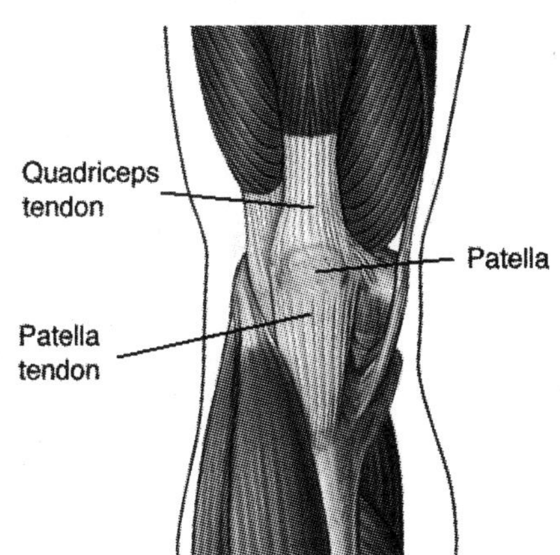

Fig. 15.16 The tendons that connect the quadriceps muscle to the tibia in the knee joint. (Copyright © 2004 Nucleus Medical Art. All rights reserved. www.nucleusinc.com.)

15.3.1 Microstructure of Tendon

Tendon is composed mainly of well-aligned Type-I collagen fibrils and ground substance interspersed with parallel rows of fibroblasts. The microstructure is shown in Fig. 15.17.

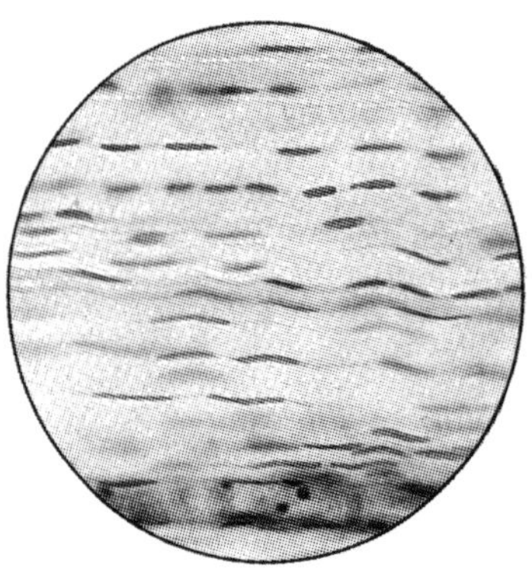

Fig. 15.17 The microstructure of tendon. (From Michael H. Ross, Gordon I. Kaye, and Wojciech Pawlina, Histology, a Text and Atlas, Lippincott, Williams & Wilkins, 1995.

The fibroblasts synthesize the collagen and the rest of the ECM. A schematic drawing of a fibroblast is shown in Fig. 15.18. The rough endoplasmic reticulum is essentially a protein factory. The outer faces of the folded sheets contain ribosomes, i.e., "bodies" (somes) that utilize ribonucleic acid (RNA) to synthesize proteins. The proteins are then stored in between the sheets until portions pinch off to form what is called a Golgi apparatus. The proteins are transported to the cell walls by way of the Golgi apparatus, and they are then secreted to the ECM.

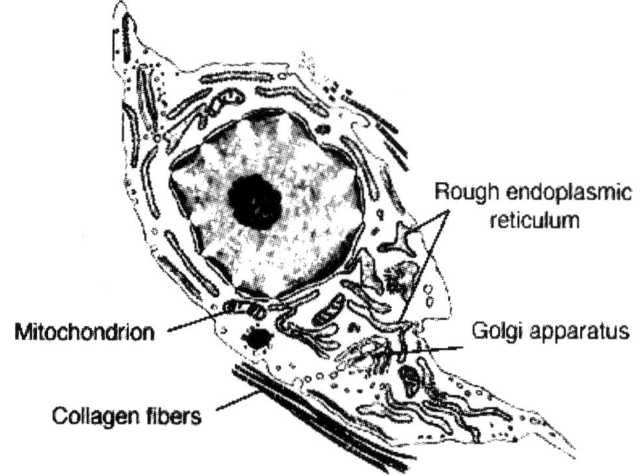

Fig, 15.18 A schematic representation of some important components of a fibroblast. (From C. Rossee and D. K. Clawson, *Introduction to the Musculoskeletal System,* Harper & Row, 1970.)

The mitochondria are the power plants of the cells in which oxidation of nutrient molecules takes place. The energy released from these reactions provides the activation energy needed for the reactions that occur in the production of proteins and other molecular species.

Different lines of fibroblasts produce the collagen fibrils and the proteoglycans. They all derive from what are called mesenchymal cells, which are cells found in the core of an embryo. (In Greek, mes means within, and enchyme means an infusion.)

The overall structure of tendon, shown schematically in Fig. 15.19, is built up from collagen molecules to microfibrils to subfibrils to fibrils, which are then bound together by glycoproteins, proteoglycans, and water to form fascicles. These are wrapped in an endotenon, which contains blood and lymphatic vessels and nerves and which permits relative movement of the fascicles. The fibrils in the fascicles are crimped. The complete tendon is made up of a parallel bundle of fascicles and is encased in an epitenon*.

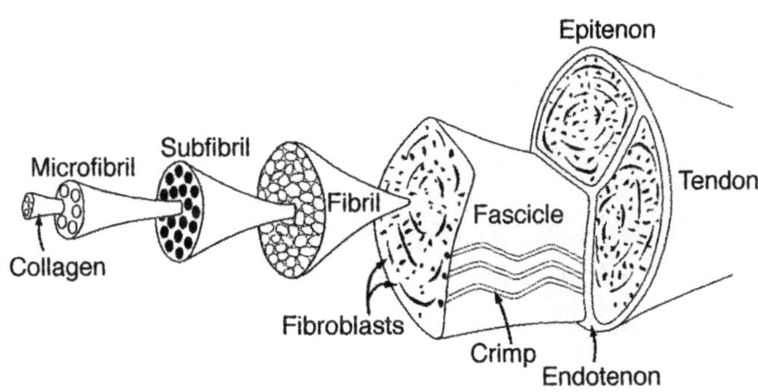

Fig. 15.19 Schematic representation of the architecture of a tendon. (Adapted with permission from J. Kastelic and E. Baer, in the Mechanical Properties of Biologic Materials, J. F. V. Vincent and J. D. Curry, eds. Cambridge University Press, 1980, pp. 397-435.)

Some tendons, like the flexor tendons in the hand, have to bend sharply around a bone. In this case, the tendon is enclosed in a sheath, which acts as a guide, and the tendon is lubricated by synovial fluid that is secreted from the wall of the sheath and by an epitenon that covers the tendon. This kind of tendon is partially avascular, and in these regions the nutrition is thought to come from the synovial fluid.

Straight tendons are wrapped in a covering called a paratenon. This contains blood vessels from the attached muscle and bone and from surrounding tissue, and these are connected to capillaries inside the tendon.

15.3.2 Mechanical Behavior of Tendon

The stress-strain curve of tendon, as shown in Fig. 15.20 starts with a "toe" region of low stiffness in which the fibrils become un-crimped, followed by a high-stiffness region in which the fibrils are loaded and begin to stretch. In humans, the ultimate stress is in the range 50 to 105 MPa. The modulus ranges from 1.2 to 1.8 GPa, which is about half of the modulus of nylon fiber. The ultimate strain, which is related to the energy absorbed, is in the range 9 to 35%.

*The terms endotendinium and epitendinium are sometimes used for endotenon and epitenon.

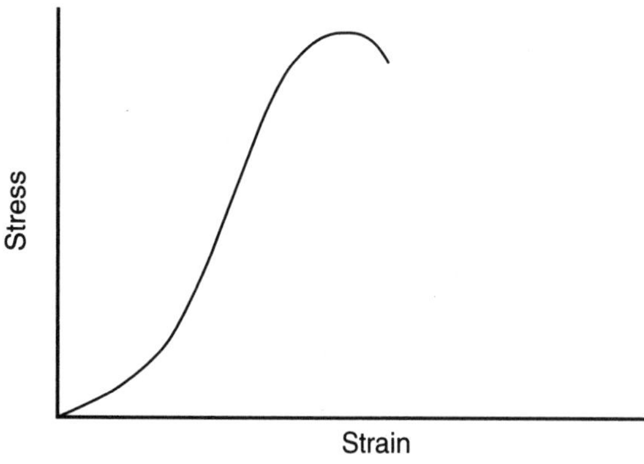

Fig. 15.20 Schematic representation of the tensile stress-strain curve of a tendon.

The mechanical properties of tendon vary with the anatomical location. For example, the flexor tendons of the human hand have different stress-strain curves, as illustrated by Fig. 15.21. The flexor tendon of the middle finger is the strongest, while that of the little finger is by far the weakest. The index and ring fingers are similar and intermediate in strength.

Tendon is viscoelastic; that is, it undergoes creep and stress relaxation; and load-unload tensile curves exhibit hysteresis, as shown in Fig. 15.22. When a muscle/tendon unit is loaded to a fixed displacement, that is, isometrically, the tendon stretches by creep. This allows the muscle to shorten, and this relaxation increases the performance of the muscle by reducing fatigue.

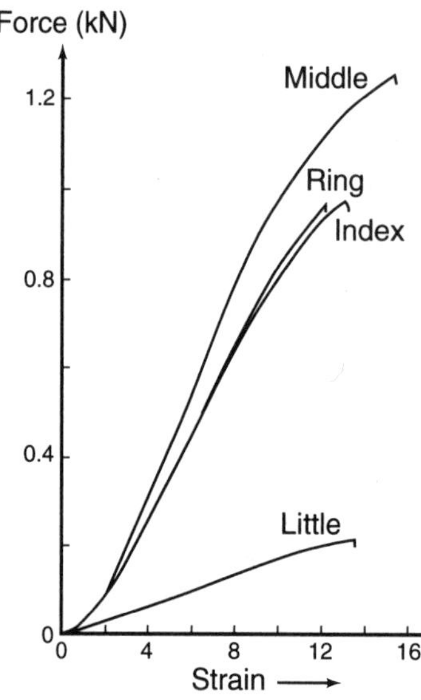

Fig. 15.21 Examples of the tensile behavior of the flexor tendons of the hand. (Reprinted from D. J. Pring, A. A. Amis, R. R. H. Coombs, *J Hand Surg* (Br) 1985, vol. 10, p. 331, with permission from the British Society for Surgery of the Hand.)

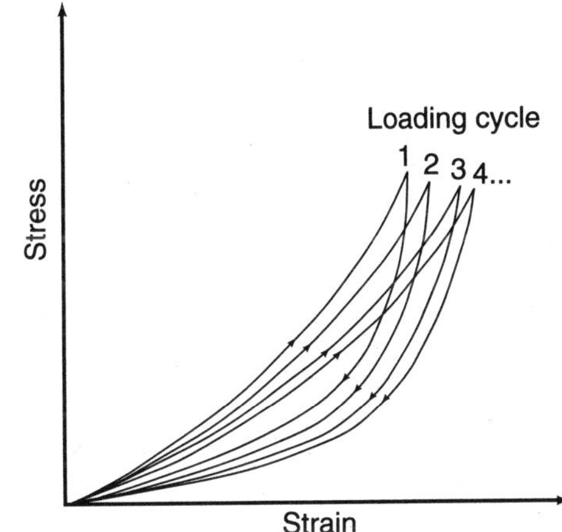

Fig. 15.22 Examples of cyclic stress-strain curves of tendon, showing hysteresis and the softening of the tissue. After 10 cycles, the curves usually converge to a steady state and become repeatable. (From S L-Y Woo, K-N An, S. P. Arnoczky, J. S. Wayne, D. C. Fithian, and B. S. Myers in *Orthopaedic Basic Science,* Amer. Acad. Of Orthopaedic Surgeons, 1994.)

Exercise improves the mechanical properties of tendon. The mass increases because of increased synthesis of collagen. The fibrils thicken, and more cross links form. This causes the modulus and the ultimate strength to increase. Cross-links also develop with age to maturity, and the stress-strain curve becomes steeper, as illustrated for the case of rat-tail tendon in Fig. 15.23.

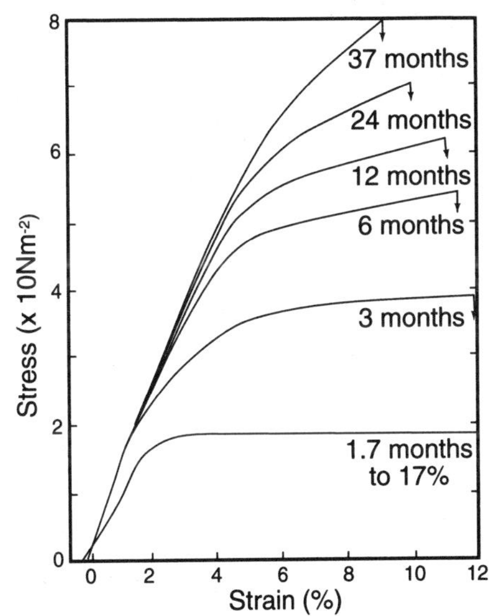

Fig. 15.23 Tensile stress-strain curves for rat-tail tendon as a function of age. (Adapted with permission from J. Kastelic and E. Baer, in the *Mechanical Properties of Biologic Materials,* J. F. V. Vincent and J. D. Curry, eds, Cambridge University Press, 1980, pp. 397-435.)

15.3.3 Injury, Healing, and Repair of Tendon

A tendon can be injured in two ways: first, by direct trauma, that is, by laceration (cutting or tearing) or by contusion (bruising), and, second, by tensile overload. The weakest parts of a tendon are at the insertion into a bone and at the connection with a muscle. Thus, overload can lead to either avulsion, where the tendon tears away part of the bone where it is connected, or to rupture of the junction between the tendon and the muscle.

The other mode of failure due to tensile overload is a rupture along the midsection. However, this is generally preceded by some kind of degenerative process, such as overuse or just normal aging. For example, rupture of the Achilles tendon is commonly found in middle-aged individuals who engage in unaccustomed strenuous exercise. Another form of degeneration is attrition caused by rubbing of the tendon against bone. For example, this can occur from rubbing of the tendon of the rotator cuff against the top of the scapula in the shoulder.

Healing of a lacerated or bruised vascular tendon can occur in the same way as healing of other vascular tissue, because it is in contact with such tissue. The healing sequence involves exudation of blood, formation of a fibrin clot, vascu-lariztion of the clot, proliferation of cells, synthesis of an extra-cellular matrix, and finally remodeling of the repair tissue. In animal experiments, healing of a cut through a tendon involves bridging of the cut faces with disorganized fibrous tissue and later remodeling in which the fibers become organized into a parallel longitudinal orientation and cross links are formed. This process is promoted by careful exercise, which is necessary to restore the scar tissue to the normal structure and function.

The healing of sheathed, or avascular, tendon is still a subject of investigation. In vitro experiments in a cell culture on partially severed flexor tendons from rabbits indicate that cells from the epitenon and endotenon can differentiate into phagocyctes, which are cells that digest damaged tissue, and later into fibroblasts, which can then fabricate collagen and ground substance. To allow this process to occur in an actual wound, the ends of a severed tendon can be brought together by special sutures, as illustrated in Fig. 15.24.

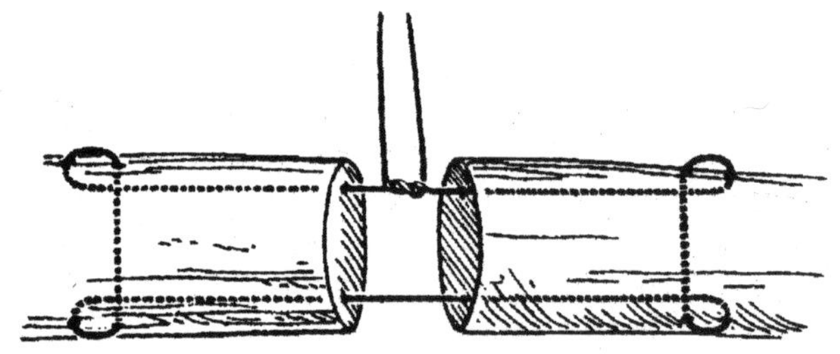

Fig. 15.24 Schematic representation of a tendon repair. (Reprinted from H. E. Klienert, S. Schepel, and T. Gill, *Surg Clin North Am,* 1981, vol. 61 p. 267, with permission from Elsevier.)

15.4 Ligament

Bone-to-bone connections are made with ligaments, which are short, dense, tough bands of fibrous tissue that are similar in appearance and microstructure to tendon. Here, we will focus on the ligaments that stabilize the knee joint. These are depicted in Fig. 15.1. The cruciate ligaments are intra-articular, i.e., within the joint, and the collateral ligaments are extra-articular. The distinction is important with respect to healing of injuries, because the collateral ligaments are next to normally vascular tissue, but the cruciate ligaments are contained within a synovial fluid.

15.4.1 Microstructure of Ligament

A ligament is made of parallel bundles of Type-I collagen in a matrix of ground substance, along with a small amount of elastic fibrous protein called elastin. Interspersed among the bundles are rows of fibroblasts, arranged in essentially the same way as shown in Fig. 15.17 for tendon. Ligament has a lower percentage of collagen and a higher percentage of ground substance than tendon does. Elastin is a protein made by fibroblasts that can form fibers of varying thickness. It has some of the same amino acids as collagen (glycine and proline). However, its polypeptide backbone is unusual in that it allows the long-chain molecules to coil randomly. In addition, some of the amino acids can form cross links between chains, and this results in the elastomeric behavior of elastin, much like vulcanized rubber.

The build-up of the microstructure of a ligament from the triple-helix collagen molecule to fascicles is similar to that of ligament, as shown in Fig. 15.19. The fascicles can be wound spirally, as in the anterior and posterior cruciate ligaments (ACL and PCL, respectively), or they can be straight, as in the medial and lateral collateral ligaments, (MCL and LCL, respectively). The fascicles can slide relative to one another within the fascicular sheath, the epitenon.

There are two kinds of connection, or insertion, between a ligament and a bone, called direct and indirect, the latter being more common. In both cases, the superficial fibrils of the ligament merge with the periosteum of the bone, and the deep fibrils insert into the matrix of the bone. In the direct insertion, the deep fibrils pass into the bone in two stages: first, a thin layer of fibrocartilage and then another thin layer of mineralized fibrocartilage, as shown in Fig. 15.25.

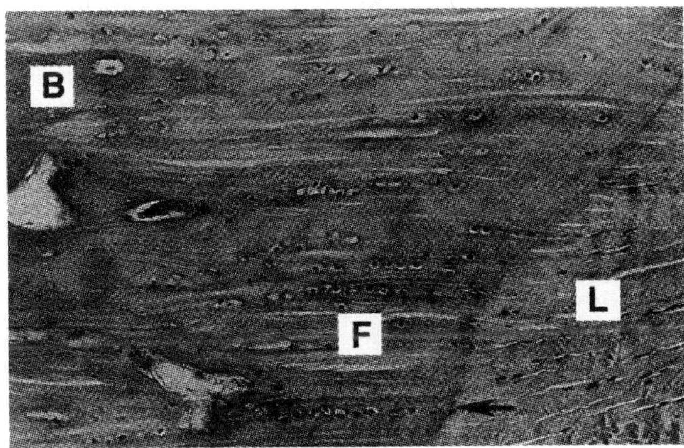

Fig. 15.25 The direct insertion of a rabbit MCL (L) into the femur (B) through a zone of uncalcified and (F) calcified fibro-cartilage. (Reprinted from S. L-Y Loo, M. A. Gomez, T. J. Sites, et al., J Bone Joint Surg, 1987, vol. 9A, p. 1200, with permission from the Journal of Bone and Joint Surgery, Inc.)

The collagen fibrils in a ligament form a somewhat irregular woven pattern; that is, they are not all parallel to the long axis of the ligament. The fibrils are also crimped in a kind of zigzag pattern. This arrangement is reflected in the tensile behavior.

15.4.2 Mechanical Behavior of Ligament

The mechanical behavior of ligament is essentially the same as that of tendon. The characteristic stress-strain curve of a ligament is similar to that of tendon, as shown in Fig. 15.20. A ligament can be gripped for a tensile test by using pieces of the bones to which it is attached, so the specimen comprises a bone-ligament-bone complex. For example, a femur-ACL-tibia complex is called an FATC.

The low-stiffness "toe" region of the stress-strain curve reflects the straightening and alignment of the collagen fibrils. After this, the curve enters the high-stiffness linear region until the ultimate stress is reached. Normal human activities take place in the low-stiffness regime, so the joint articulates readily. Extraordinarily large forces take the ligament into the high-stiffness regime. The advantage of this behavior is that excessively large displacements of the joint are thereby constrained. However, because ligament has less collagen than tendon, the modulus in the high-stiffness region is lower.

As in the case of tendon, ligament is a viscoelastic material. It undergoes creep and stress relaxation, and the load-unload tensile curve exhibits hysteresis. (This is the same kind of behavior as found in linear polymers above the T_g. It does not involve the kind of fluid flow discussed previously in the case of cartilage.) As shown earlier for tendon (Fig. 15.22), the first cycle to a given stress results in a lower strain than succeeding cycles. After some number of cycles, the curves superimpose, and the hysteresis becomes constant. Thus, the stress-strain curve is history-dependent. The tensile behavior is also strain-rate-dependent. That is, both the stiffness and ultimate load increase as the strain rate is increased.

During a period of inactivity of a joint, the fluid content of ligaments increases. When activity resumes and forces are applied to the joint, excess fluid is exuded, and the stiffness and hysteresis of the ligaments decreases with succeeding loading cycles until a steady state is reached. This is one of the reasons for the warm-up period that is recommended before exercise.

The mechanical properties of ligament vary with the anatomical location, age, and other factors. For example, the ultimate loads for the human ACL and MCL are approximately the same, between 340 and 390 N, but the PCL has about twice the ultimate (failure) load.

The effects of immobilization of a joint are decreases in the ligament stiffness, ultimate load, and energy absorbed, as illustrated by Fig. 15.26, which shows this for a rabbit MCL. It has been found that this deterioration occurs in both the substance of the ligament and in the insertions of the ligament into the bones. The major effect is in the insertions, where resorption of bone around the deep fibrils occurs. This can lead to avulsion, that is tearing away of the insertion along with some of the bone, if exercise of the joint is overdone during recovery.

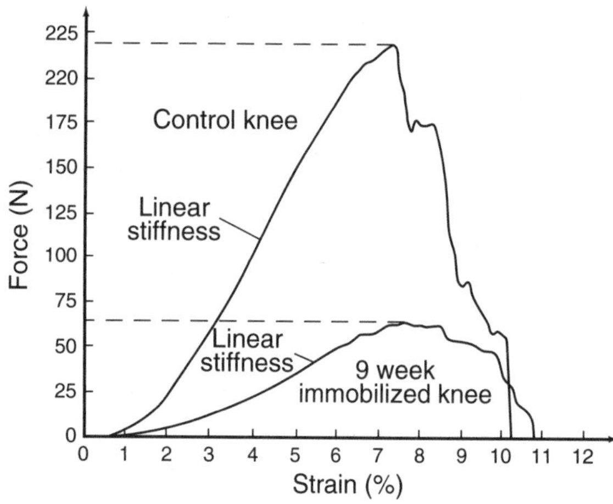

Fig. 15.26 Force vs. strain curves for a rabbit femur-MCL-tibia-complex (FMTC) from a leg that had been immobilized for 9 weeks, compared to one that had not been immobilized. (Adapted from S. L-Y Woo, M. A. Gomez, Y. K. Woo, et al., *Biorheology,* 1982, vol. 19, p. 397 with permission of IOS Press.)

The ligament substance recovers in a time period roughly equal to the period of immobilization, as shown schematically in Fig. 15.27, but the insertion site recovers much more slowly, because it requires remodeling of the affected bone. The properties of the ligament substance are improved by regular exercise, as indicated in Fig. 15.27, and exercise appears to offset the expected deterioration with age.

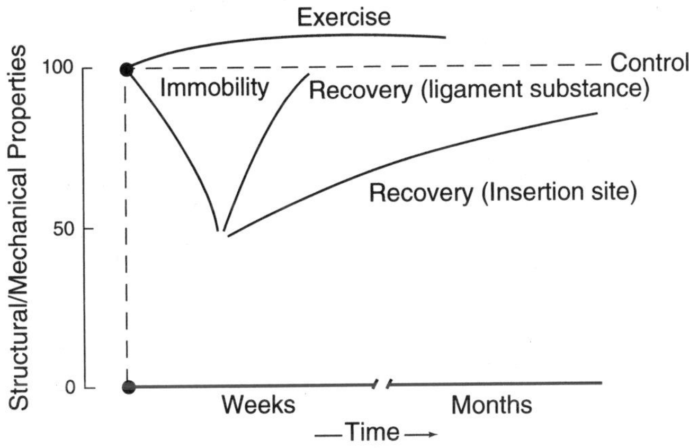

Fig. 15.27 Schematic representation of the effects of time on the structural and mechanical properties of ligaments, showing the effects of immobilization and recovery, compared with the effects of exercise. (Reprinted from S. L-Y Woo, M. A. Gomez, T. J. Sites, et al., *J Bone Joint Surg,* 1987, vol. 69A, p. 1200, with permission from The Journal of Bone and Joint Surgery, Inc.)

15.4.3 Injury and Healing of Ligament

Ligament injuries are categorized as follows:

Grade I - A mild strain caused by over-stretching; it is characterized by small hemorrhages and tears.

Grade II - A moderate sprain that shows gross tears and hemorrhage.

Grade III - Complete disruption of the ligament.

Extra-articular ligaments, like the MCL and LCL, as opposed to the intra-articular ligaments, heal like other vascular tissue, because they are in contact with such tissue. The healing sequence involves exudation of blood, formation of a fibrin clot, vasculariztion of the clot, proliferation of cells, synthesis of an extra-cellular matrix, and finally remodeling of the repair tissue. Thus, an isolated Grade-III tear of the MCL will heal by itself without surgical intervention, given enough time. For this to occur, the knee joint has to be stabilized by the ACL. If the ACL is also torn, then the treatment gets much more complicated.

An intra-articular ligament is surrounded by synovial fluid, rather than vascular tissue. Thus, a torn ACL usually does not heal. Surgical rebuilding of the joint is necessary, using some kind of graft. This can be an autograft using, say, part of the patient's own patella tendon, or an allograft from a donor, or a synthetic material. Biological tissue is much preferred, because it can be remodeled by the body after the repair. The subject of treatment of such injuries is an area in which animal studies are still being carried out.

References and Recommended Reading

1. Henry J. Mankin, Van C. Mow, Joseph A. Buckwalter, Joseph P. Iannotti, and Anthony Radcliffe, in *Orthopaedic Basic Science,* Ed. Sheldon. R. Simon, American Academy of Orthopaedic Surgeons, 1994.
2. Savio L-Y. Woo, Kai-Nan An, Steven P. Arnoczky, Jennifer S Wayne, Donald C Fithian, and Barry S. Myers, ibid.
3. Cornelius Rosse and D. Kay Clawson, *Introduction to the Musculoskeletal System,* Harper and Row, New York, 1970.
4. Christopher K. Matthews and K. E. van Holde, *Biochemistry, 2nd ed.* Benjamin Cummings, 1996.
5. Bruce Alberts, Alexander Johnson, Julian Lewis, Martin Raff, Keith Roberts, and Peter Walter, *Molecular Biology of the Cell, 4th ed.* Garland Science, Taylor & francis Group, 2002.
6. Michael H. Ross, Gordon I. Kaye, and Wojciech Pawlina, *Histology, a Text and Atlas,* Lippincott, Williams & Wilkins, 1995.
7. Lubert Stryer, *Biochemistry, 3rd ed.* W. H. Freeman and Co. 1988

Summary

We have considered here the structure-property relationships in four types of flexible connective tissue that are of critical importance in the knee, as well as other joints. The remarkable lubricating and shock-absorbing properties of articular cartilage are the result of the arrangement of Type-II collagen fibrils and proteoglycans and the water-trapping properties of this network. The menisci comprise the other shock-absorbing elements in the knee joint. They have a microstructure that is somewhat similar to that of articular cartilage, except that they employ Type-I collagen fibrils. Tendons, which connect muscle to bone, and ligaments, which act as interconnects between bones, have microstructures similar to each other, and their main structural elements are Type-I collagen fibrils. Their viscoelastic behavior plays a crucial role in absorbing shock loading in joints. These tissues have blood supplies that range from nil to ample, and this determines whether they are able to heal from injuries on their own or whether surgical repair must be carried out.

Glossary/Vocabulary - Chapter 15

Achilles tendon	The tendon of the gastrocnemius and the soleus muscles of the leg. It is used in the extension of the ankle. It sometimes ruptures in middle-aged people during unaccustomed strenuous exercise.
ACL	Abbreviation for anterior cruciate ligament. This is one of the intra-articular ligaments in the knee joint.
Alanine	One of the 20 α-amino acids.
Allograft	A graft from the body of a donor. This can be used to repair a ligament, for example.
Alpha helix	A right-handed helix. This is found in collagen fibers.
Amino group	An NH_3 group. This is found in all amino acids.
Amino acid	A residue of a protein having an amino group at one end and a carboxyl group at the other end. Amino acids are the building blocks of proteins.
Arginine	One of the 20 α-amino acids.
Articular cartilage	The hyaline cartilage on the surface of a bone in an articular joint. It is found on the epiphysis of a long bone, like the femur for example.
Asparagine	One of the 20 α-amino acids.
Aspartate	One of the 20 α-amino acids.
Autograft	A graft using tissue from one's own body. This can be used to repair a ligament.
Avulsion	A forcible tearing away, as when a tendon tears away a part of a bone to which it is attached. In the case of a tendon, the alternative type of tear is a rupture of the tendon/muscle junction or a rupture along the mid-section.
Carboxyl group	A COO group. This is found in all amino acids.
Cartilage	A tough, elastic, almost colorless structural material found in vertebrates. There are three kinds: hyaline cartilage, elastic cartilage, and white fibrous cartilage.
Chondrocytes	The cells found in cartilage. Their function is to produce the ECM.
Chondroitin sulfate	One of the GAGs found in the proteoglycans in the ground substance of hyaline cartilage. This, along with keratan sulfate, forms the bristles on the brush-like proteoglycan molecules.
Chondryle	The knob on the epiphysis of a long bone. The menisci in the knee act as cups to hold the chondryles of the femur.
Collagen	A protein, i.e., a polypeptide that is the main structural unit of many parts of the body. It is the most abundant protein found in mammals.
Collateral ligaments	The extra-articular ligaments on the inside and outside of the knee joint. Collateral means side-by-side. These are the medial collateral ligament MCL and the lateral collateral ligament LCL.
Cruciate ligaments	The intra-articular ligaments in the knee joint. Cruciate means cross-shaped. These are the anterior cruciate ligament ACL and the posterior cruciate ligament PCL.

Deep zone	The zone of articular cartilage that lies just above the subchondrial bone. The lower part of this zone is calcified cartilage.
ECM	Abbreviation for extracellular matrix. This is the tissue produced by the cells.
Elastin	This is a protein fiber that contains some of the same amino acids as collagen (e.g., glycine and proline), but its polypeptide backbone is unusual in that it can coil randomly. It has cross links between amino acids in neighboring chains, and this gives it its elastomeric behavior.
Epitenon	The fibrous sheath that envelops a tendon. It contains nerves, blood vessels, and lymphatic vessels.
Extracellular matrix	See ECM.
Fibrin clot	A mass formed by the coagulation of blood; its internal network is fibrin. Fibrin is an elastic, threadlike insoluble protein formed by the action of the thrombin in the blood.
Flexor tendon	A sheathed tendon that moves the bones of the fingers in the hand. The sheath contains a synovial fluid.
GAG	Abbreviation for glycosaminoglycan These are the polysaccharide side chains that comprise the bristles of the brush-like proteoglycan molecules in the ground substance of the ECM in flexible connective tissue.
Glutamate	One of the 20 α-amino acids.
Glutamine	One of the 20 α-amino acids.
Glycine	One of the 20 α-amino acids. This is the smallest amino acid and it allows a helix to form when it comprises every third residue in a collagen molecule.
Glysosaminoglycan	See GAG.
Golgi apparatus	A small vesicle in the cytoplasm of a cell that transports proteins from the rough endoplasmic reticulum to the cell walls for secretion into the ECM. The vesicle is formed by pinching-off of the sheets that make up the rough endoplasmic reticulum.
Ground substance	A semi-fluid gel in the ECM that contains proteoglycan molecules in a water-based fluid. The proteoglycan molecules are protein chains with polysaccharide side chains. They are strung along chains of hyaluronic acid.
Hyaline cartilage	A pearly bluish connective tissue comprising chondrocytes and an ECM of mainly Type-II collagen fibrils and ground substance. It is about 75% water. It forms the prototypes of the bones in the fetal skeleton, as well as the articular cartilage in joints.
Hyaluronic acid	A long-chain disaccharide polymer. Also called hyaluronate. The proteoglycan molecules in ground substance are attached to chains of hyaluronic acid.
Hydroxylation	The addition of one or more hydroxyl groups to a molecule. For example, hydroxylation of proline yields 4-hydroxyproline.
Keratan sulfate	One of the GAGs found in the proteoglycans in the ground substance of hyaline cartilage. This, along with chondroitin sulfate, forms the bristles on the brush-like proteoglycan molecules.

LCL	Abbreviation for the lateral collateral ligament. This is the outer extra-articular ligament on the side of the knee joint.
Leucine	One of the 20 α-amino acids.
Ligament	A flexible connective tissue that connects one bone to another. The microstructure comprises fibroblasts and an ECM of mainly Type-I collagen fibrils, elastin, and ground substance.
MCL	Abbreviation for medial collateral ligament. This is the inner extra-articular ligament on the side of the knee joint.
Meniscus	A pad of cup-like connective tissue on the plateau of the tibia. There are two of them in the knee joint. They distribute the load of the femoral chondryles on the tibial plateau.
Mesenchymal cells	The primitive cells found in the core of an embryo. They can differentiate into a variety of cells, including fibroblasts, chondroblasts, osteoblasts, myoblasts, etc.
Methionine	One of the 20 α-amino acids.
Middle zone	The central 40-60% of the thickness of hyaline cartilage. The collagen fibrils here are randomly arrayed and less densely packed than in the STZ and in the deep zone.
Paratenon	The wrapping of a straight tendon.
Patella tendon	The tendon that connects the patella to the tibia. It forms part of the unit: quadriceps tendon/patella/patella tendon.
PCL	Abbreviation for posterior cruciate ligament. This is one of the intra-articular ligaments in the knee joint.
Phagocytes	Cells having the ability to ingest and destroy various kinds of debris like bacteria, damaged cells, protozoa, etc. They include macrophages and leukocytes (white blood cells).
Polypeptide	A polyamide formed by the reaction of the amino groups and carboxyl groups of amino acids. Proteins are polypeptides.
Proline	One of the 20 α-amino acids.
Proteoglycan	A protein chain to which is attached side chains of polysaccharides called GAGs. These are attached to chains of hyaluronic acid in ground substance.
Quadriceps muscles	The group of four muscles in the front part of the thigh that acts as the extensor of the lower leg. They are the rectus femoris, vastus lateralis, vastus medialis, and the vastus intermedius.
Quadriceps tendon	The tendon that connects the quadriceps to the patella. This is part of the unit: quadriceps tendon/patella/patella tendon
Residue	An amino-acid unit in a polypeptide chain. The residues are connected by peptide bonds.
Ribosomes	The bodies (somes) in the cytoplasm of cells in which proteins are synthesized by ribonucleic acid (RNA). The ribosomes are located on the outer faces of the rough endoplasmic reticulum.

RNA	Abbreviation for ribonucleic acid. It differs from DNA in that its sugar is ribose, instead of deoxyribose, and one of its four bases is uracil, rather than thymine. RNA controls protein synthesis in all living cells.
Rough endoplasmic reticulum	The folded sheets in the cytoplasm of cells on which proteins are synthesized. The synthesis is carried out by ribosomes located on the outer faces of the rEPR.
Serine	One of the 20 α-amino acids.
STZ	Abbreviation for the superficial tangential zone. This is the region just below the articular surface of articular cartilage. It comprises 10-20% of the thickness of the cartilage.
Subchondral bone	The bone just below the articular cartilage in a joint.This is a layer of compact bone that covers the spongy bone of the epiphysis.
Synovial fluid	A viscous, yellowish white fluid that resembles egg white. (Ovum means egg in Latin.) It comprises mainly blood plasma and chains of hyaluronic acid.
Synovial joint	A joint that is encased by a synovial membrane and moves freely. The knee is a synovial joint.
Synovial membrane	The membrane that encloses a synovial joint. It is vascular connective tissue, laid up in folds, and its inner surface is lined with the cells that make the synovial fluid.
Synovium	Another name for the synovial membrane.
Tendon	A fibrous connective tissue that connects muscle to bone. Its microstructure mainly comprises well-aligned fibrils of Type-I collagen in a matrix of ground substance, interspersed with parallel rows of fibroblasts.
Tropocollagen	The long-chain proteins that are used to make collagen fibrils. They are twisted in a triple helix to make rods 300nm long and 1.5nm in diameter.
Type-I collagen	A fibrous type of collagen comprising triple helical chains of tropocollagen. This is the type of collagen fibril that is found in the meniscus, ligament, tendon, bone, and skin.
Type-II collagen	A fibrous type of collagen comprising triple helical chains of tropocollagen. This is the type of collagen fibril found in hyaline cartilage.
Zones of cartilage	The layers in articular cartilage. There are three zones: superficial tangential (STZ), middle, and deep.

Exercises

15.1 What are the main microstructural components of articular cartilage?

15.2 Explain the special mechanical properties of articular cartilage and how these depend on its microstructure.

15.3 Why do injuries to articular cartilage not heal as in most other soft tissues?

15.4 What are the similarities and differences between the meniscus and hyaline cartilage?

15.5 What is the physiological advantage of having the "toe" region in the stress-strain curve of tendons and ligaments?

15.6 What are the basic differences and similarities between tendon and ligament from the standpoint of both function and microstructure?

15.7 What changes take place in ligaments and tendons during the "warm-up" period before exercise?

15.8 Which ligaments of the knee joint will heal on their own if torn, and which will not? Explain why.

16

RIGID CONNECTIVE TISSURE: BONE

Bone is the material of the rigid skeletal framework that supports the body. It is a composite made up of strong, tough collagen fibers that resist tensile stresses in a mineral matrix of a crystalline calcium phosphate that resists compressive stresses. In this sense it is analogous to steel-reinforced concrete. However, unlike concrete, bone is a living material that is constantly being remodeled, and it serves the vital function of storing calcium and supplying it to the blood stream to maintain the proper physiological level. Bone also serves as a container for the marrow, which is the source of stem cells needed for various ongoing functions of the body.

In this chapter we will consider the long bones, as in the leg. The macroscopic structure of a typical long bone is illustrated in Fig. 16.1, with various
16010 parts labeled. The long shank is called the *diaphysis,* from the Greek dia, meaning *through* and phyein, meaning *to grow* or *bring forth.* It is the first part of the bone to calcify during development of the fetus, and growth takes place at its ends, each of which is called an *epiphysis,* epi meaning *upon.* The *metaphysis* comes in between the ends and the shaft, meta meaning *between.* The bone is encased in a membrane called the *periosteum.* The shaft is made of *compact bone,* which also covers the outside of the ends, which are made of *spongy bone,* as illustrated in Fig. 16.2. This is also called *cancellar* bone (meaning *latticework* in Latin) or *trabecular* bone (from the Latin trabis, meaning *beam*). We should note that the hollow-tube design of the diaphysis employs the same low-mass, high-moment-of-inertia geometry used in bicycle tubes.

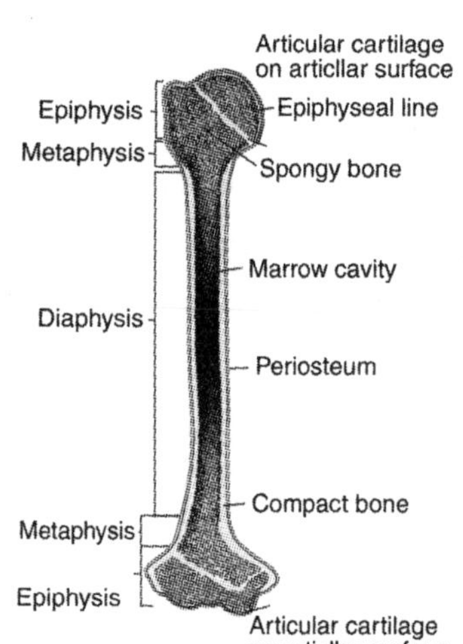

Fig. 16.1 Structure of a typical long bone. (From Michael H. Ross, Gordon I. Kaye, and Wojciech Pawlina, *Histology, a Text and Atlas,* 4th ed., Lippincott Williams and Wilkins, 2003.)

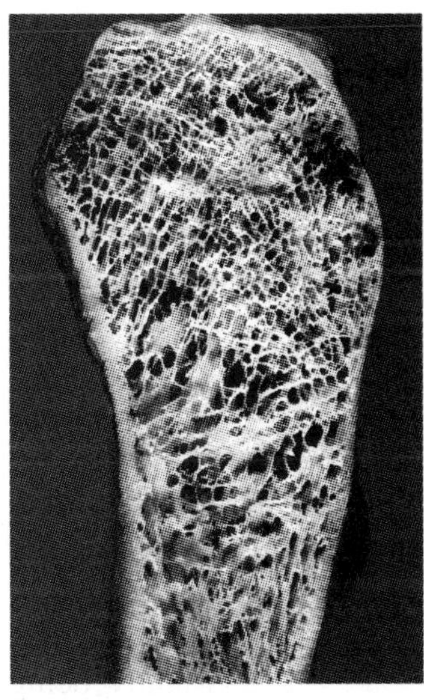

Fig. 16.2 Longitudinal section of the epiphysis of a long bone, showing a spongy bone interior encased in compact bone. (From Michael H. Ross, Gordon I. Kaye, and Wojciech Pawlina, *Histology, a Text and Atlas,* 4th ed., Lippincott Williams and Wilkins, 2003.)

16.1 Microstructure of Mature Compact Bone

As shown schematically in Fig. 16.3, it can be seen that compact bone comprises thick-walled cylinders made up of concentric shells

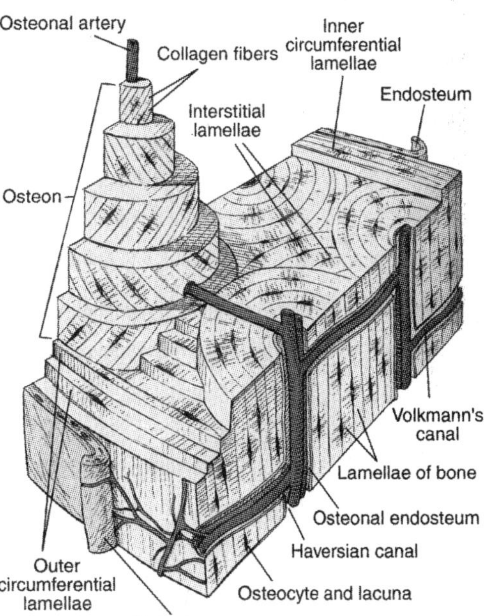

Fig. 16.3 Schematic representation of the microstructure of compact bone. (From Michael H. Ross, Gordon I. Kaye, and Wojciech Pawlina, *Histology, a Text and Atlas,* 4th ed., Lippincott Williams and Wilkins, 2003.)

In the regions between the cylinders shown in Fig. 16.3 are the remains of former cylinders; these are called interstitial *lamellae* and the cylinders themselves are called *osteons.* The inner and outer surfaces of the bone are made of circumferential lamellae. The central hole in each osteon is called a *Haversian canal,* and it contains an artery. The arteries are connected laterally by blood vessels that run through other canals, called *Volkmann's canals.* In between the shells of the osteon are cells called *osteocytes,* which lie in spaces called *lacunae.* From each of these there are projections (referred to as *processes*) that allow osteocytes to communicate with each other. This microstructure is the result of the *remodeling* process, which will be described later after we see how bone is formed on a fine scale.

16.1.1 Growth of Bone at the Cellular Level

In contrast to the growth of cartilage, which occurs by internal swelling of chondrocytes that continue to split and to secrete the ECM, most bone grows on the surface of existing bone; this is referred to as *appositional* growth. The process is illustrated schematically in Fig. 16.4. Flat, quiescent osteoprogenitor cells are contained under the fibrous connective tissue that constitutes the periosteum, and they also line the inner, or *endosteal,* surfaces.

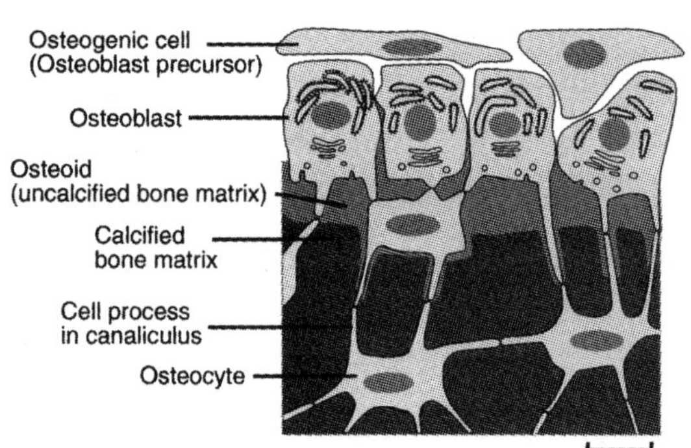

Fig. 16.4 Deposition of bone matrix by osteoblasts. (From Bruce Alberts, Alexander Johnson, Julian Lewis, Martin Raff, Keith Roberts, and Peter Walter, *Molecular Biology of the Cell,* 4th ed. Garland Science, 2002.)

During growth the osteoprogenitor cells become active as *osteoblasts,* which secrete an ECM consisting of Type-I collagen fibrils as well as some Type-V collagen and some ground substance, which consists of a small amount of GAGs, glycoproteins, and sialoproteins. Type-I collagen, which, as we have seen, is also found in tendon and ligament, is similar to the Type-II collagen found in cartilage, except that in Type I one of the polypeptide chains is different from the other two. This is in contrast to Type II, in which all three chains are the same. The principal amino acids found in Type-I collagen are glycine, proline, and hydroxyproline.

The osteoblasts also secrete vesicles that activate calcification. When an osteoblast becomes embedded in the matrix that it has produced, it is called an osteocyte. This un-mineralized material is called osteoid. The *osteoid* is gradually converted to hard bone by the formation of a hydrated form of calcium phosphate, called *hydoxyapatite.* The formula is

$$Ca_{10}(PO_4)_6(OH)_2$$

This calcification process occurs by the precipitation of small crystals in the spaces at the ends of the collagen fibrils and in between the fibrils. As noted earlier, the osteocytes send out processes, or arms, during the formation of the osteon, and these allow neighboring osteocytes to communicate chemically across gap junctions at the ends of the processes. The osteocytes participate to some extent in the regulation of the calcium-ion concentration in the blood by the resorption and re-deposition of the surrounding mineralized matrix. The microstructure of mature long bone that is described here (Fig. 16.3) is the result of remodeling, which will be described later.

16.2 Formation of Long Bones during Development

During the development of a fetus, a long bone starts out as a small-scale model made of hyaline cartilage, and it goes through the stages illustrated schematically in Fig. 16.5, always keeping the same proportions as in the scale model. After this process gets started, it is called *endochondrial ossification.*

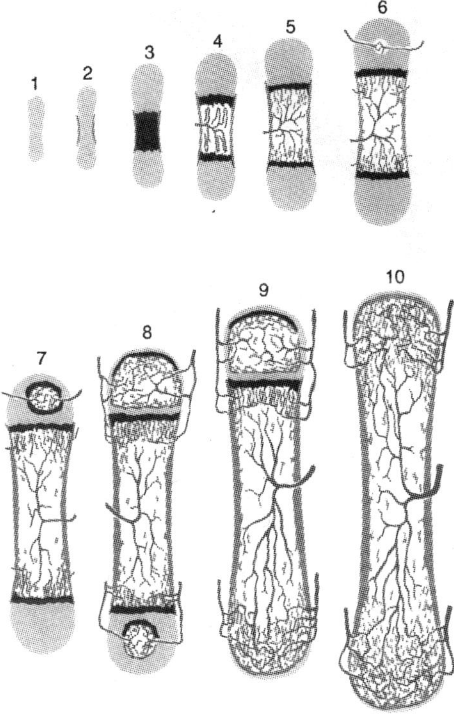

Fig. 16.5 Schematic representation of the development of a long bone. (From Michael H. Ross, Gordon I. Kaye, and Wojciech Pawlina, *Histology, a Text and Atlas,* 4th ed., Lippincott Williams and Wilkins, 2003.)

After formation of the cartilage model from mesenchymal cells that differentiate into chondroblasts and proliferate, the second phase is the formation of a bony layer around the midsection. This is the result of the differentiation of mesenchymal cells into osteoblasts in this location. In this newly formed bone, the collagen fibrils are interlaced, and the cells (now osteocytes) are randomly arranged; this immature bone is referred to as *woven* bone.

In the third phase, after formation of the bony collar around what will become the diaphysis, the chondrocytes in the interior become enlarged (hypertrophic), and they secrete alkaline phosphatase, causing calcification of the surrounding cartilage. This inhibits the diffusion of nutrients to the hypertrophic chondroblasts, and they die. This brings us to the fourth phase, in which the interior breaks down into small cavities that grow and coalesce. While this is going on, blood vessels penetrate the bony collar and vascularize the expanding cavity.

In the fifth phase shown in Fig. 16.5, primitive cells enter the cavity via the new blood vessels, and these differentiate into osteoprogenitor cells and other cells that form the marrow. At the same time, the spicules of remaining calcified cartilage at the ends of the cavity act as the sites for appositional formation of bone by the action of the osteoblasts that evolve from the osteoprogenitor cells (cf. Fig. 16.4). The un-calcified cartilage that remains at each end of the diaphysis is called *epiphyseal cartilage,* and these regions are the loci for further elongation of the bone.

In the sixth phase, shortly after birth, blood vessels invade the upper, or *proximal,* epiphysis, meaning the one closest to the center of the body, and ossification starts there in the seventh phase. The last three phases involve, first, vascularization of the lower, or *distal* epiphysis and ossification there, secondly, the disappearance of the distal epiphyseal cartilage, leaving the growth plate at the upper end to complete the elongation of the bone, and finally, after growth is completed, the disappearance of the upper epiphyseal cartilage. Each end of the bone then remains as spongy bone that is covered by compact bone, with the residual hyaline cartilage at the articulating surfaces on the ends.

The lengthening part of the growth process involves the formation of new cartilage at the *epiphyseal plate* and the formation of new bone under this plate, which pushes the epiphysis away and extends the diaphysis. The diameter of the diaphysis increases by formation of new circumferential lamellae of compact bone underneath the periosteum, and resorption of bone occurs on the inner (endosteal) surface, so that the marrow cavity expands.

16.3 Remodeling of Bone

After the woven bone is formed, the remodeling process transforms the immature woven bone into the osteonal (or Haversian) structure described earlier. This process begins with the action of *osteoclasts,* which are cells with multiple nuclei that are related to macrophages, the cells that eat up invading matter at an injury (phagean means *to eat* in Greek). Osteoclasts attach to an endosteal surface, as shown in Fig. 16.6, and begin to digest the organic part of the bone and to cause dissolution of the calcium phosphate by secreting hydrogen ions.

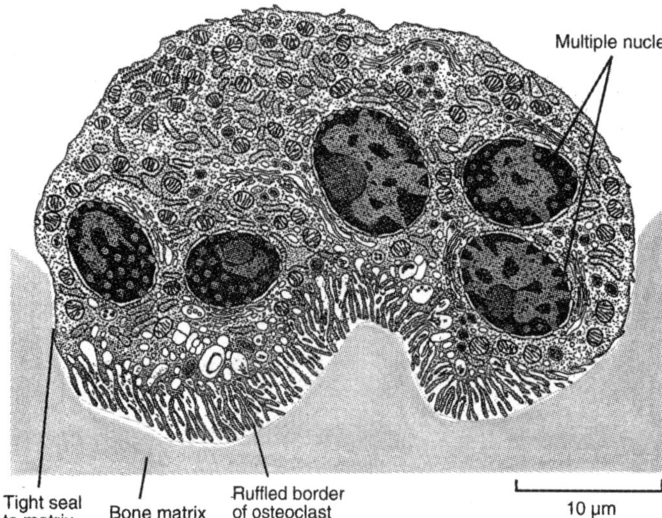

Fig. 16.6 The cross section of an osteoclast. (From Bruce Alberts, Alexander Johnson, Julian Lewis, Martin Raff, Keith Roberts, and Peter Walter, *Molecular Biology of the Cell,* 4th ed. Garland Science, 2002.)

The osteoclasts get together and bore a tunnel into the bone, as shown in Fig. 16.7, and a blood vessel surrounded by loose connective tissue follows in behind. The walls of the tunnel become lined with osteoblasts, which begin to lay down a new layer of osteoid on the walls. The osteoblasts become buried within the osteoid, and mineralization gradually occurs.

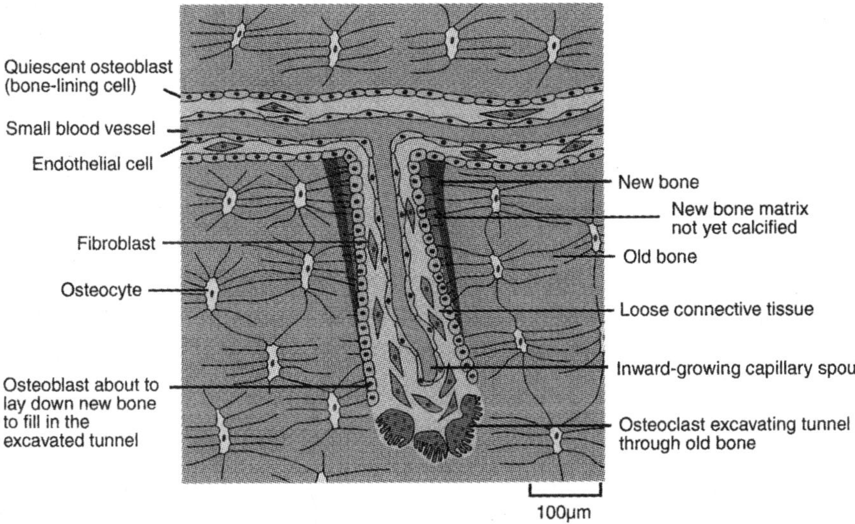

Fig. 16.7 Tunneling by osteoclasts and formation of new lamellae by osteoblasts during the process of remodeling of bone. (From Bruce Alberts, Alexander Johnson, Julian Lewis, Martin Raff, Keith Roberts, and Peter Walter, *Molecular Biology of the Cell,* 4th ed. Garland Science, 2002.)

The whole process of forming a new osteon is depicted schematically in Fig. 16.8, and the cross section of a new osteon is shown by the photomicrograph in Fig. 16.9.

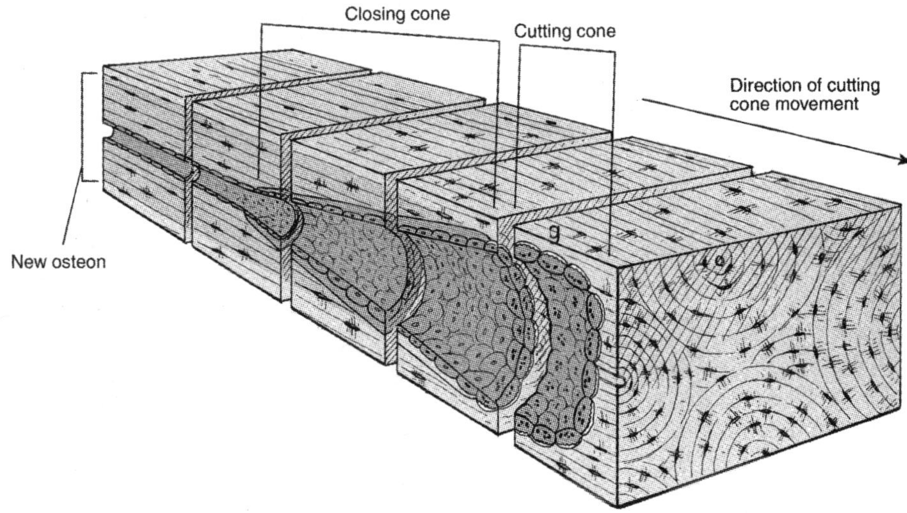

Fig. 16.8 Diagram of a bone-remodeling unit. (Adapted from Michael H. Ross, Gordon I. Kaye, and Wojciech Pawlina, *Histology, a Text and Atlas,* 4th ed., Lippincott Williams and Wilkins, 2003.)

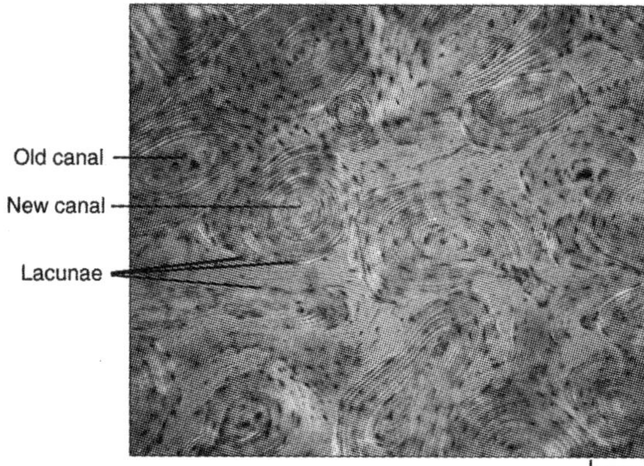

Fig. 16.9 Photomicrograph of a transverse section of a long bone. (From Bruce Alberts, Dennis Bray, Julian Lewis, Martin Raff, Keith Roberts, and James D. Watson, *Molecular Biology of the Cell,* Garland Publishing Co. 1983.)

The remodeling process is part of the system that regulates the calcium ion concentration in the blood. That is, bone serves as a reservoir for calcium in the body. The resorption by osteocytes is stimulated by a hormone from the parathyroid gland and is regulated by calcitonin from the thyroid gland. Thus, these glands serve to maintain the proper calcium level in the body.

It is possible to differentiate between osteons of different ages by making an x-ray radiograph through a thin transverse section of bone, as shown in Fig. 16.10. The oldest, most highly mineralized regions appear white, because they are very dense and thus absorb the x-rays. The youngest regions are the darkest, because, being only lightly mineralized, they do not absorb x-rays very much. The Haversian canals, of course, are totally black.

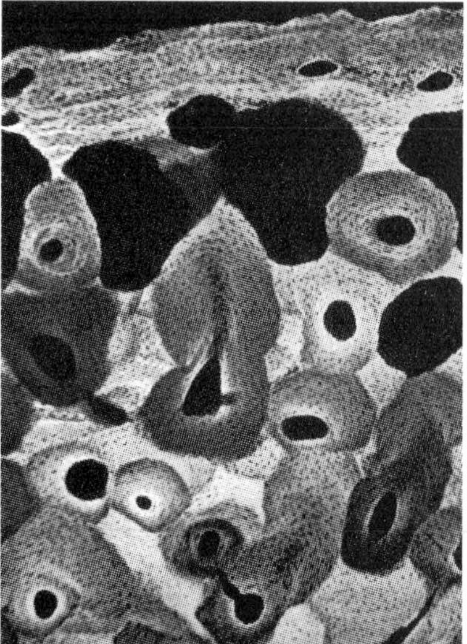

Fig. 16.10 Microradiograph of the cross section of a bone. (From Michael H. Ross, Gordon I. Kaye, and Wojciech Pawlina, *Histology, a Text and Atlas,* 4th ed.,Lippincott Williams and Wilkins, 2003.)

16.4 Mechanical Behavior of Bone

We will focus mainly on the femur, the largest bone in the leg, as illustrated by Fig. 16.11. As a long hollow shaft loaded mainly in compression by contact forces, it is somewhat analogous to the seat tube in a bicycle frame. However, because of the configuration at the top (Fig. 16.11a), the vertical force applied at the hips results in a bending moment, as do the forces from the muscles that are attached at the joints. The net bending moment produces a tensile stress on the
outer (*lateral,* as opposed to *medial,* or inner) surface of the shaft. For example, 16120
it has been estimated that, when a 70-kg man walks, he applies a tensile stress on the order of 65 to 68 MPa to the lateral surface of his femur.

Torsional loading can be applied by twisting forces at the joints, but the resulting shear stresses are normally low enough to be ignored. It is possible to put a net tensile stress on the front (*anterior,* as opposed to *posterior*) surface of
the femur, because of its curvature in the sagittal plane, that is, the plane shown 16130
in Fig. 16.11b.

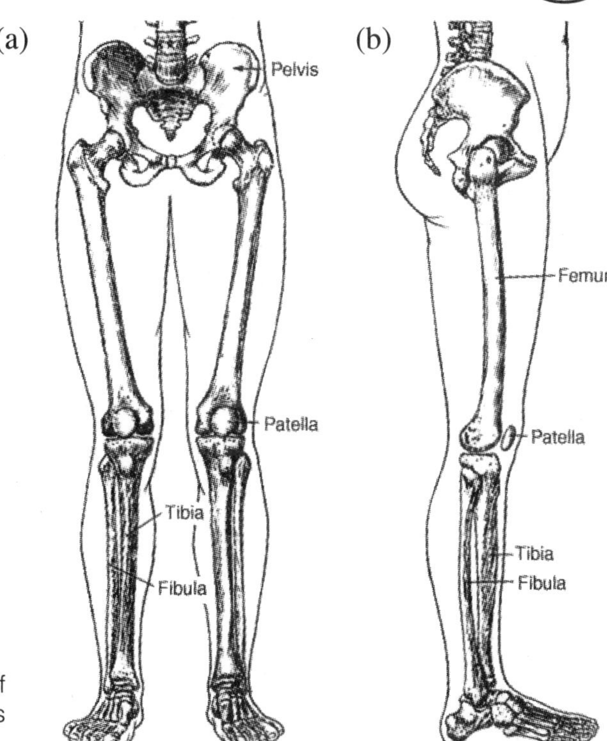

Fig. 16.11 (a) Anterior view and (b) lateral view of the bones of the leg. (From Medical Models Laboratory)

Compact bone behaves like a ceramic/polymer composite with discontinuous fibers. When loaded in tension, a specimen of this bone exhibits a stress-strain curve that is initially linear and then shows a departure from linearity that is called yielding, as shown schematically in Fig. 16.12. However, this is not the same kind of yielding that occurs in metals or polymers. Rather, it is characterized by microstructural damage that is actually the beginning of fracture, which finally occurs after a further increase in stress. Thus, there is a certain amount of toughness in compact bone, partly due to the collagen fibrils, which can stabilize microcracks in the mineral phase until their number becomes overwhelming. However, the apparent toughness (energy absorption in fracture) is the result of accumulation of damage.

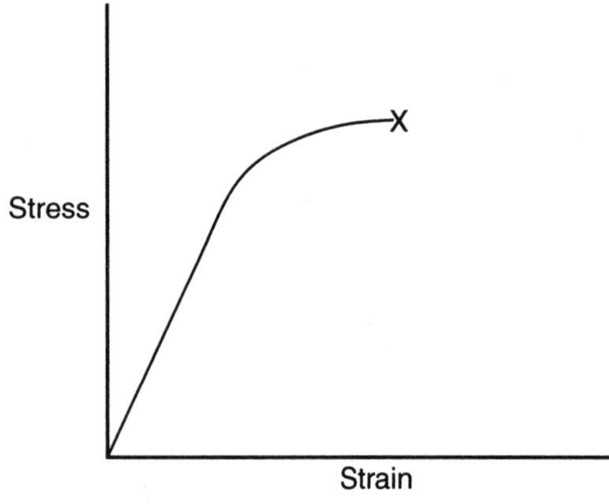

Fig. 16.12 Schematic representation of the tensile stress-strain curve of compact bone.

Compact bone (which is also called *cortical* bone) exhibits viscoelastic behavior, by virtue of its polymer component, and this is reflected in the strain-rate dependence of the stress-strain curve, as shown for bovine cortical bone in Fig. 16.13. Clearly, the yield stress and fracture stress both increase with increasing strain rate. The strain-to-fracture increases somewhat at lower strain rates, but then decreases as the strain rate is increased further (which allows the applied stress to increase to levels where microcracks can propagate to failure). Failure occurs mainly by pullout of osteons as a result of cracks having been deflected into the interfaces between the osteons and the interstitial bone. This is somewhat analogous to the failure in a carbon-fiber-reinforced bicycle tube(cf. fig. 13.28).

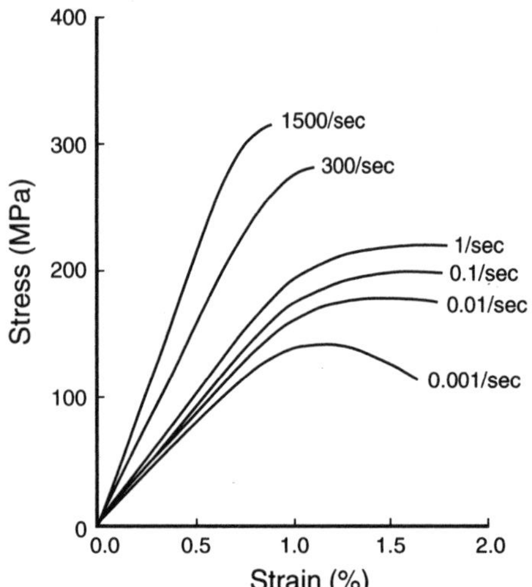

Fig. 16.13 Effect of strain rate on the tensile stress-strain curve of compact bone. (Reprinted from J. H. McElhaney, *J. Appl. Physiol* 1966, vol. 21, p. 1231; used with permission.)

In the example shown in Fig. 16.13, the elastic modulus increases from about 14 to 20 GPa in the range of strain rate between 10^{-3} and 1 per second, and it rises to around 40 GPa for the fastest loading. However, the modulus is known to be a strong function of the apparent density of bone, so these numbers should not be taken as general material constants for compact bone.

Compact bone is much stronger in compression than in tension with regard to both yielding and fracture, as shown in Fig. 16.14. This is because micro-cracking is suppressed by the compressive loading. Both yielding and fracture in compression occur by shear at roughly 45° to the osteons.

Because of its oriented structure, compact bone is considerably weaker when loaded in transverse tension. Although this might be thought to be a highly unusual type of loading, it does occur when the stem of a hip prosthesis is forced into the marrow cavity at the top of a femur (from which the head has been removed).

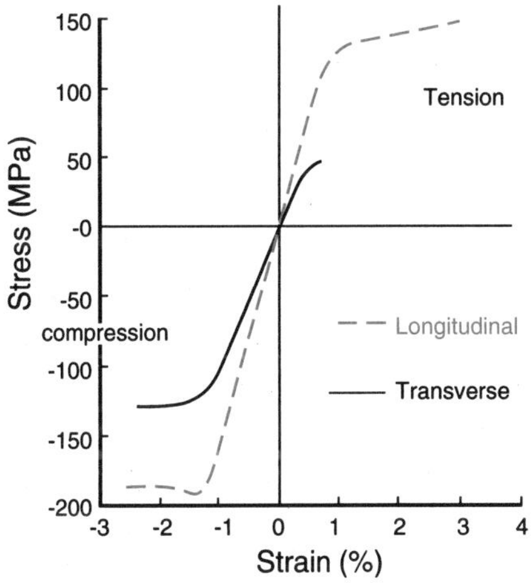

Stress (MPa)
150
100
50
-0
-50
-100
-150
-200
Tension
compression
Longitudinal
Transverse
-3 -2 -1 0 1 2 3 4
Strain (%)

Fig. 16.14 Stress-strain plots for human compact bone in tensile and compressive loading. (From L. J. Gibson and M. F. Ashby, *Cellular Solids: Structure and Properties,* Cambridge University Press, 1988.)

Again because of its viscoelastic nature, compact bone undergoes creep deformation under long-time loading. The creep curves look like those of other kinds of structural materials, as shown schematically in Fig. 16.15. The stress and strain to fracture by creep decrease with the time over which the load is applied, as shown in Fig. 16.16. This is typical for structural materials, but the increased creep strength in compression is again the result of the effect of compressive loading inhibiting the propagation of microcracks.

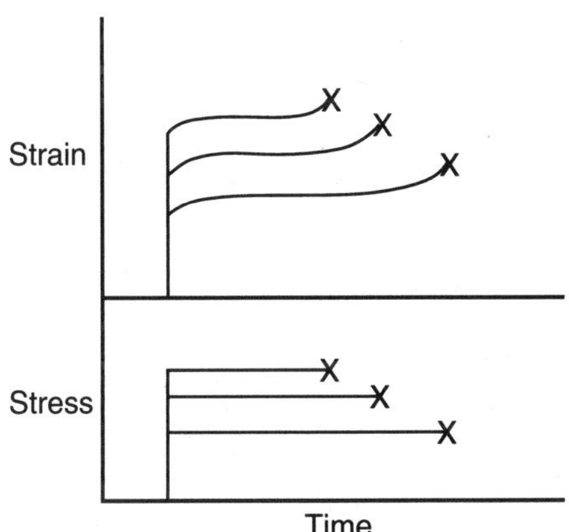

Fig. 16. 15 Schematic representation of strain vs. time (creep) curves of compact bone given a constant load.

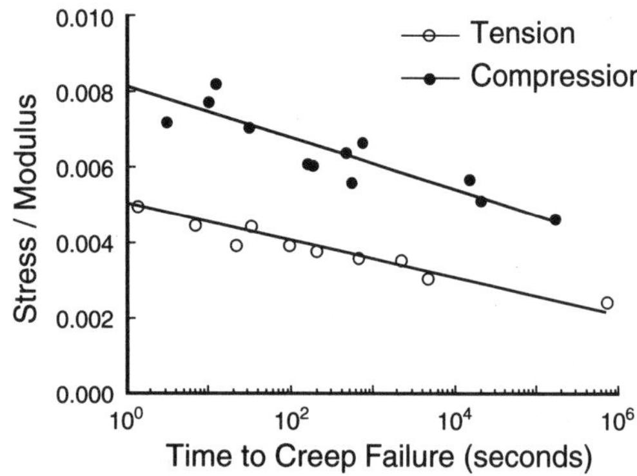

Fig. 16.16 Variation of creep-fracture stress of human compact bone with time to failure. (Reprinted from W. E. Caler and D. R. Carter, *J Biomech* 1989, vol. 22, p. 625, with permission from Elsevier.)

The fatigue behavior of bone is obviously important, because cyclic loading is a constant fact of life. So-called *stress fractures* that are common in distance runners and other athletes are, in fact, fatigue cracks. If the applied stress is high enough, the same kind of microstructural damage found in monotonic loading (i.e., tensile or compression tests) occurs in cyclic loading. As with metals, the stress needed to produce fatigue damage is well below the yield stress. Accumulated fatigue damage may be the cause of apparently sudden fractures of the hip or spine in elderly people who have lost bone density with age.

The special feature of bone as a living structural material is the ability of remodeling to repair microstructural damage and to arrange the microstructure to resist future damage. Thus, if the rate of damage accumulation is low enough, the amount can be kept to an innocuous level by remodeling.

The propensity for bone to grow in a manner that responds to applied loads has been expressed as what is known as *Wolff's law,* which essentially states that bone is resorbed in regions of low stress and becomes thicker in regions of high stress. This may be a result of the piezoelectric properties of bone. The piezoelectric effect occurs in materials in which the centers of positive and negative charge are separated, for example in the unit cell of a crystal. The application of a stress that changes this separation thereby changes the electric-field gradient within the crystal, and this can cause the flow of current in a circuit around the crystal. In bone, not only is the crystalline hydroxyapatite phase piezoelectric, but so are the biopolymers, including collagen. The exact mechanisms of the growth of bone in response to stress are still being studied, but it may involve the transport of ions like Ca^{2+} in response to the electric field gradients that result from the piezoelectric response.

Compact bone has been shown to follow *Coffin-Manson* behavior; that is, the strain-range* needed for failure varies inversely with the log of the number of cycles to failure, as shown in Fig. 16.17. Also indicated are the approximate strain ranges for various exercises, showing that as the stress level goes up, the number of cycles to failure decreases. This is a reflection of the inability of remodeling to keep pace with high rates of damage. Remodeling is time-dependent, and running produces not only higher stress levels, but also a greater cyclic frequency. Military recruits are known to suffer stress fractures because of running that amounts to 1000 miles during training, which lasts on the order of six weeks.

*expressed as stress range divided by the modulus

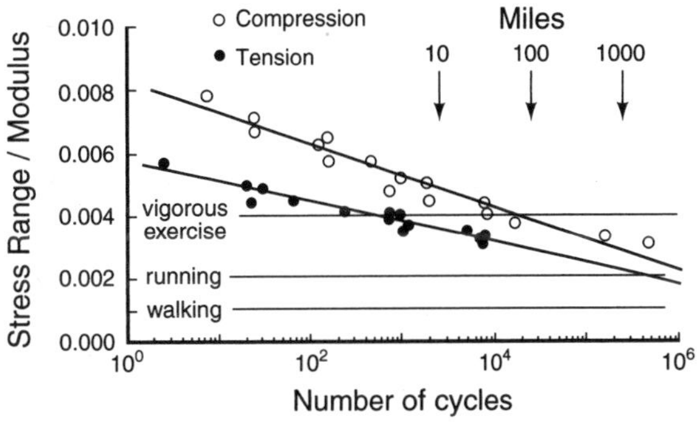

Fig. 16.17 The increase in fatigue life with decreasing strain range for compressive and tensile cyclic loading of human femoral compact bone. Typical strain ranges for various activities are shown. (Reprinted with permission from D. R. Carter, W. E. Caler, and D. M. Spengler, *Acta Orthop Scand* 1981, vol. 52, p. 481.)

As in other structural materials, fatigue cracks tend to nucleate at stress raisers, which in the case of bone are discontinuities in the microstructure like Haversian canals, lacunae, and canaliculi. Fatigue cracks form as a result of link-up of microcracks, and they tend to propagate along interfaces such as the "cement lines" between osteons and between lamellae. These interfaces deflect cracks away from the plane of high tensile stress, so the oriented nature of this composite gives a measure of resistance to fatigue crack propagation.

Spongy bone, being an open cellular structure, is much better suited to compressive loading than to tensile loading. As a result of continuous remodeling, the orientation of the plates and rods tends to become such as to give maximum resistance to the forces experienced over time. Therefore, spongy bone is mechanically anisotropic, as shown by the dependence of the modulus on both density and specimen orientation in Fig. 16.18. Note that the values of the modulus are more than an order of magnitude lower than for compact bone.

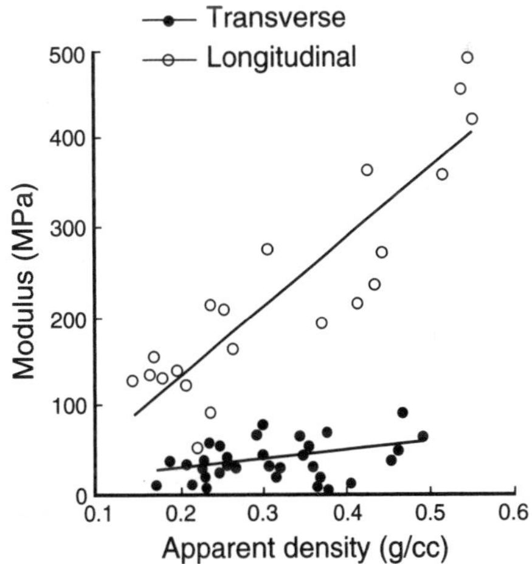

Fig. 16.18 Modulus for compressive loading of spongy bone subjected to loading in the transverse and longitudinal directions. (From J. L. Williams and J. L. Lewis, *J Biomech Eng,* 1982, vol. 104, p. 50. Reproduced with permission.)

A comparison of the compressive stress-strain curves of spongy vs. compact bone is shown in Fig. 16.19. Although the yield stress is much lower, the strain to complete fracture is much higher, as a result of the cellular structure. Initially, the bone behaves elastically, but yielding starts at low stresses by fracture of individual rods and plates. This carries on until the cavities begin to fill up with debris, whereupon the curve starts to rise before complete collapse occurs.

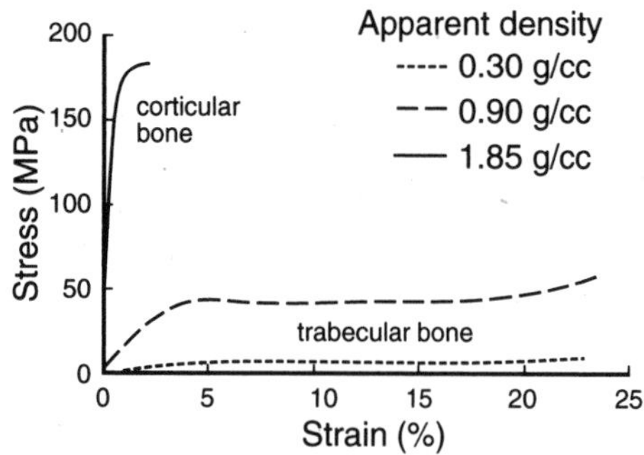

Fig. 16.19 Examples of compressive stress-strain curves for spongy bone and compact bone for different apparent densities. (From T. M. Keaveny and W. C. Hayes, in *Bone,* B. K. Hall, ed., CRC Press, 1993, vol. 7, p. 285.)

When loaded in tension, the stress at which yielding occurs (by fracture of rods and plates) is extremely low, as shown in Fig. 16.20. (Compare the stress scale of this curve with that in Fig. 16. 19.) Here, there is no range of stable deformation; fracture occurs under a falling load just after yielding. Obviously, this is not a material suited for tensile loading.

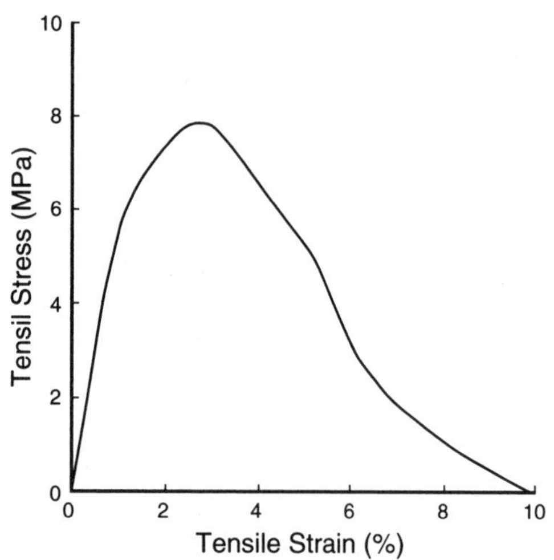

Fig. 16.20 Tensile stress-strain behavior of spongy bone. (Reprinted with permission from D. R. Carter, G. H. Schwab, and D. M. Spengler, *Acta Orthop Scand,* 1980, vol. 51, p. 733)

16.5 Effects of Aging

The overall bone mass of a person starts to increase rapidly with the adolescent growth spurt, and it reaches a maximum around age thirty. After that, it decreases continuously, as shown in Fig. 16.21. The rate of formation of new bone stays about the same, but the resorption rate increases. In general, the porosity of bone increases, and the density and mineral content per unit volume decrease.

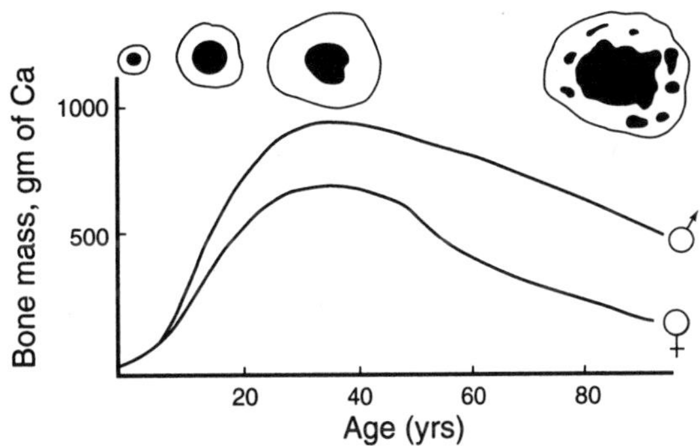

Fig. 16.21 The relationship between bone mass and age for both genders. (From F. S. Kaplan, W. C. Hayes, T. M. Keaveny, A. Boskey, T. A. Einhorn, and J. P. Ianotti, *Orthopaedic Basic Science,* Ed. S. R. Simon, American Academy of Orthopaedic Surgeons, 1994.)

The age-related remodeling of cortical bone can be illustrated schematically by the changes in cross-section of the diaphysis of the femur, as shown in Fig. 16.22. Both the outer (periosteal) and inner (endosteal) diameters increase after the third decade. Even though the thickness of the wall (the *cortex*) decreases, the moment of inertia is increased by the increase in the diameter, and this partly offsets the decrease in density with age, as far as the fracture strength is concerned.

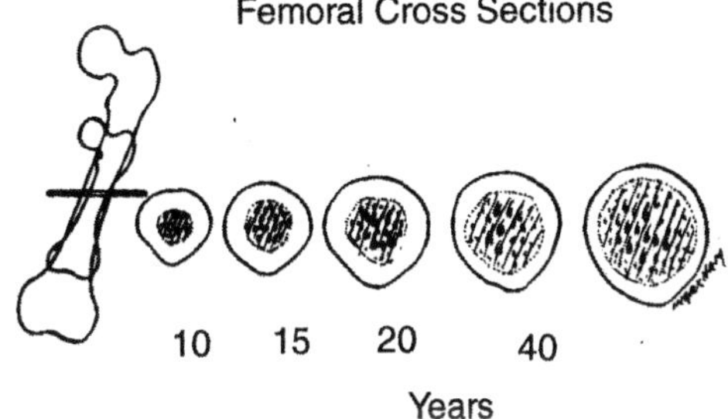

Fig. 16.22 Effects of age on the femoral diaphysis. (From F. S. Kaplan, W. C. Hayes, T. M. Keaveny, A. Boskey, T. A. Einhorn, and J. P. Ianotti, *Orthopaedic Basic Science,* Ed. S. R. Simon, American Academy of Orthopaedic Surgeons, 1994.)

The decrease in density and mineral content with age are reflected in the tensile modulus and ultimate tensile strength of compact bone, both of which decrease approximately linearly after about age 20, as shown in Fig. 16.23. The area under the stress-strain curve, which relates to energy absorption at fracture, also decreases at the rate of about 7% per decade.

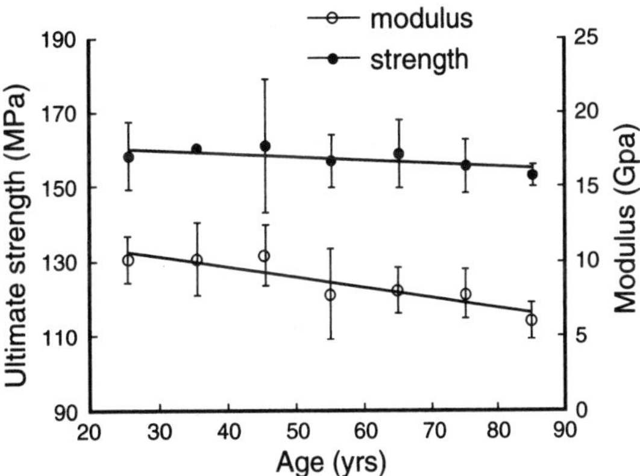

Fig. 16.23 Effects of age on the longitudinal tensile modulus and the ultimate tensile strength of human femoral compact bone. (Reprinted from A. H. Burstein, D. T. Reilly, and M. Martens, *J Bone Joint Surg,* 1976, vol. 58, p. 82, with permission from The Journal of Bone and Joint Surgery, Inc..)

The effects of aging on trabecular bone, as in the spine and the femoral head, for example, are much more serious than in compact bone. As shown by the example in Fig 16.24, both the number and thickness of the trabeculae in the femoral head decrease with age. The loss of trabeculae is particularly serious, because it is irreversible, since formation of new bone can only occur on the surface of existing bone. When vertical trabeculae become fewer, thinner, and longer, the crushing strength obviously decreases, and this can be a particular problem in the spinal vertebrae.

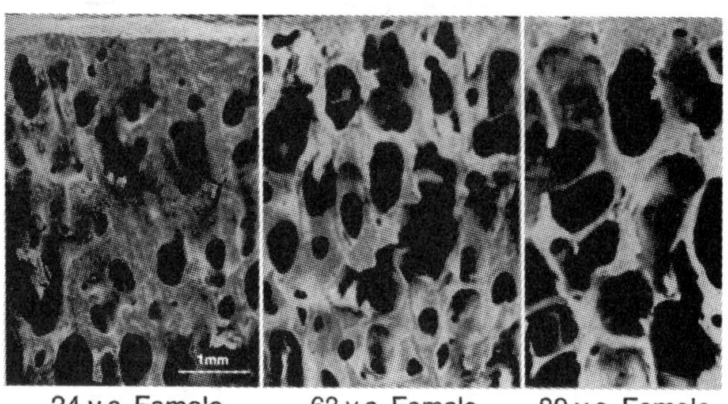

Fig. 16.24 Age-related changes in human trabecular bone from the femoral head. (Courtesy of Marc D. Grynpas, Ph.D.)

16.6 Fracture and Repair

It should be no surprise that bone fractures like the composite material that it is. The departure from linearity in the stress-strain curve shown in Fig. 16.12 does not represent plastic flow by shear as in the case of metallic materials. Rather, yielding is known to involve the early stages of fracture, in which damage accumulates under a rising load to the point at which catastrophic fracture occurs. The reason the load continues to rise after the damage has begun is that the combination of a critical-size flaw and a sufficient stress for its unstable propagation has not yet been reached. Thus, the formation of damage occurs as the strain in the bone increases, and the final catastrophic fracture occurs when a sufficient stress has been reached.

A recent study by Nalla et al. has illuminated the stages of the fracture process. They cut a specimen out of human compact bone in the form of a four-point-bend specimen and put two identical notches in the central region, in which
16270 the bending moment is uniform. When loaded to failure, the specimen fractured at one of the notches, as indicated schematically in Fig. 16.25.

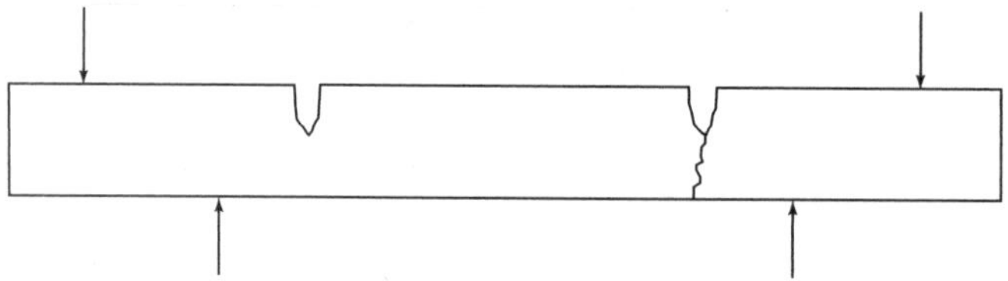

Fig. 16.25 Double-notched four-point-bend specimen used by Nalla et al.

The other notch obviously must have been on the verge of fracture, and they made microscopic observations there to study the damage that led up to the final fracture. They did this in specimens with the notches oriented so that the final crack would propagate either along or across the long axis of the osteons. Figure 16.26, taken from their work, illustrates their results.

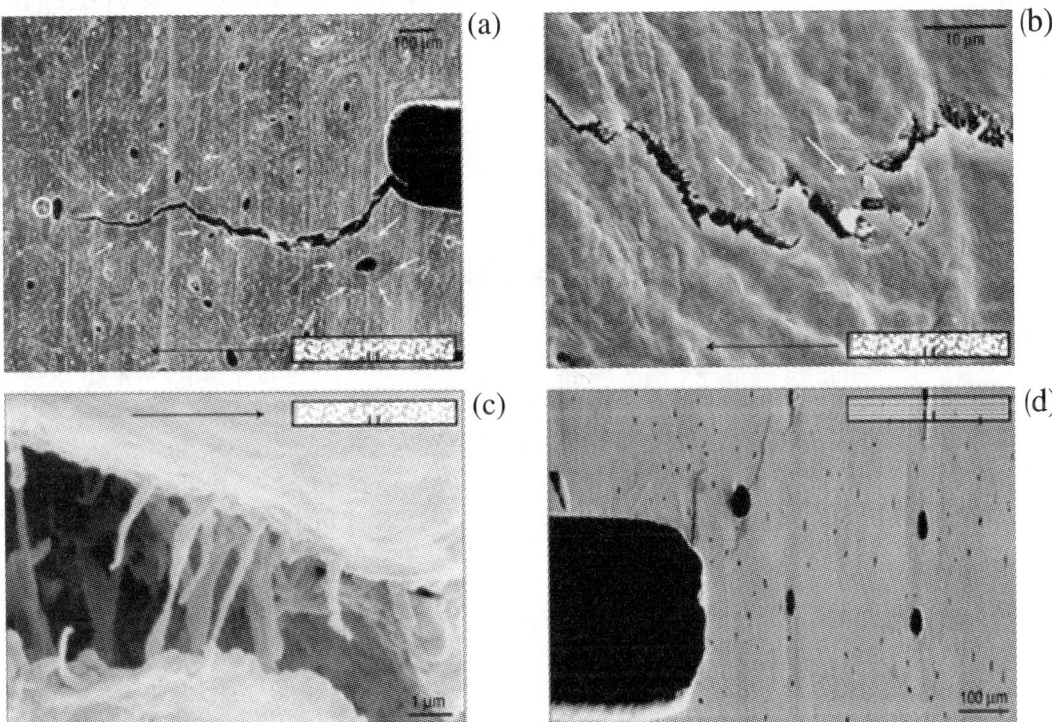

Fig. 16.26 (a) Crack running between osteons from the tip of a notch that runs longitudinally along the bone. That is, the long axis of the bend specimen is transverse to the long axis of the bone. Osteons indicated by white arrows. (b) Area indicated by the white circle in (a) at higher magnification. (c) Same crack at still higher magnification, showing bridging of the crack by collagen fibrils. (d) A different specimen, having its long axis parallel to the long axis of the bone, with the notch running across the osteons, showing cracking along the long axes of the osteons. (From R. K. Nalla, J. H. Kinney, and R. O. Ritchie, *Nature Materials,* 2003, vol. 2, p. 164.)

Fig 16.26(a) shows a crack emanating from a notch and running on a surface that is parallel to the long axis of the osteons, three of which are denoted by the white arrows. The crack runs both across and between the osteons. The region within the white circle is shown at a higher magnification in Fig. 16.26(b), which shows two bridges that are not entirely cracked through (arrows), meaning that there is still some bony material holding the crack faces together. These are referred to as un-cracked ligaments. At still higher magnification in Fig. 16.26(c), one can see stretched collagen fibrils bridging the crack. Figure 16.26(d) shows another notch, this time oriented so that the crack should run across the long axis of the osteons. Here, we see the initial cracks running along the boundaries of osteons, indicating that this is a region of weakness. This weak interface thus tends to deflect cracks away from the plane of maximum tensile stress.

From these micrographs we can see three reasons why a crack in bone has difficulty in propagating, at least initially. One is the existence of un-cracked ligaments (Fig. 16.26b); another is the bridging of crack faces by collagen fibrils (Fig. 16.26c), and the third is the weak-interface effect that tends to deflect the crack away from the plane of maximum stress (Fig. 16.26d). It is not until the load becomes high enough that these crack-inhibiting factors can be overcome.

After a fracture has occurred, the debris at the site is cleaned up by macrophages, and loose connective tissue containing fibroblasts and capillaries forms there. After that, dense connective tissue forms in this matrix and grows into a callus that bridges the fracture site and helps to hold the fractured ends in place. Osteoprogenitor cells from the periosteum differentiate to osteoblasts and start to deposit new bone on either side of the fracture, and a bony sheath grows over the callus. New osteoblasts move inward from the sheath and convert the fibrous/cartilaginous callus to a bony callus.

Bone formation across the fracture also takes place internally from cells that originate in the endosteum. The fracture site is then filled with spongy bone that is gradually replaced with compact bone. The bony callus is removed by osteoclasts, and remodeling ultimately restores the bone to the original shape and microstructure. This takes six to twelve weeks in a healthy person, depending of the severity of the fracture. Healing can be accelerated by fixing the fractured ends in place by means of internal pins, screws, or plates, or externally by a cast or other kinds of fixtures.

References and Recommended Reading

Orthopaedic Basic Science, Ed. Sheldon. R. Simon, MD, American Academy of Orthopaedic Surgeons, 1994.

Michael H. Ross, Gordon I. Kaye, and Wojciech Pawlina, *Histology, a Text and Atlas, 4th ed.,* Lippincott Williams and Wilkins, 2003.

Bruce Alberts, Alexander Johnson, Julian Lewis, Martin Raff, Keith Roberts, and Peter Walter, *Molecular Biology of the Cell, 4th ed.* Garland Science, 2002.

Summary

Bone is a living composite structural material that is the inverse of a tire in that it has a rigid matrix and a compliant set of fibers. As such, it is optimized for compressive loading, rather than for tension. The brittle mineral matrix of hydrated calcium phosphate is subject to microcrack formation under tensile loading. However, if this cracking does not accumulate too rapidly, it can be repaired by the continuing process of remodeling. This process involves the formation new osteons by the removal of old bone by osteoclasts and the deposition of new layers of bone by osteoblasts that follow behind. Remodeling also serves the physiological function of storing and releasing calcium as required in the rest of the body.

Bone has viscoelastic properties by virtue of its component of Type-I collagen fibrils. This results in the kind of strain-rate sensitivity one would expect, as well as creep deformation under a static stress. The fatigue behavior of bone follows the classical Coffin-Manson law. Crack growth in either cyclic or monotonic loading is inhibited by the collagen fibrils that bridge microcracks and by the un-cracked ligaments that are found between microcracks. These give bone some apparent fracture toughness, which, of course, is important in that it allows some damage to occur without catastrophic failure.

Glossary/Vocabulary - Chapter 16

Appositional growth	The growth of bone on the surface of existing bone. This is the way that most bone growth occurs.
Calcitonin	A hormone produced by the human thyroid gland. It is important for maintaining a dense bone matrix and for regulating the blood calcium level.
Callus	The dense connective tissue that bridges a fracture site. It holds the fractured ends together until the fibrous/cartilaginous callus can be converted to a bony callus.
Canaliculi	The small channels in which the extensions of osteocytes (called processes) lie. They extend out from the osteoclasts in all directions.
Cancellous bone	Another word for spongy bone. Cancellous means lattice-like in Latin.
Cement lines	The outer boundaries of osteons. These are surfaces of relative weakness in compact bone.
Chondroblast	The cell type that forms cartilage. These differentiate from mesenchymal cells.
Coffin-Manson behavior	This is the fatigue "law" to the effect that the number of cycles to failure decreases linearly (on a log scale) as the cyclic-plastic strain range increases. In metals, where this originated, this relates directly to the plastic-blunting model for fatigue-crack growth.
Compact bone	The bone formed by the remodeling process that produces osteons. The microstructure comprises cylindrical layers around a central (Haversian) canal.
Cortical bone	Another name for compact bone.
Diaphysis	The shaft or central part of a long cylindrical bone. Growth takes place at the ends of the diaphysis.
Distal	The opposite of proximal. That end or side of a body part farthest from the center of the body, i.e., from a medial line or from the trunk.
Endochondrial ossification	The process of formation of a bone from the cartilaginous model during the development of a fetus. It starts with the formation of a bony collar around the central portion of the model.
Endosteal surface	An internal surface in a bone. This is where the remodeling process begins.
Epiphyseal cartilage	The un-calcified cartilage on either end of the diaphysis during growth of a long bone. This is where elongation of the diaphysis takes place.
Epiphysis	The knobby end of a long bone. It comprises spongy bone encased in a layer of compact bone.
Femur	The long bone between the hip and the knee; the thigh bone. This is the longest and strongest bone in the body.

Glycoprotein	A combination of a sugar and a protein.
Haversian canal	The canal that runs along the center of an osteon. This is what remains of the tunnel that is formed during remodeling.
Hydroxyapatite	The hydrated calcium phosphate that comprises the mineral phase in bone. It forms by the precipitation of crystals in the spaces at the ends of, and in between, collagen fibrils.
Hydroxyproline	The product of hydroxylation of proline. This is one of the principle amino acids found in Type-I collagen.
Interstitial lamellae	The lamellae of old osteons that lie in among newer osteons. They are left over after remodeling has occurred.
Lacunae	The spaces occupied by osteocytes in compact bone. They lie between the lamellae of osteons.
Lamellae	The layers of bone that form during each stage of remodeling. They are laid down by the osteoblasts that line the wall the tunnel formed by osteoclasts.
Lateral surface	The surface of a body part, like the femur, for example, that is away from the mid-plane of the body. Walking produces a net tensile stress on the lateral surface of the femur, because of the way it is curved.
Macrophage	A cell that disposes of old or abnormal cells and cellular debris, as well as pathogenic organisms. Phagean means "to eat" in Greek.
Marrow cavity	The hollow interior of a bone that contains the marrow. For example, the hollow part of the diaphysis of a long bone contains yellow marrow. Red marrow occupies the cavities of spongy bone. It produces white and red blood cells and fragments of cells called platlets.
Medial surface	The surface of a body part that is nearer to the central plane of the body. The medial surface of a femur faces the opposite leg.
Metaphysis	The small section of a long bone that lies between the diaphysis and the epiphysis. It lies at the end of the marrow cavity and is the region where growth takes place.
Osteoblast	The type of cell that produces osteoid and the mineral phase of bone. Osteoblasts lay down new bone on the surfaces of existing bone.
Osteoclast	The multinucleated cell that digs a channel into bone in the process of remodeling. It also removes damaged bone in the repair of fractures. It digests the organic part and causes dissolution of the mineral phase by secreting hydrogen ions.
Osteocyte	The name given to an osteoblast after it becomes buried in hard bone. It remains metabolically active and helps to maintain bone as living tissue. Osteocytes lie in spaces called lacunae along the interfaces between lamellae.
Osteoid	The un-mineralized material that is produced first by an osteoblast. It is later converted to hard bone by the precipitation and growth of crystals of hydroxyapatite.
Osteon	The cylinder of compact bone formed during the process of remodeling. It comprises concentric lamellae around a hollow core.
Osteoprogenitor cell	Flat, quiescent cells that later become active as osteoblasts. They are contained under the periosteum and along endosteal surfaces.

Parathyroid gland	A small endocrine gland located behind and at the lower edge of the thyroid gland, or embedded within it. It secretes the parathyroid hormone that stimulates the resorption of bone by osteocytes.
Periosteal surface	The outer surface of a bone. The periosteal diameter increases during the whole life of a bone.
Piezoelectric	A property of a material in which an electric current is caused to flow in response to the application of a stress. In bone, both the hydroxyapatite phase and the collagen fibers are piezoelectric.
Proximal	The opposite of distal. That end or side of a body part closer to the center of the body.
Remodeling of bone	The process of resorption of bone and the formation of a new osteon. Osteoclasts dig a tunnel, and osteoblasts lay down new lamellae on the sides of the tunnel.
Resorption	The process of dissolution or digestion of body tissue.Osteoclasts cause resorption of bone during remodeling.
Spongy bone	The porous bone found in the metaphysis and epiphysis of long bones. It is also found inside small bones like the vertebrae.
Stress fracture	A crack in bone caused by cyclic loading. It is actually a fatigue crack.
Tibia	The shin bone of the leg. It lies in front of the fibula.
Trabecular bone	Another name for spongy bone. Trabis means beam in Greek. It can be viewed as a cellular structure made of plates and rods.
Wolff's law	The statement that bone is resorbed in regions of low stress and becomes thicker in regions of high stress. It is a consequence of the piezoelectric properties of bone.
Woven bone	Compact bone that has not undergone remodeling. It is composed of interlaced collagen fibers with randomly arrayed osteocytes.

Exercises

16.1 Consulting Fig. 16.3, explain how the microstructure of mature compact bone is designed to resist a bending force. What other types of composite materials encountered in this book use this principle?

16.2 What are the three main types of cells found in bone, and what are their functions?

16.3 What type of bone is first formed during the development of a long bone in a fetus? How is this different from mature bone?

16.4 What functions are served by the process of remodeling of bone?

16.5 What kinds of mechanical test would manifest the viscoelastic nature of bone?

16.6 What is the process by which a "stress fracture," i.e., a fatigue crack in a bone, heals with time?

16.7 How is the process of "yielding" in bone different from yielding in metals and linear polymers?

16.8 How is the age-related thinning of the cortex of a long bone partly compensated for as a person ages?

16.9 What is the reason why there is stable growth of a crack in compact bone before catastrophic fracture occurs?

17

SKELETAL MUSCLE

Skeletal muscle, which comprises more than 40% of human body weight, is an active structural material that can act as an ATP*-driven molecular engine capable of producing joint motion and locomotion. The power unit is a cylindrical structure about 2.5 micrometers in length called a *sarcomere,* within which two sets of nanoscale protein filaments overlap and self assemble into a hexagonal array. These filaments interact in such a way that the sarcomere can contract and generate the substantial forces needed to operate the body. Our goal here is to understand how this engine operates, because this knowledge is important for any intervention that one would want to make in the neuromuscular system, as well as for the optimization of the performance of that system.

17.1 Muscles and Muscle Fibers

Figure 17.1 shows a few of the important muscles in the human leg. The basic unit of muscle architecture is the muscle fiber, which is, in effect, a long single cell formed during development of the body by the fusion of small cells called *myoblasts.* As shown in Fig. 17.2, the muscle fibers may run along the axis of the muscle, or they may lie at an angle to this axis. The fibers can vary in length from a few millimeters to nearly a meter.

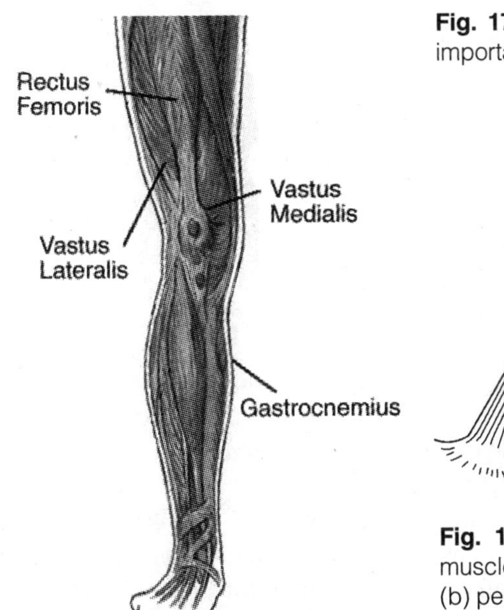

Fig. 17.1 The human leg, with a few of the important muscles indicated.

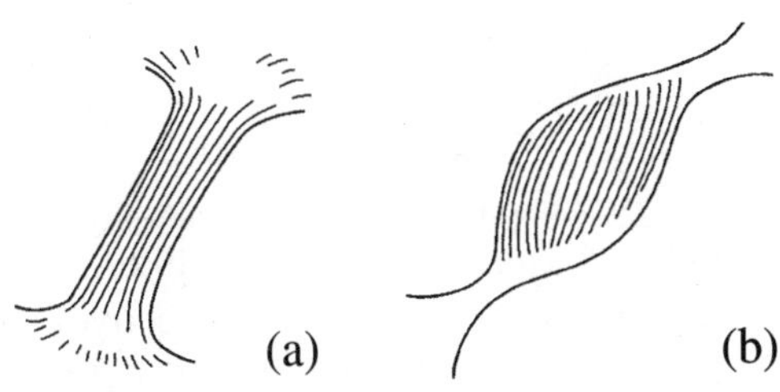

Fig. 17.2 Examples of the arrangement of muscle fibers in a muscle body: (a) parallel, (b) pennate (from the Latin penne for *feather*), and (c) bi-pennate.

* ATP is adenosine triphosphate, which is the source of energy for muscle contraction.

The strength of a muscle, that is, the maximum force it can exert by its contraction, is proportional to the cross section of the muscle. So muscles used for high-strength purposes, like the biceps of the arm, tend to have relatively short fibers running at an angle to the long axis of the muscle. On the other hand, where a rapid and large contraction is needed, as in the fingers of the hand, the fibers tend to be relatively long and lying parallel to the long axis of the muscle.

17.2 Microstructure of Muscle

As shown in Fig. 17.3, the muscle cells, or fibers, are arranged in groups called fascicles, and each fiber contains an internal structure of sets of filamentary proteins that are arranged in *myofibrils.* Each myofibril consists of a chain of sarcomeres, and, as noted earlier, it is the action within these sarcomeres that is responsible for muscular contraction.

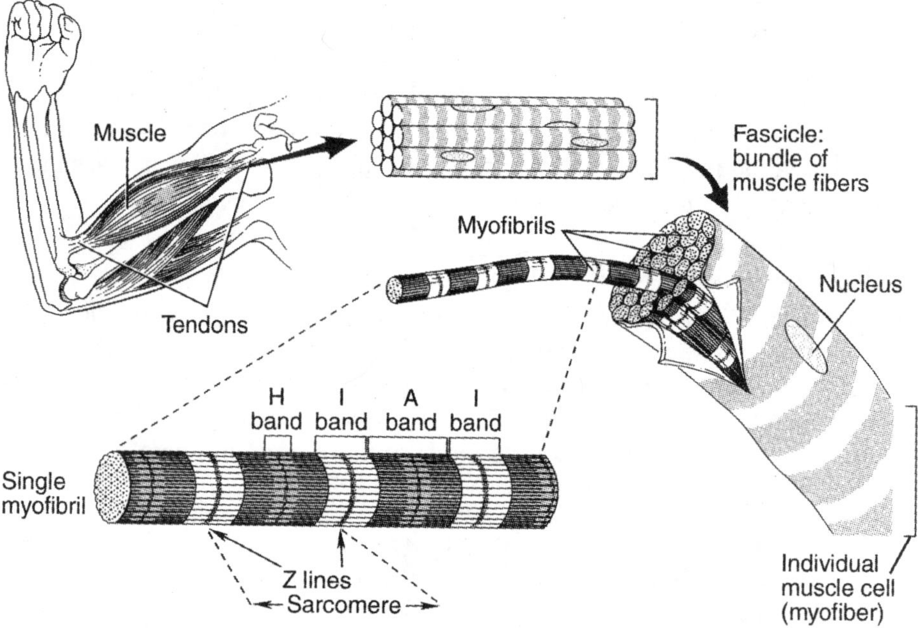

Fig. 17.3 Levels of organization in skeletal muscle. (From *The World of the Cell,* 2nd. ed., by W. M. Becker and D. W. Dreamer Copyright © 1991 by The Benjamin/Cummings Publishing Company, Inc. Reprinted by permission of Pearson Education, Inc.)

17.2.1 Muscle Fibers

Figure 17.4 shows an optical micrograph of a transverse section of parts of three fascicles; the fibers are packed together in an array that resembles the cross section of a cellular material, like a polycrystalline metal. Each fiber is surrounded by a membrane of connective tissue called the *endomysium.* This membrane contains fine capillaries and branches of neurons. Each fascicle is surrounded by a thicker membrane of connective tissue called the *perimysium;* this contains larger blood vessels and nerves. The fascicles are bound together by a sheath of dense connective tissue called the *epimysium;* the major blood vessels and nerves go through this sheath.

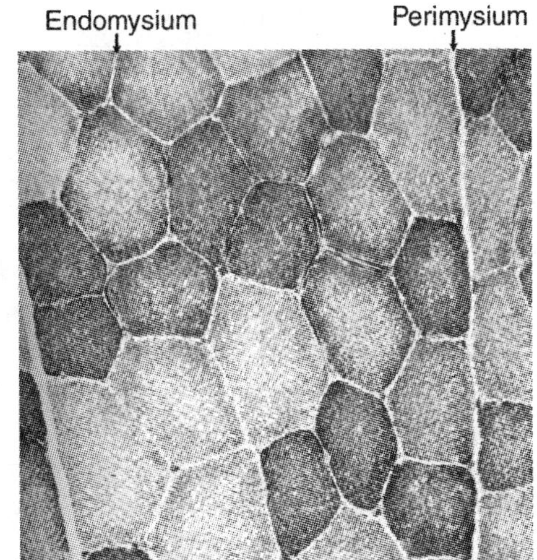

Fig. 17.4 Photomicrograph of the cross section of parts of three bundles of muscle fibers. The deeply stained fibers, called red-muscle fibers, contain more mitochondria and more of the oxygen-binding protein called myoglobin than the lighter, white-muscle fibers. See Section 17.4 for more details. (From Michael H. Ross, Gordon I. Kaye, and Wojciech Pawlina, *Histology, a Text and Atlas,* Lippincott, Williams & Wilkins, 1995.)

Through any cross section of skeletal muscle fiber, the sarcomeres are in register, so a muscle fiber can be thought of as comprising a stack of discs. In the optical microscope, using polarized light, one can see light and dark bands along each fiber; this gave rise to the term *striated* muscle. The light bands were deemed to be isotropic, so they were called I-bands; the dark bands, being anisotropic, were called A-bands. (cf. Fig. 17.3.)

When a longitudinal section of skeletal muscle is examined with an electron microscope, the fine structure is revealed, as shown in Fig. 17.5. The dark bands between the sarcomeres are called Z-lines (from the German word zwischenscheibe, meaning *between discs*). In the center of the A-band is a light region called the hell (German for *light*) band, or H-band, and in the center of the H-band is a thin dark band called the mitte (*middle*) line, or M-line.

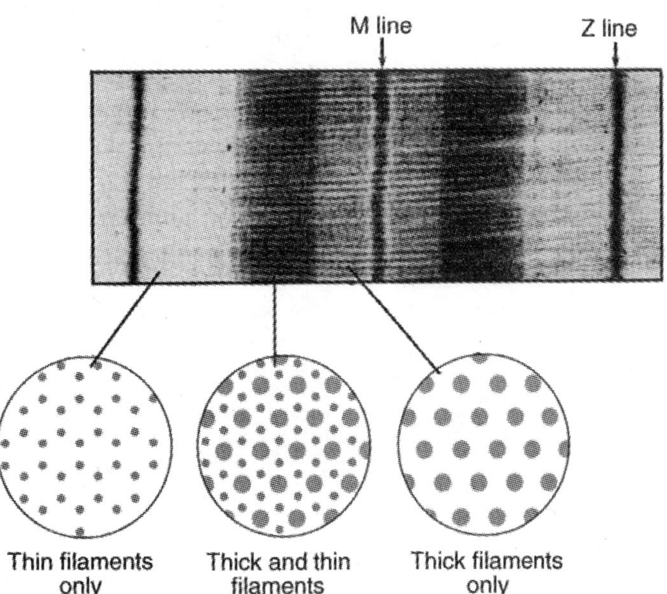

Fig. 17.5 Transmission electron micrograph of a sarcomere in skeletal muscle. (From *Biochemistry, 2nd ed.* by Christopher K. Matthews and K. E. Van Holde. Copyright © 1996 by the Benjamin/Cummings Publishing Company, Inc. Reprinted by permission of Pearson Education, Inc.)

17.2.2 Sarcomeres

Each sarcomere is made up of an ordered arrangement of thick and thin filaments that interdigitate, as shown in Fig. 17.6(a). Muscle contraction occurs when the overlap of the thick and thin filaments increases, and extension occurs when the overlap decreases, as shown in Fig. 17.(b) and (c).

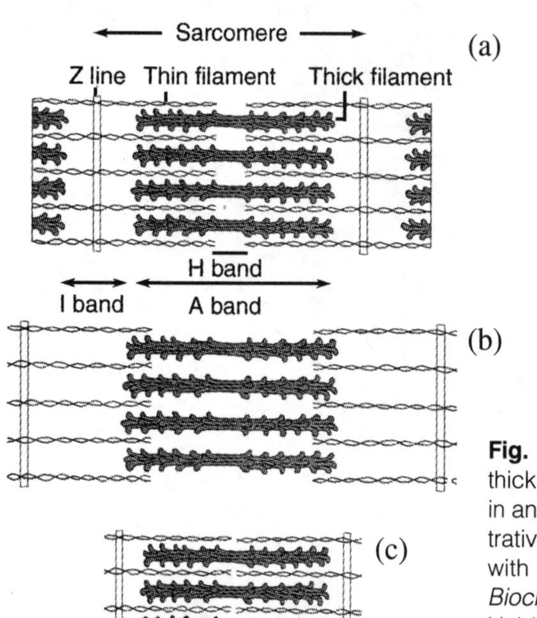

Fig. 17.6 (a) Schematic representation of the arrangement of thick and thin filaments in a sarcomere. (b) and (c) Arrangement in an extended and a contracted muscle, respectively. (For illustrative purposes, the thick filaments are shown much shorter and with many fewer chains than is the actual case.) (From *Biochemistry, 2nd ed.* by Christopher K. Matthews and K. E. Van Holde. Copyright © 1996 by the Benjamin/Cummings Publishing Company, Inc. Reprinted by permission of Pearson Education, Inc.)

The thin filaments in a sarcomere are anchored at the Z-lines and are made of two helically wound chains of polymerized *actin,* an extremely common protein. The diameter is about 9nm. As shown in Fig. 17.7, the grooves of the helices of actin contain other long-chain proteins called *tropomyosin.* Attached to the tropomyosin, and spaced at 38.5nm intervals along the thin filaments, are clumps of three proteins called the *troponin complex.* One of these (called TnT) bonds the troponin complex to the tropomyosin, and another (called TnI) bonds it to the actin. The third protein, called TnC, binds to Ca^{2+} ions and is active in the muscle-contraction process.

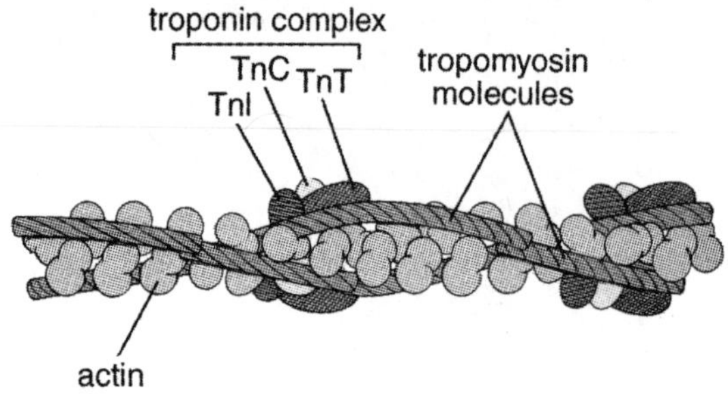

Fig. 17.7 Schematic representation of the double-helical actin chain with tropomyosin molecules in the groove and a troponin complex on a tropomyosin molecule. (From Michael H. Ross, Gordon I. Kaye, and Wojciech Pawlina, *Histology, a Text and Atlas,* Lippincott, Williams & Wilkins, 1995.)

The thick filaments are made up of myosin molecules*, which comprise six polypeptide chains, depicted schematically in Fig. 17.8. There are two so-called heavy chains, 230 kDa each**, and four light chains of about 20 kDa each. The heavy chains are wound in a helical coil and have a globular region at one end. The globular-head region, or motor domain, of each heavy chain has a binding site for actin and one for ATP.

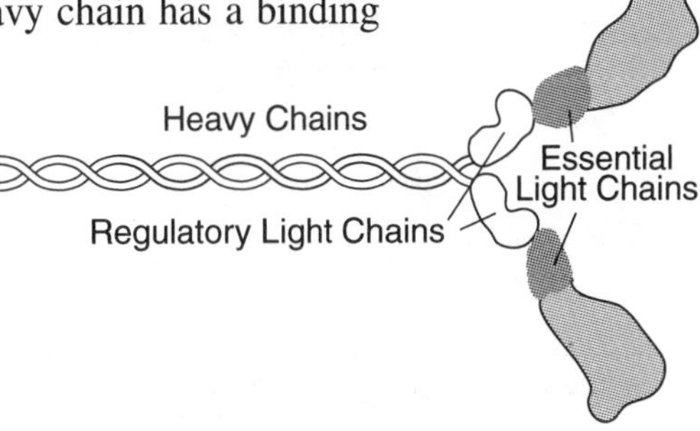

Fig. 17.8 Structure of the end of a myosin chain, showing the head region that contains the motor domain and the light chains and the tail region. (Adapted from Y.E. Goldman and E. Homsher in *Myology, Basic and Clinical, 3rd ed.* vol. 1, Eds. A. G. Engel and C. Franzini-Armstrong McGraw-Hill, 2004)

The thick filaments are 16nm in diameter and about 1.6μm long. They are joined tail-to-tail at the M line, and the thick and thin filaments are arrayed in interlocking hexagonal patterns, as indicated in Fig. 17.5. The globular heads of the thick myosin filaments can form cross bridges, spaced 14.3nm apart, to the six neighboring actin chains.

The sarcomeres are embedded in the *sarcoplasm,* the cytoplasm of the muscle cell. A net-like membranous structure called the *sarcoplasmic reticulum* encases the system of sarcomeres, as shown in Fig. 17.9. The sarcoplasmic reticulum (SR) is composed of repeated units that join along the junctions of the A- and I-bands. Calcium ions are stored in sacs of the SR called terminal cisternae, and muscle contraction starts when the calcium ions are released into the sarcoplasm. The transverse tubules are formed by invaginations of the plasma membrane, also called the *sarcolemma,* that surrounds the muscle cell, i.e., the muscle fiber. It is the depolarization (see Fig 17.20) of the walls of the t-tubules that causes the release of calcium ions through the "feet" of the terminal cisternae.

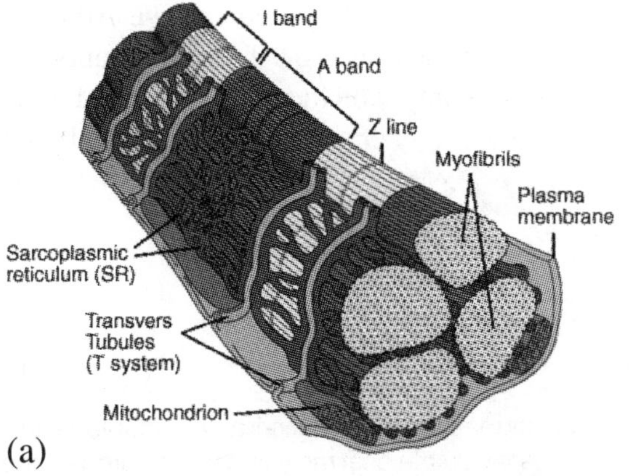

(a)

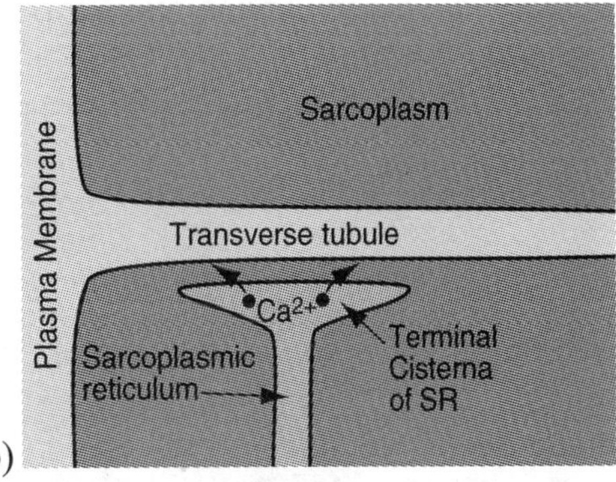

(b)

Fig. 17.9 (a) The structure of a muscle fiber, showing the sarcoplasmic reticulum that surrounds each myofibril. (From *The World of the Cell,* 2nd. ed., by W. M. Becker and D. W. Dreamer Copyright © 1991 by The Benjamin/Cummings Publishing Company, Inc. Reprinted by permission of Pearson Education, Inc.) (b) Schematic representation of the gap between a foot of the terminal cisternae and a part of a t-tublule.

* Called myosin II, because it has two globular heads.

** 230 kDa (kilodaltons) means a molecular weight of 230,000 g/mol.

17.3 Contraction of a Muscle Fiber

The source of energy for the contraction comes from ATP, which is one of the most important energy-storing compounds in the body. It provides the energy needed for many functions. The hydrolysis of ATP converts it to adenosine diphosphate, ADP, and an inorganic phosphate, P_i, with a release of 31kJ/mol, as shown schematically in Fig. 17.10.

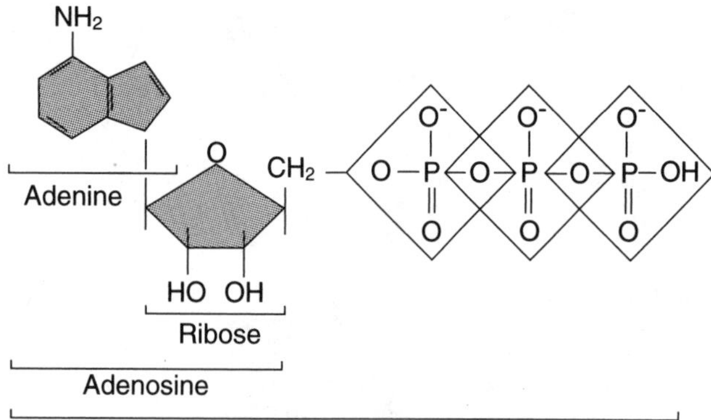

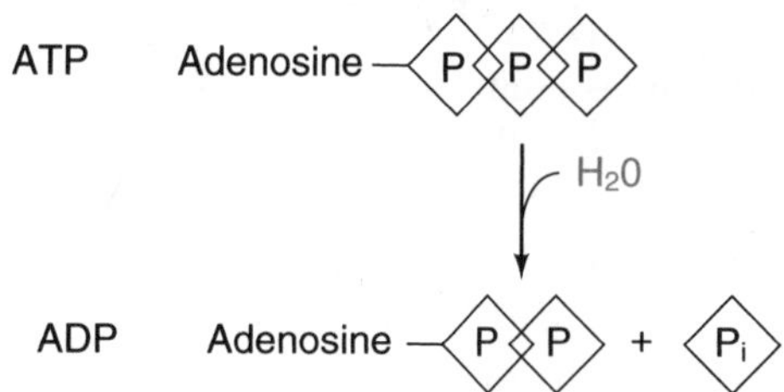

Fig. 17.10 Schematic representation of ATP and of its hydrolysis to ADP that releases the energy used in muscle contraction. (From *Biochemistry, 2nd ed.* by Christopher K. Matthews and K. E. Van Holde. Copyright © 1996 by the Benjamin/Cummings Publishing Company, Inc. Reprinted by permission of Pearson Education, Inc.)

When the Ca-ion concentration in the sarcoplasm exceeds a certain value, the Ca^{2+} ions can bind to the TnC molecules of the troponin complexes on the actin filaments (cf. Fig. 17.7). This changes the configuration of the troponin
17150 complexes in such a way that the myosin binding sites on the actin chains are uncovered. This allows the heads of the myosin chains to bind to the actin, as shown in Fig. 17.11.

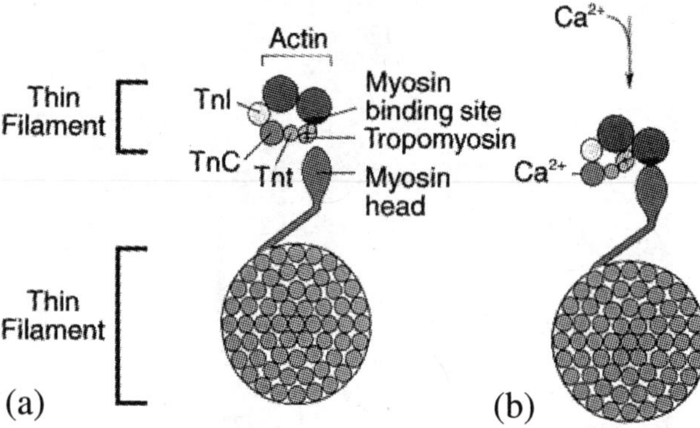

Fig. 17.11 (a) In a relaxed muscle, the configuration of the tropomyosin and the troponin complex block the myosin head from binding to the actin. (b) At the beginning of muscle contraction, the rearrangement of the thin-filament components makes available the myosin-binding site on the actin. (From *The World of the Cell,* 2nd. ed., by W. M. Becker and D. W. Dreamer Copyright © 1991 by The Benjamin/Cummings Publishing Company, Inc. Reprinted by permission of Pearson Education, Inc.)

The present hypothesis for the contraction cycle can be described as follows (Ref. 7): 17170

When the muscle is relaxed the myosin heads are separated from the actin filament, and a molecule of ATP is bonded to each head. The ATP is undergoing a reversible hyrolysis to ADP + P_i, and the head is free to wobble.

ATP ⇄ ADP + P_i

Relaxed state

When the change in the configuration of the troponin complex allows it, the head binds to the actin.

ADP + P_i

Attachment

Dissociation of the P_i causes the head to swivel toward the m line, forcing the actin and myosin to slide past one another. This is called the power stroke.

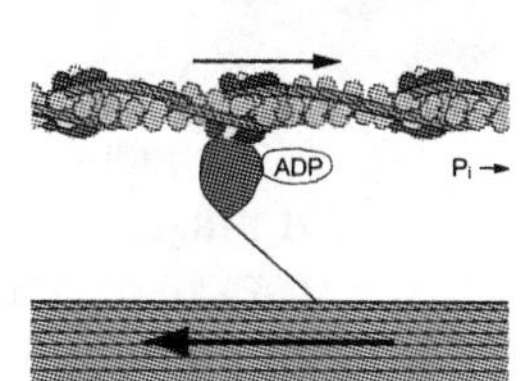

Power stroke

When the ADP departs from the head, and a new ATP binds to it, the head is detached from the actin, and the muscle is again relaxed. After this, the cycle can begin again.

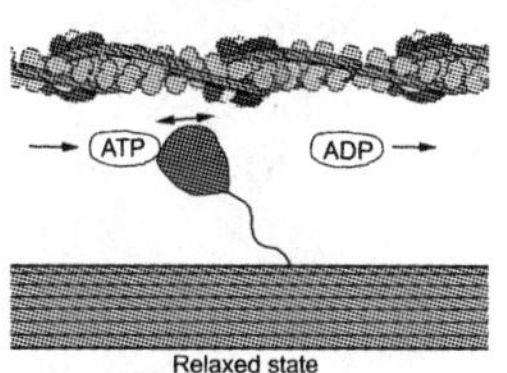

Relaxed state

While this process is going on, the calcium ions are pumped back into the channels of the sarcoplasmic reticulum and are ready to be released again when another nerve impulse (see Section 17.5.3) is received. As this cycle occurs at the many myosin heads on each thick filament, the result is the decrease in length of the sarcomeres (Fig. 17.6) and the overall contraction of the muscle. Each thick filament has about 300 heads at each end, and each head cycles about 5 times per second during a rapid muscle contraction. A sarcomere in fast skeletal muscle can shorten by about 10% in about 1/50th of a second.

17.4 Energetics of Muscle Contraction

As we have seen, the energy for the shortening of the sarcomeres that results from the myosin-actin interaction comes from the hydrolysis of ATP molecules. Therefore, in order for a muscle to continue to function, these molecules must be replenished. It has been estimated that, without any replenishment, there is enough energy available in the stored ATP for a person to run about 50 yards. More ATP can be produced by the combination of two ADP molecules to make one ATP and one AMP (the monophosphate) and from the reaction of ADP with creatine phosphate to make ATP and creatine.

$$ADP + ADP \rightarrow ATP + AMP$$

$$ADP + CP \rightarrow ATP + Creatine$$

$\overset{+}{N}H_3$ — $HN{=}C$ — $H_3C{-}N{-}CH_2{-}COO^-$

Creatine

$H_2\overset{+}{N}{-}P(=O)(O^-){-}O^-$ — $HN{=}C$ — $H_3C{-}N{-}CH_2{-}COO^-$

Creatine phosphate

Using all these immediate sources, the estimate can be extended to a run of about 200 yards. For more prolonged exercise, ATP must be replenished by either anaerobic or aerobic metabolism of some nutrient.

The anaerobic mechanism is used when a lot of energy is being expended quickly, and it involves the *glycosis* (sugar-splitting) of stored *glycogen* (sugar-former). Glycogen is animal starch, a polymer chain of d-glucose molecules, that is the storehouse for sugar in the body. The anaerobic process starts with the hydrolysis of glycogen:

$$\underset{\text{glycogen}}{(C_6H_{10}O_5)n} + n\ H_2O \rightarrow \underset{\text{d-glucose}}{n\ C_6H_{12}O_6}$$

It goes through a number of steps employing various enzymes and ends with the reaction:

$$C_6H_{12}O_6 + 2\ \text{phosphate} + 2\ \text{ADP} \rightarrow 2\ \text{lactic acid} + 2\ H_2O + 2\ \text{ATP}$$

The lactic acid is somewhat toxic, and it causes acidosis and muscle fatigue, so it must be removed in the blood and rebuilt into glycogen.

As indicated schematically in Fig. 17.12, the anaerobic mechanism is only good for relatively short bursts of high-intensity activity. For prolonged exercise at lower intensity, the aerobic (or oxidative) metabolism of either glucose or fat is used to replenish ATP. (In unusual situations, proteins can be also used.) In the case of glucose metabolism, ADP is converted to ATP by a process having the following overall reaction:

$$C_6H_{12}O_6 + 6O_2 + 38\ P_i + 38\ \text{ADP} \rightarrow 6\ CO_2 + 6\ H_2O + 38\ \text{ATP}$$

Since you get 38 ATP per glucose, instead of two, this is obviously a more productive use of glucose than the anaerobic mechanism. The glucose would come from the diet in the form of carbohydrates.

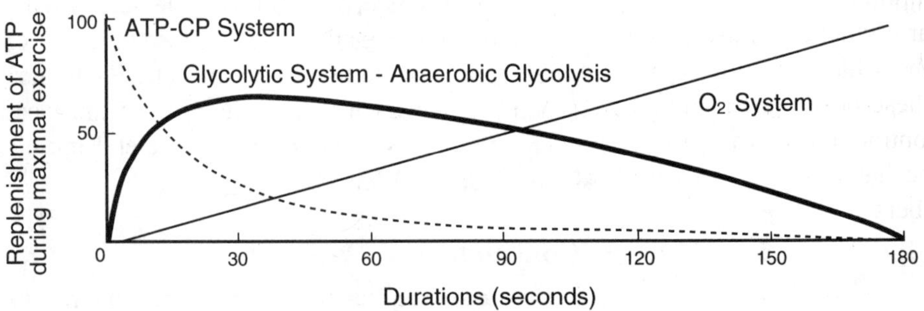

Fig. 17.12 Schematic representation of the different systems that can be used to replenish ATP during muscle activity. (Redrawn from William E. Garrett, Jr. and Thomas M. Best, in *Orthopaedic Basic Science*, ed. Sheldon R. Simon, American Academy of Orthopaedic Surgeons, 1994.)

The other aerobic process is the oxidation of fats, which are usually stored as triglycerides. These can convert a variable amount of ADP to ATP, depending on the length of the carbon chain in the fatty-acid molecule. According to Garrett and Best (Ref. 2), a 16-carbon chain when fully oxidized can convert 129 molecules of ADP to ATP. In prolonged exercise, the glucose and serum triglycerides tend to get used up first, because they are more readily available. After that, body fat (adipose tissue) provides the fuel supply. To burn a significant amount of body fat, it is thought that the exercise must be extended beyond the half-hour range.

The anaerobic metabolism takes place in the sarcoplasm of the muscle fiber, whereas the aerobic metabolism occurs in the mitochondria.

There are two general types of motor unit (see next section) in skeletal muscle: Type I, or slow twitch, and Type II, or fast twitch. Type II is broken into subgroups A and B. The characteristics are as follows:

Type I – slow twitch	**Type IIA – fast twitch**	**Type IIB – fast twitch**
Slow tension and relaxation	Fast tension and relaxation	Fastest tension and relaxation
Low strength	High strength	Highest strength
Fatigue resistant	Fatigable	Most fatigable
Small motor units	Large motor units	Largest motor units
Uses oxidative reactions	Uses both oxidative and glycolytic reactions	Uses only glycolytic reactions during contraction

During exercise the Type-I motor units are recruited first, followed by Types IIA and B as the intensity and speed of the exercise increase.

The different types of muscle fibers are revealed by staining that is sensitive to the content of oxidative enzymes that are found in the mitochondria. This is shown in Fig. 17.4, in which the smaller fibers that stain deeply are the red, slow-twitch, Type-I fibers; these have the highest concentration of mitochondria and the oxygen-binding protein called myoglobin, and the oxidative reactions are greatest in these fibers. The red fibers dominate in the limb muscles of animals and in the breast muscles of migrating birds, where great resistance to fatigue is important. (Birds that do not fly much, but spend their time on their legs, like farm chickens, have a dominance of red fibers in their legs.) The larger, white fibers have the fewest mitochondria; they are the fast-twitch, Type-IIB fibers. These develop the highest peak muscle tension, and they are adapted to rapid contractions and precise movements, as required, for example, in the fingers of the hand. The fibers of intermediate size and staining response are Type-IIA fibers.

17.5 The Stimulus for Muscle Contraction

17.5.1 Motor Neurons

To understand the whole process of muscle contraction, one must consider how it is wired up to the central nervous system. This is done by means of motor neurons, one of which is illustrated schematically in Fig. 17.13(a). A neuron can receive inputs from other neurons by connections to its dendrites or its cell body, and it delivers its output through its single axon. Near the muscle, an axon typically branches and forms connections with a number of muscle fibers, as shown in Fig. 17.13(b). The combination of an axon and all the muscle fibers that it innervates is called a *motor unit*. Each branch connects with only one muscle fiber by an array of bulbs, called boutons, as shown in the photomicrograph in Fig. 17.14. This collection of boutons is called the *motor end plate.*

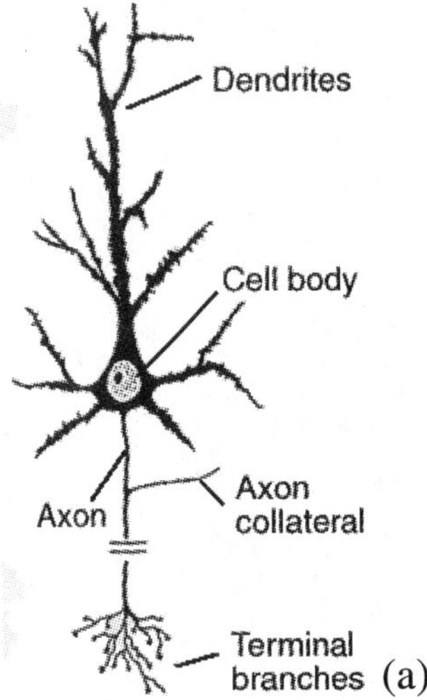

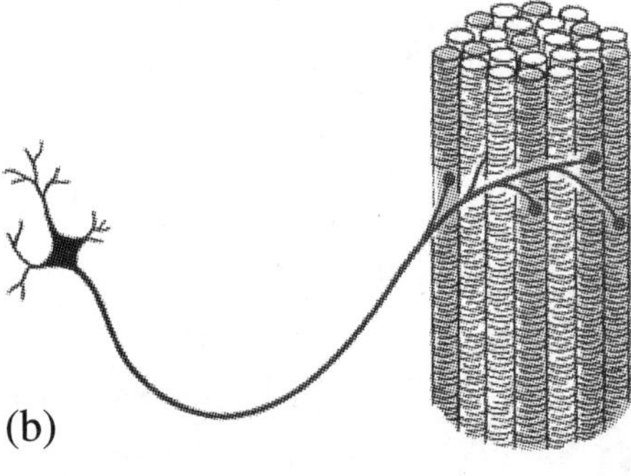

Fig. 17.13 Schematic representation of (a) a motor neuron and (b) its connection to a bundle of muscle fibers. (From Per Brodal, *The Central Nervous System, Structure and Function,* Oxford University Press, 1992.)

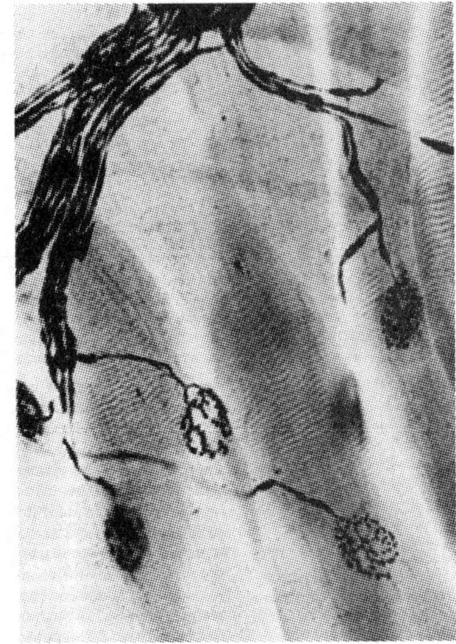

Fig. 17.14 Photomicrograph of muscle cells and a bundle of nerve fibers that innervate the cells, showing motor end plates. (From Per Brodal, *The Central Nervous System, Structure and Function,* Oxford University Press, 1992.)

Some details of a neuron are shown schematically in Fig. 17.15. Of particular interest is the wrapping of the axon by the *myelin sheath*, which is there to insulate the axon and accelerate the transmission of the nerve impulse along the axon. This sheath is formed by the action of *Schwann cells;* as shown in Fig. 17.15. These encase the axon and generate multiple layers of phospholipid and protein called *myelin.* Of equal importance are the periodic gaps between the Schwann cells, known as the *nodes of Ranvier.* These play an important role in the transmission of the electrical impulse down the axon, as will be described later.

The junction between a bouton and a muscle fiber is called a *synapse,* as shown schematically in Fig. 17.16, and this is where the signal from the axon is transmitted to the muscle fiber. Along with the mitochondria, which supply the energy for the process, the bouton holds vesicles that contain the neurotransmitter *acetylcholine.* It is the release of acetylcholine molecules from the *presynaptic membrane* of the bouton into the *synaptic cleft* and the migration of these molecules across to receptors on the *postsynaptic membrane* that begins the muscle contraction. This acetylcholine release comes as a response to an *action potential,* or nerve impulse, that travels down the neuron. The transmission of the impulse takes place by changes in the potential of the membrane of the axon.

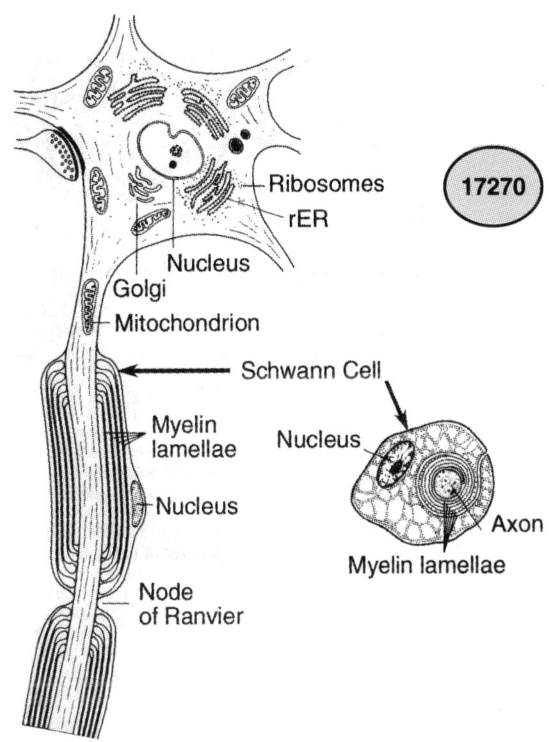

Fig 17.15 Component parts of a motor neuron and its axon, including the Schwann cells and the insulating myelin sheath. (Adapted from Per Brodal, *The Central Nervous System,* Structure and Function, Oxford University Press, 1992.)

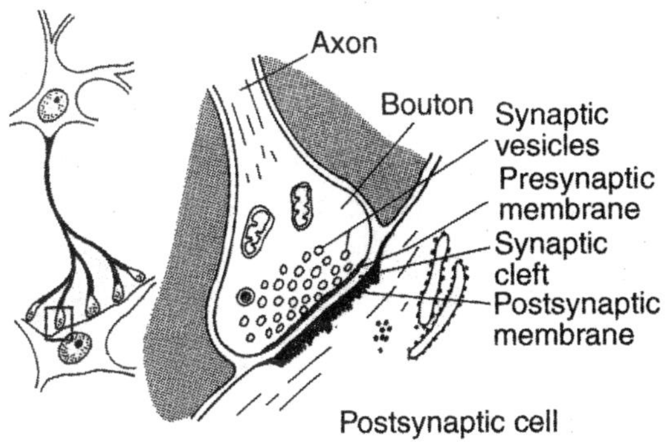

Fig. 17.16 Schematic representation of a synapse at the junction of a bouton and a muscle fiber. (Adapted from Per Brodal, *The Central Nervous System, Structure and Function,* Oxford University Press, 1992.)

17.5.2 The Membrane Potential

The action potential involves the movement of ions through the cell membrane along the axon and the short-range diffusion of some ions within the axon. The ions of most interest are Na^+, K^+, and Ca^{2+}. These ions move in and out of the axon through *ion channels,* as shown schematically in Fig. 17.17. These are special protein structures that extend through the cell membrane and open or close in response to one of two kinds of stimuli. Some ion channels are voltage-gated. That is, they respond to changes in the *membrane potential.* This is the voltage gradient that arises from the unequal concentrations of positively charged and negatively charged ions on either side of the cell membrane (Fig. 17.17). Other ion channels are transmitter-gated (or ligand-gated); that is, they respond to the binding of a transmitter molecule to a receptor.

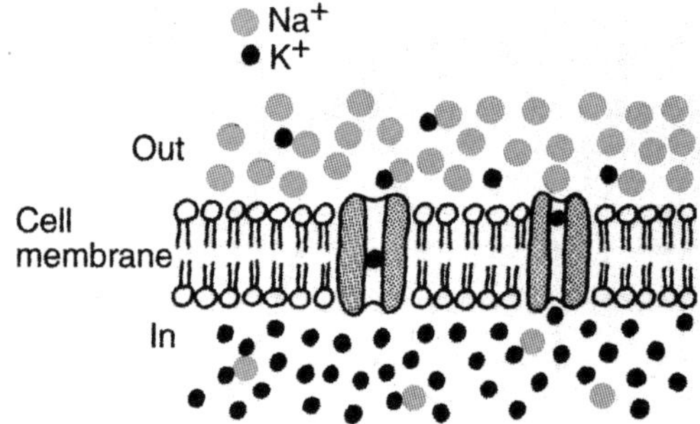

Fig. 17.17 Schematic representation of a voltage-gated ion channel (From Per Brodal, *The Central Nervous System, Structure and Function,* Oxford University Press, 1992.)

The flux of ions through the ion channels occurs in response to both the concentration gradients and the voltage gradient, that is, the membrane potential. For example, the concentration of K^+ ions inside the cell is greater than that outside, but there is an excess of negative charge (anions) inside compared with the outside. As indicated in Fig. 17.18, the K^+- ion concentration gradient tends to drive the K^+ ions out, but this is opposed by the voltage gradient, which tries to pull K^+ ions in.

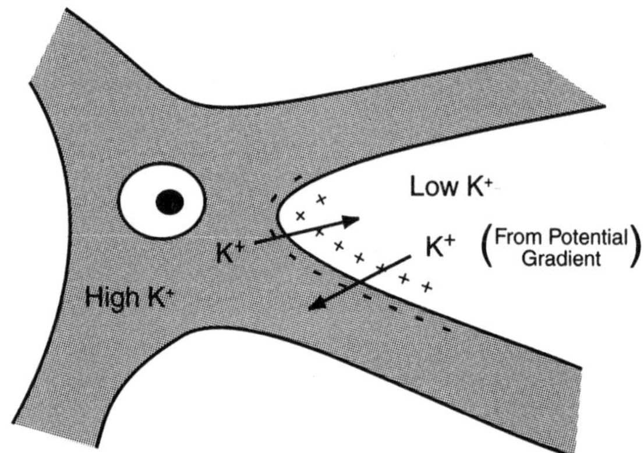

Fig. 17.18 Forces acting on K^+ ions. (From Per Brodal, *The Central Nervous System, Structure and Function,* Oxford University Press, 1992.)

The potential gradient does the same for Na^+ ions, which are concentrated on the outside more than on the inside, in contrast to the K^+. However, the permeability of the resting cell membrane for Na^+ ions is only around 2% of the permeability for K^+ ions. Because of the excess of anions inside the cell, the resting membrane potential is around –60 mV (+/– about 15 mV, depending on the type of nerve cell).

The negative membrane potential comes from the concentration of negatively charged protein molecules (Prot $^-$) inside the cell; these stay put, because they cannot pass through the cell membrane.

The concentration gradients of the K^+ and Na^+ ions tend to drive the K^+ ions out and the Na^+ ions in. (A one-for-one exchange would not change the membrane potential.) Over time this would erase the gradients were it not for the fact that another set of membrane proteins called *sodium-potassium ion pumps* actively maintain the steady-state concentrations of these ions inside and outside. This pump is illustrated by Fig. 17.19. It is energized by the hydrolysis of ATP, which binds to a site on one of the proteins on the inside of the channel. For each molecule of ATP expended, 3 Na^+ ions are moved outward and 2 K^+ ions move inward. (This is a common phenomenon that occurs in cells in general to maintain the proper ion concentrations.)

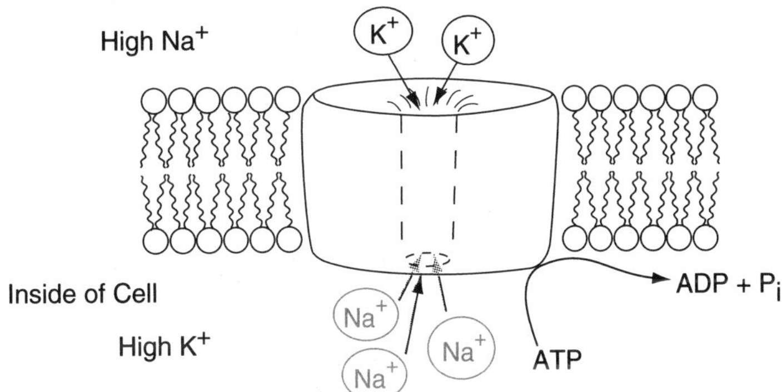

Fig. 17.19 Schematic representation of the sodium-potassium ion pump.

17.5.3 The Action Potential

A nerve impulse is initiated by the action of neurotransmitter molecules on transmitter-gated Na^+ channels, which open to admit Na^+ ions into the cell (driven by both the concentration gradient and the membrane potential). This reduces the membrane potential from the resting potential of around -60 mV; that is, it sends the membrane potential toward a positive value. This process is called *depolarization.* Once the depolarization reaches a threshold value, voltage-gated Na^+ ion channels open up, and more Na^+ ions rush in. As shown in Fig. 17.20, this sends the membrane potential up toward +55 mV, which is the theoretical equilibrium value for Na^+-only.

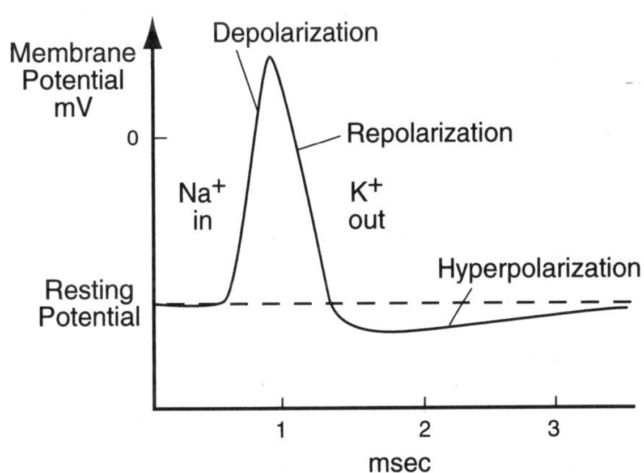

Fig. 17.20 The action potential. (From Per Brodal, *The Central Nervous System, Structure and Function,* Oxford University Press, 1992.)

As the depolarization reaches into the positive range, K^+ ions move out, driven by both the newly reversed membrane potential and the concentration gradient. Once depolarization has reached a threshold value, voltage-gated K^+ channels also open up, and the out-flux of K^+ ions and the concomitant repolarization accelerates and ultimately overshoots the resting potential (Fig. 17.20). Until this hyperpolarization dissipates, the cell is in a refractory, or inactive, state. The time span for all this is on the order of a few milliseconds.

The ion pumps work to re-establish the proper ion concentrations (Na^+ out and K^+ in), but the percentages of ions that move in one impulse are small. A nerve cell can produce several thousand impulses before the concentration gradients become so small that the cell can no longer be excited.

An action potential is not transmitted by the motion of ions all the way along an axon, like the flow of electrons along a copper wire. The ion concentration is too small, and the axon is too narrow for this. Also, ions can be lost through the cell membrane, and the membrane can store a certain amount of charge, acting as a capacitor. Thus, each impulse would move only a small distance before it would die out. What actually happens is the following: The impulse starts near the cell body, where the membrane is depolarized by the influx of Na^+ ions. The local buildup of positively charged ions causes a potential gradient that causes the excess ions to migrate away along the axon. This causes a wave of depolarization to propagate along the cell membrane. When this wave reaches the first node of Ranvier, voltage-gated ion channels open up in the locally bare membrane and produce a new action potential, as indicated schematically in Fig. 17.21. This continues along the axon in a pulsing fashion until it gets to the motor end plate.

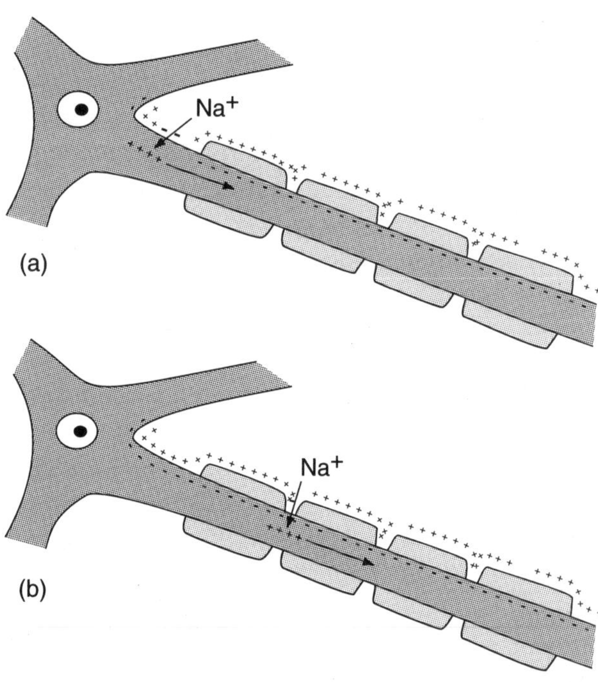

Fig. 17.21 Schematic representation of the conduction of an action potential down the axon of a motor neuron.

17.5.4 Synaptic Transmission

When an action potential reaches the terminal bouton at the neuromuscular junction, as shown in Fig. 17.22(a), it causes a change in the membrane potential there. This opens ion channels in the membrane and allows Ca^{2+} ions to flow into the bouton from the extracellular space (Fig. 17.22b). Inside the bouton the increase in the Ca-ion concentration causes the synaptic vesicles, each of which contains thousands of molecules of acetylcholine, to move to the membrane, fuse with it, open the membrane, and expel acetylcholine molecules into the synaptic cleft (Fig. 17.22c)). These neurotransmitter molecules diffuse across the cleft to the plasma membrane of the muscle fiber where there are acetylcholine receptors. The binding of the acetylcholine to the receptors changes the potential of this post-synaptic membrane, and this causes ion channels in the membrane to open and to allow Na^+ ions to flow from the extracellular space into the muscle cell (Fig. 17.22d). This influx of Na^+ ions causes rapid depolarization of the plasma membrane of the entire muscle fiber, including the walls of the t-tubular system that penetrates deep into the muscle fiber. This change in potential in turn causes channels in the walls of the sarcoplasmic reticulum to open and release stored Ca^{2+} ions into the sarcoplasm of the muscle cell.

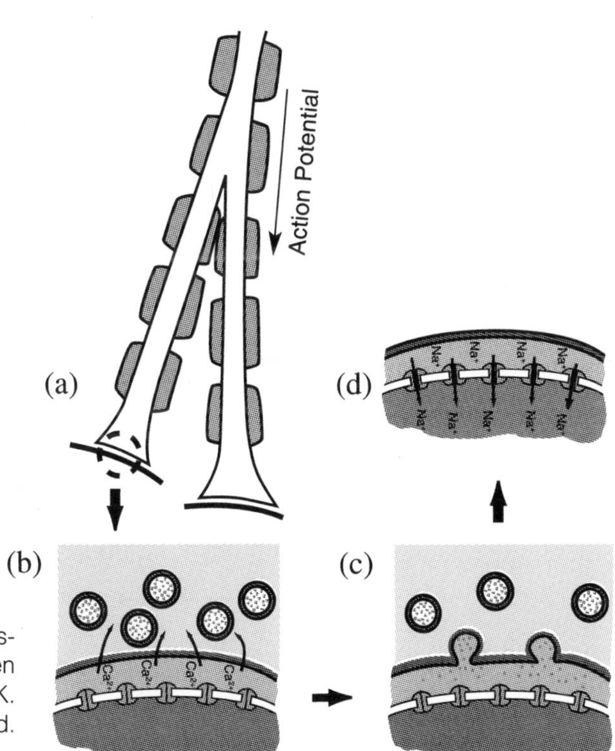

Fig. 17.22 Schematic representation of the transmission of an action potential across a synapse between a bouton and a muscle cell. (Adapted from C. K. Mathews and K. E. van Holde, *Biochemistry,* 1st ed. Benjamin Cummings, 1990.)

The stimulus from a single nerve impulse would cause a rise in the tension generated by a muscle to a maximum, followed by a decrease in the force to zero. This is called a muscle *twitch* as illustrated by Fig. 17.23. If another stimulus arrives at the neuromuscular junction before the force from the preceding one has decreased to zero, then the maximum tension rises above the preceding maximum. If the stimuli continue and the frequency of the stimuli increases, the maximum tension continues to rise toward an ultimate maximum, as shown in Fig. 17.23. This maximum is called a *fused tetanus,* or a complete tetanus (from the Greek word tetanos, meaning *spasm*). On the way up to the maximum, the tension-curve passes through a range of un-fused (or incomplete) tetanus. The overall maximum tension depends not only on the frequency of the stimuli, which can reach several hundred Hz, but also on the amount of recruitment of additional motor units for the exercise. It appears that both the increase in frequency and recruitment occur together as the maximum tension is approached.

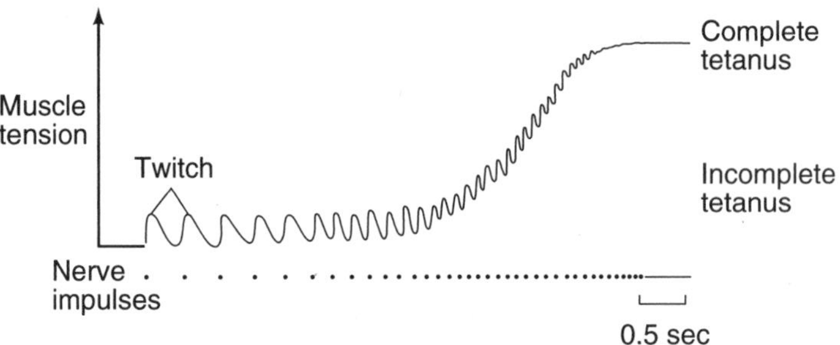

Fig. 17.23 Schematic representation of the increasing tension in a muscle as the frequency of nerve impulses increases. (From Per Brodal, *The Central Nervous System, Structure and Function,* Oxford University Press, 1992.)

17.6 Mechanical Behavior of Muscle

A muscle is joined at its end to a tendon at what is called the *myotendinous junction.* As shown in Fig. 17.24, this junction comprises a highly folded membrane, such that the muscle tissue and tendon tissue interpenetrate deeply. This arrangement allows the area of the junction to be very large, and it also means that the stresses at the junction that are imposed by a force along the muscle are shear stresses, rather than tensile stresses that would tend to tear the interface apart. Thus, this junction employs the principles that engineers use in adhesive joints, as we have seen previously.

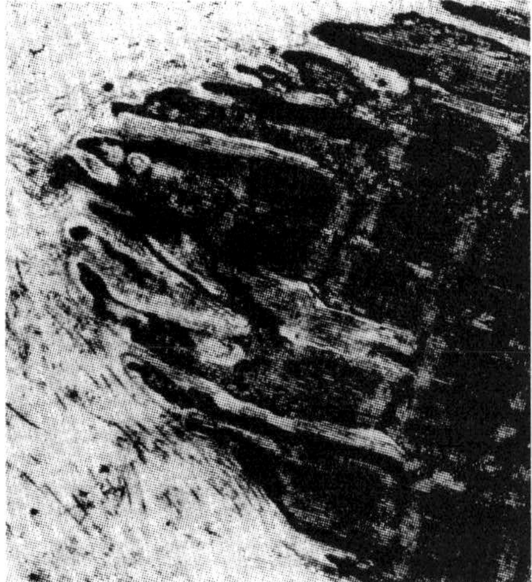

Fig. 17.24 Electron micrograph of a myotendinous junction (Reprinted from J. G. Tidball, *Exp Mol Pathol* 1984, vol. 40, p. 1. with permission from Elsevier)

The stress-strain curve for unstimulated, or passive, muscle tissue is similar to that for tendon and ligament as discussed in Chapter 15. This is the response of the connective tissue that encases the fascicles and the muscle body. The early stages show a low, but increasing, slope - the toe region - as the collagen fibers straighten and become aligned, and then a linear range before failure.

The more interesting behavior is the plot of tensile force *vs.* length of a stimulated muscle. As shown schematically in Fig. 17.25, the curve goes through a maximum, which occurs at an optimum length. As the length is increased beyond the optimum, the amount of overlap between the thick and thin filaments is reduced, which therefore limits their interaction. As the length is shortened from the optimum, the thick filaments start to pile up against the Z-lines, and again the strength of the interaction is reduced.

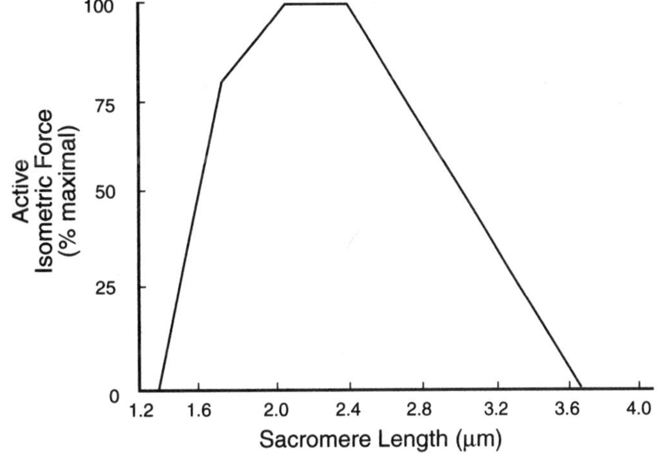

Fig. 17.25 Schematic representation of the variation of the isometric tension that can be exerted by a muscle as a function of its length. (Adapted from Y.E. Goldman and E. Homsher in *Myology, Basic and Clinical, 3rd ed.* Eds. A. G. Engel and C. Franzini-Armstrong vol. 1, McGraw-Hill, 2004.)

The skeletal muscles of interest here operate by causing rotation of, say, an arm or leg around a joint. The quantity of operational interest is the torque that is exerted at that joint, which is given by the tension in the muscle times the moment arm, which is the perpendicular distance from the line of action of the muscle to the axis of the joint. Thus, the torque depends both on the tension-*vs.*-length curve of the muscle and on the length of the moment arm, which changes with the angle of rotation at the joint. For example, when the arm flexes, the biceps muscle shortens and the moment arm goes through a maximum at about the mid-point of the process, as shown schematically in Fig. 17.26. The maximum force exerted by the muscle also goes through a maximum at about that stage, as the length is decreasing, so that is where the torque reaches a maximum, for example, in an arm-curl exercise in weight lifting.

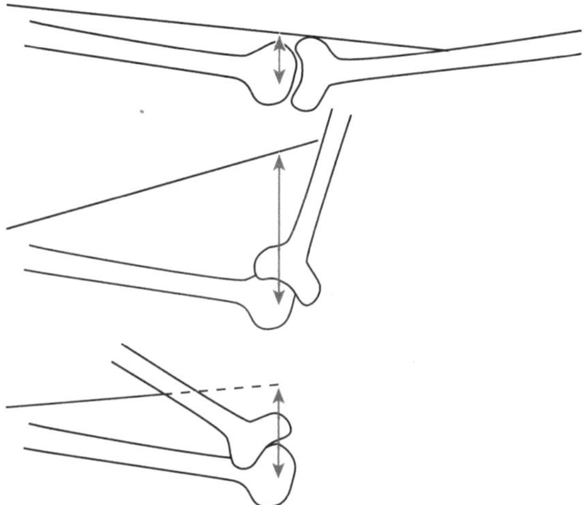

Fig. 17.26 Schematic representation of the variation in the moment arm of the force exerted by a muscle as it flexes and moves a bone around a pivot point.

17.7 Training Effects

Muscle tissue and performance can be modified by different kinds of training. Strength training involves exercises that contract the muscles against a level of resistance that is increased over time. The resistance should be high enough that fatigue prevents more than a relatively small number of repetitions during one set of a given exercise. The strength increase is found to be directly related to an increase in the cross-sectional area of the muscle. Most of this increase in size is believed to be due to an increase in the diameter of individual fibers (hypertrophy), rather than an increase in the number of fibers (hyperplasia), although some of the latter does occur. An example of this is shown in Fig. 17.27, in which the staining treatment has made the Type-II fibers dark, which is the opposite of that shown in Fig. 17.4.

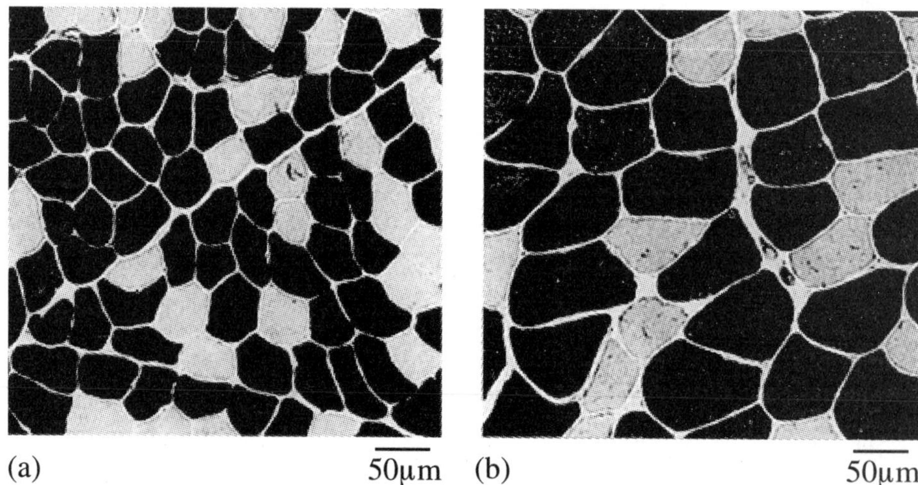

Fig. 17.27 Photomicrographs that show a comparison of the sizes of muscle fibers in (a) a "normal" person and (b) a weight lifter. (From Per Brodal, *The Central Nervous Sustem, Structure and Function,* Oxford University Press, 1992.

The increase in fiber size is accompanied by an increase in the content of contractile proteins, i.e., actin and myosin. Type-II fibers are reported to show greater hypertrophy than Type-I fibers. Another change that results from strength training is an increase in the number of motor units that can be recruited for a given exercise. This is thought to be the result of changes in the ability of the central nervous system to fire the motor neurons in a way that gives better synchronization of muscle activation.

In contrast with strength training, which involves an increase in muscle size, endurance training, also called aerobic training, does not involve working muscles against high resistive forces. The effects have to do with the supply and utilization of energy, specifically with regard to blood circulation and oxidative metabolism. The size of the heart increases so as to produce a greater stroke volume, and the number of capillaries in the muscles increases with extended endurance-type exercise. (Because of the greater stroke volume, the resting heart rate decreases.)

The increase in oxidative metabolism is accomplished in part by an increase in the size and number density of the mitochondria in the muscle fibers. In addition, there is an increase in the enzymes that are involved in the energy conversion process, including those used to process fatty acids in the mitochondria. One result of endurance training is an increase in the proportion of fatty acids that are used for fuel, as opposed to the use of glycogen. However, an increase in stored glycogen through an increase in carbohydrates in the diet for a few days before testing or competition can have a significant effect on extending endurance, meaning postponing fatigue.

17.8 Injury and Healing of Muscle

There is still much to be learned about how muscles heal after injury. A number of studies have been done with laboratory animals, mainly rats and rabbits, but our knowledge is still far from complete. There are two general types of injury: direct, involving laceration or contusion, and indirect, involving a partial or complete tear, which is also referred to as a pull or a strain. A laceration can mean a complete transection of the muscle body or an incomplete cutting of the muscle. In a complete transection, partial healing can be accomplished after suturing the cut faces, mainly by the formation of a dense scar of connective tissue. It has been reported that a small number of myotubes can penetrate across the scar. These are constructed from undifferentiated cells that exist in muscle fibers and that form myoblasts after the injury. They can fuse into myotubes, which may later coalesce into muscle fibers. Complete restoration of strength and the original amount of possible contraction are rarely, if ever, achieved after a complete transection. The extent of recovery after partial laceration is proportional to the extent of the laceration, and it depends on the degree to which revascularization and reinnervation occurs.

The other kind of direct injury, contusion, is caused by a blunt impact that does not penetrate the muscle tissue. In rat studies, healing starts with an inflammatory reaction and hematoma, followed by the formation of a scar consisting of dense connective tissue. The rate of healing depends on the rate of vascular ingrowth in the damaged area. It has been found that the recovery of full function is more rapid if the muscle is mobilized during healing. Sometimes, the healing process is accompanied by the formation of bone within the muscle, called *myositis ossificans.* This bone formation, which can be detected by x-ray examination, can occur periostially on existing bone, or it can be completely remote from existing bone, out in the muscle body, in which case it is called *heterotopic* bone. The formation of heterotopic bone is more likely after repeated contusions in the same area, and the heterotopic bone may or may not be resorbed with time. The presence of heterotopic bone appears to delay healing, but it does not appear to prevent the ultimate restoration of full function of a muscle.

Complete tears have been studied in rabbits by pulling the muscle-tendon unit to failure. Slightly more force is required if the muscle is actively stimulated. The failure is usually located at, or very close to, the junction of the muscle and tendon. Remember that the ends of tendons penetrate well into the muscle tissue by reason of the folded nature of the junction (cf. Fig. 17.24). The sarcomeres in the region tend to be stiffer than elsewhere, and this limits the ability of this region to accommodate stretching, so stress tends to intensify there.

Incomplete tears are much more common in humans. In rabbit studies they are found to occur at or near the muscle-tendon junction, and the healing involves some hemorrhaging, inflamation, edema, and formation of scar tissue. The return of essentially full function took more than a week in one study cited by Garrett and Best. In humans, this process can be followed by CT scans or MRI
17430 studies. The most common sites for tears are the hamstrings, the rectus femoris, and the gastrocnemius (cf. Fig. 17.1). These muscles cross more than one joint, and the muscle-tendon junction extends particularly far into the muscle; in the case of the hamstrings it goes from one end of the muscle belly to the other. As pointed out earlier, this kind of joint is well developed to resist failure by overload, and these muscles presumably evolved this way because they can be particularly subject to over stretching.

Although it is not properly called an injury, *per se*, disuse or immobilization of a muscle causes degeneration in terms of size, structure, and metabolic processes. Disuse can occur as a response to some painful condition, or during bed rest, or during exposure to low-gravity conditions. Immobilization can be part of the treatment of some injury or disease. Both have similar effects, including atrophy of individual muscle fibers, accompanied by a decrease in muscle mass, cross section, and strength. The atrophy occurs most rapidly in the early stages, and the rate decreases with time. The rate also varies among muscles; for example, studies of suspended animals have shown that the muscles used to resist the force of gravity atrophy faster than others. The ability to resist fatigue also declines in unused muscles, and this is related to decreased energy supply, increased lactic-acid production, and decreased ability to use fats in aerobic exercise. It has been found that muscle immobilized without tension suffers more than a muscle that is stretched during immobilization. For example, the quadriceps lose strength more than the hamstrings when a person is immobilized with the legs straight. The stretch has the result of synthesis of new contractile proteins and the addition of sarcomeres at the end of the existing fibrils, and this partially offsets the loss of muscle cross section from atrophy of fibers.

Another kind of quasi-injury is the delayed muscle soreness that can follow intense exercise, usually starting after several hours and reaching a maximum in a few days. It is usually accompanied by some firmness and swelling of the affected muscles and a loss of isometric strength. It has been found to be exacerbated by forceful jerky movements, particularly in people unaccustomed to such exercise. The soreness appears to be the result of structural disruption of sarcomeres, edema, and increased pressure caused by changes in ion concentrations in muscle fibers, along with the breakdown of some connective tissue. The damage appears to be repairable, and muscle training can increase the resistance to this type of damage.

Finally, a common phenomenon that is not yet well understood is cramping of muscles. This is the result of spasmodic contractions that begin when a muscle is in a shortened condition, and it can be relieved by stretching the muscle. It can occur when a person is resting or even sleeping, or as a result of fatiguing exercise, particularly in the presence of dehydration. The susceptible muscles include the gastrocnemius, the hamstrings, and the abdominal muscles. Cramping is thought to be associated often with disturbance of the electrolyte balances, and athletes are often advised to drink fluids that replace sodium ions when these can be lost by perspiration.

References and Recommended Reading

1. The Johns Hopkins *Atlas of Human Functional Anatomy*, ed. George. D. Zuidema, Johns Hopkins University Press, 1997.
2. William E. Garrett, Jr. and Thomas M. Best, in *Orthopaedic Basic Science*, ed. Sheldon R. Simon, American Academy of Orthopaedic Surgeons, 1994.
3. Christopher K. Matthews and K. E. van Holde, *Biochemistry, 2nd. Ed.*, Benjamin Cummings, 1996.
4. Bruce Alberts, Alexander Johnson, Julian Lewis, Martin Raff, Keith Roberts, and Peter Walter, *Molecular Biology of the Cell, 4th ed.* Garland Science, 2002.
5. Michael H. Ross, Gordon I. Kaye, and Wojciech Pawlina, *Histology, a Text and Atlas,* Lippincott, Williams & Wilkins, 1995.
6. Per Brodal, *The Central Nervous Sustem, Structure and Function*, Oxford University Press, 1992.
7. Y. E. Goldman and E. Homsher in *Myology, Basic and Clinical, 3rd ed.,* Eds. A. G. Engel and C. Franzini-Armstrong, *Vol. 1,* McGraw-Hill, 2004.

Summary

Although skeletal muscle is "structural" in that it carries loads of various kinds, it is actually as much a "functional" system as it is structural. The basic functional unit is the sarcomere, in which a set of two filaments, actin and myosin, operate to contract the sarcomere and thereby to shorten the myofibrils that are made up of chains of sarcomeres. The heads on the myosin filaments act as molecular motors to pull the myosin along the actin filaments. The energy for this comes from the hydrolysis of adenosine triphosphate, ATP, which must be recycled in order for the muscle to continue to operate. For short-time exertions this is done anaerobically by the hydrolysis of glycogen (stored animal starch). For long-time exertions aerobic metabolism (using oxygen) is required. Slow-twitch (Type-I) muscle fibers are optimized for aerobic metabolism, and fast-twitch (Type-II) fibers for anaerobic metabolism.

A muscle contraction is initiated by an action potential that propagates down the axon of a motor neuron to a bundle of muscle fibers, each of which is a long, single, multinucleated cell. (Each fiber contains many myofibrils.) The action potential causes a release of neurotransmitters, which ultimately leads to the release of calcium ions into the sarcoplasm of the fibers, and this initiates the shortening of the sarcomere.

Glossary/Vocabulary - Chapter 17

A-band — The dark band seen in the middle of a sarcomere of a muscle fiber when viewed under polarized light in an optical microscope. A for "anisotropic." The A-band is the region occupied by the thick filaments.

Acetylcholine — The neurotransmitter that is used by motor neurons to induce a muscle contraction. It is an ester of choline, which is an amine, $C_5H_{15}NO_2$. The univalent acetyl radical is CH_3CO. It is carried in the synaptic vesicles to the pre-synaptic membrane and then released into the synaptic cleft.

Actin — One of the two contractile proteins that make up the sarcomeres in muscle fibers. The thin filaments of muscle fiber comprise two helically wound chains of polymerized actin.

Action potential — A nerve impulse that travels down the axon of a neuron. It constitutes a wave of depolarization of the membrane of the axon.

Aerobic metabolism — The oxidative metabolism of either glucose or fats that is used to replace ATP. It occurs in the mitochondria of cells. This is highly efficient metabolism, because each glucose molecule is used to convert 38 ADP to ATP.

ADP — Abbreviation for adenosine diphosphate. This is one of the reaction products from the hydrolysis of ATP. The other product is inorganic phosphate.

Anaerobic metabolism — The mechanism of replenishment of ATP that starts with the hydrolysis of glycogen to make glucose and involves various enzymes in a number of steps to convert ADP to ATP. It occurs in the sarcoplasm of muscle cells. It converts only two ADP to ATP for each molecule of glucose.

ATP — Abbreviation for adenosine triphosphate, a compound of adenosine (a nucleotide containing adenine $C_5H_5N_5$ and ribose $C_5H_{10}O_5$; a pentose sugar) and 3 phosphate acid groups. The hydrolysis of ATP provides the energy for a number of functions in the body, including muscle contraction.

Axon — The long extension of a nerve cell (neuron) along which the action potential (nerve impulse) travels. In a motor neuron it runs from the cell body down to the boutons that connect to muscle fibers.

Bouton` — One of the bulbs in an array at the end of the terminal branch of an axon. Each array of boutons at the end of a terminal branch connects with one muscle fiber in the motor end plate.

Cramping of muscle	A condition involving painful spasmodic contractions of a muscle. It is often associated with electrolyte imbalance caused by dehydration. It can be relieved by stretching the muscle.
Creatine	An amino acid. Creatine phosphate can react with ADP to produce ATP plus creatine; this helps to replenish ATP in anaerobic metabolism in muscle.
Depolarization	The change of the membrane potential of a cell from its resting value of about – 60mV in the positive direction that occurs when Na-ions are admitted into the cell. This initiates an action potential in a neuron, for example, and the nerve impulse is transmitted as a wave of depolarization down the axon.
Endomysium	The membrane of connective tissue that surrounds a muscle fiber. It contains fine capillaries and the branches of neurons.
Epimysium	The sheath of dense connective tissue that binds the fascicles of muscle fibers together. The major blood vessels and nerves go through this sheath.
Fascicle	A bundle of muscle fibers. In a microscopic cross section it looks like a typical cellular structure, like a polycrystalline metal.
Fast-twitch fiber	A Type-II muscle fiber that uses either both oxidative and anaerobic reactions (Type IIA) or only anaerobic reactions (Type IIB). They are faster acting but more fatigable than Type I.
Glycogen	A polysaccharide commonly called animal starch, literally, a "sugar-former." It is the storehouse for sugar in the body. Hydrolysis of glycogen, or glycolysis (sugar splitting), gives glucose.
H-band	The light band in the center of the A-band of a sarcomere when viewed via TEM. This is the region between the ends of the thin filaments in which only the central regions of thick filaments are seen. H is from the German hell, meaning light.
I-band	The light band seen between the A-bands of a sarcomere of a muscle fiber when viewed under polarized light in an optical microscope. I for "isotropic." The I-bands are the regions that do not contain thick filaments. They are optically isotropic because they contain only one type of filament.
Ion channel	A special protein structure that provides a passage for ions through the lipid bilayer of a cell membrane. A channel opens or closes in response either to a change in the membrane potential (voltage-gated ion channel) or to the binding of a transmitter molecule to a receptor (transmitter-gated or ligand-gated ion channel).
Ion pump	A mechanism for the passage of ions through the lipid bilayer of a cell membrane that operates to maintain the steady-state ion concentrations on either side of the membrane. A sodium-potassium ion pump sends three Na^+-ions out for every two K^+-ions sent in.
Lactic acid	One of the by-products of the anaerobic metabolism of glucose. The buildup of lactic acid is associated with muscle fatigue.
Membrane potential	The voltage gradient that arises from unequal concentrations of positively and negatively charged ions on either side of a cell membrane. The membrane potential changes when various ions move through ion channels in the membrane.
Mitochondria	Cell organelles, rod- or oval-shaped, that contain the enzymes for aerobic metabolism. The "power plants" of cells. This is where the production of ATP occurs.

M-line	The thin dark band in the middle of the H-band of a sarcomere. M is from the German mitte, meaning middle. This is the line marking the center of the thick filaments.
Motor end plate	The collection of boutons at the end of a terminal branch of the axon of a motor neuron. Each terminal branch and its collection of boutons connects with only one muscle fiber.
Motor neuron	A nerve cell that innervates a bundle of muscle fibers. The action potential, or nerve impulse, travels down the axon of a motor neuron.
Motor unit	The combination of an axon of a motor neuron and the muscle fibers to which it is attached. The motor units of Type-I muscle fibers are recruited first, followed by those of Type II.
Muscle fiber	A muscle cell. This is a multinucleated tubular cell formed by the fusion of myoblasts.
Myelin sheath	The covering of the axon of a neuron. It comprises multiple layers of phospholipid and protein. The myelin sheath is formed by, and contained in, the Schwann cells.
Myoblast	The embryonic cell that fuses with other myoblasts to form a muscle fiber. Myoblasts originate from mesenchymal cells.
Myofibril	A long cylindrical organelle made of the filamentary contractile proteins, actin and myosin, and other structures inside a muscle fiber. It is essentially a long stack of sarcomeres, each of which is surrounded by a sarcoplasmic reticulum.
Myosin	The polypeptide chains that make up the thick filaments in sarcomeres. There are two heavy chains, 230kd each, helically wound, and four light chains, about 20 kd each. Each heavy chain begins with a globular head.
Myositis ossificans	The formation of bone tissue in a muscle that is healing from a contusion. If it forms in the muscle body, away from existing bone, it is called heterotopic bone.
Myotendinous junction	The junction between a tendon and a muscle. This is a highly folded membrane, so that the stresses on the junction are mostly shear stresses applied to a large area.
Node of Ranvier	The space between two Schwann cells along the axon of a neuron in which there is no myelin sheath. At this point, the axon lacks electrical insulation and can emit and receive ions from the surroundings.
Perimysium	The membrane that surrounds each fascicle in a muscle fiber. It contains blood vessels and nerves.
Postsynaptic membrane	The membrane of the down-stream side of a synapse that contains the receptors for the neurotransmitters.
Presynaptic membrane	The membrane on the bouton of a terminal branch of an axon on the up-stream side of a synapse. The neurotransmitters are released through this membrane.
Recruitment	The addition of motor units in a muscle fiber as the force exerted by a muscle increases. The slow-twitch motor units are the first to be recruited.
Sarcomere	The unit that is repeated along the length of a myofibril in a muscle fiber. It comprises interdigitated thick and thin fibers (myosin and actin) and other proteins. The shortening of the sarcomere is the mechanism of muscle contraction.

Sarcoplasm	The cytoplasm of a muscle cell. This is where the anaerobic replenishment of ATP occurs.
Sarcoplasmic reticulum	The tubular network structure that surrounds each sarcomere in a myofibril of a muscle fiber. It is the storehouse for Ca-ions that start muscle contractions.
Schwann cell	The insulating cells that lie along the axon of a nerve cell. These produce and contain the myelin sheath that insulates the axon from its surroundings.
Slow-twitch fiber	A Type-I fiber that uses oxidative metabolism and is fatigue resistant. Type-I motor units are recruited first. They are most important for sustained exercise.
Striated muscle	Muscle made of long fibers filled with myofibrils composed of sarcomeres. Skeletal muscles are striated muscles.
Synapse	The junction between the end of an axon and its neighboring cell. In a motor neuron the junction is between a bouton and the muscle fiber.
Synaptic cleft	The space between the pre-synaptic and post-synaptic membranes. This is the space through which the neurotransmitter passes to the receptors on the post-synaptic membrane.
Synaptic vesicle	The small sac that holds the neurotransmitter molecules in the bouton at the end of a terminal branch of an axon. In a motor neuron, the neurotransmitter is acetylcholine.
Terminal cisternae	Extensions of the sarcoplasmic reticulum into the muscle fiber in which calcium ions are stored.
Tetanus	The maximum in the force *vs.* time curve for a muscle fiber. As the rate of stimuli increases, the twitches occur faster and the curve becomes smooth and flattens out.
Transverse tubule	The part of the cell membrane around a sarcomere that invaginates into the muscle fiber where the depolarization occurs that causes Ca^{2+} ions to be released from the terminal cisternae of the sarcoplasmic reticulum. The Ca-ion release begins the contraction of the sarcomeres.
Tropomyosin	Long-chain proteins that lie along the grooves of the helically wound actin chains in the thin fibers of sarcomeres. The troponin complexes are attached to the tropomyosin chains at 38.5 nm intervals.
Troponin complex	The cluster of three proteins attached to tropomyosin chains along the thin filaments of sarcomeres. One of the proteins, TnT, binds to the tropomyosin. Another, TnI, binds the troponin complex to the actin chain, and the third, TnC, binds to Ca-ions and is active in the process of muscle contraction
Type-I muscle fiber	See slow-twitch muscle fiber.
Type-II muscle fiber	See fast-twitch muscle fiber.
Z-line	The dark band that lies between sarcomeres in the myofilaments of muscle fibers. They are discs to which the ends of the actin chains are attached. Z is from the German zwischensheibe, meaning literally "between discs."

Exercises

17.1 What is the difference between a muscle fiber and a myofibril?

17.2 What is the unit of microstructure of a myofibril?

17.3 In this unit, what is the "motor protein," and how does it function?

17.4 What is the role of the node of Ranvier in a motor neuron?

17.5 How do calcium ions act to begin the cross-bridge cycle?

17.6 What provides the energy for the power stroke in this cycle?

17.7 How is this energy source replenished in anaerobic and aerobic exercises?

17.8 Why do farmyard chickens and migratory birds have red meat and white meat in different places in their bodies?

17.9 What is special about the design of the junction between a muscle and a tendon?

Appendix 1

Conversion of Units

Length

1 Å = 10^{-10} m = 10^{-8} cm = 0.1 nm = 3.937 x 10^{-8} in

1 cm = 10^{-2} m = 0.3937 in

1 ft = 12 in = 0.3048 m

1 in = 0.0254 m = 2.54 cm = 25.4 mm

1 μm = 10^{-6} m

1 nm = 10^{-9} m

Volume

1 cm^3 = 0.0610 in^3

1 in^3 = 16.3x10^{-6} m^3

1 gal (US) = 3.78x10^{-3} m^3

Mass

1 g = 0.602x10^{24} amu = 2.20x10^{-3} lb_m

1 kg = 2.20 lb = 10^3 g

1 lb_m = 0.454 kg

1 oz (Avoirdupois) = 0.0625 lb_m = 28.37 g

Density

1 g/cm^3 = 62.4 lb_m/ft^3 = 10^3 kg/m^3 = 1 Mg/m^3 = 1 mg/mm^3

1 lb_m/ft^3 = 16.0 kg/m^3

1 lb_m/1in^3 = 27.68 g/cm^3 = 27.68x10^3 kg/m^3

Energy or Work

1 Btu = 1.06x10^3 J

1 gram cal = 4.18 J

1 eV = 0.160x10^{-18} J

1 ft·lb_f = 1.355 J

1 in·lb_f = 0.113 J

1 dyne·cm = 10^{-7} J

1J = 1N-m

Force

1 N = 0.224 lb_f = 98.0 g_f

1 lb_f = 4.44 N

1 dyne = 10^{-5} N = 2.24x10^{-6} lb_f

Stress or Pressure

1 Pa = 1 N/m^2 = 0.145x10^{-3} lb_f/in^2

1 lb/in^2 = 6.89 kPa

Appendix 2

Physical Constants

atomic mass unit (amu) = $1.66 x 10^{-27}$ kg = $1.66 x 10^{-24}$ g

Avogadro's number (N) = $6.022 x 10^{23}$ atoms or molecules/mole

Boltzmann's constant (k) = $13.8 x 10^{-27}$ J/K = $8.63 x 10^{-5}$ eV/K

Gas constant (R) = Boltzmann's constant x Avogadro's number = 8.31 J/K·mole

electronic charge (q) = $0.16 x 10^{-18}$ Coulombs

Bohr magneton (magnetic moment of one electron spin) = $9.27 x 10^{-24}$ $A \cdot m^2$

electron volt = $0.160 x 10^{-18}$ J

acceleration of gravity (g) = 9.80 m/sec^2

Appendix 3

SI Prefixes

10^9	giga	G
10^6	mega	M
10^3	kilo	k
10^{-3}	milli	m
10^{-6}	micro	μ
10^{-9}	nano	n
10^{-12}	pico	p

Appendix 4

Physical Properties of Common Metals and Semiconductors (Room Temperature)

Element	Atomic Number	Atomic Mass (amu)	Atomic Diameter (Å)	Density (g/cm³)	Crystal Structure
Ag	47	107.87	2.89	10.5	fcc
Al	13	26.98	2.86	2.70	fcc
Au	79	196.97	2.88	19.32	fcc
Be	4	9.01	2.28	1.85	hcp
Cd	48	112.40	2.96	8.65	hcp
Co	27	58.93	2.50	8.9	hcp
Cr	24	52.00	2.50	7.20	bcc
Cu	29	63.54	2.56	8.92	fcc
Fe (α)	26	55.85	2.48	7.88	bcc
Ge	32	72.59	2.44	5.35	diamond cubic
Li	3	6.94	3.04	0.534	bcc
Mg	12	24.31	3.22	1.74	hcp
Mn	25	54.94		7.2	complex
Mo	42	95.94	2.73	10.22	bcc
Ni	28	58.71	2.49	8.90	fcc
Pb	82	207.19	3.50	11.34	fcc
Pt	78	195.1	2.78	21.45	fcc
Sc	14	28.09	2.36	2.33	diamond cubic
Sn	50	118.69		7.31	diamond cubic
Ti(α)	22	47.90	2.93	4.51	hcp
V	23	50.94	2.63	6.11	bcc
W	74	183.85	2.73	19.4	bcc
Zn	30	65.37	2.78	7.14	hcp
Zr	40	91.22	3.24	6.51	hcp

Appendix 5

Elastic Constants of Common Metals

Metal	Young's Modulus E GPa	Poisson's Ratio ν	Shear Modulus G GPa
W	345	0.28	134
Ni	214	0.31	75
Fe	210	0.28	82
Cu	110	0.35	41
Ti	116	0.36	45
Al	70	0.34	26
Mg	45	0.29	17
Pb	14	0.45	4.8

Appendix 6

Ionic Radii (Å)

ion	CN=4	CN=6	CN=8
Al^{2+}	0.46	0.51	
Co^{2+}		0.99	1.02
Cl-		1.81	1.87
Cr^{3+}		0.63	
F^{-}	1.21	1.33	
Fe^{2+}	0.67	0.74	
Fe^{3+}	0.58	0.64	
K^{+}		1.33	
Li^{+}		0.68	
Mg^{2+}	0.60	0.66	0.68
Mn^{2+}	0.60	0.66	0.68
Na^{+}		0.97	
Ni^{2+}	0.63	0.69	
O^{2-}	1.28	1.40	1.44
OH^{-}		1.40	
P^{5+}		0.35	
S^{2-}	1.68	1.84	1.90
Si^{4+}	0.38	0.42	
Ti^{4+}		0.68	
Zn^{2+}	0.67	0.74	
Zr^{4+}		0.79	0.82

CN=Coordination number

Appendix 7

Specific Modulus Values

Bulk materials	Density, ρ g/cm[3]	Modulus, E GPa	E/ρ
Al	2.7	70	26
Fe (steel)	7.8	250	26.9
Mg	1.7	45	26
soda-lime glass	2.5	76	30.4
softwood	0.4	11	26
hardwood	0.6	17	27
PVC	1.3	4.5	22
Reinforcing Materials			
Al_2O_3	3.9	400	100
B	2.3	400	170
Be	1.9	300	160
BeO	3.0	400	130
C	2.3	700	300
SiC	3.2	500	160
SiN	3.2	400	120

Appendix 8

Properties of Some Engineering Materials

Material	Density g/cm^3	Thermal Conductivity $(W/mm^2)/(K/mm)$	Thermal Expansion Coefficient K^{-1}	Electrical Resistivity ohm-m	Elastic Modulus GPa
Al alloys	2.7	0.16	$22x10^{-6}$	$45x10^{-9}$	$70x10^3$
brass (70-30)	8.5	0.12	20	62	110
grey cast iron	7.2	—	10	—	140
Cu	8.9	0.40	17	17	110
Fe	7.8	0.072	12	98	210
steel 1020	7.8	0.05	12	170	210
steel 1040	7.8	0.05	11	171	210
steel 1080	7.8	0.04	11	180	210
stainless steel	7.9	0.015	16	700	210
Mg	1.7	0.16	25	45	45
Al_2O_3	3.8	0.029	9	10^{12}	350
concrete	2.4	0.001	13	—	14
brick	2.3	0.006	9	—	—
glass					
window	2.5	0.0008	9	10^{12}	76
silica	2.2	0.0012	0.5	>1015	76
Vycor	2.2	0.0012	0.6	10^{18}	76
graphite	1.9	—	5	10^{-5}	7
MgO	3.6	—	9	—	205
quartz	2.65	0.012	—	10^{12}	310
SiC	3.17	0.012	4.5	—	—

GLOSSARY LOCATOR*

% elong 2
%RA 2
6061-T6 aluminum alloy 10
8-N rule 9
A-band 17
Abrasive wear 9
Accelerated vulcanization 14
Acetylcholine 17
Achilles tendon 15
ACL 15
Actin 17
Action potential 17
Activation energy 5
Addition polymerization 12
Adhesive bonding 11
Adhesive wear 9
ADP 17
Aerobic metabolism 17
Alanine 15
Allograft 15
Allotropic transformation 7
Alloy steel 11
Alpha helix 15
Amino acid 15
Amino group 15
Anaerobic metabolism 17
Anionic polymerization 14
Anisotropic 13
Annealing 5
Annealing twins 9
Anodic reaction 1
Anodizing of aluminum 11
Appositional growth 16
Arc welding 11
Arginine 15
Articular cartilage 15
Asparagine 15
Aspartate 15
Aspect ratio 13
α-stabilizer 11
Atactic 12
ATP 17
Austenite 6
Autograft 15
Avulsion 15
Axon 17
Bainite 8
Bakelite 13
Beads 14
Belts 14
Bending-moment 11
Bending-moment diagram 11
Benzene ring 12
Binding-energy curve 2
Body-centered cubic, BCC 1
Body-centered tetragonal, BCT 8
Bonded joints 11
Boundary lubrication 9
Bouton 17
Bragg's Law 4
Branched polymer 12
Bravais lattice 3
Brazing 7
Bridging oxygens 9
Bright-field technique 4
Brittle fracture 6
Brittleness 9
β-stabilizer 11
Buckling 11
Burgers vector 4
Butadiene 12
Butted tubing 11
Butyl rubber 14
Calcitonin 16
Calendering 14
Callus 16
Canaliculi 16
Cancellous bone 16
Capillary action 7
Carbon black 14
Carbon fiber 13
Carbon-fiber reinforced plastic, CFRP 13
Carboxyl group 15
Carburization 9
Cartilage 15
Case hardening 9
Cast iron 8
Casting 11
Cathodic reaction 1
Cation 9
Cationic polymerization 14
C-curve 8
Cellulose 13
Cement lines 16
Cementite 6
Ceramic 9
Chemical potential 7
Chloroprene 12
Chondroblast 16
Chondrocytes 15
Chondroitin sulfate 15
Chondryle 15
cis-Polyisoprene 12
Cleavage fracture 6
Climb 4
Close-packed direction 3
Close-packed plane 3
Coarsening 5
Coefficient of friction 9
Coffin-Manson behavior 16
Coherent interface 10
Cold drawing (metals) 8
Cold-drawing of a linear polymer 13
Cold welding 9
Cold work 5
Collagen 15
Collateral ligaments 15
Compact bone 16
Component 7
Composite elastic modulus 13
Compositional component of γ 10
Compounding 14
Condensation polymerization 13
Conjugated diene 12
Contact angle 7
Continuous transformation-(CT) diagram 8
Cooling curve 7
Coordination number 1
Copolymer 14
Core of a dislocation 4
Coring 7
Cortical bone 16
Covalent bonding 9
Crack arrest 13
Cramping of muscle 17

* Chapter numbers indicated

Creatine 17
Creep 12
Critical radius 10
Cr-Mo steel 11
Cross slip 4
Cross-linking 12
Cruciate ligaments 15
Crystal lattice 3
Crystal symmetry 6
Curing agent 13
Curvature of a beam 11
Cyclic loading 1
Dark-field technique 10
Dashpot 12
Deep zone 15
Deformation processing 2
Deformation twinning 9
Degree of polymerization 12
Dendrite 7
Depolarization 17
ΔG^* 10
Diamond-pyramid hardness, DPH 5
Diaphysis 16
Diffraction contrast 4
Diffusion coefficient (diffusivity) 9
Dilational stress 4
Dilatometer 8
Dimer 9
Direction indices 3
Discontinuous fibers 13
Dislocation 2
Dislocation density 4
Dislocation energy 4
Dislocation glide 2
Dislocation interactions 4
Dislocation loop 4
Dislocation multiplication 4
Dislocation-solute interactions 4
Distal 16
Double cross slip 4
Drawing of glass fibers 13
Driving force 5
Ductile-brittle transition 6
Ductility 2
ECM 15
Edge dislocation 4
Effect of grain size on strength 5
Elastic limit 2
Elastic modulus 2
Elastin 15
Elastomer 12
Emulsion polymerization 14
Endochondrial ossification 16
Endomysium 17
Endosteal surface 16
Energy of formation 5
Energy of motion 5
Energy-dispersive x-ray analysis 13
Engineering strain 2
Engineering stress 2
Entanglement 12
Enthalpy 5
Entropy 5
Epimysium 17
Epiphyseal cartilage 16
Epiphysis 16
Epitenon 15
Epoxy adhesives 13
Equilibrium 5
Equilibrium in a cellular network 5
Eutectic alloy 7
Eutectic divorcement 7
Eutectic reaction 7
Eutectoid reaction 8
Eutectoid steel 8
Extensometer 2
Extracellular matrix 15
Extrusion 10
Face-centered cubic, FCC 1
Fascicle 17
Fast-twitch fiber 17
Fatigue crack nucleation 6
Fatigue life 6
Fatigue limit 6
Femur 16
Ferrite 6
Fiber pull-out 13
Fiber-reinforced composite 13
Fibrin clot 15
Fick's second law 9
Filament 14
Finite-element method 13
Flexor tendon 15
Flux 7
Force on a dislocation 4
Fracture mechanics 9
Free radical 12
Frictional force 9
Furnace brazing 11
GAG 15
Galvanic series 1
Gauge length 2
Gibbs free energy 5
Glass transition 12
Glutamate 15
Glutamine 15
Glycine 15
Glycogen 17
Glycoprotein 16
Glysosaminoglycan 15
Golgi apparatus 15
Grain boundary 3
Grain boundary pinning 5
Grain growth 5
Grain-boundary energy 3
Griffith equation 9
Ground substance 15
Guinier-Preston (G-P) zones 10
Gutta percha 12
Habit relationship. 8
Hardenability 9
Hardening of steel 9
Hardness test 5
Hard-sphere model 1
Haversian canal 16
H-band 17
Heat-affected zone, HAZ 11
Heterogeneous nucleation 10
Hexagonal close-packed, HCP 9
High-density polyethylene, HDPE 12
Homogeneous nucleation 10
Hooke's law 2
Hot isostatic pressing (HIP) 9

Hot working 5
Hyaline cartilage 15
Hyaluronic acid 15
Hydrodynamic lubrication 9
Hydrostatic compression 4
Hydroxyapatite 16
Hydroxylation 15
Hydroxyproline 16
Hypereutectic alloy 7
Hypoeutectic 7
Hysteresis 12
I-band 17
Incoherent interface 10
Incorporation 14
Injection molding 12
Interfacial energy 10
Intermetallic compound 7
Internal energy 5
Interstitial diffusion 6
Interstitial lamellae 16
Interstitial solute 6
Investment casting 11
Ion channel 17
Ion pump 17
Ionic crystal 9
Isotactic 12
Isothermal-transformation (IT) diagram 8
Isotropic 2
Jominy bar 8
Keratin sulfate 15
Kevlar 13
Kinetics 5
Lack-of-penetration defect 11
Lactic acid 17
Lacunae 16
Lamellae 16
Lamellar 7
Lateral surface 16
Latex 14
Lattice parameter 3
LCL 15
Leucine 15
Lever rule 7
Ligament 15
Line tension 4
Linear polymer 12
Liner 14
Liquidus line 7
Low-alloy steel 11
Low-density polyethylene 12
Lubricant 9
Lug 11
Macrophage 16
Marrow cavity 16
Martensite 8
Maxwell solid 12
Maxwell-Boltzmann distribution 5
MCL 15
Medial surface 16
Membrane potential 17
Meniscus 15
Mer 9
Mesenchymal cells 15
Metallic bonding 9
Metallography 3
Metaphysis 16
Metastable 10
Methionine 15
M_f temperature 8
Micelle 14
Microhardness test 11
Middle zone 15
Miller indices 3
Miscible 7
Mitochondria 17
Mixed dislocation 4
Mixing of rubber 14
M-line 17
Modifier 14
Molybdenum disulfide 9
Moment of inertia 11
Monomer 9
Motor end plate 17
Motor neuron 17
Motor unit 17
M_s temperature 8
Muntz metal 7
Muscle fiber 17
Myelin sheath 17
Myoblast 17
Myofibril 17
Myosin 17
Myositis ossificans 17
Myotendinous junction 17
Natural rubber 14
Necking 2
Necking criterion 2
Network modifiers 13
Network polymer 12
Neutral axis 11
Newtonian viscosity 13
Noble vs. active 1
Node of Ranvier 17
Non-equilibrium solidification 7
Normal stress 2
Normalized steel 8
Nucleation and growth 5
Nylon 13
Octahedral site 6
Ordered precipitate 10
Orowan mechanism 10
Orthorhombic 8
Osteoblast 16
Osteoclast 16
Osteocyte 16
Osteoid 16
Osteon 16
Osteoprogenitor cell 16
Overaging 10
Packing density 1
Parabolic hardening 4
Paraffin 12
Paratenon 15
Parathyroid gland 16
Passivated surface 1
Patella tendon 15
Patenting of steel 13
Pauli exclusion principle 9
PBD 14
PCL 15
Pearlite 6
Peierls stress 4
Perfectly plastic material 9
Perimysium 17
Periosteal surface 16
Periosteum 15
Peritectic reaction 7
PET 14

Phagocytes 15
Phase 1
Phase rule 7
Photomicrograph 3
Piezoelectric 16
Pinning 4
Pitting corrosion 1
Plain-carbon steel 8
Plane strain 9
Plane stress 9
Plane-strain fracture toughness, K_{Ic} 9
Plastic blunting 6
Plastic constraint 2
Plastic strain 2
Plasticizer 14
Plies 14
Point defect 5
Poisson's ratio 2
Polyacrilonitrile, PAN 13
Polyamide 13
Polybutadiene 14
Polycrystalline material 3
Polydiene 14
Polyester 14
Polyethylene terephthalate 14
Polyethylene, PE 12
Polymerization 12
Polymethylmethacrylate, PMMA 12
Polypeptide 15
Polystyrene 12
Polytetraflouroethylene, PTFE 12
Polyvinylchoride, PVC 12
Porosity 11
Postsynaptic membrane 17
Precipitation hardening 9
Pre-impregnated tape, "prepreg" 13
Presynaptic membrane 17
Primary constituent 7
Primary slip plane 4
Proeutectoid ferrite 8
Proline 15
Proteoglycan 15
Proximal 16
Quadriceps muscles 15
Quadriceps tendon 15
Quench cracking 9
Radiography 11
Random walk 12
Rayon 13
Reaction bonding 9
Reactivity ratio 14
Recalescence 8
Recovery 5
Recruitment 17
Recrystallization 5
Regulator 14
Remodeling of bone 16
Reptation 13
Residual stress 9
Residue 15
Resorption 16
Retained austenite 8
Ribosomes 15
RNA 15
Rough endoplasmic reticulum 15
Rule of mixtures 13
Rupture 2
S- curve 5
Sacrificial anode 1
Sarcomere 17
Sarcoplasm 17
Sarcoplasmic reticulum 17
SBD 14
SBR 14
Scanning-electron microscope, SEM 13
Schmid factor 2
Schmid law 2
Schwann cell 17
Scorch 14
Screw dislocation 4
Secondary hardening 9
Segregation of solute atoms 5
Self diffusion 6
Semi-coherent interface 10
Serine 15
Shear modulus 2
Shear strain. 2
Shear stress 2
Shot peening 6
Sialoprotein 16
Silica glass 13
Silicon nitride, Si_3N_4 9
Sintering 9
Slip 2
Slip band 2
Slip system 4
Slow-twitch fiber 17
Small-scale-yielding approximation 9
Soldering 7
Solid solubility 7
Solid solution 1
Solid-solution hardening 10
Solidus line 7
Solute segregation 6
Solution polymerization 14
Solution treatment 10
Solvus line 7
Spheroidization 8
Spherulitic crystallization 12
Spinnerette 13
Spongy bone 16
Spring constant 2
Stabilizer 14
Stacking-fault energy 9
Stainless steel 1
Stored elastic energy 2
Stored energy of cold work 5
Strain gauge 2
Strain hardening 2
Stress concentration 6
Stress field of dislocation 4
Stress fracture 16
Stress intensity factor 9
Stress relaxation 12
Stress softening 14
Stress to bow a loop 4
Stress-concentration factor 6
Stress-strain curve 2
Striated muscle 17
Structural component of γ 10
Structure of carbon black 14
Styrene-butadiene rubber 14
STZ 15
Subchondral bone 15

Substitution transformation 5
Substitutional diffusion 6
Supersaturated solid solution 10
Surfactant 14
Synapse 17
Synaptic cleft 17
Synaptic vesicle 17
Syndiotactic 12
Synovial fluid 15
Synovial joint 15
Synovial membrane 15
Synovium 15
Tacticity 12
Temper designation 10
Tempering 9
Tendon 15
Tensile test 2
Terminal solid solution 7
Tetanus 17
Tetragonal distortion 6
Tetrahedral site 6
Thermal activation 5
Thermal analysis 8
Thermal stresses 9
Thermocouple 7
Thermodynamics 5
Thermoplastic 12
Thermoplastic elastomer 14
Thiol 14
Ti-3%Al-2.5%V 11
Ti-6%Al-4%V 11
Tibia 16
Tie line 7
TIG welding 11
Tire cord 14
Toughness 9
Trabecular bone 16
Transfer length 13
trans-Polyisoprene 12
Transverse tubule 17
Triblock copolymer 14
Tropocollagen 15
Tropomyosin 17
Troponin complex 17
True strain 2
True stress 2
Twinning 9
Type-I collagen 15
Type-II collagen 15
Ultimate tensile strength (UTS) 2
Undercooling 8
Unit cell 3
Vacancy 5
Vacancy concentration at equilibrium 5
Valence band 9
Valence electrons 9
Van der Waals bonding 9
Vinyl polymers 12
Viscoelastic modulus 12
Viscoelasticity 12
Voight solid 12
Vulcanization 12
Weld metal 11
Wetting 7
Widmanstätten ferrite 8
Wire drawing 2
Wolff's law 16
Woven bone 16
Wrought product 2
X-ray analysis by diffraction 7
X-ray diffraction 4
X-Y recorder 2
Yarn 14
Yield stress 2
Young's modulus 2
Zones of cartilage 15

INDEX

Abrasive wear, 198
Accelerated vulcanization, 361
Acetylcholine, 431, 435
Actin 424
  binding sites, 426
Action potential,
  depolarization, 433-435
  repolarization, 433-435
Activation energy, 88
  for diffusion, 210
  for substitutional diffusion, 120, 209
Active metal in corrosion, 2
Addition polymerization, 294, 359ff
Adenosine diphosphate (ADP), 426
Adenosine triphosphate (ATP) 426
  hydrolysis of, 426, 427
Adhesive bonding, 271, 332ff
Adhesive joints, design of, 333
Adhesive wear, 196, 198
Aerobic metabolism, 428ff
Age-hardenable aluminum alloys, compositions, 248
Aging of rubber, 303, 361, 362
AISI/SAE system of steel designation, 181
α- Si_3N_4, 220
α–stabilizer in titanium alloys, 272
Allotropic transformation
  in iron, 174
  in tin, 163
  in titanium, 272
Alloy carbides in tempered steel, 204
Alloy elements
  Cr and Mo in steel frames, 261ff
  in steel, hardenability, 202ff
Alloy steel
  in bicycle frames, 258ff
  AISI 4130, 204
  AISI 4340, 203
  AISI 52100, 201
  vs. carbon steel tubing, strength comparison, 264
Alpha carbon, 377
Alumina, 214
Aluminum alloy 6061
  heat treatment, 249
  microstructure (TEM), 249
  phase diagram, 249
Aluminum-lithium alloy, 237
Amino acids, 377, 378
Amorphous polymer, 297
Anaerobic metabolism, 427ff
Anelastic strain due to interstitial motion, 121
Anionic polymerization, 357, 370
Anisotropy, 16
Annealing, 87ff
Annealing twins, 223
Anode
  in corrosion,1,
Anodic reaction, 1
Anterior vs psoterior, 407
Antioxidents in rubber, 361
Appositional growth of bone, 402
Arc welding, 266
Aromatic polyamide (Kevlar), 324 352
Arrhenius equation, 92
Articular cartillage, 376ff
Aspect ratio of a fiber, 321
Asperities (in friction), 197, 213
Atactic, 300, 309
Austenite
  decomposition of, 165ff
  in stainless steel, 5
  in carbon steel, 174
  stabilizer, 188, 202
Austenitic stainless steel
  composition, 5
  crystal structure, 5
Axon of motor neuron, 429ff
Bainite, 179, 184, 268
Bakelite, 330
Bamboo bicycle frame, 256
Band model of solids, 196
Banded microstructure in an alloy steel, 268
Beads in tires, 350, 351
Beam, pure bending of, 277ff
Bending, 14
  vs. axial loading, 282
Bending moment, 14, 272
Bending moment diagram, 277
β-SiAlON, 220
  microstucture (TEM), 221
Bias-ply tires, 350
Bicycle frames
  comparisons of different materials, 259
  nomenclature of components, 256
  wooden, 257
Bicycle wheel, 7ff, 340
Binding-energy curve and the elastic modulus, 21, 22
Body-centered-cubic crystal, BCC, 5
  slip systems in, 116
Body-centered-tetragonal, BCT
  unit cell, 133, 163
  in martensite 187, 189
Body diagonals in cubic crystals, 5, 48
Boltzmann's constant, 92
Bone, 400ff

anisotropy of, 409
degree of mineralization, 406
development of, 403
effects of cyclic loading on, 410
effects of strain rate on, 408
effects of aging on, 412ff
elastic modulus of, 408
fracture and repair of, 414ff
callus formation, 416
mechanical behavior of, 407ff
remodeling of, 404ff
spongy vs compact, 411, 412
stress fractures (fatigue cracks) in, 410
stress-strain curves of 408, 409, 412
viscoelastic behavior of, 409
creep of, 409, 410
yielding of, 407, 408
Bonded joint
in composite frame, 333ff
in Al-alloy frame, 272
Bonding in ceramics, 215
Boundary lubrication, 199
Bouton of motor neuron, 430, 435
Bragg's law, 63, 78
Braiding of rope, 316
Branching in polymers, 291
Branching of a polyethylene molecule, 291
Bravais lattices, 132, 133
Braze welding, 161
Brazed bicycle frames, carbon steel *vs.* alloy steel, 261ff
Brazing, 138ff
alloys, 160
Bridging oxygens, 216, 327
Brittle fracture
in carbon steel, 130
in ceramics, 213
in CFRP tubing, 338
Bubble growth, 97
Bubble raft, 43
Buckling of a thin strut under axial compression, 283
Burgers vector, 56
of a screw dislocation, 56
of an edge dislocation, 56
Butadiene, 301, 354ff
Butted tubes, 269
Butyl rubberr, 359
Calcitonin in bone, 406
Calendering, 367
Cancellar bone, 400
Carbon black, 361ff
structure of, 362
C-curve, eutecoid steel, 178
Capillarity
in brazing, 138, 140
in sintering, 218
Carbide-forming elements in steels, 206
Carbon fibers
elastic modulus, 325
PAN precursor, 325
Carbon-carbon bond, flexibility, 290
Carbon steel *vs.* stainless steel spokes, 1ff
Carbon steel in frames, 258ff
Carburization, 207
Cartillage, 376ff
creep in, 383
injury to, 383
mechanical behavior of, 382ff
microstructure of, 376
zones of, 380ff
Case depth, 208
Case hardening, 207ff
Cast irons, 173
Cathode
in corrosion, 1
Cathode:anode area ratio, 3
Cathodic reaction, 1
Cavities in a tensile specimen, 29
Cellulose, 315, 321
acetate, 321, 352
Cementite
in carbon steel, 103
stucture of, 174
Cement lines in bone, 411
Ceramic
bearings, 213ff
Ceramics
charge neutrality in, 214
dislocation mobility in, 215
CFRP (carbon-fiber reinforced plastic), 333
tape, 338
tube, tensile behavior, 339
tubes, 333ff
Chemical potential, 158, 165
Chloroprene, 301
Chondrocytes, 377
Chondroitin sulfate, 381, 382
Chromium plating, 3
cis-Polyisoprene, 302
Clay, 217, 364
Climb of dislocations, 95
Clincher-type tires,328
Close-packed direction, 53

Close-packed plane, 44, 45
Coarsening
  of cementite, 105
  of precipitates, 239
Coefficient of friction, 197
Coffin-Manson behavior of bone, 410, 411
Coherent precipitates, 244
Cold welding, 197, 213
Cold-drawing of a linear polymer, 323
Cold-worked state, 87
Collagen, 315, 377ff
Collateral ligaments, 375, 384, 390-392
Compact bone, 400ff
Components in phase diagrams, 141ff
Composite
  frames, 333ff
  materials, 315ff, 321
  wheels, 340ff
Composites
  elastic modulus, upper and lower bounds, 319
  load distribution, 317
Compressive stress, 13
Condensation reaction, 322, 352
Conjugated dienes, 301, 354ff
Constant-temperature solidification, 148
Constituents of a microstructure, 149
Contact angle in brazing (wetting), 138
Continuous-fiber composites, 317ff 350ff
Continuous-transformation diagram, 179ff
  for a 1040 steel, 183
  for eutectoid steel, compared with IT diagram, 180
Contrast in optical microscopy, 42
Cooling curves for phase diagram determination, 147
Coordinate systems, Cartesian *vs.* cylindrical, 65
Copolymers, 304, 354ff
Copper-zinc alloys for brazing, 160
Core
  of a dendrite, 157
  of a screw dislocation, 57
Corrosion current, 3
Corrosion of iron, 1
Corrosion protection of carbon steel
  sacrificial anode, 2
  chromium plating, 3
Cortex of bone, 413
Cortical bone, 408
Covalently bonded ceramics, 213
Crack arrest in composites, 318
Creatine, 428
Creep
  of a viscoelastic material, 299
  of solder, 159
Critical radius of particle, 240
Critical stress for fracture, 225
Cross-bridge cycle, 427
Cross slip, 57, 73
Cross-links, 292
  in vulcanization of rubber, 303, 364ff
  in collagen, 380
Cruciate ligaments,n375, 384, 390-392
Crystal structure
  of silicon nitride, 219
  of ceramics, 214
Crystal symmetry, 132
Crystallization
  of polyethylene, 294
  of rubber, 293
Crystalline regions in polymers, 291
CT diagram, eutectoid steel, *vs.* IT diagram, 180
Cubic crystals, 46
Curing agent, 331
Curvature of a beam, 280
Cyclic loading of spokes, 8
Cylindrical tube as a beam, 278, 281
Dangling bonds
  in ceramics, 214
  in polymerization, 293
Dark-field TEM, 237
Dashpot, 298
Decarburization and fatigue, 128
Deformation of a beam, grid pattern, 278
Deformation twins, 224
Degree of polymerization, 294, 355
Degrees of freedom in the phase rule, 158, 164
Dendrites, 145, 154
  in Cu-Sn and succronitrile, 154
Dendritic solidification, explanation of, 154
Densification in sintering, 216ff

Diamond-cubic crystals, unit cell and covalent bonds, 163, 214
Diamond frame of a bicycle, 256
Diaphysis of a long bone, 400
Dienes, polymerization of, 354ff
Diffraction contrast, 62
Diffraction of xrays and electrons by crystals, 78
Diffusion coefficient, diffusivity 208
Dilational stress terms, 66, 67, 79
Dilatometer, 179
Dimensional stability in heat-treated steels, 206
Direction indices, 48
Disc wheels, 340ff

Discontinuous fibers, 320
Dislocations
  by-passing of particles, 238
  bowing, shear stress for, 72
  cell structure, 96
  climb, 95
  concept, 25
  core
    stresses in, 66
    of a screw, 117
  cutting of particles, 237
  density, 69, 74
  energy, 67
  glide, 56
    resistance to, 61, 215
  imaging of, 62
  line, 55
  loop, 59, 72
  mobility
    in BCC crystals, 117, 130
    in ceramics, 215
  multiplication, 72
    need for, 70
  pinning, relation to fatigue limit, 120, 128
  positive *vs.* negative, 59, 60
  source, 73
  types, 55ff
Disorder *vs.* order, 89
Displacement transducer, 19
Distal vs proximall, 404
Dot product of vectors, 50
Double cross slip, 73
Double-butted tubing, 269
Driving force
  for austenite decomposition, 176
  for coarsening, 105
  for grain growth, 97, 100
  for precipitation, 240
  of a reaction, 88
  for recovery, 95
  for recrystallization, 90
Ductile-to-brittle transition, 117, 130
Ductility, 5, 30, 215
Edge dislocation, 25, 55
Elastic modulus, 14
  physical basis, 21
  of composites, 317ff, 364
  of fibers, 326
  of tendon, 387
Elastic
  stiffness, 14
  strain, 14
Elastin, 390, 391
Elastomer, 292
Elastomeric behavior, 293, 304
Electrochemical nature of corrosion, 1
Emulsion polymerization, 355ff
  gel formation in, 357
Endochondrial ossification, 403
Endomysium, 422
Endostial surface of bone, 402
Endotenon, 387
Energy band, 196
Energy-dispersive x-ray analysis, 335
Energy of a dislocation, 67ff
Engineering stress, (tensile or compressive), 16
  stress-strain curve, 28
  strain, 16
Enthalpy, 89
Entropy, 89
  in crystals, 109
  in polymers, 290
  in rubber, 304
Epimysium, 422
Epitenon, 387
Epoxy group, 331
Epoxy resins, 330
  formation reaction, 331
  in adhesive bonding, 272
Epiphysial cartilage, 404
Epiphysial plate, 404
Epiphysis of long bone, 400
Equilibrium state of a system, 87
  criterion for, 89
Equilibrium defects in crystals, 121
Equilibrium of surface tensions
  in brazing, 139
  in grain growth, 99
Error function, 209
Etching, 44
Eutectic composition, 141
  constituent, 150, 155
  divorcement, 156
  point, 141
  temperature, 141
Eutectoid
  reaction, in Fe-C, 174, 176
  steel wire, 328
Excess free volume in grain boundaries, 43, 44, 100
Extensometer, 19
Extracellular matrix (ECM), 376
Extra half-plane of an edge dislocation, 55, 95

Extrusion
of wheel rims, 247
of rubber, 367
Face diagonals in FCC crystals, 6, 49
Fascicle
of tendon, 387
Of ligament, 391
Fast-twitch (Type II) muscle fiber, 429
Fatigue, 8, 122ff
carbon steel *vs.* stainless steel spokes, 128, 129
crack growth, 122
crack initiation,122
fracture surfaces, 123, 127
life, scatter of, 125
limit, 128
of tires, 364
resistance, 125
Face-centered-cubic crystal, FCC, 5
Fe-C phase diagram, 173
Femur, bending moment in, 407
Ferrite (BCC iron), 103, 173
Ferrite-stabilizing alloy elements in steels, 262
Fiber/matrix interface strength, 320
Fiber-pullout, 322, 339
Fiber-reinforced composites, 315ff,349ff
Fibers
for composites, 322ff
for tires, 351ff
with carbon backbones, comparison of, 326
Fibroblasts, 386
Fick's first law, 208
Fick's second law, 209
Filler metal
in welding, 266
in epoxy resin, 336
Fillers in tires, 351
Fillet brazing, 161, 162
Finite-element method, 340, 342
Firing of ceramics, 217
Flaws in brittle materials, 213, 225
Flexor tendons, 387, 388
Flow stress, 68
Fluctuating dipoles, 310
Flux in brazing and soldering, 140
Force on a dislocation, 71
Forsterite, 216
Fraction transformed
in recrystallization, 93
in austenite decomposition, 178
Fracture mechanics, 211ff
Fracture toughness, 212, 225
of CFRP composites, 338
Frame geometry, road bike, 256
Frank-Read process, 73
Free energy, 89
Free-body, 14
Free-radical polymerization, 294, 354ff
Friction, 196ff
Frictional force, 197
Fully annealed carbon steel, 106
Furnace brazing, 161
Furnace-cooled *vs.* air-cooled carbon-steel spokes, 184
Galvanic series, 2
Gas constant, 92
Gauge section, 19
Gibbs free energy, 89
Gibbs phase rule, 158ff, 164ff
Glass fibers
elastic modulus, 328
drawing of, 328
Glass transition, 300
temperature, 301
of epoxy resins, 331
Glass-transition temperature in tire rubbers, 357ff, 360
Glassy state, 297
Glide
of a dislocation, 26
of a mixed dislocation, 58
of a screw dislocation, 57
of an edge dislocation, 56
Glucose metabolism, 428
Glycine, 377, 378, 380, 391
Glycogen, 428
Glycosaminoglycans (GAGs), 381
Golgi apparatus, 386
Grain boundary, 43
energy, 43, 98, 99, 100
mobility, 100
motion in grain growth, 98
Grain growth, 97ff
effects of impurity atoms and particles, 100, 101
kinetics of, 99
Graphite
as a lubricant, 199
fibers, 325
structure and bonding of, 170
Graphitization of PAN, 325
Griffith crack, 225, 318
Griffith equation, 225
Ground substance, 381, 382
Guinier-Preston (GP) zones, 243ff
Gutta percha, 302

Habit relationship, 186
Hand brazing, 160
Hard-sphere model, 5, 21, 45, 53, 54
Hardenability of steel, 212ff
Hardened steel, applications in the bicycle, 210ff
Hardening
  effect of grain size, 102
  of rubber (by vulcanization), 303, 362
  of steel, 185
Hardness
  of martensite, 201
  decrease during tempering, 203
  tests, 108
Haversian canal, 401
Heat of fusion, 148, 152
Heat treatment of steels, 186, 205ff
Heat-affected zone (HAZ), 267, 269, 276
Heterogeneous nucleation, 241
Hexagonal close packed crystal, HCP, 223, 224
Homogeneous nucleation, 241
Hooke's law
  in compression, 13
  in shear, 15
  in tension, 22
Hot working, 102
Hot-isostatic-pressing (HIPing), 220
Hot-pressing, 220
Hyalauronic acid, 381,382
Hyaline cartillage, 376
Hydrodynamic lubrication, 199
Hydrogen bond
  in water, 143, 307
  in nylon, 320, 322
  in Kevlar, 320, 322
  in polypeptide, 378, 379
Hydrostatic compression, 64
Hydroxyapatite, 402
Hypereutectic, 147
  lead-tin alloys, 157
Hypoeutectic, 147
  lead-tin alloys, 153
Hysteresis
  in an elastomer, 293, 362
I-beam, 277
Initiator in polymerization, 293
Injection molding, 291
Interfaces
  coherent, semi-coherent, incoherent, 242, 244, 245
Interfacial energy
  in precipitation hardening, 239, 242
  in sintering, 218
Intermetallic compounds, 143
Internal energy, 89
Interstices, 4
Interstitial solute, 4
  diffusion, 120
  in a BCC lattice, 118
Investment casting, 264
Ion channels, 431, 432
Ionically bonded ceramics, 213
Ion pump, 433, 434
Iron-carbon phase diagram, 173ff
Isobutylene, 359
Isomers, 301
Isoprene, 301
Isotactic, 300, 308
Isothermal transformation diagram, 179
  for 1040 steel, 181
  for eutectoid steel, 178
Isothermal transformation in a eutectoid steel, 175ff
Isotropy, 16
Jominy end-quench test, 202
Jominy hardness curves 1040 *vs.* 4340 steels, 203
Keratan sulfate, 381, 382
Kestral monocoque CFRP frame, 338
Kevlar, 324
  fibers, structure of, 324
  elastic modulus, 326
Kinetic energy of a particle, 92
Kinetics
  of grain growth, 99
  of recovery, 95
  of recrystallization, 91
  of vulcanization, 365, 366
Knee joint, 375ff
Lack-of-penetration defect, 268, 271
Lacunae in compact bone
  interstitial, 401
  circumferential, 401
Lamellae in compact bone, 401
Lamellar morphology
  of a eutectic, 155
  of a eutectoid, 175, 181
Large plastic strains, 17
Latent heat of fusion, 148
Lateral vs medial, 407
Latex, 302, 356
Lath *vs.* plate martensite, 203
Lattice parameter, 46
Lattice vacancies, 87, 94
  equilibrium concentration of, 109
Lattice-friction stress, 251

Lead-tin alloy system, 147ff
Leathery behavior in a polymer, 299
Lignin, 315
Linear polymer, 289
Lever rule, 145ff
Ligament, 390ff
  grafts in 393, 394
  immobilization of, 392
    recovery after, 393
  injury and healing of, 393
  insertions of, 391,393
  mechanical behavior of, 391ff
  microstructure of, 390, 391
  sprain of, 393
  viscoelastic behavior of, 392
Line tension of a dislocation, 72
Linear elastic fracture mechanics, 212, 225
Liquid-phase sintering, 217
  of Si_3N_4, 221
Liquidus lines, 146
Living ends of polymer chains, 357, 370
Load cell, 19, 33
Long bones, 400ff
Longitudinal strain in bent beam, 278
Longitudinal stress in bent beam, 277
Longitudinally stressed fibers, 317ff
Lost wax process, 264
Lotus monocoque pursuit bike, 340
Lubricants, 199
Lubrication, 199
Lugged joints for brazing, 160
Lugs, investment cast *vs.* fabricated, 264
Macrophages, 404
Magnesia, 214
Mandrel
  for tube drawing, 269,
  for CFRP tubing, 336
Marrow of bone, 400
Martensite, 176, 179
  defects in, 186, 201
Martensitic transformation, 185ff, 188
Martensite-start temperature, 188
Martensite-finish temperature, 188
Maximum stress in a beam, 280
Maxwell solid, 298
Maxwell-Boltzmann distribution, 91
Medial vs lateral, 407
Membrane potential, 431ff
Meniscus, 384ff
  injury to, 385
  mechanical behavior of, 385
  microstructure of, 384
Mesenchymal cells, 386
Metal-matrix composites, 315
Metallic bonding, 196
Metallographic
  examination, 40ff
  microscope, 42
  specimen, 40
Metaphysis of long bone, 400
Metastable precipitates, 243ff
Methane, 290
Mica, 217
Microcracks
  in bone, 411, 415
  in steel, 130
Microhardness tests, 267
Microstructure
  of a brazed joint, 161
  of a partly martensitic steel, 187
  of Al-Li (TEM), 237
  of Al-Si casting, 334
  of a eutectic Pb-Sn alloy, 148
  of a hypereutectic Pb-Sn alloy, 158
  of a hypoeutectic Pb-Sn alloy (10% Pb), 156
  of a hypoeuthectic Pb-Sn alloy (30% Pb), 155
  of carbon steel spoke
    fully annealed, 106
    recrystallized, 104
  of cold-drawn carbon-steel spoke, 103, 185
  of quenched 1.4%C steel, 187
  of tempered 4130 steel (TEM), 204
  of the CFRP tubing, 337
  of the pin from a bicycle chain, 206
  of triblock copolymers, 369, 371
Microstructures
  in hypothetical simple eutectic system, 144
  of titanium alloy Ti-3Al-2.5V, 274
  of weld joint, alloy-steel frame, 267
  of weld joint in titanium-alloy frame, 275
  carbon-steel spoke, furnace-cooled *vs.* air-cooled, 172
Miller indices, 46
Mitochondria, 386, 429, 430
Mixed dislocation, 58
Mixing of tire components, 366
Mobility of dislocations related to bonding, 61, 62, 215
Molecular weight
  of a polymer, 294
  of a rubber, 355
Molybdenum disulfide, 199
Moment arm, 14
Moment of inertia of beam, 279ff

Moments of inertia, various cross sections, 280ff
Monocoque CFRP frames, 338
Monomer, 216, 355ff
Motor end plate of motor neuron, 430
Motor neuron, 429ff
Motor units in skeletal muscle, 429
Mountain bikes, 260ff
Muscle contraction, 424, 426ff
  energetics of, 427, 428
Muscle fibers, 422ff
Muntz metal, 160
Myelin sheath, 430, 431
Myoblasts, 421, 439
Myofibrils, 422
Myoglobin, 429
Myosin, 425
  heads of, 426
  binding to actin, 426
Myotendinous junction, 436
n-alkane, 280, 293
Necking, 29
Necking criterion, 33
Nerve impulses, 436
Network modification in silica, 317
Network modifiers, 317
Network polymers, 292, 330
Neurotransmitter, 431, 435
Neutral axis of beam in pure bending, 277
Newton's law of viscous flow, 298, 327
Nodes of Ranvier, 430, 431, 434
Non-equilibrium solidification, 156
Non-equilibrium solidus, 157
Nucleation and growth,
Number-average molecular weight, 294
Number-average degree of polymerization, 294
Nylon, 322
  as tire cord, 352
Nylon 6.6, formation reaction, 323
Nylon, elastic modulus, 326
Octahedral site
  of a BCC lattice, 118
Optical metallography, 40
Optical microscopy, 40
Order *vs.* disorder, 89
Ordered precipitates, 250
Organically based fibers, 322
Orowan mechanism, 238
Osteoblast, 402
Osteoclast, 404ff
Osteocyte, 401
Osteoid, 402
Osteon, 401
Overaging, 239, 247
Oxide films
  as lubricants, 199
  in passivation, 3
Ozone, effect on rubber, 303, 360, 361
Parabolic
  grain-growth law, 100
  strain hardening, 74
Paraffin, 290, 293
Paratenon, 387
Parathyroid hormone, effect on bone, 406
Passivation
  in corrosion, 3
  of stainless steel, 3
Patella tendon, 385
Patenting, 328
Pauli Exclusion Principle, 196
Pearlite in carbon steel, 106, 173
Peierls stress, 251
Percent elongation, 30
Percent reduction in area, 34
Perfectly plastic material, 197
Perimysium, 422
Periosteum, 375, 391, 400
Permanent dipoles, 306
Phase diagram
  aluminum-copper, 236
  aluminum-silver, 243
  copper-silver, 160
  copper-zinc, 160
  hypothetical simple-eutectic system, 142ff
  iron-carbon, 173
  lead-tin, 147
Phase diagrams
  NaCl and $CaCl_2$, 141
  terminal solid solutions, 142
  Ti-Al and Ti-V, 273
  use of composition axis, 141
Phase rule, 158ff
  derived, 164ff
Phase, defined, 4
Phenol-formaldehyde reaction, 330
Photomicrograph, 42
Piano wire, 328, 354
Plain carbon steel, 181
Plane strain, 212
Plane stress, 212
Plastic deformation, 23, 26
  process summarized, 77
Plastic-blunting mechanism of fatigue-crack growth, 123

Plastic
  constraint, 30
  instability in tension, 29, 33
  strain, equation for, 70
  work in fracture, 227
Plasticizer, 322
Plywood, 320
Point defects, 87, 94, 109
Poisson's ratio, 21
Polyamide, 322, 377
Polycrystalline aggregate, 42, 99
Polycrystalline material, 42ff
Polyester, 351
Polyethylene, 290, 293ff
  crystal structure, 295
  crystalline spherulites, 295
  elastic modulus, 326
  low density *vs.* high-density, 296
  molecular structure, 293
  properties, 296
Poltethylene terephthalate (PET), 352
Polymer
  architecture, 308
  stabilizers, 303
Polymer-matrix composites, 315ff
Polymerization of dienes, 354ff
Polymers, general characteristics, 289ff
Polymethylmethacrylate, 308
Polymorphs of Si_3N_4, 219
Polypeptides, 387
  residues in, 378
Poly(p-phenylene terephthalamide (Kevlar), 324
Polystyrene, 299, 308, 354
Porosity
  in castings, 265
  in ceramics, 218
Posterior vs anterior, 407
Postsynaptic membrane, 431
Precipitation hardening, 236ff
  in tempered steel, 204
  heat treatment, 248
  mechanism, 238ff
  requirements for, 238ff
  stages of, 246
Precipitation of a second phase, 146, 155
Precipitation-hardened aluminum alloys, 248
Prepolymer for epoxy resin, 330
Presynaptic membrane, 431
Primary phases, 153
Processes of osteocytes, 401
Pro-eutectoid ferrite, 181ff
Proline, 378, 391
  hydroxylation of, 380
Proteoglycans, 381, 382
Proximal vs distal, 404
Pure shear, 65
Quadriceps tendon, 385
Quench cracking, 206
Radial tires, 350
Radius of curvature of beam, 279ff
Random solid solution, 119
Random walk, polymer chain configuration, 290
Rate of substitutional diffusion, 120
Rayon, 322, 352
Reaction bonding, 219
Reactivity ratios of monomers, 358
Recalescence, 185
Recovery, 94ff
Recrystallization, 90ff
  temperature, 93
Relative amounts of phases, 144
Remodeling of bone, 404ff
Reptation, 332
Resistance strain gauge, 33
Resolved stress components, 27
Restoring force
  in a spring, 13
  in rubber, 304
Retained austenite, 187, 188, 206, 207
Ribosomes, 386
Road bikes, 260
Rocksalt, 214
Rope, 316
Rubber, 290, 354ff
  compounding of, 360
  procewssing of for tires, 366ff
Rubber elasticity, role of entropy, 304
Rubbery behavior of a polymer, 299
Rupture by void formation and coalescence, 29, 225
Rust pit, 3
S-N curve, 124ff
S-shaped curve, 92, 177
Sacrificial anode, 2
Sagittal plane of body, 407
Salt-water phase diagrams, 141
Sarcolemma, 425
Sarcomeres, 422ff
  A-band in, 423
  H-band in, 423
  I-band in 423
  M-line in, 423
  thick filaments, 424

thin filaments 424
Z-line in, 423
Sarcoplasm, 425
Sarcoplasmic reticulum (SR), 425, 435
Scalar product of vectors, 50
Scanning electron microscope, 335
Scatter in the fatigue life, 125
Schmid's law, 27
Schwann cell, 430, 431
Scorch, in vulcanization, 365
Screw dislocation, 56ff
Screw dislocation
core of, 117
stress field of, 64
Secondary bonding, 306
Secondary hardening, 204
Second moment of area, 279
Segregation of solutes
to dislocations, 119ff
to grain boundaries, 100
Seizing (cold welding), 197
Self diffusion, 95, 119
Semicoherent precipitates, 244
Shear modulus, 15
relation to Young's modulus, 21
Shear strain, 15
Shear stress, 15
Sheet-like silicates, 217
Shrinkage porosity in castings, 265
SiN_4^{8-} tetrahedron, 219
Silica-based glass, 327
Silica in tires, 363, 364
Silicate structures, 216
Silicon carbide, 214
Silicon nitride, 219ff
Silly Putty, 298
Simple cubic lattice, 46, 133
Sintering, 216ff
SiO_4^{4-} tetrahedron, 216
Size, for coating fibers, 328
Skeletal muscle, 421ff
architecture of, 422
contusion of, 439
cramping of, 441
effects of immobilization, 440
heterotopic bone in, 440
injury and healing of, 439ff
laceration of, 439
maximum force in, 422
mechanical behavior of, 436ff
microstructure of, 422
soreness in, 440
training effects on, 438, 439
Sliding friction, 197
Slip, 23
and close-packed directions, 53
and close-packed planes, 58
dislocation motion, 25
in FCC crystals, 53ff
lines in deformed brass, 24
step, 24
system, 55
vector, 56
Slow-twitch (Type I) mscle fiber, 429
Small-scale deformation, 16
Small-scale-yielding approximation, 212
Soap-bubble model for grain growth, 97
Soap micelles in emulsion polymerization, 356
Soft solder, 147
Softening during recrystallization, 90ff
Softening during grain growth, 102
Soldering, 138ff, 148
Solid lubricant, 199
Solid/liquid interface stability, 153
Solid solubility, 142
factors that control, 151
in Pb-Sn alloys, 150
Solid solution, 4
in phase diagrams, 142ff
Solid-solution hardening, 117
Solid-state sintering, 218
Solid-state *vs.* liquid-state transformations, 173
Solidus lines, 146
Solubility limit, 143
of sugar in water, 143
Solute atom/dislocation interactions, 67, 76, 117
Solution treatment, 238
Solvus line, 143
experimental determination of, 152
Space lattice, 132
Spheroidization of pearlite, 177
Spherulites in polyethylene, 295
Spinnerette, 323
Spokes
corrosion of, 1
stress-strain curves of, 19
tensioning of, 8
Spongy bone, 400
Spring constant, 13
Stability of a particle, 240
Stabilizers in polymers, 303, 361
Stacking fault, 223

Stacking-fault energy, 223
Stainless steel
  passivation, 3
  vs. carbon steel for spokes, 1ff
Stages of annealing, 90
Static friction, 197
Steel
  plain carbon, 181
  wire cord for tires, 354
    brass plating of,
  1040, 181, 183, 203
  4130, 214
  4340, 213
  52100, 21
Stem cells in marrow of bone, 400
Stiffness
  of bicycle frames, 258ff
  of rubber, 303, 364
Stored elastic energy, physical basis, 22
Stored energy of cold work, 90
Strain, 14
Strain energy per unit length of a dislocation, 68
Strain gauge, electrical resistance, 19, 33
Strain hardening, 25, 29, 32, 52ff, 74ff
  in wire drawing, 32
  mechanism of, 74
Stress at a point in a stress field, definition, 63, 64
  components, 63, 64
Stress concentration
  factor, 212
  in fatigue, 122, 124, 126
  in a plate, 211ff
Stress field of a dislocation, 63
  of a mixed dislocation, 67
  of a screw dislocation, 64ff
  of an edge dislocation, 66, 79, 80
Stress relaxation in a viscoelastic material, 299
Stress, bending *vs.* axial loading, 282
  types, 13
Stress-concentration factor, 211, 212
Stress fracture of bone, 410
Stress-intensity factor, 212, 225
Stress-strain curves, 28ff
  annealed *vs.* cold-drawn spoke, 32
  carbon steel *vs.* stainless-steel spoke, 20, 53
  parabolic hardening, 74
  of fibers, 329
  of filled rubbe, 363
  of ligament, 392
  of tendon, 388, 389
Strip-chart recorder, 28
Styrene butadiene rubber, 357ff
Substitution transformation, 92
Substitutional solute, 4
  diffusion, 119ff
  interaction with dislocations, 117
  solid solution, 4
Substrate of precipitate nucleation, 241
Superficial tangential zone (STZ), cartillage, 380, 383
Surface energy
  in fracture, 226
  in sintering, 218
  in wetting, 138ff
Surface hardening, 207ff
Surface tension
  in brazing, 139
  of a bubble, 97
Synapse of motor neuron, 430
Synaptic cleft of motor neuron 432, 432
Syndiotactic, 308
Synovial
  cells, 375, 376, 387, 393
  fluid, 375, 376, 387, 393
  membrane 375
Synthetic rubbers, 304, 354ff
Tacticity, 300, 308
Transmission electron microscopy, TEM, 62
Temper designations for aluminum alloys, 248
Tempering of a hardened steel, 188, 203ff
Tendon, 385ff
  architecture of, 387
  avulsion of, 389
  degeneration of, 389, 390
  injury, healing, and repair of, 389ff
  mechanical behavior of, 387ff
  microstructure of, 386
  viscoelastic behavior of, 388, 389
Tensile
  strain, 14
  stress, 13
  test, 18ff
Tensioning of spokes, 8
Terminal cisterae in SR, 425
Terminal solid solutions, 150
Tetanus in muscle, 436
Tetragonal distortion
  in BCC crystals, 118
  in martensite, 187
Tetragonal unit cell, 133
Thermal
  activation, 88
  analysis, 150

energy, 91
shock, 327
stresses
in quenched steels, 205
in quenched Al-alloy bicycle frames, 270
Thermoplastic behavior of polymers, 291, 297
Surfactant, 355
Thermoset, 292
Three-phase equilibrium, 159
Tie line, 144ff
TIG welding, 266
Tin, crystal structures, 163
Tire cord, 323, 351ff
Tires, 315, 349ff
belts, 350ff
cord, 351ff
liners, 350,351, 359
molding of, 368, 369
plies, 351
reinforcement of, 351
rolling resistance, 362
sidewalls
tear resistance, 362
tread, 349ff
wear resistance of, 362, 363
wet-skid resistance, 362
Titanium-alloy frames, 258ff, 272ff
Torque from muscle contraction, 437, 438
Toughness, 5, 225
of rubber, 364
Trabecular bone, 400
trans-polyisoprene, 302
Transfer length, 321
Transverse compression in a wire-drawing die, 31
Transverse tension in a necked tensile specimen, 30
Transversely stressed fibers, 318
Transverse tubules (T-tubules) in SR, 425
Triblock copolymers, 369
Tropocollagen, 379, 380
Tropomyosin, 424, 426
Troponin complex TnT, TnI, TnC), 424, 426
True strain, 17
True stress, 17
Tube geometry in bicycle-frame design, 258
Twinning in crystals, 223ff
Type I (slow-twitch) muscle fiber, 429
Type II (fast-twitch) muscle fiber, 429
Two-phase equilibrium, 145ff
Undercooling
eutectic, 155
eutectoid, 178
Unit cell, 46, 133
of polyethylene, 295
Ultimate tensile stress, UTS, 28
of tendon, 387
Vacancy, 87, 94
concentration, 109
migration, 95
Van der Waals bonding, 306
Vinyl-type polymers, 299, 308
Viscoelasticity, 297ff
Viscoelastic modulus, 299, 304
Viscosity
of a lubricant, 200
of polymers, 290
of silica glasses, 327, 328
Viscous flow, 328
Voight model, 298
Volkmann's canal in compact bone, 401
Vulcanization, 290, 302, 364ff
Wear, 198
Welding of bicycle frames, 266ff
Welding defects, 268, 271
Wetting in brazing, 138ff
Wheel rims, 247
Wheels
bicycle *vs.* wagon, 7
open spoke (aerodynamic), 337, 338
Widmanstätten α in TiAlV, 273
Widmanstätten ferrite, 183
Wire drawing, stresses in the die, 31
Wöhler curve, 124ff
Wolf's law, 410
Wood-frame bicycle, 256
Workability of glass for fibers, 327
Woven bone, 403
X-ray
analysis, 152
diffraction
Bragg's law, 78
from rubber, 304
map, 335
scattering, 78
X-Y recorder, 19
Yield stress, 17
characterization of, 19
Young's modulus (see also Elastic modulus), 14
of various materials, table, 18
Zinc on carbon steel, 2
Zipp monocoque CFRP bicycle frame, 339
Zones of articular cartillage, 380ff
superficial tangential zone (STZ), 380, 383

Periodic Table of the Elements

IA	IIA	IIIB	IVB	VB	VIB	VIIB	VIII			IB	IIB	IIIA	IVA	VA	VIA	VIIA	VIIIA
1 *h* **H** 1.008																	2 *h* **He** 4.003
3 *b* **Li** 6.94	4 *h* **Be** 9.01											5 *h* **B** 10.81	6 *c* **C** 12.01	7 *h* **N** 14.01	8 *c* **O** 16.00	9 **F** 19.00	10 *f* **Ne** 20.13
11 *b* **Na** 22.99	12 *h* **Mg** 24.31											13 *f* **Al** 26.98	14 *d* **Si** 28.09	15 *c* **P** 30.97	16 *o* **S** 32.06	17 *t* **Cl** 35.45	18 *f* **Ar** 39.95
19 *b* **K** 39.10	20 *b* **Ca** 40.08	21 *h* **Sc** 44.96	22 *h* **Ti** 47.90	23 *b* **V** 50.94	24 *b* **Cr** 52.00	25 *c* **Mn** 54.94	26 *b* **Fe** 55.85	27 *h* **Co** 58.93	28 *f* **Ni** 58.71	29 *f* **Cu** 63.54	30 *h* **Zn** 65.37	31 *o* **Ga** 69.72	32 *d* **Ge** 72.59	33 *r* **As** 74.92	34 *h* **Se** 78.96	35 *o* **Br** 78.91	36 *f* **Kr** 83.80
37 *b* **Rb** 85.47	38 *f* **Sr** 87.62	39 *h* **Y** 88.91	40 *h* **Zr** 91.22	41 *b* **Nb** 92.91	42 *b* **Mo** 95.94	43 **Tc** (98)	44 *h* **Ru** 101.07	45 *f* **Rh** 102.91	46 *f* **Pd** 106.4	47 *f* **Ag** 107.87	48 *h* **Cd** 112.40	49 *t* **In** 114.82	50 *t* **Sn** 118.69	51 *r* **Sb** 121.75	52 *h* **Te** 127.60	53 *o* **I** 126.90	54 *f* **Xe** 131.30
55 *b* **Cs** 132.91	56 *b* **Ba** 137.34	57 *h* **La** 138.91	72 *h* **Hf** 178.49	73 *b* **Ta** 180.95	74 *b* **W** 183.85	75 *h* **Re** 186.2	76 *h* **Os** 190.2	77 *f* **Ir** 192.2	78 *f* **Pt** 195.09	79 *f* **Au** 196.97	80 *r* **Hg** 200.59	81 *h* **Tl** 204.37	82 *f* **Pb** 207.19	83 *r* **Bi** 208.98	84 *m* **Po** (210)	85 **At** (210)	86 *f* **Rn** (222)
87 *b* **Fr** (223)	88 **Ra** (226)	89 **Ac** (227)															

58 *f* **Ce** 140.12	59 *h* **Pr** 140.91	60 *h* **Nd** 144.24	61 *h* **Pm** (147)	62 *h* **Sm** 150.35	63 *b* **Eu** 151.96	64 *h* **Gd** 157.25	65 *h* **Tb** 158.92	66 *h* **Dy** 162.50	67 *h* **Ho** 164.93	68 *h* **Er** 167.26	69 *h* **Tm** 168.93	70 *f* **Yb** 173.04	71 *h* **Lu** 174.97
90 *f* **Th** 232.04	91 **Pa** (231)	92 *o* **U** 238.03	93 **Np** (237)	94 **Pu** (242)	95 **Am** (243)	96 **Cm** (247)	97 **Bk** (247)	98 **Cf** (249)	99 **Es** (254)	100 **Fm** (253)	101 **Md** (256)	102 **No** (254)	103 **Lw** (257)

c=cubic
f=face-centered cubic
b=body-centered cubic
r=rhombohedral
d=diamond cubic
h=hexagonal
m=monoclinic
t=tetragonal
o=orthorhombic